CHORUSES, ANCIENT AND MODERN

Choruses, Ancient and Modern

Edited by
JOSHUA BILLINGS, FELIX BUDELMANN,
AND FIONA MACINTOSH

OXFORD
UNIVERSITY PRESS

UNIVERSITY PRESS

Great Clarendon Street, Oxford, OX2 6DP,
United Kingdom

Oxford University Press is a department of the University of Oxford.
It furthers the University's objective of excellence in research, scholarship,
and education by publishing worldwide. Oxford is a registered trade mark of
Oxford University Press in the UK and in certain other countries

Published in the United States of America by Oxford University Press
198 Madison Avenue, New York, NY 10016, United States of America

British Library Cataloguing in Publication Data

Data available

Library of Congress Control Number: 2013937377

ISBN 978-0-19-967057-4

Printed and bound by
CPI Group (UK) Ltd, Croydon, CR0 4YY

Links to third party websites are provided by Oxford in good faith and
for information only. Oxford disclaims any responsibility for the materials
contained in any third party website referenced in this work.

Acknowledgements

We are most grateful to the Mellon Foundation, the Faculty of Classics and St Hilda's College, Oxford, as well as to the British Academy and the Society for the Promotion of Hellenic Studies, all of whom have supported us in various ways during the preparation for this book. We also thank OUP for assistance with picture costs. We warmly thank all those who attended our 'Choruses, Ancient and Modern' Conference, 13–14 September 2010, and especially the theatre director Claudia Bosse, who ably and with much good humour led the delegates in a practical workshop on chorus-making in the Jacqueline du Pré Building at St Hilda's College.

Particular thanks are due to the following: the Archive of Performances of Greek and Roman Drama (APGRD) Archivist/Administrator, Naomi Setchell for her excellent organization of the conference and for all her help and advice with the pictures; Emelen Leonard for very kindly agreeing to help with the bibliography; and Lucy Jackson for very helpfully reading everything at short notice. As ever, the support of all our current colleagues at the APGRD has been immeasurable: Peter Brown, Cécile Dudouyt, Edith Hall, Stephen Harrison, Justine McConnell, Naomi Setchell, Oliver Taplin, and Tom Wrobel. At OUP, we thank Hilary O'Shea again for her continued support and enthusiasm, Taryn Das Neves for all her efforts on our behalf, Kizzy Taylor-Richelieu and Hilary Walford for their hard work on this volume. Finally, we thank our indexer, Jane Horton, who worked to an unpredictable timetable with enormous efficiency and good humour.

Contents

Part III. Shadows

Part IV. Community

List of Illustrations

List of Contributors

Christian Biet is Professor of Theatre History and Aesthetics at the Université de Paris X-Nanterre. His numerous publications include *Miroir du Soleil* (1989), *Œdipe en monarchie, tragédie et théorie juridique à l'âge classique* (1994), *Racine ou le Passion des larmes* (1996), *La Tragédie* (1997), *Henri IV, la vie, la légende* (2000), and *Qu'est-ce que le théâtre?* (with C. Triau 2006).

Joshua Billings received his doctorate from Oxford in 2011 and is Assistant Professor of Classics and Humanities at Yale University. Research interests centre on tragedy, intellectual history, and the classical tradition, and his first book on Greek tragedy and German philosophy around 1800 is forthcoming.

Felix Budelmann is University Lecturer in Greek Language and Literature at the University of Oxford. He is the editor of the *Cambridge Companion to Greek Lyric* (2009), and is currently preparing an edition with commentary of selections from Greek lyric. He also works on cognitive approaches to Greek tragedy.

Laurence Dreyfus performer and musicologist, is Professor of Music at the University of Oxford and a Fellow of Magdalen College. He is author of *Bach's Continuo Group* (1986) and *Bach and the Patterns of Invention* (1996). His latest book, *Wagner and the Erotic Impulse*, was published by Harvard University Press in 2010.

Cécile Dudouyt is Postdoctoral Research Fellow at the APGRD and Junior Research Fellow at New College, Oxford. Her doctorate (Oxford/Paris X) was on 'Sophoclean Revenge: Renaissance and Enlightenment Rewritings'. She is currently working on early modern translations of ancient drama and a study of Freud's engagement with Greek and Shakespearian tragedy for the Freud edition of Plon's dictionary series.

Zachary Dunbar is Senior Lecturer in Music Theatre and Classical Acting at Central School of Speech and Drama, University of London. He has chapters in *Theorising Performance: Greek Drama, Cultural History and Critical Practice* (2010), *Theatre Noise: The Sound of Performance* (2011), and *Studies in Musical Theatre* (2011). He is a concert pianist and freelance theatre director/writer, and his original works have been staged in the UK and in Europe.

Helen Eastman writer and theatre director, is Artistic Associate of the APGRD. After studying Classics and English at Oxford, Helen trained as a theatre director at LAMDA and was Producer of the Onassis Programme for the Performance of Ancient Drama at the University of Oxford from

2005–2011. Recent directorial credits include *Agamemnon* for the Cambridge Greek Play (2011) and Jane Griffiths' *Sappho . . . in 9 fragments* (Oxford and Greenwich Theatre 2012).

Erika Fischer-Lichte is Director of the Institute for Advanced Studies on 'Interweaving Cultures in Performance' (since 2008) and spokesperson of the International Doctoral School 'InterArt' (since 2006) at the Freie Universität Berlin. Among her many publications are *Theatre, Sacrifice, Ritual: Exploring Forms of Political Theatre* (2005) and *The Transformative Power of Performance: A New Aesthetics* (2008).

Simon Goldhill is Professor of Greek at Cambridge, where he is also Director of the Centre for Research in Arts, Social Sciences, and Humanities, Director of the Cambridge Victorian Studies Group, and Fellow of King's College. He is also Fellow of the American Academy of Arts and Sciences.

Constanze Güthenke is Associate Professor of Classics and Hellenic Studies at Princeton University. She is the author of a book on the relationship between Germany and modern Greece in the Romantic period, and she is currently working on a study of the rhetoric of German classical scholarship in the long nineteenth century.

Edith Hall is Professor of Classics at King's College London. She is Co-Founder and Consultant Director of the APGRD. Her most recent publications include *The Return of Ulysses* (2008), *Greek Tragedy: Suffering Under the Sun* (2010), and *Adventures with Iphigenia in Tauris* (2012).

Eleftheria Ioannidou is Lecturer in Drama at the University of Birmingham. After a doctorate in Oxford, she held a Humboldt Postdoctoral Fellowship at the Freie Universität Berlin. Her doctorate on postmodernism and Greek tragedy will be published next year in the Oxford University Press Classical Presences Series.

Fiona Macintosh is Director of the APGRD and Fellow of St Hilda's College, University of Oxford. Her recent publications include *Sophocles' Oedipus Tyrannus* (2009) and *The Ancient Dancer in the Modern World: Responses to Greek and Roman Dance* (edited 2010).

Sheila Murnaghan is the Allen Memorial Professor of Greek at the University of Pennsylvania and the author of *Disguise and Recognition in the Odyssey* (2nd edn, 2011). Her current projects include a co-authored study of Classics and childhood 1850–1965, a commentary on Sophocles' *Ajax*, and further investigations of the tragic chorus.

Anastasia-Erasmia Peponi is Professor of Classics at Stanford University. She teaches and writes on Greek aesthetics in poetry and philosophy. Her book

Frontiers of Pleasure: Models of Aesthetic Response in Archaic and Classical Greek Thought was published in 2012 by Oxford University Press. She has also edited a volume on *Performance and Culture in Plato's Laws*, published by Cambridge University Press.

Martin Revermann is Associate Professor of Classics and Theatre Studies at the University of Toronto. His publications include *Comic Business* (2006), *Performance, Iconography, Reception* (co-edited with P. Wilson, 2008), *Beyond the Fifth Century: Interactions with Greek Tragedy from the Fourth Century BCE to the Early Renaissance* (co-edited with I. Gildenhard, 2010). He is currently writing a monograph on Brecht and Greek tragedy.

Ian Rutherford teaches in the Classics Department at the University of Reading. He is the author of *Pindar's Paeans: A Reading of the Fragments with a Survey of the Genre* (2001), and many other publications on Greek poetry and religion. He is particularly interested in contact between Greek culture and other ancient civilizations, especially Anatolia and Egypt.

Roger Savage Honorary Fellow of the University of Edinburgh, has staged several seventeenth- and eighteenth-century operas for professional and amateur groups, broadcast on things related for BBC Radio Three, and published essays on the history of opera production, on Renaissance staging and its classical backgrounds, and on works of Purcell, Pope, Rameau, and Metastasio.

Richard Seaford is Professor of Ancient Greek at the University of Exeter. His numerous papers range from Homer to the New Testament. His books include Euripides *Cyclops* (1984), Euripides *Bacchae* (1996), *Reciprocity and Ritual* (1994), *Money and the Early Greek Mind* (2004), and *Cosmology and the Polis* (2012). In 2009 he was President of the Classical Association.

Helen Slaney is currently the Joanna Randall McIver Junior Research Fellow at St Hilda's College, Oxford. She has been affiliated with the APGRD for the past three years and has recently completed a D.Phil. thesis on the performance reception of Senecan tragedy.

Note on Nomenclature, Spelling, and Texts

Our policy has been to use the names as they appear in the text/programme/ publicity for modern adaptations/versions of the ancient plays. But with the names and characters of the ancient plays and their abbreviations, we have adopted the Latinized versions of Greek proper names where those are well established, broadly in line with the practice of the fourth edition of the *Oxford Classical Dictionary*.

Abbreviated references to ancient works and editions of ancient works are those of the *Oxford Classical Dictionary* where possible.

When referring to the ancient authors in the original language, we have used the most recent edition published in the Oxford Classical Texts series.

Introduction

Joshua Billings, Felix Budelmann, and Fiona Macintosh

For even this is music for the wretched, to sing their troubles without chorus [ἄτας κελαδεῖν ἀχορεύτους].

Euripides, *Trojan Women*, 121

For the Greeks, to be 'without chorus' (ἀχόρευτος) was to be lacking something essential. Long before Plato's assertion—too often taken for granted—that 'the uneducated man is one without choral experience' (ἀπαίδευτος ἀχόρευτος) (*Laws* 654a), the word could be used in a negative sense to mean 'unmusical' and hence 'joyless'. To be without choral experience was not only to be uneducated, but to be cut off from a major form of social interaction, of religious worship, and of aesthetic pleasure. Where we today tend to understand these spheres of action as separated, the Greek chorus had a tendency to make them blend into one another, visible equally in Spartan choruses of unmarried girls, paeans performed at Delphi, and the dramatic choruses of Athenian tragedy and comedy. Though these and other choruses served substantially different functions in heterogeneous societies, they all took part in what has been called Greek 'song culture'—or better, song-and-dance culture. The etymology proposed (perhaps facetiously) in Plato's *Laws*, connecting *choros* to *charis* (grace, joy), demonstrates, whatever its historical truth, the value of choral song and dance to Greek culture. To take part in a chorus was to be embedded in a social texture and to have a share in the pleasures of community.

Choruses *mattered* in ancient Greece in a way they largely have not done in the modern western world. Except in musical theatre, the modern western world could be said to be broadly 'without chorus'—though there has been a renewed interest in choruses in certain quarters in recent decades. Choral song and dance today tend to divide realms of experience that coexisted in the Greek chorus. The chorus as performance (most often in theatre, but also in dance and music concerts) and the chorus as social ritual (in liturgical settings, in spontaneous song) more often than not have only a tenuous link to one another today, while they were organically and essentially linked in ancient Greece. In a single festival, the choruses onstage in tragedy would have been mirrored by dithyrambic choruses, and in turn again by song and dance in the processions and cultic rituals surrounding the competitions. These choruses, though appearing in different contexts and performing different songs, would have been recognizably kindred (as reflected in the many points of contact between tragic and lyric choral song). In the West today, few choruses outside musical theatre sing and dance in the choreographed unison of the ancient Greek chorus. Consequently, it is not surprising that modern notions of the chorus have tended to focus on ancient theatrical, and especially on tragic, choruses. Though only one of many ancient choral phenomena, the tragic chorus has been seized on as the representative choral form for modernity. The atomism of modern choral experience brings into focus discrete elements of ancient choruses, while the broad importance of the Greek chorus sheds light on the social forms and priorities of modern cultures.

The relative absence of modern choral experience, along with the ostensible genealogical descent of modern from ancient choruses, makes the rich choral texture of ancient Greek culture particularly alluring. As the realities of the ancient Greek chorus have receded from view, modern imaginations have filled the chorus with even greater potential and mystery. The modern Western tradition has viewed the ancient chorus with a powerful sense of desire and nostalgia. The present volume locates itself at the intersection of choral practice and choral (re)imagination. It juxtaposes choral contexts in ancient and modern cultures to understand better the enduring fascination of the chorus. Because of the self-consciousness so deeply embedded in ancient choral texts, the chorus is a particularly fruitful ground for thinking about the dialogue between ancient and modern experiences. Choruses, ancient and modern, have a striking tendency to focus conceptions of political, artistic, and social existence, and thus serve as media for exploring similarity as well as difference, and for tracing continuity and rupture alike. Despite the gap between ancient and modern choruses, there nevertheless exist points of significant commonality that allow for reciprocal illumination.

There are many different choruses contained in this volume, but all— ancient and modern—are bound by an *idea* of the Greek chorus. This idea, to be sure, is itself mediated by the choruses of Roman drama, by liturgical choruses, by the *corps de ballet*, and by the visual arts (to name just a few). The Greek chorus has been diffused and refracted through many later phenomena, yet the chapters in this volume show the persistence of its power over the modern imagination. The fascination with the primal quality of the chorus begins in antiquity. From the earliest choral texts we have, choruses often reflect on their relation to an originary moment of choral song and dance. Ancient choruses are both actions themselves and representations of action, *praxis* and *mimesis*, and resist any single temporal frame: performing in the present, choruses look to the past and future. There may be an inherent nostalgia to choral representation, and this elegiac quality is most pronounced in modern choruses, but it is by no means limited to them. The juxtaposition of 'original' and modern choruses in this volume mirrors the polarities of choral song. In so far as this volume presents an image of the chorus, it is a protean one, constituted by a play of here and beyond, now and then, identity and alterity.

We treat the chorus in this volume as a phenomenon of classical reception or tradition, rather than of anthropology. All the chapters collected here relate in some way, more or less directly, to the ancient Greek chorus, and do not attempt to cover the range of choral forms outside the Graeco-Roman tradition. This is not at all to deny the value of anthropological approaches to choruses (which have contributed substantially to understandings of the Greek chorus), but we are focused here not on independent instances of choruses, but on the dependent relation of modern choruses to their Greek forebears. The transhistorical focus allows the volume to take in a broad spectrum of choral phenomena, which are nevertheless united—or haunted—by their relation to the Greek past.

Though our questions are defined in the first instance by scholarship on the classics and classical reception, they reach far beyond, to theatre and dance studies, musicology, intellectual history, and literature in modern languages. One of our aims, indeed, is to place the thinking about choruses that has gone on within various disciplines in dialogue with each other. We believe there is much to be gained from taking fuller account of transhistorical choral practice and theory, not least for those interested in the ancient Greek chorus, which so often is taken as the unmarked point of reference for work on choruses more broadly. In the most general terms, we suggest, the effect of confronting such diverse phenomena is to *defamiliarize* the chorus.

The chorus outside Greek antiquity brings with it a sense of challenge and even strangeness that creates a strong contrast to the Archaic and Classical chorus, which is usually studied as embedded in the texture of the cultural and social lives of individuals and communities. Again and again choruses since the Renaissance have presented difficulty—not always and not equally in all genres—but nevertheless with considerable regularity. Many modern theorists have treated the chorus as a problem to be solved, both within and beyond academia. In drama, choruses have been the exception rather than the norm after antiquity, and even writers drawn to choruses, like Voltaire and Schiller, found themselves wrestling with them. And, of course, where choruses were and are a success, the success is understood to be the product of hard work by directors, choreographers, conductors, and performers, moulding a group of individuals into a unified group: choruses do not come naturally to modern Western theorists and practitioners.

As the chapters in this volume demonstrate, the challenge posed by choruses has not just been a cause of struggle and even avoidance of choruses altogether, but has also prompted creative responses—and these responses again point to contrasts with antiquity. This is most explicit when thinkers such as Schiller or Nietzsche use the chorus as the basis on which to build theories about the distance between antiquity and modernity. In a rather different way, the contrast comes to the fore when choruses are fitted into non-ancient aesthetics. Brecht, for instance, one of the few twentieth-century Western dramatists who found the chorus a useful medium to work in, employed choruses by shaping them in ways explicitly opposed to ancient practice. Other powerful modern models of choruses are equally aberrant in ancient terms. The notion of choruses as revolutionary bodies, which became particularly powerful before and after the French Revolution, is not one at home in most accounts of ancient choruses, which, on the whole, tend to see the chorus as harmoniously aligned with cosmic, social, and political order. Even the weaker notion, which makes an appearance in various modern periods, of utopia-seeking choruses, while closer to standard models of ancient chorality, nevertheless is at odds with them because of the gap it programmatically opens up between the chorus and the current state of the world.

These contrasts can be productive and can point up avenues of investigation for ancient choruses, as three examples may help to suggest. The casting of many ancient tragic choruses as non-citizens and their often difficult relationships with other characters in the play, for instance, looks less particular when considered in the light of the uneasy fit between many modern choruses and their surroundings. Might there be something to be gained from revisiting the issue of choral identity in tragedy in terms not of politics or genre but of a fundamental question of choral experience: can a chorus, theatrical or otherwise, ever fully mesh with its context?

A second example is the conceptual question of what in fact constitutes a chorus. The diversity of modern choral phenomena as well as of discourses about choruses raises difficult questions about what makes a chorus. Does it require music? Does it require movement? How many performers are needed? Is it a question of discourse more than fact, or of reference back to the ancient chorus as the ur-model? Is there room for contestation: performing groups that see themselves as choruses but are labelled mere dancers or crowds by their detractors? By contrast, classicists by and large feel secure about what constitutes a chorus, aided by the fact that *choros* is, of course, a Greek word; but even for antiquity there must be a case for a focused interrogation of the ideological as well as the real boundaries between chorus and dance, between processionary and stationary choruses, between rehearsed and impromptu choruses, and so on.

Thirdly, the juxtaposition of ancient and modern offers material for reflection on the vantage point from which one looks at Archaic and Classical Greek choruses. The sense of challenge that accompanies much modern chorus-making has created a strand of chorality that places choruses in the imagination. As the perfect chorus is unattainable, the chorus becomes an idea, something that is appealed to, longed for, or imagined, rather than real. This is the topic of Part III, populated by echoes of earlier choruses, imaginary choruses, choruses that cannot be seen. In a different way, it characterizes the position of anybody who tries to come to terms with ancient choruses today while being conscious that in our own world the kind of choral experience reconstructed for the Greeks is simply impossible. Scholars are engaged in creating imaginary choruses, and it is worth asking whether there is an element of nostalgia here too. At a minimum it would be productive to think through the notion that already in Archaic and Classical Greece choral songs demonstrate a hankering for the impossible (note the habit of Greek choral texts to imagine performances by other, often mythical, choruses), and that already in Archaic and Classical Greece there was a consciousness of the sheer difficulty of the chorus as a medium. Ancient and modern choruses are too different from each other to give any reliable direct comparison, but in their very difference there is the potential for broadening the range of questions scholars ask.

Modern approaches to the chorus, the chapters collected here suggest, have been defined by a certain residual idealism, which can broadly be traced to Germany around 1800. As this volume amply demonstrates, our language of the chorus is very often predetermined by theoretical formations that are relatively recent. In general terms, this has meant that modern notions of the chorus place a strong emphasis on choral essence or identity (as opposed to choral participation), on the chorus's reflection of contemporary religious, political, and philosophical concerns (instead of seeing it as an empty and outmoded form), and the practice of staging Greek choruses or choruses in a Greek manner as an urgent dramaturgical issue (where previously it had been a largely moot, though occasionally discussed, point). Though none of these ways of thinking is genuinely *new* around 1800, all gain greatly in importance and explanatory prestige. The conclusions drawn by Idealism can seem quaint today, but the questions being asked are largely still open and definitive for modern approaches to the chorus. Much the same, to be sure, can be said of conceptions of tragedy generally, but the particularity of the chorus within Idealist thought is that its theorization is almost completely independent of Aristotle's *Poetics*, the text that has determined the framework for so much thought on tragedy (even when, as in Idealism, this framework is unacknowledged or explicitly denied). The chorus represented a kind of theoretical vacuum, which Idealist thinkers filled with notions that have remained powerful and influential.

The theoretical approaches of Idealism have proved remarkably tenacious for understandings of the chorus. August Wilhelm Schlegel's much-misquoted

and misunderstood judgement that the chorus represents 'the idealized spectator' (*der idealisierte Zuschauer*) echoes, perhaps surprisingly, in the first
pages of Jean-Pierre Vernant and Pierre Vidal-Naquet's *Myth and Tragedy
in Ancient Greece*, which describes the chorus as 'an anonymous and collective
being whose role is to express, through its fear, hopes, and judgments, the
feelings of the spectators who make up the civic community' (Vernant and
Vidal-Naquet 1990: 24). The chorus for both represents a reflection of the
viewers watching the work, and is intimately connected to the community of
Attic tragedy. By contrast, earlier discussions, including Aristotle's, are far
more functionalist, seeing the chorus in terms of its interventions in the
dramatic action, and less as an independent body requiring conceptual explanation. Idealism has proven most powerful for modern notions of the
chorus in that it has defined *the chorus as a problem*.

The extent of this influence has become particularly apparent in recent
years, with the explosion of studies of classical reception. Very often, these
have pointed to the chorus as an intellectual and conceptual challenge for
moderns. Of course, within ancient Greek contexts, the chorus requires no
explanation—much more than the dramatic form itself, choral song and dance
were familiar from other realms of existence. In societies, however, that do not
share this choral culture (but that often have long dramatic traditions), the
dramatic chorus appears as an anomaly demanding justification. This perpetual theoretical lacuna has to be traced back to Aristotle's *Poetics*, which
expends only a few, famously unhelpful words on the chorus. From Aristotle,
modern thought inherited vocabulary for conceiving varieties of dramatic
narratives and characters—while the only measure of the chorus to be found
in the *Poetics* is the extent to which they 'participate'. Yet, as is patently
obvious in the choral odes, Aristotle does not exhaust the chorus's contribution. The sense of inadequacy has been continually frustrating but continually
productive for efforts to conceptualize the chorus.

The chorus has remained a conceptual problem in recent years, but there are
two important developments, one in the theatre and the other within classical
scholarship, which between them help make this a timely volume. Several
factors have conspired to stop many modern theatre practitioners perceiving
the chorus to be the insurmountable hurdle that it so often was. In 1952 Peter
Halmos wrote an essay on 'The Decline of the Choral Dance' and argued that
this was a symptom of a decline in our bio-social life. In the theatre at this
time, the star system was still dominant; the chorus, if it existed at all, was
synonymous with the mechanized, commodified chorus line that had much in
common with the factory workers on the industrial production line, or, as
Billy Wilder's *The Front Page* (1974) makes clear, the stenographers in the
1920s typing pool.

In recent years, theatrical practice has increasingly come to value the chorus, and, with the demise of the star system, the chorus/ensemble has been recognized as a compelling medium of presentation. Initially, this came about from the increasing exposure in the Western world to non-Western theatrical traditions, notably from Asia and Africa, where choral traditions are still very much alive. Two productions in particular were striking for their use of a singing and dancing chorus: Yukio Ninagawa's Japanese *Medea* (1984), which transformed the kabuki chorus into a sixteen, all-male, singing/dancing chorus; and Yael Farber's slightly less high-profile, South African adaptation of the Oresteia, *Molora* (2008). Both of these productions furnished audiences in the Western world with analogues that enabled them to apprehend the centrality of the singing/dancing chorus of Greek tragedy in performance. Moreover, the rise to prominence of non-hierarchical theatre companies in the 1980s, notably Ariane Mnouchkine's Théâtre du Soleil in Paris and Włodzimierz Staniewski's Gardzienice near Lublin, allowed the chorus/ensemble to be recognized as the engine of the company from which actors would occasionally, and temporarily, step out in order to perform individual roles. It is, perhaps, not surprising that coincident with this new prominence granted to the chorus in performance has been a resurgence of interest in ancient choruses among theatre historians as well as classicists.

Research in cognitive science, which sheds new light on the relationship between spectator and performer, has significant implications for the study of choruses in particular. Challenges by neuroscience to the Cartesian mind/body dualism have shown incontrovertibly that there can be no viewing without some degree of participation. When a spectator watches the movements of others, the same sets of neurons are activated in the observer as in the performer (Meltzoff and Prinz 2002). Research with dancers, moreover, has indicated that, the more expert the viewer, the better the evocation of the feeling of the movement pattern (Calvo-Merino et al. 2005). This discovery, in particular, may well explain how societies with rich choral traditions also have deeply satisfied spectators. The ancient chorus, from this perspective, is less the 'idealized spectator' than 'the surrogate participant', who literally provides, through singing and dancing, an active way into the performance.

This new interpretation of performance dynamics made possible by developments in neuroscience has been mirrored by reconsiderations of the relationship between spectator and the ensemble. As Bernard Dort argued in *La Représentation émancipée* (1988), and later Jacques Rancière in *The Emancipated Spectator* (2009), there is no real divide between spectating and participating in the action, only authority figures that make people believe they are merely passive consumers. Institutional divisions in the theatre from the end of the seventeenth century may well have severed the long-standing link between the spoken word, song, and dance, once separate venues were established for 'serious' drama and for opera and ballet. But it was only in the mid-nineteenth century that theatre audiences, newly confined to a darkened auditorium, were also expected to remain quietly in their seats throughout the performance. Members of the hectoring proletariat were finally removed from the parterre to the gallery and eventually banished to the music hall and tavern. Even anecdotal evidence, however, would suggest that it is hard to suppress muscular response to a favourite sporting event, even when confined to the sitting room and watching it on TV. Viewing and participation differ in degree rather than kind and vary according to political and social contexts. This understanding of performance dynamics between spectator and the ensemble has been labelled in France 'choralité'. Even though, as the name implies, the ancient chorus has become a point of reference rather than the end point for this new mode of theatrical performance, it has become, in a very real sense, impossible to ignore in both contemporary theatre theory and practice.

The renewed importance of the chorus in the creative arts has a counterpart, though as yet without much direct interaction, in a kind of renaissance that the chorus has enjoyed in classical scholarship. The sense that choruses are challenging remains unchanged, but in recent years this sense of challenge has been productive rather than debilitating. There now seems to be a particular urgency to thinking about choruses, especially Greek lyric choruses (for example, Rutherford 2001; Kowalzig 2007a; Athanassaki and Bowie 2011; Peponi 2013c; formative for lyric choruses generally is Calame 1997, originally published in 1977). From this interest, scholarship on drama has become newly sensitive to the interconnections between different choruses in ancient Greece (as in Golder and Scully 1994/5; Perusino and Colantonio 2007; Swift 2010) and has considered the unique role of the chorus within comic and tragic *mimesis* (Ley 2007; Bierl 2009a, originally published in 2001; Gagné and Hopman 2013). Broadly speaking, an attention to the political, social, and institutional contexts of choruses distinguishes these recent studies from their more formalist forebears (a paradigmatic study of these contexts is P. Wilson 2000 on Athens). The present volume seeks to build on the growing consciousness of the variety of choral performance and experience in Greece as well as the growing interest in choruses among certain theatre theoreticians and practitioners by connecting ancient and modern choral phenomena. It is distinguished from other treatments of the reception of the chorus (sections in Riemer and Zimmermann 1998; Macintosh 2010; Rodighiero and Scattolin 2011; Gagné and Hopman 2013) by its prismatic perspective, which brings together expertise from numerous disciplines to investigate the many manifestations of choruses in the Greek and modern traditions. Where previous research into modern choruses has been defined mainly by questions relating to the ancient chorus, we begin with the choral tradition as a whole and pose questions that we believe are applicable to antiquity and modernity.

We propose four contexts in which choruses, ancient and modern, might be situated: conceptual and historical understanding ('Scholarship'), formal and artistic questions ('Aesthetics'), expressions of temporal distance and nostalgia ('Shadows'), and social and political cohesion ('Community'). A chapter on the ancient Greek chorus opens each section, and establishes concerns that will be common to the chapters on modern choruses following. We have continually found there to be a productive tension between ancient and modern contexts of the chorus, and we hope to illuminate this tension itself, in the process drawing attention to the particular difficulties for understanding that choruses present. This thematic focus distinguishes our volume from much previous work in classical reception (especially work dealing with ancient as well as modern sources), and creates provocative juxtapositions of various choral contexts. The gaps between the chapters may be as suggestive as the correspondences.

'Scholarship' considers the various ways that the chorus has been understood in conceptual discourse through time, and the often-surprising ways that such discussions have resonated beyond their original formulations. A first chapter on ancient accounts of the chorus compares and synthesizes Plato, Aristotle, and scattered later discussions to point out some of the major challenges and divisions in thinking about the chorus in antiquity and beyond (Anastasia-Erasmia Peponi). It is followed by two chapters focusing on the nineteenth century (Simon Goldhill and Constanze Güthenke), which, it is argued, forms a turning point in post-classical conceptions, with changes echoing throughout the last 200 years of scholarship. From the late nineteenth century, anthropology's observation of choral phenomena in non-Western societies has offered ways of thinking about the chorus as a constant of collective existence, which provides a model for understanding the ancient Greek chorus (Ian Rutherford). Collectively, these chapters show how attempts to grasp the chorus have consistently challenged conceptual frameworks and prompted thinkers to develop new and speculative theoretical models.

'Aesthetics' focuses on the ways that choruses have been employed and conceptualized within different artistic contexts. The first chapter considers the paradoxical status of Archaic and Classical Greek festival choruses as both of and not of the occasion at which they were first performed (Felix Budelmann). Seneca's choral practice, it is argued, creates a metaphysical 'hyperspace', which can be understood through the analogy with ancient pantomime (Helen Slaney). From the Renaissance onwards, operatic and dramatic choruses sought alternatively to overcome or to exploit the distance of the chorus, as the *coro mobile* of 'polymorphic' choruses and the *coro stabile* of 'purist' choruses existed side by side in stage practice (Roger Savage). Around the end of the eighteenth century, though, a change in the valuation of the otherness of the chorus is visible across Western Europe, which has important consequences for theory and practice of tragedy in Germany (Joshua Billings). The section closes with a look at the unique choral practice and theory of Bertolt Brecht, whose aesthetic of the chorus, though formulated in direct opposition to German Idealist and Aristotelian dramatic theory, nevertheless finds the chorus an important and powerful medium (Martin Revermann). These chapters point to the diverse formal roles that choruses have fulfilled throughout Western history, and to the artistic challenges they have consistently posed.

'Shadows' examines reflections on choruses of the past, and experiences of nostalgia and longing connected to the ancient chorus. In tragic choruses of old men, nostalgic recollection and urgent questioning of choral participation go hand in hand as groups reflect on the actions of their leaders (Sheila Murnaghan). The absence of a chorus in early modern French drama reflects a collective riven by religious tensions and therefore unable to constitute any kind of choral group (Christian Biet). Under the absolute monarchy of the eighteenth century, the public fictional spaces created within Voltaire's stage works afford a kind of 'phantom' chorus, through which the linking of citizenry and the king can be gestured (Cécile Dudouyt). Another transfigured chorus is found in Wagner's music dramas, which assign the choral role programmatically to the orchestra as a means of translating the Greek chorus's relation to truth and prophecy into purely musical form (Laurence Dreyfus). After these heavy precedents, the Broadway musical of the twentieth century struggles to reinvigorate the chorus as an essential element in a newly individualistic context (Zachary Dunbar). In changing times, the ancient chorus has proved a fixed point for diverse reflections, which often emphasize absence and discontinuity in more or less elegiac fashion.

'Community' discusses collective performance as a means of social constitution. The first chapter explores the political valences of the chorus in ancient Greece, with particular attention to the relation between mystic choral performances and civic institutions (Richard Seaford). Jumping to the eighteenth century, a tension between notions of the collective and conceptions of modernity is traced in reflections on the political and social dimensions of the chorus (Edith Hall). In the nineteenth century, the *corps de ballet* was often considered antithetical to Greek drama, yet is shown to have grown originally out of attempts to revive ancient choruses during the revolutionary period, as a means of constructing and reflecting community at a time when the star system dominated within the theatre (Fiona Macintosh). In the twentieth century, the chorus was politicized more emphatically than ever with the rise of militant fascism, as demonstrated in a chapter on Nazi-era Germany, in which choruses could be a means of enforcing social conformity (Eleftheria Ioannidou, using rare archival materials from the Leyhausen Collection). Reacting to this troubled legacy, the 'choric theatre' of late-twentieth-century

German drama has brought the tension between social collective and individual choice to the fore (Erika Fischer-Lichte). Finally, the past twenty years have seen a new and highly original interest in chorus-making in British theatre, which has rejected static staging of the collective for freer and more physically engaged modes (Helen Eastman). Together, these chapters emphasize the persistent political and social potencies of the chorus, which have made it a privileged medium for thinking through tensions within and between communities.

Part I

Scholarship

1

Theorizing the Chorus in Greece

Anastasia-Erasmia Peponi

Despite its uncertain etymology, the Greek word for chorus, *choros* (χορός), appears to have quite clear semantics. In some of its earliest attested usages, especially in Homeric poetry, the word denotes either public areas designated for dance or the dancing activity itself, the latter usually performed by a group. In some cases the two meanings are hard to distinguish, the communal space for dance and the dance itself appearing to be culturally, and thus notionally, interdependent.[1] The cultural importance of public areas demarcated for dance is reflected in the frequent early poetic use of the compound adjective *euru-choros*, which is usually attributed to whole cities and understood originally to mean 'having spacious dancing-places'.[2]

Certainly, the best-known meaning of *choros* is that of a dancing and singing group. This semantic nuance, which is prevalent in the classical period and thereafter, is often implicit in early usages of the word, but it is also made explicit in archaic compositions such as the *Shield*—attributed to Hesiod in antiquity—where performing choruses (*choroi*, in plural) are described as participating in a wedding procession.[3] Although descriptions of choral activity where either the kinetic or the vocal component is singled out occur in several Greek texts, it is clear from our sources that, for the most part, *choroi* performed a combination of both components in various forms. Both poetic and philosophical evidence indicates that in choral practices the alliance of body and voice was considered essential to the group's overall coordination, even in cases where the performance seemed to require a distribution of the kinetic and the vocal action between its members.[4]

---

[1] See, e.g., *Il.* 3.393; *Od.* 6.157, 12.4. See also Chantraine (1999: s.v. χορός) for both the semantics and the uncertain etymology of the word.

[2] *Il.* 23.299; *Od.* 4. 635; 11.265; Hes. *Fr.* 37.17 MW.

[3] [Hes.] *Sc.* 277.

[4] For *choreia* as the whole of vocal and kinetic activity, see, e.g., Pl. *Leg.* 654a–655a; 816a–b; Pratinas *PMG* 708; Ar. *Ran.* 241–249.

Theorizing designates here processes of conceptualizing, of suggesting and shaping perceptions and interpretations about a given phenomenon. More specifically, this chapter aims at exploring ancient perceptions about Greek *choreia*, the combined activity of song and dance, and will focus predominantly on the way sources external to poetry meditated upon, or commented on, things choral in antiquity. It is important to note, however, that it is primarily thanks to extant archaic and classical Greek poetry—epic, lyric, and dramatic—that we can have today a satisfactory idea both about the way Greek choruses presented themselves and about the way choral performances were perceived and, in a few cases, evaluated.[5] As poetry both reflected and contributed to the formation of intellectual, emotional, and cultural attitudes in archaic and classical Greece, the way in which the chorus, an integral part of cultural life, was depicted within poetic discourse is a good illustration of the overall way in which chorality was conceptualized over these periods. On the other hand, the cultural importance of chorality (the term is used here to denote the entire phenomenon of choral practices in Greece along with the various principles and ideologies embedded in them) prompted discourses outside poetry to engage with it. From evidence scattered in later authors one receives the impression that things choral were part of political, moral, and aesthetic discourses.[6] A lost treatise *On the Chorus*, attributed to Sophocles, indicates that issues pertaining to *choreia* might have already been systematized in written form in the fifth century BC.[7] This chapter discusses important instances in which the Greek chorus and the broader phenomenon of Greek chorality are theorized in surviving philosophical, interpretative, and critical discourses in antiquity.

PLATO'S CHORAL VISIONS

The earliest surviving and, as it turns out, particularly influential of such instances occur in Plato's works. Plato's hostility against the ways in which *mousikê* was practised in Athens is well known and, though much discussed, still provides ample room for further deliberation. As Greek *mousikê*, originally referring to the activity of the Muses, comprised all possible instantiations or combinations of vocal, instrumental, and kinetic activity within the widest range of genres of performance, its practice embraced, among other kinds of

---

[5] *Il.*18.590–606 and *Hymn. Hom. Ap.*156–64 are the most representative examples of the way in which *choreia* was perceived and evaluated in early poetry.

[6] See, e.g., Hdt. 5.67; 6.129; Thuc. 3.104.

[7] *Suda* s.v. *Sophoklês.*

performance, the three poetic genres encountered today under the name of epic, lyric, and dramatic poetry. From the all-encompassing domain of *mousikê*, however, it is Plato's explicit and repeated criticism against epic and tragic poetry that has usually been noticed and discussed. His references to the various non-epic and non-dramatic types of performance have received less attention, to some extent because of their obliqueness and ambiguity. As choral poetry and performance are considered part of the broader domain of lyric, Plato's references to chorality are to a large extent contingent upon his quite complex attitude towards lyric types of performance, named *melic* in his times.

If the level of popularity that certain genres of *mousikê* enjoyed in Athens was indeed a decisive factor for Plato's attack on contemporary musical trends, it is quite odd that a well-established and popular choral genre on the Athenian musical scene, the dithyramb, has very rarely been the explicit target of his criticism.[8] If one takes into account the festival of the city Dionysia in Athens alone, dithyrambic performances required that one thousand individuals every year participated in the twenty competing dithyrambic choruses, ten choruses of men and ten of boys, each chorus comprising fifty members and representing one of the ten Athenian tribes.[9] Surprisingly, though, Plato's discussion of this choral genre is remarkably limited, his references to the dithyramb being usually parenthetical and numbering no more than a dozen throughout his dialogues. In several of these cases one can sense an ironic tinge, hinting either at the exaggerated complexity of dithyrambic language or at the genre's ecstatic fervour.[10] Brief ironic references to the poets of the dithyramb in *Gorgias* and in the *Apology* are essentially a reiteration of Socrates' overall criticism of the poets' lack of real knowledge and of their interest in nothing other than pleasing their audiences, their success in poetic composition being attributed to divine inspiration alone.[11]

Interestingly, in the above cases it is mainly the verbal aspects of dithyrambic poetry, not the genre in its glamorous performative practice, that Plato targets. In other words, even though the genre's effectiveness in Athens lay precisely in the communal character and the profoundly social prestige of its chorality, Plato seems uninterested in this prominent aspect of the dithyrambic genre. This becomes clearer in a well-known passage of the third book of the *Republic*, where the dithyramb is mentioned as a genre presented through the recital of 'the poet himself', thus differentiated from other genres such as tragedy and comedy, which, according to Socrates, take place wholly

---

[8] About Plato's attacks on poetry and 'mass media' culture, see Nehamas (1999).
[9] See, e.g., Csapo and Slater (1995: 103–8).
[10] *Cra.* 409c; *Ion* 534c.
[11] *Ap.* 22a–b. See also *Grg.* 501e–502c.

'through mimesis'.[12] There have been various suggestions regarding the meaning of the quite obscure expression 'recital of the poet himself' as opposed to 'mimesis', but for our purposes it is worth noting that the customary public performer of the dithyramb, the singing and dancing chorus, is completely passed over in silence here.[13] Even if Plato was thinking of dithyrambic poems in which the characters of the narrative had no direct speech, thus creating the impression that one was hearing the poet's own 'voice', he nonetheless avoided any mention of the actual agent enacting the poet's 'voice'—namely, the chorus. It is the singing voice of the dithyrambic chorus that an audience would customarily hear in the Athenian festivals, not that of the dithyrambic poet, a fact that certainly rendered the mimetic status of the dithyrambic performance more complex than Plato was willing to address in this fundamental passage for the theory of genres.

And, yet, Plato seems to have contemplated chorality with more perception and more creatively than any other Greek thinker. It is less when Plato analyses the existing culture of Athens and more when he conceives of *mousikê* as deeply embedded in the structure of the cosmos that we find the most interesting Platonic visions of *choreia*. The major instances come in the tenth book of the *Republic*, in the myth of the soul in the *Phaedrus*, and, finally, in his last work, the *Laws*. Whereas the first two are part of Plato's metaphysics, the last one is attached to his vision of an alternative model of culture, where the chorus is given a central role.

Let us start with Plato's choral metaphysics in the *Republic*. Close to the end of the tenth book of the *Republic* Socrates narrates the story of Er, a man from Pamphylia who, after apparently having been killed in battle and while lying on the funeral pyre, was revived and enabled to tell the story of his after-life journey. The relevant section of Er's tale includes the description of the universe and its motions, as seen when the souls reach a straight beam of light that, stretched through the heaven and the earth, holds together the entire cosmic sphere. It is from there that the spindle of Necessity is hung, by which eight circles, depicted as the circular rims of eight hollow whorls, turn round. A Siren stands on top of each of the eight revolving circles, each Siren emitting a single sound (*mian phônên*), a single pitch (*hena tonon*), while carried around with the revolution.[14] From these sounds, eight in all, is made the concord of a single *harmonia*. In addition, three Fates, sitting round about at equal distances, sing to the *harmonia* of the Sirens, each one of them having a different subject: Klotho sings 'what is', Lachesis 'what has been', Atropos

---

[12] *Resp.* 394b–c. For implicit Platonic references to the New Dithyramb's extravagant experimentations in performance, see esp. *Resp.* 397a.

[13] On this passage, see, e.g., Adam (1902: ad loc.); Koller (1954: 47); Vicaire (1960: 237–2); Cross and Woozley (1964: 272–3); Else (1986: 29); Belfiore (1984: 141–2); Murray (1996: ad loc.); Peponi (2013a).

[14] *Resp.* 616b–617c.

'what will be'. At the same time, Klotho touches the outer circumference of the spindle and helps its rotation, pausing from time to time, Atropos does the same to the inner circles, and Lachesis does both.[15]

With its likely Pythagorean origins and its many substantial alterations throughout antiquity, Plato's cosmic vision had a remarkable impact in later thought, with Kepler's theory of the *Harmony of the World* a glorious moment in its long history. It has been repeatedly suggested that the conception of the octave scale underlies the Platonic depiction of *harmonia* deriving from the eight Sirens' vocal pitches.[16] In his times, however, Plato's cosmic model would also evoke associations deeply rooted in choral traditions, an aspect usually underestimated in scholarship. *Harmonia*, for instance, related to the verb *arariskein* (to fit together), was a key concept to the Greek chorus, as the coordination of vocal multiplicity was central to its aesthetics.[17] Furthermore, the Sirens were an integral part of the Greek choral imaginary. Varying in number according to different sources, these demonic creatures are often presented in earlier Greek poetry as an archetypal musical model identical or opposite to, but nevertheless often as authoritative as, that of the chorus of the Muses. Choruses of young women are repeatedly assimilated to, or even supposed to enact, the Sirens' voices.[18] The Fates were also occasionally imagined as a chorus.[19] The three Fates singing of three different temporal domains (past, present, and future) sound like an intriguing twist on the trio's choral genotype.[20]

Thus, by envisioning cosmic music as the product of the complementary vocal and kinetic activity of the Sirens and the Fates, Plato elaborated on, and at the same time transformed, inherited perceptions of chorality. The background of cultural associations permits fuller appreciation of Plato's cosmic model and its novelty. For not only must the imaginary stagecraft of the rotating universe have exceeded in fancy the latest high-tech stage machinery of fourth-century Athenian theatre, but even the specifics of his choral arrangement must have sounded like a striking innovation. Athenian audiences were quite familiar with performing semi-choruses, yet Plato's conception of an antiphonal singing of two distinctive choruses, performing each its own

---

[15] *Resp.* 617c–d. Much of the diction used here is based on the translation of the passage by Barker (1984: ii. 56–8).

[16] On this and other interesting aspects of Plato's musicological endeavour, see Barker (1984: ii. 56–9) and Petraki (2008).

[17] In Hesiod, for instance (*Theog.* 39), the archetypal divine chorus of the nine Muses sing while 'fitting together their voices', and, in one of the most revealing lines of Greek choral criticism, the exquisite chorus of the Deliades is praised for their 'beautifully fitted together song' (*Hymn. Hom. Ap.* 164). See also Budelmann, Chapter 5, this volume.

[18] Alcm. *PMGF* 1.96–100; *PMGF* 30; Pind. fr. 94b M.

[19] See, e.g., Calame (1997: 35).

[20] It should be noted that Plato's Fates sound here like a transformation of yet another chorus, that of the Muses in Hesiod *Theog.* 31–4.

vocal routine while one modulates the kinetics of the other, is an extraordinary piece of orchestration and choreography compared to what we otherwise know from that era.[21]

Although both ancient commentators and modern scholars, preoccupied with the broader issues raised by the Platonic text regarding astronomy, mathematics, and musical science, consistently overlooked this aspect of Er's myth, Renaissance culture capitalized on it. The interludes for Girolamo Bargagli's *La Pellegrina*, presented in Florence in 1589 to celebrate the wedding of Ferdinando I de' Medici and Christine of Lorraine, offered a musical extravaganza that became an early landmark in the evolution of opera and prominently featured elaborations on the Platonic choral fantasy.[22]

While the stagecraft of Plato's celestial music in the *Republic* seems like a twist on the rich choral imagery to be found in Greek poetic texts, a different model of *choreia* is dreamt up in the *Phaedrus*, in yet another myth or allegory, that of the soul-chariot. The soul here is likened to a chariot attached to two winged horses and driven by a charioteer.[23] Whereas the gods' chariots, Socrates says, are equipped with two perfect horses, everyone else's chariot is yoked to one beautiful and good horse and to one ugly and unruly one, which makes chariot driving particularly challenging and painful. Grouped into eleven sections and led by eleven gods, all soul-chariots fly high in the air while patrolling the heavens.[24] In key moments of the Socratic narrative the soul-chariots, thus divided, are designated either with the collective attribute *choros* (chorus) or with the individual attribute *choreutês* (member of a chorus).[25] The souls of the gods, who operate as chorus leaders in Plato's vision, 'take their stand on the high ridge of heaven, where its circular motion carries them around as they stand while they gaze upon what is outside the heaven'.[26] It is in this extra-celestial realm that the Forms, the abstract and immaterial archetypes of the physical word, exist. Among the other soul-chariots only the ones who follow the god most closely can see the Forms, Socrates says.[27] Their charioteer, striving to balance the two horses, can raise his head up and glance at the Forms while being carried around in the circular

---

[21] Quite close to this model but not identical is the case of the Nereids and the Muses lamenting in *Od.* 24.57–61. The choral metaphysics of the tenth book of the *Republic* is a fully-fledged elaboration on the motions of the heavenly bodies (imaginatively addressing both the visual *and* the acoustic) assimilated to *choreia* elsewhere in Plato. On these heavenly motions, see esp. *Timaeus* (40c) and the most recent analysis by Kurke (2013) with further references and bibliography.

[22] For a detailed account on the Interludes for *La Pellegrina* and their contemporary reception, see Treadwell (2008); and cf. Savage, Chapter 7, this volume.

[23] *Phdr.* 246a–b.

[24] *Phdr.* 246c–e.

[25] *Phdr.* 247a, 250b, 252d.

[26] *Phdr.* 247b–c, trans. Nehamas and Woodruff (1995: 33).

[27] *Phdr.* 248a.

motion along with the gods' chariots. This celestial journey of the souls and
their eventual ritual viewing (*theoria*) of the Forms is soon to be linked to the
way one associates oneself with the beloved on earth—more particularly with
the restrained and essentially contemplative manner in which one is supposed
to respond to the beauty (*kallos*) of the beloved.[28]

Since the terms *choros* and *choreutês* are explicitly employed by Plato in key
moments of his narrative, the circular rotation of the soul-chariots cannot but
evoke the formation of the circular dances practised in Athens, to a large
extent identical with the dithyrambic performances mentioned previously.[29]
Yet, while this familiar nexus of choral associations is at work for an Athenian
audience, Plato introduces defamiliarizing novelties. First off, 'choruses' of
chariots as such are hard to find in Greek literature.[30] Furthermore, instead of
actually dancing, the chorus of soul-chariots is in fact 'being danced', for they
are stationed on the rim of heavens, which itself rotates. At the same time,
unlike actual dancers who are themselves a spectacle for their audiences
(especially in Athenian theatrical choral culture), his peculiar heavenly
choruses, stationary and rotating at the same time, are here turned into the
very spectators of the marvellous spectacle that lies in front and beyond them,
that of the Forms.

In sum, an eccentric and idiosyncratic chorality, a peculiar mixture of
remotely familiar and utterly unfamiliar features, with imagery and terminology that evoke both mystical initiation and choral initiatory rites, seems to
be essential to the viewing of the Forms in the *Phaedrus*. Unlike the *Sympo-
sion*, where the young man's gradual ascent towards the Forms appears in
Diotima's doctrine to be quite solitary, the process of an orderly 'choral'
viewing of the Forms in the *Phaedrus* might indeed represent an experiment
on Plato's part to reimagine the potential of the chorus as an initiatory institution.[31] Thus, a subtle affirmation of choral practices as a mode of aesthetic
training and moulding might occur in this dialogue, but with a vision of
chorality that is far removed from Athenian reality, or, to put it another
way, wholly transferred to a world of fantasy.

The potential of a thoroughly reimagined and refashioned chorality is deftly
implied rather than explicitly articulated in Plato's celestial imagery, both in
the *Republic* and in the *Phaedrus*. In his last work, however, the *Laws*, the

---

[28] On *theoria* in this part of the *Phaedrus*, see Nightingale (2004: 157–68).

[29] On the imagery of the Athenian dithyramb in the *Phaedrus*, see Belfiore (2006: esp. 205–6),
who also makes other interesting associations with the broader area of drama. The suggestion
made here, however, is that, even in cases where familiar choral imagery could be evoked in
this passage of the *Phaedrus*, there is always a defamiliarizing aspect that turns Plato's
choral imaginary into a remarkable oddity.

[30] Perhaps Hom. *Il.* 23.1–16 can be used as a remote parallel to the chariot-chorus in the
Phaedrus.

[31] *Symp.* 210a–212a.

chorus is openly and extensively discussed as a constitutive cultural component of Magnesia, the imaginary colony to be established in the south of Crete
under the control of Knossos. While the three interlocutors, the Cretan
Cleinias, Megillus from Lacedaemon, and the anonymous Athenian, converse
about the proper principles and institutions with which to organize a new
polis, a wide range of choral matters arises, with particular emphasis in books
2 and 7. For instance, a clear definition of *choreia*, not encountered in any
other extant source from antiquity, is given in the second book of the *Laws*.
Choreia, the Athenian says, is the whole of dance (*orchêsis*) and song (*ôidê*)
and one without chorus-training (*achoreutos*) is a person with no education.[32]
Choreia thus emerges as fundamental for the education of young people, an
idea not to be found in any other Platonic dialogue, even though issues
relevant to the musical education of the young do come up in other dialogues.[33] The importance of choral training for the formation of what seems to
be the intersection of sensation and judgement is clearly articulated.[34] What is
clearly suggested is a well-ordered cultural system founded on a Spartan-
inspired model of three choruses, to be applied across-the-board based on
age-class (children, those under 30 years old, those between 30 and 60).[35]
Unlike Plato's *Republic*, which is preoccupied with the education of the
exclusive class of the guardians, the *Laws* embraces the whole of the community and explores the ways in which the 'correct' musical education becomes
the founding principle of all-participatory cultural practices, with the chorus
at their core. Here it is the entire polis, in its most inclusive manifestation, that
sings and dances. 'Every man and child, free and slave, female and male—
indeed the whole city', the Athenian says, 'should never cease chanting to (and
enchanting) the entire city, itself to itself, these things we have described,
which must in one way or another be continually changing, presenting variety
in every way, so that the singers will take insatiable desire and pleasure in their
hymns.'[36]

Do, then, the mimetic poetry and music expelled from the city of the
Republic gloriously return to the city of the *Laws*? One soon realizes that,
although the mimetic aspect of choral performance is explicitly acknowledged
and affirmed in the *Laws*, choral mimesis is to be practised and judged on
the basis of its essentially moral content. A principle of 'correctness' (*orthotês*)

---

[32] *Leg.* 654a–b.

[33] *Resp.* 386a–403c; *Prt.* 324d–328d. On issues of musical education in the *Republic* and in the
Laws, see Mouze (2005: 112–45, 222–42).

[34] *Leg.* 653a–d; 655a–b; 657b; 659d.

[35] *Leg.* 664c–d. On the three choruses, as well as on the fourth group, that of men over 60, see,
e.g., Morrow (1960: 315–18); Brisson and Pradeau (2007: 32–6); Panno (2007: 135–54); Calame
(2013).

[36] *Leg.* 665c, trans. Pangle (1980: 46), with modifications.

is supposed to determine any practice of *mousikê* in the polis. The all-encompassing chorality of Magnesia, practised by all ages and classes, is the result of a strict system of ideological and aesthetic control, where both content and form, as well as all technical and logistical details regarding the organization of musical competitions and performances, are well under the control of those who are considered to possess the proper experience and knowledge.[37] And, although the Athenian stipulates that the songs sung by the choruses be 'continually changing', the range of innovation allowed by the authorities seems to be limited. Not accidentally, in other parts of the *Laws* we learn that innovation, if not totally eliminated, should be limited, the ultimate model of unchanging musical perseverance being Egyptian musical culture.[38]

Why, then, does the chorus appear to be so dominant in the culture of the *Laws*, especially since, as we saw, it is only sporadically mentioned in the rest of Plato's works? The answer probably lies in the emphasis that Plato put, in his last dialogue, on culture as a decisive tool of manipulation and social cohesion.[39] The chorus, envisioned by Plato with all the restrictions mentioned above, emerges as a most effective vehicle of communal discipline, solidity, and stability, promoting and reproducing established ideological doctrines from and for the entire dancing and singing community. Above all, the all-participatory but well-controlled and immutable chorus of the *Laws* seems to function as the antipode of what Plato perceived to be the decline of Athenian musical culture, its *theatrocracy*—namely, a cultural regime where the audience dictates and encourages constant musical experimentation with the sole criterion of pleasure.[40]

ARISTOTELIAN DIVERSIONS

Was this vision of an enhanced chorality shared among other intellectuals in the fourth century? In the case of Aristotle, at least, the answer should probably be negative. Certainly, the surviving part of Aristotle's *Poetics* engages mainly (though not exclusively) with the tragic genre; thus one has to take into consideration his references to the tragic chorus in particular. Yet his overall approach to musical culture, as it emerges in the *Politics* as well, is quite different from Plato's, this difference affecting his views on the role and the function of the chorus.

---

[37] *Leg.* 655c–660a.   [38] On this issue, see, most recently, Rutherford (2013*b*).
[39] On the conceptualization of choral and social cohesion in the *Laws*, see especially Kurke (2013).
[40] *Leg.* 700–701b. On this issue, see Peponi (2013*b*).

Nonetheless, it is quite striking that in the Aristotelian quantitative divisions of tragedy every section of the play is defined in relation to the chorus's
dramatic presence. Tragedy's quantitative elements, Aristotle says, can be
listed as: prologue, episode, exodus, choral section (*chorikon*), the latter
appearing in its two versions, as the chorus's processional entrance into the
theatre (*parodos*) and as choral action in the *orchestra* (*stasimon*).[41] Furthermore, the *prologue*, Aristotle tells us, is the portion of tragedy that precedes the
choral entrance; an *episode* is an entire portion of tragedy between complete
choral odes; the *exodus* is the portion of tragedy that follows the *final choral
ode*.[42] Is this description, then, a sign of a still-surviving perception about the
key role of the chorus in tragedy? Or is the chorus used here as a mere
technical marker, as a punctuation device in the sequence of dramatic action?
Whether this labelling of the parts of tragedy reflects Aristotle's own taxonomical pursuits or a fourth-century BC theatrical vernacular is not possible
to say, yet one would be justified in imagining that, in the early stages of
the evolution of the genre, at the end of the sixth century BC and the beginning
of the fifth, such quantitative divisions would have reflected opposite trends.
The chorus would have been the all-pervasive agent, its musical action
punctuated by the intervention of individual agents in the form of chorus-
leaders (*exarchontes* or *choragoi*), eventually to morph into dramatic actors
(*hupokritai*).[43]

Likewise, Aristotle's qualitative approach to tragedy leaves open key questions regarding the role of the chorus. Certainly, the chorus is by implication
included in his famous definition of tragedy. 'Tragedy is a representation of an
action which is serious, complete, and of a certain magnitude', Aristotle says,
'*in language which is garnished* in various forms in the different parts'.[44]
Inasmuch as he defines *garnished* language as 'language that has rhythm and
melody', there is no question that Aristotle takes into account the chorus's
lyrics as essential parts of the tragic genre. The reader of this section of the
Poetics will soon see that verbal style and song-and-music (*lexis* and *melos*) are
considered the media of tragic mimesis and are listed along with plot structure
(*muthos*), character (*ethos*), reasoning (*dianoia*), and spectacle (*opsis*), all six
of them designated by Aristotle as the qualitative elements of the genre.

The chorus, therefore, is clearly addressed in Aristotle's *Poetics*, both as a
quantitative and as a qualitative constituent of the genre. If there is a problem
with Aristotle's theoretical treatment of the chorus in the *Poetics*, it is to be
found in the inadequate way in which he touches on what should be

---

[41] *Poet.* 1452ᵇ14–27.

[42] The English translation here relies heavily on Halliwell (1987: 43–4), emphasis added.

[43] On the evolution of the tragic genre from the *exarchontes* of the dithyramb, see *Poet.* 1449ª.
On the origins of Greek tragedy, see, e.g., Pickard-Cambridge (1962: 60–131) and Nagy (1990:
384–413).

[44] *Poet.* 1449ᵇ24–28, trans. Halliwell (1987: 37), emphasis added.

considered its role in the tragic play—namely, its chief dramatic function. Later on in the treatise Aristotle mentions that the chorus 'should be handled as one of the actors; it should form an integral part of the whole and should be actively involved—not as in Euripides but as in Sophocles'.[45] Given the philosopher's understanding of tragedy as a genre the essence of which lies predominantly in achieving structural faultlessness on the level of the 'arrangement of events', this quite opaque desideratum can be interpreted as Aristotle's way of restoring the chorus's role in the tragic play, which by his times was marginalized to performing musical interludes between the acts.[46]

Yet, even if the chorus is an integral part of the plot, thus participating in the dramatic action as one of the actors, the distinctive medium it employs differentiates its mode of participation from that of the actors. How, then, do the different 'garnishings' (*hêdusmata*) of tragedy, according to Aristotle's own vocabulary, achieve the main goal of the tragic play, which is *katharsis* through the arousal of pity and fear? In the case of the chorus, how does its marked musicality affect its dramatic, and by extension cathartic, effectiveness?

Without doubt, Aristotle was fully aware of the importance of this question. In his *Politics*, for instance, while discussing the general role of music in education and leisure, not only does he mention *katharsis* as one of the functions of music but he also seems to refer to the *Poetics* for a more extensive discussion of this subject.[47] Besides, the fact that pity and fear are mentioned, if parenthetically, in this passage of the *Politics* is quite indicative of the way Aristotle was thinking of issues relevant to both projects. The gap between the *Politics* and the *Poetics*, then, as far as the dramatic force of *melopoiia* (music and song-making) is concerned, could have been bridged by a discussion of the way in which song and music affect the audience's cognitive and emotional experience of dramatic structure in particular.[48] Yet, whether or not and in what way the medium of lyric song and music may function as an aesthetic catalyst (especially if the chorus actively participates in the plot as Aristotle suggests) remains unanswered in the surviving part of the *Poetics*.[49]

Nor can we know whether Aristotle touched on this issue elsewhere. That the chorus as a cultural formation still had deep roots in the social consciousness and, one may add, in the collective unconscious of the era in which

---

[45] *Poet.* 1456ª25–32, trans. Halliwell (1987: 52).

[46] The *embolima* are explicitly mentioned *Poet.* 1456ª29–32. For an extensive discussion of this broader issue, see Mastronarde (2010: 88–152).

[47] *Pol.* 1341ᵇ40. On this issue, see Kraut (1997: 209). See also Ford's extensive discussion of music and *katharsis* in the *Politics* in Ford (2004).

[48] On *melopoiia* as including both lyric song and music in the *Poetics*, see Halliwell (1986: 239–40). On the broader issue of pity and fear in the tragic chorus, see Visvardi (forthcoming).

[49] On the quite problematic status of the chorus in the *Poetics*, see Halliwell (1986: 238–52; 1987: 153–4).

Aristotle flourished seems to be quite certain. An under-explored area in classical scholarship is the way in which chorality appears as a metaphor or analogy in discussions and arguments not directly related to *mousikê*. In Aristotle's *Politics*, for instance, the chorus surfaces in handy examples used to illustrate concepts such as those of political virtue or excessive individual glamour. 'The goodness of all the citizens is not one and the same', Aristotle says, 'just as among the members of a chorus the skill of the head dancer is not the same as that of the subordinate leader'.[50] Elsewhere, a defence of the institution of ostracism for citizens who become exceedingly powerful prompts analogies from the realm of arts: 'Nor yet will a trainer of choruses allow a man who sings louder and more beautifully than the whole chorus to be a member of it,' Aristotle says.[51]

That Aristotle was well aware of the chorus's cultural pervasiveness is precisely what makes the lack of any explicit reference to the chorus in the sections of the *Politics* that are expressly dedicated to *mousikê* even more remarkable. What underlies this silence is a cultural vision that is located at the other extreme from Plato's last dialogue. As we saw earlier, the *Laws* propounds an all-encompassing and all-participatory civic *choreia*, transcending gender, age, and class divisions. By contrast, Aristotle's *Politics* seems to advocate a polis where the pleasure of music is to be enjoyed by a musically sensitive, yet generally non-performing, audience, with performance to be handed over to people of lower standing.[52] The surviving works of the fourth century BC, then, leave us with two major philosophers struggling against an over-theatrical musical culture that encourages what they conceive to be vulgar pleasure. While the former looks for the antidote in a chorally hyperactive city that sings and dances under the auspices of political and cultural authorities, the latter strives for a complete separation between professional performers and an audience of citizens, a separation that does not seem to provide enough room for a vibrant and pivotal civic *choreia*.

POST-CLASSICAL MOMENTS

Extant theoretical or critical thought about the chorus after the fourth century BC is sparse. This is not to be attributed to a total eclipse of choral performances. On the contrary, a wide variety of literary sources, in both prose and poetry, along with epigraphic material, indicate that choruses kept performing, in one form or another, all over the Hellenistic and Graeco-Roman

---

[50] *Pol.* 1277^{a}12–13, trans. Rackham (1932: 189), slightly modified.
[51] *Pol.* 1284^{b}11–13, trans. Rackham (1932), slightly modified.
[52] See esp. *Pol.* 1339^{a}27–b10 and 1340^{b}20–1341^{b}33. On this issue, see also Peponi (2013*b*).

world.[53] Yet newer discourses about cultural phenomena are more likely to flourish when the phenomena themselves are important to current ideologies and trends. One wonders whether over these centuries the civic chorus instead survived largely as a vehicle of tradition, a default and perfunctory institution to be practised by various local communities. If this is true, then Plato's ideal of a traditional and fundamentally unchangeable civic *choreia* might have ended up being the predominant way the institution survived, musical experimentations and true cultural debate having been transferred to other performance genres. One of these genres was the pantomime, an art form that became particularly popular in the Roman Empire between the first century BC and the second century AD, but with roots that can be traced back to the fourth century BC in Greece and with numerous signs that it persisted in the East well into the sixth century AD.[54] Pantomimic performance regularly involved a remarkably skilled solo dancer *and* a singing chorus, the latter apparently serving merely as the canvas on which the silent dancer, the centrepiece of the performance, enacted a rich repertoire often drawn from Greek poetry, principally tragedy.[55] While the mimetic priorities of the pantomimic genre are evident in the term *pantomimos* (meaning the one who 'mimics' everything and originally referring to the dancer himself), it is worth noting that on a morphological level the genre juxtaposes and at the same time splits the vocal and the kinetic components, the two components that Greek *choreia* traditionally combined in a variety of forms.[56]

Can, then, pantomime performance be seen, partly at least, as evolving from a culture pervaded for centuries by the various forms of *choreia*? Or can *choreia* be seen as having morphed in some way or another into pantomime dance? Instead of just emphasizing the undeniable divergences between the two performance genres, it might be worth considering their possible points of intersection and especially the way aesthetic and, more generally, ideological discourses about the former might have been transfused into discourses about the latter. Since older discourses on the dance component of *choreia*, likely to have emerged in the fifth and fourth centuries BC, are lost to us, it is not easy to

---

[53] For choral performances as described and discussed in post-classical times and especially in the imperial period, see Bowie (2006: 61–92), who discusses issues of reception of the earlier choral tradition in later authors and references to their contemporary choral practices. See also Rutherford's extensive discussion of the dithyramb and discourses about the genre at Rome in Rutherford (2013*a*).

[54] Lada-Richards (2007: 19–25). Slaney, Chapter 6, this volume, considers the possible influence of pantomime on Seneca's chorus.

[55] Lada-Richards (2007: 32–7). For solo singers accompanying pantomimic dance, see Lada-Richards (2007: 42 and n. 23). For explicit evidence on the presence of the singing chorus in pantomimic performances, see Lucian *Salt.* 63 and Lib. *Or.* 64, paras 87, 88, 91–3, 95–7.

[56] The term regularly used in Greek texts for the pantomimic dancer was the unmarked term *orchêstês* (dancer), *pantomimus* being the term used in Latin. See Molloy (1996: 81–5) and esp. Lucian *Salt.* 67.

trace a shared conceptual apparatus between such discourses and later discourses on pantomime dancing. Yet there are several instances in both
Lucian's *On Dance* and later in Libanius' *On the Dancers* that seem to be in
explicit or implicit dialogue or even debate with at least one inherited tradition, the origins of which we are actually able to identify: Plato's works. In
Lucian's treatise, for instance, behind Crato's detestation for the pantomime
dancer as the 'girlish fellow who plays the wanton with dainty clothing and
bawdy songs and imitates love sick minxes . . .', it is possible to sense Plato's
anxieties when discussing the morally proper dancing postures and melodies
in the *Laws* and asking whether a manly person and a cowardly one would
represent a fictive character beset by troubles with the same verbal utterances
and dancing postures.[57]

Similarly, in Libanius' remarkably emphatic assertion that 'dancing is not
made complete by songs, rather it is for the sake of dancing that the songs are
worked out' one might see more than just the obvious fact that in pantomime
performances the kinetic component was more important than the vocal
one.[58] In fact, a deeper conflict between the tradition underlying Libanius'
argument and the Platonic vision of an idealized *choreia*, where the kinetic
component essentially depends on the verbal one, may be at work here.[59] In
actual choral practices of the archaic and the classical periods issues concerning the relationship between the kinetic and the verbal were probably handled
in a less ideological and more empirical manner. According to Athenaeus, for
instance, Aeschylus was personally involved not only in the choreography but
also in the training of his choruses, a practice that may indicate established
ideas both about the inextricability of the verbal and the kinetic and about the
ad hoc adaptability of either one to the other.[60] Furthermore, remarks such as
the one also by Athenaeus regarding Telesis or Telestes, Aeschylus' dancer,
who was apparently able to make clear the action of the *Seven against Thebes*
simply by dancing, regardless of the accuracy of their details, indicate that a
discussion about the relationship between the verbal and the kinetic and the
priority of either one to the other was likely to have had deep roots well into
the fifth century BC.[61] Interestingly, Plutarch, who also engages with this issue
in the ninth book of his *Table Talk*, quotes lines from a *hyporchema* he

---

[57] Lucian *Salt.* 2 and *Leg.* 654e–655a. Not accidentally, Crato is soon explicitly to mention
Plato, along with Chrysippus and Aristotle (*Salt.* 2).

[58] Lib. *Or.* 64.88 in Molloy's translation ad loc. It should also be noted that Libanius' oration
poses as a refutation of a (now lost) work by Aelius Aristides (Lib. *Or.* 64.4–5), in which the latter
might have been engaged as well in the discussion about the relationship between the verbal and
the kinetic components in pantomime dancing and possibly in Greek dance in general. See also
Molloy (1996: 86–7). On various aspects of pantomime dancing see Hall and Wyles (2008) and
Webb (2008).

[59] On the kinetic component being essentially dependent on the verbal one, see esp. *Leg.* 816a.

[60] Ath. *Deipn.*1.21e, with explicit reference to Chamaeleon as his source.

[61] Ath. *Deipn.* 1.21f–22a. On this issue, see, e.g., Lawler (1954: 155–6); Golder (1996: 2–3).

attributes to Pindar in order to illustrate the intense osmotic action between poetry and dance, so that the 'two arts taken together effect a single work'.[62]

If we can trust such evidence, we might be moving closer to early models of *choreia*, in which an established and unaltered priority of the verbal over the kinetic is indeed questioned. Those priorities most likely were alternating both in actual choral training and in the way different types of choral performances were perceived by their audiences and theorized in intellectual circles. In this case, views developed in the era of pantomime dancing, such as the one reflected in Libanius' discussion, might have been closer than is usually thought to the ones developed in the golden era of Greek *choreia*, despite the undeniable differences between the two genres.

An exegetic vernacular intermixed with anecdotes about all things to do with performances, including choral performance, is likely to have arisen throughout antiquity. To what extent such lore might have imbued (now mostly lost) treatises of cultural history that were later used by intellectual figures such as Athenaeus and Plutarch is, of course, hard to say. In the works of both one encounters numerous useful and revealing pieces of information relevant to the broader area of Greek chorality, such as the ones just mentioned, but they are often disconnected and sometimes unassimilated.[63] One can perhaps find more substantial evidence about modes of understanding and conceptualizing Greek choral poetry and performance in two other distinctive types of discourse, the usually brief scholia and the extensive treatises on literary style.

Given that most of the scholia (explanatory comments written on the margins or between the lines of texts) extend from a couple of words to a couple of sentences, they are by definition sketchy. Still, they often seem to reflect inherited or current interpretative tendencies and as such they occasionally represent conflicting approaches. In this regard it is worth mentioning the two different sets of scholia, both dating from the first century AD, on Alcman's Louvre *Partheneion*, the oldest surviving piece of Greek choral poetry from the seventh century BC. *Scholia A* are written by three different hands in the intercolumnar spaces and the margins of the Louvre papyrus that preserves the poem, whereas *Scholia B*, though fragmented, are clearly part of a full running commentary.[64] Some divergences between the two sets of scholia indicate varying interpretations of key words, which have prompted quite substantial conflicts in modern scholarship as well. For instance, the two different meanings of the word *pelêades* in line 60, whether *doves* or the cluster

---

[62] *Quaest. Conv.* 748a–c, trans. Sandbach (1961: 295). See also Lawler (1954); Lada-Richards (2007: 26).

[63] For a discussion of Plutarch's references to *choreia*, see Bowie (2006).

[64] For the scholia on Alcman's *Partheneion*, see more recently Tsantsanoglou (2006). For discussion of some of the interpretative problems in Alcman's Louvre *Partheneion*, see Budelmann, Chapter 5, this volume.

of the *Pleiades*, drastically change one's whole understanding of both the poem's semantic nexus and the role of the choral agents within it.[65] More importantly, a remarkable interest not only in the meaning of specific words but also in the poem's original setting as an actual performance can be seen in some of *Scholia A*, where one of the scholiasts seems to be commenting on possible successive alternations of both the performing choral speaker(s) and their manner of oral delivery in different sections of the poem.[66] The existence or lack of such alternations affects one's whole perception of issues relevant to choral mimesis and choral identity in early performance practices. But it is an open question whether these issues were ever explicitly addressed and discussed by ancient scholars as broader theoretical problems rather than just as ad hoc exegetical remarks.

In this regard, the scholia on Pindar's epinician odes are revealing. The vigorous debate within classical scholarship in the last decades about the identity attached to the first-person singular, which often appears in the Pindaric odes, has raised broader issues pertaining to the representation of the 'self' in ancient lyric poetry as well as to notions of genre in antiquity and the way these might affect modes of performance. The basic question behind these much broader issues is whether one should understand several obscure first-person singular utterances in Pindar as referring to the poet himself or to a performing chorus. The answer to the question affects our understanding of the odes as choral or monodic pieces.[67] Interestingly, the Pindaric scholia often reflect a similar uncertainty as to who the speaker of the odes might be, but at the same time they display a remarkable flexibility. We find phrases such as 'the speech is of the chorus or of the poet' and in a few cases the issue is addressed in more detail.[68] For instance, in the beginning of the second strophe of *Nemean 1* (ll. 20–4) a first-person singular voice says: 'And I have taken my stand [*estan*] at the courtyard gates of a generous host as I sing [*melpomenos*] of noble deeds, where a fitting feast has been arranged for me, for this home is not unfamiliar with frequent visitors from abroad.'[69] The scholiast thinks that 'it is uncertain whether this is the poet or the chorus. The chorus could say this properly on its own [*kuriôs . . . eph' heautou*] but Pindar could also say this metaphorically'.[70] In a couple of other cases the scholiast suggests the possibility of a shifting identity behind the first-person utterances

---

[65] On this issue and for further bibliography, see, e.g., Calame (1977b: 72 n. 52; 1983: 313, 331–2); more recently, Ferrari (2008: esp. 77–103).

[66] Tsantsanoglou (2006: esp.11–12).

[67] On this issue, see, e.g., Lefkowitz (1963, 1991); Heath (1988); Burnett (1989); Carey (1991); Heath and Lefkowitz (1991); Morgan (1993); D'Alessio (1994).

[68] See, e.g., *Σ Pyth.* 5.96a, *Pyth.* 6.1a. In other cases, such as schol. *Ol.* 9.11a and *Ol.* 9.163b, the option refers to a second-person addressee, being either the chorus or the poet himself.

[69] Trans. Race (1997: 7).

[70] Schol. *Nem.*1.29a.

within the same ode, sometimes referring to the poet, other times to the chorus.[71] One wonders, then, whether in the Pindaric scholia this overall openness to ambiguity is the result of simple uncertainty on the part of the scholiasts, as it often sounds, or a sign of an existing and much broader interpretative agenda. Since the scholia seem to be unconcerned about whether an individual or a collective speaker might affect the generic taxonomy of the odes, the question is rather whether such an interpretative agenda would have ever engaged in broader questions about the mimetic and rhetorical diversity of the first-person speaker in Pindar's odes and the way such diversity would be communicated to an audience in performance.

On the whole, a critical question concerning ancient Greek scholarship on the chorus is the extent to which choral texts were contemplated in their three-dimensional potential. A chorus in actual performance brings up parameters that one would tend to ignore when preoccupied with a written choral text. Quite a few poetic passages, for instance, suggest that choral voices, joined in a unified and evidently loud whole, added to the visual impact of the chorus a profound auditory experience further stimulated by the rhythmical noise of many dancing feet hitting the ground. Even when not seen, that is, choruses echo, their echoes repeatedly described in poetic texts as reverberating and resounding all over.[72] Recent scholarship has shown persuasively how acoustics affected the very formation of a performing chorus in the history of the ever-popular dithyramb. The harshness of the sibilant sound 's' and the natural difficulty it presented for a large chorus in synchronizing its pronunciation was better handled in a wide circular choral formation facing inwards towards the pipe-player (aulete) than in a linear one. Apparently resolved in this effective way by Lasus in the sixth century BC, this issue was mentioned in various treatises throughout antiquity.[73]

How extensively and systematically such technical and theoretical issues regarding the chorus were discussed in ancient treatises is not clear. Still, issues of choral acoustics emerge unexpectedly in discourses of popularized wisdom, such as the pseudo-Aristotelian *Problems*. To the question 'why the voice of drunken people is more broken than that of sober people', the answer of the Aristotelian speaker is that 'they break their voice quickly because they are filled', the evidence being drawn from the realm of performance: 'For neither choruses nor actors practise after breakfast, but when fasting,' the speaker says, so, 'as people are fuller when drunk, it is reasonable that they break their voices more'.[74] Choral training provides here a common field of reference, as shared lore. Representative of such tendencies is the following question: 'Why, when

---

[71] Schol. *Nem.* 7.123a.

[72] See, e.g., Hes. *Theog.* 38–42; Sappho 44V.24–34; Alcaeus 130bV.17–20; Pind. *Ol.*10.76–7.

[73] On this fascinating issue, see D'Angour (1997).

[74] [Arist.] *Pr.* 11.46, trans. Mayhew (2011: 389).

the *orchestra* is covered with straw, are choruses less able to be heard?', to which the answer is given that the voice in this case strikes rough, less unified ground. 'For it is not continuous,' the Aristotelian speaker says, 'just as the light too shines more on smooth surfaces because it is not interrupted by impediments'.[75] Such examples, drawn from palpable everyday experience, imply a vivid and culturally infiltrating choral world to which one could handily refer to clarify otherwise abstract and quite complex notions.

Such a world of choral sounds and echoes, reflecting in various ways accustomed contact with the somatic presence of performing choruses, seems to be missing from treatises of literary criticism that nevertheless show profound interest in the acoustics of verbal compositions. Since treatises such as Longinus' *On the Sublime* and Plutarch's on *How to Study Poetry* do not provide extensive discussion of choral works, we will conclude this chapter with the first-century BC literary critic Dionysius of Halicarnassus while also quoting an actual choral piece. Dionysius' treatise *On Literary Composition* is a representative instance of ancient criticism's interest in describing and classifying arrangements of the different phonetic qualities of vowels and consonants. Structure in this case is studied not as relating to the sequence of represented events, as Aristotle had put it in the *Poetics*, but to the sequence of individual words, their interlacing perceived as creating different sonorities, in turn affecting an author's mode of signification. In aspiring to this type of literary analysis, Dionysius' critical thought moves freely across discourses generically diverse, such as poetry, oratory, historiography, and philosophy. When he discusses what he calls the 'polished' style, for instance, he examines sonorousness in the arrangement of words in Sappho's poetry and in Isocrates' speeches.[76] For the 'austere' style, he analyses passages from both Pindar and Thucydides.[77] The 'austere' style, Dionysius says, is not at all florid; it is magnanimous, outspoken, unadorned. Words stand firmly on their own feet and occupy strong positions; parts of the sentence shall be at considerable distances from one another, separated by perceptible intervals; harsh and dissonant collocations do happen; grammatical sequence can be neglected; the construction of the length of the various periods has no concern for the speaker's breath.[78] Dionysius illustrates this with the beginning of a dithyramb by Pindar (fr. 75 M):

> Come join our chorus, Olympians [*Deut' en choron Olympioi*],   1
> and send over it glorious grace, you gods
> who are coming to the city's crowded, incense-rich navel

---

[75] [Arist.] *Pr.* 11.25, trans. Mayhew (2011: 371).
[76] Dion. Hal. *Comp.* 23.
[77] Dion. Hal. *Comp.* 22.
[78] All references to Dionysius' analysis are taken from the English translation of his treatise by Usher (1985).

in holy Athens
and to the glorious, richly adorned agora.   5
Receive wreaths of plaited violets and the songs
plucked in springtime,
and look upon me [*idete*] with favour as I proceed from Zeus
with splendour of songs secondly
to that ivy-knowing god,
whom we mortals call Bromios and Eriboas   10
as we sing of the offspring of the highest of fathers
and of Kadmeian women.
Like a seer, I do not fail to notice the clear signs,
when, as the chamber of the purple-robed Horai is opened,
the nectar-bearing flowers bring in the sweet-smelling spring.   15
Then, then, upon the immortal earth are cast
The lovely tresses of violets, and roses are fitted to hair
And voices of songs echo to the accompaniment of pipes
And choruses come to Semele of the circling headband.[79]

Dionysius expresses confidence that everybody 'with moderately well-developed literary sensibility' can attest 'that these lines are powerful, robust and dignified and possess much austerity'. They are 'rough and harsh upon the ear, but not excessively so', he continues. It is not possible to go through his close reading of the entire Pindaric quotation, yet his analysis of the first line is representative of his overall approach to this choral piece:

The first clause consists of four parts of speech—a verb [*deute*] a connective [*en*], and two appellatives [*choron, Olympioi*]. Now the verb [*deute*] and the connective [*en*] have produced a not unpleasing combination by mingling and fusing together; but the juxtaposition of the appellative [*choron*] and the connective [*en*] has produced a junction of considerable roughness, for the words *en choron* are dissonant and not melodious, since the connective ends with the semivowel *n*, while the appellative begins with the voiceless consonant *ch*. These letters cannot by their nature be combined and united, for it is not natural to *n* to precede *ch* in the same syllable. Hence, when they form the boundaries between successive syllables, they do not produce a continuous sound, but there is bound to be a pause between the two letters, and this keeps their sounds distinct. That, then, is how the first clause is roughened by the arrangement of its words.[80]

Certainly, this analysis displays fascinating attention to the phonetic texture of words.[81] But, while thoroughly absorbed by the sonorous effects of words

---

[79] Trans. Race (1997).

[80] Trans. Usher (1985: 177). His 'melodious', however, should read '*not* melodious' (*ouk euepes*); the typographical error is corrected in my quotation.

[81] On Dionysius' approach to the sound of language in the broader context of similar interests in antiquity, see Porter (2010: esp. 235–48). On the broader ideological parameters and the normative aesthetics of Dionysius of Halicarnassus, see the extensive monograph by Wiater

throughout this choral poem, including the mere word *choros* in the first line, does Dionysius' reader sense how Pindar's *choros* emerges throughout these lines as a vibrant and electrifying communal organism? For it is not just the words' sonorities that are a key to the acoustics of this poem, but the entire synaesthetic network that creates an exuberant scene whereby the chorus calls attention to its own corporeal presence. In a crescendo of sensual associations—choral sounds and sights blurred with the sights and fragrances of a blooming spring—this chorus begs to be seen and heard. Such synaesthetic voluptuousness, freely mingling singing voices, the sound of pipes, and tresses adorned with sweet-smelling flowers, could regularly be achieved by the Greek chorus when it flourished as a living cultural entity. No amount of later literary analysis or theorizing could hope to capture the reality of such total events.

(2011: esp. 226–77). On physicality in Greek lyric poetry (both monodic and choral), see E. Jones (forthcoming).

2

The Greek Chorus: Our German Eyes

Simon Goldhill

This chapter poses an apparently simple question: what is the influence of German Idealist thinking on the modern conceptualization of the chorus? It is a question that immediately spreads in several directions, however. First, it proposes to investigate an intellectual history, not just of how a group of influential German thinkers reflected on the chorus of Greek tragedy as a dramatic form, but also of how this theoretical reflection takes shape between tragedy and opera, word and music, the self and politics. The interest in the ancient Greek chorus is an enquiry not so much into ancient performance models, as into modern ideas of the self, action, and the state. Second, we need to investigate how the philosophical writing of the German Idealists also informed theatrical performance traditions (which will again need a detour through opera). Hegel never saw a performance of an ancient tragedy; by the end of the century, when Hegel's writing on tragedy had become a major influence on writers such as A. C. Bradley, reconstructions of Greek tragedy had become part of the cutting edge of modern drama. The increasing influence of German Idealist writing on tragedy is coextensive with the reinvention of tragedy on the modern stage.[1] Third, Schlegel in particular, often in the most jejune form, entered not just the higher levels of criticism but also school textbooks, and handbooks for outreach lectures in working men's educational institutions. Writing the history of the influence of German Idealist thought also requires a careful recognition of how it was popularized as well as debated; debased as well as lauded.

A more developed version of these arguments is published in Goldhill (2012). Thanks to the editors and Miriam Leonard for helpful discussion, and to Josh Billings and Constanze Güthenke for fruitful interactions on this topic.

[1] See Flashar (1991); Hall and Macintosh (2005).

ESTABLISHING A FRAMEWORK

There are four elements of background that are essential to pursuing such a project. The first concerns the status of tragedy within the tradition of German Idealist philosophy. The tyranny of Greece over the German imagination throughout the nineteenth century is well known.[2] For the generation after Kant, the thinkers who had such an impact on the continuing intellectual and political life not just of Germany but of the whole of Europe—Schelling, the Schlegel brothers, and, above all, Hegel, along with the self-consciously rene-gade Schopenhauer, and his two most passionate readers, Wagner and Nietzsche—Greek tragedy held a uniquely privileged place even within their philhellenic idealism. Greek tragedy was the supreme art form. What is more, tragedy was integral to the *philosophical system* of each of these writers, and each lavished many pages on it as a genre.[3] Tragedy revealed something essential about conflict within the world, and, above all, about the *Sittlichkeit*, the ethical self-positioning, of human actors within the world. And within the supreme art form, integral to philosophical system, Sophocles stood at the apex. The discussion of the chorus of Sophocles takes place always within this framework: and the chorus thus carries a heavy load within such philosophical schemas.

The second background narrative concerns the political. Tragedy prompted a debate around inner freedom and external necessity, and this was not just an aesthetic or philosophical issue, but played directly into the political under-standing of the period. The era I am discussing is mapped by the fixed beacons of 1789, 1848, and 1914. Through these political upheavals, there is a changing sense of what community, the crowd, the collective, the voice of the people, can mean, and this dynamic inevitably affects the conceptualization of the chorus, not just by virtue of a potential politicization of its group dynamics, but also, and perhaps more stridently, by virtue of the insistent impact of ideals of the freedom of the individual on the understanding of the heroes of tragedy in relation to the chorus.[4] How does the celebration of *das Volk* in national history relate to the chorus as the voice of the people? When we turn, say, to Reinhardt's celebrated production of *Oedipus Tyrannus* at the begin-ning of the twentieth century, where the massed ranks of his chorus were perceived both as a discomforting manifestation of the 'primitive', 'ritual' crowd and as a precursor of Nazi rallies, it is important to recognize that

---

[2] See E. Butler (1935); also Silk and Stern (1981); Morrison (1986); Gossman (1994); Potts (1994); Marchand (1996); Lincoln (1999); D. Schmidt (2001); Gildenhard and Ruehl (2003); Goldhill (2011: ch. 4).

[3] For exemplary discussions with further bibliography, see Pillau (1981); Silk and Stern (1981); D. Schmidt (2001).

[4] See McLellan (1969); Nauen (1971); Kain (1982); Ritter (1982); Beckman (1999); Moggach (2006); each with further bibliography.

there is a long history behind this moment, a history of how the representation of the chorus in public culture enters a domain of politics. When I say that the chorus goes to the heart of modern ideas of the self, action, and the state, it is because the chorus is conceptualized within this broad political framework.

The third narrative concerns performance and the parallel medium of opera. The history of the performance of Greek tragedy is wholly intertwined with the history of opera. From Monteverdi to Wagner, opera has seen itself as the reinvention of Greek tragedy, and the modern performance of tragedy repeatedly draws on opera for its performance tradition.[5] Throughout the nineteenth century, opera was a battleground for modernist aesthetics and politics, and it made the chorus a centrepiece for debates about what modern theatre should be—just as the same debates were taking place in drama itself, starting with Schiller's *Bride of Messina*. Yet the chorus of the Idealist philosophers was not easy to put onstage, and was not easy for an audience to see. The tension between the intellectual conceptualization of the chorus and its staging in performance becomes central to its reception. The chorus in performance in opera and theatre became a battleground of what modernity itself is.

The fourth background brings together two unlikely bedfellows: first, the opposition of words and music, and, second, religion. Here, Schopenhauer, and his influence on Wagner and Nietzsche, are crucial. Schopenhauer argues that music reaches a truth of meaning that mere words cannot:

The internal relation that music has to the true nature of all things can also explain the fact that, when music suitable to any scene, action, event, or environment is played, it seems to disclose to us its utmost secret meaning and appears to be the most accurate and distinct commentary on it.[6]

This credo is quoted and discussed at length by both Nietzsche and Wagner.[7] So, is it the music or the words of the chorus that reach the truth of commentary that the Idealist philosophers seek? How, then, is this argument about the truth of music related to religion? Most simply put, because of the role of the oratorio and the chorale and community choirs within the church.[8] Schelling and Schopenhauer found in the Mass the trace of ancient musical ideals— while the church itself struggled both with its classical heritage and its antipathy to grand music obscuring the truth of the word of god. Wagner's search for the perfect music drama self-consciously set his project against what he saw as the bourgeois oratorios of Mendelssohn. The search for the musical

---

[5] See Brown and Ograjenšek (2010) (with further bibliography).

[6] Schopenhauer (1958: i. 262).

[7] Nietzsche (1956: 98–101).

[8] For a stimulating discussion of the immediate eighteenth-century precursors, see Hamilton (2008). I have learned here from the work of Josh Billings, well represented in Chapter 8 in this volume. For the exemplary story of the specific rediscovery of the Matthew Passion of Bach, see Geck (1967).

essence of the chorus became a pressing question in part in relation to Schopenhauer's and Wagner's search for absolute musical experience, in part in relation to the burgeoning practice of choral performance in contemporary society.[9] How, in short, did the Greek chorus relate to the choirs all around in Victorian civic life?[10]

ESTABLISHING THE CASE

Now, these four background narratives intertwine in fascinating ways, and I have only given the briefest of outlines for each, but they are essential framings for my central questions. There is certainly no space here for a full doxographical account of the German Idealist approach to the chorus. Rather, I want to emphasize certain main lines of argument in which the problem of the chorus is formed.

Let me begin with a general observation, which is fundamental but quite unnoticed by commentators.[11] The chorus is integral to Idealist thinking on tragedy, but in the hundreds of pages by Hegel on tragedy barely a dozen treat the chorus. Schlegel is the most quoted authority throughout the nineteenth century. He writes no more than two pages on the chorus. Schelling similarly has but a couple of pages in his lengthy discussions of tragedy. Even Nietzsche barely discusses the form of the tragic chorus. The chorus is profoundly central but barely discussed. How can this be so? The bluntest answer is that the overwhelming interest of all these philosophers is on the individual—the individual, that is, as a moral agent, as a site of moral conflict, and as a political figure: the hero's *Sittlichkeit*. And, as Schelling states paradigmatically, the individual is 'the negation of the larger group'.[12]

Schelling is exemplary of how the chorus is marginalized by the focus on the individual. For Schelling, the 'innermost spirit of Greek tragedy'[13] is located in the struggle and fate of the hero. It is in the hero that we perceive the tension between inner freedom and the external necessity that sums up why tragedy is such a powerful representation of the *Sittlichkeit* of humans. 'This is the most sublime idea and the greatest victory of freedom: voluntarily to bear the

---

[9] Smither (1977–2000: iv).

[10] The historian Droysen, whom we will meet later, wrote that the oratorio 'belongs not only to art and its history, rather, as the true purpose of art can only be, to the community, to the nation [*das Volk*]' ('Deutsche Oper in Paris', *Berliner Allgemeine Musikalische Zeitung*, 6 (1829), 205).

[11] The only discussion of the chorus in this light is Silk (1998). See the work of Billings, Chapter 8, and Güthenke, Chapter 3, this volume.

[12] Schelling (1989: 69).

[13] Schelling (1989: 254).

punishment for an unavoidable transgression in order to manifest his freedom precisely in the loss of that very same freedom, and to perish amid a declaration of free will.'[14] For Schelling, the individual hero is the *only* location of such moral sublimity: 'This is also the only genuinely *tragic* element in tragedy'.[15] The hero achieves his sublime state by calmly bearing the disasters fate sends him, and it must be *necessity* and not mere bad luck or misfortune that faces him:

The hero of tragedy, one who nonetheless calmly bears all the severity and capriciousness of fate heaped upon his head, represents for just that reason that particular *essential nature* or unconditioned and absolute in his person ... It is essential that the hero be victorious only through that which is not an effect of nature or chance, and hence only through inner character or disposition, as is always the case with Sophocles.[16]

Sophocles is the perfect example of tragedy because of his focus on the individual hero and his travails. The chorus, therefore, is secondary; it sets the hero in a more idealistic, more symbolic light. The chorus responds to the hero, but, because it anticipates the spectator's own reaction, it also blocks the spectator from a free response, but rather encourages through art a higher form of reflection in the audience:

The chorus acquired the function of anticipating what went on in the spectator, the emotional movement, the participation, the reflection, and thus in this respect, too, did not allow the spectator to be free, but rather arrested him entirely through art. To a large extent the chorus represents objectivized reflection accompanying the action.[17]

By displaying its own pain, the chorus mitigates the audience's pain, and reaches a calmer, more serene reflection of the hero's condition: 'the spectator was guided toward more serene reflection and thereby relieved, as it were, of the feeling of pain by that feeling being placed into an object and presented there as already mitigated'.[18] The chorus is thus primarily *functional*. It is a device to enable the audience to reach a more serene reflection of the hero: it is a glass through which our perspective is focused. The chorus is integral to tragedy, but only in so far as it mediates the crucial relationship between the spectator and the hero. As Schiller puts it, by blocking passion 'the chorus restores to us our freedom'.[19]

Such generalizations about the chorus can be paralleled throughout German Idealist thinking. One consequence of such generalizations about the individual and the chorus is that it is hard to find in any of the Idealist philosophers any description of any specific chorus in any particular play.

---

[14] Schelling (1989: 254).   [15] Schelling (1989: 254).
[16] Schelling (1989: 89).   [17] Schelling (1989: 259).   [18] Schelling (1989: 260).
[19] Schiller (1841: 13). On Schiller, see Billings, Chapter 8, this volume, and Barone (2004: esp. 164–205).

There are barely any analyses either of individual odes or of the action of any chorus within a play. *A* chorus is of minimal concern, only *the* chorus deserves attention.

It is in this light that we should look at the most famous, most quoted, and least comprehended generalization about the chorus, Schlegel's 'That is, the chorus is an idealized spectator'.[20] It is a phrase that has launched a hundred essays, and many hundreds of sniffy comments: it is cited in handbook after handbook. But it is rarely understood. Notice first it is a restatement of what has preceded it: 'That is,' it begins. What has preceded it? The assertion that the chorus represents 'first the common mind of the nation, then the general sympathy of all mankind'.[21] That is, what makes the chorus an ideal spectator is first of all its rootedness in *national* thinking, and second the relation of this national thinking to a more universal *human sympathy*. The representation of general 'human sympathy' is predicated on the ability of the chorus to 'incorporate statements' of the poet, who speaks 'as a spokesman of the whole human race'[22]—the well-known (self-)promotion of the Romantic artist as a spokesman for mankind. Behind this appeal to the universal lies a nationalism, however. Schlegel is full of nationalist fervour throughout his lectures, which end with an appeal to the unity of his audience as Germans. He is assertive that there is an especial affinity of Germans to the highest art form, tragedy, because of the 'peculiar character of the nation', its 'German national features'. There is something especially *vaterländisch* about the chorus.

What makes the chorus ideal, then, is its ability to represent something uniquely Greek (which will be especially appreciated by the German nation, its descendants). The chorus is not an idealized spectator because it watches and gets things right. It is idealized because it links the *Geist* of the national character with the profundity of poetic authority. Schlegel is not saying that the chorus simply gets things right, and serenely watches, and thereby tells us how to react. Rather, he is contributing to what he thinks an ideal engagement with art looks like, an engagement from a nationalist perspective that finds in tragedy an authoritative statement about the world. The chorus for Schlegel is a 'personified reflection of the action';[23] as with Schelling, it has the function of 'elevat[ing the real spectator] to the region of contemplation'.[24] It does so by virtue of its national and universal sentiment: it is this that makes it ideal, within an ideal model of tragedy. He offers an ideal chorus to explore our artistic ideals, not to describe the genre of Greek tragedy comprehensively.

Here, then, is my first conclusion: the chorus is discussed in the most lapidary form in the German Idealist tradition, and is discussed primarily as

---

[20] Schlegel (1846: 70). Sometimes *idealisierte*, 'idealized', is translated 'ideal', which aids miscomprehension.
[21] Schlegel (1846:, 69–70).   [22] Schlegel (1846: 69–70).
[23] Schlegel (1846: 66).   [24] Schelling (1989: 260).

an ideal form, separate from any performance and separate from any particular chorus and without reference to any particular set of choral stanzas. The focus on the individual hero as the locus of tragic conflict and ethical or political freedom repeatedly reduces the chorus to a functional role in constructing this focus. The functional role establishes the chorus primarily as a mediator between the spectators and the heroes, rather than as figures in dialogue with the heroes. Its role is to raise the spectators to a level of profound reflection. This generalized chorus will reappear often in later discussions, both in the intellectual tradition of scholarship on tragedy and in the theatrical tradition. But, because the chorus is conceptualized in such a generalized form, when it comes to the instantiations of the model in the messiness of specific performance, what the audience repeatedly recognizes is the gap between the model and what is embodied onstage. From this dynamic, the 'problem of the chorus' onstage takes shape. Simply put, the more ideal the chorus in the imagination, the less satisfying the real chorus onstage is likely to be.

THE INWARDNESS OF MUSIC AND DANCE

My second and briefer set of questions concerns music and dance, media that are integral to the chorus in performance and in conception. My first section focused at one level on how the chorus becomes a problem for modernity by virtue of its collectivity: how can the community be represented? What is the value of the community's mediation of individual striving, and what wisdom is encapsulated in the reflection of the group? Music and dance form the second great problem for modernity's thinking on the chorus. As productions of Greek tragedy come to be staged with more regularity, the chorus becomes the most vexing difficulty for directors and audiences alike, a difficulty not just of the conceptualization of the collective onstage but its very form of performance and voice: singing and music, or chant, or speech? Dance, rhythmic movement, or stillness? Collective singing and speaking, or individual voices? How can the intimacy and personal violence of the exchanges of tragedy be played out in front of an apparently inactive group of spectators, constantly onstage?

The intellectual background to these issues is no less rooted in Idealist philosophy. Perhaps the key term, linking the theory of music, the tragic, and performance, is *das Musikalische*, 'musicality'.[25] When Nietzsche entitled his provocative volume *The Birth of Tragedy from the Spirit of Music*, his connection of tragedy and music was not as shocking as it might seem. Not only was

---

[25] The term is pervasive (see n. 26): especially influential is Hanslick (1854), a book that went to many editions and set the agenda for much of music criticism's aesthetics.

the assumption that tragedy developed out of Dionysiac choruses a common-place, in line with Aristotle's authoritative history of the genre in the *Poetics*, but also German philosophy had discussed the conceptualization of music, with specific reference to ancient tragedy, for fifty years and more. There is one particular line of argument that runs through Hegel, Schelling, and above all Schopenhauer, and that leads via Nietzsche and Wagner into the practice of performance with profound effect in theatre and opera house. It is a place where the connection between abstract theory and staging is especially vivid and insistent.

It is music's power to reveal *Innerlichkeit*, 'the inner', 'inwardness', that fascinates the German Idealists. As Lydia Goehr, who has explored these ideas most pertinently, puts it: '"musicality" connotes some sort of pure *Innerlich-keit*, or powerful preconceptual or predeterminate expressivity, an emotional energy or drive of deep aesthetic, moral, cultural, religious or social significance'.[26] So, for Hegel, music's proper element 'is the inner life as such ... music's *content* is constituted by spiritual subjectivity in its immediate subjective inherent unity, the human heart, feeling as such'.[27] For Schelling, the chorus is fundamental in this search for the inward: or rather, its musicality provides the inner, ideal face of drama. The essential role, he writes, of the ancient chorus is to draw outer attention to what is inner, within the total symbolic appearance of the artwork. Schopenhauer, however, offers the fullest account, which has its most long-lasting effect by enabling the separation of *das Musikalische* from the chorus. We have already cited this passage:

> The internal relation that music has to the true nature of things can also explain the fact that, when music suitable to any scene, action, event, or environment is played, it seems to disclose to us its innermost secret meaning and appears to be the most accurate and distinct commentary on it.[28]

Music—by virtue of its relation to the nature, the innermost Will, of the world—has the power to reveal something otherwise concealed to the spectators. Music is the route to a transcendent insightfulness. The chorus's role as commentator and as medium for an audience to reach a new level of reflectiveness has been taken over by music itself. Music aims, not at specific, particular, definite feelings, but at feelings '*themselves* to a certain extent in the abstract, their essential nature, without accessories, and therefore without their motives'.[29] Music should escape from mere representation to become the most spiritual of the arts. Indeed—most grandly: 'We could just as well call the world embodied music as embodied will.'[30]

---

[26] Goehr (2008: 50 (following Johnson 1991); see also Dahlhaus (1989); Krausz (1993); Goehr (1998); Parret (1998).

[27] Hegel (1975: 626).   [28] Schopenhauer (1958: i. 262).

[29] Schopenhauer (1958: i. 261).   [30] Schopenhauer (1958: i. 262–3).

I have raced through here what could be explored at far greater depth, because it seems to me that, for my current argument, the importance of this line of thinking about music's revelation of inwardness is not its philosophical depth so much as its influence on both Nietzsche and Wagner, and the impact it turns out to have in the theatre itself.[31] For Nietzsche, the link between philosophy and music is fundamental: 'To what does this miraculous union between German philosophy and music point', he exclaims, 'if not to a new mode of existence, whose precise nature we can divine only with the aid of Greek analogies?'[32] Music and philosophy have a 'miraculous' interrelationship, and this must be understood both as a national phenomenon (it is true of *German* philosophy and music) and as a genealogical imperative: it needs the analogies of ancient Greece to be comprehended. But, for Nietzsche, the choral, Dionysiac experience of collectivity is not secondary to the tragic hero's individuality, but is superior to it. 'Music alone allows us to understand the delight felt at the annihilation of the individual.'[33] So: 'For a brief moment we become, ourselves, the primal Being, and we experience its insatiable hunger for existence.'[34] Indeed our wild joy in Being is not as individuals but as part of something collective and greater: 'Pity and terror notwithstanding, we realize our great good fortune in having life—not as individuals, but as part of the life force with whose procreative lust we have become one.'[35] Where for Hegel the chorus is an ineffective voice of commonality to be transcended by the hero's self-consciousness, for Nietzsche it is precisely the loss of such self-consciousness that constitutes Dionysiac wisdom. Nietzsche's appropriation of Schopenhauer leads through music's transcendent expressivity to a revaluation of the chorus as the true inwardness of the Dionysiac within tragedy. Nietzsche's provocation consists thus not in stepping outside the tradition of German thinking on tragedy but on using its resources to reverse what was—as he himself notes—becoming commonplace opinion, and thus turning the chorus from spectator to prime participant in the experience of the tragic.

Wagner, who, as Nietzsche said, 'summed up modernity', also read Schopenhauer avidly. And it led him to a particular performance-based solution to the problem of the chorus. Wagner wrote how the orchestra took on the role of the chorus in modern music—and the *Ring* indeed, unlike Wagner's earlier operas and *Parsifal*, has no real chorus. The music of the orchestra provided, as Schopenhauer demanded, the revelation of the innermost secrets of things and a commentary on the action onstage. He constructed the Festspielhaus at Bayreuth with the orchestra concealed beneath the level of the stage in a 'mystic abyss', so that the music emerged, disembodied, as it were, pure and

---

[31] See Silk and Stern (1981).   [32] Nietzsche (1956: 120).
[33] Nietzsche (1956: 101).   [34] Nietzsche (1956: 102).
[35] Nietzsche (1956: 103).

abstract, without the visual distraction of its actual means of production.[36] Wagner's reading of Schopenhauer led to the removal of the chorus as a physical, staged presence in music drama, while yet claiming that the full force of the tensions of tragedy obtained. Wagner inherited a tradition that declared the operatic chorus to be the new embodiment of the ancient chorus of tragedy, and he contested it in the same terms. He made it possible to have a chorus without a chorus.

There is a tension within Wagner's thinking between the chorus as a potentially idealized form of the voice of the People, linked intimately to the nationalist ideals of *das Volk*, and the ideal of absolute music as an expression of the true inwardness of emotion.[37] Art and revolutionary politics go together. 'Public art' was for the Greeks 'the expression of the deepest and noblest principles of the people's consciousness'; this has been lost in contemporary bourgeois society. 'Greek tragedy' was 'the entry of the artwork of the People [*das Volk*] upon the public arena of political life', and it 'flourished for just so long as it was inspired by the spirit of the People [*Volksgeist*]'.[38] His commitment to the people—a combination of early socialism and later Herderian notions of the race—does not lead to a direct representation of the people onstage, however, but rather to an abstracted, ideal form of musical expression. The collectivity of the people becomes the collective of the orchestra. It would be hard to overemphasize the importance of Wagner for the nineteenth century's obsession with its own modernity and the role of theatre and the arts in the (self-)expression of it. Wagner is a paradigm for how the chorus as an aesthetic concept is deeply embroiled in political and philosophical agendas—agendas with a fierce commitment to an ideological modernism, a progressivism linked, as with Schlegel's understanding of the idealism of the chorus, to a specifically German nationalism. My second conclusion, then, is that aesthetic debates about the musicality of the ancient chorus and about its modern instantiations in opera and onstage are fully part of a German Idealist tradition, which linked, in the aftermath of the French Revolution, aesthetic modernism with political nationalism. The chorus became a privileged site for the self-proclamation of modernity's modernism.

STAGING INWARDNESS

Schiller's *Bride of Messina* (1803), with its preface that discusses the modernity of the chorus, is an influential starting point for the tradition to which Wagner

---

[36] For the history of Wagner's performance, see Carnegy (2006). In general, see Müller, Wapnewski, and Deathridge (1992) for the best overall introduction, and Deathridge (2008).

[37] See Foster (2010). For a criticism of Foster, see Dreyfus, Chapter 13, this volume.

[38] Wagner (1892–9: i. 135–6). On *Volksgeist* as a term, see Stocking (1996).

declares himself to be the teleological apex.[39] For Schiller, the ancient chorus, even if unobtainable today, is ideal because it bars access to realism or naturalism. But it is Mendelssohn's *Antigone* (1841) that provides perhaps the most influential instantiation of German Idealist thought in the theatre (not least because, unlike Schiller's play, it was a huge hit and widely performed for many decades).[40] Indeed, this production came right out of the centre of German Idealist thinking, where the director Tieck was friends with the Schlegels;[41] Mendelssohn had been to Hegel's lectures, and was related to the Schlegels by marriage; and the first performance in Potsdam was conceived and produced as a statement of German philhellenism as a proclamation of the new German spirit. It was a production (self-consciously) from the (self-appointed) centre of the German-speaking cultural world. My third brief section will trace how German Idealist thinking found its way from the philosophical lecture hall into the theatre and to a new audience.

For *Antigone*, Mendelssohn composed settings of the stasima for a chorus of sixteen male voices, scored with a small orchestra including brass. He initially considered using 'Greek' instrumentation (flute, harp, tuba (*aulos, kithara, salpinx*)), but found the restriction wholly debilitating: finally the addition of a harp to the orchestration is the one sign of 'Greek' coloration. He used sixteen voices because he believed, incorrectly, that the chorus of fifteen was augmented by the chorus leader. He also included recitative or melodrama: a bare musical accompaniment to the actors' voices, especially carefully marked for the transitions between stasima and scenes. There are also solo parts for Antigone and Creon in the *kommoi*. The chorus sings in unison, in two half choruses, and in quartets and with solo voices (in the style of the oratorios that were so popular in the nineteenth century), but the musical line is always simple and single; there are no overlapping polyphonic harmonies and no verbal repetitions. Rousseau, followed by many Romantics, claimed harmony was a modern barbarism.[42] The direct melodic line of Mendelssohn's *Antigone* is part of its historically self-aware classicizing.

Mendelssohn wrote of the script that 'the moods and the prosody are so genuinely musical throughout that one does not have to think about the individual words and only needs to compose those moods and rhythms; then the chorus is finished'.[43] In this letter we can hear striking echoes of Schelling and Schopenhauer. The poetry is 'echt musikalisch', and this comes via 'Rhythmen'. But the music is not representative, imitative: rather, the

[39] See Kain (1982); Pillau (1981: 155–90); and Billings, Chapter 8, this volume.

[40] See Steinberg (1991); Seaton (2001); and, in particular, Geary (2006), reprised in Geary (2010). For the European distribution, see Boetius (2005: 262–79); for the English productions, see Hall and Macintosh (2005: 318–50).

[41] Paulin (1985).

[42] Rousseau (1969: 242); see Dalhaus (1989: 48).

[43] Droysen (1959: 72).

specific words are subordinated to a *Stimmung*, a voice, a mood. The music, that is, brings out the true inner meaning of the chorus. Mendelssohn's *Antigone* was perceived, and sometimes celebrated, as an attempt to recover the music of antiquity, not in an imitative manner—the orchestration makes this clear enough—but in a manner mediated through German Idealist philosophy.

There were famous productions of *Antigone* in London and elsewhere.[44] It made the performance of Greek tragedy trendy. But, as the century progressed, the score came to be most widely reperformed by oratorio societies and amateur groups as a separate set of choruses, for which a piano score was published. The price of four shillings priced it for the extremely broad, largely middle-class, domestic market, accustomed to piano reductions of oratorios as well as other orchestral pieces. It is in this form that 'to most lovers of music Mendelssohn's *Antigone* is too familiar to permit any word of comment here', as Jebb put it in 1888, two generations after the Potsdam opening.[45] The music itself is so like oratorio and part-song familiar from other Christian environments that the success of the music was due to its recognizability as much as its modernity. By the end of the century, Mendelssohn was very old hat indeed, especially to self-conscious modernists:[46] what began as an experimental and informed engagement with German philhellenism eventually circulates in British culture as a thoroughly domesticated musical experience.

Through Schiller, Mendelssohn, and Wagner we have begun to see how German Idealist conceptualizations of the chorus have moved from theoretical material into a performance tradition, to a good degree through the interface of theatre and music. And here we have my third conclusion: when tragedy came to be staged, the chorus emerges as a problem, and perhaps could not have appeared otherwise. No production of tragedy can escape the three great questions posed by the German Idealist tradition and its reception through opera. Can the chorus be modern? Can it be ideal? Can it be musical? In short, will the very staging of the chorus inevitably result in it falling short of its Idealist imagining?

PERFORMANCE AND PHILOSOPHY

This influence of German philosophical thinking on dramatic performance could certainly be extended. As Mendelssohn himself became unfashionable

---

[44] Hall and Macintosh (2005: 318–50).
[45] Jebb (1888: pp. xli–xliii).   [46] Eatock (2009: 115–50).

(however popular he remained in England), the theatre itself began to produce performances of Greek tragedy to challenge the opera house. In particular, if Mounet-Sully's celebrated performance of *Oedipus Tyrannus* appears fully to fulfil an audience's expectations of the instrumental chorus, aiding the audience's emotional response to the hero, just as Schelling and Hegel expected, Reinhardt's *Oedipus* was constructed in such a way as to challenge such assumptions.[47] Reinhardt's chorus was huge; it invaded the audience's space; it dominated the action. John Sheppard, a classicist whose love of performance and eccentric personality made him a more distinguished Provost of King's College, Cambridge, than a renowned scholar, commented tellingly: 'Reinhardt's actors... raged and fumed and ranted, rushing hither and thither with a violence of gesticulation which, in spite of all their efforts, was eclipsed and rendered insignificant by the yet more violent rushes, screams, and contortions of a quite gratuitous crowd.'[48] Reinhardt's chorus, 'to add to our discomfort', was directed 'to utter meaningless yells and to clash strange cymbals and other instruments of brazen music. The appeal was to our senses.'[49] At one level, Sheppard is recording his deep discomfort at the thoroughly Unwinckelmannian performance: this was the opposite of calm dignity, of sublime restraint, of profound simplicity. But, at another, more pointed level, Sheppard's physical distaste—matched by many reviewers—to the chorus's invasion of the audience space is because it destroyed the rule of the chorus as a 'living wall', in Schiller's terms, between the audience and action: it broke down the wall, it disturbed the physical calm of the spectators: it was, in this sense, thoroughly, unideal.[50] The commitment to Nietzsche's view of the Dionysiac crowd, with an admixture of the anthropology of primitivism that followed Nietzsche, is evident in Reinhardt's staging, and evidently disturbed Sheppard as it did many of the English audience—and did so in part at least because it went against the inherited theory of the chorus from the German Idealist tradition.

In this fourth and final section, however, I want to trace how a scholar like Sheppard came into contact with German Idealism and how it formed his views: for it started well before he became a professional classicist. Sheppard

[47] On Reinhardt, see Braulich (1969); Styan (1982); Jacobs and Warren (1986); Marx (2006) with further bibliography. Macintosh (2009a) is good on this performance history.

[48] Sheppard (1920: p. ix).

[49] Sheppard (1920: p. ix). See also Macintosh (2009a).

[50] 'The introduction of the chorus... serve[s] this end—namely to declare open and honourable warfare against Naturalism in art... a living wall which Tragedy had drawn around herself, to guard her from contact with the world of reality, and maintain her own ideal soil, her poetical freedom' (Schiller 1841: 7).

was taught by Arthur Gilkes at Dulwich School. Gilkes (1849–1922) was a pioneering educationist in the mould of Thomas Arnold of Rugby, who linked a strong social conscience, formed by his passionate Christianity, with a belief in classical learning.[51] He wrote and published his *School Lectures on the Electra of Sophocles and Macbeth* in 1880, while teaching at Shrewsbury. As a set of school lectures, it is an especially clear guide to what one might expect to be said about the play, a summation of the critical views thought suitable for young men to absorb. Gilkes clearly knew his way round the German tradition, probably by reading August Schlegel (whose lectures had been translated as early as 1815, and reprinted many times), perhaps indirectly from university days. So, he tells his pupils, the chorus's 'office is the same always, namely, to direct the minds of the spectators to the thoughts which are most proper to each situation'; the chorus 'constantly, as the action proceeds, passes upon it the judgment that would suggest itself to the highest human authority, to the educated man'; he even sees the chorus, more daringly, in the modern world as 'an orchestral accompaniment', as if he had been reflecting on Schopenhauer or Wagner.[52] Edmund Morshead, the assistant master at Winchester, in his school edition of Sophocles (1895), takes much the same line, with the added regret that, if only they could act—with the vigour of an English schoolboy— the chorus would not be so reflective: 'the chorus is . . . an "ideal spectator" . . . their words represent . . . the unuttered thoughts that would pass through our minds at a crisis, if our hands were tied.'[53] A plucky English lad, given a free hand, would not faff like the chorus of the *Agamemnon* or stand with eyes averted like the chorus of the *Medea*.

   The schoolboys of England are fed a version of German Idealist thinking that is divorced from German nationalist ideals and from the political agendas that underlie the analysis of the hero's *Sittlichkeit*. The question of the chorus has become a largely formal issue. The distaste for the chorus's inaction that Morshead reveals is taken to a further level by the renegade Irish classical scholar J. P. Mahaffy, who clashed repeatedly and publicly with his countryman Jebb (central to the institution of classics and its dignity).[54] Mahaffy adds a striking twist to the orthodoxy from Schlegel: 'The chorus . . . was . . . by Sophocles degraded to be a mere spectator of the action—sometimes an accomplice, sometimes a mere selfish, sometimes an irrelevant observer.'[55] The word 'mere', along with 'selfish' and 'irrelevant', sniffily undermines the idealistic model of the chorus, and attacks the claim, from Aristotle onwards, that Sophocles treated his chorus like an actor. Mahaffy is constructing an argument against the privileged position of Sophocles as a moral beacon in the

[51] Leake (1938).   [52] Gilkes (1880: 39–40, 40, 42).
[53] Morshead (1895: 7, 8).   [54] Stanford and McDowell (1971).
[55] Mahaffy (1983: i. 317).

ethical development of mankind—but he does so still through a redrafting of German Idealist thought.[56]

J. P. Sandys, the Cambridge don, fulsomely recommended Gilkes's volume for undergraduates too, as 'a book which ought to be in the hands of all who desire to read [*Electra*] with profit'.[57] It duly appears in the bibliography of an undergraduate mentored by Sandys, L. G. Horton-Smith, whose prize essay in Latin, comparing Greek and Shakespearian tragedy, was published in 1896.[58] The essay was reviewed in turn by the Professor of Greek at Glasgow, Lewis Campbell, who singled out Horton-Smith's comments on the chorus for specific praise (although his views are probably closer to those of Mahaffy than Gilkes).[59] Schlegel in particular is cited in the standard handbooks in France, Germany, and England throughout the nineteenth century. Patin's guide to tragedy went through several editions in France—and it is liberally laced with quotations from Schlegel.[60] Back in Cambridge, Verrall edited Kitchin's translation of the guide to Greek literature by the German scholar Munk, because his views 'represent very fairly the current opinion'.[61] Munk quotes whole pages of Schlegel on tragedy. From schoolteacher to pupil to undergraduate to don to professor, we find the same commonplaces, usually decontextualized and trivialized, offering a formal view of the chorus as a sympathetic but ineffectual observer of the action of tragedy. Shepherd's distaste for Reinhardt's production was in this way absolutely typical: his expectations had been formed in a remarkably uniform intellectual atmosphere where the chorus of Greek tragedy and of Sophocles in particular had a role to play in a view of Sophocles that linked and bonded all levels of British educated society.

Nor is it surprising that Horton-Smith compared Shakespeare and Greek tragedy. *Unser* Shakespeare was an icon for German writing as much as for English, and it is not by chance that perhaps the most influential of Shakespearian studies, A. C. Bradley's *Shakespearian Tragedy*, is also the most instrumental book in introducing Hegel to an English critical tradition.[62] Bradley's Hegelianism influenced more than one generation of scholars in the twentieth century, and the key arguments about tragedy in recent years have often found their focus in later examples of the genre, for all that a debt to Greece is repeatedly acknowledged. While classicists in the twentieth century have in general been slow to recognize how academic debates around the chorus and choral performance traditions have been formed in response to German Idealist questions and concepts, the influence of such a critical

---

[56] See Goldhill (2012: ch. 8).   [57] Sandys (1880: p. lxii n. 1).
[58] Horton-Smith (1896); see also Goldhill (2012: ch. 8).
[59] Campbell (1897: 119).   [60] Patin (1841–3).   [61] Verrall (1891: p. v).
[62] A. C. Bradley (1904); see also Cooke (1972). For most explicit discussion of Hegel, see A. C. Bradley (1909).

tradition on the broader discussions of tragedy has been explicit and pervasive. Peter Szondi, George Steiner, Terry Eagleton—to take three exemplary theorists of the tragic—each places his work explicitly in line with Schiller, Schlegel, Schelling, Hegel, Schopenhauer, and so forth.[63] A German Idealist framework has thus been further reimported into classics, often without recognition, by the adoption of 'the tragic' as a unifying generic concept from modern criticism.[64]

Yet, in a final twist of the story, when we turn specifically to the chorus in such modern writing, a surprising fact emerges. Szondi does not discuss the chorus at all, Eagleton never mentions the word, and even Steiner does little but note ruefully and wrongly that the chorus has been 'essentially lost to spoken drama', before moving rapidly on.[65] It is as if their commitment to modernism aligns them with Schopenhauer, Wagner, and, say, Hofmannsthal, with his chorus-free *Electra*, in removing the chorus as a form. It is particularly surprising that both Eagleton and Szondi, writing from within a Marxian tradition, resist articulating the dramatic form through which the people, the masses, the state had been embodied according to the theorists with whom they are affiliating themselves. Perhaps this strategy is best seen as an attempt to uncover a sense of the tragic that transcends the particularities of dramatic form, or even as an implicit modernist politics that resists such representations of a social collective. But it is hard not to hear this silence about the chorus as a wilful partiality in their comprehension of the German Idealist tradition.

My fourth conclusion, then, is that German Idealism articulated a set of questions and concepts that have defined the debate about the chorus in modern criticism. But not only does this influence spread throughout the different but interrelated arenas of performance and teaching and critical study, but also the form in which these ideas have spread has often been indirect and oversimplified, for all their power and pervasiveness.

Three final conclusions emerge. First, the German Idealists needed to theorize the chorus in order to construct their accounts of the theatrical experience, their concept of the community and the importance of the individual as a historical subject, and their ideas of musicality as an expressive medium. The chorus is integral to German Idealist writing about tragedy.

Second, this tradition of thinking was hugely influential in writing about tragedy, theatre, and opera across the nineteenth and twentieth centuries. Schlegel's construction of the chorus as idealized spectator finds its way into the standard handbooks on the history of literature; Hegel's influence is pervasive across a range of literary criticism. Schopenhauer had a particular

---

[63] Szondi (1961, 2002); Eagleton (2003) (see also Eagelton 1990); Steiner (1984) (see also Steiner 1996, and the influential Steiner 1961).
[64] See the exemplary Silk (1996).   [65] Steiner (1984: 167).

influence on thinking about music and thus the choral role as the embodiment of musicality in tragedy. From Nietzsche and Wagner, both of whom affiliate themselves to Schopenhauer, two quite different (if related) lines emerge: for Nietzsche, the chorus becomes the embodiment of the Dionysiac within tragedy, the potential loss of individuality in the group, the ecstatic experience of the life force through music (and, in modern times, Wagner's music); yet, for Wagner, in his prose and more tentatively in his operas, the chorus is replaced by the orchestra, articulating a commentary, a narrative, a journey of meaning that is interwoven with the actors' voices and actions onstage. Two contrasting productions of Reinhardt, the *Oedipus* and Hofmannsthal's *Electra*,[66] are iconic theatrical expressions of these two lines of comprehending the chorus as a form for modernity. Huge embracing chorus; or no chorus at all.

Third, it is hard to trace single lines of influence from the philosophical tradition to particular productions. Not only are theatre practitioners often magpies who pick up elements of contemporary and past thought without any requirement of system, but also the audiences who came to the shows brought different ranges of expectation and knowledge. Yet, as we have seen, one narrative that is essential to understanding the development of tragedy in the nineteenth century is articulated by the tension between philhellenic idealism (as developed by German Idealist philosophy and nationalist claims of genealogical authority from the classical past) and the challenge to that idealism by a further self-conscious modernism (also fostered by a German-speaking intellectual tradition that would include the philosophy of Nietzsche,[67] the psychology of Freud,[68] and the anti-humanist anthropology of the Berlin group,[69] for all that each has its own engagement with antiquity as a privileged model). The chorus—its presence or absence, its construction as a group or as individual voices, its relation to music and to speech—is one focalization of this tension. The chorus thus becomes a battleground of modernism.

This account of the modern conceptualization of the chorus, along with the intertwined performance histories of opera and theatre, reveals how *over-determined* the discussion of the chorus is. The broad dissemination of strands of German intellectual understanding of the chorus, and the wide circulation of the literature and productions deeply influenced by such thinking, mean that, when we look at the chorus of Greek tragedy, then and now, we are always viewing through German-tinted spectacles.

---

[66] Also directed by Reinhardt; see Goldhill (2002: 108–70; 2012: ch. 7).
[67] See Silk and Stern (1981).
[68] See Rudnytsky (1987); Armstrong (2005).
[69] See, e.g., Stocking (1996); Zimmerman (2001).

3

The Middle Voice: German Classical Scholarship and the Greek Tragic Chorus

Constanze Güthenke

From around 1800, tragedy in Germany became linked to articulations of modernity, at a time when classical knowledge in Germany received new impetus from two directions: from philosophy, literature, and the arts; and from the establishing of classical philology as a normative institutional practice. We have tended to examine these newly 'modern' discourses on the tragic mainly in the light of philosophical and artistic thought, with philological historicism and positivism as, at best, its dustier 'other', thus following Nietzsche in highlighting the gap between radically modern thinking and dull disciplinary myopia.

Philologists are not beyond self-criticism, and Nietzsche's invective against a certain (stereo-)type of scholar has had its attractions, especially outside Germany, where the German tradition has been and still is in equal parts revered and satirized. But it is useful to uncouple nineteenth-century scholarly engagement with tragedy from Nietzsche's account and to look at its history before and beyond the dominant association with Nietzsche.[1] Within this engagement, I suggest, the tragic chorus is a privileged site where discussions of tragedy are keyed to reflections on the role of classical scholarship and of classical scholars in relation to and in distinction from the thinking of poets and philosophers.

Our standard impression is that tragedy as a barometer of (German) modernity is the domain of philosophers and poets, and not of scholars. In an obvious sense, though, common ground between tragic thinking inside and outside the boundaries of disciplinarity is not hard to imagine: both are making the individual and individual subjectivity a central, modern concern,

---

[1] For the early modern period up to and including the eighteenth century, Michael Lurje's run-through of the longue durée (Lurje 2004) of scholarly thinking on tragedy, especially on tragic guilt, is extensive.

the toggle, so to speak, between modernity and tragedy. Classical scholarship, after all, taps deeply into the discourse of *Bildung*, as the formation of the individual, as the central term to connect the development of antiquity and its own *Bildung* with that of the modern individual arising out of it, both historically and in terms of the process of gaining classical knowledge. That tragedy, individuality, and the modern are linked, and that this linkage involves structured acts of understanding—in other words, that tragedy has to do with hermeneutics—is a proposition that scholars as well as poets and philosophers could agree on.

If a theoretical concern with individuality, and the historical consciousness of a break between the ancient and the modern, were shared territory between the spheres of philosophy, of poetry, and of philology, so to speak, then it may be the very boundary separating the scholar from the others that requires elucidation and that can account for some of our perceived differences. Ulrich von Wilamowitz-Moellendorff's famous reaction to Nietzsche's *Birth of Tragedy*, the angry essay 'Zukunftsphilologie!' of the same year (1871), is a particularly good example of such policing of the boundaries.

His main point of criticism comes right at the start: 'Indeed, the book's main offence lies in its tone and tenor. Herr Nietzsche in no way presents himself as a scholar and scientific researcher: insights gained by intuition are presented as a form of *raisonnement* that is part pulpit, part familiar from journalists, those "paper slaves of today"'.[2] And indeed, in the preface to the 1886 re-edition of *Birth*, Nietzsche agrees with Wilamowitz's reproach that he did indeed, deliberately, not write as a scholar.[3] In many ways, the acrimonious debate over the scholarly voice as a guarantor of classical knowledge sounds like the culmination of what Glenn Most has described as the forking of the paths of literature and philology around 1800: in a recent history of German literature, arranged by events, he presents a vignette of Goethe listening, from behind a curtain, to Wolf's lectures on Homer, in the summer of 1805.[4] Most reads this curtain as the protective veil for poetry against the growing monopoly of scholarship to elucidate antiquity, as the Homer of the poets and of the scholars are setting off on separate ways, after a brief walk side by side. And yet, *pace* Most, while the paths certainly diverged, that veil within which poetry was enveloped was never a wall; as much as poetry sought out its

---

[2] Wilamowitz-Moellendorff (1969: 29). For the invective and its ambivalent understanding of philology in the dispute, see Danneberg (2007), who makes a good case that the firm final distinction between 'art' (*Kunst*) and 'science' (*Wissenschaft*) was in place only by about 1900. Ugolini (2003) makes a detailed argument for Nietzsche's thorough philological knowledge, which he brought to the *Birth of Tragedy* even though not signposting it through its expected markers. The sources of the Nietzsche–Wilamowitz quarrel are collected in Gründer (1969).

[3] In the short essay 'Attempt at Self-Criticism' ('Versuch einer Selbstkritik'), repr. in Nietzsche (1994: 97–108).

[4] Most (2004).

proper sphere, it is possible to see the attempt to pin down a modern, scholarly voice as troubled by the proximity of the arenas of poetry (and also philosophy) outside the scientific sphere, and the other kinds and practices of classical knowledge they may have offered.

The tragic chorus, I suggest, is one particular area in which a preoccupation with the proper scholarly voice is reflected in classical scholarship. Goldhill, in his contribution to this volume, comments on the challenge the chorus posed to nineteenth-century audiences, thinkers of various stripe, and theatre practitioners: if tragedy in the Idealist tradition was essentially about the heroic individual, then what place was assigned to the chorus?[5] The choric voice as ostensibly collective and usually as less 'tragic' seemed to render the position of the chorus in the action and development of tragic thought less obvious. In order to integrate the chorus into modern readings of tragedy, the answer advanced by dramatic theory was either to bypass the issue and claim that there could be no place for the ancient chorus any longer, or to put emphasis on its reflective role, its focusing and shaping of the audience's responses, and its encouragement of higher forms of reflection in the audience themselves.[6]

This is a workable genealogy that looks primarily to Germany while also taking account of the larger European ramifications that followed. (German) Idealist interpretation of tragedy, or at any rate what passed for Idealist interpretation before a broader audience, can be captured well in the catchphrase of the heroic struggle between individual or notional freedom and external force or necessity (*innere Freiheit und äussere Notwendigkeit*), dutifully repeated across all standard scholarly accounts by mid-century.[7] The pairing was popularized by August Wilhelm Schlegel's series of *Lectures on Dramatic Art and Literature* (1809), even though its traces and versions—or to be accurate a web of diachronic and synchronic references—infuse the writings of many of the Idealist, post-Kantian thinkers, among them Schelling, Schiller, and Hegel in their philosophical aesthetics.[8] Schlegel's *Lectures*, incidentally, are of course themselves a good example of the overlap between academic scholarship and the world of poetry and philosophy outside institutional frameworks: like his brother Friedrich, August Wilhelm was a philosopher, writer, and translator, as well as a university teacher, and his *Lectures*

---

[5] Goldhill, Chapter 2, this volume.

[6] With particular reference to the writings of Schelling, Schiller, Schlegel, and Hegel, see also the overview in Goldhill (2012: 174–81); further Silk (1998); in much greater detail Billings (forthcoming), and Billings, Chapter 8, this volume.

[7] Ast (1808: 111–22) and Boeckh (1877: 632–44) may be representative for widely read 'encyclopaedias', meaning summaries of the discipline's form and content. Even though Boeckh's was published only posthumously in 1877, it was based on a series of introductory lectures he had given regularly over the space of thirty years at Berlin, thus training several generations of scholars.

[8] Billings (forthcoming) offers a new genealogy of the tragic in those writers and thinkers; for specific attention to the choral element, see Billings (2013).

became not only a standard reference for German scholarship on ancient drama, but met with quick and considerable success across Europe, especially in France, Italy, and England.[9]

Aside from the distinction between inner freedom and external necessity, Schlegel's *Lectures* are also to blame for the omnipresent phrase that would be rolled out at any opportunity to sum up the challenge posed by the chorus: that of the chorus as the 'idealized spectator'—a phrase to which I will return just below. On a practical level, that is on the level of a developing performance tradition, Goldhill is certainly right to ask what was one to do with an idealized spectator put onstage, individually or as a group? His emphasis on the practical difficulties that the chorus posed leads him to point out the subsequent lack of specific, rather than generalized, discussions of its role and of its manifestation in a range of Greek tragedies by writers and practitioners across Europe. I want to suggest, though, that it is actually when we turn to classical scholarship that we find a group ostensibly much more comfortable with finding a place for the chorus—and that this was so because the chorus as a reflective, distanced voice, functionally mediating between the tragic hero and the audience, and speaking on behalf of the poet, had considerable overlap with the self-image of the modern classical scholar.

Schlegel, to repeat his catchphrase more fully, saw the chorus as, 'in short, the idealized spectator [*der idealisierte Zuschauer*]', who

mediates or ameliorates [*lindert*] the impression of a profoundly disturbing or moving representation, in so far as it offers to the actual audience their own emotions already expressed lyrically, that is musically, and moves the audience upwards to the realm of contemplation [*indem er dem wirklichen Zuschauer seine eignen Regungen schon lyrisch, also musikalisch ausgedrückt entgegenbringt und ihn in die Region der Betrachtung hinaufführt*].[10]

That the chorus, in this understanding, offers a form of reflection that is qualitatively different from the raw emotion of the audience, and that in effect shepherds the audience on towards a higher and freer form of reflection, is echoed, as I said, in the writings of Schelling and Schiller. Especially Schiller, who was well read and also well received in classicists' circles, was known for his own dramatic experiment with restaging the classical chorus in his play *Die Braut von Messina* (1803), to which he appended an introductory essay 'On the Use of the Chorus in Tragedy'.[11] However successful or unsuccessful his attempt to stage a modern chorus may have been (his contemporaries were by

---

[9] Billings (forthcoming); Goldhill (2012: 202–17) for a case study of Schlegel's popularity in British readings of Sophocles.

[10] A. W. Schlegel (1966: 65).

[11] For more detail on Schiller's play and his conception of the chorus, with further references, see Billings, Chapter 8, this volume.

and large doubtful), one of his central claims, that the tragic chorus is essentially a breaker of illusion, is a motive that finds parallels in the classical scholarship of the time. It is, for example, repeated by Schiller's correspondent Wilhelm von Humboldt, even though he is difficult to pin down as a classical scholar only, in his introduction to a long-gestating translation of Aeschylus' *Agamemnon* (1816), or by the Leipzig professor of philology Gottfried Hermann, to whose writings on the Greek tragedians, Aristotle's *Poetics*, and Greek metrics Humboldt had certainly looked.[12] For Schiller, the chorus's function lies in creating distance and closeness at the same time: as a prompt to reflection, it creates the characteristically modern distance that allows for *Bildung*, and a certain 'ennobling' of the audience's pleasure, in short a form of freedom (certainly in Schiller's understanding of the term).[13] At the same time, the chorus as a fundamentally 'alien' element is also the only one that might allow us any insight and way into understanding ancient tragedy, which by definition resisted the illusion familiar from more recent dramatic practice—in other words, it allows us, moderns by necessity, to take the foreignness of Greek drama by its horns. In addition, he claims, ancient tragedy as a genre arose out of choric and lyric song, wherefore the chorus still bears the traces of that origin while in and of itself offering the promise of its own, and tragedy's, interpretation. Schiller calls the ancient chorus a 'judging witness' (*richtender Zeuge*), who adjudicates and evaluates, an attitude that was not lost on the scholars' understanding of Greek tragedy either.[14]

A. W. Schlegel himself claimed in the *Lectures on Dramatic Art and Literature* that he objected to Schiller's attempt not only in practice, but also on the level of Schiller's basic premises—namely, those of creating a work of art that is both ancient (in form) and Romantic (in content).[15] But it seems fair to say that the understanding of the ancient chorus as a mediating body of reflection was widely available, and generally agreed upon, in the intellectual climate of the time. Still, this is not to suggest that there is an easy line to be drawn from the rational, reflective chorus to the reflective, interpretative scholar; instead, it is to argue that it is precisely the *ambivalence* of the Idealists' (and classicists') chorus that makes it significant for the self-perception of scholarly identities, as it skirts and explores that boundary with the non-(institutional-)scholar. It is important to remember that it is a tempered, *artistic* form of reflection offered by the chorus that makes it functional

---

[12] Humboldt (1816: esp. pp. xiii–xv); for Hermann, see his essay 'de tragica et epica poesi commentatio' appended to his edition of and commentary on Aristotle's *Poetics* (1802), especially the last section 'de choro tragico', 267–70, where he talks about the chorus's ostensible lack of necessity and action, and its function to interrupt and divert the minds of the audience; also Köchly (1879: 32–3). Thanks to Joshua Billings for pointing out this passage to me.

[13] Schiller (1996: 282).

[14] Schiller (1996: 290).

[15] Schlegel, as quoted in Schiller (1996: 717).

in the first place. It is also this role of mediator that brings the chorus close to the Romantic artist, at least as envisaged by the core group of Romantics affected by and implicated in German Idealist thought. The artist as mediator between the real and ideal, between the sensible and intelligible, did not only put interpretation and hermeneutics, the communicating of something other, at the core of Romantic poetics; Friedrich Schlegel states that the poet, 'if he wants to be an expert and understand his fellow citizens in the realm of art, has to be a philologist as well' (*will er Kenner sein und seine Mitbürger im Reiche der Kunst verstehen, muss auch Philolog sein*).[16] Being the Young Turk he was, Schlegel highlighted what was otherwise latent: that the boundaries between poetry, philosophy, and philology (the latter understood as the skill and method of reading and interpreting texts and linguistic sources) were more porous than the self-image of a discipline coming into focus suggested. His radical programme may not have reflected common or comfortable beliefs of institutionalized scholarship, busy at that moment building its disciplinary framework.[17] But the Romantic and Idealist language of mediation and of interpretation both as deeply reflective and as potentially artistic and creative had a place in the language of dramatic criticism and literary history that, most prominently through A. W. Schlegel's *Lectures*, became a staple of classical scholarship. Thus, scholarly literature, too, picks up on that double function or oscillation of the controlled and the expressive voice.

K. O. MÜLLER'S *EUMENIDES* (1833)

Karl Otfried Müller's important edition, translation, and commentary of Aeschylus' *Eumenides* (1833) illustrates the point well. Müller's edition is known today, if at all, as the trigger of one of the more protracted cases of the German *Philologenstreit*, after it provoked strong words from, and equally strong responses once more in turn to, Gottfried Hermann. Rather than file this episode under the opposition between *Sachphilologie* (Müller) and *Wortphilologie* (Hermann)—that is to say, the opposition between a historical–contextual–archaeological interpretation and a strictly philological–linguistic one—Most has suggested we would be better served to realize that Müller's real provocation rested in advancing in the first instance a literary translation (however successful or unsuccessful) geared towards a larger readership, and

---

[16] Athenaeum fragment 255 (to the extent that we can identify the author of individual fragments in this joint project).

[17] Though see Poiss (2010: 152–7) (based in turn on Körner 1929) for the claim that Friedrich Schlegel's thought, by way of Schleiermacher's hermeneutics, ultimately reached into a broadly conceived task for philology as developed by August Boeckh.

in his attempt to advance new literary interpretations through historical contextualization.[18] What is more, Hermann himself may have felt a kind of monopoly on being the scholar of choice when it came to the artistic interest in tragedy: Goethe had consulted his works and editions of tragedies with admiration and corresponded with him, and Humboldt had gladly, despite initial doubts, shared some of Hermann's theories on tragic metre with Schiller.[19]

Müller's substantial commentary opens with a long exposition on the chorus and its number, in his view split into several main and ancillary choruses and involving a large part of the citizenry in a well-oiled and elaborate hierarchy.[20] To be precise, though, the commentary section begins with Müller's claim that the actual dramatic prize awarded by the state to the winning trilogy went not as such to the poet as poet, but to the poet as chorus master, *Chormeister* (χοροῦ διδάσκαλος), as the teacher and instructor of the citizen chorus.[21] Müller stresses that the chorus has both lyrical and speaking parts, which gives it a double function (even though not one that would map neatly onto generic or metrical differences): as structurally organizing, reflect-ive, and contained, on the one hand, and as emotional and expressive of tension, on the other hand. This is in fact not so unlike Schiller's conceptual-ization of the chorus as a locus both of calm and reflection and of 'active passion'.[22] Here is Müller:

The choric singing of ancient tragedy can generally be divided into two kinds, a distinction that is altogether fundamental: there are songs by the entire chorus, mainly the stasima, and songs sung by individual members.... The stasima structure the tragedies into acts, creating moments of calm [*Ruhepunkte*], motivating the entrance of new characters and pointing to the passage of time; their inner meaning is to allow the mind to collect itself and to adopt a sublime composure, which ancient tragedy attempts to maintain even within the greatest excitement of emotions [*ihrer*

---

[18] Most (1998: 350–8).

[19] Michel (2010); also, in the same volume, Poiss (2010) on the easy misconstrual of the quarrel as between neatly separated objects of philological enquiry.

[20] K. O. Müller (1833: 71–83). Müller's answer to the problematic question of the size of the chorus in Aeschylus—ancient testimonia claim both the numbers 15 and 50—was a complicated calculation based on the mathematics of staging and the logistics of choreography that left him with the number 48; his cultural–social argument runs to the effect that each play of the trilogy would have had its own citizen chorus, who would each be responsible for a manageable amount of choreography to learn, in addition to silent chorus players making up the numbers of other figures such as slave women, etc. That the number of the chorus was an obvious topic of discussion in German scholarship can also be seen in Boeckh (1808: 35–46), with reference to Hermann (maybe evidence in scholarship of what Billings in this volume calls the 'choral craze' of the early nineteenth century). A later piece by Boeckh (1874 [1843]) suggests that the number of chorus members remained generally a topic of choice.

[21] K. O. Müller (1833: 71).

[22] 'handelnde Leidenschaft', thus in a letter to Körner, 10 Mar. 1803, quoted in Schiller (1996: 693).

innerlichen Bedeutung nach dienen sie dazu, dem Geiste die Sammlung und erhabene Fassung zu geben, welche die alte Tragödie auch in der grössten Aufregung der Gefühle festzuhalten sucht].[23]

By contrast, he characterizes the *kommatika*, or passages of enhanced lyrical dialogue thus:

they contribute essentially to the continuation and motivation of the plot in so far as they express most vividly the commotion of will, passionate striving, and tendencies and intentions either at odds or supporting each other [*indem sie Willensbewegungen, leidenschaftliches Begehren, miteinender kämpfende oder einander unterstützende Neigungen und Bestrebungen auf das lebendigste ausdrücken].*[24]

Where Schiller's chorus, in repose, is the one 'standing on safe land while the ship is battling in the waves',[25] Müller's chorus is a token of the spectator (quite literally) who is taken from land to sea back to dry land:

Given its origin and development among the Greeks, this is the most essential element [*das Wesentlichste*] of tragedy: that in it sensations and emotions arise which by their nature and strength force the soul out of its calm balance and throw it to a storm of contradicting winds, while at the same time through continuity and development they purify and elevate themselves [*sich selbst läutern und erheben*], so that they leave the soul in a state of calm, composure and ennobled harmony [*in Ruhe und Gefasstheit und einer höhern und veredelten Stimmung*].[26]

AUGUST BOECKH'S *ANTIGONE* (1843)

August Boeckh's writings on tragedy, my second example, present at face value a much more controlled chorus, though again one, standing in for the poet himself, that is absolutely central in helping us understand what the 'whole', the unity of tragedy is about. His *Antigone* (1843) was not simply a translation plus commentary, but a composite volume of new and older materials that came on the heels of an influential, state-approved and -sponsored production of the play in Potsdam (just outside Berlin), with music by Felix Mendelssohn-Bartholdy. The text was accompanied by two substantial essays based on lectures Boeckh had delivered at the Royal Academy of Sciences in Berlin in 1824 and 1828, now revised not merely to be a publication for scholars, but to have the potential to reach a larger and more popular audience.

The chorus according to Boeckh, who has read his Schlegel, is also one that reflects and mediates, though this time between the emotional excesses of the

---

[23] K. O. Müller (1833: 84).   [24] K. O. Müller (1833: 84).
[25] Schiller (1996: 693).   [26] K. O. Müller (1833: 191).

heroic, tragic individual and the broader audience. Boeckh's aim is to single out the 'basic idea [*Grundidee*] through which the unity of the whole is revealed [*das Ganze als in seiner Einheit aufgeht*]; it is only from this point that the particular, too, can be grasped completely'.[27] To this end, the chorus is of prime importance:

The allusions of the chorus are of special importance here. The chorus stands above the passions of the actors and formulates a general judgement for the spectator [*das allgemeine Urtheil für den Betrachtenden zieht*], articulating the spiritual content of the action, as the organ of the poet who is only too well aware of its function [*als Organ des seines Zweckes sich wohl bewussten Dichters*].[28]

By his suggestion, the chorus of old men, of perfectly balanced and measured commentators, is an embodiment of what he identifies as the basic idea of the play—namely, that hubris and any passionate striving that exceeds its measure lead to downfall, while rationality (*Vernunft*) is the 'the highest good of happiness' (*das Beste der Glückseligkeit*). At the same time, this chorus is the perfect mediator of the poet's own voice and judgement: 'Here, too, the chorus of calm old men possessed of true measure [*im Besitze der wahren Besonnenheit*] expresses the poet's judgement.'[29] To present the chorus as such a clear and moreover successful embodiment of the poet's voice, Boeckh has to tread a fair amount of water, though. He is honest enough to refer to A. W. Schlegel's 'clever' (*geistreich*) comment about the weakness of this chorus of elders marked by their submissiveness and their ostensible lack of support for Antigone. Boeckh's own explanation lies in reinterpreting the poet's purpose of the entire play, which is not about evaluating Antigone as positive or negative, but rather about the wish to explore the larger link between history and tragedy in the specifics of causality, origins, and filiation. The chorus as a conduit for such a poetic intention is in fact not so far removed from the challenge of studying history faced by the classical scholars.

In Boeckh's vision, the chorus is a fully functional mediator and interpreter, both of the dramatic author himself, and of the dramatic action onstage, whose material plot is a symbolic representation of a higher idea, always involving the conflict between freedom and necessity. What is more, just as Schelling's or Schiller's choruses were meant to encourage free reflection, by blocking unfiltered emotion, Boeckh's teacher–interpreter chorus is also a site of artistic mediation. Whether or not we agree with his assessment (we may well not), Boeckh was himself involved with the Potsdam production of the *Antigone* both as a scholar consultant and as a kind of dramaturge or artistic director tasked with checking, modifying, and approving the

---

[27] Boeckh (1843: 159).   [28] Boeckh (1843: 159).   [29] Boeckh (1843: 165).

translation by J. J. C. Donner that was used for the staging.[30] In this way, he too finds, or at least seeks, a way of squaring an artistic, poetic gesture with the figure of the scholar–interpreter.[31]

WILAMOWITZ'S ACTOR–PHILOLOGIST

My last example is Ulrich von Wilamowitz-Moellendorff, who may be the most extreme both in his deep nostalgia for the poetic side, and in his insistence that a cleaving to scientific standards, *Wissenschaftlichkeit*, must, at the end of the day, always be maintained. (Strong) individuality—and often one that had to struggle to assert itself against a restraining environment—was a central parameter for Wilamowitz's understanding of antiquity and of studying antiquity. In truth, he saw in classical writings a disappointing overall absence of real insight into individuality, with two exceptions: Plato and tragedy. For tragedy created 'entire human beings who let us experience how they became who they are' (*ganze Menschen, bei denen wir empfinden, wie sie so werden mussten*).[32]

Equally, he claims that 'the specific task [*Aufgabe*] of philology altogether lies in grasping another's individuality [*das Erfassen einer fremden Individualität*]. We want to immerse ourselves in another soul [*sich in eine fremde Seele zu versenken*], be it that of a man or a people.'[33] How then does the chorus relate to this individuality that finds release mainly in tragedy? While certainly not identical with the tragic hero, the chorus ought to be localized within the same framework.

His chorus, too, is a reflection of the poet's voice; but it is also the site of critical distance, of appearing behind a mask, of being other. Not least, for him the chorus as we know it mirrors increasing reflectivity and mediation in a historical sense. His *Introduction to Greek Tragedy* (1907) suggests a historical development of tragedy out of choral lyric and more specifically out of a mimetic type of dithyramb, whose subject matter is heroic myth (*Heldensage*),

[30] The stage translation was that of J. J. C. Donner, with some additions, especially of choric passages, by Boeckh. Boeckh's 1843 Greek and German edition of the text features his own complete retranslation.

[31] It is worth mentioning that Boeckh himself had, if not literary ambitions for sure, at least strong links into literary circles. In the early 1800s, he had close contact with the group of writers now referred to as the Heidelberg Romantics, both during his time in Heidelberg and in Berlin; see Ziolkowski (2008).

[32] Wilamowitz-Moellendorff (1972: 124). For Wilamowitz's understanding of ancient individuality, see further Güthenke (forthcoming).

[33] Wilamowitz-Moellendorff (1889i/1907: 257).

perfected in the context of the Athenian polis.[34] This historical trajectory, if we look closely, allows him to postulate that the longer arch is in fact one that leads from Homer's heroic epic, through lyric and tragedy, to Plato's Socratic dialogues—themselves dramatic forms of sort in which the poet speaks only indirectly, and whose hero is Socrates.[35] It is not irrelevant that one can also make a case for Wilamowitz's understanding of Plato as an almost perfect mirror of the modern scholar: as someone preoccupied with education, interpretation, *Bildung*, and the activity of the teacher–philosopher, overcoming an earlier inclination towards the poetic.[36] In other words, for Wilamowitz there is an eventual trajectory that leads from tragedy and Plato to the modern scholar as its closest embodied mediator—and it is the chorus as speaker who articulates that trajectory.

Wilamowitz's tragic poet puts on a mask—that for him is the central element, and it is therefore possible for him to make almost no distinction between choral speaking and tragic speaking, nor between the voice of the author and the voice of the tragic actors—choral or heroic.[37] In fact, he uses the terms choric song (*Chorlied* or also *Chorgesang*) and tragedy interchangeably throughout, since the development of single actors is for him an organic offshoot from or distillation of the mimetic poetry implied in tragic choral song. The chorus captures the mediated voice of the poet—just as mediation and interpretation are also the work of the scholar.

As tragedy as a genre progresses, the choric voice potentially loses in specific individuality, yet *gains* in taking on the voice of the author, who Wilamowitz of course claims has himself a strongly individual voice.[38] In other words, the chorus rather progressively modulates the kind of individuality it takes on. It may be revealing that Wilamowitz spells out one such example, apropos the chorus of old men of Euripides' *Heracles*, by way of an associative and

---

[34] The *Introduction to Greek Tragedy* is mostly a reprint of the four long sections that, under the heading 'Introduction to Attic Tragedy', form volume i of his edition of Euripides' *Heracles* (1889). That it exists as an independent edition of 1907 is testament to its popularity as a general introduction to tragedy. I am in what follows referencing the work, whose pagination is the same in both editions, as Wilamowitz-Moellendorff (1889i/1907).

[35] This is a trajectory of cultural and literary history similar to that suggested by Hegel, even though the latter includes comedy as an intermediary between tragedy and philosophy.

[36] Güthenke (forthcoming).

[37] 'the characteristic of choral lyric of the 6th century is that the chorus as such disappears while the poet appears. In drama, it is the poet who disappears, who speaks not only through the mouth of another but through another person. This is a contrast, and all similarity of form cannot make us forget, that a drama without μίμησις δρώντων, without putting a mask in front of the poet's face [*ohne die Vornahme einer Maske vor das Antlitz des Dichters*] is not a drama'; Wilamowitz-Moellendorff (1889i/1907: 81).

[38] 'given that the individuality of the chorus becomes increasingly dim in outline [*immer schattenhafter wird*]' (Wilamowitz-Moellendorff 1889: ii. 99, with reference to Euripides, *Heracles*, ll. 236–7).

anecdotal excursus about Gottfried Hermann as both editor of tragic texts and as scholarly individual:[39]

With the vow that is expressed here to serve the Muses and Charites despite old age and never to give in to *amousia*, Euripides becomes even more extreme; it won't do here to think only of the Attic chorus, which, as an old man, is still wearing a mask: we are dealing with the properly individual sentiments of the poet [*ganz individuelle Empfindung des Dichters*], who allows us a glimpse into his soul. The strange desire for a second life, especially for someone who has not wasted his, loses much of its strangeness when it happens to a man who struggles and strives with his mind [*dem geistig ringenden und strebenden Manne*] and feels the tyranny of the physical body all the more; when G. Hermann celebrated his anniversary in 1843, he expressed and motivated his own desire for a second lifetime in almost those same words as Euripides uses not quite here but in the parallel passage *Hik.* 108: that one would need a second life to correct the mistakes of the first when mature and with experience [*die Fehler des ersten nach der reiferen Erfahrung wieder gut zu machen*] . . . there is no question that in these stanzas we recognize the individual expressions of a tragedian, which we can use as reliable testimony of his life and opinions [*ein zuverlässiges Zeugnis für sein Leben und seine Gesinnung*].[40]

For Wilamowitz, the understanding of tragedy in the modern age needs the involvement of the philologist as the key-holder of historical hermeneutics:

the entire historical development of the Greeks tends towards this period [*strebt auf diese Zeit zu*], the entire development of Greek poetry tends towards tragedy. In this way tragedy is not only a historical object that is singularly meaningful [*rein geschichtliches Objekt von ganz einziger Bedeutung*], but every theoretical analysis of dramatic and altogether of all poetry will be miserable patchwork [*jämmerliches Stückwerk*] if it fails to understand Attic tragedy. No analysis can do that just on the basis of tragedy, however hard it tries. But philology will squander its privilege to reject unfounded arrogance and shallow wit [*kenntnislose Hoffart und flache Geistreichigkeit zurückzuweisen*] if it does not do its duty to communicate correct historical insights to philosophical speculation, which can then employ them freely [*das rechte, das geschichtliche Verständnis der philosophischen Betrachtung übermittelt, auf dass diese dann in voller Freiheit damit schalte*]. Because he alone holds the keys to Attic tragedy (as to many other treasures), the philologist will be indispensable to poetry and

---

[39] Wilamowitz's general admiration for Gottfried Hermann as a past master of philological skill was noticeable, and positive references to the older scholar, who died the same year Wilamowitz was born, are found across his writings and letters. A good example is Wilamowitz's eulogy of Hermann in his account of the *Eumenidenstreit* between Hermann and Müller—as a charismatic philologist who taught the 'living interaction' (*lebendiger Verkehr*) with ancient writers, whose manly and quasi-military virtues helped establish German scholarship vis-à-vis other nations, and who did for the re-evaluation of Greek tragedy on the part of textual criticism what Goethe had done for it on the artistic side; Wilamowitz-Moellendorff (1889i/1907: 235–43).

[40] Wilamowitz-Moellendorff (1889: ii. 175).

philosophy for all eternity [*werden Poesie und Philosophie in alle Ewigkeit des Philologen nicht entraten können*].[41]

Wilamowitz hastens to point out that the scholar and *Wissenschaftler* is not and should not be a poet ('we philologists as such have nothing of the poet or prophet, though the historian has to have some degree of that'[42])—even though the dividing line between philologist and historian seems thin; on the other hand, the true scholar has to be an artist of some sort no less, and Wilamowitz, who repeatedly pointed out scattered across his publications how important his experience of acting in school was to him, here sees the best paradigm for the work of scholarship:

we, however, must have some of the actor in us, not of the actor as virtuoso, who shapes a part according to his own lights, but of the true artist, who infuses the dead word with the life of his own heart's blood [*vom echten Künstler, der dem toten Worte durch das eigene Herzblut Leben gibt*].[43]

In his introduction to a translation of Aeschylus' tragedies, likewise, he speaks of his attempt to gain understanding that leads him 'to the point of complete physical and psychological exhaustion'.[44] The modern classical scholar embodies the characteristics of ancient tragedy; he performs the interpretation of ancient tragedy, as an active, artistic participant, above and beyond, yet also because of his scientific role. That Wilamowitz dreamed, consciously or not, of such an embodiment of scholar as artist carries across in the revealing way he closes his *Introduction to Greek Tragedy* and his reflection on the scholar as stage actor: once more with the image of Gottfried Hermann, this time in a reminiscence of the great scholar figure intoning Greek tragic choral lyric:

We achieve this best through the living word [*das lebendige Wort*]: when Gottfried Hermann read choral lyric, the ancient rhythms would rush with all their might [*dann rauschten die alten Rhythmen in voller Stärke*]—the ears of those who had the occasion to hear him are still ringing. But the word's echo is lost, and we need to rely on its imperfect surrogate: writing. And yet, even the biggest commentary is justified only if it furthers our understanding of drama, that it unlocks for the studious reader full enjoyment of the poetry, an enjoyment that can of course only be had at the price of hard and serious work [*einem Genusse, der freilich nur um den Preis ernster Arbeit feil ist*].[45]

---

[41] Wilamowitz-Moellendorff (1889i/1907: 119).

[42] Wilamowitz-Moellendorff (1889i/1907: 257).

[43] Wilamowitz-Moellendorff (1889i/1907: 257).

[44] Quoted in Görgemanns (1985: 143), though according to him merely as proof of Wilamowitz's 'long and intimate familiarity' with Aeschylus, just like his habit of constant recitation of some of his choric songs.

[45] Wilamowitz-Moellendorff (1889i/1907: 257).

What tragedy scholarship needs, so Wilamowitz concludes, is excellent linguistic knowledge combined with historical interpretation of the poet's voice. As is often the case, Wilamowitz's scholarly voice, though extreme, is symptomatic. If we assume that modernity and tragedy are in the German nineteenth century linked by the notion of individual subjectivity in relation to art and history, a subjectivity that is modern in so far as it is conscious of and confronted with a rift needing mediation, then we see a spectrum opening up, on which rational, scientific thought and poetic, artistic expression alike are movable entities. The scholar's voice, no less than that of the poet and philosopher, seeks to understand itself in relation to the same terms.

If the collective voice of the chorus poses a challenge to the heroic individual, the oscillation between the individual and the universal is also the precinct of the historical scholar. The ambivalence of the chorus as lyrical and prosaic, so to speak, as removed commentator and direct participant, is picked up by the ambivalence of scholarship as scientific and expressive, as objective and subjective: these are the two sides of the chorus's reflexivity, which the Idealist tradition of reading tragedy held high.

Wilamowitz was undoubtedly disturbed by more than one aspect of Nietzsche's *Birth of Tragedy*. As much as the author's unscholarly tone, and his less than enthusiastic account of Euripides, Wilamowitz's favourite, as the rationalist who spells the death of tragedy, Nietzsche's suggestion of an unfettered Dionysian chorus may also well have upset the younger philologist: it was at odds with (though maybe also too close to) the controlled artistry and exhausting interpretation that Wilamowitz read into tragedy. In his *Introduction to Greek Tragedy*, Wilamowitz refers in passing to past grandees in the field of textual scholarship as *Koryphäen*. In this he reflects linguistic usage still current in German now: a *Koryphäe* is a specialist, a leader of his field, especially in the sciences and arts. If we look at historical dictionaries of the nineteenth century, though, it might not be coincidental that this is a usage that comes about only as the nineteenth century progresses. Whereas around 1800 the *coryphaios* appears in learned dictionaries solely as the Greek chorus leader, it is only from the middle of the century that the meaning comes to include any leader in the arts or sciences.[46] As the role of the scholar develops, so the meaning of the chorus leader expands. We have come full circle to Schiller's choric voice as that of an 'adjudicating witness': the chorus could, indeed, speak for the nineteenth-century attitude to Greek tragedy, be it in poetry or in the science of philology.

---

[46] Zedler (1731–50); Campe (1804); Brockhaus (1809); Pierer (1849); Grimm and Grimm (1854); Herder (1855).

4

Chorus, Song, and Anthropology

Ian Rutherford

Dancing has long been a concern of anthropology, but the sorts of questions it asks and the answers it has found have varied greatly, just as the discipline of anthropology itself has changed. The questions asked by anthropologists in the first decades of the twentieth century are very different from those asked by them in the last few decades, and there are also huge differences between the lines of enquiry coming from social or cultural anthropology and those emerging from the field of physical anthropology, which is concerned with human evolution.

THEORIES OF INITIATION: 1900–1920

When, starting in the second half of the nineteenth century and continuing into the first years of the twentieth, anthropologists and ethnographers begin to describe and analyse tribal cultures, they could hardly avoid the topic of dance, because it is so pervasive in them. A good example is the ethnography of the Kikuyu people of Kenya by the husband and wife team William Scoresby Routledge and Katherine Routledge published in 1910. This includes a fourteen-page section on dancing, which distinguishes a total of twelve different dances, arranging them by the performers (I reproduce their synoptic table in Figure 4.1).[1] Notice that two of the dances are linked to male initiation into adulthood, and in fact one of these, the Mam-bú-ra, is regarded by the authors as of central importance and is described earlier in the book in a section on 'ceremonies of initiation into the tribe'. In emphasizing initiation, the Routledges were following one of the dominant anthropological paradigms

---

Thanks to audiences in Oxford and New York.

[1] Routledge and Routledge (1910: 179).

DIFFERENT DANCES 179

KIKÚYU DANCES[1]

Dances of Uncircumcised Boys—

(1) Ke-boi-i-a . . . . A dance by young boys with a special dress, and body as if tattooed.

(2) N'goi-i-sa . . . . A dance by big boys wearing maize-cob decorations.

(3) Mam-bú-ra . . . . The dance at the great ceremony of initiation.

Dances of Men only—

(1) N'dor-ó-si . . . . A festival of youths lately initiated (mu'-mo), and other young warriors.

(2) Ki-bá-ta . . . . A spectacular dance given by warriors.

(3) A peculiar dance on the completion of the maize harvest. Special description given.

Dances of Men and Women together—

(1) Mui-goí-o . . . . A social dance.

(2) Ke-chú-ki-a . . . . The principal social dance. This dance is always started by the warriors and young women at any large gathering.

(3) Ke-o-na-no . . . . No notes available about this dance.

(4) Ku-i-ne-né-ra . . . . A social dance. The men form the outside ring; the girls inside by themselves in groups.

Dances of Women only—

(1) Ge-ti-ro . . . . Dance of elder women at betrothal of a daughter.

(2) N'dú-mo . . . . No detailed notes on this dance.

Fig. 4.1. 'Kikuyu Dances', from W. S. Routledge and K. Routledge, *With a Prehistoric People: The Akikiyu of British East Africa* (London: Routledge, 1910), 179. Courtesy T & F Royalties Department. Image courtesy of the Bodleian Library, University of Oxford; taken from volume classmark 570 L1

of the time. Looking back from the start of the twenty-first century, Arnold Van Gennep's *Les Rites de passage*, published in 1909, seems to inaugurate the study of 'rites of passage', but actually Van Gennep was simply synthesizing ethnographic work, and to some extent theoretical discussions, dating back half a century.

In this period, the relationship between Classics and the broader intellectual tradition was quite close. Classicists, particularly those of the so-called

Cambridge School seem generally aware of what is going on in other disciplines, and, perhaps more surprisingly, the other disciplines show signs of taking notice of what is going on in Classics. In *Les Rites de passage* Van Gennep actually cites Jane Harrison's work, for example.[2] Harrison herself, who was of roughly the same generation as the Routledges (1850–1928), made a memorable connection between rites of passage and dance. This was in her work on the so-called Hymn to the Kouros from Palaikastro in eastern Crete, sensationally discovered in 1904, in the course of which a figure called the 'Kouros', apparently the young Zeus, is asked to 'leap' (*thore*) into 'our cities, ships, citizens and into justice (Themis)'.[3] This appealed to Harrison because she had already declared in print (in *Prolegomena* from 1903) that the myth of how the so-called Kouretes, primeval shield-clashing warriors, protected the baby Zeus from his father should be interpreted as a ritual of tribal initiation, where a new recruit to the *Männerbund* had to undergo a symbolic death.[4] In a paper published in 1909 ('The Kouretes and Zeus Kouros: A Study in Pre-Historic Sociology') she argued that the Hymn to the Kouros was itself an integral part of an initiation ritual, and the performers were members of a primitive secret society who represented themselves as the primordial Kouretes. In that paper she refers to anthropological scholarship, not to Van Gennep at this stage, but to Hutton Webster's book *Primitive Secret Societies* (1908);[5] the revised version of the argument, which appeared in *Themis* (1912), adds references both to Van Gennep (1909) and to Routledge and Routledge (1910).[6]

Partly as a direct result of Harrison's work on the Hymn to the Kouros, the rites-of-passage model went on to have a huge influence in Classics. It gave a title to Henri Jeanmaire's book *Couroi et courètes* (1939), which discusses rites of passage in African tribal societies, including the role of dance.[7] And we can follow it right through to Angelo Brelich and Claude Calame (of whom more later). It is only recently that people have begun to think the emphasis given to the rites-of-passage model by twentieth-century scholarship has been excessive.[8] It may well be that some ancient Greek choral dancing is connected with initiation or rites of passage or rites of maturation or aggregation, though

---

[2] Van Gennep (1960: 87–8).   [3] For the text, see West (1965).

[4] J. E. Harrison (1903). Palaikastro Hymn: Ἰώ, μέγιστε Κοῦρε, | χαῖρέ μοι, Κρόνειε, | παγκρατὲς γάνος, βέβακες | δαιμόνων ἀγώμενος | Δίκταν εἰς ἐνιαυτὸν | ἕρπε καὶ γέγαθι μολπᾷ ('O, greatest Youth, I greet you, son of Cronos! Almighty splendour, you have come, leading your spirits. Come to Dikte at the turn of the year and rejoice in our song').

[5] J. E. Harrison (1908–9; 1912: 24): 'instruction among savage peoples is almost always imparted in more or less mimetic dances', citing H. Webster (1908: 50–1), who refers to Enright (1899).

[6] H. Webster (1908: 50–1); Harrison (1912); van Gennep (1909); Routledge and Routledge (1910).

[7] Jeanmaire (1939: 190, 440); Brelich (1969); Calame (1977*a*).

[8] See Dodd and Faraone (2003).

it is not clear that there is any reason to think that the Hymn to the Great Kouros itself is anything but a simple cult song. In particular, the name 'Kouros' need not imply a rite-of-passage ritual involving Kouretes imperson-ators, but forms a unit with the adjective *Kroneios*, i.e. 'son (of Kronos)'.[9]

Harrison was not the only scholar in the general milieu of the Cambridge Ritualists who made use of anthropological data about choral dancing. An-other was William Ridgeway, whose *The Dramas and Dramatic Dances of Non-European Races in Special Reference to the Origin of Greek Tragedy* (1915) aimed to make a contribution to theories about the origin of drama, specific-ally by demolishing one theory and arguing for another. The thesis demol-ished is the Cambridge Ritualist thesis that Greek drama has a ritual origin in the schema of the dying vegetation deity, and the one argued is that it came from commemoration of the ancestors, which he claims to be a widespread function of dramatic dance in tribal societies, and to that end he marshals data from a wide range of cultures.[10] Although the book completely fails to provide a convincing theory for the origin of Greek drama,[11] it succeeds in establishing that commemoration of ancestors through dance is a common pattern. Scholars today would probably want to look for the reasons that motivate people to sing about their ancestors, and how this activity provides a focus for group identity.

DANCE AND SOCIAL ANTHROPOLOGY: 1920–1980

What we miss in the ethnography of the Routledge and Routledge type, and in its adaptation by classicists in this period, is any attempt to understand dance itself. Here the big breakthrough came in 1922, when Alfred Radcliffe-Brown published his ethnography of the Andaman Islands. Radcliffe-Brown had had the benefit of reading the works of the French sociologist Émile Durkheim, whose *Elementary Forms of Religious Thought* had been published a decade before in 1912. Durkheim had tried to show how human cultures use religion as a device to generate social cohesion, but had not said a great deal about dance *per se*. Radcliffe-Brown filled in the gap.

In the dance the individual submits to the action upon him of the community: he is constrained, by the immediate effect of rhythm as well as by custom, to join in, and he is required to conform in his action and movements to the needs of common activity. The surrender of the individual to this constraint or obligation is not felt as painful, but

---

[9] For alternative interpretations, see Perlman (1995) and Alonge (2005).

[10] Cornford (1914).

[11] 'In strict logic Ridgeway was weak. In support of a theory, of the truth of which he was convinced, he would use all kinds of evidence, strong and weak alike . . .' (Conway 2004).

on the contrary as highly pleasurable. As the dancer loses himself in the dance, as he becomes absorbed in the unified community, he reaches a state of elation in which he feels himself filled with energy or force immediately beyond his ordinary state. In this way the dance produces a condition in which the unity, harmony and concord of the community are at a maximum, and in which they are intensely felt by every member. It is to produce this condition, I would maintain, that is the primary social function of the dance . . . The well-being, or indeed the existence, of the society depends on the unity and harmony that obtain in it, and the dance, by making that unity intensely felt, is a means of maintaining it.[12]

This is a powerful, if idealized, statement that still reverberates today. However, not all contemporary anthropologists saw dance quite this way. Another young British anthropologist with a bright future, Edward Evans-Pritchard, published a paper on African dance in 1928 that embraced Radcliffe-Brown's position, but pointed out that in reality things were often a lot messier, and that collective dance is an environment that lends itself to intense sexual attraction between participants and consequently outbreaks of violence.

As children grow up into boys and girls they will never miss a dance. To both sexes it is a means of display which becomes intensified at puberty. The dance is one of those cultural milieux in which sexual display takes place and selection is encouraged. The sexual situations of the dance are not very obvious to the observer. Boys and girls come to the dance to flirt, and flirtation often leads to sexual connexion, but society insists that neither the one nor the other shall be indulged in blatantly. At the same time society permits these sexual incidents so long as they occur with discretion and moderate concealment. A boy who openly approached a girl would be reprimanded and abused, but if he catches her attention whilst she is dancing with her friends, gives her a little nudge perhaps, and when he sees that his advances are reciprocated says *mu je gude* (come on kid!) no one will interfere. They go quietly into the bush or into a neighbouring hut and have intercourse. It is a different matter with married women. Their husbands are always jealous of them going to dances and generally accompany them. Men are also frightened to flirt with married women since they will have to pay heavy compensation to the husbands and in the past risked the severe punishment of mutilation.[13]

In this context it is also worth mentioning Margaret Mead's great classic *Coming of Age in Samoa*, also published in 1928, which has a whole chapter on dance, showing its role in the education of the young and their socialization. However, Mead sees its function as first to develop individuality and second to compensate for repression in other spheres of life. Her implicit target seems likely to be Radcliffe-Brown's analysis of Andaman dance.[14]

---

[12] Radcliffe-Brown (1922: 252–3). See Humphreys (1978: 102). The social analysis of dance was developed by Hambly (1926).
[13] Evans-Pritchard (1928: 457–8).   [14] Mead (1928: 101).

In the following decades anthropologists continued to be interested in dance, though they looked for ways of making Radcliffe-Brown's rather broad formulation of its relation to society more precise and nuanced. One example is Roy Rappaport's classic work *Pigs for the Ancestors* (1967), which studied the social economy of the Maring culture of New Guinea, looking in particular at the intermittent Kaiko festival, key elements of which are the lavish sacrifice of pigs and elaborate dancing by members of neighbouring groups, who have been invited to attend.[15] Applying terminology that comes ultimately from zoology,[16] he suggests we see these dances as having two functions: 'epigamic' and 'epideictic'. To call dance 'epideictic' means that it is 'for display'—that is, it is a means by which one settlement shows off its manpower to the others, with the intention of averting military conflict. To call dance 'epigamic' means that it is the purpose of marriage—that is, to attract the attention of potential marriage partners. Rappaport says: 'it would be difficult to conceive a more economical means for communicating information about the availability of males than the sample presentation of the dance.'[17]

Another contribution from the same period is Maurice Bloch's classic paper 'Symbols, Songs, Dance and Features of Articulation: Is Religion a Form of Traditional Authority?' (1974). Bloch's subject was the initiation ritual of the Merina people of Madagascar, and he showed how elders use song and dance to instil respect for traditional authority. This was basically the Durkheimian approach again, though with emphasis on the use made by one social group—the elders—to dominate another. Bloch sums the situation up in five words: 'You cannot argue with a song!'[18]

By this point, a synthesis was badly needed, and this came with Paul Spencer's edited volume *Society and the Dance*, published in 1985. The collection consists of seven essays preceded by an analytic introduction by Spencer. The papers include Adrienne Kaeppler on 'Structured Movement Systems in Tonga', which describes complex choral performances on the occasion of the Kava ritual. Another is Andrew Strathern's account of the Melpa of New Guinea, who have various forms of dance, including a special type of circular dance where the audience are in the centre, which is exactly where the audience ought to be, if circular dance symbolizes the community. And Spencer himself has a study of the Samburu of Kenya, describing the dances of the so-called moran, men in their twenties who for a number of years live outside the settled farming communities, and whose performances typically involve the threat of conflict with the established order.

---

[15] Rappaport (1967). Rappaport's account of this festival was used as a case study by Ulf (2006), an important paper exploring what contribution anthropology can make to understanding Greek festivals.

[16] Wynne-Edwards (1962: 193).   [17] Rappaport (1967: 193).

[18] Bloch (1974: 71) = Bloch (1989: 37).

Spencer's helpful introduction sets out seven 'themes' in the papers:

Theme 1. 'Dance as a safety valve: the cathartic theory.'

Theme 2. 'The educational role of dance and the transmission of sentiments' (this corresponds to Maurice Bloch's 'You cannot argue with a song').

Theme 3. 'Interaction with the dance and the maintenance of sentiments' (this is basically Radcliffe-Brown).

Theme 4. 'Dance as a cumulative process: the theory of self-generation' (this is mostly about the feeling of transcendence, including the feeling of being possessed by a deity).

Theme 5. 'The element of competition in dance: theories of boundary display' (that includes Rappaport's 'epideictic' function).[19]

Theme 6. 'Dance as ritual drama: the theory of communitas and antistructure' (these are Victor Turner's terms, and the idea that in dance normal social hierarchies vanish; we are all the same).

Theme 7. 'The uncharted deep structures of dance' (which is supposed to be about the relationship between the forms of dance and the deep structures of the human mind).

I would draw attention to two striking features of the typology. First, there is no sign of rites of passage or secret societies, which belies their importance in the subject seventy years earlier. In fact, these are not excluded, but merely incorporated under the educational role of dance. Secondly, notice that the only reference to religion seems to be under theme 4, which is supposed to include cases where dancers feel that a god possesses them. The low profile of religion will surprise students of ancient Greece, where it was rare for a choral performance not to take place under the sign of religion. Social anthropology, at least of this period, tends to sideline religion, in a way that Durkheim did not.

In fact, most of these 'themes' are models of how dance reflects society. I would distinguish five of them:

- confirmation of your sense of belonging to the community (theme 3);
- losing yourself, becoming one with the dance (i.e. 'communitas' in Victor Turner's sense) (theme 6);
- feeling energized by it: transcendence (theme 4);
- becoming a member of society and learning its principles (theme 2);
- showing off to other people: boundary display (theme 5).

---

[19] P. Spencer (1985*a*: 40) illustrates this theme with N. Chagnon's account of the Yanomano of Venezuela: Chagnon (1968: 109–11).

Radcliffe-Brown's cruder Durkheimian approach has thus been broken down and sifted to make five more nuanced approaches.

These developments in social anthropology between the 1920s and the 1980s were largely ignored by scholars of ancient Greece. Take, for example, the case of one of the pioneers of the early study Greek dance, the American scholar Lillian Lawler (1898–1990), whose two monographs on dance appeared in 1964, but who was already publishing papers on the subject from the 1930s. Some of her early work shows an engagement with ethnographic literature, such as her piece on the so-called dance of the *pinakides* (1940), which she interprets as a dance in which flat pieces of wood are clapped together, a practice widely attested in different parts of the world. She does something similar in a paper on fish dances from 1941.[20] But her work does not attempt to apply the general theories of dance that were emerging from social anthropology.[21]

The study of Greek chorality really starts with Claude Calame's work on Alcman's partheneia or maiden songs in the 1970s. Calame is absolutely clear that in cultures like archaic Sparta choral performance has a central political role,[22] and that in particular the partheneia are part of a religious occasion that doubles as maturation rituals for girls—a plausible interpretation given what we know from the ethnographic data. At the time it was published, the book was received by the Classics community as radical and controversial, but, looking at it from the point of view of the development of the anthropological theory of dance, it might be better characterized as on the conservative side.[23] Calame is usually seen as linked to the Durkheim-inspired Annales School and was better qualified as an anthropologist than most scholars who have worked on Greek religion—his most recent book mentions fieldwork he himself did in New Guinea.[24] In view of that, it is surprising that he mentions comparative material on dancing rather little—one reference to Mead in the original edition, and a reference to a paper in Spencer's *Society and the Dance* in the

---

[20] Lawler (1940); the dance of the *pinakides* is referred to by Athenaeus 14.629f; Lawler (1941). Her paper on the Delian geranos (1946*b*) seems less successful, arguing that it is a form of snake-dance, using comparative material assembled by Sachs (1937: 151–9). Lawler might have made use of contemporary work being done on maze-dances among the Malekula people of Vanuatu by John Layard: Layard (1936) and Layard (1942: 340–1, 652–3), who himself seems to have been helped by the Latinist W. F. Jackson-Knight (1936).

[21] The same criticism can be made of other work from this period, such as Bowra (1962), although Bowra had read widely in ethnographic literature. Mention should also be made of the important *Dances Sacrées* volume from 1963, which covers dance in several ancient and modern civilizations, though not Greece.

[22] Cf. Calame (1977*a*: 277). Ahead of his time, as often, was Herman Koller, who in 1955 argued that the notion of ἐγκύκλιος παιδεία (origin of the word encyclopaedia) incorporates the metaphor of the circular dance.

[23] The same criticism could perhaps be made of Bierl's rites-of-passage interpretation (2001) of the Aristophanic chorus.

[24] Calame (2009*b*: 123–9); see also Calame (2003).

English translation.[25] To be fair, he may be assuming knowledge of earlier works such as Angelo Brelich's *Paides e parthenoi* (1969) and Jeanmaire's *Couroi et courètes* (1939), both of which have ethnographic surveys.[26]

The first book by a classicist that tries to make extensive use of Spencer's *Society and the Dance* was, as far as I know, Stephen Lonsdale's *Dance and Ritual Play in Greek Religion* from 1993, which is one of very few monographs to have attempted an overview of Greek choral culture. Some of the chapters in the book follow the categories identified by Spencer.[27] So Chapter 2, entitled 'Ordering force', corresponds to themes 2 and 3 in Spencer, while chapter 3, 'Disruptive force', is more like his themes 1 and 4. Lonsdale also deserves credit for pointing out how much we can learn about Greek chorality from Plato's *Laws*, where it is advocated as a means of inculcating the correct values.[28]

Probably the most innovative recent work on the subject is Barbara Kowalzig's *Singing for the Gods*, which came out in 2007. Kowalzig makes surprisingly little explicit use of anthropological material, at least anthropological material about communal dancing, but the whole thrust of her argument is that in archaic Greece choral performance is used as a way of representing and in some cases creating political communities. A number of other scholars have recently pursued similar lines reflecting individual poems or performances.[29] One particular interest in recent years has been Plato's use of choral performance, where Anastasia-Erasmia Peponi has taken a leading role.[30]

EVOLUTIONARY ARCHAEOLOGY

The general view these days is that the pivotal period in the development of civilization in Western Asia and Europe was somewhere around 9000 BC, when the first towns and villages develop. This accompanies the simultaneous development of agriculture, which is supposed to have originated in south-east Turkey and Syria. If choral dancing has to do with defining communities, then

---

[25] Mead is cited in Calame (1977*a*: 445–6, n. 187); cf. translation Calame (1997: 261, n. 187). Calame adds a reference to Strathern (1985).

[26] See Calame (1977*a*: 32, n. 71, and 38, n. 128).

[27] The chapters of Lonsdale (1993) are: 1. Laws; 2. Ordering force; 3. Disruptive force; 4 Divine prototypes; 5, Manhood; 6 Women's transitions; 7. Courtship; 8. Death; 9. Pan and private worship.

[28] Lonsdale (1993: 40) cites Spencer (1985*b*) for play.

[29] Dougherty (1994) on Pindar, *Paean* 2 (a composition that Ridgeway would have found useful, since it celebrates a dead ancestor), Rutherford (2004) on choral performance at common sanctuaries, which draws on parallels with Andean dance traditions as described in Sallnow (1987).

[30] Peponi (2013*c*); see also Kowalzig (2004) and Peponi, Chapter 1, this volume.

we might expect to find evidence of dancing from around the same time. In fact, evidence for exactly this has been presented by the Israeli archaeologist Yosef Garfinkel in his book *Dancing at the Dawn of Agriculture* (2003). Garfinkel observed that the motif of dancers, usually dancing in a circle, appears a great deal in material culture from the period 8000–4000 BC in the Near East and southern Europe. It is found on various media: rock carvings, pottery, and towards the end of the period seals. Garfinkel's reasonable conclusion is that choral dancing became very important in this period.

Ancient villagers conceived dance as the most significant cultic activities whose essence as a religious experience was expressed by the circle of dancers. The uniformity of the figures in the circle gives ideological expression to the equality of members of the community. Moreover all the figures have the same role in the ceremony. Even if other people such as shamans or priests were present at the ceremony, they are not more important in cognitive terms . . . Dancing together creates unity, provides education, and transmits cultural messages from one generation to the next.[31]

Meanwhile, evolutionary anthropologists have attempted to push the birth of chorality back even further, in fact to the dawn of humanity.[32] There seem to be two main theories. First, in 2000, Björn Merker, a Swedish biomusicologist, argued that 'synchronous chorusing' might be an evolved phenomenon in humans. As is well known, the ability to chorus synchronously is an ability that humans share with many species of birds and insects. In the case of birds and insects, Merker believes that the aim of synchronous chorusing is to attract a mate, and he thinks this could be true of humans as well. To be more precise, Merker's hypothesis is that, if there was a need for early humans to attract a mate from outside the immediate family group—that is, from some distance—a loud singing chorus of young men or women would have an advantage. Indeed, anthropologists have, as I have already mentioned, observed that sexual liaisons have a tendency to happen in the context of choral dancing; this is also something known to the Greeks, as we know from traditional narratives in which a love affair starts at a sanctuary, such as the story of Acontius and Cydippe.[33]

The second theory is that collective singing and dancing are something that holds early human societies together. This was argued in 2003 by Edward Hagen and Gregory Bryant, in their paper 'Music and Dance as a Coalition Signaling System'. The idea here is that song and dance developed as way of holding large groups or 'coalitions' of proto-humans together. Song–dance performance serves the dual purpose of holding the coalition together and marking its territory and defining themselves against others. Hagen and Bryant were in fact anticipated by a few years by Robin Dunbar, who in his

---

[31] Garfinkel (2003: 100).   [32] See Mithen (2005) for a survey.
[33] Callimachus frs 67–75.

Grooming, Gossip and the Evolution of Language (1996) suggested that choral performance might have developed to keep groups together. He also proposed that this might have facilitated the development of speech and that the initial stimulus to language might have 'been the emotional uplift of the Greek chorus'. If I understand him correctly, the hypothesis is that humans sang before they could speak, and they sang in chorus, or antiphonally, before they could sing individually.[34] (It is interesting to see here anthropology drawing on ancient Greece for its inspiration, just as in an earlier time Van Gennep made use of Jane Harrison).

If the coalition-building theory seems familiar, it is maybe because it is so similar to what the social anthropologists had long been saying. The only difference is that, for the social anthropologists, the chorus is a device that tribes use for the purpose of social cohesion, building a group identity and everything else, while for the evolutionary anthropologists the ability to perform in a chorus is hard-wired into our DNA. For the latter, it comes down to nature, and, for the former, it is a matter of culture. This hypothesis invites us to revise the way we look at Greek choruses: a chorus need not be merely a representation of a community; rather, it could be a primal form that early human communities and coalitions took. In looking at a Greek chorus, we are thus glimpsing the origins of humanity.

To recapitulate, it would seem that dance, having been of marginal concern to ethnographers, assumed a much more important role in the social anthropology of the 1920s, and nowadays many see it as a dynamic component of early human societies. Scholars of early Greek dance can be seen to have seasoned their work with references to anthropology and ethnography from the beginning, but until quite recently there seems to have been little appreciation among classicists of the true importance of choruses as a social phenomenon. The work done on the subject to date has barely scratched the surface, however, and it is to be hoped that in future years anthropological theory will play an even greater role in guiding the imagination of classicists working on dance and the chorus.

---

[34] Dunbar (1996: 146, 150).

Part II

Aesthetics

5

Greek Festival Choruses in and out of Context

Felix Budelmann

It is a cumulative argument of this volume that one of the fundamental binaries of Western thinking about cultural expressions, couched in terms such as aesthetics versus social function, and art versus ritual, finds particularly sharp articulation in modern perceptions and uses of the chorus. Since at least the eighteenth century there has been a deep gulf between, on the one hand, choruses as an art form, in opera, in choral music, in theatre; and, on the other, choruses as a ritual practice, above all among non-Western peoples, studied by travellers, ethnographers, and anthropologists. Of course, the divide can be crossed, in church music, for instance, and above all in dance, the term used in preference over 'chorus' in the anthropological tradition, and of all modern genres that use choruses the one that has created most suspicion. But, on the whole, it is difficult to deny that in modernity choruses have tended to be looked at *either* as products of high art *or* for what they do for their performers and their society.

This chapter explores a version of this binary for what I shall refer to as the canonical festival choruses of Archaic and Classical Greece: compositions by what were, or with hindsight came to be, high-profile poets, such as Alcman, Pindar, and Bacchylides, in choral genres regularly performed at civic festivals, like paean, dithyramb, prosodion (processional song), and partheneion (maiden song).[1] Non-dramatic ancient choruses are less familiar to non-classicists than their tragic and comic counterparts, even though for the

I am grateful to my fellow editors and to Peter Agócs, as well as an audience in Cambridge, for helpful comments on earlier versions.

---

[1] That is to say, I do not discuss epinician, a genre that, whatever its actual circumstances of performance, often positions itself on the cusp between solo and choral and between private and public. Nor do I discuss Stesichorus, who raises too many unanswerable questions about the mode of performance and the nature of his songs.

Greeks they were the default, and have not prompted the same amount of theorizing; but for that very reason they deserve attention here. The hope is that the discussion will broaden the sometimes narrow base non-classicists use for thinking about ancient choruses, and vice versa that for experts in Greek lyric it will underline the usefulness of placing their understanding of these choruses in thinking about choruses more broadly.

Exactly because they are so central to modern intellectual traditions, the terms 'art', 'aesthetics', and 'ritual' carry many associations that are notoriously counterproductive in work on antiquity, not least the sense that 'art'/ 'aesthetics' and 'ritual' are mutually exclusive, and I shall therefore use them only sparingly until I confront those associations head on near the end. The binary that will instead do most of the work revolves around the notion of occasion that has been central to recent work on Greek lyric: canonical festival choruses as both of and not of the occasion, as, on the one hand, performing at and for the occasion for which they were composed, and, on the other hand, transcending that occasion already in their original performance.

The occasional–functional perspective needs no justification. A large body of recent scholarship has brought these difficult texts to life by reconstructing their often intricate relationships with the contexts in which they were performed. In their different ways, Alcman's partheneia, Pindar's paeans, or Bacchylides' dithyrambs are meticulously designed tools that enable specific sets of performers and specific communities to communicate with the divine, to define and promote themselves, to mould memories of recent or less recent history for the needs of the current moment, to celebrate, to mourn, to create identities. Canonical festival choruses reflect, serve, and shape the occasion for which they are commissioned, be it one specific occasion or a type of recurrent occasion. Yet at the same time they also encourage a rather different perspective, one in which they are songs that are performed and listened to in their own right. Canonical festival choruses travelled beyond their original contexts (that is how they became canonical), and, already at their first performances, they encouraged responses that are not adequately described in terms of the song's occasion-specific function. Most obviously, as is often pointed out, audiences were encouraged to admire the skill of performers qua performers and to savour the aural and visual pleasures of their performance. They were also encouraged to admire the skill of the poet as a poet; and they were made to engage with engrossing and wide-ranging interpretative questions and were taken off into worlds of the imagination far away from the here and now. The choruses performed not just songs for the gods or songs for the polis but also songs as songs.

The thrust of the discussion will be twofold. The first two of three parts, devoted respectively to re-performance and original performance, are empirical and textual in that they use the texts of Greek canonical festival choruses, together with external evidence, to illustrate some of the value of a

performance-for-its-own-sake perspective, not to take issue with the occasional–functional perspective, but to show how much the texts do to demand a
well-developed occasion- and function-independent viewpoint side by side
with it, a viewpoint that maximizes the autonomy of the poet in shaping the
song and the autonomy of each listener in responding to the song. In this
respect the chapter aims to contribute in its own way to the recent revival of
interest in matters of aesthetics in early Greece, showcased in the work of
scholars such as James Porter, Anastasia-Erasmia Peponi, and Richard Neer.

The third part is more conceptual and discusses the relationship between
the two perspectives. Returning to the modern unbridgeable divide between
'art'/'aesthetics' and 'ritual'/function and the modern history of the chorus
from which I started, I shall defend the benefit of keeping the two viewpoints
distinct also for the festival choruses of early Greece, despite the risk of
anachronism. The close interrelation of the two perspectives in early Greece
may be a paradox above all because of modern cultural traditions, but it
nevertheless is a paradox of undeniable power, which we must acknowledge
and with which we must engage.

I

Much early Greek lyric was composed for a particular occasion, but it was re-
performance across an increasingly connected, 'panhellenic' world, together
with written texts that ensured its survival and eventual inclusion in the
Hellenistic editions. Festival choruses are no exception, as Chris Carey and
Thomas Hubbard have recently emphasized for Alcman and Pindar, respectively.[2] For our purposes, one needs to distinguish between two overlapping but
essentially distinct scenarios. One is, typically regular, re-performance in the same
or similar settings. For instance, it is plausible, as has repeatedly been suggested,
that Alcman 1 (in the numeration of Page and Davies), the *Louvre Partheneion*,
was not composed for a one-off performance, but was performed at a recurring
festival, maintaining much of its function unchanged from year to year.[3]

The other type of outing beyond the original occasion, the one that is of
interest here, is one that takes the song into an altogether different context
from that of the original commission, be it through re-performance or through
use of written texts. Our earliest evidence comes mostly from dramatic texts of

---

[2] Carey (2011) and Hubbard (2011). On Alcman, see also Hinge (2006: 282–304, 339–40). In
general, on the importance of pan-Hellenism for the transmission of early poetry, see Nagy
(1990: chs 2 and 3).
[3] Most influentially, Nagy (1990: 345–9); and see the articles in the previous note. Much could
be said, of course, about how the effect of certain aspects of the text, such as personal names,
would subtly change over time, even at a recurring occasion.

the second half of the fifth century, which testify to widespread knowledge in Athens not just of names like Alcman, Stesichorus, or Simonides, but also of individual choral compositions of non-Athenian origin. Perhaps the most powerful instance is the patent allusion in the parodos of the *Antigone* to Pindar's *Paean* 9, composed for original performance at the Theban Ismenion sanctuary a good number of years earlier.[4] The invocation ἀκτὶς ἀελίου ('beam of the sun') that opens both songs establishes the connection, which is then developed in a number of ways, above all through the Theban setting of both works and the hoped-for delivery from danger: in Pindar's case protection against an eclipse, which the chorus pray will not turn out a portent of catastrophe, and in the *Antigone* the defeat of the besieging army, which in characteristic tragic fashion turns out anything other than the end of all woes. One might go even further and contrast the jubilant τὸ κάλλιστον ... φανέν ... τῶν προτέρων φάος ('most beautiful light of all that shone before', *Ant.* 100–2) with the anxious ἐλαύνεις τι νεώτερον ἢ πάρος ('do you drive a newer course than before?', l. 6), or compare (as Armand D'Angour does) the worried insistence on newness in Pindar—apart from l. 6 there is also the 'new race of men' potentially presaged by the eclipse—with the 'new ruler' that emerges from the 'new events of the gods' after Sophocles' parodos (ll. 155–8). One could point out further (with Ian Rutherford) that the sun's beam in Pindar is a 'driver of horses' (l. 7) and in Sophocles drives away the enemy with a bridle (ll. 108–9), and that later in Pindar's ode we hear of the oracle of Teneros and in Sophocles' play of the seer Tiresias. As ever, the extent of intertextuality is a matter of judgement, but it is evident that Sophocles expected at least a portion of his audience members to know Pindar's Theban paean, and know it well.

Other testimonies to familiarity with canonical cult songs in different contexts as early as the fifth century are not quite as rich as the parodos of *Antigone*, but the cumulative case is unassailable, and not just for Pindar.[5] For Alcman, an especially interesting text is the Spartan's song that closes Aristophanes' *Lysistrata* (1296–1321). As scholars have long been aware, the similarities with the surviving fragments of Alcman's Spartan partheneia are numerous and must constitute some form of allusion, though perhaps generally to Alcman's output in this genre rather than specifically to any one song.[6]

---

[4] *Paean* 9 Maehler = A1 Rutherford. See the discussions by Rutherford (2001: 199–200) and D'Angour (2011: 46–8). *Paean* 9, or at least its opening, remained famous in later centuries: see the testimonia in the standard editions.

[5] See esp. Alcm. 26.3 *PMGF* (genre uncertain), adapted by Ar. *Av.* 250–1; Pind. frs 76 and 77 M, alluded to at Ar. *Ach.* 637–9 and *Eq.* 1329; Pind. fr. 89a M, parodied at Ar. *Eq* 1264; Pind. *Paean* 14.35–7 M, apparently envisioning reperformance elsewhere. Carey (2011: 457–60) and Hubbard (2011: 348–9) cite further texts.

[6] See Bierl (2011). More broadly on Athenian knowledge of Spartan partheneia, see Swift (2009: 425–6).

Thanks to their re-performance, supported probably by an incipient culture of reading, festival choruses could transcend the limits of their first performance.

In the context of the argument here it is important to stress that this is not just an episode in the history of transmission but also says something about the nature of the songs. As the intricacy of Sophocles' play with Pindar's text shows, these compositions were such that Athenian audiences, and presumably readers too, took an interest in them even though they belonged to a different place and/or time. Various things will have contributed to this interest: Carey, for instance, points to dialect, myth, genre, and the projection of the poet as features that are not configured strictly locally even in as locally grounded a poet as Alcman.[7] What I want to explore here is an aspect of the texts that helps them to travel not by lessening their ties to the occasional, but paradoxically by exploiting them. To a greater or lesser degree the surviving texts of canonical festival choruses contain a set of prompts that permit imaginative re-enactments of the original occasion by later audiences and readers.[8]

The two texts mentioned above, Pindar's ninth *Paean* and Alcman's first *Partheneion*, will continue to serve as examples. *Paean* 9 opens with an arresting scene. Insistent questions addressed to the sun, followed by an urgent request, produce at the same time a sense of emergency, a ritual moment, and an easily comprehensible setting; an eclipse has caused fear in Thebes, and makes the chorus pray (ll. 1–10):[9]

Beam of the sun! What have you contrived, observant one, mother of eyes, highest star, in concealing yourself in broad daylight? Why have you made helpless men's strength and the path of wisdom, by rushing down a dark highway? Do you drive a newer course than before? In the name of Zeus, swift driver of horses, I beg you, turn the universal omen, lady, into some painless prosperity for Thebes.

After further questions in the antistrophe and a large gap in our text of the epode, there comes a shift at the opening of the second surviving triad (ll. 33–8):

I have been ordained by some fateful [noun missing] near the immortal bed of Melia to link noble voices by means of the *aulos* (pipes) and the counsels of my mind for your sake. I beseech you, far-shooter . . .

These lines contextualize the performance further. It takes place not anywhere in Thebes, but more specifically 'near the bed of Melia', for now a mysterious statement with what may be little resonance outside Thebes. Less mysterious is the notion that the song is the response to a divine prompt (whatever is lost in the gap). This kind of statement about the motivation for the song is included in some of the framing paratexts that introduce paeanic inscriptions in later

---

[7] Carey (2011: 441–4).   [8] Cf. D'Alessio (2007: 96, 104–5).
[9] All *Paean* 9 translations are Rutherford's, slightly adapted.

centuries.[10] Here it subtly changes the dramatic moment in the course of the
song itself, shifting the now from the moment of the eclipse to sometime
after—enough time, that is, to compose and rehearse this song. Finally, at the
end of our preserved text, a myth helps non-Theban audiences and readers
identify the 'bed of Melia' as the oracular shrine of the little-known local
prophet Teneros, son of the Oceanid Melia.

What all this adds up to is a memorable evocation of an unsettled community using song to reach out to the divine. To be sure, the picture has an
element of haziness—who, for instance, are the performers, and what sort of
occasion should we imagine beyond the choral performance itself?—but there
is enough there for non-Theban listeners and readers to imagine a gradually
unfolding choral event as they take in the text.

The best-preserved section of Alcman's first *Partheneion*, constituting
almost two thirds of what survives (ll. 39–101), insistently refers to the chorus
itself, with a plethora of deictic articles and pronouns guiding the actual or
mental gaze, and so a complex picture emerges of the girls of the chorus, their
outfits, their actions, their sentiments, especially vis-à-vis their leaders Hagesichora and Agido. The section is too long to print here in its entirety, but the
following extract is a good illustration (ll. 64–77):[11]

> For abundance of purple is not sufficient for protection, nor intricate snake of solid
> gold, no, nor Lydian headband, pride of dark-eyed girls, nor the hair of Nanno, nor
> again godlike Areta nor Thylacis and Cleësithera; nor will you go to Aenesimbrota's
> and say, 'If only Astaphis were mine, if only Philylla were to look my way and
> Damareta and lovely Ianthemis'; no, Hagesichora wears me away.

There is plenty in these lines and elsewhere in the text to stimulate vivid
impressions of the girls, their looks, and their feelings. One is even led to think
of a specific time of day, around dawn (ll. 40–3, 60–3, 87–8). And, as in *Paean*
9, a number of addresses and requests extend the scene to include personages
beyond the chorus, present as well as absent, human as well as divine. The
picture that emerges is manifold and even hazier than that developed by *Paean*
9 (more on that in the next section), but, as the enormous amount of
scholarship on the poem shows, it is all the more intriguing for it. Wave
after wave of pictorial detail allows later audiences and readers to catch
glimpses of that occasion back then in distant Sparta.

Rather than shed their original occasion, then, both *Partheneion* 1 and
Paean 9 take it with them. Their attraction to audiences and readers divorced
from the original occasion rests not simply in universal applicability, in the
manner of, for instance, Ariphon's hymn to Health or the Erythraean paean,
which contain hardly any features that link them to their origins, but to a

---

[10] E.g., Makedonios' paean: *IG* II² 4473 = *SEG* 23 126.
[11] All Alcman 1 translations are Campbell's, slightly adapted.

considerable degree also in their ability to conjure up dramatically a specific place and specific time.[12] It is not an accident that Sophocles alluded to *Paean* 9 in a play set in Thebes and that Aristophanes puts the exodus of *Lysistrata* in the mouth of a Spartan.

As is often emphasized, this characteristic of canonical festival choruses is exploited by Hellenistic authors, above all Callimachus in his mimetic hymns, who developed the representational tendencies of Archaic and Classical cult songs into self-standing texts that few scholars believe were composed for cultic purposes.[13] Such Alexandrian texts evoke a performance occasion without being grounded in one, yielding in this respect little for the kind of occasional–functional perspective that is so powerful for the Archaic and Classical material. The argument of this section is that this development had reached more than its halfway point already in fifth-century (and probably earlier) uses of the songs away from the original occasion. Unlike Callimachus' readers, Athenians listening to or reading Alcman's partheneia or Pindar's *Paean* 9 were imaging an occasion that resembled one that was once real, and what is more we should reckon with the possibility that, unlike Callimachus' mimetic hymns, festival choruses still carried a ritual charge when re-performed in Athens: at one level, *Paean* 9 was simply *a* paean and the *Louvre Partheneion* simply *a* partheneion, ready for appropriation and ritual reuse elsewhere. However, at another level, like Callimachus' readers, Athenians listening to or reading Alcman's partheneia or Pindar's *Paean* 9 were conscious they were imagining an occasion that was far removed from their own here and now: *Paean* 9 may have been *a* paean but it was not *their* paean, and the *Louvre Partheneion* was not *their* partheneion. It is frustrating that we know nothing about the contexts in which Athenians re-performed foreign festival choruses—civic festival or private? in honour of the same or a different deity? in sacred space? in a competition? with a political point, stressing Athens's attitudes vis-à-vis the city that produced the song?—but on any scenario it stands to reason there will have been a sense of at least partial autonomy, of a song that stands by itself, at a certain distance from its new surroundings.[14]

Scholarship on Attic drama likes to point out that it is a feature specific to tragedy and comedy that they routinely remove lyric genres from their appropriate cult settings and make use of that distance. This is at the very least an overstatement; Athenians were used to this kind of removal also from the re-performance of canonical festival choruses, and, as in the case of drama, part of the effect of such performances will have turned on that removal.

---

[12] *PMG* 813, 934.

[13] See, e.g., Fantuzzi (1993); D'Alessio (2004: 292–4).

[14] Our ignorance is particularly frustrating for the partheneia, because of the well-known lack of evidence for a culture of female *choreia* in Athens.

II

Re-performance provides salient material for suggesting that canonical festival choruses could be emphatically *not* of their occasion. The next question is whether any comparable considerations apply also to the original perform-ances. To what degree does it make sense to say that original audiences might respond to the songs as things in their own right, as self-standing, abstracted from their occasion?

To begin with there are some obvious yet important performance-related points to be made. Every powerful performance, even a priest wielding a sacrificial knife, has the potential to arrest the viewers' attention and to make them focus on the performance *qua* performance rather than on its context or purpose. This is particularly apparent in the case of elaborate choruses, which were carefully choreographed and rehearsed, and were judged and admired for their skilled singing and dancing.[15] Our fullest and most famous Archaic description of a choral performance, the Delian Maidens in the *Homeric Hymn to Apollo*, is useful testimony (ll. 156–64).

And besides, this great wonder, the fame of which will never perish: the Maidens of Delos, the servants of the Far-shooter, who, after first hymning Apollo, and then in turn Leto and Artemis profuse of arrows, turn their thoughts to the men and women of old and sing a song that charms the peoples. They know how to mimic all people's voices and their babble; anyone might think it was he himself speaking, so well is their singing fitted together.[16]

The Delian Maidens are described both as mediators of worship and as skilful performers. Especially the last phrase, 'so well is their singing fitted together [συνάρηρεν]', highlights skill, the fitting-together of song. The Delian Maidens use this skill in praise of Apollo and Artemis at the Delian festival, but they are in their own right, through the quality of their performance, a 'great wonder, the fame of which will never perish'. Occasional–functional and self-standing perspectives have equal prominence and intermingle.

These and similar observations about the pleasure generated by choral performance are regularly made, but they are less regularly developed further at the level of poetics, and are thus at risk of getting displaced by a purely occasional–functional focus when individual compositions are discussed. I shall, therefore, return to texts, and pick up where I ended the previous section, by examining the passages evoking an occasion, not because those are the only textual feature that could be profitably looked at—other candidates

---

[15] The aural and visual pleasures of choral performance are, in different ways, emphasized throughout the ancient tradition. Discussion in Peponi, Chapter 1, this volume.

[16] The text and translation (West's in the Loeb, except for the last two words) are uncertain in some places. See in particular Peponi (2009) on the alternative readings κρεμβαλιαστύν and βαμβαλιαστύν in 162, and the meaning of μιμεῖσθ' in l. 163.

include artful narration of myth, thought–provoking links between mythical and non-mythical sections, patterning of sound, and often elaborate metrical structures—but because they constitute a hard case: it is obvious that such passages are designed to prompt occasional–functional responses, very strongly so. I want to illustrate how much there is to be said for a different approach even here. These passages go out of their way to make their audiences work, to prompt them to produce readings, to fill gaps, to make connections, to reflect. In addition to the aural and visual pleasures of the performance, the texts provide the kind of pleasures that derive from the encounter with a rich and challenging poetics. They do so partly by creating elaborately complex relationships between text and context—the pragmatic gap that has been the subject of much recent work (though not always from an audience perspective).[17] At least as important is the complexity of the texts in their own right, a complexity that helped to make even the most overtly occasional passages absorbing and stimulating objects of poetic interpretation and appreciation, kinds of interpretation and appreciation that an occasional–functional perspective by itself cannot adequately capture.

Paean 9 starts by transporting its Theban audience back to their experience of the eclipse, and then, in the second triad, goes on to situate itself in a space and time closer to what we assume are the actual circumstances of the performance. The text moves the audience along mimetically, perhaps with a certain psychological efficacy, as it allows them first to relive their fears, before adopting a calmer tone in the second part, with a statement of the motivation for the composition and a mythical narrative.[18] The shift is, however, a harsh one, as Rutherford points out: 'the two triads do not cohere very well, and it almost seems as if an apotropaic παιάν has been welded on to a cult παιάν to Apollo and Tenerus.'[19] In fact the incongruence is so systematic that one may justifiably detect a poetic strategy. The first triad addresses the sun; the second, in the same metrical position, addresses Apollo. The first triad is Panhellenic, mentioning Thebes in the context of the universal (πάγκοινον) reach of the eclipse (ll. 9–10) and speculating about the eclipse as a cataclysmic cosmic event that presages the birth of a new generation of men (ll. 19–20); the second is thoroughly local, with a local myth, a local shrine, and possibly an address of the (Theban) audience or chorus (l. 37: 'for your sake', plural).[20]

There is then a captivating open-endedness to the way the song presents its own occasion, which offers audiences different ways of framing the eclipse. More than that, the extensive emphasis on signs and interpretation throughout

---

[17] See, in particular, the special issue of *Arethusa*, 37 (2004); as well as Fantuzzi (1993: 941–5); Bonifazi (2001); D'Alessio (2007); and the overview in D'Alessio (2009).

[18] Psychological efficacy: Stehle (1997: 51).

[19] Rutherford (2001: 198).

[20] See Rutherford (2001: 196) for the different possible interpretations of ὑμετέραν χάριν.

paves the way for a more pointed reading. The song challenges its audience to think about how best to bring together the two different but corresponding parts—corresponding in metre as well as certain textual features—to contemplate the Sun and Apollo both as the same and as different gods, and, ultimately, to contemplate the genre paean. By juxtaposing two rather different modes of paeanic song, at the same time as producing a cult song, Pindar engages in his own manner in the kind of thing for which tragedy is well known in its own use of choruses: self-conscious play with a genre of cult song.[21]

Continuing in this vein, note the phrase 'I beseech you, far-shooter, as I dedicate your oracle to the arts of the Muses' (Μοισαίαις ἀν[α]τιθεὶς τέχνα[ι]σι χρηστήριον) (ll. 39–40). One would have expected something like 'as I dedicate the arts of the Muses to your oracle', and the reversal of the dative and accusative objects emphasizes the song as an artistic product.[22] Rather than *mousikê* celebrating the oracular shrine, the oracular shrine becomes a place of *mousikê*. Several other aspects of the text point in the same direction. The 'I' in 'I have been ordained to compose a noble song' brings to mind the poet, among other options, and the phrase σοφίας ὁδόν ('path of skill/wisdom') near the beginning suggests poetry. The scenarios in ll. 13–20 of what the eclipse might portend are not just self-consciously hyperbolic but end with a nod to Hesiod's myth of the races. And above all the theme of the eclipse itself puts the song into a literary tradition. Plutarch refers to *Paean* 9 alongside compositions about eclipses by Mimnermus, Archilochus, Stesichorus, and Cydias.[23] Pindar, one suspects, composed a poem that aimed to be a particularly powerful treatment of an eclipse, to be held against others. There is plenty, then, in this poem that is not captured by an occasional–functional perspective, and not just in re-performance.

Alcman 1 does some comparable things in a different way. The considerable difficulty we have in elucidating this text is commonly regarded as the result of our lack of knowledge about the context. Indeed, it would be silly to deny that much that is obscure to us will have been clear, or clearer, to Alcman's Spartan audience, but the search for the context in which the song makes most sense should not stand in the way of appreciating the inherent and purposeful complexity of its poetics.

The chorus of Alcman 1 spends a notoriously large amount of time talking about itself, 62 of the surviving 101 lines (ll. 39–101), but much of what they are talking about is partly or wholly a matter of the imagination. As Peponi has demonstrated, the chorus's description of Hagesichora and/or Agido in terms of the sun, in terms of beautiful horses, and possibly in terms of doves, and

---

[21] For tragedy see most fully Swift (2010).

[22] Rutherford (2001: 196, n. 21): 'Pindar reverses the "natural" hierarchy of direct and indirect objects.'

[23] *De fac.* 931e.

their description of themselves as lavishly dressed are not really descriptions but rather reconfigurations of the actual performers.[24] The text does not so much reflect what the audience sees as tell it what to see. Following Peponi's lead but going beyond the performers' appearance, one finds oneself contemplating what the chorus are described as doing in lines 39–101. In actuality, the audience is watching a chorus of girls dancing and singing, but what scene does the text project onto this chorus in performance?

The question permits no simple answer, except to say that this scene is elusive and ever-shifting, and that is the point. Intermittently, as one might expect, a choral performance is evoked. 'I sing of the brightness of Agido,' the chorus sing (ll. 39–40), a properly self-referential statement of choral activity, and there are one or two other such statements. But these are just fleeting moments, which need to be seen in the context of many lines that seem to detract from any notion of a chorus-in-performance: the girls' talk of their anxieties and inadequacies and their feelings towards their leaders; references to the movements and whereabouts of Agido and Hagesichora, but no such references for the chorus; the naming of what appear to be individual chorus members, something that is highly unusual for the unison body that is the chorus (the closest parallel is perhaps the names of the performers on the *post-performance* scene of the Pronomos vase).[25] Bringing all the divergent visions together into a coherent picture of the chorus's (imaginary) activity and situation is one of the major challenges this text poses to its audiences, and it does so prior to any considerations about the gap between this picture and reality.

This elusiveness and mobility of the setting from which the choral voice emerges are not just elusiveness and mobility for their own sakes but part of a poetic strategy that allows the chorus to extend the remit of its song-dance to other ritual acts at the festival, at least some of which were outside the spatio-temporal frame of its actual performance. The strongest candidate (not a certain candidate) for a reference to a ritual performance here and now is the chorus members' passing description of themselves as carrying a robe for Orthria (l. 61).[26] By contrast, Hagesichora's and Agido's prayers to the gods (l. 82) are offered elsewhere (ll. 78–9) and, while just conceivably taking place in parallel to the choral performance, make better sense as an earlier or later part of the festival sequence. The same holds even more obviously for what is perhaps 'our sacrificial feast' ($\theta\omega\sigma\tau\acute{\eta}\rho[\iota\acute{a}\ \tau$'] $\check{a}\mu$', l. 81).[27] Exactly because the song gives

---

[24] Peponi (2004).

[25] See Seaford, Chapter 15, this volume, for a different—political—take on the use individual names. Aristophanes too occasionally names (some) chorus members, e.g. *Ach.* 609–12 and *Lys.* 254 ff., in both cases generic names, charcoal-y and old men, respectively.

[26] 'Robe' translates $\phi\hat{a}\rho o\varsigma$. The interlinear gloss $\alpha\rho o\tau o$ seems to advocate the meaning 'plough', but garments are far more common than ploughs as gifts for deities.

[27] The translation 'feast' is based on the etymological connection with $\theta o\iota\nu\acute{\eta}$, $\theta o\iota\nu\alpha\tau\acute{\eta}\rho\iota o\nu$, $\theta\acute{\omega}\sigma\theta\alpha\iota$. The scholion glosses 'festival', which makes only a limited difference for the argument here.

the audience only a blurry and refracted picture of the chorus itself, it is able to bring the entire festival into view as part of the same blurry and refracted picture. What is more, the lack of clear or stable focus also enhances the audience's freedom for associative connection-making. As scholarly discussions demonstrate in detail, the song can prompt extensive tracing of, and reflection on, poetic themes, such as order, pairs, beauty and desire, horses, or fighting. In short, Alcman's text uses the whirring chorus as a phantasmagorical machine that spins a kaleidoscopic panorama out of nowhere. Already for Spartan audiences this must have been a text that was hard to pin down, and for that very reason a text that was almost inexhaustibly resonant.

After several decades of intense scholarly work the case for an occasional–functional interpretation of Alcman 1 no longer needs to be made, even if the detail is greatly contentious.[28] At every level this text had rich ties with the occasion, doing work for the performers, their contemporaries, their families, and the entire audience. The themes listed in the previous paragraph, all of which will have been richly meaningful for both the girls and Sparta at large, are a case in point. So is there anything to be said for looking at the song without the occasional–functional lens? The answer must be yes, and I shall draw three points out of my discussion of the poetics of the song.

First, there is the substantive amount of interpretation, filling of gaps, and making of connections that the text requires, not just in linking the song to the context but also in making sense of the song in its own right. It is a text that already made its first audience do considerable hermeneutic work, investing in the audience's engrossing encounter with the song *qua* song.

Secondly, there is the way the surviving section of the text—the lost opening may or may not have been different (compare Alcman 3)—expresses its relationship with the festival, not situating itself in it as one aspect of the larger whole but pulling the large whole into its own remit. To overstate for effect, but not by much: like *Paean* 9, which dedicates the sanctuary to the arts of the Muses, Alcman 1 is not content with contributing; instead it absorbs, making the wider world, including the whole festival, part of its own fantastic universe. It is, in that sense, self-standing, demanding to be viewed as all-encompassing.

Thirdly, the text prompts reflection on the chorus *qua* chorus. It is impossible to miss the prominent references to artistic skill and artistic judgement, as the girls concern themselves with the quality of their own as well as their leaders' abilities as performers, expressing anxiety about the former and

---

[28] The secondary literature is vast. I would highlight: Griffiths (1972); Calame (1977*a*, *b*); Robbins (1994); Stehle (1997: 30–9, 73–88). Apart from Peponi's work mentioned above, closest in some aspects to my approach here, despite substantial differences, are Hutchinson (2001: 76–102) and Ferrari (2008).

admiration for the latter (esp. ll. 85–7, 96–101). And there may be more, for which, more tentatively, I return one last time to the elusive choral scene that is painted in ll. 39–101, to put forward what I consider the most persuasive way of forging the various fleeting images into one picture. Arguably, the scenario that best accommodates the paucity of references to the chorus's performance (little song and no dance), the many individual names, and the emphasis on Hagesichora and Agido, is that of a set of individual chorus members who are (pretending they are) not currently performing but giving voice to their thoughts and anxieties as they are watching their leaders. Compared to the song of the Delian Maidens in the *Homeric Hymn to Apollo*, the song of Alcman's maidens is, as far as the text is concerned, not just not 'beautiful' but not even 'fitted together'.[29] Attention to individual girls and their attainments, as well as a self-depreciating voice, make good sense, of course, in a song performed by marriageable girls, and the use of a pre-performance perspective within the performance text is well attested in ritual, all of which is to say that an occasional–functional perspective on the chorus's self-presentation is certainly available. But the unusual length to which the surviving text goes in presenting a chorus that is not really a chorus, combined with the insistent language of aesthetic judgement, also invites the audience to contemplate the difficult art of chorus-making, as practised by the girls and their leaders as well as in the abstract.

III

The argument so far has tried to bring out just how far canonical festival choruses went in encouraging not just an occasional–functional but also a stand-alone perspective, even in respect of what might seem to be their most pronouncedly occasion-specific aspects, but it has had nothing to say about the relationship between the two perspectives. That relationship will be the topic of this final section. In this difficult area one thing is clear, even commonplace: the two perspectives are not mutually exclusive. The modern sense of separation between two incompatible spheres with which I started the chapter, often associated with terms such as 'aesthetics' or 'art' versus 'ritual' or 'religion', is an inheritance that we owe to a tradition that may have its origins as early as Plato and that today carries the imprint of eighteenth- and

---

[29] It is not 'fitted together' also in the abrupt shifts in its train of thought, so much so that is has been suggested that the text was performed by two half choruses (see esp. Péron 1987). That suggestion has on the whole not carried conviction, but the fact it could even be made is an indicator of the non-linear progression of the text.

nineteenth-century thought, but that is profoundly misleading for the periods under consideration here.[30]

In the case of canonical festival choruses, the compatibility and indeed interweaving of the two perspectives can be expressed in various ways. One well-established idea is that of the song as a beautiful offering. The gods like a good show, a predilection represented at the Athenian City Dionysia by the Priest of Dionysus' seat on the edge of the *orchestra*. In their tastes they are an idealized human audience, and everything that makes the song attractive *qua* song to humans makes it attractive also to gods. The thing in itself is also an *agalma* for the gods and thus has a function within the religious economy of early Greece.[31] What is more, the gods' delight in beautiful song in turn opens up a political dimension. A song that is perceived to be pleasing reflects well on the whole community that produced it, and so aesthetic, religious, and political concerns mesh closely together.

A less frequently explored yet arguably no less powerful way of thinking about how the two perspectives interrelate starts from the observation that religious experience, even in early Greece, is a matter not just of action—beautiful offerings—but also of the mind. When the texts pull festival-goers into a world of the imagination, this is as real and as central an aspect of their festival experience as any other, and indeed it shapes their understanding of the festival more broadly.[32] Festivals were after all multifaceted events, where participants wove together action and imagination, being themselves and play-acting.[33] Perhaps one could even point out that it takes only one step to advance from gaps, disconnects, and difficulty to mystery and the numinous.[34] On this line of thinking, the high degree of poetic challenge inherent in the texts discussed here might be seen to be appropriate to the heightened states of mind of festival-goers making contact with divinity.

Now, if the two perspectives are as tightly interwoven as these and other models suggest, one cannot help asking whether there is in fact any point in talking about them as distinct in the way I have been doing. Should we not simply accept that they merge to the point of becoming for all intents and purposes inseparable? There is an obvious attraction in that position—it

---

[30] The most important treatment of these issues for early Greece, well informed also on the later tradition, is Porter (2010). Note also the argument (pointed out to me by Leslie Kurke) of Elsner (2007: 1–26) that antiquity conflated two modes of visuality, one ritual-centred and one mimetic. The genealogy of 'religion' and 'ritual' is traced by Bremmer (1998). The introduction and some of the chapters in Yatromanolakis and Roilos (2004) pick their various ways through the theoretical issues raised by the co-presence of ritual and aesthetics in ancient Greece.

[31] The best treatments are Depew (2000) and Day (2010).

[32] Cf. the discussion of the interaction between poem and context in Kurke (2005: esp. 1–5).

[33] Parker (2011: 200), 'The participants in festivals oscillate between being themselves and acting a role'. See also Connor (1987).

[34] There is a considerable body of work in anthropology that examines the different characteristics of ritual and ordinary speech acts. See in particular Bloch (1974) and Tambiah (1985).

certainly avoids anachronistic use of modern categories—but I nevertheless believe adopting it would be a mistake, and will use the remainder of the chapter to develop two, rather different, sets of considerations in support of the usefulness of studying festival choruses with those two perspectives in mind, treating them as intricately interlaced but conceptually distinct.

First, the particular balance between the two perspectives varies, tellingly so, and it would be reductive to ignore this variation. There is, to begin with, the variation discussed earlier between first performance and re-performance, and between re-performance in similar and in different circumstances from those of the original commission. There is, next, variation between performances within and outside competitions. Competition does not void ritual embedding, but it does insistently prompt considerations of skill and comparison with other songs: it makes a difference to the balance.[35] Then there is variation between periods. When *Paean* 9 is more explicit than Alcman 1 in pointing to its own artifice and unlike Alcman 1 might be said to be playing with genre, then this is, among other things, a reflection of the changes in poetic culture: the self-standing perspective imposes itself with more urgency as time goes on, not just from the Classical to the Hellenistic period, but also within the Archaic period.

In limiting itself to compositions that became canonical, this chapter implicitly foregrounded above all a further, difficult, yet intriguing type of variation: that between, on the one hand, compositions by high-profile composers—in the case of Pindar and the fifth century often composers that were celebrities already at the time, in the case of Alcman and the seventh or early sixth centuries conceivably composers that became celebrities only later on— and, on the other, traditional cult songs linked in antiquity with names such as Olen and Tynnichus. The idea of the traditional song is a slippery one, since what is a song composed by a famous composer for a special occasion today may be a traditional song tomorrow, but some such distinction was evidently operational in antiquity, as we can see from the anecdote of Aeschylus refusing to compose a paean for the Delphians on the grounds that Tynnichus' was just fine, and that his composition would fare no better than new statues side by side with ancient ones.[36] The distinction must at least in part be to do with the degree to which audiences look at the song as a song. At the extreme ends one can imagine the scenario of the long-awaited premiere of the latest composition by a Panhellenic composer that has created considerable excitement in

---

[35] Bremer (2000) may be going too far towards treating competition and ritual as mutually exclusive. The contrary view is expressed by Wilson (2007: 169–71) and Calame (2009*a*: 177). Rutherford (2004: 88) in interpreting the 'Sandwich Marble' on Delos (*IDélos* 98.94) contemplates the possibility that the inscription talks about separate choruses for cult and competition.

[36] Plato, *Ion* 534d and Porphyry, *On Abstinence* 2.18. For traditional songs, see also Hdt. 4.35 on Olen and the 97BC inscription *FD* 3.2.48 = *Syll.*[3] 711L, which features performance of 'the ancestral [*patrios*] paean'.

advance, and the performance of an anonymous and short yet resonant cult song as part of a prescribed ritual routine.[37]

All this is uncertain terrain on our evidence, but the general point is beyond doubt. Individual texts and performances are, in part, characterized by the specific way in which the two perspectives relate to one another, and for that alone the distinction deserves to be maintained. To be content with the notion of an indistinct blend would be to flatten out the landscape of early Greek festival choruses.

The second set of considerations in support of working with the distinction turns on the very anachronism of the modern intellectual traditions that inform our thinking on the issue. Exactly because choruses as art and choruses as ritual practice are so often kept apart in Western thought and chorus-making, the conceptual divide between 'ritual' and 'aesthetics' or 'art' is even harder to bridge for choruses than for many other literary forms, such as drama or solo song.

Partly, the issue is one of limitations. The position of choruses in the West puts considerable obstacles in our way when we try to imagine the two perspectives as intermingled in antiquity. We soon get pulled in either direction, forced to subordinate one viewpoint to the other. Maintaining both at the same time, even-handed, is extremely difficult or even impossible with the conceptual tools at our disposal. Chorus-as-art and chorus-as-ritual resemble the rabbit and the duck in the famous illusion: we can make our cognitive apparatus perceive only either one at a time even though we know both are there.

But there is perhaps a further risk to guard against: the risk of overcompensation and idealization in imagining a culture we know to be distant and other. Made from the vantage point of a world in which choruses tend to inhabit this sphere or that, any statement about the interrelation, let alone merging, of the two perspectives in early Greece (a period for whose poetic culture we have precious little evidence beyond the poetic texts) contains an inevitable element of postulation. The point is not that we should not try, but that we need to proceed with caution and guard against swapping the error of anachronism for that of romanticizing. We need to approach canonical festival choruses with the acknowledgement that we are wrestling with a phenomenon that is, from where we sit, difficult to grasp.

This leads on to the tradition of thinking about choral lyric specifically, which is usefully thrown into relief by comparison with work on that other major Greek choral form, drama. Within scholarship on drama, especially tragedy, there is a long history of thinking and arguing about versions of the binary under consideration here. Mark Griffith recently made this the first of

---

[37] Such as the Erythraean paean, performed together with the sacrifice offered in thanks of incubation.

twelve 'paradoxical paired principles' for studying Greek tragedy: 'Tragedies in Athens were performed both (*a*) as part of a *polis*-organized Dionysian ritual and (*b*) as theatrical entertainment.'[38] Gilbert Murray, to give an earlier and even more high-profile example, concluded his 'Excursus on the Ritual Forms Preserved in Greek Tragedy', printed in the 1912 edition of Jane Harrison's *Themis*, with a statement that grapples with the same kind of issue:

> An outer shape dominated by tough and undying tradition, and inner life fiery with sincerity and spiritual freedom; the vessels of a very ancient religion overfilled and broken by the new wine of reasoning and rebellious humanity, and still, in their rejection, shedding abroad the old aroma, as of eternal and mysterious things: these are the fundamental paradoxes presented to us by Greek Tragedy. The contrasts have their significance for other art also, perhaps for all great art. But aesthetic criticism is not the business of the present note.[39]

The terminology, theoretical apparatus, and precise focus have been ever-changing, but broadly some such paradox has in different guises been producing intense debate in scholarship on tragedy since at least the nineteenth century, and has been the engine of influential readings as well as advances in theorizing about tragedy and tragic choruses.

Arguably, the same is true to only a lesser degree for non-dramatic choral song (with the exception of epinician). Choral lyric has had its share of context-independent or weakly contextualized readings over the years, but a far smaller share than tragedy. New Criticism, for instance, which for a long time dominated work on tragedy, made far fewer inroads into non-epinician choral lyric. And on the whole—and it is trends that matter here[40]— scholarship on choral lyric has tended to be more relaxed than scholarship on tragedy about applying the term 'ritual' to its texts without counterbalancing it along the lines of Griffith's statement cited above, or to subordinate 'entertainment', 'aesthetics', and so on to an overall functionalist viewpoint. As a result, statements that we make about the ability of choral lyric to combine ritual and aesthetics, or politics and entertainment, or function and artistry, while no less true, do not evoke quite the same depth of scholarly tradition as do similar statements about tragedy, like Murray's or Griffith's; and this relative lack of depth further strengthens the case for regarding the art-and-ritual paradox as a challenging conundrum rather than a simple truth.

Of course tragic and non-dramatic choruses differ in important respects, and these differences go a certain way towards accounting for the variation in emphasis between the two scholarly traditions. Above all tragedy embeds its choruses in dramatic narratives and thus invites with more insistence than

---

[38] Griffith and Carter (2011: 2).
[39] Murray in J. E. Harrison (1912: 363).
[40] Counter-examples are, of course, easy to list, some in nn. 24 and 28.

choral lyric a perspective that looks at them in isolation from their performance contexts. But the two genres also share much ground, and it is that
common ground that has proved important at various points in this chapter.[41]
The texts of both lyric and tragic choruses are full of gaps that require an active
audience that supplies connections and interpretations, of the texts themselves
in their multifarious richness as well as of their relation with their contexts,
and thus both lyric and tragic choruses prompt reflection on the ritual actions
they describe at the same time as they carry out ritual actions. Tragedy does so
often ironically, while festival choruses characteristically maintain a celebra-
tory and affirmative, or in any case hopeful, tone. The kinds of gap, vagueness,
and complexity that bode disaster in tragedy are evocative and stimulating in
lyric. But, for all the differences in tone, the poetic strategies that characterize
the two genres have much in common. An implication of the argument of this
chapter is that so should the assumptions, conceptual frameworks, and ways of
reading we adopt when studying them.

---

[41] This common ground is stressed, in ways very different from one another and from
the position adopted here, by, e.g., D'Alessio (2007); Kowalzig (2007*a*: 395–6); Ferrari (2008:
106–26); Swift (2010).

6

Seneca's Chorus of One

Helen Slaney

Senecan choruses are notoriously detached from the plays' dramatic action, resisting standards of consistency and integration derived from Greek proto-types. Instead, what they deliver is a wholly distinct lyric counterpoint. The spatial, mythological, or ethical dimensions they unfold do not constitute part of the play's ostensible plot, but nevertheless constitute the play's actual subject matter, and in doing so challenge modern assumptions of dramatic structure and mimetic unity. D. E. Hill attributes Senecan choral anonymity to a deliberate revision of choral function, arguing that 'it is their message, not their identity that matters . . . the chorus's task is to enunciate ideas'.[1] As groups, Seneca's choruses have no positive identity, and minimal presence within the acts (the two exceptions being the *Trojan Women* and the second-ary chorus of Trojan captives in the *Agamemnon*, both of which are strongly marked in the text). Attempts to pinpoint the requisite number needed for a Senecan chorus have proved inconclusive.[2] I would like to propose an alter-native: most of Seneca's choruses, and particularly the complex *Prunkstücke* or show-stoppers such as *Medea* 301–79 (the Argonautic voyage), *Phaedra* 736–823 (the perils of beauty), and *Thyestes* 789–884 (universal apocalypse), invite physical interpretation by a solo performer, albeit supported by vocal and instrumental accompaniment.

This is not an arbitrary proposition. Recent scholarship has made intriguing connections between some idiosyncratic aspects of Senecan dramaturgy and the concurrently prevalent performance medium of Roman pantomime.[3] I would, therefore, like further to consolidate these connections and test the hypothesis that Seneca's choral odes, just as much as his soliloquy-driven scenes, respond to the cult of the soloist and the permissiveness of a

---

[1] Hill (2000: 569, 577).

[2] Sutton (1984) posits a full double chorus for *Hercules Furens*; Calder (1975: 33) allocates 'between three and seven members' to *Ag*.

[3] Zanobi (2008); Zimmermann (2008).

non-representational dramatic form. Seneca represents an alien dramaturgy, one that does not fit the conventional parameters even of ancient tragedy, and it therefore pays to keep an open mind. Most readings assume for Seneca a straightforward, linear, mimetic performance mode (or, conversely, its lack);[4] altering this initial standpoint relaxes such assumptions, and may enable a more flexible reading of the works in their capacity as performance texts. Sutton, for example, expresses unease at the idea of choral re-entry, as it 'requires us to think...that these plays were performed under quite non-uniform conditions'.[5] Information on first-century Roman theatre is so scanty that it is dangerous to assume any default, and 'non-uniform conditions' may in fact be closer to a Senecan norm. Because no texts unequivocally identified as pantomime libretti remain extant, their precise characteristics are not known, but the work of Virgil, Ovid, Statius, and Lucan, among others, is attested as having provided libretti in some capacity, and references to 'dancing a tragedy' suggest that dramatic texts were regularly utilized for pantomime.[6] Jory concludes that, despite late antique deprecation, early pantomime libretti 'were frequently valuable literary works, adapted from the best epic or tragic poets of the past or freshly composed by the best poets of the age'.[7] It is, therefore, not at all unlikely that the works that have come down to us identified by medieval scholars as Seneca's 'tragedies' may represent the verbal component of this otherwise ephemeral theatrical form.

WHAT IS A CHORUS?

To support the claim that an individual may function as a chorus, the definition should be clarified. Choruses—ancient and modern—perform manifold functions, but overall these may be divided into two categories. In some instances, the chorus is solidly present in the primary fictional or

---

[4] Positive exponents include Sutton (1986), P. Davis (1993), and Marshall (2000); the same default has been turned against Senecan dramaturgy by, for instance, Zwierlein (1966), Fantham (2000), and Mayer (2002). Kohn (2004: 165) proposes: 'Since the Senecan tragedies can be performed by only three actors...with a fourth used in two cases, *let us imagine them produced in such a way*' (emphasis added).

[5] Sutton (1984: 304).

[6] According to Lucian (*Salt.* 61), the dancer 'will not be ignorant of anything that is told by Homer and Hesiod and the best poets, and above all tragedy'. Virgil's *Aeneid*: Suet. *Nero* 49; Ovid's *poemata*: *Trist.* 2.519; Statius' (lost) *Agave*: Juv. *Sat.* 7.86–7. Vacca's *Vita Lucani* 65 mentions that Lucan composed a number of *salticae fabulae*. For discussion, see relevant chapters in Hall and Wyles (2008). Hall (2008) proposes the 'Barcelona *Alcestis*', a fourth-century 'compressed Greek tragedy' in hexameters, as an alternative model.

[7] Jory (2008: 161).

'mimetic' space of the play.[8] They become opaque, their bodies and voices and (most importantly for Attic drama) their collectivity occupying the same imagined site as the protagonists, affecting its spatial dynamics: surrounded by the suffering citizens of Thebes, Sophocles' Oedipus conducts a necessarily public investigation. In other instances, the chorus members suppress their status as characters and function as an instrument for conveying extra-scenic information. They become transparent, their physical actions gesturing beyond the literal to evoke another, diegetic space tangentially related to that of the plotted action: through the sequence of stylized movements implied by their words, Aeschylus' chorus relates Iphigenia's sacrifice prior to Agamemnon's arrival. Within the odes, this transparency arguably predominates; as David Wiles argues, 'the primary function of the chorus is to offer an alternative, transformative mode of seeing'.[9] The bare *orchestra* need not always be regarded as a fixed setting.[10] In the absence of naturalistic scenery, transformation (or transportation) may be accomplished with the minimal stimulus of an image-rich phrase and its accompanying choreography. A blend of both states, transparency and opacity, is employed to particularly poignant effect in the counterfactual πόθος-odes of *Iphigenia in Tauris*, *Trojan Women*, and *Hippolytus*: Ἰδαῖά τ' Ἰδαῖα κισσοφόρα νάπη | χιόνι κατάρυτα ποταμίαι (*Tro.* 1066–7) ('And Ida, Ida ivy-valed, | trickling snow-melt'), sing the exiles, constructing an absent homeland from purely imaginative resources, a *mise-en-abime* in which the spectator is briefly engulfed. The distinctively theatrical dyadic tension between what is absent and what is present, usually experienced by an audience as *double* vision, the pleasurable confluence of two ontological states, suddenly becomes *triple*, a chord-like triad as Athenian men dance Trojan women, dancing a threnodic resurrection of imaginary Ida. The choral body represents not only itself, but also the content of the ode.

The political properties of the Athenian tragic chorus have been discussed extensively.[11] In the context of participatory civic ritual, as an expression and extension of the ideology sustaining the democratic state, the value of having a homogeneous group displayed onstage before the mass gaze of the community seems obvious. A crucial dynamic operating throughout Greek tragedy is the relationship of the collective to the individual: citizens to ruler, suppliants to saviour, sympathizers to sufferer, collaborators to criminal, even (as in *Prometheus Bound*, or Euripides' *Iphigenia at Aulis*) incidental witnesses drawn into the orbit of personal catastrophe. The constant presence of the group

---

[8] Issacharov (1981: 215–22) divides dramatic space into 'mimetic' (visible onstage) and 'diegetic' (mediated by discourse).

[9] Wiles (1997: 123).

[10] Wiles (1997: 115–23). On scenic effects available in the Athenian theatre, see Kuntz (1993: 153–61).

[11] E.g. Vernant (1990: 24); Foley (1993).

imposes openness on the space, so that their cooperation must be solicited and even the most secretive plotting (as in *Electra*, *Orestes*, or *Helen*) must be conducted in the blinding light of the public eye.[12] The group, the representative multitude, possesses inalienable presence and power.

Compare this, then, to a counter-example, the etiolated 'Chorus' of Shakespeare's *Henry V* ('O for a muse of fire', etc.). Appearing only between the acts, and played by a single figure, this Chorus takes no part whatsoever in the ensuing action, providing instead a channel for visualization and the erection of verbal scenery:

> The king is set from London, and the scene
> Is now transported, gentles, to Southampton:
> There is the playhouse, now, there you must sit;
> And thence to France shall we convey you safe
> And bring you back.
>
> (II, Pro. 35–39)

Here we find no doubling, let alone tripling, of referents, but rather a form of epic narrative that effaces the speaker in favour of the sensory data conveyed by the spoken word. The motif of transportation is one crucial element in this Chorus's role, and he self-consciously foregrounds it with typical early modern meta-theatrical reflexivity;[13] the change in location is predicated exclusively upon his verbal direction. Another element is the diminution (or promotion) of Shakespeare's Chorus to a solitary individual, reflecting a shift in the image of authority. The theatre, like a royal progress, follows the movements of the king as articulated by the Chorus, to Southampton and thence to France. In this play, which likewise features a monarch's relationship to his subjects, the pro-England, pro-Harry, Chorus mirrors in corresponding fashion the locus of political power.[14] Members of the public certainly appear on Shakespeare's stage, but, unlike a Greek χορός, they never unite into an instrumental unit. This is reserved for the Chorus, the soloist, the virtuoso whose monologue disseminates impressions of battlefields, navies, multitudes, siege warfare, and triumphal pageantry. Because the early modern theatre drew so heavily upon Seneca, finding ingenious ways of realizing components of these texts that arose from an entirely different set of performance

---

[12] D. M. Carter (2007: 79–81) points out that marginalized groups may not necessarily represent the *demos*, but, according to Calame (1999: 151), audience identification occurs 'notwithstanding differences of social status and of gender'.

[13] See Lopez (2003: 35–96) on early modern meta-theatre.

[14] According to Craik (1997: 65), the chorus's numerous imperatives 'encourage the audience to be imaginative as well as patriotic'. E. Smith (2002: 83) records that the 1997 Globe production had the actor playing Henry deliver the Chorus's lines. Lopez (2003: 81) comments that 'exposition works on some level to extend one's feeling of mastery to the realm of things that occur offstage'.

constraints, it provides for Senecan dramatic form an inter-text at least as useful as fifth-century tragedy.

All evidence for the performance of Seneca's drama in first-century Rome remains circumstantial, but the hints are tantalizing. Full-scale productions of tragedy cease to be attested for Rome after the Augustan period, after which they splinter into numerous coexistent media: recitation, private theatricals, *tragoedia cantata* (climactic episodes, generally delivered competitively), and *tragoedia saltata* (a type of solo ballet, more commonly known as 'pantomime').[15] Pantomime filled the immense, sumptuous public theatres of the early empire, and acquired pre-eminence not only as a popular diversion but also as a serious art form. Ancient pantomime has received considerable scholarly rehabilitation in recent years, and most pertinent to the present discussion is Alessandra Zanobi's article discussing the influence of pantomime on Seneca's tragedies.[16] Zanobi attributes to pantomime some of the unusual features of Senecan dramaturgy, such as its 'characteristically loose dramatic structure, the presence of "running commentaries", and lengthy narrative set-pieces'.[17] Although mentioning Seneca's treatment of the chorus among them, she does not, however, examine this aspect in detail; I would like to suggest that the conjectural (and brilliantly plausible) link between Seneca and pantomime may also be applied to Senecan choral lyric, and that considering the odes in this light may help to free them from artificial criteria of consistency, character development, or motivation.

The *Latin Anthology* contains an anonymous description of the pantomime dancer:

> ingressus scaenam populum saltator adorat.
>   solerti tendit prodere gesta manu.
> nam cum grata **chorus** diffundit cantica dulcis
>   quae resonat **cantor**, motibus ipse probat.
> pugnat, ludit, amat, bacchatur, vertitur, adstat.
>
> (*Anth. Lat.* 100.3–7)

Entering the stage, the dancer addresses his public, | extending an expert hand to produce his gestures. | For when the chorus pour out their pleasant song | he affirms with movement whatever echoes in the singer's voice: | he fights, he plays, he loves, he raves, he pirouettes, he stops.

Webb identifies this alternation of fluid movement and sudden freeze as the essential rhythm of pantomime, the dancer's transition between different characters being as vital to his art as the studied portrayal of each

---

[15] For a useful summary of forms of theatre available in first-century Rome, see Beacham (1999: 233–7).

[16] Zanobi (2008). See also Lada-Richards (2007), Webb (2008), and Macintosh (2010).

[17] Zanobi (2008: 228).

figure in turn.[18] According to Lucian, a cultivated audience could tell (like ballet buffs today) if a foot or even a finger happened to be out of place.[19] Nevertheless, as Webb argues: 'The performance of actions in pantomime . . . can never have been "literal", but must have been circumscribed by the artistic constraints of the genre.'[20] It utilized a sophisticated stylized movement vocabulary, not mimetic in the sense of representational but rather affective, acting upon the bodies of the spectators through corporeal and neurological sympathy.[21] The music, the *cantor's* melodic line, passed like an electric current through dancer and audience alike, galvanizing the one into well-trained, finely tuned motion, and compelling the other to vibrate, albeit inarticulately, in response. The power dynamics articulated by pantomime may thus be construed as a three-way nexus of body, voice, and gaze, in which the dancer's body hangs upon the sound, absorbing the lyric line and flinging it back out into the *cavea* redoubled as kinetic energy. In true multimedia fashion, the audience/spectators receive two complementary but only laterally related sets of stimuli, glutting their eyes on the mobilized body while being themselves simultaneously penetrated by the mobilizing soundtrack.[22]

The *Anthologia* poet mentions a *chorus* and a *cantor* in the same breath. The singular may be chosen to fit the metre,[23] or it may imply that the libretto is split between soloist and choir. Other sources are divided as to whether one or more singers accompanied the pantomime dancer.[24] The likeliest solution, and incidentally one that is congruent with Senecan practice, suggests a group of singers out of which a solo vocalist could periodically emerge to speak or sing. Lucian refers to the elusive *hypokrites*, who has been variously identified as an assistant dancer, an interlocutor, or an actor playing minor roles; it may

---

[18] Webb (2008: 60–85).   [19] Lucian, *Salt.* 80.   [20] Webb (2008: 75).

[21] 'Neuropsychological experiments demonstrate that when individuals observe an action done by another individual their motor cortex becomes active, in the absence of any overt motor activity' (Rizzolati and Craighero 2004: 174). On the neurology of watching dance, see Calvo-Merino et al. (2005). This phenomenon was also observed in antiquity. Libanius, for example, asks: 'What old man or what lazy man . . . would not be inspired to move by the dancer's leaping?' (64.117). Webb (2008: 87–90) describes pantomime as 'synaesthetic' and 'an all-absorbing experience for spectator and performer, sometimes bordering on trance'.

[22] On what Lada-Richards (2007: 73–4) calls the 'cultural logic' of vision and power, see Benton (2002) and Barton (2002), with counter-argument by Webb (2008: 168). Barton (2002: 219) notes that the eyes, like the genitals, were conceived as 'both extremely vulnerable and extremely aggressive'.

[23] This is unlikely, however, because *quae resonant voces* or *quae cantores sonant* would also fit, had the author been concerned to retain the plural.

[24] For soloists, see *Anth. Pal.* 16.287, 9.542. Lucian, *Salt.* 63, mentions choral backing, but later contrasts the ὑποκριτοῦ εὐφωνίαν ('fine voice of the actor') and the ἀδόντων ὁμοφωνίαν ('harmony of the singers') (*Salt.* 68). Kelly (1979) also supports some combination. Webb (2008: 62) provides further late antique evidence for this, both textual and iconographic. The panto-mime chorus, and the relationship of pantomime with *choreia*, are also discussed by Peponi, Chapter 1, this volume.

equally be a term for a vocal soloist.[25] Regardless of whether one voice or several—or a combination—were responsible for the soundtrack, however, its coils and convolutions were still brought to bear on a single point, the body of the *saltator*.

SENECA'S CHORUSES AND PANTOMIME

Turning now to Seneca, we may examine a selection of the major choral odes with this performance mode in mind, and then briefly compare the exceptional group activity found in *Agamemnon* and *Trojan Women*. Overall, it should be reiterated that Seneca's choruses play little part in the action between odes, which has provoked much discussion about their possible exits and re-entrances.[26] The occasional announcement of a character's arrival (*Oed.* 202–5, 911–14 ; *Phaed.* 833–4, 889–90, 1154–5) and a single instruction to the grieving Theseus (*Phaed.* 1244–6) hardly constitute regular interactive dialogue. The chorus's cooperation is never solicited, its opinion never requested. On two occasions (*Thy.* 626–748 and, more briefly, *Med.* 879–90), choruses supply interrogative interjections that prompt the respective *Nuntii* to deliver their accounts. In *Oedipus*, the chorus provides a real-time account of Jocasta's onstage suicide.[27] Although it could be interpreted as helpful commentary for the benefit of the blinded Oedipus, this seems an unnecessarily literal reading. Verbal representations of characters or events supposedly also present onstage are delivered by chorus and characters alike.[28] At *Oedipus* 1040–1, the chorus performs its 'transparent' function, imprinting on the auditor a visceral image of Jocasta's death: *vulneri immoritur manus | ferrumque secum nimius eiecit cruor* ('Her hand itself dies from the wound it inflicts | and excess blood spews out the sword along with it') (ll. 1040–1). The chorus is not at all the focus of this line; instead, invisible as a camera, it forces a slow-motion, close-up replay of Jocasta's wound in almost pornographic detail.

Descriptio of this kind falls to the Senecan chorus elsewhere as well, providing pantomime-style commentary on characters either within the play or in mythological proximity to the events portrayed. *Medea* 849–65, for example, which closely resembles the Nurse's commentary on Medea's frenzy at ll. 382–96, is singled out by both Zanobi and Bernhard Zimmermann as a

---

[25] For discussion of the *hypokrites*' role, see Jory (1998: *passim*) and Lada-Richards (2007: 42).

[26] P. Davis (1989, 1993); Sutton (1984, 1986).

[27] Although not identified by Zimmermann (2008: 223–4), this brief passage fits his category of 'short pantomimic commentary'.

[28] E.g. *Trojan Women* 945–68 (the reactions of Polyxena and Hecuba), *Hercules Furens* 1002–53 (the murder of Megaera and the children), *Oedipus* 303–83 (the bull sacrifice), and *Medea* 382–96 (Medea's rage).

pantomimic passage.[29] *Quonam cruenta maenas praeceps amore saevo /
rapitur*? the Chorus asks:

> Flagrant genae rubentes,
> pallor fugat ruborem.
> Nullum vagante forma
> servat diu colorem.
> Huc fert pedes et illuc,
> ut tigris orba natis
> cursu furente lustrat
> Gangeticum nemus.

(ll. 858–65)

Her cheeks burn crimson | then pallor flushes it out. | She keeps no colour for long, |
appearance in flux, | pacing back and forth | like a tiger bereaved of her cubs | takes her
furious course | through the Indian jungle.

In particular, the *vagante forma* with which Medea confounds her onlookers
may be related to the pantomime's protean aspect, his ability to shift with
heady rapidity from one state to another. Instructions for movement—pacing
here and there, the frantic dash (*cursu furente*), and the predatory steps of the
tiger give clear physical, as well as figurative, shape to the dancer embodying
them. Other instances of choral commentary on a present protagonist, also
among those listed by Zanobi and Zimmermann, include *Agamemnon* 710–19,
which picks out choice aspects of Cassandra's entry into prophetic delirium;
and *Hercules Furens* (*The Madness of Hercules*) 1082–1121, which draws its
subject out of madness and into restless sleep, going on to predict the ferocity
of an impending grief that will boom through the Underworld.[30] In all of these
passages—two within lyric odes, and one (*Agamemnon*) integrated into the
trimeter—the chorus operates as a mechanism facilitating richer insight into
the states of quasi-delirium suffered by individual characters. In one respect,
the character is thereby elevated, acquiring greater stature and connotative
density; but at the same time she sacrifices autonomy, subject to a construction
of her identity from without, dancing like a human marionette suspended on
the vocal line.[31]

One can add to these episodes a number of others that lend themselves to
the dynamics of concurrent *descriptio*. In these instances, the *saltator*'s role
shifts from direct representation of the protagonist to representing a gallery of
associated figures. *Phaedra* 296–352 illustrates the irresistibility of Eros with a

---

[29] Zimmermann (2008: 221–2) mentions this passage as an example of 'actual pantomime',
but does not discuss it in detail. Zanobi (2008: 233) lists it along with several others, making no
distinction between descriptions delivered by the chorus and descriptions delivered by other
characters.

[30] Zimmermann (2008: 221–2). Zanobi (2008: 233–8) discusses Cassandra.

[31] Cf. Plutarch's description of the puppet-like *hyporchema* in *Moralia* 748c.

series of increasingly burlesque vignettes: Apollo's *servitium amoris*, Jupiter's several disguises, Hercules' transvestism, and a whole menagerie of animals on heat. Lucian attests that pantomime frequently depicted 'the love affairs of all the gods, and especially those of Zeus' (*Salt.* 59). It is easy to envisage a pantomime artist exercising his protean skill to pose as Apollo in love, just as the Augustan dancer known as Hylas famously showed an Agamemnon deep in thought, or bringing the house down as an effeminate Hercules (one of the *saltator*'s disturbing qualities, for the early Christian moralists, was his androgyny, his supple male body that could become pliant and flirtatious).[32] Displaying the visual iconography of each character in turn assists in distinguishing them among a catalogue whose density could otherwise suppress their specificity. The second ode of the *Phaedra*, a profound meditation on the fragility of *forma* (beauty, perfection, but also shape or wholeness), shares this preoccupation with male physicality, focused in this instance on Hippolytus. The chorus compares him first of all to elemental forces, to an *insanae procellae* and a comet (ll. 736–40), and then to another catalogue of divine *exempla*: Phoebe, Lucifer, and Bacchus, each of whom would, according to Lucian, possess a distinct, readily identifiable pantomimic persona.[33] This is followed by a Salmacis-like scene in which *Naïades improbae* lure the attractive youth into a deceptively limpid pool (ll. 776–84), and finally an encomium addressed to Hippolytus himself, imagined as a marble statue with the physique of Mars or Hercules, adopting a quick succession of virile poses (riding, hunting, archery). None of this invites group enactment. On the other hand, it powerfully suggests a single performer slipping from role to role like a *tableau vivant*, his gestures not literally illustrative but complementarily suggestive of the vain Bacchus, the wilting meadow, the lascivious nymph, the Parthian archer. The group has no role other than the provision of a vocal line, reflecting the auditors' attention unswervingly back to Hippolytus, the cynosure, the avatar of *forma*, whose beauty—like Jocasta's hand—will become the unconscious agent of its own undoing.

Two other typically Senecan attributes add further support to this conjecture. First, the catalogue effect, which is prevalent throughout his dramatic corpus, arranges multiple episodic images around a given subject, frequently in the form of similes. These often feature a single mythological archetype (such as Bacchus) or a natural phenomenon in motion (a lightning bolt, a lily *languescens*). This technique provides the *saltator* with his verbal score, a sequence of clear suggestions acting as a mould for plastic interpretation.

---

[32] Anecdote from Macrob. *Sat.* 2.7.13–14. On the dangerous effeminacy of pantomime dancers, see Webb (2008: 77–9) and Lada-Richards (2007: 69–70). On 'Apollo in love' as a pantomime subject, see Lucian, *Salt.* 45 and Ingleheart (2008: 212).

[33] Lucian, *Salt.* 37–61. *Salt.* 19 describes Proteus as the archetypal *saltator*, able to imitate fire, water, and trees as well as various animals, 'just like the dancers of today'.

Whereas the more extended descriptive passages allow for the development of a single emotional state, these short bursts appeal to the other noted attribute of pantomime, its rapid transitions from frame to frame. Secondly, Seneca's choral odes are not strophic; nor, with the exception of a couple of early experiments, are they even polymetric.[34] Although it remains unclear precisely how Greek choral metre related to Greek choral choreography,[35] it is evident that by Seneca's time this relationship has dissolved altogether. Deprived of the strong rhythmic impulses provided by strophic structure, Seneca's choruses rely wholly on verbal imagery, and this has far less to offer a uniform group of dancers than it offers to a soloist whose articulate instrument can pick up and transmit a subtler register of poetic activity.

Further examples may be found in *Medea* and *Oedipus*. *Medea* 301–79 fashions a miniature version of the *Argonautica*, a myth of overreach and self-destructive avarice into which the Roman play is far more tightly woven than the Greek.[36] The *audax* Argo is a Roman—more specifically, a Horatian—trope, whipped up by Seneca to gale force. The narrative portion of the ode commences with Tiphys the helmsman, representatively described as *ausus* and *avidus*, performing a montage of nautical activity:

> **nunc** lina sinu tendere toto,
> **nunc** prolato dede transversos
> captare notos,
> **nunc** antemnas
> medio tutas ponere malo
> **nunc** in summo religare loco.
>
> (ll. 321–5)

[He dared] now to extend the sheet to full sail, | now paying out the line | to catch the cross-wind, | now fixing the sail-yards | safely in mid-mast, | now making them fast to the highest point.

Each repetition of *nunc . . . nunc* suggests a change in corresponding gesture or posture, and this again seems more appropriate for a solo performer than a whole group of identical sailors.[37] The Argo then encounters the Symplegades, provoking even *audax* Tiphys to turn pale, and Orpheus' hand to fall silent from the strings (ll. 346–9). This is followed by two vignettes from the Argo's

---

[34] Tarrant (1985: 31). Fitch (1981: 305–6) dates the polymetric odes in *Oed.* and *Ag.* to early in Seneca's career.

[35] On responsion in Greek choral choreography, see T. B. L. Webster (1970) and Wiles (1997: 87–113).

[36] M. A. Davis (1990) discusses the Roman application of the Argonautic myth to imperialist expansion.

[37] Cf. also Zanobi's remark: 'The visualization of the actions performed is facilitated by the use of parallel statements, which describe the character's movements in a very simple and arguably unpoetic way' (2008: 238).

return voyage, both also character-focused: rabid Scylla foaming at her many jaws, and the Sirens captivated in their turn by Orpheus *citharoedus*. Finally, the Chorus asks, 'What was the *pretium* [price/prize] of this voyage?' and the dancer's limbs melt in response, morphing implacably, impeccably, back into Medea, as she rises like a goddess from the eastern sea: *merces prima digna carina*. Similarly, the second half of *Medea's* third ode (ll. 607–9), where the metre changes from regular sapphics to extended hendecasyllabic stanzas,[38] likewise incorporates Argonautic material, enumerating the fate of each Argonaut in turn: the now-familiar Tiphys succumbing to disease, Orpheus dismembered, Hercules poisoned, Meleager burning,[39] Hylas drowned, and an epic host of others. The catalogue of death bounces so rapidly from one to another that it becomes less of a dirge and more of a litany, reaching the same degree of surfeit as the catalogue of sex in *Phaedra*. Merely sung, the individual figures blur; projected onto a *saltator*, however, they become an opportunity for him to display tremendous versatility as the palpable tremors of death after death roll over him.

Almost every choral ode in *Oedipus* affords similar, if variant, possibilities. Instead of mythological figures, *Oed.* 110–201 proceeds through the collocation of generic *exempla*, which may be divided into four sections: ethnic *effigies* illustrating the (over)reach of Theban/Roman power (ll. 110–22), various victims stricken by plague (ll. 132–59), a procession of *monstra* emerging from the Underworld (ll. 160–79), and the awful symptoms of the plague itself (ll. 180–201). Each of these crystallizes repeatedly around images that form and dissolve, creating Seneca's trademark kaleidoscopic effect, each image spearheaded by a distinctive noun (*Parthi, sacerdos, serpens, ignis*) and/or by a physically evocative verb (*labimur, rupere, tremuisse, rigant*). *Oedipus'* second chorus, the ode to Bacchus, may be regarded as unproblematic for pantomime, in that it represents a single divine figure moving through a mythological narrative, supplemented on occasion by cameos such as that of Agave's anagnoresis and the Ovidian transformation of pirates into dolphins. Like *Medea* 607–69 or *Phaedra* 296–352, its tone is much less sombre than the surrounding action, suggesting that Roman audiences were as capable as their early modern counterparts of coping with wild swings of dramatic mood, facilitated perhaps by this attested pantomimic mercuriality. *Oedipus'* third ode (709–63) treats a number of episodes from the Cadmean dynasty,[40] and the fourth (ll. 882–910) uses Icarus to illustrate a preference for moderation. Once again, graphic descriptive strokes are used to cast the attention of the audience onto the content of the odes, content that concentrates on individual

---

[38] Costa (1973: *ad loc.*).

[39] Suggested by Ingleheart (2008: 213) as a subject for pantomime derived from Ovid's *Metamorphoses*.

[40] All of which episodes are mentioned by Lucian, *Salt.* 41.

mythological figures performing definite, characteristic actions, precisely in the manner described by Lucian and later commentators on Roman pantomime.

This type of Senecan set piece, then, appears to fit the pantomime bill extremely well. According to fourth-century dance enthusiast Libanius, as well as representing people and emotions, the *saltator* could also represent landscapes:

In any kind of picture, what meadow is a more pleasant sight than that of the dance and the dancer when he leads the spectator around into the groves, and lulls herds of cattle to sleep under the trees, placing goats at pasture, flocks and shepherds in charge of the animals, some working at their tasks to the syrinx, others to the aulos? (64.116).[41]

Compare the pastoral pastiche found in the first lyric passage of *Hercules Furens*:

> Pastor gelida cana pruina
> grege dimisso pabula carpit
> ludit prato liber aperto
> nondum rupta fronte iuvencus;
> vacuae reparant ubera matres;
> errat cursu levis incerto
> molli petulans haedus in herba.

> (ll. 139–46)

The shepherd, having sent his flock abroad | gathers fodder iced with white frost. | The calf, forehead not yet split by horns, | plays free on the open meadow. | His mother, drained of milk, attends to her udder. | Lightly, on his impulsive course, the kid | strays impetuously in the soft grass.

The chorus then shifts focus to a sailor, who like Tiphys entrusts his fragile craft to the ocean currents, and a fisherman casting his line from the rocks. If we accept that pantomime could express not only the qualities of people but also the qualities of places, whole vistas of Seneca's text open up for this kind of performance. Greek tragedy establishes a precedent for choral activity that functions as a medium for depicting significant landscapes, prime examples being the catalogue of conquered islands in Aeschylus' *Persians* (ll. 880–96) and the 'Colonus' ode in Sophocles' *Oedipus at Colonus* (ll. 668–93). The Roman version of choral scene-setting simply dispenses with the filter of the group and selects particular aspects of the landscape, which may be impressed, sequentially and cumulatively, upon the malleable and unaffiliated limbs of the *saltator*.

---

[41] Libanius' oration 'On Behalf of the Dancers', in Molloy (1996). See also Lada-Richards (2007: 48).

If it is possible further to expand spatial coverage, this technique could equally apply to *Thyestes* 789–884, the 'Zodiac' ode. After Atreus murders his nephews, a supernatural darkness descends which the chorus interprets as the onset of *ekpyrosis*. The shaken universe will collapse in on itself, engulfing mortals and gods alike in formless chaos (ll. 830–3). The chorus goes on to recognize each constellation in the zodiac as they plummet burning down the sky to be extinguished in the tomb-like ocean. Cosmic ecphrasis is not unknown in Greek choral and narrative discourse (for example, Euripides' *Electra* 451–75 or *Ion* 1141–65),[42] but Seneca grounds it firmly in *Thyestes'* ethical bedrock, utilizing dramatic convention to support a key thematic and philosophical point. Ecphrases typically function meta-textually, providing a microcosm of the poem within which they occur. Senecan tragedy, as Alessandro Schiesaro has shown with particular reference to *Thyestes*,[43] is fond of this type of meta-theatrical game, and it is no stretch to suppose that the choral interludes operate in much the same way. The Zodiac Ode introduces universal cataclysm into what would otherwise remain a domestic tragedy following a centripetal trajectory that comes to rest in the bodily interior of its victim. Unlike the static depictions in *Ion*, *Electra*, and elsewhere, which strive to compose disparate elements into an orderly unity, Seneca's entropic momentum rips this unity asunder. A disordered cosmos entails disorder in the state, which is realized as a disordered individual body.[44] According to Senecan cosmology, human evil has cosmic repercussions; the individual is a microcosm of the universe, a site where natural forces converge.[45] This becomes especially evident when Senecan verse is staged as pantomime. For a single performer to attempt to contain and express the end of days might seem absurdly hubristic, but this replicates in a particularly concentrated form the self-aggrandisement that pervades the action of the play. Like Atreus, who styles himself in the next scene as 'equal to the stars, surpassing everything, grazing the highest pole with my towering crown' (ll. 885–6), the *saltator* who dances the Zodiac Ode makes manifest Seneca's Stoic philosophy of the whole expressed in the one.

After the echoes of Armageddon have died away, the chorus poses a question not altogether rhetorical:

> **Nos** e tanto visi populo
> digni, premeret
> quos everso cardine mundus?
> in **nos** aetas ultima venit?

> (ll. 875–8)

---

[42] See further Csapo (2008), who identifies connections between Pythagorean 'cosmic harmony' and choral dance.

[43] Schiesaro (2003).

[44] Sklenář (2008) discusses this in relation to *Oedipus*. See also Poe (1969: 373–6; 1983).

[45] T. G. Rosenmeyer (1989).

Do we seem worthy, out of so many | civilizations, to be crushed | by the downfall of the universe? | Has the final age arrived with us?

The first-person plural may be read as evidence that the chorus must here be conceived of as a group, but this is not necessarily the case. *Nos* does not only refer to its speaker/s, but reaches out to include the audience as it articulates the irrational eschatological fear of every generation with misgivings about its abuse of power, or the rapidity of progress. Whereas the preceding passage directed attention towards the heavens, conceivably utilizing the gestures of a *saltator* in whom a dying starscape could be personified—many of these constellations, after all, such as the Twins (l. 853), the golden Ram (ll. 850–1), the Nemean Lion (ll. 855–6), and Chiron the centaur (ll. 860–2), are mythological figures in their own right, which to judge by Lucian's catalogue were codified into the gestural system of pantomime—these concluding verses prompt self-examination among the audience. The dancer finishes his frenetic solo as Arctophylax crashes down beneath the icy waves, and the question rings out in the post-apocalyptic hush: Is this the end of the world? *Are we responsible?*

EXCEPTIONS AND COMPLICATIONS

At times, however, a Senecan chorus demonstrably participates in dialogue, as in the scene following *Thyestes* 546–622. This ode has attracted critical attention because of its apparent inconsistency: the chorus should know that Atreus' reconciliation is duplicitous; therefore, 'its' celebration of fraternal *pax* is scarcely plausible. Reading the ode with pantomime in mind dissolves this problem. Opportunities for the *saltator* within the ode include preparations for siege warfare succinctly encapsulated in representative archetypes (a frightened mother, a resolute watchman, and so on), and a multifaceted simile comparing immanent human conflict to various manifestations of a troubled sea (ll. 577–95). These opportunities are succeeded by a more reflective passage, arguably a *cantor*'s solo, which includes a direct address to the audience warning those who rule the world to beware of complacency (ll. 607–9). It is possible that this suspension of pantomimic discourse enables the *saltator* to change his mask or cloak in preparation for his next role: as *Fortuna* revolves (*rotat*, 618), so does the *saltator*, entering the wild spinning (*turbine versat*, 622) that will carry him into the Nuntius' electrifying entrance: *Quis me per auras turbo praecipitem vehet | atraque nube involvet?* ('What whirlwind will snatch me headlong into the sky | and twist me up in black cloud?') (ll. 623–4).[46] The ensuing scene contains the greatest number of choral interjections anywhere in Seneca's corpus. I suggest that these may be delivered by the *cantor, in propria persona*. As a theatrical device, the Senecan chorus has no identity or presence within the fictional world of the play. D. E. Hill compares it to the soundtrack of a film; nobody asks where the musicians are, or wonders how they know what mood to evoke, or expects them to intercede.[47] An alternative (live) comparison might be made to the pianist in a music hall. His primary—self-effacing—function is to provide accompaniment, but he is nevertheless capable of asserting his presence musically or vocally and engaging in banter with the performers with no detrimental effect on the routine; indeed, such exchanges highlight the skill of both parties. In *Thyestes*, a member of the otherwise transparent ensemble breaks out of his customary anonymity to perform the role of interlocutor, prompting the reluctant Nuntius to disclose horror after horror. Greedy for more obscene details, he wants to know *an ultra maius aut atrocius | natura recipit* ('Does Nature hold any even greater atrocity?') (ll. 745–6). Seneca manipulates theatrical convention in order to make a point about perpetually unsatisfied desire.

Similar manipulations may account for the handful of instances in which a Senecan chorus is unambiguously referred to as a group. *Medea* 56–115 is a hymeneal hymn, suggesting that the *iuvenes* called upon in l. 107 are to be identified with the chorus itself. This ode, however, is already a representation of a performance, a poeticized rendition of the kind of public ceremony staged for any state occasion. A dozen official singers singing a hymeneal chorus are playing a dozen official singers singing a hymeneal chorus: illusion collapses. At *Hercules Furens* 827–9, Theseus announces the approach of a large crowd (a *densa turba*) crowned with laurel and singing an epinician for the victorious Hercules. There are a number of peculiarities here, however, which have led Sutton to propose the entrance of a secondary chorus (as in the similarly problematic *Agamemnon*). First, the chorus is apparently already onstage.[48] Secondly, such a strongly marked entry occurs only here and at *Ag.* 586–8.[49] Finally, the anticipated epinician does not in fact commence until l. 875, some forty lines later; the intervening stanzas contain a melancholy and oddly meta-theatrical account of the crowds streaming down to the Underworld, resembling the public who rush *ad novi ludos avidus theatri* ('avidly to the spectacle

---

[46] On potential enactment of *Thyestes*' messenger-speech as pantomime, see Zanobi (2008: 242). *Anth. Pal.* 16.289 mentions a *saltator* performing the *angelos* among other roles from the *Bacchae*.

[47] Hill (2000: 587).

[48] P. Davis (1993: 19) argues for an exit at l. 592.

[49] It also occurs in the pseudo-Senecan *Hercules on Mount Oeta*, 581–2; for discussion, see Sutton (1984). Ferri (2003) suggests that the pseudo-Senecan *Octavia* may also have a secondary chorus, but its entrance is not marked in the same way.

at some new theatre') (l. 839). I suggest that perhaps, rather than the entrance of a second chorus, such self-referentiality represents a sudden, quite unprecedented, and quite shocking focus turned on the choral singers themselves, emphasizing their solidity and presence and rendering their bodies opaque, a rupture in convention as disorienting in its way as a voice from the orchestra pit.

Such calculated disruption may also explain the contradictory views of death expressed by the chorus of the *Trojan Women*, which is the only complete Senecan tragedy named for its chorus rather than its protagonist.[50] In their notorious second ode (ll. 371–408), which dismisses the afterlife as a mere *fabula*, the singer or singers are purely functional, transparent, a conventional vehicle for the philosophical position expressed. The third ode (ll. 814–57) speculates as to where the captives will be sent. A geographical catalogue, it whips with the dexterity of a patter song through some thirty place names in forty lines (Euripides' equivalent passage (*Tro.* 196–229) mentions only five). Whether or not these place names or their associated characteristics—a sinuous coastline, a hurrying river, Chiron reclining in his cave—could be represented using the gestural system of pantomime, the focus of this ode appears predominantly to be the rolling montage of Greek landscapes, not the attitude of the singer/s.

The *parodos*, however (ll. 67–163), in which the chorus joins Hecuba in a formal lament for Hector and Troy, affords the singers a uniquely coherent collective identity and a uniquely material corporeality. The simplicity of the choreography and its verbal representation in the text may also function as directions given to a group of non-professional dancers required to perform outside their comfort zone. Hecuba addresses them as *turba captivae mea* (l. 63) and goes on to emphasize their femininity, their physical movement, and their semi-nudity:

> Solvite crinem.
> Per colla fluant maesta capilli
> tepido Troiae pulvere turpes.
>
> .   .   .   .   .
>
> Paret exertos turba lacertos:
> veste remissa substringe sinus
> uteroque tenus pateant artus.
> Cui coniugio pectora velas,
> captive pudor?

> (ll. 83–91).

Loose your hair. | Over your neck let it flow in your grief, | grimed with the warm ash of Troy . . . Let the group prepare its arms for movement: | remove your clothing, tuck

---

[50] *Phoenician Women*, ironically, contains no choral passages.

in the folds, | expose your body right down to the womb. | What wedding-night are you saving your breasts for, | chastity enslaved?

It must be stressed that nowhere else does a Senecan chorus receive this kind of visual attention. The disembodied agents of the vocal track are turned into the objects of both the text and the gaze, eroticized in their removal of garments and loss of *pudor*, their loose hair and dishevelment combined with a stagy masochistic revelry in self-harm: *iam nuda vocant pectora dextras* ('now my naked breasts are crying out to be beaten') (l. 106).[51] This inversion, which places individual choral members at the mercy of the audience's gaze, represents an extraordinary departure from Seneca's usual practice. In first-century Rome, to sing in a chorus was significantly less humiliating than to display one's body openly as an actor;[52] here, Seneca not only makes the emotional suffering of his chorus unusually central, but marks it definitively in the exposure and degradation of the female body. Thematically, of course, this is *Trojan Women's* primary motif, and Seneca uses a twist on the theatrical resources at his disposal to facilitate a reversal of fortune at the most fundamental level. Perhaps it is significant that the only other instance of a Senecan chorus with a secure group identity is also a group of Trojan captives, the 'secondary' chorus of the *Agamemnon* who accompany Cassandra. Again, I would suggest that switching the focus with such abruptness from the content transmitted by choral odes to the human medium of these transmissions commits a deliberate violation of the Senecan choral role itself. *Non est lacrimis, Cassandva, modus*, this chorus sings, *quia quae patimur vicere modum?* (*Ag.* 691–2). ('Our suffering breaks all boundaries'). When suffering overflows not only the limits of endurance but the limits of form, the form must crack. Agony pours through the breach in theatrical contract.

To speak of a Senecan choral solo, then, is not strictly accurate. I hope to have shown, however, that many of Seneca's choral lyrics lend themselves to pantomime, with everything that this implies for the power dynamics articulated within the theatre. The early empire was notorious for its 'aestheticization of politics' and for the mutual dissembling that maintained the emperor as locus of absolute power.[53] The solo star performer replaced the ensemble cast at roughly the same time as republican oligarchy gave way to autocracy. Much has been written on the slippage between emperor and actor, particularly with reference to Nero's histrionic ambitions, and pantomime fits into the same paradoxical scheme. Reliant on public adoration but simultaneously

---

[51] Benton (2002: 31) argues that 'a sadomasochistic dialectic may be useful for understanding the staging of violence and gender in *Troades*'. Her discussion centres on characters rather than chorus.

[52] Acting was considered shameful in Rome because it involved displaying the body. Edwards (1997); Benton (2002).

[53] On Nero's obsessive self-dramatization, see Bartsch (1994: esp. 1–35), and Beacham (1999) on the culture of spectacle during the early Principate. It is Beacham (1999: 118) who applies Benjamin's phrase 'the aestheticization of politics' to imperial Rome.

exercising control over his spectators, elevated to superstar status but simultaneously exposed to mass scrutiny, the *saltator* theatricalizes the relationship between the *Princeps* and the people. Seneca's imperial tragedies no longer have a role for collective authority. Instead, Senecan tragic lyric is mediated by the individual, and this individual is mute, animated by language directing him from without. This radical concentration of energy is entirely appropriate for a socio-political context in which the citizen group has no authority, but absolute imperial power is vested in one man. It is also appropriate for a theatre containing characters who subsume the universe, and a universe that will devour us all.

7

'Something like the Choruses of the Ancients': The *Coro Stabile* and the Chorus in European Opera, 1598–1782

Roger Savage

In 1747, an operatic spectacular on the Phaeton myth was premiered in London: *Fetonte*, with a text by Francesco Vanneschi and music by Domenico Paradies. The opera's wordbook included a prefatory 'discourse' by the poet and translator John Lockman, and it has interesting things to say about *Fetonte*'s use of the chorus: 'As judicious Writers on Tragedy wish for something like the *Choruses* of the Ancients, the present Drama is therefore intermixed with Choruses which, though they may not imitate those of the *Greeks* and *Romans*, may perhaps remind many Spectators of them.'[1] Lockman, eager to set the new piece in a classical tradition that would appeal to a discerning audience yet careful to avoid laying claim to what might nowadays be called 'authenticity', is himself part of a tradition: the recurring concern through much of the seventeenth and eighteenth centuries to place the procedures and conventions of ancient drama (the ever-present chorus or *coro stabile* among them) beside those of modern opera, with a view to revealing parallels and divergences, precedents and influences, relative merits and demerits.

Linkages of this sort were being made as early as opera's first decade, 1598–1608. Claims were lodged then that, with its 'new songs', opera would allow audiences to 'admire the ancient honour of the Argive stage', and that it would 'come close to the so celebrated tragedies of the ancient Greeks and Romans' if given proper support by talented artists and generous princes. The novel dramatic monody for solo voices at its heart was thought by some to have been foreshadowed, and so perhaps justified, by the delivery of the speeches in ancient drama, which (if the influential savants Girolamo Mei and Francesco

---

[1] Lockman in Vanneschi (1747: p. xvi): spelling and punctuation modernized.

Patrizi were to be believed) had been wholly sung.[2] As for its choruses, the pioneering librettist Ottavio Rinuccini drew attention to 'the service that the chorus had been to the ancients and the importance it has in similar works'; and some of the choric procedures in antiquity were certainly reflected in the new operas. Thus, in modern opera as in Greek tragedy, the big lyrics that separated the episodes of dramatic action were sung, and in both they performed the same double function: providing a perspective on the progress of the drama that differed from that of the principal characters, and suspending normal time so that more events could be imagined as taking place offstage than would be possible during the actual minutes a choral lyric took to sing. Further, choric practice *c.*1600 could be seen as following the precepts of the two most revered ancient writers on the poetics of drama, Aristotle and Horace. In Aristotle's view, a choric group should be regarded 'as one of the actors' and as 'taking part in the action'; and, in Horace's, a chorus should 'sustain the part . . . of an actor, and sing nothing . . . that does not advance and fitly blend into the plot'.[3] True to precept, the first operatic choruses at Florence and Mantua were always choruses 'of ' something (of nymphs, fishermen, spirits, or whatever); what they sang was always in some sense apt to the situation, and they quite often tangled with the principal singers, joining in celebrations, interrogating messengers, grieving with protagonists.

Yet there were important aspects of the Greek tragic chorus that were reflected only occasionally in early opera or were not reflected at all. An aspect seemingly never reflected was the *manner* of ancient choric singing. Musicians of the time knew very well—Girolamo Mei had told them—that the odes in Greek tragedy were sung throughout in un-harmonized unison. The settings were 'truly a plainchant', Mei wrote, 'in every song a single air, such as we hear today in church in the recitation of the psalmody of the Divine Office'.[4] Yet the new operatic choruses were always sung in harmony: homophonically at first but quite soon blossoming into polyphony on occasion. This was a case of recent local traditions supplanting ancient faraway ones, for the choric numbers in the most prestigious classically linked shows of the late sixteenth

---

[2] 'New songs': O. Rinuccini, prologue to *Arianna*, in Solerti (1904–5: ii. 148). 'Celebrated tragedies': M. da Gagliano, preface to *Dafne*, trans. in Carter and Szweykowski (1994: 49). (Translations in this chapter are mine except where indicated, as here.) Mei and Patrizi: see Hanning (1973: 249–52), Palisca (1994: 453–56; 2006: 111–14).

[3] Rinuccini: quoted in T. Carter (1989: i. 142). Aristotle, *Poetics*, 1456ᵃ25–9, trans. in Russell and Winterbottom (1989: 74). Horace, *Ars Poetica*, vv. 193–5, trans. in Fairclough (1929: 467). For three essays of the period on choruses old and new—one in Nicolò Rossi's *Discorsi* of 1590, one attributed to Giovanni Bardi, and one in the anonymous *Il corago* of *c.*1630—see respectively Weinberg (1970–4: iv. 109–11), Palisca (1989: 140–51), and Savage and Sansone (1989: 503). For the sixteenth-century conflation of Aristotle and Horace on choruses, see Herrick (1946: 93–5). For aspects of the early operatic chorus, see T. Carter (1989: i. 142–5, 168–74), Grout (1963: *passim*, esp. 153–9), and Hanning (1980: 131–54, esp. 139–40).

[4] Trans. in Palisca (1989: 63, 57).

century had all used harmony: for example, Andrea Gabrieli's severely homo-phonic choruses for the otherwise spoken Italian *Oedipus Rex* mounted at Vicenza in 1585, and the more elaborate polyphony of the choral numbers that were often part of the spectacular all-sung mythological playlets or *intermedii* that interspersed the acts of spoken dramas when presented on festive occasions. (The *intermedii* attached to Girolamo Bargagli's comedy *La pellegrina* in Florence at the big Medici–Valois wedding of 1589 were the apogee of up-to-date multimedia spectacle and had choruses to match.) The choruses in opera followed suit. 'Classical' they may have been, but they wore their classicism with an audible difference.

An aspect of the Greek chorus reflected only on occasion was its being what Humanist writers called a *coro stabile*:[5] a group of singer–dancers who made their entrance after a play's prologue and did not leave again until the very end, adopting one corporate role throughout, helping to frame the action and providing a link or buffer between the audience and the principal players. Even aside from bold antiquarian revivals like the Vicenzan *Oedipus*, the later sixteenth century had encountered a body with some resemblance to a *coro stabile* in the scripts (and on occasion the performances) of courtly pastoral drama: its presence perhaps deriving from that of similar choric groups in the Latin tragedies of Seneca, themselves much read, sometimes staged, and quite often emulated at the time. However, the *stabile* idea had a powerful antagon-ist in the fashionable *intermedio*. Part of the allure of the sets of *intermedii* performed on festive occasions was their polymorphism, their restless shape-shifting in matters of scenery, character, and costume: something that in the case of *La pellegrina* involved the chorus singers' impersonating in succession panicky peasants, triumphant muses, piratical sailors, the sad denizens of Hades, and blessed spirits from beyond the moon. And this polymorphism nudged some early operas away from allegiance to a notion of the stable 'Greek' chorus towards the idea of the choric troupe as a pool of performers who would be happy to come and go, changing character and costume between one appearance and the next if the action required it.[6]

---

[5] The Latin terms *chorus stabilis* and *chorus mobilis* become current in the 1560s—see, e.g., J. C. Scaliger's *Poetices Libri Septem* (Scaliger 1561: 19a1 and Index s.v. 'Chorus')—probably reflecting the frequent use of the adjectives in Petrus Victorius' discussion of Aristotle's 'stasima' and 'parados' (*Poetics* 1452[b]18) during his pioneering *Commentarii in Primum Librum Aris-totelis de Arte Poetarum* of 1560. The Italian term *coro stabile* is being discussed in *Camerata* circles a couple of decades later (Palisca 1989: 148–9); and in the 1590s Angelo Ingegneri uses both terms in Italian in his treatise on practical stagecraft, *Della poesia rappresentativa* (Marotti 1974: 281, and (mentioning 'Pier Vittorio') 307). A hundred years later they appear in Andrea Perrucci's *Dell'arte rappresentativa* (Perrucci 1961: 153–4); and, half a century later still, Pietro Metastasio refers to the 'coro stabile' in his commentary on Aristotle (see n. 16). For a modern view of Aristotle's original 'stasima' and 'parados', see Dale (1969: 34–40).

[6] For a discussion in 1598 of choric contributions to spoken drama—the formal Sophoclean chorus a necessity in tragedy but choruses optional in pastoral and comedy (where they are

That is certainly the case in *Il rapimento di Cefalo* ('The Abduction of Cephalus'), the heavily *intermedio*-influenced opera of 1600 with text by Gabriele Chiabrera and music largely by Giulio Caccini, which in succession fields choruses of huntsmen, marine deities, cupids, signs of the zodiac, yet more deities, and finally huntsmen again. As for the choruses in other more 'regular' operas of the period, their creators sometimes chose to sample both the stable and the polymorphous modes. Thus the earliest operas on the Orpheus and Euridice myth, Jacopo Peri's *Euridice* of 1600 to a text by Rinuccini and seven years later the *Orfeo* of Claudio Monteverdi and Alessandro Striggio, both make a point in their extensive early scenes of presenting one rooted rustic chorus, but later shift the location to Hades, replacing the Grecian nymphs and shepherds with a group of philosophical spirits, only to shift it back eventually to the woods and fields above ground, where in the Peri the earlier rustics are on hand to celebrate the hero's and heroine's wedding, while in the Monteverdi the group from Acts I and II reappears just in time to rejoice at Orpheus' final translation to the heavens. (In Striggio's draft-text a third choric group, a scary bevy of Bacchantes, had arrived to frustrate any such happy ending.)

Choric polymorphism and eclecticism did not have it all their own ways, however. A more purist emulation of the classical *coro stabile*—keeping the chorus in one role throughout, keeping it on stage for all the action, and keeping it integrated with that action in one way or another—is to be found in some early libretti, especially some by Rinuccini himself. For instance, in his *Dafne* (set by Jacopo Corsi and Jacopo Peri in 1598 and reset, somewhat revised, by Marco da Gagliano ten years later) he experiments with a stable group of nymphs and shepherds, singing all together sometimes, sometimes in smaller groups, sometimes in solos. Though they inhabit a world quite close to that of such sixteenth-century pastoral plays as Guarini's *Pastor Fido* and the *Aminta* of Torquato Tasso, they are much more consistently alert, forthcoming, and involved in things than are their equivalents there. Beyond several quite lengthy strophic lyrics, they exchange views among themselves and take part in every scene as participants in the dialogue or reflective observers. They also tangle with mythological figures in the way that Tasso's and Guarini's choric groups do not. Rinuccini later takes this idea of a permanent chorus further in his longer, more ambitious libretto on the Theseus–Ariadne–Bacchus myth, *Arianna*, performed in 1608 with a score by Monteverdi, and after that in *Narciso*, his tragedy of Echo and Narcissus, also offered to Monteverdi but not set by him (or seemingly by anyone else). In *Narciso* there is a group of nymphs that the librettist specifically labels 'coro stabile' in his manuscript.[7] They enter at the end

---

replaceable *ad lib.* by *intermedii*—see Ingegneri. *Della poesia rappresentativa*: Marotti (1974: 279–83; cf. 306–9).

[7] Solerti (1904–5: ii. 190). For other aspects of Rinuccini's relationship with classical drama, see Hanning (1973: *passim*).

of the first scene and stay onstage thereafter, singing as commentators, celebrators, interlocutors, interrogators, and elegists, conversing quite extensively with one another and with the lead singers. Given the preparedness of courtly audiences like Rinuccini's to see themselves on occasion as idealized pastoral folk, the poet is presumably hoping here for an association of audience and chorus analogous to that on the ancient Athenian stage.

Arianna has one stable choral group too: a company of fishermen on the island of Naxos. After a quasi-Greek prologue, they come onstage and stay there throughout, and, although two other *cori* also appear—one at the start associated with Theseus, the other at the end with Bacchus—they are subordinate groups, like the troop of hunters who make brief appearances in Acts II and V of *Narciso*. Rinuccini could have cited ancient precedent for such secondary choruses (the hero's hunting companions at the beginning of Euripides' *Hippolytus*, for instance); but it is the fishermen who form the group that counts in *Arianna*. They get more and more involved in the action as the opera goes on, both in their big lyrics and in their exchanges with Ariadne's confidante and with a couple of news-bringers; and they gain real classical credibility by giving vocal support to the deserted heroine during her climactic lament: the fine and famous plea to the fates to let her die, 'Lasciatemi morire'. Indeed, if we look at the libretto, we can see this as resembling the formal lyric exchange of a Greek *kommos*; so it is particularly sad that only the music for Ariadne's contribution to it has survived.[8]

The loss of Monteverdi's music for the fisherfolk in that *kommos* could stand as a symbol of the later seventeenth century's dwindling interest in Rinuccini's classicism. True, there were some classicizing choric moments in the decades that followed, but they were few and far between. Still, the form's first thirty years did give the growing number of people mounting opera in the court theatres of northern Italy and at Rome (the Rome of the Barberini particularly) the choice of polymorphism or of a classicist purism where choruses were concerned.[9] The dice were loaded against the latter, however, by the century's passion for spectacular scene changes on proscenial stages. As the wing-flats and backdrops at a well-appointed court playhouse changed

---

[8] For Rinuccini's texts, see Solerti (1904–5: ii). We do, however, have a setting by Severino Bonini of the relevant lines from Rinuccini's *kommos*, which was made for salon use about five years later and which includes the fishermen's interjections as well as the heroine's grieving. For this, see (and hear) Anthony Rooley's LP-anthology, *Lamento d'Arianna* (Deutsche Harmonia Mundi, 1984). For Rossi on the *kommos* in his *Discorsi* of 1590, see Weinberg (1970–4: iv. 109–10).

[9] Around 1640, Giovanni Battista Doni stages a related debate—should the acts of spoken plays be separated by choruses integral to the drama or by spectacular, diverting but arguably alien *intermedii*?—in the third 'Lezzione' of his *Della Musica Scenica* (Doni 1763: ii. 187–8). For Rome, see Murata (1981: 179–84; 1984: *passim*).

from, say, the Palace of Jupiter to a stormy seascape and then to the Temple of Minerva, a *coro* with ambitions to be *stabile* would be reduced to scuttling from the one to the other; and only the Furies in the *Oresteia* could bring that off convincingly! A versatile polymorphous group, on the other hand, could do well under such conditions. Given adequate costume-changing facilities, it could present vivid and arresting cameos of an assembly of gods at Jupiter's Palace, then of personifications of raging winds in the sea scene, and finally of a chapter of priests in Minerva's Temple.

That sequence of three comes from Antonio Cesti and Francesco Sbarra's enormous court show *Il pomo d'oro* ('The Golden Apple') for Vienna in 1668, by which date court opera of course had a rival: public opera as established in Venice around 1640. Predictably perhaps, fidelity to antique dramaturgy did not come high on *its* list of priorities: witness the preamble of an anonymous poet to his Venetian–Virgilian opera on the marriage of Aeneas, *Delle nozze d'Enea in Lavinia*, which had a setting (now lost) by Monteverdi.

The chorus . . . was an integral part of the old tragedies, entering not only as a character but singing mainly between the acts with gestures and dancing . . . But in the modern [tragedies] it is made less important, being seen in some for very little other than the division of the acts. Just as I have introduced still more choruses in the middle of the same acts, so I have not availed myself of them at their end, for since the entire tragedy is sung, the chorus singing [at the end] as well would become too tedious.[10]

Moreover, in Venice as in the other cities that came to welcome public opera, the number of choruses of whatever sort began to shrink. One reason for this was economic. If you were one of the new breed of impresario mounting opera for paying audiences as a commercial proposition, you had to try to be cost effective; and a way to be that in an age when solo arias were getting more crowd-pullingly elaborate and their singers commensurately more expensive was to encourage your librettist to cut back wherever possible on choruses. He was welcome, if he liked, to field numbers of *comparse*: those silent supernumeraries impersonating citizens, senators, priests, pages, and soldiers (vigorously combatant soldiers sometimes) who served to fill out a scene and 'dress the stage'. *Comparse* came relatively cheap—you could hire four for the price of one stagehand in Venice in the 1650s[11]—and in the main they needed little rehearsal, which was not the case with any of the old types of chorus. So those were under threat.

It was a threat compounded by a new aesthetic that was running alongside the new economics: one as relevant to the Intendant of a court opera as to the impresario of a commercial venture. 'Verisimilitude', *vraisemblance*, the

---

[10] Trans. in Carter and Szweykowski (1994: 173).

[11] Glixon and Glixon (2006: 221); productions often fielded around forty of them. For the absent Venetian chorus in the seventeenth century, see Rosand (1991: 54–5).

watchword of much late Renaissance literary theory, was beginning to connect with opera; and it tended to see a chorus not as a many-headed single consciousness in the Greek way but as a gathering of 'real people'. Considered as real people, of course, choruses could not plausibly deliver quantities of high and erudite speech unanimously as the Greek choruses had done, or even such stanzas of elegant meditation, celebration, and supplication, as Rinuccini and Striggio had presented to their composers. So the texts for choruses in the Italian and Italianate opera, as it moved towards the *opera seria* mode that developed in the very late seventeenth and early eighteenth centuries, tended to become short as well as infrequent.[12] 'Likelihood' was threatened particularly by the *coro stabile*, of course. Would consequential people really discuss issues of state or family intimacies in the presence of such a motley crew? Its presence was also a hindrance to the sort of psycho-realism embodied in the soliloquy—and by extension in the reflective aria. As the theorist of spoken drama Hédelin d'Aubignac wrote in his *Pratique du théâtre* of 1657, if he has a chorus onstage with him, a character 'cannot with verisimilitude speak out loud about secret matters without being overheard', while, 'if he were made to speak very quietly and pensively, as soliloquies always suppose, the chorus would have to think him insane'.[13] Of course, one might move a *coro stabile* offstage during such soliloquies, but that would be difficult, and anyway it was rarely done in Greek tragedy. Better for a modern dramatist to dispense with that sort of chorus altogether.

People with classical tastes attracted to Italian *opera seria* yet nostalgic for the weightiness of the Athenian choric odes might on rare occasions be consoled by singular pieces like the Vanneschi/Paradies *Fetonte* of 1747, which, as we have seen, John Lockman described as 'intermixed with Choruses which, though they may not imitate those of the *Greeks* and *Romans*, may perhaps remind many Spectators of them'. Or they might be placated by the view of some eighteenth-century savants and librettists, Ranieri de' Calzabigi in his *seria* phase among them, that the alternation of recitative-scene and time-arresting aria in *opera seria* was a happy mutation out of the alternation of sung dramatic episode and meditative choral lyric in ancient tragedy, so

---

[12] They tended too to be set and cast in fairly utilitarian ways, except on the rare occasions when it was a matter of making a splash with a big inset choric–choreographic celebration: see, e.g., R. Strohm in Brown and Ograjenšek (2010: 173–6). If a 'choric' number had to be sung in connection with a battle, a hunt, a royal occasion, or whatever, it might well be delivered by the solo singers in consort, while the group lyrics that rounded off many an *opera seria* and that tended to be labelled 'cori' in the printed libretti (when all the plot's loose ends had been tied up and the all-but-inevitable happy ending achieved) were very often so sung. See Dean (1969: 147–8), and cf. Freeman (1981: 240–51).

[13] D'Aubignac (2001: 315–16). Giraldi Cinthio had made the point about issues of state a century before in a letter to Ercole II d'Este discussing his tragedy *Didone*: Weinberg (1970–4: i. 477). Horace's assurance (*Ars Poetica* 200) that a good chorus will 'keep secrets' was clearly not enough for him.

that in retrospect the noble corpus of Greek choruses could be viewed as resembling 'a union of many of our arias': arias that were 'nothing other in essence than parts of the chorus'.[14] But the nostalgists had to acknowledge that there was no putting the clock back, however much certain people with a measure of influence over the making of Italian libretti would have liked to do so: the 'Arcadian' theorist Giovanni Crescimbeni, for instance, who regretted the lapsing of the *stabile* chorus characteristic of the 'best ancient taste' and who warmly recalled Agostino Manni and Emilio de' Cavalieri's use of it in their century-old *Rappresentazione di animo et di corpo* ('The Play of the Soul and the Body'), that bold blend of opera and traditional religious drama from Rome in 1600.[15] Such retrogressions, however, were very firmly ruled out by the prime librettist of *opera seria* in the eighteenth century, Pietro Metastasio, whose twenty-seven full-length texts written between 1727 and 1771 were extraordinarily widely set. In his lively and often approving commentary on Aristotle, the *Estratto dell'Arte Poetica*, Metastasio adopts an evolutionary model for the chorus that sidesteps Aristotle's precepts:

As a flower or fruit emerges from its covering, so the [Greek] drama emerged from the bosom of the chorus ... Though so very different a thing, it could never quite detach itself from that covering ... because the cult of Bacchus and the god's praises sung in chorus formed the principal object of the festivals, and the drama newly grown out of this was only to be considered as an ornament added to the song of the chorus.

But further growth of the fruit meant that the choric husk should be discarded. Hence erudite modern authors—Metastasio may have had Crescimbeni in mind, or his own tutor Gianvincenzo Gravina—would be misguided if they

persisted in considering the *coro stabile* as an essential and principal part of the drama ... For it is a wholly unnatural improbability that all the people constituting a permanent chorus should spontaneously conceive and put into words exactly the same similes, descriptions, lengthy historical narratives, subtle arguments to persuade and dissuade, prolix congratulations, interminable condolences ...

—the building blocks, that is to say, of many Greek tragic odes. Not that the dismissal of the *coro stabile* meant that

all sorts of choruses ought to be banned indiscriminately from the stage. For then the theatre would lose the opportunity of using them with dignity, verisimilitude, and pleasing effect in sacrifices, triumphs, festivals ... where, since it is likely that what is

---

[14] Calzabigi (1994: i. 30–1).

[15] Crescimbeni (1730–1: i. 295–6, 311–12); cf. Freeman (1981: 21). The general lack of such choric effects in early eighteenth-century opera outside France should not give the impression that the period was short of big, often dramatic and on occasion 'philosophical' choruses in a narrative context. Their home, though, was the Handelian concert-oratorio and the Lutheran church Passion. The period's English 'masque' and continental *festa teatrale* should be mentioned too as shorter 'borderline' forms: staged or semi-staged but sometimes with oratorio-type choruses.

being sung was premeditated, it is quite natural for a great number of people to give voice simultaneously to the same sentiments and words.

It was *so* natural indeed that very brief choral lyrics growing out of formal occasions like these can be found in almost half Metastasio's own libretti. (In his entry on the 'Chœur d'Opéra' for the *Encyclopédie* in the 1750s, Jean-François Marmontel found a label, the 'chœur appris', for such premeditations, pairing them with the other type of chorus acceptable to *vraisemblance* and approved by Metastasio, the brief cry of shared emotion: 'Hurrah!', 'Look out!', 'Oh my God!' This Marmontel labelled the 'chœur impromptu'.)[16]

In Marmontel's homeland there were certainly the physical resources to pursue a choric purism *à l'antique*. From its establishment around 1670, French lyric theatre (soon very much under the thumb of Jean-Baptiste Lully) had a strong choral element, which it retained all through the Enlightenment and beyond. Its originating body, the Académie Royale de Musique, was an arm of the monarchy, and its continued connections with the state ensured that it went on having the sort of opulence that had characterized opera in princely Italy. So big choric effects remained central. In *La Danse ancienne et moderne* of 1754, Louis de Cahusac looked back chauvinistically across seventy-five years to the mould-creating chorus work of Philippe Quinault, Lully's librettist–collaborator:

The choruses, which the Greeks had used only ineffectually and which the Italians . . . did not know how to use, were skilfully and precisely placed by Quinault, and frequently furnished him with scenes of great spectacle, general activity, ravishing sounds, striking *coups de théâtre*, and occasionally the most exquisite pathos.[17]

But our *coro stabile* really did not stand much of a chance. For one thing, there were those scene changes: an Italian taste that had quite quickly spread across the Alps. For another, *tragédie lyrique* not only called on its choruses to play several roles in connection with the main plot: roles that, given the mythological cast of so much of the French genre (as opposed to the quasi-historical focus of most *opera seria*) might feature supernatural beings as well as mortal ones. It also called on them to be involved with the inset *divertissements* that the genre delighted in and that in part derived from the sequences of vivid *entrées* for exotic, symbolic, and allegorical characters central to the older French *ballet de cour* and its offshoots. In all, then, the range of roles taken by the chorus in any one opera at Paris or Versailles was likely to be wide,

---

[16] Metastasio (1943–54: ii. 1059–62); trans. based in part on Weiss (1982: 393); cf. Calzabigi (1994: i. 32–3), and see Strohm (1997: 205, etc.). (Metastasio's evolutionary model is foreshadowed, as he acknowledges, by that of the late Latin commentator Aelius Donatus: see Lawton (1949: 7).) Gravina and the need for choruses: Gravina (1973: 575–81). Marmontel on *chœurs*: Diderot and D'Alembert (1969: v. 348).

[17] Cahusac (1754: bk 3, ch. 5, p. 67); trans. in Wood and Sadler (2000: 45). See pp. 52–63 of Cahusac for a justification of his criticism of Greece and Italy in this matter.

stretching from the peoples of various distant nations through heavenly and subterranean beings to ghosts and genies, seasons and hours, planets even.

The musical and theatrical structures deploying these choruses could be powerful and impressive, especially in the *tragédies lyriques* and related works of Jean-Philippe Rameau—so impressive that the critics suggested classical parallels. 'The most astonishing things we are told about the choral songs of the ancients', said the *Mercure galant* in 1764, 'no longer seem so when we consider several of M. Rameau's.' Rameau may have relished the compliment. After all, the devisers of French opera in the 1670s had not been short of reminders that the Greeks' use of choruses was one of the most beautiful and rational achievements of *their* drama;[18] and it may be that Lully and Quinault, and the partners who succeeded them at the Paris Opéra from the 1690s to the 1750s, felt that, with the elaborate constructions of sung solos and duets, choruses and dances in their own inset festivities, rites and pageants, they were creating equivalents to the extended bursts of choric and coryphaeic song and dance in Aeschylus, Sophocles, and Euripides. But the choric groups in Rameau and the others were far too on-and-off-the-stage, too what-new-role-will-they-play-next, fully to serve an ancient function. Too passive also. One of Aristotle's requirements, that the chorus should be 'taking part in the *action*', had been largely overlooked, and this was beginning to irritate some visitors to the Opéra by the middle of the eighteenth century. Partly it was a matter of action—or rather the lack of it—in the purely physical sense. Enlightenment wits found the Opéra chorus reminiscent of so many organ pipes ranged statically around the edges of the stage (see Figure 7.1); and Cahusac noted tartly in his 'Chœur' entry for the *Encyclopédie* that, though in an earthquake scene the ladies and gentlemen of the chorus sang that the ground was collapsing beneath their feet, they themselves remained on one spot and displayed perfect composure.[19] And then there was action in the wider sense of moving an opera's plot forward musically and through vivid characterization. French composers and librettists had very largely been content that the chorus should be a *re*active body rather than a proactive one: that it should furnish *divertissements*, ceremonies, visions, and such when principal characters needed them, that it should be on hand to express dismay when things took a turn for the worse, and should generally show itself able to second a

---

[18] Astonishing things: quoted in Masson (1930: 288). (See all of Masson 1930: ch. 5, esp. 287–98.) Reminders: see Gabriel Gilbert and Charles de Saint-Evremond (writing in the 1670s) in Becker (1981: 121, 137).

[19] Organ pipes: Lesure (1984: i. 245, ii. 135–6). Cahusac: Diderot and D'Alembert (1969: i. 573). For aspects of the attitude of the Encyclopedists to opera generally, see Oliver (1947: chs 3, 4, 9). An uninvolved coldness on the part of the chorus was certainly a recurrent criticism of the Opéra in the 1750s and 1760s—see Jacobshagen (1997: 62–3, etc.)—but there is some evidence that the *chœurs* were not wholly inert: see Banducci (1993: 186–8), and M. Cyr in Bauman and McClymonds (1995: 108–15).

Fig. 7.1. Principal and Chorus in finale of *Atys* (Lully/Quinault); engraving by François Chauveau after the drawing by Jean Bérain; staged 1676 at Saint-Germain-en-Laye. Frontispiece to the libretto (1676)

motion, so to speak, but not that it should offer an independent view, a challenge, or a new idea. Enlightenment critics wanted more proactivity.

Enlightenment musicians too, among them the celebrated Chevalier Gluck. Gluck and several contemporaries working around Europe (the composers Niccolò Jommelli and Tommaso Traetta, for instance, the writers and ideologues Giacomo Durazzo, Mattia Verazi, and Calzabigi in his post-*opera seria* vein) were having fresh ideas about the writing and staging of choric scenes: one aspect of the attempt of parts of international music theatre in the 1750s, 1760s, and 1770s, focused first on Vienna and then on Paris, to move opera forward by way of an integration of the best of current Italian and French modes. A decade or so before, Charles de Brosses had caricatured the modes at their worst, pillorying the 'monotonous construction' of aria-dominated Italian operas where 'there are no trios or choruses, unless you count the feeble little chorus at the end of the final act', and protesting too at those parts of French *tragédie lyrique*, where, when 'the action has most deeply moved your soul, you find it distracted from such feelings, since the eyes are now occupied with a dance and the ears with a song' (that is, with yet another choric–balletic *divertissement*).[20] It was for Gluck, Jommelli, Traetta and their poets to take the choral element in opera beyond Italian feebleness and French ineptitude;[21] and it was Gluck who, making an astute choice of librettists during his Parisian years in the 1770s, found himself becoming the movement's (rather elderly) poster-boy—and found himself a myth-figure too when an anonymous article in the *Journal de politique et de litterature* in 1777 hailed him as the Prometheus who 'shook his torch' so that 'the statues came to life'. The statues were the members of the chorus at the Opéra, whom Gluck made an active part of a drama that was true to 'nature' both in the music he wrote for them and in matters of stage movement, where he was a tireless and exhausting rehearser. And this was done not only in the spirit of Aristotle's *Poetics* but often under a Greek star-sign in other ways too: a case of neoclassicism asserting, in Alexander Pope's phrase from earlier in the century, that 'Nature and Homer were the same'—or rather, in the case of 1770s Paris, that Nature and Greek tragedy were. Writing his operatic manifesto in a letter to the revered Padre Martini, the *Gluckiste* François Arnaud hailed the composer's effect on operatic choruses:

The Chevalier Gluck was the first to put them in action, and by simple, natural and true harmony has . . . stamped the drama with extraordinary movement. Each time I hear them I see myself thrown back to ancient Athenian times and believe I am in the audience for performances of the tragedies of Sophocles and Euripides.[22]

Of Euripides especially. Gluck and his librettists made notable operatic adaptations (at one or two removes) of Euripides' *Alcestis*, *Iphigenia in Aulis*, and *Iphigenia in Tauris*, and in all three the 'natural and true harmony' sung by the

---

[20] De Brosses: *Lettres familières*, trans. in Wood and Sadler (2000: 50–1). Cf. French scorn in the 1780s for all Italian choruses and much Parisian *divertissement*: Lesure (1984: i. 245, ii. 39, 146–7, etc.). For integration, see B. A. Brown (1991: esp. ch. 11), and M. McClymonds in Bauman and McClymonds (1995: 119–32). For 'the feeble little chorus at the end of the final act', see above, n. 12.

[21] For instances in Traetta and Jommelli, see Heartz (2004: 306–12), and McClymonds (1980: 256–7). For the increase in care called for in the casting and rehearsing of choruses in these new situations, see M. R. Butler (2006: *passim*).

[22] *Journal de politique*: Lesure (1984: i. 107). Gluck rehearsing: see Jacobshagen (1997: 65). Pope: v. 135 of *Essay on Criticism*. Arnaud: Lesure (1984: i. 245).

choruses compliments their being integrated into the action and activity of the plot. In *Alceste*, with one fairly brief exception, the *chœurs* play only King Admetus' citizens, and do so in all three acts. They have a solicitous, inter-active relationship with the king, and their breaking down quite often into small subgroups humanizes them further. Near the beginning of *Iphigénie en Aulide* a chorus of critical Greeks berates the high priest Calchas, then another of admirers of the heroine sings an extended ode to her; after which the opera's choric groups are mainly concerned to get their views across forcefully to the generals who command the action.[23] But the most intriguing of Gluck's Euripidean series from the choric point of view is the tightly constructed rescue-opera *à l'antique* of 1779, *Iphigénie en Tauride*, written to a text by Nicolas François Guillard. This, the 'dramatis personae' declares, has four chorus groups: the heroine's fellow priestesses, rough Scythians of Tauris, the men of the expeditionary force that has come from Greece with Orestes and Pylades, and a pack of Furies who torment Orestes when they get him on his own. Polymorph-ism might seem to rule; but if one looks closer it is clear that, as in Rinuccini's *Arianna* for Monteverdi 170 years before, one of the choral groups dominates. Here it is Iphigenia's priestesses who attract and hold the attention, coming quite close indeed to forming a *coro stabile*. As the *Journal de Paris* noted in 1779 in its 'Annonce de l'Opéra d'Iphigénie en Tauride', choruses in opera,

so vital in the performance, have almost always been defective up to now, slowing the action and chilling the interest. [But here] Monsieur Guillard, who has drawn his subject from the Greeks, has followed *their* manner. The Greek women, priestesses under Iphigenia, share her duties, her feelings, her regard for the family of Agamem-non, and are her sole confidantes.

They are on stage in each of the acts and for almost two-thirds of the action. They mourn; they pray; they sing hymns. Either *en masse* or through two *coryphées* they solace, exhort, advise and wait on the heroine, and at one point, when the news seems to be that Orestes the Deliverer is dead, they take part with her in what amounts to a *kommos*. It is even given them to provide the final clinching piece of evidence ('It is she whom Diana saved!') at the climactic moment of realization that the hero and heroine are in fact brother and sister. Their presence and their choric songs 'following the manner of the Greeks' are a major contribution to an opera that an early review in *Les Mémoires secrets* called 'a genuine tragedy, a Greek tragedy . . . One can only applaud Chevalier Gluck for having discovered the secret of the Ancients.'[24]

---

[23] At the very end they have what is musically the most authentically 'Greek' number of any opera of the first 200 years of the form in the war song of the confident army departing for Troy: pure monody, with all the singers and orchestral instruments (one drum apart) cleaving to the same unison melodic line throughout.

[24] *Journal de Paris*: Lesure (1984: i. 427). *Mémoires secrets*: quoted in Howard (1995: 199). For the Gluck *Iphigénie en Tauride* and Euripides, see Ewans (2007: ch. 3, esp. 44–6). (An interesting

With all those choric effects so tellingly deployed in *Iphigénie en Tauride*, the way might seem open to a sequence of full-scale operatic revivals of sung Greek tragedy and of other myths treated in a similar way, each with something approaching an active and engaged yet also lyrical and reflective *coro stabile* that would encourage a revived Athenian chorality. And Gluck himself seems to be moving further in that direction in his next—and last—opera, the collaboration with Ludwig von Tschudi on *Echo et Narcisse*, with its unit set and single chorus of nymphs and swains. However, librettist and composer here give the chorus disappointingly little to do: much less than Rinuccini's *coro stabile* in *his* Narcissus libretto of 1608. Far bolder in pushing things forward in a *stabile* direction is an opera of 1782 by Jean-Baptiste Lemoyne, *Electre*, to a text by *Tauride*'s Nicolas Guillard. 'One was very satisfied with the *chœurs* in this opera', noted a reviewer in the *Almanach musical*, 'which are almost always on stage';[25] and, since the score deploys only one visible choral group, 'le Peuple', the People find themselves playing a major role. A stage direction near the climax of Act III points this up: '*Electra holds the urn; she is at one side of the scene; Orestes and Pylades are at the other; the chorus occupies the middle of the stage.*' Entering first in the fourth scene of Act I, they are in evidence in twelve of the opera's remaining sixteen scenes. Fiercely loyal to Electra, they converse with her several times. They share her 'cruel sorrows', lament the 'ever-fatal race' of the Argives in a set-piece lyric, keep a distasteful distance from Clytemnestra, implore death to strike them down at the seemingly bad news of Orestes, mourn the noble dead of his family and veer round joyfully at the revelation that he is alive, celebrating 'a day of triumph and happiness' in his honour and swearing an oath to him. This is the 1780s: you feel that they might well storm the Bastille if he so commanded (though, since Lemoyne's opera is dedicated to Marie Antoinette, it is not likely that the call will come).[26]

However, though Gluck's operatic influence was widespread in several respects, it was not to be so in this matter of onstage choruses, pieces like *Electre* notwithstanding. It was the watchword of Leblanc du Roullet, librettist of *Iphigénie en Aulide*, that one should follow the Greeks 'as far as the

analogue is the *Iphigénie en Tauride* of Gluck's 'rival' Niccolò Piccinni, to a text by du Congé Dubreuil, first staged in 1781. In this, plot-connected choric groups of priestesses, royal guards, and Scythian citizens are quite often in evidence and occasionally utter, being joined near the end by silent Greek soldiers and then sailors; but there is no sense of any group being *stabile*, and for most of the time the singing groups content themselves with duplicating the words of the soloists.)

[25] Quoted by Jacobshagen (1997: 71).

[26] For big operatic oath-scenes involving choruses in the years of the French Revolution, see Bartlet (1992: 137–53). In 1793 Lemoyne and Guillard would themselves collaborate over one in their *Miltiade à Marathon*. On the 'phantom' theatrical choruses at this time, see Dudouyt, Chapter 12, this volume.

difference of the age and the stage permits'[27]—a piece of prudent classicism that recalls John Lockman saying of the London *Fetonte* that its choruses may remind spectators of ancient drama 'though they may not imitate those of the *Greeks* and the *Romans*'. Stage- and age-differences seem not to have permitted the establishment of a full-fig *coro stabile* in the 1780s.

It was André Grétry who, around the same time as Gluck's *Tauride*, wrote an opera (also in part Euripidean, also involving a fury-tormented Orestes on a fateful voyage) that had much more of the choral future in it—which was ironic, since Grétry had hoped to be assigned Guillard's Taurian text to set. Instead, he set a libretto based by Louis-Guillaume Pitra on Racine's *Andromaque*. Orestes loves the Greek Hermione, who loves King Pyrrhus of Epirus, who wants to marry the troubled Trojan widow Andromache—an imbroglio that is made the more vivid by the leading characters each being given a semi-chorus of followers: Epirot courtiers and soldiers for Pyrrhus, groups of companions for Hermione and Andromache, and a deputation of princes of Greece supported by Greek soldiers and sailors for Orestes. The rather tight-lipped Epirots apart, these groups are all very vocal in advice, encouragement, solicitude, and news-bearing, and, when they make musical gestures in support of their particular lead-character, the effect can be powerful, especially when two or more of them are at it at the same time, as happens at least once in each act. It is not surprising that some critics at the premiere were disconcerted that there were 'choruses without number', that the opera was 'an almost continual chorus'.[28]

Where do Grétry and Pitra's semi-choruses come from? Their being so forthcoming musically of course links with the whole French operatic tradition and their attaching themselves to particular operatic principals connects with the confidants of Racine's original tragedy, some of whose lines Pitra borrows for them. But how has it got into their heads to be *multi-voiced* confidants? Perhaps it is a simple multiplication by four of Iphigenia's priestesses in Gluck's Taurian piece, or an extension to the whole opera of those very brief moments of highest tension in both his *Iphigénies* (in each case just before the *dea ex machina* descends) when two choric battalions bark memorably at each other: Agamemnon's Greeks and Achilles' Thessalians in *Aulide*, the Scythian guards and Pylades' men in *Tauride*. Or could it be that the semi-choruses derive from the Italian tradition of *comparse* that goes back at least as far as the spectacular theatre of the late sixteenth century: those groups of normally silent guards, soldiers, retainers, and so on attached to particular leading roles in *opera seria*—characters we tend to forget except when we are reminded of them by paintings of those operas in performance

---

[27] Lesure (1984: ii. 160).
[28] Grétry and *Tauride*, and critical response to *Andromaque*: Brenet (1884: 120–4; 143–4; cf. 142–8).

Fig. 7.2. Francesco Battaglioli's scene from *Nitteti* (Conforto/Metastasio) as staged at the Buen Retiro Theatre, Madrid, 1756. Marble Hill, courtesy of English Heritage

(see Figure 7.2). Have Pitra and Grétry, after two centuries, at last given the *comparse* the chance to open their discretely closed mouths? But wherever they came from, it is clear where these semi-choruses are headed to, and that is nineteenth-century Grand Opera, with its big ensembles quite often involving multiple choral groups: the double chorus of Scandinavians and Caledonians in one scene of Le Sueur's *Ossian* of 1804 and the chorus of Bards, Virgins, Ghosts, and the Offspring of Heroes in another; the Vestals and the Roman Citizens in Spontini's *La Vestale* of 1807; the Aztecs and Conquistadors in his *Fernand Cortez* of 1809–17, and on from these to the sons of the three cantons in Rossini's *Guillaume Tell*, the crews of the Norwegian and Dutch ships in Wagner's *Der Fliegende Holländer*, and the groups of Wedding Guests, Seigneurs, Protestant Soldiers, and Catholic Students heard all together at one point in Meyerbeer's *Les Huguenots*. The polymorphs will have it very much their own way for many decades. The advocates of the *coro stabile* will lie very low—or they will pursue their ends by other means.[29]

---

[29] See Billings, Chapter 8, this volume.

8

'An Alien Body'? Choral Autonomy around 1800

Joshua Billings

The polarity of actor and chorus is one of the defining features of ancient Greek tragedy. The two were distinguished in performance by appearance, diction, and (to some extent) space, were selected by separate mechanisms, and served broadly complementary dramatic functions. Commentators on Greek tragedy, ancient and modern, have often elided these differences, viewing the chorus through the lens of the protagonists. A brief passage in Aristotle's *Poetics* has been decisive for modern discussions: 'the chorus should be treated as one of the actors, it should be a part of the whole and join in the action [μόριον εἶναι τοῦ ὅλου καὶ συναγωνίζεσθαι], not as in Euripides, but as in Sophocles' (Arist. *Poet.* 1456ᵃ).[1] Horace's *Ars poetica* consolidated this Aristotelian injunction with its declaration, 'let the chorus maintain the part of an actor and the manly office' (*actoris partis chorus officiumque virile | defendat*, Hor. *Ars P.* 193–4). Modern considerations of the tragic chorus have generally followed these discussions in understanding the tragic chorus primarily as a participant in the action of tragedy. Aristotle's and Horace's normative prescription—the chorus *should* be integrated into the plot—was (mis)understood as a descriptive judgement on the role of the chorus in tragedy—the chorus *is* fundamentally a part of the action. This integrationist viewpoint informed most discussions of the tragic chorus through the eighteenth century. Around 1800, though, changing intellectual currents, some internal and some external to thought on Greek tragedy, began to produce an interest in the non-integrationist potential of the Greek chorus, which is articulated most influentially in the writings of German Idealist thinkers. Theories of the chorus move away from the neo-Aristotelian account

---

[1] All translations my own; standard modern editions, where they exist, are cited (and spelling from older editions is standardized).

by emphasizing the chorus's *difference from* rather than *similarity to* the protagonists. Though the conclusions drawn around 1800 can seem slight and idiosyncratic from present perspective, their difference from previous discussions is substantial and enduring.[2] The consequences of this shift in perspective are profound, and can be seen in many if not most modern studies of the chorus, which assume that choral experience in tragedy demands a critical approach different from that demanded by the protagonists.[3]

French writing on the tragic chorus of the eighteenth century illustrates the Aristotelian approach that broadly prevailed before 1800.[4] It often points to a dual quality: the chorus *qua* character provides a witness to the action, offering an interested though often detached viewpoint on the events of the play; the chorus *qua* collective, on the other hand, takes part in the dramatic economy of the piece by connecting episodes with its songs. Both of these functions are founded on the logic of French dramatic theory of the period, which seeks, in neo-Aristotelian fashion, to establish *vraisemblance* ('likelihood'). Aristotle's description of drama as *mimesis* provided the foundation for an approach that sought to ensure the *vraisemblance* of all dramatic action—though what this meant in practice was highly contested. The chorus was valued primarily in so far as it contributed to this end. Because the action of Greek tragedy takes place in public, the presence of a mass of people on stage appeared as a realistic element, reinforcing the mimetic quality of the action. 'One might say,' André Dacier writes in his influential translation of the *Poetics*, 'that it is the chorus that creates all the likelihood [*vraisemblance*] of tragedy'.[5] At the same time, the choral odes represented a technique for preserving the unities of time and space, and keeping the stage occupied throughout the piece. Justifying his choral practice in *Athalie*, Racine writes that he has used the chorus to preserve 'that continuity of action which makes it so that their [the Greeks'] theatre is never left empty, and the intervals of the acts are not indicated except by the hymns and moralities of the chorus'.[6] Here, too, the chorus is subject to the law of *vraisemblance*, which dictates that the content of the odes 'express [the chorus'] sentiments or those of the spectators by the desires and fears to prepare the events to come'.[7] Though

---

[2] The state of affairs from Idealism forward is sketched by Goldhill (2012: 166–200) and Goldhill, Chapter 2, this volume. My chapter describes the fundaments of the approach of which Goldhill investigates the consequences.

[3] To choose only the most recent examples, Gruber (2009), Swift (2010), and the essays on 'choral mediations' in Gagné and Hopman (2013), Gagné and Hopman's introduction begins with the programmatic statement that 'there is something distinctive about choral *mimesis* in Greek tragedy'.

[4] See Dudouyt, Chapter 12, this volume, for a more nuanced view. I am attempting a thematic synthesis of a varied—though largely continuous—discussion.

[5] Dacier (1692: 312); cf. Brumoy (1730: i, p. xvii).

[6] Racine (1999: 1012).

[7] Brumoy (1730: i, p. lxxvi).

going far beyond the *Poetics'* lapidary prescription, French thinkers around 1700 internalize Aristotle's mimetic principle and integrationist perspective, assimilating the functions of the chorus to those of more familiar elements of tragedy.

The question of the chorus in France is emphatically one of practice, and often carries a normative aim, either to re-establish the chorus within modern drama, or to argue for its lack of utility. Such prescriptions could again draw on Aristotle for their authority, especially his rejection of *embolima*, choral songs unrelated to the action that were often inserted into tragedies in the fourth century. A parallel practice had established itself in French theatre of the seventeenth and eighteenth centuries, in which the periods between acts were generally filled with musical interludes performed by a group of strings. Corneille had approved of this practice because, unlike a choral song, it allows 'the spirit of the auditor to relax'.[8] Dacier, in contrast, preferred choral songs precisely because they are linked to the action, and do not break the concentration of the spectators.[9] Dacier's text was published at the height of the dispute known as the *Querelle des anciens et des modernes*, and took quite a dogmatic line on ancient practice. In his preface, he argued that the reintroduction of the chorus, as Racine had done recently in *Esther* and *Athalie*, would be a way of re-founding theatre on moral principles.[10] The implication, that contemporary theatre largely failed to live up its moral calling, was effectively a broadside against the *Modernes*, and particularly their favourite tragedian, Corneille. By following Aristotelian principles, Dacier argued, tragedy could again attain its moral and aesthetic acme.

In the very same year, the equally dogmatic Charles Perrault took aim at the Greek chorus in the third volume of his *Parallèle des anciens et des modernes en ce qui concerne les arts et les sciences*, deploring the ostensible moral utility of their *sententiae*:

> I do not believe that there is anything on earth so distasteful or so boring as the choruses about which you speak. I am persuaded that the ancient poets had not invented them except to insert various commonplaces that they had in their pockets on the necessity of dying, the instability of human affairs, on the discomforts of royalty, on the happiness of innocence, on the miseries that menace criminals and other similar materials.[11]

The *Querelle* generally had the effect of polarizing viewpoints on ancient literature, and echoes clearly in Voltaire's sixth *Lettre sur Oedipe*, which finds the Greek chorus boring and unnecessary, and justifies a practice that preserves a chorus in name but not in function. Pierre Brumoy's position, ten years after Voltaire, is generally conciliatory, and notes both the benefits of the

---

[8] Corneille (1987: 181).   [9] Dacier (1692: 315).
[10] Dacier (1692: p. xvi).   [11] Perrault (1692: 199–200).

chorus in antiquity and its apparent incongruity on the modern stage, where the actions of tragedy tend to take place in private. When in his widely read *Théâtre des Grecs* it is time to compare ancient and modern theatre against one another, Brumoy finds the chorus a point that cannot be decided one way or the other: 'Because the chorus has its advantages and inconveniences, it is a matter that one ought to exclude from comparison.'[12]

The most extensive eighteenth-century French discussion of the chorus is that of the Abbé René Vatry, whose *Dissertation où l'on traite des avantages que la Tragédie ancienne retiroit de ses chœurs* was published in 1733 (though it was based on a paper delivered to the Académie des Inscriptions five years previously). Vatry's essay consolidates contemporary theories of the chorus but introduces a twist by emphasizing the sensory and affective power of the singing, dancing chorus. This strand was suggested by Jean-Baptiste Dubos's *Réflexions critique sur la poesie et la peinture*, which had pointed out the composite character of ancient Greek song, while at the same time downplaying the musical element of tragic choruses by describing them as declamation.[13] Vatry takes the point about the enlarged sense of music in ancient Greece, but, according to him, tragedy was closer to what moderns consider music: 'I admit', he writes, 'that everything that concerns ancient music is full of difficulty, and that one does not know well if the song of tragedies was a true music like ours. It has, however, the appearance, that the music of the scenes resembled what we call *recitatif* in operas, and the music of the choruses was what we call arias.'[14] The analogy of ancient tragedy and modern music drama is as old as opera, but Vatry's argumentative strategy in the essay is radical: assuming this analogy, he draws consequences for our understanding of the ancient chorus: 'That which ought to convince us of the great effect of ancient choruses is the success of our operas.'[15] The circularity of this argument did not prevent it from being constructive: by analysing the ancient chorus through the modern lens, Vatry finds its core in the emotional power it exerts over the spectators, a step away from the formalism and moralism of previous discussions.

Vatry describes three functions of the chorus, of which the first two are largely familiar from Dacier and Brumoy, relating to the chorus's formal role in guaranteeing the unities and varying the scenes, and to its character as a collective observing the important actions of the protagonists. The third, and most important, function, though, is 'the pathetic that they produced', which for Vatry is linked inextricably to the moral aim of tragedy: 'That noble and majestic tragedy took from morality its most beautiful maxims, authorized itself by religion, and embellished itself with its most august ceremonies. And deploying all the charms that poetry has to ravish the spirits and touch the

---

[12] Brumoy (1730: i, p. clvi).   [13] Dubos (1719: i. 400).
[14] Vatry (1733: 203).   [15] Vatry (1733: 210).

hearts, tragedy joined to it moreover all that can enchant the senses.'[16] The choral songs constitute an appeal to the senses, without which the teaching of their poetry would be lacking in visceral power. The poet, in setting his maxims in the songs of the chorus, gives 'a new force to the sentiments that the dialogues of the protagonists have excited'.[17] At the same time, 'in offering to the spectators other spectators, so to speak, [who are] strongly affected', the poet creates an identification between the audience and the chorus, which will increase the audience's emotional participation.[18] Vatry's argument points to two foci of later, Romantic discussions of the tragic chorus: the media of choral performance (language, music, dance), which have a power that surpasses language alone; and the parallel with the audience (recognized but rarely emphasized in earlier discussions), which gives the chorus's reactions a privileged connection to the emotions of the spectators.

Vatry's essay does not seem to have had any immediate effect on choral theory or practice. The *Encyclopédie* entry on the chorus, though citing Vatry's essay, contains no trace of his interest in the emotional effect of the chorus.[19] A few experiments at hybridity notwithstanding, spoken tragedies continued to eschew choral song and dance, and commentators continued to debate the utility of the chorus in tragedy, though without adding substantially to the discussions of Dacier and Brumoy.[20] It was much more on the operatic stage that choral practice developed, especially in the works of Christoph Willibald Gluck. In his collaborations with the choreographer Jean-Georges Noverre of the 1760s and 1770s, the chorus gained a new importance and integration into the drama.[21] This was often experienced as a genuine revival of Greek tragedy.[22] Yet there remained an important difference between the two: the Greek chorus was on stage from the parodos to the exodos, and remained the same character throughout; Gluck's choruses, though often spending much of the opera on stage, generally had different identities and dramatic functions in each act. They are employed very much as one of the characters, defined by their participation in the plot. This is never entirely the case with Greek tragic choruses, which, whatever their role in a particular play, always have a degree of abstraction from their dramatic character. Gluck's choral practice employs *choruses*, but never *the chorus*.[23]

---

[16] Vatry (1733: 209).   [17] Vatry (1733: 209).
[18] Vatry (1733: 209).   [19] Mallet (1753).
[20] Two exceptions are particularly interesting: the works of Jean-Jacques Lefranc de Pompignan, a translator of Aeschylus, whose works for the stage often included choruses; and the 1782 adaptation of Sophocles' *Electra* by Guillaume Dubois de Rochefort, a translator of Homer and Sophocles and collaborator on the 1785 *Théâtre des Grecs*. On Lefranc, see Macintosh (2009*b*).
[21] See Savage, Chapter 7, this volume, as well as Betzwieser (2000).
[22] See Goldhill (2011: 90–7); Jacobshagen (1997: 119–24).
[23] Schiller (1988–2004: v. 290) makes the point: 'when on the occasion of Greek tragedy I hear talk of *choruses* instead of a chorus, I begin to suspect that one does not really know of what one speaks.'

Both in theory and in practice, Germany was late in coming to the chorus. Discussions until the 1780s are largely derivative (as is the case for most writing on Greek tragedy), but interest in the chorus does seem to have grown quite quickly, inspired perhaps by the social valences that created parallel interest in *Volk* forms.[24] The first edition (1771–4) of Johann Georg Sulzer's *Allgemeine Theorie der schönen Künste* (*General Theory of the Fine Arts*), a central reference work for late eighteenth century, includes a substantial article on the chorus, which follows Vatry in seeing opera as the 'closest imitation' of ancient tragedy, and advocating the reintroduction of the chorus into spoken tragedy.[25] Vatry's essay, curiously, was translated, without acknowledgement, by Peter Wolster in 1786, and published in that year's *Theaterkalender*, suggesting some interest in the ancient chorus.[26] Yet practice remained largely indifferent: the two most important adaptations of Greek tragedy of the period, Wieland and Schweitzer's *Alceste* (1773) and Goethe's *Iphigenie auf Tauris* (original version 1779; revised version 1787), both do away with the chorus, though preserve echoes of its role in a confidante character (Wieland) and songs inserted into the dialogue (Goethe's famous 'Song of the Parcae').

Interest in the chorus in the 1770s and 1780s could both draw on and contribute to an increasing acceptance of Aeschylus' works, which presented choruses that patently do more than 'join in the action'. As long as discussions of Greek tragedy were oriented to Sophocles and Euripides, the neo-Aristotelian understanding of the chorus as a kind of secondary character was plausible enough. In this fashion, the chorus of *Antigone* or *Hippolytus* could be seen in terms of a dual function, playing a minor role in the action and serving to ensure dramatic unity. For the more substantial choral practice of Aeschylus, this consensus was patently inadequate: not only is the chorus usually the largest speaking part, but it could also play a central role in the action (as in the *Eumenides* and *Suppliants*). The very flexibility of the choral role in Aeschylus' drama may have contributed to a sense that the neo-Aristotelian normative structure needed rethinking. The first translations of Aeschylus into French and English reflect a growing interest in the chorus: Jean-Jacques Lefranc de Pompignan's 1770 *Tragédies d'Eschyle* points out and lauds their importance to the action, while Robert Potter's 1777 *Tragedies of Aeschylus* describes the chorus as 'always grave, sententious, sublime, and ardent in the cause of liberty, virtue, and religion'.[27]

---

[24] Herder is the most important advocate, especially his collections of *Volkslieder*. See Oergel (2006: esp. 52–64) on the connection between literary thought and concepts of national culture.

[25] Sulzer (1771).

[26] Wolster (1786).

[27] Lefranc de Pompignan (1770: 431–3); Potter (1777: p. xii).

German commentators turn still more passionately to the Aeschylean chorus, using it as a rallying cry for a reform of (presumably French) theatre. Though there was no complete translation available until 1808, there was a substantial interest in Aeschylus in the 1780s, which saw translations of the *Prometheus*, *Persians*, and two of the *Agamemnon*. The perceived lack of a strong literary tradition may have made Germans more open to adopting the Greeks and the tragic chorus as a path for creating a national literature. Both Johann Georg Schlosser's 1784 *Prometheus in Fesseln* and Daniel Jenisch's 1786 *Agamemnon* include substantial polemics against the lack of moral instruction in modern, particularly French, theatre.[28] For both authors, introducing elements of Greek choral practice appears as a means of restoring the moral basis that tragedy had in ancient Athens.[29] Similarly, the Stolberg brothers (who were at the time translating Sophocles and Aeschylus) published a volume of *Schauspiele mit Chören* in 1787, plays containing major choral roles and concerning struggles for freedom against tyranny, ancient and modern.[30] This is entirely consistent with their other writings, which emphasize revolutionary and patriotic themes. German writers had often interpreted Greek tragedy in a democratic light, but the 1780s show a new concentration on the chorus's songs as the locus of tragedy's political content.

Jenisch's *Agamemnon* asserts that 'the τραγικοτατον [*sic*; 'the most tragic'] of Greek tragedy are the choral songs'.[31] The chorus is the essence of Greek tragedy for Jenisch because it differentiates dramatic from epic and lyric poetry, and, even more importantly, Greek from modern tragedy. The chorus is perhaps the starkest reminder of Greek tragedy's difference from modern works, and can suggest that the ancient and modern forms are more divergent than similar. Jenisch was writing in a period of growing historical consciousness, when the assumed continuity of the genre of tragedy was explicitly being questioned. Herder's 1773 essay 'Shakespeare' had famously found Sophocles and Shakespeare more different than alike: where Greek tragedy developed from the ritual chorus and was essentially a work of elaboration, Shakespearian tragedy developed from representations of history, and consisted in condensation and crystallization. Subjecting modern tragedy to 'rules' derived from a fundamentally different form of drama seemed a restricting and fruitless enterprise. With the rejection of Aristotle's normative influence on creation, his critical assumptions about Greek tragedy could equally be abandoned. From this vantage point, Greek tragedy could seem to be an *essentially*

---

[28] Schlosser (1784: 13); Jenisch (1786: 134).
[29] Schlosser (1784: 3); Jenisch (1786: 133). The model for both, though, is Thomson's *Agamemnon*, which includes only a very minor choral role. Their advocacy of the chorus may be more of a rhetorical point than a dramaturgical one.
[30] Hempel (1997: 117–23).   [31] Jenisch (1786: p. xvi).

choral form, and the chorus a point of fundamental difference from modern works.

By 1790, then, the Greek chorus is already embedded in discourses of national and historical identity. These contexts will become more urgent with the French Revolution, which brings a sense of disorientation and crisis to German thinkers, most of whom initially were sympathetic. Yet a new, aesthetic, context becomes important with the 1790 publication of Immanuel Kant's *Kritik der Urteilskraft* (*Critique of the Power of Judgement*). Though Kant's highly complex treatise has little to say about works of art, two of its consequences are particularly important for approaches to the tragic chorus, both elements of the doctrine known today as 'aesthetic autonomy'. First, Kant distinguishes the beautiful from the good and the pleasing (*das Angenehme*), arguing that the judgement of beauty, unlike the others, is 'without interest', made not on the grounds of any desire, but solely on the basis of the pleasure afforded.[32] This ostensible removal of morality from the judgement of art made typical instrumentalizing perspectives on the tragic chorus (as a patriotic inspiration or a moral teacher, for example) untenable. Aesthetic appreciation, for Kantians, does not contribute directly to morality or civic order.

This impression, though, is modified by another passage, which argues that 'the beautiful is the symbol of the morally good [*das Schöne ist das Symbol des Sittlich-guten*]'.[33] The concept of the symbol, for Kant as for his followers, represents a bridge between the worlds of sense and intellect, and so suggests that the judgement of beauty has its foundation in morality, even though it is not a means to morality. Indeed, beauty appears, dimly and tentatively, as a means of reconciling the realms of sense and intellect, affording an insight into 'the supersensory [*das Übersinnliche*], in which the theoretical power is bound to the practical into unity by a common and unknown way'.[34] The extraordinary importance that this passage affords to beauty as a reconciliation of the two epistemological domains of Kantian philosophy made aesthetics a privileged subject for the generation that came after. The description of beauty as a sensory insight into what lies beyond sense was particularly fruitfully applied to tragedy by German Idealism. For those thinking about the chorus, Kant's notion of aesthetic autonomy offered a way of making sense of the choral role as both independent of the action (without interest in its outcome) and as tragedy's means of symbolizing a higher, moral truth. The chorus became the aesthetic instance within tragedy, the element that raised it above the particular concerns and conflicts of the protagonists into the higher realm of the ideal.[35]

---

[32] I. Kant (1908: 209–11(§5)).   [33] I. Kant (1908: 353 (§59)).
[34] I. Kant (1908: 353 (§59)).
[35] On the chorus's ideality, see Goldhill, Chapter 2, this volume, and Goldhill (2012: 174–81).

From 1800, efforts to theorize Greek tragedy have approached the chorus as a *problem* in a way they largely did not before. Operatic choruses notwithstanding, there was no real analogy through which to understand the choral role of Greek drama, and this lacuna spurred thinkers to new approaches. An early hint of this preoccupation with the chorus as problem comes in a 1795 letter of Friedrich Schlegel to his brother August Wilhelm:

I flatter myself to know what the Greek chorus is [*was der Griechische Chor ist*], which none of those who have written has known. A knowledge that gives infinite perspective [*unendliche Aussicht*] on tragedy and poetry in general, and that loosens the most difficult knots.[36]

What Schlegel believed himself to have discovered can be only very conjecturally reconstructed,[37] but the simple framing of the question shows his distance from previous approaches: Schlegel considers the role of the chorus in the abstract, without reference to its participation in dramatic action, and as the source of a unique insight into the genre of tragedy. Schlegel's perspective disassociates the normative question of modern practice from the descriptive question of ancient practice—effectively breaking the circle of analogies that had been so powerful in conceptions of the chorus. For Schlegel and choral theorists around 1800, Aristotle's normative and integrationist perspective is inadequate to the problem of the chorus, which must be grasped on its own unique terms.

August Wilhelm Schlegel, perhaps influenced by his brother's lost ideas, announced his approach to the chorus in his 1798 Jena *Vorlesungen über philosophische Kunstlehre* (*Lectures on Philosophical Art-Theory*). The lectures were not published in Schlegel's time, but widely circulated in manuscript, including to F. W. J. Schelling, whose own 1802–5 lectures on the *Philosophie der Kunst* (*Philosophy of Art*) show the clear influence of Schlegel, not least in their pages on the chorus.[38] Schlegel's account of the chorus is explicitly directed against integrationist theories, calling the chorus's participation in the action a 'side issue [*Nebensache*]', in comparison with their primary role as 'the expression of general participation [*Ausdruck der allgemeinen Teilnahme*]'.[39] In these early lectures, the chorus's importance for Schlegel is primarily affective, but he transforms Vatry's argument that it increases the pathetic effect of drama. For Schlegel, in contrast, the chorus serves to moderate the audience's affective participation:

---

[36] F. Schlegel (1958–: xxiii. 267 (23 December 1795)).

[37] There are sketchy indications in F. Schlegel (1958–: xi. 201–9), which describe the chorus repeatedly as a spectator (*Zuschauer*), and so may suggest some of the background to August Wilhelm's theory.

[38] Schelling (1859: 705–7).

[39] A. W. Schlegel (1989: 87).

It is a primary means to ensure that the emotions brought up never cross over into serious tones [*in ernstlichen Akzent übergehen*], but remain always a poetic play [*ein poetisches Spiel*], when the tragic poet brings the general human participation [*die allgemeine menschliche Teilnahme*] in the fate portrayed and the observation of it into the sphere of his ideal representation, and this is the significance of the chorus in Greek tragedy, whose contingent origin does not concern us in this respect.[40]

The chorus, however affected by the action of the play, should retain its 'ideal' and 'general' character, and thus help to maintain a degree of emotional distance in the audience. The participation of the chorus enters 'the sphere of ideal representation' in that it acts symbolically: not as a figure who shares the fate of the protagonists, but as a disinterested, though sympathetic, observer. The description of spectatorship as 'poetic play' is a Kantian–Schillerian element, and implies a way of viewing that maintains the degree of abstraction necessary for contemplating suffering without intense emotional participation. Too much sympathy, Schlegel suggests, would destroy the aesthetic impression of tragedy. Schlegel assumes a commonplace choral function, that it links the audience and the protagonists emotionally, but places the chorus outside the integrationist framework that had conditioned previous ways of understanding. The effect of the chorus is no longer assimilated to that of the protagonists, but contrasted to it.

The other point of emphasis in Schlegel's discussion is political. Here, his perspective is somewhat more conventional, and taps into the republican valences of the chorus that commentators had long noted, and that had been particularly celebrated in Germany. 'According to their [the Greeks'] republican spirit,' he writes, 'to the completeness of an action belonged also the public of such an action'.[41] Schlegel adopts the integrationist logic of *vraisemblance* in arguing that the chorus was necessary to tragedy as the representation of the republican collective. Though Schlegel recognizes a political context of the chorus, he does not draw particular interpretive consequences from it, as many earlier critics had done; the republican state explains the presence of the chorus, but not in any meaningful sense its character. This relatively apolitical perspective distinguishes Schlegel (and Schiller as well) from the contemporary theories of Hegel and Hölderlin, both of whom see the chorus's republican constitution as vital to its role, and seem to be working out their own relation to the French Revolution through theories of the chorus.[42] Schlegel understands the function of the chorus in terms of a general economy of drama, rather than as a participant in

---

[40] A. W. Schlegel (1989: 87).

[41] A. W. Schlegel (1989: 725) from the 1802–3 Berlin lectures; cf. p. 87 (from the Jena lectures) and A. W. Schlegel (1966: 49). The republicanism of the chorus features also in Friedrich's notes: F. Schlegel (1958–: xi. 208–9).

[42] See Billings (2013). On operatic choruses under the Revolution, see Bartlet (1992).

any individual work. This is nicely illustrated by the comparison of Greek tragedy to a temple, in which the chorus provides the walls while the protagonists are the columns holding up the 'weight of necessity'.[43] The chorus, 'as the surrounding of the whole which is not especially distinguished in itself', defines the space of the drama in which the protagonists act.[44] This division of the drama into two fundamentally different spheres is definitely non-Aristotelian, and has a striking affinity to Hegel's discussion twenty years later in the lectures published as *Vorlesungen über die Ästhetik* (*Lectures on Aesthetics*).[45]

The major elements of Schlegel's enormously influential theory of the chorus in the 1808 Vienna *Vorlesungen über dramatische Kunst und Literatur* (*Lectures on Dramatic Art and Literature*) are already present in the earlier lectures. His famous description of the chorus as 'the idealized spectator' seeks to integrate the political and affective significances of the chorus, seeing its collective quality as the guarantee of its power of emotional abstraction:

> Whatever in particular it [the chorus] may be and do in a single piece, it represented first of all the national common spirit, then the general human participation [*stellte er überhaupt den nationalen Gemeingeist, dann die allgemeine menschliche Teilnahme dar*]. The chorus is in a word the idealized spectator [*der idealisierte Zuschauer*]. It eases the impression of a deeply shocking or moving representation, in that it brings back to the real spectator his own emotions expressed lyrically, musically, and leads him into the region of contemplation.[46]

Schlegel's words are often mistranslated and misremembered as describing an 'ideal' spectator, rather than an 'idealized' one.[47] This may seem a trivial difference, but it points to a central tenet of Schlegel's understanding of the chorus: it is a form of mediation between the spectator's empirical response and a desired aesthetic one. This process of idealization is described in the following sentence: the chorus's poetic and musical expression transforms the powerful emotions of tragedy into a more abstracted contemplation. As in the earlier lectures, the chorus serves to moderate the spectator's response, initiating a dialectic between affective participation and cognitive distance. Leading from individual, affective response to 'general human participation', the chorus universalizes Greek tragedy by raising it above particular incidents and national characteristics.

Despite the idealizing terms of Schlegel's discussion, he is keenly aware of the historical nature of the Greek chorus. Unlike most of those sympathetic to the ancient chorus, he does not argue that it should be revived in modern

---

[43] A. W. Schlegel (1989: 727).   [44] A. W. Schlegel (1989: 727–8).
[45] Hegel (1970: iii. 542).
[46] A. W. Schlegel (1966: 65); cf. A. W. Schlegel (1989: 725).
[47] Nietzsche, among others, makes this mistake in *Birth of Tragedy*, §7, which leads him to caricature Schlegel's theory of the chorus despite its closeness to his own (which draws heavily on Schiller).

drama. He criticizes efforts to introduce choruses into theatrical cultures that have no musical or choreographic idiom for them, rejecting comparisons with opera.[48] Closing his discussion of the chorus, Schlegel declares that Greek tragedy will 'remain an alien plant, which one can hardly expect to flourish even in the greenhouse of learned artistic practice and contemplation'.[49] At the time, these words would have been unsurprising: Greek tragedy was performed very rarely in translation, and the few experiments with it were largely unsuccessful.[50] Schlegel's conviction that ancient tragedy could best be experienced as closet drama was widely shared, and may reveal wounds still smarting from his own failed adaptation (without chorus) of the *Ion* in 1802.[51] The Greek chorus for Schlegel is both an intellectualizing and a purely intellectual entity.[52]

Schlegel's interest in the Greek chorus in his Jena and Berlin lectures seems to have struck a chord in other thinkers and writers. A new interest in the chorus spread to Idealist philosophers such as Hegel and Schelling as well as to Romantic writers such as Ludwig Tieck and Zacharias Werner, both of whom wrote choral dramas in the early years of the nineteenth century. The furthest echo of it may come in the Third Act of Goethe's *Faust II*, which was conceived around this time and includes a time-and-space-travelling chorus.[53] The most substantial product of this minor choral craze, though, is Friedrich Schiller's 1803 *Die Braut von Messina oder die feindlichen Brüder: ein Trauerspiel mit Chören* (*The Bride of Messina or the Enemy Brothers: A Tragedy with Choruses*) and its preface 'Über den Gebrauch des Chors in der Tragödie' ('On the use of the chorus in tragedy'). If Schlegel's tendency was to disassociate choral theory from practice, Schiller's was the opposite. His use of the chorus in *Braut* and his theory of the chorus in the preface have a crucial interrelation: though the essay was written after the play was completed, it lays out fundaments of Schiller's dramatic theory that are implicit throughout his later works. The *Braut* preface is the last theoretical text he ever published, and appeared eight years after he had effectively given up philosophy to turn back to poetry. In the interim, he had studied Greek tragedy closely, and he seems to have been especially indebted to his reading of the newly published translation of Aeschylus by Friedrich Leopold Graf zu Stolberg (1802). Schiller believed that, in writing *Braut*, he was appropriating elements of Aeschylean practice,

[48] A. W. Schlegel (1966: 59, 66).
[49] A. W. Schlegel (1966: 66).
[50] See Goldhill, Chapter 2, this volume. On Goethe's 1809 staging of the *Antigone* and other contemporary experiments, see Flashar (2009: 47–57).
[51] See Reichard (1987).
[52] Güthenke, Chapter 3, this volume, ascribes this character to an identification between the critic's role and that of the chorus.
[53] See Petersen (1974: 92–106) on the early version.

using motifs of fraternal hatred and family guilt that would have been suggested by the *Seven against Thebes*.[54]

Braut can seem a bewildering pastiche of elements from Greek and modern tragedy. In some respects, it adheres quite closely to the formal dramaturgy of Greek tragedy: the work includes a prologue, metrically differentiated choral parodos, odes, and exodos, stichomythia, monodies, and amoibaia (lyric exchanges with the chorus).[55] Schiller's chorus departs from Greek practice in that it enters and exits through the piece, as was common in operatic practice, and necessary for Schiller's changing settings. The chorus, in another formal liberty, is divided into two semi-choruses (perhaps loosely following the *Eumenides*), which nevertheless merge for much of the action. Though the construction of the work is classicizing, the story is not classical. It is set in medieval Sicily, concerns a love triangle, and portrays characters motivated by Christian-tinged concepts of guilt and atonement. Debates about how to explain this coexistence of ancient and modern elements persist to this day, but a first indication might be found in the subtitle, '*Trauerspiel* with Choruses'. The words *Tragödie* and *Trauerspiel* are not strongly differentiated for Schiller, but there is a subtle nuance in their usage: *Trauerspiel* suggests a modern work, while *Tragödie* is generally used for the ancient genre.[56] *Braut*, as a '*Trauerspiel* with Choruses', presents itself as a modern work to which a classical element, the chorus, has been added—not an effort at a thorough revival of Greek drama.[57] Indeed, Schiller understands his choral practice as fundamentally different from that of the Greek tragedians, and as the heart of a self-consciously modern aesthetic programme.[58]

Schiller describes his use of the chorus largely through a polemic against what he calls 'the common concept of the *natural*'—that is, an aesthetic based on correspondence between the world of the senses and the world of drama.[59] Instead, art should portray reality symbolically, as the instance of a higher form of truth, which is glimpsed through the medium of aesthetic representation. Concretely, this calls for a dramaturgy that would be decisively set off from the everyday. Schiller's dramas of this period, known as his 'classical' works, are all written in verse, take place in alien times or places, and concern figures of high status. Schiller's polemic against naturalism is in essence a call for drama on the classical model, but at the same time opposes neoclassical practice. Schiller rejects the doctrine of *vraisemblance* as too bound to the real world, replacing the criteria of likelihood or believability with his own of 'poetic

---

[54] Schiller (1988–2004: xii. 626).   [55] See Zimmermann (2011).

[56] The preface is entitled 'on the use of the chorus in *Tragödie*' and its first paragraph notes that in *Trauerspiel* the chorus can appear out of place: Schiller (1988–2004: v. 281).

[57] One can, admittedly, find letters in which Schiller seems to blur this distinction; the intention, at any rate, is clear in the preface.

[58] Latacz (1997: 246–7).

[59] Schiller (1988–2004: v. 284).

truth'. As a highly stylized element, the chorus increases the drama's distance from the everyday and its symbolic potential:

The introduction of the chorus would be the last, the decisive step—even if it only served for this—openly and honestly to declare war against naturalism in art. It should be for us a living wall, which tragedy draws up around itself, in order to cut itself off purely from the real world and to protect its ideal basis, its poetic freedom [*So sollte er uns eine lebendige Mauer sein, die die Tragödie um sich herumzieht, um sich von der wirklichen Welt rein abzuschließen und sich ihren idealen Boden, ihre poetische Freiheit zu bewahren*].[60]

The chorus's performance is a stark reminder of the poetic quality of dramatic representation, and so secures the freedom of the author to create an imaginative world. For Schiller, this is not an act of escapism, the creation of a mere illusion, but the basis of a symbolic insight into the truth hidden behind sensible reality.[61] To penetrate to this ideal world, aesthetic representation must establish itself as lying beyond and above the real world—here, through the 'living wall' of the chorus. Schiller's theory, like Schlegel's (which may well have been an influence), sees the chorus through the lens of post-Kantian philosophy, as a means to ensuring the autonomy of aesthetic experience.

Like Schlegel, Schiller links aesthetic and emotional autonomy in his description of the chorus. Just as the chorus ensures the dramatist's poetic freedom, so too it ensures the audience's affective freedom by moderating the pathos of tragedy. The choral odes provide the audience with a salutary distance on the events of the drama:

If the blows with which tragedy meets our heart followed on one another without interruption, suffering would triumph over action. We would become wrapped up in the material and no longer float above it [*so würde das Leiden über die Tätigkeit siegen. Wir würden uns mit dem Stoffe vermengen und nicht mehr über demselben schweben*]. In that the chorus holds the parts together, and steps between the passions with its calming observations, it gives us back our freedom, which would be lost in the storm of feelings.[62]

Schiller understands the affective economy of tragedy as an alternation of passion and reflection—ironically, not far from Corneille's argument *against* the chorus (and in favour of an even further abstracted instrumental interlude). The choral odes represent a moment of rest and recovery from the main action, and so oppose the dominant, pathetic, impression of tragedy. For Schiller, the chorus is doubly exceptional: as a stylized body, it establishes the dramatic world as opposed to reality; as a reflective body, it counters the effect of tragedy on the audience within the dramatic world. Both of these strands aim at ensuring varieties of freedom (poetic, emotional), and are

---

[60] Schiller (1988–2004: v. 285).   [61] Hinderer (2009: 316).
[62] Schiller (1988–2004: v. 289).

predicated on a Kantian understanding of disinterested spectatorship. As thinkers were coming to grips with Kant's rigorous notion of autonomy, the chorus appeared an illustration of ideal aesthetic experience.

Schiller's choral practice, it should be noted, does not seem wholly congruent with his theory. Where Schiller's preface emphasizes the chorus's distancing role, *Braut*'s chorus is notably engaged and partisan over long stretches of the play. The semi-choruses are each attached to one of two feuding main characters (the 'enemy brothers' of the title), and take part in substantial and hostile exchanges in the choral sections. Though they can merge and reflect as a whole, they are just as often divided and engaged in the action. Schiller's preface, while emphasizing the autonomous nature of the chorus, recognizes a dual function: the chorus both 'takes part in the action [*mithandelt*] as real person and as blind mass' and at the same time remains 'as an ideal person always one with itself'.[63] Such an oscillation in the chorus's participation is, of course, common in Greek tragedy, but *Braut* is actually relatively light on moments of choral reflection, with most of the chorus's time on stage taken up in dialogue with the protagonists or immediate responses to the situation.[64] There seems to be a gap between Schiller's dramaturgical instincts, which tend towards involving the chorus as a central part of the action, and his theory of the chorus as a part of the larger economy of tragedy, which sees its role as more autonomous. This discrepancy—noted again and again by commentators—may be inevitable in modern appropriations of the chorus, in so far as they seek to sow the 'alien plant' of the chorus in the soil of modern drama.

Schiller's preface, whatever its explanatory or justificatory value, is uniquely reflective in differentiating the roles of the chorus in antiquity and modernity. In effect, he takes up Schlegel's point that the chorus, though essential to Greek dramaturgy, is alien to modern works. It is for Schiller precisely this alienness that makes the chorus valuable in modernity. The chorus can be a 'living wall' separating artifice from reality only because it is out of place in modern culture. In ancient Greece, the chorus was a necessary element of any important action: 'ancient tragedy, which originally concerned itself with gods, heroes, and kings, needed the chorus as a necessary accompaniment, it found the chorus in nature, and needed it, because it had found it'.[65] This natural choral integration seems as irrecoverable to Schiller as it did to Schlegel. The modern chorus, in contrast 'becomes an artificial organ [*Kunstorgan*], it helps *to bring forth* poetry [*die Poesie hervorbringen*]'.[66] This chorus opposes its contemporary reality by recalling the natural age of the

---

[63] Schiller (1988–2004: v. 290).   [64] See Müller (1987).
[65] Schiller (1988–2004: v. 286).   [66] Schiller (1988–2004: v. 286).

Greeks, 'transform[ing] the common modern world into the old poetic world'.[67] The modern chorus creates an effect of alienation from historical reality, an entirely different effect from the ancient chorus, which reflected its idyllic world. This leads to a surprising consequence: the chorus, for Schiller, is even more necessary for moderns than it was for ancients.

For all his enthusiasm for the chorus, though, Schiller is acutely conscious of the problems of putting a chorus on the modern stage.[68] Ancient tragedy, Schiller reminds us at the very beginning of his preface, was a complex art form of words, music, and movement: 'The poet gives only the words; music and dance must be added in order to animate them.'[69] Schiller understands the chorus only secondarily as literature; it is first and foremost a performance, and cannot be experienced fully in reading. For the original staging, Schiller hoped for musical accompaniment, but in the end this proved impractical, and he settled for some form of (unaccompanied) declamation. Still, Schiller's attention to the complete impression of choral performance is unusual for its time, and reflects his strong practical orientation as a dramatist. When presented without its 'powerful sensory accompaniment', he writes, the chorus can appear only 'as a foreign thing, an alien body, and a delay [*als ein Außending, als ein fremdartiger Körper, und als ein Aufenthalt*], which interrupts the action, which destroys the illusion, which leaves the viewer cold'.[70] Though Schiller recognized the danger of a lifeless choral performance, his work could not avoid it: reactions to the chorus were divided, and became more and more negative with revivals that did not reproduce Schiller's careful direction. *Braut*'s chorus has been judged 'an alien body' for 200 years, and is rarely performed today.

It should be clear that Schiller's *Braut* is an appropriation much more than an approximation of the Greek chorus. Indeed, this is accounted for in Schiller's preface, which sets out differing roles for the chorus in ancient and modern tragedy. Schiller's choral theory is a construction that emerges from his dramaturgical and philosophical preoccupations. It is not intended to describe the Greek chorus (as Schlegel's is), but, rather, to formulate the programme for a self-consciously modern choral practice. The *brisance* of Schiller's thought, here as elsewhere, lies in its argument that being modern necessarily entails reflection on the difference from antiquity. In the history of theatrical returns to antiquity, Schiller's is unique for placing the gulf separating antiquity and modernity at the heart of a classicizing programme. His choral practice in *Braut* seeks *to represent temporal difference*, using the alienness of antiquity to alienate modernity from its own historical condition. The extraordinary ambition of this theory was probably impossible to realize in practice, and brings us to the heart of the modern 'problem' of the chorus: it

---

[67] Schiller (1988–2004: v. 286).   [68] See Sergl (1998).
[69] Schiller (1988–2004: v. 281).   [70] Schiller (1988–2004: v. 281).

is both the most distinctive element of ancient tragedy, and the one most alien to modern drama.[71] Though the chorus's foreignness to modern drama had been recognized for centuries, its exceptional character within ancient tragedy first comes into focus around 1800, laying the foundation for much modern discussion. Schiller attempts to embody both the choral nature of Greek tragedy and the alienness of the chorus on the modern stage. There seems, however, to have been a mismatch between theories of the chorus and practical execution. The 1841 Potsdam *Antigone* was probably the first production convincingly to present Greek choral practice, but each generation since has had to confront the problem anew, even as theoretical understandings of the chorus have remained comparatively circumscribed. Though he could not himself close the gap in *Braut*, Schiller seems at least to have recognized it: 'a poetic work', the preface begins, 'must justify itself. And where the deed does not speak, the word will not help much.' For *Braut*, it did not.

[71] See Silk (1998).

9

Brechtian Chorality

Martin Revermann

Not 'the Brechtian chorus' but 'Brechtian chorality': this is an idiosyncratic choice of a title, to be sure. It may be best to start by outlining why it was chosen, for this will lead to the core of some of the issues I wish to deal with. There certainly are 'Brechtian choruses' in the common sense of a distinct singing collective, a fair number of them even: the 1930 opera *The Rise and Fall of the City of Mahagonny*, by Brecht and Kurt Weill, has various important moments of choral singing. So does *The Threepenny Opera*, albeit on a significantly smaller and musically less sophisticated scale. The plays *St Joan of the Stockyards*, *The Mother*, as well as *The Measure* and the two 'school operas' (in Brecht's words) *The Yes-Sayer* and the *Nay-Sayer* all feature choral singing in a variety of contexts, some extensively so.[1] To these choruses created by Brecht the dramatist need to be added those by Brecht the lyricist, who, for instance, wrote, in collaboration with the composer Hanns Eisler, a collection of 'Lieder Gedichte Chöre' ('Songs Poems Choruses') designed for group delivery.[2] It contains existing and new songs like the 'Hitlerchoräle' ('Hitler Choral Songs'), vitriolic and cynical poems set to the music of six Christian hymns, which are among the most popular and, to the present day, most commonly sung hymns in the German Lutheran church.

This very basic introductory survey leads to a few important general observations. First, Brecht is one of the very few theatre artists of the twentieth century who resorts to choruses as a means of theatrical expression independently and out of his own choosing as an artist—that is, in situations where

I wish to thank Adriana Brook, Alysse Rich, and Bernd Seidensticker for helpful comments.

[1] The play *Der Brotladen* (*The Bread Shop*) (BFA 10.565–659, cf. also Knopf (2001: 238–42)), which Brecht worked on in 1929 and 1930 but never completed, also had a chorus (consisting of the unemployed). The preserved fragments were put together for the stage by the Berlin Ensemble and performed in 1967. All Brecht citations refer to the Berliner und Frankfurter Ausgabe (BFA): B. Brecht, *Bertolt Brecht, Grosse kommentierte Berliner und Frankfurter Ausgabe*, ed. W. Hecht et al. 30 vols (Berlin and Frankfurt am Main, 1988–2000).

[2] They were published, with Eisler's scores, in France in 1934 (= BFA 11.199–254).

there is no generic or traditional pressure to use a chorus (pressure that, most notably, exists in the case of adaptations of Greek tragedy and of Japanese Noh). The list of other twentieth-century Western theatre artists with particular interest in choruses is a distinguished but not particularly long one: it includes Meyerhold, Reinhardt, Beckett, Weiss, Stein, Heyme, Mnouchkine, and Schleef.[3] For Brecht choruses are an autonomous part of his regular creative repertory, and their use need not be triggered by appropriating established and traditional choral art forms such as Greek tragedy or Noh.

While this unusually independent artistic choice and preference in itself justifies the inclusion of a piece on Brecht in a volume entitled 'Choruses: Ancient and Modern', it also calls for an explanation, precisely because of the lack of a straightforward genealogical link with Greek drama. I use the term 'genealogy' (as opposed to 'equivalence', another key concept that I will turn to shortly) in cases where there is a conscious and clearly signalled reference by one work of art or artistic device back to another, creating a nexus between the two not unlike family relationships. One result of this missing genealogical link (or kinship, if you will) is the great variety of works that feature choruses, spanning opera and music theatre, parodic drama, didactic plays, and one play, *The Mother*, in which Brecht comes as close as he ever got to 'Socialist realism'. This broad range of works and genres already insinuates that we are dealing with a complex phenomenon that is likely to resist any monolithic approach. It will, therefore, be wise to cast the net wide and keep our minds open and flexible. Last but not least, the plays and operas just mentioned fall into a temporal cluster, the period between 1927 and 1933. This is a critical, indeed life-changing, period for Brecht personally, ideologically, and aesthetically, as well as a crucial turn in German history, from the final years of the Weimar Republic into the abyss of Nazi rule and totalitarianism. Neither before nor after this period did Brecht resort in any similarly sustained way to the theatrical chorus, with the important exception of Brecht's *The Antigone of Sophocles* (1948). A tentative explanation for this clustering will be given below as part of my third major conclusion.

While the Brechtian chorus proper (that is, a distinct singing or chanting onstage collective) is essentially confined to the temporal cluster from 1927 to 1933, song itself is, of course, a strikingly prominent element that pervades the whole Brechtian *œuvre*, from the very beginning in the late 1910s/early 1920s until Brecht's death in 1956. His natural affinity to musicianship and solo performance probably has its fair share here: in the 1910s the adolescent Brecht singing songs to his guitar was a familiar sight to his circle of friends

---

[3] An excellent first exploration of choruses in the twentieth century is Baur (1999), a monograph that has not received the attention it deserves. Schmidt (2010) provides an extensive discussion of Schleef and his 'choral theatre'. See further Fischer-Lichte, Chapter 19, this volume.

and in the taverns of his native Augsburg. Autobiographical aspects, in the form of lack of personal interest and skill, may similarly be part of the explanation for the conspicuous near-absence of dance in Brechtian play-writing and directing (the dancing at the end of the *Caucasian Chalk Circle* (BFA 8. 91 and 184) being a notable exception[4]). Brechtian choruses do not dance: even the chorus of *The Antigone of Sophocles* appears to have been either entirely or mostly static under Brecht's direction in 1948, with the chorus members delivering their songs while holding in front of them sticks with their propped-up masks (big and 'primitive'-looking as they were).[5]

Brechtian songs are often monodies, sometimes duets, and sometimes songs performed by a very small group of people. Hence they do not, or not necessarily, fit any narrow formal definition of the chorus and choral singing as a *collective* activity. But, setting aside the sheer number of singers as a criterion, much, in fact most, singing in Brecht done by individuals or very small groups is characterized by a significant amount of (self-)reflexivity and of 'tapping into' collective wisdom, collective experience, and collective au-thority—all of which are, of course, features typically seen in the choruses of ancient Greek drama, especially tragedy (and, one might add, in the choruses of Japanese Noh drama). A crucial distinction, therefore, needs to be intro-duced at this point: that between the *physically choral* (= a singing collective) and the *conceptually choral*, which is singing characterized by such 'tapping-into' collective experiences and a high degree of (self-)reflexivity.[6] Only with this distinction in mind, I submit, is it possible to describe and analyse adequately the nature, function, scope, and ideology underlying songs and singing in Brecht. This is because only the broader mindset of looking for the conceptually choral enables the analyst to register the complexity of Brechtian song, and to grasp how it aims to transcend the individual and particular and to move towards highlighting the typical, the situational, and the societal conditions under which characters act and make decisions in the first place. Hence also my insistence, in the title of this paper, on the term 'chorality' instead of the narrower and restrictively formalist term 'chorus'. My case studies and the more general conclusions I will draw at the end will, I hope, help to clarify and substantiate this important point.

Not only does Brechtian drama help to destabilize reductively formalistic definitions of the choral versus the monodic and the collective versus the

---

[4] Mittenzwei (1987: i. 138) relates a pertinent anecdote that illustrates Brecht's personal aversion to dancing.

[5] This is suggested by Brecht's remarks on the chorus in his *Antigonemodell 1948* (BFA 25.94, 96, 98, 102, 112, 120, 150, 152, and 158).

[6] One helpful analogy may be the chorus in Shakespeare's *Henry V*, which shows the conceptually choral but, being played by a single actor (see Stern 2009: 112–17), is not physically choral. Note, however, that this chorus neither sings nor recites but speaks in the register of normal poetic speech (blank verse), which is where the analogy breaks down.

individual. Of at least equal interest is the fact that, since Brecht uses chorality autonomously as part of his artistic repertory and normally without appropriating the ancient Greek tradition of dramatic choruses, classicists in particular (but not exclusively) are forced to ask themselves questions to do with equivalence. I use this concept in a rather specific way: equivalence, as opposed to the previously discussed term genealogy, denotes a relationship between two works of art (or artistic devices) A and B where A and B serve similar functions or have similar effects on recipients, *without* there *necessarily* being the conscious and clearly signalled reference (or nexus) that is characteristic of genealogical relationships. My usage of the term equivalence therefore differs from the way it is now most commonly used, in Translation Studies (and certain areas of Comparative Literature), to describe the relationship between a source text and a target text.[7] In a translation, the relationship between a source text and a target text is, of course, always fundamentally genealogical (B is always specifically a translation *of* A), and questions of equivalence are superimposed onto this pre-existing genealogy. In my usage, on the other hand, equivalence and genealogy *can* be entirely separate. Some of those questions to do with equivalence, while beyond the scope of this chapter, nonetheless should be articulated in the present context: how do Brechtian songs compare to the choral songs of Greek drama? If there are no genealogical links between a Brechtian work and a Greek drama, can we nonetheless meaningfully and fruitfully discuss equivalences between Brecht and Greek drama, equivalences that may, ideally, shed some light on Brecht and Greek drama alike? And precisely what kinds of equivalence are we talking about here: formal, functional, ideological, other?

My remarks on Brechtian chorality are, therefore, also an attempt to move the study of the reception of Greek drama beyond what I call the 'genealogical approach'—looking at adaptations/reperformances of Greek tragedy and their performance history—towards the 'comparatist approach', where there are no or very few genealogical links but clearly equivalences of some sort.[8] This comparatist approach is exemplified by the first and third of the three brief case studies, or vignettes rather, to which I now turn.[9] These are parts of a scene from the Brecht/Weill opera *Rise and Fall of the City of Mahagonny* (first performed in 1930) and a song from *Mother Courage* (first performed in 1943 and then in 1949). Genealogy, the focus of traditional reception studies, features in my second vignette: any discussion of the topic would be

---

[7] See Pym (2010: chs 2 and 3).

[8] I have advocated such an approach in Revermann (2008). Worth (2004) (on Beckett and Greek tragedy) is a good example of how it can be pursued.

[9] The vignettes will be presented in German followed by my own English translations. These translations tend to be foreignizing in that I attempt to adhere to German word order and diction. Naturalizing translations of Brecht, on the other hand, can be found in most volumes of the Methuen *Collected Works* edition (by John Willett, Ralph Mannheimer, and others).

inadequate if it failed to engage with Brecht's *The Antigone of Sophocles* (1948), Brecht's adaptation of Sophocles' *Antigone*, which remains his only genealogical contact and sustained artistic engagement with Greek tragedy (or any literary work of Greco-Roman antiquity, for that matter).[10]

AN OPERATIC PARODY

CHORUS *from the distance.*
    Haltet euch aufrecht! Fürchtet euch nicht!
    [Keep upright! Fear not!]
[*end of scene 11*]

Scene 12
[In the following minutes of performance time the hurricane makes a detour around the city of Mahagonny.]

CHORUS: girls, men
    O wunderbare Lösung
    Die Stadt der Freude ward verschont.
    Die Hurrikane gingen vorüber in grosser Höhe
    Und der Tod tritt in die Wasser zurück.
    O wunderbare Lösung!

    [O wonderful resolution | The city of joy has been saved. | The hurricanes went by high above | And Death went back into the waters. | O wonderful resolution!]

AND FROM NOW ON THE MOTTO OF THE PEOPLE OF MAHAGONNY WAS 'YOU MAY', AS THEY HAD LEARNED IN THAT NIGHT OF HORROR.

Scene 13
MAHAGONNY IN FULL SWING, ABOUT A YEAR AFTER THE GREAT HURRICANE.
The men approach the ramp and start singing.
CHORUS. Erstens vergesst nicht, kommt das Fressen
    Zweitens kommt der Liebesakt
    Drittens das Boxen nicht vergessen
    Viertens Saufen, das steht im Kontrakt.
    Vor allem aber achtet scharf
    Dass man hier alles dürfen darf.

[First eating, don't forget! | Second is the act of love | Thirdly, don't forget boxing, | fourth is booze, that's in the contract. | But most of all, take good care that one is allowed to be allowed anything here.]

---

[10] Note, however, Brecht's contact with Aristophanic comedy (*Wealth*) in his never-finished 'Pluto Revue' (BFA 10.824–31). I hope to discuss this project in more detail elsewhere.

The scene is the turning point of this 1930 opera (music by Weill, libretto by Brecht). By the ridiculous miracle of a hurricane deciding to take a detour, the city of Mahagonny has survived the ultimate tragic situation of helpless exposure to a lethal threat (emphasized in Weill's score by execution drums). Now the men and young women of that depraved city are united in a song of thanks and celebration. 'O wunderbare Lösung' activates a highly poetic and solemn linguistic register, with clear references to the one intertext that for Brecht is the most important of all, the Bible (!):[11] death parting back into the sea (compare the people of Israel fleeing from Pharaoh at Exodus 14) and, earlier on, the solemn choral admonition, from a distance, not to be afraid (compare the archangel Gabriel addressing Mary at Luke 1:30). In this parody of biblical motifs as well as the *deus ex machina* scheme familiar from Greek tragedy, the mixed chorus sing music that is the most tender, harmonic, enchanting and, as Brecht and Weill would put it, 'culinary'[12] of the whole opera: a solemn and tranquil piece, suitably accompanied by solo guitar. Dominated by D minor, the song is, ultimately and after some tension created by chromatic and dominant-seventh chords, resolved into a soothing A Major. The final line (the repeated 'O wunderbare Lösung') evolves into a charming two-voice canon, closing in that soothing A Major mode. In a large-scale 2007 production of *Mahagonny*, at the Los Angeles Opera, the choral nature of the collective was further emphasized visually by letting the singers hold torch-lights underneath their chins, which gave them mask-like facial features.[13]

By the time the city has been converted to unrestrained hedonism along the new motto 'Du darfst' ('you may'), the chorus members (now only men in the LA production) have put on sunglasses (this is accompanied by a costume change of Begbick from veiled mourner in black into mature glamour woman). Their sung reflections on the new 'Du darfst' motto are decidedly rational: note the structure 'first' (eating), 'secondly' (love-making), 'thirdly' (boxing), 'fourthly' (drinking), all nicely subsumed under the principal 'Du darfst' slogan mentioned last. This serves not just as an evaluative and prioritizing structure but also as a narrative principle that organizes the subsequent scenes of the opera. The collective voice of the chorus therefore bundles, elevates, reflects, evaluates, rationalizes, prioritizes, and structures.

---

[11] Esslin (1959: 91–105) remains the most perceptive, if brief, discussion to date of Brecht's relationship with the Bible.

[12] In the very important *Anmerkungen zur Oper 'Aufstieg und Fall der Stadt Mahagonny'* of 1930 (BFA 24.74–86).

[13] The LA production (featuring Audra McDonald, Patti Lupone, and Anthony Dean Griffey, conductor: James Conlon) is available on DVD (euroarts). Also note the DVD of the 1998 Salzburg production by director Peter Zadek (Arthaus Musik), which is not as strong in terms of acting but, unlike the LA production, does not omit the difficult 'crane duet'.

THE UNWISE ELDERS OF THEBES

KREON. So fällt jetzt Thebe.
Und fallen soll es, soll's mit mir, und es soll aus sein
Und für die Geier da. So will ich's dann.
Creon off with the maids.

DIE ALTEN. Und wandte sich um und ging, in
Händen nicht mehr als ein blutbefleckt
Tuch von des Labdakus ganzem Haus
In die stürzende Stadt hin.
[*First chorus member*] Wir aber
Folgen auch jetzt ihm all, und
Nach unten ist's. [*Second chorus member*] Abgehaun wird
Dass sie nicht zuschlag mehr
Uns die zwingbare Hand. [*Third chorus member*] Aber die alles sah
Konnte nur noch helfen dem Feind, der jetzt
Kommt und uns austilgt gleich. [*Fourth chorus member*] Denn kurz ist die Zeit
Allumher ist Verhängnis und nimmer genügt sie
Hinzuleben, undenkend und leicht
Von Duldung zu Frevel und
Weise zu werden im Alter.

[CREON: So falls Thebe now. | And it shall fall, shall fall with me, and it shall be over | And for those vultures. Thus I want it then. | [Exit Creon with the maids.]
THE ELDERS: And he turned around and went, in | His hands not more than a blood-stained | Cloth of Labdacus' whole house | Into the collapsing city. [First chorus member] But we | Follow him now too all, and | Downwards it is. [Second chorus member] Cut off | So that it can no longer hit | Our forcible hand. [Third chorus member] But she who saw everything | Could only help the enemy who now | Comes and will extinguish us presently. [Fourth chorus member] For short is the time | All around is disaster and never is it enough | To live along, unthinking and easy | From endurance to sacrilege and | To become wise in old age.]

As fascinating and sometimes bizarre as it is undervalued, Brecht's *The Antigone of Sophocles* (1948) is a curious hybrid of a translation, an adaptation, and a new play. About 400 of the *c.*1,300 verses are taken directly from Hölderlin's 1804 translation, an (in)famous work that, at different times and by different people, has been considered both the work of a mad man and the product of pure genius.[14] Its idiosyncrasies attracted Brecht's interest, especially the regional tone of the German and Hölderlin's extreme boldness

---

[14] Schadewaldt (1957) continues to be an excellent, thorough, and thought-provoking discussion of this translation (and that of *Oedipus the King*). For an incisive and informative survey, see Böschenstein in Kreuzer (2002: 278–89).

with regards to word order.[15] Beside fundamental changes to the plot—in Brecht's version Creon attacks Argos out of greed for its natural resources— the chorus is the most striking Brechtian innovation. Complicit in Creon's crimes, the chorus is a group of perpetrators as much as victims (the parallelism with the guilt of the German people under Hitler is impossible to miss). In a telling move, Brecht does not represent the four men who make up the chorus as old (unlike Sophocles, whose choice is in sync with a bias of the genre): wisdom, argues Brecht in the 'model book', has nothing to do with age, and 'to make wars one does not have to be old but must only belong to those in power'.[16] The same passage from the 'model book' (*Antigonemodell 1948*, first published in 1949), which grew out of Brecht's 1948 production in Chur (Switzerland), also contains the idiosyncratic proposition that the double function of the choral persona between commentator and agent is not all too important, since the chorus is best described as just lending itself to those in power and 'because wisdom in thought and baseness in action often go hand in hand'. No intricate oscillations of choral identity in this conception of Greek tragedy!

The choral passage selected as a case study is the very ending of the play. Its formal features alone are remarkable. The initial comment on the departing Creon is spoken by all four chorus members[17] in the third person and the past tense—that is, in the 'epic' mode of narrative. It therefore takes on the form of *Brückenverse* ('bridge verses'), which Brecht also used in the Prologue, in the 'model book' as well as in the rehearsal process with his actors.[18] Subsequently, the collective choral voice splits up into those of the four individuals, each of whom departs after his bit.[19] The physically dissolving chorus nicely embodies the moral erosion we are made to witness: this is the tragic abyss in its most blunt, brutal, and disillusioned form, a downward spiral lacking any redemptive features. The chorus's acknowledgement of its continued complicitness is just about the only insight this tragic chorus has to offer. Anticipating its own annihilation—a notable departure from Greek tragic choruses, which are always the designated survivors of the tragic catastrophe—this fading chorus pronounces a message as fatalist as it is nihilistic: nothing has been learnt, and there is no capacity of (self-)reform in view of all the suffering (past, present, and future). The section is entirely Brechtian, and its blunt message radically inverts that of Brecht's source text, Hölderlin's translation: Hölderlin, for all

---

[15] As Brecht remarks in his journal (16 December 1947) (BFA 27.255, cf. BFA 8.49).

[16] BFA 25.102 (from the *Antigonemodell 1948*).

[17] In Brecht's play the chorus always speaks, either unaccompanied or with percussion-like piano accompaniment. The mechanics of this accompaniment are detailed in the *Antigonemodell 1948* (BFA 25.120).

[18] *Antigonemodell 1948* (BFA 25.79–80).

[19] This feature of the performance is not indicated in the published text, but outlined by Brecht in the *Antigonemodell 1948* (BFA 25.158). In the text I mark the individual speakers using square brackets and italics.

his mistakes and idiosyncrasies, did preserve the Sophoclean notion of a chorus that has acquired wisdom in old age.[20] Brecht, by contrast, deprives his chorus not just of old age—but of all wisdom.

THE SHIFTS IN MOTHER COURAGE'S CAPITULATION

[*End of Scene 4* MOTHER COURAGE SINGS THE SONG OF THE GREAT CAPITULATION]

[R] Einst, im Lenze meiner
jungen Jahre
Dacht auch ich, dass ich was
ganz Besondres bin.
[Sp] (Nicht wie jede beliebige Häuslertochter, mit meinem Aus-
sehn und Talent und meinem Drang nach Höherem!)
[R] Und bestellte meine Suppe ohne Haare
Und von mir, sie hatten kein Gewinn.
[Sp] (Alles oder nix, jedenfalls nicht den Nächstbesten, jeder is
Seines Glückes Schmied, ich lass mir keine Vorschriften ma-
chen!)
[Sg] Doch vom Dach ein Star
Pfiff: wart paar Jahr!
  Und *du marschierst* in der Kapell
  Im Gleichschritt, langsam oder schnell
  Und bläsest einen kleinen Ton:
  Jetzt kommt er schon.
  Und jetzt das Ganze schwenkt!
  Der Mensch denkt: Gott lenkt
  Keine Red davon!

[[R] Once, in the spring of my young years | I too thought that I was something uniquely special. | [Sp] (Not like any old cottager's daughter, with my looks | And my talents and my drive towards Higher Things!) | [R] And I ordered my soup without hairs | And from me they had no profit. | [Sp] (All or nothing, definitely not just the next one available, each | Man for himself, no one tells me what to do!) | [Sg] But from the roof a starling | Whistled: wait a few years! | And you'll be marching with the band | In step, slowly or fast | And you'll be blowing a small tone: | Now it's coming already. | And now the whole company turns! | Man thinks: God's in charge | No talk of that!]

[R] Und bevor das Jahr war abgefahren
Lernte ich zu schlucken meine Medizin.
[Sp] (Zwei Kinder aufm Hals und bei dem Brotpreis und was alles

---

[20] 'Grosse Blicke aber | Grosse Streiche der hohen Schultern | Vergeltend, | Sie haben im Alter gelehrt, zu denken'. There are gross misunderstandings of the Greek here, but the notion of wisdom in old age is Sophoclean (*Antigone* 1353: *gêrai to phronein edidaxan*).

verlangt wird!)
[R] Als sie einmal mit mir fix und fertig waren
Hatten sie mich auf dem Arsch und auf den Knien.
[Sp] (Man muss sich stelln mit den Leuten, eine Hand wäscht die
Andre, mit dem Kopf kann man nicht durch die Wand.)
[Sg] Und vom Dach der Star
Pfiff: noch kein Jahr!
Und *sie marschiert* in der Kapell
Im Gleichschritt, langsam oder schnell
Und bläset ihren kleinen Ton:
Jetzt kommt er schon.
Und jetzt das Ganze schwenkt!
Der Mensch denkt: Gott lenkt
Keine Red davon!

[[R] And before the year had gone | I had learnt to swallow my medicine. | [Sp] (Two children on my hands and what a price for bread and the kind of things people are | Asking of you!) | [R] Once they were completely done with me | They had me on my ass and on my knees. | [Sp] (You have to arrange yourself with people, one hand washes the | Other, you can't bang your head against a brick wall. | [Sg] But from the roof a starling | Whistled: not even a year! | And she'll be marching with the band | In step, slowly or fast | And she'll be blowing her small tone: | Now it's coming already. | And now the whole company turns! | Man thinks: God's in charge | No talk of that!]

[R] Viele sah ich schon den Himmel stürmen
Und kein Stern war ihnen gross und weit genug.
[Sp] (Der Tüchtige schafft es, wo ein Wille ist, ist ein Weg, wir
Werden den Laden schon schmeissen.)
[R] Doch sie fühlten bald beim Berg-auf-Berge-Türmen
Wie doch schwer man schon an einem Strohhut trug.
[Sp] (Man muss sich nach der Decke strecken!)
[Sg] Und vom Dach der Star
Pfeift: noch kein Jahr!
Und *sie marschiern* in der Kapell
Im Gleichschritt, langsam oder schnell
Und blasen ihren kleinen Ton:
Jetzt kommt er schon.
Und jetzt das Ganze schwenkt!
Der Mensch denkt: Gott lenkt
Keine Red davon!

[[R] Many I saw storm heaven | And no star was big and far away enough for them. | [Sp] (Industry prevails, where there's a will there's a way, we'll | Get things done after all.) | [R] But soon they started feeling, while piling mountain on mountain | How difficult to carry even straw hats were. | [Sp] (One has to cut one's coat according to one's cloth!) | [Sg] But from the roof a starling | Whistles: not even a year! | And they'll be marching with the band | In step, slowly or fast | And they'll be blowing their small tone: | Now it's coming already. | And now the whole company turns! | Man thinks: God's in charge | No talk of that!]

Mother Courage's 'Song about the Great Capitulation', which concludes the early scene four of the play, is one of the best-known Brecht songs and, like the play as a whole, firmly associated with Helene Weigel in the title role of the famous, even legendary, Berlin production of 1949. Weigel's rendering of the song (composed by Paul Dessau in 1946) is available both on CD as an audio version and as part of the 1960 movie by Peter Palitzsch and Manfred Weckwerth (filmed on the basis of the Berlin production).[21] In this scene a soldier who had saved the captain's horse is set to complain about not having been rewarded for his deed. Mother Courage, who also wants to bring forward a complaint, points out to him that his anger is not 'long enough', and that soon he too will conform to the system like everyone else.

Formally a monody, this song exemplifies what I have called the 'conceptually choral', which is characterized by 'tapping into' collective experiences and by a high degree of (self-)reflexivity. This is most obvious in the way in which the subjective autobiographical narrative is, from the very start, deflected and displaced into the realm of the more general and universal, especially through the increasing use of one of the most blatant means of 'tapping into' collective experience: the gnomic wisdom of proverbs, which are quoted in abundance and to an ironizing effect.

Notable in this context is the shift in performative register (not indicated in the script but very palpable in the recordings): all three stanzas show the same pattern of two lines in recitative (which I marked above as [R]), two lines of speech (marked as [Sp]), a repetition of two lines of recitative and speech respectively, and then the song proper (marked as [Sg]). The song takes the form of a nine-line refrain, although there is one small yet crucial change: this is the shift from the second-person singular in the first stanza ('Du marschierst') via the third-person singular in the second stanza ('sie marschiert') to the third-person plural in the final stanza ('sie marschiern') (I have emphasized those sections in the text above). The genesis of those shifts is instructive. Brecht had intended two soldiers to start joining Mother Courage in the refrain, beginning with the second stanza. Hence the shifts. This intention is documented in the complex tradition of the performance script for this play—but the addition of the two soldiers was never implemented on stage, and it did not make it into the printed text either.[22]

That the shifts were kept is indeed telling: clearly, they continued to feel right both to Brecht and to his alert star performer Helene Weigel even when

---

[21] The CD is no. 7 of the 20-CD set 'Bertolt Brecht Werke: Eine Auswahl', published in 1997 by BMG Musik (Berlin).

[22] Hennenberg (1984: 433). The details of the textual history are well documented in Olsson (1981: 88–92), where the four variants of the play script are juxtaposed.

performed by Mother Courage alone. This is no doubt because they are indicative of the overall programmatic move from the individual situation of Mother Courage to the universal human condition that this song demonstrates and exposes. The song, therefore, personalizes and generalizes at the same time, with Mother Courage herself functioning as a negative mythical exemplum of sorts. Embedded in the plot yet detachable from it, this monody has the larger conceptual scope so typical of many choral songs encountered in Greek tragedy, including the metaphysical dimension that in Brecht takes the form of a radical anti-theology: 'Der Mensch denkt: Gott lenkt | Keine Red davon!' There is, however, a fascinating twist: while Greek choruses tend to be ultimately ineffectual and unable to influence the turn of events—a kind of marginality and lack of agency that has provoked much discussion since the 1990s[23]—Mother Courage *is* effective. But it is *negative* capability: as a result of the song, the soldier capitulates, as does Mother Courage herself. Instead of inspiring transformative action, the song effects resignation.

The harsh, punctuated, and percussion-dominated music by Dessau gives the whole song a strong military feel, quite the opposite of 'culinary' comfort music. Weigel makes no attempt whatsoever to hide the fact that her voice is untrained and that of an amateur. On the contrary, the lack of craft seems to be emphaszed to authenticate both performance and message, and to pre-empt, by formal means, any possibility of an audience member's enchantment or empathy (which one may be lured into by the mere content of the song). Similar dynamics operate throughout the many songs of this play. The chorus formed by Mother Courage and her three children, together with the cart they are pulling, is the one element of the play that not only structures it and holds much of it together (especially with its anthem-like theme song) but that illustrates, in a moving way, the workings of the plot: *Mother Courage* can plausibly be described as a play not so much about one prominent individual but about a nuclear-family chorus (notable for the absence of a father) that perishes, one by one, with only its chorus leader surviving—not to tell the story but to continue the downward spiral created by greed and violence. The sole choral survivor, Mother Courage, has witnessed everything, and learnt nothing. Deluded in her belief that one of her sons is still alive, she leaves the stage headed even deeper into the abyss of personal catastrophe. All this makes the family chorus of *Mother Courage* an 'anti-chorus' if measured against the benchmark of Greek tragedy, where choruses (who, it would appear, seldom shared the bond of kinship[24]) survive collectively and in full number to bear

---

[23] The best entryway into this extensive and still ongoing debate is Gould (1996) (with Goldhill's rejoinder).

[24] The choruses of Aeschylus' *Suppliants* and *Eumenides* as well as the chorus of the *Prometheus* are such kinship collectives (but only the first, of course, is a collective of humans).

witness, to remember, and to pass on their wisdom painfully derived from watching the catastrophe unfold before their eyes.

SOME CONCLUSIONS

It is time to wrap up and present broader conclusions, some of which will require integrating, rather casually at this point, other works by Brecht, like *The Measure* or *St Joan of the Stockyards*, which space constraints prevent me from discussing in any detail. I have organized my conclusions into five separate sections.

(1) Brecht's attraction to chorality in its own right, without Greek tragedy looming in the background as a catalyst, is rooted both in his theatre aesthetics and in his political and ideological position (two areas that for Brecht, of course, cannot possibly and reasonably be separated). One of the pillars of Brechtian theatre aesthetics, from its very inception, is a relentless emphasis on theatrical transparency, on exposing theatre as theatre, that is, as an artificial, constructed mode of communication, an adjustable tool for representing reality rather than attempting to replicate it somehow (as Naturalism had set out to do). Within such aesthetics the chorus fits excellently as an anti-naturalistic and anti-realistic stage device, on a par with the half curtain, the visible musical accompaniment, or the brightly lit stages. In particular, for Brecht the singing chorus is one of the many theatrical devices capable of achieving *Verfremdung*. This is explicitly stated in Brecht's much-quoted 1936 essay 'Verfremdungseffekte in der chinesischen Schauspielkunst' and, with specific reference to the ancient Greek dramatic chorus, in the preface to the *Antigonemodell 1948* (first published in 1949).[25]

In view of all this, it is perhaps initially surprising that the chorus is under-theorized in Brecht, both in the plays themselves and especially in the extensive theoretical writings. This sets Brecht apart from the Greek playwrights of the fifth century (Aristophanes certainly, but also Sophocles, who is said to have written a treatise entitled 'On the Chorus'[26]), as well as other playwrights, who both used and theorized choruses: Schiller in his preface to *Die Braut von Messina*, but also Shakespeare (note the chorus at the beginning of *Henry V*: 'And let us, ciphers to this great account, | On your imaginary forces work'— that is, work as a magnifier and stimulator of the imagination)—not to speak of non-practitioners like Schlegel or Nietzsche. The under-theorized chorus is a feature Brecht does, however, share with Aristotle, in whose *Poetics* the chorus is notoriously sidelined. Yet the reasons for this shared lack of attention are

---

[25] BFA 22.207 and 25.75 respectively.   [26] Bagordo (1998: 11–12).

diametrically opposed: Aristotle's near silence on the chorus is a result of its insignificance within the Aristotelian conceptualization of tragedy along the lines of plot construction, plot intelligibility, and character configuration.[27] Here the unwieldy chorus collective with its fuzzy boundaries of impersonation, both within and somehow outside the action, does not quite fit in. Within Brechtian theatre aesthetics and theory, however, the chorus fits in all too well—so well, in fact, that it requires only cursory discussion as yet another possible device to achieve *Verfremdung*.

(2) Beyond its theoretical appeal, further elements of chorality come to mind that had to appeal to Brecht and facilitated its frequent use. The banal but fundamentally important fact that the chorus is an embodied voice of the collective is surely one of them. Brechtian drama is arguably not interested in the inner life of a dramatic character or a character's inner psychology (such subjectivity is much more a feature of Brecht's extensive lyrical work). Rather, dramatic character in Brecht is contextual and situational, symptomatic of broader socio-economic factors. Hence the Brechtian actor is asked to demonstrate, rather than embody, a character in performance. Antigone, for instance, is, in Brecht's reading, not a resistance fighter of any description but serves as a character foil to help throw into relief Creon as the representative of a repressive form of government driven by greed and exploitation (fascism/capitalism—the former, for Brecht, being the extreme manifestation and logical extension of the latter). Antigone and Creon as dramatic characters cumulatively point beyond their individuality towards the systemic and structural (or *Überbau*, in Marxist terminology). Within such an aesthetic of theatre, in which the exterior is privileged over the interior, social condition over individual situation, the chorus, and the choral mode, are welcome opportunities to point *beyond* the immediacy of the characters' present actions to the larger framework that conditions and enables those actions: what set of conditions, what kind of world, *enables* the characters to act the way they do? And, if what the characters do is evidently not right and morally unjust, what needs to be done to change not those dramatic characters but that enabling larger framework?

The equivalences, as well as the crucial differences, with Greek tragic chorality are evident: in terms of commonalities, there is the conceptual extension, the 'tapping-into' collective experience and 'pointing-beyond' the here and now of the dramatic action to a larger framework, be it that of myth, of theology, or of reflections on the human condition. But Greek chorality, like Greek tragedy as an art form in general, is, in the last resort, conservative by way of reaffirming the validity of those very frameworks, thus stabilizing the status quo. This is a far cry from the transformative nature, or, better, the

---

[27] Halliwell (1998: 238–52).

transformative mandate, of Brechtian drama, which appeals to its audience not only to recognize the contradictions between how the world is and how it ought to be but, as a necessary result of such reflection, to take action towards fundamental transformation (the ending of *The Good Person of Sezuan* is a textbook example of such a transformative mandate, not spelt out but initiated and implied). This is what makes Brechtian theatre 'dialectical', whereas an art form like Greek tragedy struck Brecht as fatalistic and reactionary.

(3) Granted Brecht's general sympathy for the choral mode as a theatrical device of collective self-expression, the actual sources and inspirations for deploying this choral mode ('the triggers', so to speak) were varied. Only in the minority of cases is Brecht's use of the choral mode motivated by a literary model and generic tradition. In *The Antigone of Sophocles* the chorus was part of the literary baggage that came with adapting a Greek tragedy, as was the case when Brecht adapted the Noh play *Taniko* in the two didactic plays *The Yes Sayer* and *The Nay Sayer*. And when in 1940 he set out to adapt, very freely, Aristophanes' *Wealth* in the 'Pluto Revue', an intriguing project that remained unfinished, a chorus (of four men, as later in *The Antigone of Sophocles*) is part of the action. Yet the trigger for the choral mode can be only partially or very loosely literary. The *Mahagonny* opera, for instance, at least occasionally derives its parodic use of the choral mode from the literary tradition that associates chorality with a vague notion of 'the tragic' (that is, the archetypal tragic situation of extreme danger and agony). More important in this case, however, is the musical tradition of the operatic chorus, most influentially exemplified by some Wagner and, above all, Verdi.

A very important non-literary trigger for Brecht's use of the choral mode is its strong association with ritual, in particular its liturgical use as part of the Christian Mass. *St Joan of the Stockyards*, especially its ending with the death and canonization of the heroine, is full of liturgical choruses. While there are intertextual dynamics with one literary text—the highly choral ending of Goethe's *Faust (Part II)* celebrating the hero's redemption—the parody, even outright cynicism, of Brecht's use of chorality in this play derives its main force from liturgical associations with Christian notions of ritual worship, communal praise, trust in the supernatural, and hope for redemption. The control chorus of *The Measure*, a didactic play from 1930 justifying the execution of a communist agitator by his fellow comrades to ensure the bigger cause of revolutionary victory, similarly thrives on the liturgical associations of chorality, but puts a positive spin on them: the play, probably Brecht's most controversial, can be described in formal terms as a passion play, an oratorio almost, celebrating the justness inherent in a human sacrifice of a Christ-like figure for the welfare of the ultimate collective, humankind, and its redemption from evil (capitalist oppression, that is).

A final trigger for Brecht's use of the choral mode is its strong connection, by the 1920s, with the socialist workers' movement. Since the nineteenth century Germany had, and still has, a strong tradition of organized amateur choirs, a social phenomenon that found its most visible institutional articulation in the *Deutscher Sängerbund* (founded in 1862) and its socialist counterpart, the *Arbeitersängerbund* (founded in 1877).[28] The choral songs written by Brecht the lyricist that I briefly mentioned at the beginning are, at least for the most part, meant for these types of workers' choirs, who notoriously and for the longest time lacked a specific communist/socialist repertoire (in the early decades they would, in fact, sing more or less exactly the same repertoire of mostly popular song (*Volkslieder*) that their bourgeois counterparts were cultivating).[29] For anyone familiar with Athenian drama, this particular socio-political aspect conjures up interesting associations: Athenian dramatic chorality (and dithyramb, one might add) is, of course, also engineered to be the expression of a particular segment of Athenian society, the Athenian citizen body from which the *choreutai* and dithyrambic singers, at least at the Great Dionysia, had to be recruited, turning those choruses into proper citizen choruses and onstage representations of the citizen body.

For Brecht, the workers' chorus was, without a doubt, the consummate form of chorality: class-conscious amateur singers, recruited from the right stratum of society, committed, in some form or other, to the socialist cause and a public, propagandistic weapon of class war ('agitprop'). This, the socio-political aspect of chorality, is perhaps the one that most importantly and fundamentally underlies Brecht's use of the chorus. Among other things, it probably best explains the above-mentioned fact that choruses proper (that is, distinct singing collectives) feature prominently in Brecht only within a specific period, those tumultuous years between 1927 and 1933, when the German political scene was extraordinarily polarized and violent. Yet, as so often, Brecht's artistic patterns remain unpredictable and surprising. In only one case is this socio-political aspect of chorality given the kind of uncritically positive 'agitprop' spin one might expect. This is the play *The Mother,* a 1933 adaptation of Gorki's 1906 novel, an unusual play in that it is the closest Brecht ever got to what in the 1930s started to be labelled 'Socialist Realism' (hence its rich and long performance history east of the Iron Curtain, especially in the GDR).[30]

More often, interestingly, Brechtian choruses as socio-political agents are presented in a critical, even sinister light: note the complicit chorus of *The Antigone of Sophocles*, which is deeply implicated in Creon's crimes, or the self-destructively disoriented choruses of the *Mahagonny* opera in their

---

[28] See further Ioannidou, Chapter 18, and Fischer-Lichte, Chapter 19, this volume.

[29] This kind of communal singing (and reciting) was, after initial appropriation and support, banned by the Nazis in 1936, a decision that prompted Brecht to write the poem 'Als Hitler den Sprechchor verbot' (BFA 14.327).

[30] L. Bradley (2006).

apocalyptic circular final movements. Even the control chorus of *The Measure* does not necessarily have a positive ring to it (let alone an 'agitprop' spin), since it embodies The Party as an abstract and strangely detached entity rather than a collective of workers in the flesh.

(4) Chorality in Brecht—and Brechtian song in general—is characteristically performed by the untrained amateur singer who makes no attempt whatsoever to cover up the lack of musical training. On the contrary, the Brechtian singer may even consciously *emphasize* it (as did Weigel in her 'Great Capitulation' song). The sole exception to this is the *Mahagonny* opera, which, despite its critical and parodic position relative to traditional opera, is, of course, still an opera, hence in need of professional musicians.

The prevalent Brechtian emphasis, insistence even, on musical amateurship is chiefly motivated by the perceived need to authenticate and democratize art: anyone can, and should, be a Brechtian singer. It does, however, have at least one further repercussion, of particular interest to the classicist: Brechtian chorality cannot possibly be the site of aesthetic beauty, conventionally defined, or of artistic perfection. There is no way in which its formal, aesthetic features could ever 'enchant', 'electrify', or, as Brecht would put it, 'hypnotize' the viewer and the listener. These are deliberate artistic strategies, because the critical, alert, and unenchanted audience is a major, perhaps *the* major, objective of Brechtian drama in general. The composers working for Brecht—Kurt Weill, Hanns Eisler, and Paul Dessau—understood this very well, and matched the amateurship of the performers with music that is not only not particularly taxing technically (except for the *Mahagonny* opera) but that, more importantly, resists the label 'beautiful'. Note in particular the heavy use of percussion instruments and brass, which give the music a certain aggressive energy. The general atmosphere conveyed by this music is definitely not soothing, and, if this is ever the case, parody is usually either obvious (for example, in the *Hitlerchoräle*) or lurking (for example, in the *Mahagonny* example discussed above).

This is an extremely stark contrast with Greek drama, tragedy as well as comedy, where chorality is, of course, very much a site of aesthetic beauty and aesthetic perfection: ancient dramatic choruses, composed of non-professionals, may not always have got it right when they were singing and dancing—but they were, of course, always trying to! This is clearly indicated, not just by the considerable efforts that went into the choregic system that trained and supported choruses[31] but also by the challenging sophistication and level of complexity that, in the texts that have come down to us, can be detected in the poetic and metrical dimension of Greek chorality (a complexity

---

[31] P. Wilson (2000) is the standard large-scale discussion of the choregic system in Athens and elsewhere.

that extends, by implication, to those elements of choral performance that are essentially lost to us, music and choreography).

(5) Brechtian choruses and chorality often negatively invert patterns and motifs that are associated with Greek chorality in particular and with liturgical chorality in general. They are, therefore, for Brecht, indicative of the flaws inherent in the whole Western artistic tradition. Only within the right ideological framework, a Marxist framework, can chorality become positive and constructive, and only then can it act as a positive amplifier of the right and just cause. I reiterate, however, that such positive chorality in Brecht is surprisingly rare: it can be found in *The Mother*, in the fragments of *The Bread Shop* and, with qualifications, in *The Measure*.

Ritual is a good example. Brecht is keenly aware that choral singing traditionally has a strong ritualistic element and often features in religious and liturgical contexts: united by song, the collective refers to, and reflects on, higher levels of its reality, notably the divine. For Brecht, this ritual, liturgical, and theological dimension of chorality is nonsense, and his appropriation is correspondingly aggressive: often choral singing in Brecht becomes parodic (in part so in the *Mahagonny* opera, very much more so in *St. Joan of the Stockyards*). Alternatively, chorality can be presented as outdated, primitive, and barbarian, an inferior and unenlightened stage of humankind (thus in *The Antigone of Sophocles*).

Other typical aspects of chorality are similarly inverted: collective wisdom becomes collective ignorance, stupidity, and viciousness; the survival of the chorus—note, again, that Greek tragic choruses always survive the catastrophe—turns into the demise of the chorus (the children in *Mother Courage*, the chorus in *The Antigone of Sophocles*); meaningful and socially constructive ritual functions of the chorus become empty and ossified hyper-ritualizations. Choruses are such an attractive target for this kind of detraction because they tend to aim so high, hence can fall so deep to set a useful negative example. It is because choruses often refer to these higher levels of experience and authority (divine authority, the gnomic authority of collective wisdom, the authority of myth and historical experience) that they can be taken down so effectively. Choruses are no ordinary dramatic entities: they are big, they perform big, they think big. In addition they, yes, sing, and song is no ordinary mode of expression either. It is an extraordinary event in a play, a new modality that immediately commands a different, higher level of attention and awareness from the spectator. For Brecht, who categorically denies the value of those higher authorities regularly invoked by choruses such as divinity or received collective wisdom, choruses become ideal platforms to set up those ideals, expose them as hollow, and take them down as irrelevant and ridiculous.

All of this is, of course, in the last resort an implicit acknowledgement of the exceptional *power* of chorality and the power of song. And perhaps this is where, at least for the classicist, the true value of the project 'Brechtian chorality' actually lies. Brechtian choruses and Brechtian singers, while sharing some important characteristics with ancient chorality, are in equally crucial other aspects very much unlike ancient Greek choruses. It is clear that Brechtian choruses cannot help us to relive, let alone reconstruct, the full panorama of ancient dramatic chorality so sadly lost to us. But they do invite us to reimagine ancient Greek chorality in all its potentialities, to realize which of those potentialities the ancient playwrights did and did not actualize, and to understand the full implications of those choices. Not least of all, Brechtian choruses remind us that chorality is, and was in the ancient Greek theatre, an enormously powerful theatrical device, capable of transforming an old traditional tale into a fresh, thought-provoking, beautiful, and engaging challenge that forces, to the present day, its viewers to rethink fundamental aspects of what the world around them is, what it could be, and what it ought to be.

Part III

Shadows

10

The Nostalgia of the Male Tragic Chorus

Sheila Murnaghan

For the ancient Athenians, tragedy was a species of choral poetry, a spectacular new development within a long tradition of group performances combining song and dance. Modern discussions and receptions of tragedy have generally focused on what was added as tragedy left its purely choral roots behind: individual speaking actors impersonating the main characters of a myth. But recently critics have paid more attention to tragedy's ongoing choral element, investigating not only the particular choruses of individual plays, but also the tragic chorus's connections to non-dramatic lyric and to the ritual contexts in which most choral song was performed.[1] We are gaining a clearer understanding of what the chorus became when it appeared in tandem with the clamorous individuals who dominate tragic plots.

Athenian drama came into being as the leaders of choruses emerged from the group and began to imitate characters in the myths that were being retold. The details of this process are unknown, but by the time of our first extant tragedies, in the second quarter of the fifth century BC, two distinct actors were a standard feature of each play, and three soon after that. Outside the drama, the role of chorus leader also developed into the figure of the *chorêgos*, a rich individual who assumed the expenses of a tragic presentation, especially the funding, training, and outfitting of the chorus. Being a *chorêgos* was at once a form of involuntary public service, since this role was required by the city of its wealthiest citizens, and an opportunity for self-promotion, since the *chorêgos* gained enviable visibility and glory from a successful production.[2]

Within the drama, the chorus, which had constituted the entire personnel of the performance, was overshadowed by the actors, but never wholly

For helpful comments and suggestions on this chapter, my thanks to Felix Budelmann and Eirene Visvardi.

[1] See especially Bacon (1995), Henrichs (1995, 1996), Goldhill (1996), Gould (1996), Calame (1999), Foley (2003), Mastronarde (2010), and Swift (2010).

[2] The definitive treatment of this institution is Wilson (2000).

eclipsed.[3] Rather the chorus underwent several forms of partial displacement from its previously central and self-consciously performative role. Like the actors, it entered mimetically into the myth, taking on the role of a collective character, but never as completely. The chorus always retained elements of its previously undisguised identity as a group of singers and dancers, both in its performance mode (which included clearly demarcated episodes of formalized singing and dancing) and in its self-presentation.

In addition, the fictional identities adopted by choruses involved social displacement, in relation both to the high position of the main characters and to the real circumstances of the chorus members, who were the most privileged members of Athenian society, male citizens in the prime of life. Choruses most often represent groups of people who are socially marginal or otherwise disqualified from action: women, slaves, foreigners, the old. At the same time, choruses retain the authority to articulate central communal values, even if they sometimes speak from the more limited perspectives of their assumed identities. In this respect too, their displacement from their traditional role in non-dramatic lyric is only partial.[4]

Finally, the chorus's integration into the tragic plot entails displacement from the circumstances represented by choral performance itself. In Greek culture, choral performance was widely understood as an expression of ideal conditions: a joyful, timeless enactment of an orderly community, with vigorous participants acting in harmony and displaying just the right degree of hierarchy—with enough, but not too much, difference between leaders and followers. The performers might be singing about painful experiences and dysfunctional circumstances, but the occasion itself was affirmative. This disjunction is well illustrated by the chorus of gods in the *Homeric Hymn to Apollo*, an ideal ensemble that served as a prototype for human choruses, who embodied for their mortal communities a temporary state of Olympian joy. Led by Apollo and surrounded by dancing goddesses, the Muses 'sing all together with a beautiful voice, | of the immortal blessings of the gods | and the sufferings of mortals, which they endure at the hands of the deathless gods | as they live out their lives, witless and helpless . . .' (*Hymn Hom. Ap.* 189–92).

---

[3] It is generally assumed that the tragic chorus still had a leader, referred to in modern scholarship as the *coryphaeus*, who spoke for the group in dialogue with the actors. But that figure has no distinct identity; our sense of his presence is not secured by textual evidence, but rests on the assumption that all choruses had leaders (cf. Dem. 21.60) and the seeming unlikelihood that a group of performers spoke in unison during spoken dialogue. Wilson (2000: 134, 353 n. 92).

[4] On choral marginality and its compatibility with cultural memory and authoritative speech, see Gould (1996) and Goldhill (1996). On choral authority, see also Mastronarde (2010: 98–121). For the important point that choral identities 'are precisely the categories excluded from dancing in a chorus of citizens', see Mullen (1982: 52).

As mimesis, tragedy implicates its choruses in those mortal sufferings, drawing them into mythical scenes of conflict and disorder, removed in time and space from the annual Athenian celebration in which the plays were presented. Tragic choruses find themselves in situations in which joyful singing and dancing are impossible, in which the most appropriate musical form is the lament. Yet they go on singing and dancing, combining mournful songs with adapted versions of other, more festive genres. Their periodic formal odes respond to the mythic plot but also evoke the immediate occasion of dramatic performance. And, even though choruses enter the world of the myth, they are not directly affected by the catastrophes of the tragic plot. As perennial survivors, they retain a timeless detachment from the events they help to convey.

The interplay between the chorus's part in the tragic action and its underlying status as a group of performers is a distinctive feature of tragic style, which reflects broader cultural assumptions about particular social roles and the significance of singing and dancing. The chorus's movements in and out of character give shape to the plot and produce shifts in emphasis between catastrophic episodes of tragic pathos and the continuous social order symbolized by chorality. The doubleness of tragic choral identity has been most thoroughly studied in relation to the ritual dimensions of choral perform-ance.[5] This discussion focuses instead on the fluctuating identities of male choruses in particular and on their place in tragedy's presentation of public life, locating the tragic chorus at the intersection of musical culture and politics.[6]

Tragic choruses take on male roles somewhat less often than female roles.[7] Likely reasons for this include women's association with lamentation, trage-dy's stress on female protagonists who invite attendance by female supporters, and the social disenfranchisement of women, which makes female choruses natural outsiders. Choruses representing men are less automatically marginal than those representing women and less different from the actual performers under the masks and costumes. Their interactions with the protagonists would thus have resonated more closely with contemporary Athenian politics, in which the relationship between highly placed, often aristocratic leaders and more ordinary citizens was a central and highly charged issue.

Male tragic choruses are marginalized to some degree through age: most are cast as old men whose scope for action is restricted, with only a few portraying men of military age. The preponderance of older male choruses may have been

---

[5] Henrichs (1995, 1996). Henrichs also highlights the ironic use of choral self-referentiality to create moments of false closure, when the complications of the plot appear to be resolved but are not.

[6] This is an expansion of Murnaghan (2011: 258–64).

[7] Foley (2003: 13), with further bibliography.

a way of focusing attention on the suffering protagonists without foregrounding the issue of their pronounced distinction from everyone else. As Helene
Foley puts it in a thoughtful overview of tragic choral identity: 'Socially
marginal choruses make [awkward] issues of leadership oblique or implicit,
whereas . . . choruses consisting of soldiers potentially raise such delicate questions more directly.'[8] But, even obliquely and implicitly, the experiences of
older choruses bear significantly on the protagonists' performance as leaders.
Those choruses' assignment to a marginal position is not absolute, but vari-
able, and, as we will see, comparable to that of younger men. And both older
and younger male choruses do, at times, express a nostalgic longing for their
lost centrality, competing for sympathy with the protagonists who have
pushed them to the edges of the action.

In strictly political terms, old men are not marginal in the same way as
women or slaves: choruses of old men usually depict citizens of the community in which the play is set and are often treated as trusted advisers. But they
are limited by their unsuitability for physical action, and their age means that
they have entered the realm of time and change, which is the province of the
tragic plot, but which choral performance itself disavows. Being old means not
being able to dance, and thus having no place in the idealized community of
the chorus.

In Greek culture, advanced age was generally seen as a disqualification for
choral participation, which was physically demanding.[9] The plight of the
superannuated dancer is among the hardships of old age bemoaned in lyric
poetry. Alcman appeals to a group of young girls, such as those for whom he
wrote songs: 'No longer, o sweet-sounding, holy-voiced girls | can my limbs
carry me. Would that, would that, I was a cerylus [a male halcyon thought to
be carried on the wings of females when too old to fly]' (26 *PMG*). Sappho also
contrasts herself with girls who can still enjoy the gifts of the Muses: 'but in my
case, old age has seized my once tender body . . . my knees will not carry me |
though they once were light like fawns for dancing' (58 Voigt).

Such expressions of nostalgic regret were complemented by a popular
notion that being in choruses was rejuvenating, so that, if old people were
dancing, they were effectively no longer old.[10] This rejuvenation was linked to

[8] Foley (2003: 12). On tragedy's engagement with the Athenians' often ambivalent attitudes
towards their leaders, see Griffith (1995, 1998), stressing the people's dependence on, and
admiration for, prominent aristocrats; Seaford (1994: esp. 344–6), stressing their need to free
themselves from aristocratic domination.

[9] Foley (2003: 5).

[10] There may be hints of rejuvenation in both the Alcman and the Sappho poems. Alcman's
image of the old cerylus kept aloft by female birds suggests vicarious animation through the
dances of young girls. Bierl (2009*b*) proposes that Sappho later in the same poem redeems her
situation by identifying herself, in her role as a chorus leader, with Eos, the dawn goddess and a
mythological figure of perennial youth.

wine and the powers of Dionysus and thus forms an important theme of Anacreontic poetry, which celebrates the joys of social gatherings marked by drinking and music: 'when the old man dances | he is old if you look at his hair | but young at heart.'[11]

In Euripides' *Bacchae*, the surviving tragedy that is most directly concerned with Dionysus, this rejuvenating effect is dramatized in a scene in which two old men, the Theban king Cadmus and the blind prophet Teiresias, are inspired by Dionysus to dance (Eur. *Bacch.* 170–209). An ancient proverb, which may lie behind this episode, extends the benefits of Dionysian inspiration beyond the dancer to the entire society: 'when the old man dances, all is well.'[12] An old man dancing betokens a society that is inclusive and harmonious, in which differences of many kinds can be made to disappear. Thus the comic resolution of Menander's *Dyscolus* requires, not only a wedding that unites rich and poor, urban and rural, but a final episode in which two servants force the anti-social old grouch Cnemon to attend the wedding feast and join the dance.

The social benefit of old men dancing receives an extensive theoretical grounding in Plato's late dialogue *Laws*, in which *choreia* is identified as an indispensable source of civic health, both as an expression of social order and as the principal means of educating good citizens.[13] The three speakers who conjure up an ideal city over the course of the dialogue are themselves old men, and their city is shaped by the good sense and moderation that come with age. These attributes of the old are manifested in their dances, which involve restrained and harmonious movements and songs on uplifting subjects. To assure that such dances take place, the Athenian who leads the discussion institutes a chorus of older men, aged 30 to 60, in addition to choruses of boys and of younger men. When one of his interlocutors find this prospect *atopos*, 'out of the ordinary', the Athenian insists that the practice will maximize the good influence of the most trustworthy citizens; he also stipulates that men over 40 should be allowed greater amounts of wine to stimulate their participation in the chorus of elders, which is under the patronage of Dionysus. The conviviality that Dionysus sponsors is itself rejuvenating: 'a tonic so that we may recover our youth and, through forgetfulness of care, the temper of our souls may become softer instead of harder, like iron melting in a fire' (Pl. *Leg.* 666b7–c1).

The Dionysian chorus of elders sets the tone for the entire city. They select the most appropriate songs, 'and singing, they both themselves enjoy a

---

[11] *Anacreonta* 39.3–5; cf. 1, 7, 47, 51.53; Ladianou (2005: 51–4); P. A. Rosenmeyer (1992: 60–1).

[12] Slater (2000: 117–21).

[13] On *choreia* in the *Laws*, see Mullen (1982: 53–7), Lonsdale (1993: 21–43), and Peponi, Chapter 1, this volume.

harmless pleasure in the moment and become leaders for the younger men through their appropriate embrace of the finest manners' (Pl. *Leg.* 670d8–e1). For ordinary old men like the dialogue's three speakers, the institution of choruses for younger men still provides an opportunity for rejuvenation (in a more mediated form) and for shaping the next generation.

> While our young men are prepared to dance themselves, we old men think that we are spending our time well when we watch them, rejoicing in their fun and their festivity, since our own nimbleness is now deserting us. Longing for that and clinging to it, we propose in this way contests for those who are best able, through reminiscence, to reawaken our youth.　(Pl. *Leg.* 657d1–8).[14]

Whether the old men in question are actually dancing, or whether their nostalgia is assuaged by the dancing of others, these scenarios present young and old in perfect harmony: one generation replicates another to perpetuate a stable, unchanging, ideal community. This is a fundamentally conservative vision, in which the perennial youth of the old results from the willing adoption of traditional values by the young. In real communities, marked by factional politics and historical change, generational conflict is an inescapable fact of life and a locus for multiple forms of cultural and political division. In classical Greece, this may have been less the case in Sparta, the city on which the *Laws* is most closely based, than in Athens, the city that is addressed, however indirectly, in tragedy. In general, there is more automatic deference towards the old in oligarchic and collectivist societies than in democratic and individualistic societies,[15] and, in late-fifth-century Athens, political divisions deepened by increased wealth, empire, new forms of education, and the growing power of rhetoric were often cast in terms of a generation gap.[16] Thucydides' account of the decision to mount the Sicilian expedition of 415 provides a prime illustration of the way political conflict could be expressed in generational terms.

Thucydides presents the decision through a debate in the Athenian assembly between two leaders, the older Nicias, who argues against the expedition from a position of conservative caution, and the younger Alcibiades, who favours it from a position of imperialist expansionism, as well as personal ambition.[17] Nicias casts the issue as a conflict between sensible, unassertive elders and heedless, disrespectful youth.

---

[14] Cf. *Anacreonta* 53, where the speaker first regains youth by looking at the νέων ὅμιλον ('company of young men'), then himself 'takes wing' and dances.

[15] Falkner (1995: 152).

[16] Strauss (1993: ch, 5, esp. 145–8).

[17] On Alcibiades as the most notorious representative of unruly and insubordinate youth during that period, see Strauss (1993: 148–53).

Seeing this man's supporters sitting here, I feel alarmed. For my part, I call on the support of the older men among you. Do not be cowed, if you are sitting next to one of them, for fear of seeming weak if you do not vote to go to war. Do not, like them, fall foolishly in love with what is far off.   (Thuc. 6.13.1)

Nicias' words conjure up a dystopian image of communal division, in which men who are sitting together in the assembly are sharply opposed, and their interactions are unequal and uncivil. In his response, Alcibiades disingenuously links his own cause to the overcoming of this generational divide.

Do not be deterred by Nicias' arguments for non-intervention and his pitting of young against old; instead, in our accustomed way, like our fathers who when young, taking counsel with their elders, raised the city to its present condition, let us now in the same manner try to take it further.   (Thuc. 6.18.6).

Alcibiades' strategy is more successful than Nicias', with the result that old and young are united in the collective folly of the expedition (Thuc. 6.24.3).

This outcome reflects the deterioration of Athenian leadership since the death of Pericles fifteen years before. Alcibiades, Pericles' nephew, clearly manifests the detrimental self-seeking that, in Thucydides' view, characterized Pericles' successors, even if Thucydides portrays him less negatively than many of his other critics did (presenting Alcibiades as himself a victim of vicious rivalry and attributing the claim that Alcibiades was aiming at tyranny to public opinion). Nicias links Alcibiades' faulty advice to his excessive desire for financial gain and personal aggrandisement: 'Do not allow this person to shine brilliantly as an individual by putting the city in danger. Remember that such men harm the public interest as they spend their private wealth' (Thuc. 6.12.2). Alcibiades responds that his reputation for excess is due to envy, and his conspicuous outlays have brought glory to the city, while involving him in risks that justify his being *mê ison*, 'not on an equal footing' (Thuc. 6.16.4). Among these outlays, he includes performing the role of *chorêgos*, the funder of dramatic performances who represented, like the tragic actor, an outgrowth of the traditional chorus leader.

Numerous unsympathetic sources portray Alcibiades' behaviour in the role of *chorêgos* as aggressively self-promoting, arrogant, and abusive. They claim that he made eye-catching appearances in dazzling purple robes, used violence against his rivals, and showed disdain for the rules governing poetic competition. One accuser describes him as having struck a competing *chorêgos* during a dithyrambic contest while relying on his wealth and power to prevail nonetheless with the judges; the speaker goes on to draw an explicit connection between this and Alcibiades' other transgressive acts and the terrible things done by tragic protagonists.[18]

---

[18] Andoc. 4.23. On Alcibiades as a *chorêgos*, see Wilson (2000: 148–55).

Thucydides' account of the Sicilian debate reveals, in the context of a historical narrative with notable tragic colouring,[19] the conceptual link between an excessively prominent individual and the disempowerment and intimidation of the old. This association makes the group of old men a natural identity for the tragic chorus, whose involvement with high-placed individuals may compromise their ability to dance, or to enjoy the participation in civic life that old men dancing symbolize. The rejuvenation experienced by old men who drink and dance makes age a fluid condition that varies in intensity as choral identity also does in general. The old man who dances is a paradox that matches the two-sided tragic chorus.

A number of critics have pointed out that older figures in tragedy are not always marginalized. They can be sidelined during war or slighted by disrespectful younger men, as in Nicias' account of the Athenian assembly, but they can also be treated as respected advisers and voices of communal authority. In a recent study, U. S. Dhuga shows in detail that tragic choruses representing old men are not necessarily ineffective or uninvolved in the action. Tellingly, Dhuga finds a strong correlation between choral vitality and good leadership: 'the greatest determinant of an old man chorus' activity or passivity is the chorus' relationship to the ruler.'[20] Within the mythic plot, a responsible political leader has the same effect as Dionysus at a symposium or choral revel.

In two tragedies with idealized Athenian settings and restrained, proto-democratic leaders, Sophocles' *Oedipus at Colonus* and Euripides' *Heracleidae*, choruses of old men are active in the reception and defence of a suppliant who is also old. Their fictional identity enhances their role as sympathetic supporters of tragic protagonists whose personal misfortunes are amplified by the trials of old age.[21] At the same time, their sense of their age is also mitigated by their situation in a justly ordered city.

The chorus of the *Oedipus at Colonus* responds to Oedipus and his long sufferings with an ode on the irreversible horrors of getting older, a process in which the loss of youth first brings awareness of political strife.

> When youth has gone,
> With its blithe obliviousness,
> What trial does not follow?
> What ordeal is lacking?
> Envy, factions, strife, battles
> And slaughter. Then the hateful fate takes hold:

---

[19] Greenwood (1996: 38–9, 87, 98–107).

[20] Dhuga (2011: 9). See also the important observation that in plays with bad leaders 'old age appears in varying degrees to be a performance metaphor for inaction within political contexts that do not afford the choruses . . . strong advisory power' (p. 46).

[21] On the ordeal of old age as a tragic theme, especially in the plays of Euripides, see Falkner (1995: 169–71).

> Final, powerless, unsociable,
> Friendless old age...
>
> (Soph. *OC* 1229–37)

As citizens of Athens, however, they are themselves sheltered from the ill-effects of political conflict, and they experience a certain exemption from age that they locate in their city. Immediately after an ode in which they celebrate Colonus as a place of timeless beauty where 'revelling Dionysus always walks... nor do the choruses of the Muses shun it' (Soph. *OC* 678–9, 691–2), Creon appears. Antigone and Oedipus call on the chorus to live up to this praise with a guarantee of Oedipus' safety, and it gives a ringing answer: 'Fear not. You will have it. Even if I happen to be old | the strength of this land has not grown old' (Soph. *OC* 726–7). The chorus stands up to Creon and even tries to restrain him physically from kidnapping Antigone and going after Oedipus, until their younger king Theseus arrives to take over.

The elders of Colonus do not break the illusion of their fictional role, but they do display a physical energy linked to conditions under which old men might be expected to dance: Dionysus is present and the city is properly ordered. Among the many choruses that do break the dramatic illusion, the most famous is the contrasting chorus of Sophocles' earlier Oedipus play, *Oedipus Tyrannus*, Theban elders who respond to mounting evidence of transgression involving the royal family—oracles circumvented, a murderer unpunished—by asking τί δεῖ με χορεύειν; ('Why should I dance?') (Soph. *OT* 896).

In the *Children of Heracles*, the chorus members combine a sympathetic response to old age with countervailing references to themselves as dancers.[22] At the centre of the play is an offstage battle, in which the forces of Athens defeat an army of Argive invaders who are pursuing the children of Heracles and their aged leader Iolaus. Iolaus insists on joining the battle despite his obvious frailty, and the chorus tries to deter him, insisting that 'there is no way that you can get your youth back again' (Eur. *Heracl.* 702–8). But, as we learn from a messenger's speech, Iolaus does recover his youth during the battle, in a miraculous recapitulation of Heracles' marriage to Hebe, the goddess of youth. Onstage, the chorus subtly re-enacts Iolaus' offstage rejuvenation through shifting references to choral song. Before the battle, the chorus members sing an ode in which they promise uncompromising defence of the suppliants (in terms that make them virtual fighters) and call on Athena's aid. To secure her support, they evoke the city's unflagging worship, embodied in dances of the young:

> For the honour of many sacrifices
> Is always yours, and the waning

---

[22] On the self-referentiality of this chorus, see Henrichs (1996: 50–4).

Day of each month never lacks
Songs of the young, dances of choruses.
On the windy hillside
Sacred shouts rise up
With the beating feet of girls.

(Eur. *Heracl.* 777–83)

In a manner reminiscent of Alcman, the chorus of old men relies for support on the dancing of young girls. But when they have heard the news of the battle, they present themselves as dancers and associate the joys of the symposium with pleasure in a happy ending.

For me dancing is sweet [ἐμοὶ χορὸς μὲν ἡδύς], when the clear
Flute graces a feast,
And Aphrodite might be there.
There is pleasure to be had
In seeing the good fortune
Of friends who seemed to be without it.

(Eur. *Heracl.* 892–7)

In Euripides' *Heracles*, a chorus of old men dwells even more openly on the dynamics of dancing and old age, while contending with a tyrannical ruler, Lycus, who has usurped the Theban throne in Heracles' absence and threatens Heracles' wife, children, and old father Amphitryon. They enter the scene emphatically not dancing: they lean on staves, they compare their steps to the foot-dragging of a yoked calf pulling a wagon uphill, and they hope to revive their former vigour only so they can support one another when they fall.[23] They compare themselves to ἰηλέμων γέρων ἀοιδός . . . πολιὸς ὄρνις ('old singer of laments, the grey bird') (the swan, who sings just before death) and label themselves ἔπεα μόνον ('nothing but words') (Eur. *HF* 110–12). When they try to defend Amphitryon, Lycus turns on them and points to their further marginalization under his regime: 'you old ones . . . remember: my tyranny has made you slaves' (Eur. *HF* 246–51); they know themselves to be οὐδέν ('nothing') (Eur. *HF* 314), unable to protect Amphitryon.

But, when Heracles unexpectedly returns, the chorus's tune begins to change. It performs an ode in which the first strophe and antistrophe are devoted to the awfulness and unfairness of old age, but in which the second strophe is a declaration that it will go on singing and dancing nonetheless.

---

[23] Cf. Hecuba in Euripides' *Trojan Women*, who, in her initial monody, responds to her age and miserable circumstances by twisting her back and spine in a rocking motion that goes with crying out ἄτας . . . ἀχορεύτους ('undanceable troubles') (Eur. *Tro.* 116–21). Battezzatto (2005: 80–1). Cf. also the chorus of old men in Aeschylus' *Agamemnon*, which similarly describes itself as weak and dependent on staves (Aesch. *Ag.* 72–82). See Dhuga (2011: 75–128) for a thorough comparison of the choruses of the *Heracles* and the *Agamemnon* as old men contending with non-Athenian, tyrannical rulers.

I will not stop joining
The Graces with the Muses,
The sweetest yokemates.
May I never be bereft of music!
May I never lack for garlands!
Old singer that I am,
I still cry out to Mnemosyne,
Still I sing a victory song
For Heracles,
With wine-giving Dionysus,
With the song of the seven-stringed tortoise shell
And the Libyan flute.
Not yet will I stop honouring
The Muses, who set me dancing.

(Eur. HF 673–86)

The opportunity to sing a victory song for Heracles energizes these old men and makes them lifelong singers and dancers.[24] In the final antistrophe, their earlier swan song is recalled, but it too has been transformed and rejuvenated: instead of a lament, it is now a paean, a song of thanksgiving, equated with the paean sung by a perennial chorus of young women, the Delian maidens.[25] The chorus's next ode is performed while Heracles defeats Lycus inside the house. It announces that its songs have changed; it wants to dance; and it calls for choruses throughout Thebes, for βέβακ' ἄναξ ὁ καινός, ὁ δὲ παλαίτερος κρατεῖ ('the new ruler is gone, and the former one is in power') (Eur. *HF* 769–70). The play is only half over, and the terrible next chapter in which Heracles goes mad and kills his family is still to come; the chorus will soon revert to laments or τίν' Ἅιδα χορόν ('some dance of Hades') (Eur. *HF* 1026–7).[26] But, in a self-referential move that brings closure to the first stage of the action, they show how the right (time-honoured and legitimate) leader allows old men to defeat time, recover their youth, and dance.

The Athenians who embarked on the Sicilian expedition paid a harsh price for their willingness to be led by Alcibiades. Thucydides labels the subsequent defeat the most wretched in Greek history and a case of total destruction: 'infantry, fleet, and everything else, all was lost, and of the many who went, few returned home [ἀπονόστησαν]' (Thuc. 7.87.6). Critics have noted the epic flavour of the verb used here for returning home, *aponosteo*, which is related

---

[24] On epinician associations throughout the choral odes of the *Heracles*, see Swift (2010: 123–33).

[25] On the significance of the Delian maidens here, and the self-presentation of this chorus generally, see Henrichs (1996: 54–62).

[26] This is pointedly paradoxical, since dancing is antithetical to Hades, which is labelled ἀνυμέναιος ἄλυρος ἄχορος (wedding-song-less, lyreless, chorusless) by the chorus of *Oedipus at Colonus* (Soph. *OC* 1221–2). On the theme of 'negated music' in tragedy, see Segal (1993).

to the noun *nostos*, a key Homeric term for homecoming, the ultimate goal and reward of heroic endeavour.[27] *Nostos* is also, of course, the root of the modern word 'nostalgia', which was first coined in the seventeenth century to indicate a longing for home rather than a longing for past time such as might be inspired by political decline or a burdensome old age.[28] But temporal and spatial dislocation can go hand in hand, as is shown by the post-Periclean Athenians, who live into a time of decline, in which they are carried off to a faraway place, never to return. This connection unites the two types of male chorus found in extant tragedy: old men, such as those already discussed, and younger men of military age, who figure in two plays of Sophocles dealing with the Troy legend, *Ajax* and *Philoctetes*.

The interconnectedness of old age, nostalgia, failed leadership, and lost homecoming can be seen in another play with a chorus of old men, Aeschylus' *Persians*, our earliest surviving tragedy and one with only two actors and an especially prominent chorus.[29] The Persian elders have been left at home while all the younger men have gone to war against Greece, but they do not suffer because of their age. They are highly respected guardians (Aesch. *Pers.* 4), and they never mention the physical debilities or other humiliations of old age. They suffer because of their concern for the absent army, experiencing first an anxious longing for those who have gone, then a wrenching grief when news arrives of the devastating defeat at Salamis.[30] Their main role is to lament their departed compatriots. And yet, their suffering is nonetheless an effect of the passage of time. The Persian defeat results from a generational shift: the rash young Xerxes has taken over from his father Darius and led his subjects to their deaths.

The chorus spells out the implications of this change in Persian leadership after they and the queen have briefly reawakened the past by raising the ghost of Darius. When the ghost departs, after decrying the excesses of his heedless, overreaching son, the chorus sings a nostalgic lament for Darius' reign.

> *O popoi*, what a great and excellent
> Life of civic order [πολισσονόμου βιοτᾶς] was ours, when the old
> all sufficing undamaging invincible
> godlike King Darius ruled the land!

---

[27] Allison (1997: 512–15); Greenwood (2006: 88). Rood (1998: 242–6) points out that Thucydides' usage should be understood as reflecting the broad *nostos* tradition, as seen in tragedy and in Herodotus' *Histories*, rather than as a specific allusion to Homer.

[28] On the history of the term, see Boym (2002: 3–4); Matt (2007: 469–71).

[29] First produced in 472, *The Persians* pre-dates Thucydides and may well have influenced his reference to the failed *nostos* of most of the Athenians, as Rood (1998: 246) suggests.

[30] On the chorus's enactment of longing for the departed army as a prominent form of action in the play, see Hopman (2009).

First we proved ourselves glorious on military campaigns,
and then a system of laws [νομί(σ)ματα] steadfast as towers, regulated everything (?)
Our men returned home again from wars
successfully, uninjured and unharmed.

(Aesch. *Pers.* 852–61, trans. E. Hall)

Despite textual and interpretative problems in this passage, it is clear that the reign of Darius is presented as a time of good government and the rule of law, similar to the idealized past Athens of the *Heracleidae* and the *Oedipus at Colonus*. In a particularly pointed contrast, Darius' superior leadership is identified with the successful *nostos* of all of his followers. Furthermore, for the chorus, Darius' reign was more congenial simply because it occurred when they were young. When the ghost first appears, he addresses them as Πέρσαι γεραιοί ('old men of Persia') but also as ἥλικές θ' ἥβης ἐμῆς ('agemates of my youth'), stressing their close bond and chronological parity (Aesch. *Pers.* 681–2). Closeness in age is a common feature of non-dramatic choruses and one of the factors that promotes equal relations among their members and between their members and their leaders.[31] For the Persian elders, the reign of Darius better matches the ideal of chorality, both because Darius was an inherently better leader than Xerxes and because he was less sharply distinguished from those who followed him. Their present laments are not explicitly set against past dancing, but they do recall with regret an earlier, better time when, in the prime of life and under a better leader, they went out to fight and returned unharmed.

This image of Darius is ahistorical in general terms and specifically contradicts the account of his defeat at Marathon given elsewhere in the play.[32] But it is rhetorically effective: the nostalgia of the *Persians'* old chorus accentuates the dysfunction of Xerxes' regime by opposing it to an internal Persian past that (however improbably) echoes its external present vanquisher, thriving, democratic Athens. The chorus's relationship to this idealized past helps to naturalize the oddly hybrid tenor of their laments, which blend bitter expressions of personal loss with characterizations of Xerxes' regime that sound like Athenian patriotic rhetoric.

The Persian chorus condemns Xerxes for his failure to assure the *nostos* of his men. In their long central lament, the chorus members emphasize his agency by dwelling on his name:

Xerxes led them away, *popoi*
Xerxes destroyed them, *totoi*,

---

[31] Calame (1997: 27–9).
[32] Cf. Aesch. *Pers.* 244. For further discussion of 'the recuperation and idealization of Dareios, as perfect king-and-father, master-and-god', see Griffith (1998: 57–62).

Xerxes wrong-headedly drove everything on
in seafaring ships.

(Aesch. *Pers.* 550–4, trans. E. Hall)

They commemorate their lost countrymen in detail, causing many of their names to be sounded, first in a long introductory expression of concern (Aesch. *Pers.* 1–64), then in their encounter with Xerxes, in which they require him to specify the men he has lost (Aesch. *Pers.* 955–1006).

In the *Persians'* choral account of a justly doomed military disaster, champions of the subordinates deprived of *nostos* have a prominent voice. In contrast, the epic prototype of the *nostos* plot, the *Odyssey*, presents its story through a narrative voice aligned with Odysseus, the leader who returns from war in solitary triumph. Concern for the fate of Odysseus' men is registered in the poem, but effectively neutralized. The narrative opens with a pre-emptive claim that Odysseus tried to bring his men home, but they sealed their own fate through reckless folly (Hom. *Od.* 1.5–9). At the end of the poem, the father of a dead suitor protests Odysseus' wholesale elimination of all rivals, both the men he took to Troy and lost and the slaughtered suitors (Hom. *Od.* 24.426–9). The result is a revolt by the suitor's relatives, but this is quickly squelched through a show of power from Odysseus followed by a truce imposed by Athena. The poem ends with an ἔκλησις ('amnesty') (Hom. *Od.* 24.485), and the lost companions are officially forgotten along with the dead suitors. Odysseus' failure as a leader is revealed, but he is exempted from any consequences.[33]

The choral form of tragedy allows the ordinary men who follow a prominent leader to be heard directly, and Sophocles' two surviving Trojan War plays make use of that opportunity.[34] The chorus of Salaminian sailors attached to Ajax in the *Ajax* and the chorus of sailors attached to Neoptolemus in the *Philoctetes* are both strikingly concerned with *nostos*.[35] When the chorus of the *Ajax* realizes that Ajax has dealt with his humiliation by killing himself, their first words are ὤμοι ἐμῶν νόστων ('There goes my homecoming!') (Soph. *Aj.* 900). Throughout the play, they lament their dislocation from Greece to

---

[33] On the leader's failure to save the men who depend on him as a pervasive theme of both Homeric epics, see Haubold (2000).

[34] So, evidently, did Aeschylus' lost *Myrmidons*, which presented Achilles' withdrawal from the army and decision to return as told in *Iliad* 9 and 16–18. Surviving fragments suggest that the Myrmidons who formed the chorus were sharply critical of Achilles for his selfish inactivity, accusing him of betrayal (frs 131, 132 Radt). His response was a stark silence (famous in antiquity for its dramatic effect), which would have dramatized the complete estrangement of chorus and leader; this may have been overcome by the end of the play through shared lament for the death of Patroclus. On the play and the trilogy of which it formed part, see Michelakis (2002: 22–57).

[35] This concern with the homecoming of ordinary sailors of is one of several ways in which the play resonates with Thucydides' account of Athens in the last stages of the Peloponnesian War. Greenwood (2006: 98–107).

Troy, which is closely tied to the destructive passage of time.[36] In one ode, they contrast the unchanging nature of their near-Athenian home with the wearing length of their exile:

> Oh glorious Salamis, I know that you
> Still stand, sea-stroked, favoured by gods,
> Prominent for all to see,
> While for me time has grown old [παλαιὸς ἀφ᾽ οὗ χρόνος]
> As miserable beyond counting, I live on,
> Stuck on the grassy ground of Ida
> Worn down by time . . .

> (Soph. *Aj.* 596–605)

Like old men who feel their age, warriors on campaign are cut off from the joys of the symposium; this exclusion from festivity creates a significant contrast with the performers playing the sailors, who were dancing in Athens and were exempt from military service in order to do so.[37] In a later ode, the sailors curse the man who invented war and forced them and countless others into scenarios of proliferating trouble, πόνοι πρόγονοι πόνων ('griefs generating griefs'). 'It was he who denied me the delicious fellowship of garlands and deep cups, the sweet clanging of flutes . . .' (Soph. *Aj.* 1192–1210).

The chorus of the *Philoctetes* is distinguished by its especially tight integration into the action of the play. The sailors are closely identified with their leader Neoptolemus and offer little in the way of detached commentary or general reflection. Neoptolemus is portrayed as a young man finding his moral compass, faced with choices that will define the relationship of the younger generation to the older: as he struggles to live up to his dead father Achilles, he has to choose between two living father figures, the wronged Philoctetes and the devious Odysseus. Following Neoptolemus' lead, the chorus supports his initial choice to enact Odysseus' scheme to lure Philoctetes from Lemnos to Troy (which cannot be conquered without him); this requires pretending that Neoptolemus will take Philoctetes home to Greece. The chorus speaks up forcefully, if duplicitously, to urge Neoptolemus to fulfil Philoctetes' desire for homecoming (Soph. *Phil.* 507–18). Later, when Neoptolemus and Philoctetes have gone inside the cave and the chorus is alone on stage, they sing an ode in which they express compassion for Philoctetes and end by declaring that Neoptolemus will take him home (Soph. *Phil.* 719–29).

This passage is a critical puzzle, since the chorus is well aware that Neoptolemus' promise to Philoctetes is a ruse and he intends to take

---

[36] Tragedies with Trojan settings are 'specifically concerned with the *loss* of spatial coordinates for the chorus' (Goldhill 1996: 246).

[37] Wilson (2000: 79).

Philoctetes in the opposite direction, to Troy.[38] A possible solution stems from
the observation that the chorus seems here to disengage from the immediate
dramatic moment: they freely imagine an ending that fits better with their
sense of justice than with the exigencies of Odysseus' plot, and they speak from
a longer perspective, looking beyond the immediate aftermath of the action, to
the time when the war will be over.[39] They take a more farsightful view of
Neoptolemus as well, suggesting the fundamental decency that will later cause
him to abandon his trick and honour his promise to Philoctetes, so that the
intervention of Heracles is required to get Philoctetes to Troy.

As the actors prepare to leave for Troy, the chorus caps the action with
another premature reference to homecoming: 'let us all set off together | once
we have prayed to the salt-sea Nymphs | to come as saviours of *nostos* [νόστου
σωτῆρας]' (Soph. *Phil.* 1471). These speeches may be odd from the standpoint
of dramatic construction, but the sailors are fulfilling their identity as a chorus
both by situating the play's action within a longer span of time and by
foregrounding the goal of homecoming. *Nostos* is an appropriate concern
for them both as Homeric warriors and as choral performers, since *nostos* is
an important theme in choral lyric as well as in epic. In epinician poetry,
successful *nostos* is the occasion of performance: the song marks and facilitates
the victor's return home from the games.[40] In a play that ends with its
characters' stories unconcluded, the chorus gestures towards a stronger kind
of closure—both an end to Philoctetes' mythic adventures and a return from
the realm of myth to the time and place of performance.

Modern critics sometimes judge the choruses of the *Ajax* and the *Philoctetes*
negatively, charging them with short-sighted self-concern, as if the tragic
chorus has an obligation to be self-effacing and to direct our attention and
sympathy only to the more important and compelling actors. One of Sophocles' most sensitive interpreters describes the chorus of the *Ajax* as 'simple-
minded and self-centred' and the chorus of the *Philoctetes* as having an
attitude of 'weak pity and strong self-interest'.[41] But those choruses deserve
to be read more positively as speaking for the many who are sacrificed to the
ambitions of the glorious few.[42] Their advocacy is more muted than that of the
Persian elders; their self-seeking leaders are Greek heroes, not a barbarian
despot, and they are themselves, like all choruses, destined to survive. But they
too are living up to their identity as a chorus, making a claim for communal
well-being and reflecting, in their shifting powers as both characters and
dancers, the performance of their leaders, who fail when they leave the chorus
too far behind.

---

[38] For a survey of possible solutions, see Gardiner (1987: 31–6).
[39] Kitzinger (2008: 106–8).
[40] Crotty (1982: 104–38); Kurke (1991: 15–34); Rutherford (1997: 49).
[41] Winnington-Ingram (1980: 23, 294 n. 44).   [42] So Gardiner (1987: 76).

A 'Senecan' Theatre of Cruelty: Audience, Citizens, and Chorus in Late-Sixteenth and Early Seventeenth-Century French Dramas

Christian Biet

It is generally acknowledged that Elizabethan drama inherits from Seneca its obsession with blood, cruelty, and violence. It is less well known in critical circles that French tragedies of the same period are also terribly 'Senecan', equally obsessed with violence and able to represent this violence directly on stage.[1] In some respects, Elizabethan drama and the early French tragedies of the end of the sixteenth and beginning of the seventeenth centuries resemble each other to such a degree that they are almost identical in form and in subject, especially in their adoption of Senecan tragedy as a model. During this period, France was not as 'classical' as it would later become, if indeed French theatre has ever been as classical as certain twentieth-century critics, who have their own understanding of the term, suggest.

The adoption of the Senecan model by French dramatists also extended to their use of the chorus, which often played a significant role in the action. While the Greek chorus had represented the city in certain ways, thus providing some kind of link between the characters and spectators, this link had clearly been severed in many respects by the time of the Roman Republic. By the end of the sixteenth and the beginning of the seventeenth centuries, it had become even less secure. Where the chorus features in the printed texts of these French tragedies (largely published in Paris or in Rouen), we can be

I would like to thank Teresa Bridgeman and Cécile Dudouyt for their stylistic revisions and help in the translation of source materials.

[1] Apart from Raymond Lebègue (1954) and Forsyth (1994), only a few articles have been published on this topic. But, recently, Marie-Madeleine Fragonard, Fabien Cavaillé, Charlotte Bouteille-Meister, Corinne Meyniel, Sybile Chevallier-Micki, Tiphaine Karsenti, Mathilde Bernard, Michaël Meere, and I have been trying to recover this important corpus.

fairly certain either that the chorus's text was not performed on stage at all (because the troupes did not have enough actors to form a 'chorus' as such) or that there was a preference in performance for a single actor to declaim the words of the chorus (as has also sometimes been claimed of Senecan tragedy[2]). What is more, during the course of the seventeenth century, there was a clear lack of interest in words uttered by a collectivity—of whatever nature.

In Senecan tragedy we find a kind of equilibrium: the element of cruelty generally remains within the discourse and is not represented on stage, while the chorus provides a moral, political, or didactic interpretation of the atrocities taking place off stage. In the wake of the disasters of the sixteenth century, however, no such equilibrium seemed possible: the city could not trust those in power, indeed could not trust anyone, even the 'choric' elders. There was no political, moral, or aesthetic figure whom the spectators could trust to represent them: they now found themselves in a theatre where they were directly confronted by acts of extreme violence. How could a chorus intervene in such circumstances? The chorus seems to have gradually disappeared when faced with these onstage atrocities, which re-enacted current disasters or those of a very recent and bloody past.

Tragedy, then, could not endorse the politics of reconciliation promoted by the monarchy. Instead, it drew for its spectators a sketch of the terrible crimes that 'inhuman' humanity clearly continues to commit. The question of the chorus at this time in France, therefore, concerned not only poetics or rhetoric, but also political, religious, and social *representation*; and it was also a question of how to *represent* those facts, how to depict the violence of the world, and how to delineate the world itself. These two senses of the word *representation* (*aesthetic* and *political*) must accordingly both be taken into account when considering the increasing absence of the chorus during this period. As long as the presence of a collectivity on stage was viewed as useful and possible—in other words, as long as it was possible to translate Seneca to the stage or in a written text—the chorus could remain. But, once the theatre wished to *depict* through its action the violence, blood, and crimes of the actual world, it was no longer possible to send people out onto the stage to comment upon that violence.

TRAGEDY AS A RE-ENACTMENT OF RECENT HISTORY

In fact, these tragedies from the late-sixteenth and early seventeenth centuries function as a sort of re-enactment of the thirty years of civil and religious wars that troubled the second half of the sixteenth century. They were performed in the immediate aftermath of shocking violence and recent massacres to a

---

[2] See further Slaney, Chapter 6, this volume.

still-traumatized audience; and while, after thirty years of troubles, audiences may have rediscovered the pleasure of being inside a theatre and being a part of this very particular social gathering in conditions of relative calm, these same members of the theatrical audience also discovered a new way of seeing, observing, *and commenting on* the violent acts of the bloody years of the wars of religion that derived from their representation on stage.

This new theatre, unconstrained by the (so-called classical) rules invented by a later age, in fact left spectators free to comment on and judge its fictions. Except that the spectators did not confine themselves to commentary: they generally responded to whatever they saw and heard with a great hubbub of whistles and cries. It was as if the audience, three-quarters of whom were standing in the parterre while the remainder were seated in boxes or up in the galleries, had actively become a sort of chorus, responding to every remark, commenting on and discussing the action, creating a racket out of sheer enjoyment, for the pleasure of participating in this assembly. We could say, in short, that the chorus that formerly appeared within the tragedy was now external to it, embodied by the audience itself. The result of this shift was that the representatives of the people no longer appeared on stage; only heroes, kings, rulers and their agents, and representatives of powerful families who controlled the crowd were now to be found there. The many crimes, humiliations, and horrors that appeared on stage received no commentary from a notional 'populace'; instead they were simply portrayed, acted out in front of the spectators, who could themselves comment on and judge the actions of the historical characters. At the same time it was strikingly clear to these very varied spectators that the tragedy itself provided a commentary on events of the very recent past or, sometimes, on current events. And, if their interest was aroused by this fictional performance, there was, of course, no longer an onstage chorus to guide their views of what happened on stage.

Although the audience may have come to the theatre in a spirit of peace, abandoning the battles it had previously fought in the streets, it still came to watch, albeit at a distance, crimes and acts of violence and cruelty that recalled those fights. This same audience was free to discuss these crimes, not only as a way of consigning its experiences to a distant past, but also, paradoxically, in order to have the chance to respond to this past and the violence onstage. Some aspects of the fighting, then, were re-enacted on stage, and the spectators knew and came to watch. It would appear, then, that there was some degree of incompatibility between the attempts of the crown to promote a politics of reconciliation and the activities of the theatre. Hence, even if the kingdom and the king himself had espoused a policy intended to lead to reconciliation, or were attempting or claiming to do so, it was, at the same time, impossible to escape the dreams of retaliation, vengeance, and judgement still nurtured by the citizens of the kingdom. And what remained was an enduring fear: how could anyone prevent a recurrence of the wars of religion?

This is why Henry IV of France, in the Edict of Nantes, set out the legal requirement, following other similar ordinances or agreements, that his people should forget what had occurred, and he did so in the very first two articles of the Edict:

We (**Henry**, by the grace of God King of France and of Navarre) have, by this perpetual and irrevocable edict, established and proclaimed and do establish and proclaim:

I. First, that the recollection of everything done by one party or the other, between March, 1585 and our accession to the crown, and during all the preceding period of troubles, remain obliterated and forgotten, as if no such things had ever happened.

II. We forbid all our subjects, of whatever estate or quality, to revive its memory, to attack, resent, scold, or provoke each other with reproaches regarding past events, for whatever reason and on whatever pretext, to dispute, contest, quarrel, or to take umbrage or offence, in deed or word, but [command them] to contain themselves and live peacefully together as brothers, friends and fellow countrymen, on pain of punishment for those who contravene this order as disturbers of the peace and public rest.

Of course, this policy of oblivion or forgetting in the name of reconciliation and harmony, ordered by royal decree, extended to actors and authors. But, as the regime in France was a monarchy (and not a totalitarian state), exceptions could be made, particularly for authors who wrote for the regime, especially those who were in the process of writing the history of the new Bourbons. This is, however, the reason why authors and actors who were generally forbidden (by law) to express their views on the recent past, even through a character or role, and who were forbidden to portray this past (although it must be said that they sometimes did[3]), employed the strategy of a historical, or fictional, 'detour'. This digression through ancient or medieval history, or mythology, enabled them to recount and represent onstage, for the benefit of their audience, the horrors of a very recent past that was still vivid in people's memories. And, at the same time, the playwrights employed two theatrical devices. The first was common practice for the theatre of this period, and consisted of invoking the audience through direct and personal address. The second, more ancient, practice was increasingly rare, and involved the representation of the audience's supposed reaction, or guidance in this regard through the words of a chorus.

ENTER THE CHORUS

To examine further the devices of direct address and of choral commentary, I will examine a typical French Senecan tragedy of this period, *Scédase ou l'hospitalité violée* by Alexandre Hardy, published in 1624 and originally

---

[3] Bouteille-Meister (2011).

performed in Paris around 1604.[4] First it is important to note that, in order to comment on recent violence and events, this tragedy adopts a historical and classical turn, or 'detour', as it turns to Plutarch's *Lives of Illustrious Men* to provide an exemplary case that will enable it to stage the recent past and to pass judgement on it. Following Plutarch, Hardy constructs his drama around the story of a father—Scédase, a Leuctrian whose country is occupied by the Spartans—who leaves his two daughters at home alone, asking them to be both chaste and welcoming to foreigners; hospitable, in a word. He then departs the stage, leaving them caught in the double-bind of his paradoxical demand.

Two young aristocrats from Lacedemonia arrive, attempt to seduce Scédase's daughters, and, as they resist, rape them (this is shown onstage). As they scream, the Spartans slay them and throw them down a well. There are no witnesses. Having committed this double crime, they leave the house (the scene of the crime, which is also the stage). All these events were performed on a structure that was known at this time, in both English and French, as a 'scaffold' (*un échafaud*). At the beginning of the next act, Scédase, the father, returns, calls for his daughters, receives no answer, becomes worried, looks everywhere, makes enquiries, and finds a neighbour who has seen the two young Spartans, has heard the screams of the girls, and has seen the two men leaving, but who has not directly witnessed the crime (unlike the theatrical audience). Scédase and his neighbour then discover the two corpses in the well, and the grieving Scédase decides to accuse the two young and powerful aristocrats before the Spartan king (this trial will take place in the fifth act).

During the first four acts, the chorus of the Leuctrians, which is listed among the *dramatis personae* ('le Chœur des Leuctriens') and consequently is expected by readers to appear in the ensuing text of the play, is curiously absent. It does not appear at the end of each act, and thereby fails to perform its customary and ancient role: it does not express concern when it should, nor show indignation; and there are no lamentations following the crime and, even after the gruesome discovery, it does not speak or sing a word. So this 'chorus of the Leuctrians' does not follow the usual pattern for this period of systematically echoing at one remove the questions raised by the tragedy. It remains notably absent during the acts of violence, and, as we shall see, its echoes are only to be heard in the final act, after the trial, once the location has changed. It is only when Scédase comes back to his city that 'le Chœur des Leuctriens' finally appears to mourn and express its indignation.

The trial begins in the fifth act. Scédase builds his case, pleads well, but cannot provide sufficient evidence to prove that the two young men raped and slew his daughters. The only witness statements available to this grieving father come from his poor Leuctrian neighbours, but these defeated peasants

---

[4] Hardy (1624) in Biet (2006: 335–90).

have only heard the cries and moans and have not seen the crime. So, the king of Sparta, who is aware of the aristocratic strength of the young and powerful suspects, then asks for real and absolute proof. And it is here that a complex address is made. The king, in effect, seeks out any witness, both within the fictional world *and* among those assembled in the theatre. Since Scédase cannot find a single piece of evidence and since he is able to reiterate only the facts he has *deduced*, the king calls forward all possible witnesses (speaking directly to the theatrical audience, the spectators), asking: 'Who was witness to these murders and did nothing to prevent them?' ('Lequel ce meurtre vu précisément dépose? | Lequel fut spectateur et ne l'empêcha pas?', Act V, ll. 1165–6). The answer is, of course, the members of the audience, who are the only witnesses, who did nothing to prevent the crimes, who may even have appreciated or taken some pleasure in watching them; and who are, however, supposed to be in a different time, place, and reality from those occupied by Scédase and the king, and who therefore cannot say a word (or, in any case, whose words cannot be heard by the characters).

Our first observation is that, while the audience may be able to see, be shocked, be indignant, and even shout aloud, it cannot be heard. Our second is that it is probable that these spectators of 1604 were reminded that, some years previously, in their own lives, they or their relations witnessed crimes without taking action. They must now witness once more their past complicities. And they must, of course, be struck dumb by the situation, be unable to speak or to answer the king, but left instead to reflect on their past, their present, and themselves. The tragedy acquires the status of tragic *grand guignol*, a tragic puppet show organized according to the principles of classical dramaturgy, and following a common pattern of plays written in the aftermath of genocide, including those of the twentieth century. This pattern seizes spectators by the throat and forces them to reflect on their past conduct and behaviour and on what they have become.

In *Scédase*, then, there is no witness to speak out and no evidence. The two young Spartan aristocrats cannot, therefore, be convicted and Scédase is harshly and summarily dismissed from the trial scene. Bitter and resentful, he returns to his home, where he at last encounters the chorus of the Leuctrians; and sixteenth-century spectators, or at least those who have read Plutarch's famous text, will be aware that, in Plutarch's version, this double murder is the alleged cause of a second war, which leads to a military victory for the Thebans and Leuctrians over Sparta.

So, it is only during the fifth act, when the king and the real spectators have no opportunity to speak in the name of justice nor to act morally, that the philosophical representatives of morality at last intervene and debate moral issues. It is only during this act that the political representatives of the principal character and his people intervene. And it is only at the conclusion of this tragedy that the audience's aesthetic representatives intervene, an audience that cannot react properly to the performance and to the fiction. It is when Scédase loses his case, at the very end of the tragedy, that a dialogue begins between him and the chorus of the Leuctrians, from l. 1253 to l. 1344 (of 1366 lines). It can be divided into three sections.

First, the chorus laments the situation and weeps with Scédase, before expressing its pity for him:

> CHORUS OF LEUCTRIANS. Scédase, who deserves, it can be said,
>   The highest honours for his virtue,
>   Bears the mark of his wrath
>   Although to arouse it
>   This ancient, venerated by all,
>   Had to be told of the worst misfortune
>   Which could ever again beset
>   a poor father.
>   Two guests, monsters by nature,
>   Quenched the double flame
>   Of his chaste offspring,
>   After having consigned their honour to the tomb.
>   Oh Sun, at that hour
>   Did your course not come to an end?
>   But is this not he who returns weeping,
>   What tragedy do his tears portend?

On hearing of Scédase's desire to commit suicide, the chorus then tries to convince him to go on living:

> SCÉDASE. Friends, join this poor father
>   Who despairs of all human justice
>   Who goes to see if in eternal night
>   His rejected plea will not bear greater fruit.
>   Oh happy ones, bestow on me this final penance
>   A penance of piety rather than one filled with painful toil,
>   Like the journey whose end was the nearby tomb
>   That ravished my daughters in the flower of their youth.
>
> CHORUS OF LEUCTRIANS. Oh kindly Gods! Turn aside the wish
>   That is too clear in this regard,
>   Which conspires against his life
>   In order to find peace in that place.

Then, in the third section, the lamentation gives way to indignation:

> CHORUS OF LEUCTRIANS. How in our inaction can we allow
>   That this enraged inhuman being
>   Should commit murder
>   Against himself by his own hand?

Indignation becomes distress when Evandre, Scédase's neighbour, asks the people of Leuctria to attend the funerals. Is an armed rebellion imminent, as in

Plutarch's text? Possibly, but, just as the idea of rebellion is raised, the play comes to an end.

What, then, can be said of this tragedy? First, the crime and acts of cruelty are shown, represented on stage, including rape and murder. The audience sees that a legitimate enquiry leads to an injustice that is the consequence of the impossibility of speaking out in relation to the crimes that have just been committed. This injustice may be the result of the king's powerlessness to pass a fair judgement, but it is also the consequence of the spectators' inability to respond to the crimes they have witnessed on stage. And these spectators, therefore, are unable to testify when they are called upon to do so by the law. In a word, they are unable to prevent, oppose, or condemn the crimes because self-examination leads to the conclusion that they are cowards, whose response to violent situations is a state of shock. Before this, we have seen that the chorus, unable to fulfil its usual role, also fails to respond when faced with these crimes or to comment on them when they occurred. But, when the king and the spectators fail to pronounce and deliver justice, and when the victim needs to be helped, supported, and mourned, the chorus returns, reacts, and sings that it can provide succour.

Theatre historians would say that choruses were sometimes deleted by the theatre troupes themselves because there were not enough actors and not enough money to hire more, especially for such a limited role. Again theatre historians maintain that there were two different types of tragedy at this time, tragedies with a chorus, in keeping with humanist precepts, and tragedies without choruses, focusing on action and less inclined to put forward moral and philosophical maxims. And *Scédase* is closer to the second kind, except for its ending in choral lamentation. Here, however, the classical chorus merely laments and expresses its indignation as the principal character dies, having lost his case, his daughters, and his reason to go on living in his own country. Following on from such a catalogue of crimes, the final situation is thus in many ways analogous to that of the French people, at the beginning of the new century, as a result of their gruesome immediate past. In such circumstances, why should anybody care about a chorus that can do nothing but mourn? And, in such circumstances, it becomes clear that the chorus can be excluded from a form of tragedy in which the principal actor is crime itself.

Because the populace is in a state of uncertainty, because the representatives of the people (the chorus) are powerless to help despite their legitimacy, because the citizens can only bemoan their personal or collective guilt in the light of the events that have just occurred, there is nothing left to do but to watch the horror taking place before them, without the help of a chorus. It is a horror without mediation. And the performance, the action, is equally unmediated, without commentary. As the violence is transformed into cruelty, it is portrayed as violence into which everyone is drawn. In the absence of a mediating chorus of citizens, the characters alone have the ability to comment on the atrocities. The stage expresses the horror of the times and triggers the spectator's pity or compassion by emphasizing images of famine and the tragic consequences suffered by the victims. The fallen world of the early years of the seventeenth century is now plunged into suffering—a terrible, irresolvable, catastrophic suffering, and its general effect is to provoke indignation.

EXIT THE CHORUS, ENTER A DEVOURED ORGAN

The chorus, then, can certainly, at this time represent mourners (as in *Scédase*). It can also stand for a particular group, or the common interests of different groups, be they political, ethnic, or social. It is then a chorus divided between two hostile parties or armies, fighting each other with words and blows. We see this most clearly in *Les Portugais infortunés*,[5] in which the blacks (both men and women, 'Chœur d'Éthiopiens', 'Chœur d'Éthiopiennes') and the Portuguese (men and women too, 'Chœur de Matelots', 'Chœur de filles portugaises') appear on stage as theatrical and political groups. They are able to play a significant and spectacular part in the play (they dance and they fight) and simultaneously act to assist the black and Portuguese heroes (they comment). They do what the heroes tell them to do: they dance when they have to, fight during the staged battles, comment on the plot with general moral aphorisms, as ancient choruses do, express their fear at relevant moments in the story, and pass judgements on the characters' actions.

Les Portugais infortunés is about the shipwreck of a Portuguese vessel on the south-east coast of Africa. The Portuguese, lost in an unfamiliar landscape, search for food and meet people from another civilization who have never seen a white man before. This first encounter, marked by fears, hopes, negotiations, distrust, and misunderstandings, ends in a battle won by the blacks. The inhabitants of the savannah take everything from their enemies, even their clothes, and, victorious, leave the stage, for good. So that, during the fifth act, Portuguese men, women, and children are left mourning, starving, and dying, naked in the desert.

The four choruses of this tragedy, divided between two sides, take part in the action and, at the same time, comment on it. As they fight, triumph (for the blacks), mourn and die (for the whites) along with the main characters, they are caught inside a hopeless story of human history. The tragedy shows a world of incomprehension, doomed negotiations, loss, humiliation, and revenge, and the divided choruses take sides and become each other's enemies.

---

[5] Des Croix in Biet (2006: 711–804).

This world would have been very familiar to the audience, despite the story's location in Africa. From Aeschylus' *Persians* to *Les Portugais infortunés*, we know that the chorus can comment on the failure of the city, but here, everyone is affected by it; it becomes the failure of humanity itself, just before its annihilation, represented by the divided chorus.

Humiliation and vengeance, humiliation followed by vengeance causing fresh humiliation leading to further vengeance: in both England and France, this cycle formed the main plot of tragic drama. This dramatic, or 'drama-turgical', cycle of horror, retaliation, and humiliation also constituted a social, moral, political, and aesthetic law, a law that was at once judicial, traditional, and even anthropological in nature. But, although this ancient pattern of humiliation and vengeance is strongly present in Seneca, we have seen that, when this law was represented on stage by Elizabethan and French authors, the audience was clearly being reminded of current or recent troubles. The message of modern tragedy to audiences was that, although certain worthy Christians might have been newly converted to the concept of peace, they must still pay for their sins; while their victims had, in return, the right to react, or overreact. It is possible that conversion to a peaceful way of life might have interested the audience, but spectators were also interested in the shifting balance of the battle between claims and counter-claims and in the bloody theatrical spectacle produced by overreaction. And there was also fascination to be found in the practical and technical repre-sentation of crimes, horror, and blood. Hence the question, which was both historical and literary: was it possible to find a way to break the cycle of humiliation, to escape from this destiny of crime in which punishment never brought peace but led instead to perpetual human struggle? And tragedy generally provided no answer, or did so only at the very end by inventing a saviour *ex machina*.

But how could a character, or an author, change this traditional law of retaliation that was so much in evidence and was so in tune with the spirit of the times? These tragedies were caught up, ultimately, in a display of horror, in a theatrical world where the universal ending was cruelty and where the spectators appreciated the skilled performance of this cruelty and the fascination it exercised over them.

It was as if the recent violent troubles through which France had lived in the course of the sixteenth century had precluded, or ruled as unlawful, the possibility of any sort of mediation, whether aesthetic or political. As we have seen with *Scédase*, there was no longer a collective voice, the chorus was rejected, and the audience was no longer unified. Nor could the collectiv-ity any longer be considered to be emblematic or symbolic, or to act as a mediator; the spectators were left to face the historical and mythological facts head on. They no longer had a communal voice to shape or filter their interpretations; they had to confront fully the disgraces of their own time.

And to that end, after the representation of humiliation, retaliation, and vengeance, another figure appeared, even crueller in nature, representing the general condition of utter hunger and voracity and performing it on stage.

Tragic theatre from this period in effect introduced the state of famine into the dramaturgical pattern, representing the motif of hunger as a symptom of a more general malaise, in order to ask this essential question: what could be done in the face of hunger and voracity? And what did hunger reveal about human nature? In other words, hunger, which was initially presented as a physical reality resulting from harsh circumstances, was also metaphorical: it revealed not only a physiological hunger that must be assuaged by violence, but also an essential human hunger that could be actualized by self-devouring on a grand scale. In the tragic theatre of the late-sixteenth and early seventeenth centuries, hunger was not only a reality or a means to achieve human justice; it was also an excess, an unleashing of passions that often took the great Senecan anthropophagous banquet (*Thyestes*) as its reference, and expressed the inhumanity of the time. Such inhumanity could not be commented on by a modern chorus.

In *The Mahometan Tragedy, in which may be Seen and Observed the Disloyalty of Mahumet, Eldest Son of the King of Ottomans named Amurat, towards one of his Friends and Loyal Servants, Mahumet having made his Loyal Friend Kill his Younger Brother in order to Rule the Empire alone, and how he Handed him over to his Mother for Revenge, a most Cruel Deed,*[6] matters become more intense and take a metaphorical turn. Like many Norman and French plays, the tragedy is anonymous. It was published in Rouen in 1612, by Abraham Cousturier, and belongs to the same vein of bloody Norman theatre as *The French Tragedy of a Cruel Moor* from the same publisher. Mahumet was a topical character in contemporary history and tragedy: an infinitely cruel and furious man, an ugly, dangerous beast ruled by his passion for domination (*libido dominandi*). With the help of a Machiavellian counsellor, he disposes of all those who threaten him, including his younger brother, an infant who is also Amurat's heir. But the Sultana, his mother, discovers his crimes and opposes his tyranny in her need for revenge: Mahumet must pay for the murder of the infant. After fierce negotiations her violent maternal hunger for revenge is satisfied and appears in a magnificent and terrifying image of the act of devouring. Mahumet hands over his counsellor Moseçh to the Sultana, and she immediately tears open his side and cuts out his heart.

---

[6] Anon., *La Tragedie mahommetiste où l'on peut voir et remarquer l'infidélité commise par Mahumet, fils ayné du Roy des Othomans nomme Amurat, à l'endroit d'un sien amy et son fidelle serviteur, lequel Mahumet pour seul jouir de l'Empire fit tuer son petit frère par ce fidèle ami, et comment il le livra en la puissance de sa mère pour en prendre vengeance, chose de grande cruauté,* in Biet (2006: 603–43).

THE SULTANA. Oh, sweet contentment!
   This is nothing yet:
   I must, I must still
   Cut out his heart and devour it.

   Here she cuts out his heart and says:

   I have it at last, oh vile, atrocious heart!
   You committed the lamentable death of my son:
   O heart, how could you, more unyielding than a diamond,
   Than marble, than rock, or than any lodestone?
   I will devour you, heart! And with a strong courage
   I will cut you to pieces in cruel death.
   My beloved child, of your death I am henceforth revenged
   But I will drink a mouthful of his blood.

   Here the Sultana drinks from his blood.

THE NURSE. My Lady, enough! Cease all these efforts
   Do not inflict more wounds upon this miserable body.
   In God's name, leave it there; it no longer has the power to feel.

THE SULTANA. Oh God! My contentment is so great.
   I feel already a happy elation within me;
   Already I feel released from a horrible distress
   Which pained me earlier; I feel my lightened heart
   Leaping and fluttering:
   I feel its relief.
   Let us rest. I am, I am content.
   This greatest good has resulted from my waiting.
   But as for the king, I call upon the great gods
   Who, with vengeful lightning, will send him to the depths
   Of the Plutonian vale:
   for the gods
   Punish the inhumanities of humans.

These are the final words of the tragedy.

   In this theatre of the scaffold, Ottoman queens are capable of tearing apart
human bodies, feeding off men's hearts and drinking their blood.[7] And only a
few years earlier the Valois kings and queens have been suspected of similar
crimes. In addition to the emotion that permeates the anonymous author's
plot, culminating in the excessive hypertrophy of the last act, we cannot help
but notice a double analogy (between Constantinople and France in 1612 and
between Mahumet and tyranny), which reflects the fear that war may begin
again, that the sovereign, named after a fearful prophet, may be a tyrant, that

---

[7] The theatrical theme of the eaten heart, which was widely employed in the Middle Ages, was
a recurrent feature in *histoires tragiques*, particularly in Jean-Pierre Camus's *Horrific Spectacles*,
book I, spectacle III.

religion may be a bloody tool, and that voracious forces may once more rule the world. The name Mahumet and the title of the play highlight this aspect for the spectator and reader and emphasize the religious, fanatical, and dangerous qualities of a power defined by the name of the disloyal and reputedly bloodthirsty prophet. Behind the set, in the historical frame of Constantinople, beyond the reflecting surface, Istanbul and its prophet bathe the world in blood. But set, historical frame, image, and bloody universe, whether they are exaggerated or faithful to the spectators' own images, all still point to the future of France—a dark, devouring, self-consuming, and intolerant future.

If in *Scédase*, the chorus comes to mourn at the very end of the play, in *La Tragédie Mahommétiste*, the two choruses mentioned in the *dramatis personae* ('le premier chœur' and 'le second chœur') disappear at the end of the play. The Senecan chorus seems to have been ousted altogether from the stage by the hyper-realistically staged atrocities. In *La Tragédie Mahommétiste*, the chorus is given a very traditional function, which is probably why it disappears at the end. 'The first chorus' plays a traditional role: in the first part of the tragedy, it elaborates on a general maxim—a quiet country life is better than a city life—and hopes that the gods will help the king to be as good and kind as his father was before him. But, as usual, these reflections and wishes are contradicted—first, by the Sultana's expressions of dread, and eventually by the terrible events on stage.

When Mahumet's brothers try to escape with their nurse, the king, helped by Mosech, his counsellor, chases them, and both run offstage. It is then that 'the second chorus' appears: first, to listen to a messenger who narrates the deaths of the king's two brothers, at the hand of the counsellor; and, secondly, to express its apprehensions. The chorus typically fears for the Sultana maddened by the messenger's awful tale of crimes and heralds the last gruesome scene mentioned above.

Violence has turned into revenge and can be satisfied only by the act of devouring. This is caused by the disorder of the world, war, and tyranny. The diagnosis is that inhumanity is the essence of humanity, and that it cannot be remedied. But the issue is now cruelty itself, as an autonomous action, suddenly breaking away from causes and consequences to become an act in excess, of excess, beyond comprehension, and not susceptible to commentary by society, an act that is also supposed to amaze and fascinate the audience. This extreme representation of cruelty leaves the chorus with no ground to stand on. Formerly, 'the second chorus' had been able to express its fears and dismay during the messenger speech, but at the end everyone is left speechless, even the spectators themselves, fascinated and gripped by this ultimate act of violence.

THE CRUEL DEATH AND SUBSEQUENT
REBIRTH OF THE CHORUS

Early modern tragedy is both familiar with the Senecan tradition and draws upon it, finding there, in the first instance, a way to speak of cruelty. In the wake of the disasters of the sixteenth century, any notion of ancient order is gradually shaken: the new city cannot trust anyone any more, not even its elders, not even the usually wise members of the chorus; and the spectators are no longer in a position to trust their representatives, whether political or aesthetic. Now too we find a transposition of violence, rape, and cannibalism, from the Senecan medium of words to onstage action. Such representation on stage leaves the spectators in a state of shock and contributes to the weakening, and even the disappearance, of the chorus.

Choruses thus gradually disappeared, giving way to violence, blood, human inhumanity, and barbarity in speech and action on stage without commentary. The new citizen–spectators of this period, who had often before been faced with real-life violence, without the benefit of distance, now confronted the stage violence directly. They had to face a world operating without rules other than those of cruelty, humiliation, and retaliation. The tragedies they saw, then, worked contrary to the crown's strategy of a politics of reconciliation.

Theatrical aesthetics and practice tended to move away from the classical model with reference to the chorus since it had clearly become quite impossible for a chorus to intervene in the circumstances portrayed by the tragedies of this time. Thus, generally, the chorus disappeared in the face of the atrocities, banished from and by the disasters occurring on stage that referred to earlier, historical disasters. The chorus must henceforth be made up of the audience, the spectators, horrified by the cruel action, but able to scrutinize closely the connections between stage representations and their representations outside the theatre.

The audience formed this new heterogeneous chorus, and this audience of heterogeneous spectators watched, in an act of collective voyeurism, the fiction on stage, where power was represented on the theatrical scaffold. Then, during the performance, this *contradictory* audience could comment *contradictorily* on the horror that emerged from this image of power and could judge it without the guidance of a chorus. Choruses, hope, harmony, and unconditional happy endings soon became the ingredients of other genres, such as pastoral or tragicomedy in France and, later, the musical tragedies of Louis XIV's reign, where a reverent and enthusiastic chorus would sing of the king's power and praise its glory, but that is another story.

12

Phantom Chorus: Missing Chorality on the French Eighteenth-Century Stage

Cécile Dudouyt

> Hasten the tread of your steps with song
> Oh march on, march on in tears
>
> .   .   .   .   .
>
> Come raise the same lament once more,
> Stir up the delight that comes of much weeping
>
> (*El.* 112–13, 125–6)[1]

So sings Electra in Euripides' version of the play, effectively linking tragic pleasures, πολύδακρυν ἁδονάν, with the bruising and clawing of ritual mourners, who beat the pace of their song with pain. There is an essentially rhythmical quality to Greek tragedy, produced not only by metre, music, and dance, but also by its composition. Just as a heartbeat is a succession of diastole and systole, the Greek tragic beat alternates between two modes of performance, the episodes and the choral odes. The chorus is thus not only present in the twofold performing space of ancient theatres; it is also marking time in the tragic tempo.

Nothing could be more different from French neoclassical tragedies. Eighteenth-century French stages had no space for a chorus. They confined the performance to a narrow stretch on the stage, unified for the eye by the painted perspective of its backdrop, while the cramped orchestra, *la fosse*, hid from sight *les violons*, the musicians who played violin sonatas during the intervals. In terms of dramatic writing, the measure of a playwright's skill was precisely both his ability to sustain the action without the kind of interruption choral odes are likely to provide, and his capacity to bring about, not affecting singing and dancing, but visually striking *tableaux*.

---

[1] Kovacs (1998: 163).

CHORUS PERFORMANCE AND CHORIC FUNCTIONS

The space created by the chorus, the rhythmic suspension of narrative time it introduces, and the performance of its collective voice and body all have consequences for how spectators relate to what they are shown. Greek choruses, with their liminal position both within the *mimesis* and outside it, create a third dimension between fiction and non-fiction, both buffer zone and breathing time allowing for reflection on and detachment from what is performed by the actors. This raises aesthetic questions—when do choruses mediate and rationalize audience reaction? when do they heighten and amplify it?—as well as ethical and political ones about, among other things, the representation of power, the staging of violence, and collective responsibility.[2] It is because choruses exist and carry meaning on these different planes that the concept of chorality is especially helpful, referring as it does both to what a chorus can be (its collective dimension, expressed in performance through singing and dancing) and to what it can do (its framing function, with the potential both for didactic distancing and lyrical empathy). Far from being a mere discarded accessory, the absent chorus of the eighteenth-century plays thus throws into sharp relief the far-reaching differences between neoclassical and ancient tragedy. It is the aim of this chapter to reassess eighteenth-century reception of Greek plays in the light of this missing chorality.

In 1692, André Dacier translated and published both the *Poetics* and two tragedies intended to illustrate Aristotle's theatrical principles. His choice of Sophocles' *Oedipus Tyrannus* and *Electra* confirmed the two plays' status as figureheads of Greek tragedy and obvious targets for adaptation by authors wanting to challenge or emulate the ancient heritage. The Electra and Oedipus plays of this period will, therefore, provide the focus for this exploration of the lost choral dimension of eighteenth-century performance. Voltaire, one of the most prolific and popular playwrights of his time, rewrote both plays in 1718 (*Oedipe*) and 1749 (*Oreste*), long after Longepierre (*Electre*, 1702) and Crébillon (*Electre*, 1708) and before Houdar de La Motte (*Oedipe*, 1726), Ducis (*Oedipe chez Admète*, 1778) and Rochefort (*Electre*, 1782).[3] The reception of these two ancient plays will allow me to follow two lines of enquiry. The first concerns the removal of both chorus and choral odes. Eighteenth-century *Electras* provide a good example of the process of adaptation as amputation of

---

[2] For a discussion of these issues in the sixteenth and seventeenth centuries in France, see Biet, Chapter 11, this volume.

[3] This chapter focuses on adaptations of ancient *Electras* and *Oedipuses* performed on the eighteenth-century stage. François Melchior de Folard's *Oedipe* (1722), Brancas de Lauraguais's *Jocaste* (1781), Buffardin d'Aix's *Oedipe à Thèbes ou le fatalisme* (1784), and Bernard d'Héry's *tragédie lyrique Oedipe roi* (1786) all feature a chorus, but none of them was actually enacted. For an analysis of the aesthetic and political dimension of choruses in these plays, see Biet (1994: 117–24). For Lemoyne's *Electre*, see Savage, Chapter 7, this volume.

the chorus, leaving dramatists with a beautiful but incomplete body to which they feel the need to add prosthetic plot twists. Crucially, because ancient Electras are in many ways part of the choral dimension, modern plays leave the main character with little ground to stand on. The second point is an attempt to qualify the first. With the reception of *Oedipus Tyrannus* I would like to put forward the idea that this amputated chorality is not only missing but also missed, that it can be felt like a phantom limb, a haunting presence in eighteenth-century drama.

GREEK ELECTRAS AND THE MOURNING CHORUS

Greek choruses are characterized by collective singing (or chanting) and collective movement (dance and procession). The type of performance they introduce contrasts with that of actors who deliver speeches in iambic trimeters and bandy in stichomythia. The chorus is at one step removed from the action, witnessing and reacting to it rather than taking active part in it. Both dimensions constantly interact throughout the plays to a greater or lesser degree, but they remain spatially, and arguably essentially as well, on different planes. Whereas actors of speaking or silent parts are directly involved and active, the chorus proffers celebration or lament from the fringe of that action as an amplification or a counterpoint to what is represented. In Aristotle's account of the evolution of tragedy, actors were gradually added to a spectacle originally consisting only of a chorus.[4] Whatever the actual historical link between dithyramb and tragedy, the idea of a progressive evolution allows for a continuum between choral performance and actor performance. In this case, the Electra of the ancient versions could be seen to occupy a somewhat intermediate position between actor and chorus member. In the *Choephoroi*, she is almost one with the libation-bearers with whom she makes her entrance in the parodos; even in both later *Electras* that bear her name she retains the role of lamenting or rejoicing onlooker traditionally granted to the chorus. Her position in the three plays is liminal to the actual argument of the tragedy, to Orestes' return to Argos and his matricide, since it is Electra's part to be his witness, rejoice in his return, and edge him towards revenge.

In Aeschylus' play, the chorus of Trojan slaves sings the mourning song, which in both Euripides' and Sophocles' version becomes associated with Electra herself. The self-inflicted beat of ritual lamentation is present from the outset: '*I am come to convey libations to the accompaniment of blows* dealt swift and sharp by my hands. My cheek is marked with bloody gashes where

---

[4] Aristotle on dithyramb, 1449^{a}10; Halliwell (1995: 33).

my nails have cut fresh furrows [and later on] *the tune of grievous blows*' (ll. 22–31).[5] Electra remains in the shadow of this chorus, letting herself be guided by its strong-willed leader, who plots and schemes in her stead, luring Aegisthus home to his execution without his retinue of guards.

In sharp contrast, in both Sophocles' and Euripides' plays, Electra occupies a more strongly defined part and speaks *before* the entry of the chorus of women, in parodos-like anticipation of its entrance, with her own song of lament. In Euripides' version, Electra is first presented as character through a brief dialogue with her humble husband, before re-entering as her Aeschylean self, as a mourner, with the already quoted soliloquy, which anticipates the entrance of the chorus and associates rhythm and tragic pleasures: 'hasten the tread of your step with song | march on, march on in tears' (Euripides, *El.*, ll. 112–13).[6] She turns the song of the water-bearer into the bitter-sweet song of mourning with its thrashing beat. It is in Sophocles' play, however, that Electra achieves her strongest identity as individual character while functioning as a chorus of one, reacting and commenting rather than taking action. The play effectively concentrates on the celebration or lament that Electra utters according to the conflicting signs and tidings of her brother's return. The resonance chamber provided by the chorus thus becomes, through Electra as lyrical and choric character, the main focus of the play. For that reason, eighteenth-century adaptations of Electra are particularly revealing of the paradoxes inherent in neoclassical receptions of Greek drama.

For playwrights and theorists alike, from Chapelain to d'Aubignac, Racine or Voltaire, unity of action featured as the most prominent characteristic of Greek drama read though the lens of Aristotle's *Poetics*. Yet ancient tragedies achieve this unity precisely because the unfolding of the plot is not the sole element in the plays. In other words, Greek tragedies are whole without intricate plot lines, thanks to the presence of the chorus onstage and to the rhythmic suspension of the action during the choral odes. One of the main questions raised by adapting Greek plays in the eighteenth century is always: 'What is it that remains of the play once the chorus has been edited out?' The particular case of *Electra* further sharpens that question: what becomes of Electra's choral function when the choral dimension itself has disappeared?

THE CHALLENGES OF SIMPLICITY

To eighteenth-century sensibilities, the chorus as alternative performing mode, rhythmically punctuating the drama, seemed nothing short of an alien element, disrupting the unity of the homogeneous whole. Choral odes

---

[5] Weir Smyth (1999: 161).   [6] Kovacs (1998: 163).

were thus dropped as a matter of course. At the close of the century, La Harpe summarized opinions on the chorus in the introduction to his translation of *Philoctète* (1781), destined for reading rather than performance:

We all know what Choruses were in ancient Greece, lyrical pieces, some of great beauty, included because of their theatrical system but which added nothing to the action and at times detracted from it. I have omitted them all, as useless and out of place in a French translation which may one day be performed.[7]

Dramatists of the eighteenth century called what they admired and emulated in Greek drama 'simplicité'. The term was given its *lettres de noblesse* by Racine in the preface to *Bérénice* (published in 1671): 'What appealed to me most [in this plot] was that I found it simple to the extreme. I had long wished to try my hand at a Tragedy with such simplicity of action as the Ancients used to relish.'[8] Racine then went on to quote from Horace's *Ars Poetica* and his twofold determination of a play's scope: *simplex et unum*. The two adjectives suggest that there is more to the unity of action that mere unity—that simplicity is, so to speak, unity squared. Racine illustrates this ancient taste with, among other examples, *Philoctetes* 'of which the whole plot consists only in Odysseus' attempt to purloin Heracles' arrows', pointing at the difference there is between the simplest of modern plays and any of the ancient ones.

Yet playwrights and theoreticians of the stage admired simplicity without ever acknowledging what made it possible—namely, the choral odes that flesh out the otherwise streamlined action of Greek drama. The 'simplicity' of ancient plays is, therefore, both an ideal and a challenge to dramatists. As Crébillon put it in his 'Préface' of 1708:

The plot of *Electre* is so simple in itself that I cannot conceive how it can be used successfully without adding anything in the way of episodes. The whole play is about punishing with death Agamemnon's murderers, and in order to do it, one only waits for Orestes to return—as soon as Orestes is in Argos and Electra has recognized him, the play is at an end.[9]

This diagnosis is interesting for two reasons. First, it accurately formulates the difficulty. In the context of neoclassical drama where suspense is key, the crux of simplicity is to keep the attention of the audience alert with as little plot material as possible. But, in the case of this particular play, Crébillon points to the recognition scene between Orestes and Electra as the only event in the play before the killings themselves, implying that there is not enough material to delay the conclusion of the fiction and make the play last for five whole acts.

---

[7] La Harpe (1781: 28). Translations are my own, unless otherwise indicated.
[8] Racine (1671: p. iii).
[9] Crébillon (1819: 155–6).

The comment is interesting also because of what it overlooks: in Sophocles' play, the proclaimed model of Crébillon's *Electre*, what actually happens, besides confrontations between Electra and her sister or her mother, are her lyrical responses of either ecstatic joy or deepest despair to what she thinks means Orestes' return or his death. This rich texture of heightened emotional content clearly did not qualify as action in Crébillon's conception of drama. The challenge of 'simplicity', heightened by the absence of a chorus, is especially acute in relation to Electra's chorality.

SIDELINED ELECTRA

Longepierre's 1702 *Electre*, followed shortly by Crébillon's in 1708 and, some forty years later, by Voltaire's *Oreste* in 1749, all claim Sophocles' *Electra* as their model. Hilaire Bernard de Longepierre's version was praised *à la cour*, where it was performed three times at the Théâtre de Conti in Versailles, but its author was against having it performed *à la ville*, and the play never made it to Parisian commercial venues.[10] Crébillon's play, on the other hand, enjoyed relative success at the Comédie Française in 1708 with eight consecutive performances.[11]

Contrary to Longepierre's attempt to imitate Sophocles, Crébillon proudly advocates adaptation to modern tastes. In his 'Préface', he defends his *Electre* and the double love plot he invented to fill the emptiness of Sophocles' play. In his version, both Electre and Oreste are desperately in love with Itys and Iphianasse, respectively son and daughter of Aegisthus, their father's murderer, by a previous marriage. Voltaire, on the other hand, follows Longepierre's version very closely in his *Oreste* (while criticizing it openly) and protests virulently against Crébillon's adaptation—presenting his own play as a 'vindication of Sophocles'. However much all three playwrights claim Sophocles as their main source, none of the three dramatists seems to know what to do with Electra herself: she cannot be dispensed with like the chorus (since it remains, at least nominally, *her* play) but the 'a-chorality' of the neoclassical tragic stage leaves her with very little ground to stand on.

Without the presence of a chorus, showing Orestes' return essentially through its impact on Electra, as in Sophocles, would mean having onstage an actress standing alone or with a *confidante* for most of the play. In a context in which lamenting and reacting to Orestes' return is not considered proper 'action', as Crébillon makes quite clear, dramatists therefore retain striking fragments from Sophocles' *Electra*, such as her first speech, the confrontation

---

[10] Longepierre (1981: 10).   [11] Joannidès (1970: 194).

with Clytemnestra, and the paradigmatic Sophoclean urn scene. All three dramatists then turn to other characters to fill the gaps, staging confrontations between a disguised Orestes and Clytemnestra, adding to the part of Aegisthus and introducing new plot elements such as a murder attempt (Longepierre and Voltaire), mistaken identities, and love interests (Crébillon).

Electra's first speech is symptomatic of her problematic status in the play bearing her name. In Sophocles, revenge is introduced at first by Orestes, the Pedagogue, and silent Pylades, but immediately whisked away when Electra appears, soon followed by the chorus. From the moment of her entrance, spectators follow Orestes' return to Argos through the mediation of what she learns about it and the pain or joy those tidings bring her. Eighteenth-century versions reverse both the order of appearance of Orestes and Electra and the hierarchy between revenge (dramatic action) and mourning (lyric lamentation): Electra is given in both Longepierre's and Crébillon's play an expository function. Electra's lament comes first, functioning both as a Sophoclean signature and as an exposition to the play, but she is soon sidelined after the expository first act by Orestes' return and vengeance. Longepierre has Electra introduce herself in a first speech full of Sophoclean echoes:

> Sun . . .
> Have you ever risen without hearing my sobs?
> And whenever night brings peace back to the world,
> I, engulfed in deep sorrow,
> My breast bruised and beaten, my eyes drowned in tears,
> I denounce the harshness of hostile fates.[12]

She insists, in faithful imitation of ancient models, on her protracted mourning and helpless dependence on her brother's return: 'The gods have forgotten my father's death | they do not avenge him, I implore them in vain' (ll. 3–4) and calls for Orestes: 'let him come! Bereft in such a grievous plight | I may not bear much longer the burden of my misery' (ll. 43–4).[13] Instead of a chorus, Ismène enters, a *confidante* with a Sophoclean name, followed by Chrysothémis in close imitation of Sophocles' play. But Electra disappears during a second act devoted to Orestes, only to come back, with Ismène or on her own, at set moments: in confrontation with Clytemnestra in Act III, during the urn scene in Act IV, and when Orestes' revenge is revealed as matricide in Act V.

Crébillon's play also starts with Electra's soliloquy but on a more decisive note, with the resolution to stop mourning and start acting:

---

[12] Longepierre (1981: 26).
[13] Longepierre (1981: 26–7). 'Les dieux ont de mon père oublié le trépas, | je les implore en vain, ils ne m'entendent pas.' 'Abandonnée à de si grands malheurs | je ne puis plus porter le poids de mes douleurs.'

> Witness of the dreadful murder for which I cry revenge
> Oh Night, whose silence I have all too often troubled,
> Insentient beholder of my agony
> Electra has not come to you with tears.

(Act I, scene 1)

But her efforts towards revenge are checked in the very next scene, not by her sister Chrysotemis but by a servant she had hoped might raise an army of followers for her:

> ARCAS. Unhappy princess, alas!
>   Your fate is so worthy of pity! No hope, no friend.
> ELECTRE. Is their friendship empty in spite of what they swore?
> ARCAS. Madam, my zeal has spoken in vain
>   ... they say, let Orestes' presence
>   Bring reassurance to his friends
>   And we shall take arms for his revenge.   (Act I, scene 2)[14]

Just as in Longepierre's version, Electre the mourner fades away after the first two scenes. In Crébillon's play, she has a brand new part to play, that of the 'jeune première'. Electra is in love with and loved by Itys, the son of Aegisthus. Her duty to her father's memory forbids this union into which she is forced by Aegisthus, transforming her into a Greek Chimène or a Racinian Andromaque.

Voltaire further dramatizes the redundancy of Electra's function as mourner in his *Oreste*. The change of title is a way of distancing his play from Crébillon's tragedy, whose love plot he criticized harshly, but it also reflects the change of emphasis from Electra's empathetic and reflexive lyricism to Oresteian action.

Voltaire entrusts the exposition of the play to the old man who tends Agamemnon's grave and to Iphise, Electra's sister. This Chrysothemis figure is everything Electra should be. Sensible and discreet, she shares none of the rage, bereavement, and passion expressed by her sibling. When Electra first enters in Act I, scene 2, her stock mourning and raging soliloquy is cut short rather sharply by the old man. She is effectively told to put a stop to her rambling—which she immediately does: 'Wise and prudent old man, yes, you open my eyes, forgive me my distress and my impatience.'[15] This passage can be read as an echo to Sophocles 1326–38, when the Pedagogue scolds Electra for her imprudent display of joy upon recognizing Orestes. But, in Sophocles, Electra is silenced shortly before Orestes kills Clytemnestra a mere 200 lines before the end, not, as in Voltaire's play, from the very moment she enters the stage.

---

[14] Crébillon (1819: 161, 163–4).   [15] Voltaire (1992: 421).

INSIDE THE URN

Since the *Choephoroi*, Electra has always been the quintessential mourner, on a par with stony Niobe, who continues weeping beyond death. Sophocles further heightened this identity when he added, in his version, a scene in which Electra mourns afresh, not her long-dead father, but the reported death of her brother. After Sophocles, the funeral urn brought to her by a disguised Orestes became Electra's hallmark and identifying prop. The power of the scene is due to the irony that Electra mourns an empty urn in front of her living brother. Mistaking the urn as final proof of Orestes' death is the last and most harrowing of Electra's trials, which form the progression of Sophocles' play from the signs of Orestes' return (Clytemnestra's dream told by Chrysothemis, the lock of hair and libation on Agamemnon's grave, which Chrysothemis also reports having seen) to the increasingly objectified false proofs of his death (the pedagogue's story and finally the urn itself).

The spectators are well aware that the urn is not what Electra takes it to be, a fact chosen by Mark Ringer in *The Empty Urn* as the metaphor of Sophoclean meta-theatricality:

Electra sees the empty vessel and, like a skilled actor, begins to fill it with meaning ... she holds an empty urn, a 'prop' in both the fictive world of the story and in the performing environment of the play ... As an 'empty' vessel, it also symbolizes the phenomenon of metaphor itself. It serves as a metaphor of metaphor.[16]

The tragic irony of the scene arguably jolts spectators from the immediacy of the action and allows them to enjoy what they are shown as spectators rather than as imaginary participants. This moment of theatricality, when a prop is used as a prop by characters within the fiction, loses its centrality in eighteenth-century adaptations. It exists as a *morceau de bravoure* and a Sophoclean signature, but this moment of lament is shortened, amputated along with the chorus, and does not lead to a recognition.

Voltaire further divests the urn scene of its Sophoclean function. In his play the urn is not simply used as a prop by Orestes; it is a *bona fide* funeral urn containing the ashes of Aegisthus' son, who was sent by his father to murder Orestes and got killed in the attempt. This radically changes the irony perceived by spectators. Electra mourns a brother who is alive in front of her, but this moving situation is obscured by another irony at cross purposes with the first: distraught Electra is shown lavishing tears on her enemy's ashes. This scene is interrupted by Egisthe himself who unwittingly goes on to gloat over the ashes of his only son. In this he becomes the inverted mirror image of

---

[16] Ringer (1998: 87, 189).

Electra, but his situation is by far the more tragic of the two. When he fills Sophocles' empty urn, Voltaire reclaims it for the storyline and adds an episode to Orestes' revenge, which transforms Electra's lament into something resembling a slightly distasteful accident.

KILLING BECOMES ELECTRA

From her stunted first speech in Act I, scene 2, to the mildly embarrassing urn scene in Act III, scene 2, Voltaire is not kind to the choral dimension of mourning Electra. The next couple of scenes show that he has other plans for her. As in Longepierre's adaptation, Voltaire's Electra decides to kill the man she takes to be her brother's murderer. It is only when she pounces on him with a sword that Orestes reveals his identity. The recognition scene is not brought about by a harrowing song of lament but obtained at sword point after a short climactic scene: 'Here he stands alone, let us strike . . . die . . . traitor . . . I cannot' (Act IV, scene 5). The alexandrine line is broken up, and language becomes a prop used to prolong a unique moment. The imagery of language is suspended in order to create a living picture framed by the stage curtain.

In contrast with Greek rhythmical composition, French neoclassical traged- ies are climactic. They hinge on a moment of near perfect dynamic stillness: the tableau. The emphasis on climactic pauses goes hand in hand with an evolution in acting styles, in which, as an occasional director, Voltaire had numerous occasions to participate: images should spark from the body of the actor, rather than from the words he or she delivers. In the 'Préface de l'édition parisienne' of *Les Scythes* (published in 1767), Voltaire praised the 'paintings full of life and animation' that iconic actors of the Compagnie such as Le Kain and Melle Clairon came to develop when acting in his tragedies. He then gives as an example the urn scene:

Who before Melle Clairon would have dared to perform the urn scene in *Oreste* in the way she did, who would have painted the very image of nature as she did when she fell in a swoon holding the urn in one hand and letting the other fall inert and lifeless beside her . . . that is real theatrical action. The rest is mere conversation, however animated at times.[17]

---

[17] Voltaire (1877: 268): 'qui aurait osé avant Melle Clairon jouer dans *Oreste* la scene de l'urne comme elle l'a jouée? Qui aurait imaginé de peindre ainsi la Nature, de tomber évanouie tenant l'Urne d'une main, en laissant l'autre descendre immobile et sans vie? . . . c'est là en effet la veritable action théâtrale. Le reste était une conversation parfois passionnée.'

ACT IV, SCENE 5.
ÉLECTRE (avance vers Oreste) : "LE VOILA SEUL FRAPPONS ... MEURS... TRAÎTRE ... JE NE PUIS"

Fig. 12.1. Voltaire's *Oreste*, Act IV, scene 5; Electra with a sword. Engraving by Jean-Michel Moreau in Renouard's edition of selected *Œuvres de Voltaire* (Paris, 1801–4). Photo: by permission of the Voltaire Foundation, University of Oxford

Revealingly, however, when Moreau was given the task of illustrating an edition of Voltaire's selected works in 1805,[18] he chose to represent Electra with a sword, favouring the moment of interrupted utterance and climactic visual action (see Figure 12.1) over the traditional depiction of Electra as lyrical mourning figure. The fact that, in the two closest adaptations of

---

[18] Voltaire (1819: 154).

Sophocles' *Electra* in the eighteenth century, Electra's defining prop becomes not the urn but the blade aptly illustrates how the part has been altered to suit the taste of the time, not for the articulated laments of the mourner but for the visually striking pose of the avenger.

1780s: CHORALITY RECLAIMED

The return of choruses to favour in the 1780s coincides with Electra's return centre-stage in the eighteenth-century adaptation closest to Sophocles' *Electra*, Guillaume de Rochefort's *Electre*, first performed in Versailles on 19 December 1782.[19] In the preface, Rochefort emphasizes not only the simplicity with which the action unfolds but also the beauty of the character of Electra, and in his text he sets out to follow the ancient model very closely. Indeed, in the first four acts, this translator of Sophocles, who was to play a central role in completing Brumoy's *Théâtre des Grecs* from 1785 to 1789, follows the ancient text with minor additions, such as supplying Pylades with a speaking part. Although Rochefort left out choral odes, he replaced them not with action and plot twists but with instrumental music and silent processions.[20]

The symphonic music between the acts is given an illustrative function. For instance, instead of translating Sophocles' description of dawn and the singing of the birds (ll. 17–18), Rochefort explains in the first stage direction: 'I thought it would be better to let the musician depict it.'[21] In later descriptions of musical intermissions, the author similarly directs the music as if it were an actor. Acts I and IV end with silent processions to the sound of expressive symphonic music, Acts II and III with Electra prostrate while the music gives voice to her grief. Rochefort indicates that here 'instruments are to play pleasant music, where long moans can nonetheless be heard at intervals'. Only Act V, and thus the play, ends in silence. Rochefort also keeps Voltaire's adaptation of Sophoclean stage design. The play is not set, as in Longepierre's or Crébillon's version 'In Mycenae, inside the palace of its kings', but outside the palace, surrounded by the divine presence of Apollo: 'The scene is set in Mycenae in front of the royal palace. On one side, we see the city and the

---

[19] For an overview of the political import of the chorus of Theban elders from Voltaire's *Oedipe* to Lacroix's and a discussion of the return of choruses, see Macintosh (2009*a*: 73–81).

[20] Interestingly, Rochefort's play with processions and expressive musical intermissions is performed and published in the same year as an opera by the same title, Lemoyne's *Electre*, discussed by Savage, Chapter 7, this volume.

[21] Rochefort (1782: 3): 'Cette circonstance du chant des Oiseaux au lever de l'Aurore a été exprimée par Sophocle dans de beaux vers, mais j'ai cru qu'il vallait mieux la laisser peindre au musicien.'

temple of Apollo, on the other side a sacred wood and an altar, and at the back stands the portico of the palace with a statue of Apollo'.[22] Chorality, and Electra with it, thus reclaim the public space represented onstage in the last pre-revolutionary adaptation of Sophocles' play.

HIGH HOPES AND THEORIES

If adapting Greek drama in the eighteenth century involves *de facto* amputation of the chorus, adaptations of *Electra* illustrate the fact that, beyond the physical disappearance of the chorus, its very functions, as a relay for empathy and *mise en abîme* of spectatorship, are banished as well. The character of Electra illustrates the disappearance of chorality most prominently in its lyrical dimension. With the loss of the chorus, beyond this dismissal of the lyric chorus, lies one of the most fundamental questions of eighteenth-century reception of Greek tragedy: is it opera or theatre that truly does justice to ancient tragedy?

Voltaire liked to claim that he and his prestigious seventeenth-century predecessors, Corneille and Racine, had retrieved the essence of Greek tragedy. In the *Dissertation sur la tragédie ancienne et moderne*, first published in 1749 with his play *Sémiramis*, he resorts to an architectural metaphor to contrast his conception of theatre with contemporary French operas. Whereas, according to him, French tragedies translate the spirit of Greek drama, 'Operas are the copy and the ruin of ancient Greek tragedies'.[23] Lyric tragedies feature choruses, music, ballets, and machines, all the 'pomp' of ancient performance, yet, for Voltaire, the essence of Greek tragedy was not to be found in what he viewed as the quirks of its original performances but in the verisimilitude achieved by the dramatization of a unique action. In the context of the enduring popularity of French opera, he thus presents his own tragedies as preserving the soul of Greek tragedy—implicitly casting operas, with their singing and dancing choruses, as its walking corpse.

Yet Voltaire has an interest in choruses from the first. His first, hugely popular play, *Oedipe*, featured a speaking chorus without choral odes. His correspondence shows that he was asked a number of times to add choral odes to his play but he never did. From 1738 to 1785, most separate editions of *Oedipe* bear the title *L'Oedipe, tragédie avec des chœurs*, so choral odes seem to

---

[22] Rochefort (1782: 2): 'La scène est à Mycène devant le palais des rois. On voit d'un côté la ville et le temple d'Apollon de l'autre un bois sacré et un autel dans le fond le portique du palais avec une statue d'Apollon.'

[23] Voltaire (1992: 148–9): 'Ces tragédies opéra sont la copie et la ruine de la tragédie d'Athènes.' 'Heureusement, la bonne et vraie tragédie parut en France avant que nous eussions ces opéras, qui auraient pu l'étouffer.'

have been felt as a selling point by editors. However, Voltaire did not write them: 'I have to thank the duchess of Villeroi for sparing me the effort of writing choral odes for *Oedipe*. I would not have been successful in this; we rarely do well the things we do not enjoy; and I have no taste for music mingled with declamation. It seems to me that one always destroys the other.'[24] Voltaire's distaste for the coexistence of speech and song aside, these choral odes would not easily have made it to the Comédie Française. The monopoly awarded to the Académie de Musique in 1669 prevented the Comédiens Français from adding music and dancing to their plays. The revised statutes of 1672 allowed for a strictly limited number of violins and two singer–actors on stage, but a singing chorus would not have been permitted.[25] Even if it had, the actors would very likely not have wanted the choral odes. After the first run of performances, the Comédiens Français had omitted even the speaking chorus.[26]

If the chorus is problematic in terms of performance and in its lyrical dimension, both for aesthetic reasons and because of the politics and economics of the entertainment market of the time, the chorus remains throughout the first half of the eighteenth century highly tempting for a number of different reasons. It had an appeal on a theoretical level, first because of the authority of the Ancients and at least potentially for the chorus's other moral, religious, and didactic functions. But also in practice, since Racine's *Esther* and most of all *Athalie* provided prestigious examples of spoken tragedies with music and choruses, offering an alternative to lyrical tragedies, however doomed by the monopoly accorded to the Académie de Musique.

Choruses, while persistently failing to be revived on professional stages, were still discussed favourably in theoretical writings on theatre. Dacier's reaction to d'Aubignac's *Pratique du théâtre* gives the tone for later discussions on the chorus: the chorus he calls for is an elegant solution to the difficult equation of theatre. He effectively combines two problems in order to create a solution: on the one hand, it is difficult to deal with Greek choruses, however integral to Greek tragedies; on the other hand, the moral and religious consensus reached at the end of the seventeenth century dictated that theatre was essentially immoral. Dacier uses the first issue to address the second: according to him, Greek choruses had the function of delivering the dangerous theatrical *pharmakon* safely into the body politic of the audience in order to purify it.

---

[24] Voltaire (2001: 129–30): 'Je dois remercier madame la duchesse de Villeroi de m'avoir épargné le soin de faire des chœurs à Oedipe. Je n'y aurais pas réussi; on fait mal les choses qu'on n'aime pas; et j'avoue que je n'ai pas de goût pour la musique mêlée avec la déclamation. Il me paraît que l'un tue toujours l'autre.'

[25] For a discussion of the rivalry between the Opera and the Comédie Française, see Serre (2008: 85).

[26] Voltaire (2001: 130).

He thus manages the *tour de force* of arguing both that choruses increased verisimilitude and that they allowed for a quantum of reflexive distance.

Dacier's account of Greek choruses and their function is both echoed and qualified forty years later by another translator of Greek drama: le Père Brumoy. Pierre Brumoy is the Jesuit Hellenist to whom the eighteenth century owes, in 1730, *Le Théâtre des Grecs*, the first selection of translated Greek tragedies, re-edited and completed between 1784 and 1789 to comprise a translation of every extant Greek tragedy and comedy.[27] Brumoy's princeps edition comprised only three tragedies by Sophocles and four by Euripides, with summaries of the others and all of Aeschylus' extant plays. The work was introduced by 'dissertations', which served as a 'reader's companion', providing a cultural context to the plays. In the first one, entitled 'Discours sur l'origine de la tragédie', Brumoy, too, rationalizes ancient choruses through a study of their function, even if he does not stress the same features as Dacier. He presents choruses as 'between the acts' interludes serving two crucial purposes.

The first concerns performance: choral odes separate the different acts and allow spectators to recover from the intensity of the tragic action. But, unlike eighteenth-century violins, this intermission also brought continuity (one of the obsessions of neoclassicism was that the stage should not be left empty). The continuous presence of the chorus onstage is praised for this reason: that the performing space remains occupied even between the acts, when the fictional 'action' of the play is supposedly going on behind the scenes. Not only is the scene occupied; it is occupied with the same subject matter as the tragedy itself, so that the intermission is a continuation of the play through other means, an integral part of the whole. The second strong point in favour of the chorus lies, according to Brumoy, in the added *vraisemblance* it brings, since there are occasions in which the presence of a large onstage attendance to the action is expected. Both Dacier and Brumoy thus defend the theoretical legitimacy of a chorus onstage, but what kind of chorus do they advocate?

While he insisted on the redeeming effects of the chorus for theatre, André Dacier forcibly condemned the choral combination of acting, singing, and dancing as mere 'superstition': 'I have often striven to understand what reasons made such skilled and refined men as the Athenians add music and dancing to the tragic action . . . I then realized that they had but followed their inclination and tried to satisfy their superstitious natures. The Greeks were of all men the most superstitious and prone to singing and dancing.'[28] This is one

[27] For a survey of the successive editions of *Le Théâtre des Grecs* from 1730 to 1826, see Pascal (2011: 113–31).

[28] Dacier (1692: 85). 'J'ay souvent tâché de comprendre les raisons qui avoient obligé des hommes aussi habiles et aussi délicats que les Athéniens, d'associer la musique et la danse aux actions tragiques . . . j'ai trouvé qu'ils avoient suivi en cela leur naturel, et cherché à contenter leur

of the few occasions in which this fierce 'Ancient' abandons ancient playwrights to modern censure. Dacier's chorus clearly does not dance or sing; it
stands as a collective actor, belonging to the same sphere and submitted to the
same laws of *vraisemblance* as any other character.

Brumoy echoes this dismissal of the singing and dancing chorus in a
distinctly more developed way. He presents embellished imitation as the
'secret solution to the opposition between art and nature'.[29] On the one
hand, 'music and dance contribute to the pleasure of the spectator, while
they also soothe the audience with a softer continuation of whichever emotion
was already elicited'.[30] But music and dancing differ from truth, and imitation
is lost for the benefit of aesthetic pleasure. On the other hand, too realistic an
imitation defeats the purpose of theatre: 'too true an imitation in tragedies
would act as the sight a lifeless corpse, more likely to frighten than to produce
the true pleasure to be expected from art.'[31] Verse and declamation are,
therefore, the solution: more beautiful than speech, they remain more natural
than singing.

Brumoy introduced on that ground a hierarchy between song and dance.
The eye is easier to shock than the ear: 'this explains that nowadays we can
endure operas (even if one can scarcely abide some passages which should be
chanted rather than sung). What would it be if dance was to be added? The
ridicule would be complete.'[32] Chorus members in a tragedy should thus move
and speak in as realistic a way as possible, and appear only when consistent
with verisimilitude.

A third angle on the musical potential of Greek choruses is developed in the
third dissertation of Dubos's *Reflexions critiques sur la poésie et sur la peinture*
(1770). Quoting Aristides Quintilianus' *On Music*, Dubos stresses that the
ancients called music not only the sound of instruments and voices but also
poetry, and the overall *actio* ('manner of delivering') as a music of the body.
This is an illuminating way to look at ancient theatre, not as a medley of
heterogeneous elements but as so many ways of 'composing music': through
sounds, words, and movement.[33]

---

superstition. Les grecs étaient les hommes du monde les plus superstitieux et les plus portez à la
danse et à la musique.'

[29] 'L'imitation embellie.' 'Le nœud secret de l'art et de la nature' (Brumoy 1749: 127).

[30] 'La musique et la danse contribuent à ce plaisir du spectateur, sans compter qu'elles
délassent en continuant doucement l'impression déjà commencée' (Brumoy 1749: 129).

[31] 'Une ressemblance trop vraie dans la tragédie serait comme un corps inanimé, plus capable
d'effrayer que de produire le véritable plaisir qu'on attend de l'art' (Brumoy 1749: 129).

[32] 'De là vient que l'on souffre de nos jours les Opéra, on a pourtant quelque peine à entendre
certains morceaux qui devroient être plutôt déclamés que chantés. Que serait-ce si la danse s'en
mêlait? Le ridicule serait accompli' (Brumoy 1749: 127).

[33] 'La musique des Anciens était une Science bien plus étendue que ne l'est notre Musique…Dans l'antiquité, l'art poëtique était un des arts subordonnés à la Musique, et par

His reading of ancient music as something that subsumes all the elements of the performance is in stark contrast with the main eighteenth-century paradigm for theatre, which is the art of painting. Aesthetic theories of the time divide the arts between visual, mimetic arts (painting in particular) and musical arts. Theatre is thus conceived mainly in visual terms as a succession of striking *tableaux* (there is, for example, a clear emphasis on the visual rather than on the acoustics in theatre building at the time). Dubos's approach proposes what is *de facto* another opposition between painting and music: painting, on the one hand, is static and spatial, while music develops in time and allows for movement. Yet Dubos does not reach the conclusion that choruses should therefore be able to dance and sing—he deduces from his insight that the singing and dancing of ancient choruses were in actual fact nothing but stately declamation and gestures, so that he de-musicalizes Greek choruses rather than allow for a view of the whole theatrical experience of ancient Greek as 'musical' in the extended sense he so interestingly unearths.[34] The chorus praised, advocated, or tolerated by theorists is a non-singing, non-dancing entity submitted to the same rules of *bienséance* and *vraisemblance* as the rest of the cast.

According to Dacier and Brumoy, the only remaining function that prevents choruses from being just another actor is that of delivering the odes (which bridge the gap between the acts). Brumoy writes: 'since the invention of true tragedy the chorus has never sung anything that was not to do with the whole play.'[35] The idea that choral odes should allude to the plot or situations of the play sounds intellectually satisfying: but what does a practitioner have to say about this? In the Sixth Letter on *Oedipe*, containing a discussion on choruses, published with the first 1719 edition, Voltaire rather debunks theoretical enthusiasm for choral intermission. The chorus can speak only about what has just happened, what is about to happen, or something entirely different: in any case 'it was bound to be boring'.[36]

---

conséquent c'étoit la Musique qui enseignoit la construction des vers de toute figure' (Dubos 1993: 291).

[34] 'Il paroît donc évident que le chant des pièces dramatiques qui se récitoient sur les théâtres des Anciens n'avoient ni passages, ni ports de voix cadencés, ni tremblemens soutenus, ni les autres caractères de notre chant musical: en un mot que ce chant étoit une déclamation comme la nôtre' (Dubos 1993: 321).

[35] 'Depuis l'invention de la véritable tragédie ... il [le chœur] ne chantait rien qui ne fût lié à tout l'ouvrage' (Brumoy 1749: 120).

[36] Sixième lettre, qui contient une dissertation sur les chœurs. Voltaire (2001: 374).

THE CHORUS MOCKED

If it is not for the continuity and constant occupation of the stage, or the moral reflection that they can provide, what purpose can choruses possibly serve? Are chorus members, according to Voltaire, nothing but glorified stage extras? When the playwright dismissed choral odes as useless, he had just received great acclamation from the incredibly popular production of his first play, *Oedipe*, featuring, as it happens, a chorus. In the Sixth Letter on *Oedipe*, he actually defends what he thinks is the only possible way of having a chorus: 'I transformed the chorus into a character, appearing at its proper rank, as the other actors, and sometimes showing itself without speaking, in order to add more interest to the scene or more pomp to the show.'[37] What is this 'proper rank' of the chorus? The main problem encountered by Voltaire was that, if a chorus can sing together, it cannot really speak together. He accordingly singles out two chorus characters (*personnages du chœur*) thus giving his chorus a voice without destroying the idea of a collective entity.

This arrangement, even if it might not sound overly daring, nonetheless provoked laughter and taunts from spectators. In the *Discours sur la tragédie*, appended to the first edition of *Brutus* in 1731, Voltaire explains that the ridicule was prompted by the unskilled declamation of the *personnage du chœur*.[38] This in itself seems surprising: the 'chorus' was composed, as far as one can gather from the registers of the *Comédie*, by men and women who belonged to the *Comédiens Français*. The audience may actually have jeered at the lines themselves, since close to half of the first eight lines delivered by the two members of the chorus begin with the lyrical 'ô' (which stands as a fair estimate of the percentage of 'ô' sentences pronounced by the chorus throughout the play). It gives a clue as to what the 'proper rank' of the chorus might be. The term 'rank' has been taken so far in an aesthetic sense: what is the proper place for a chorus that has no apportioned time and no dedicated space in the performance? It is merely a cumbersome actor. But rank implies first and foremost a social hierarchy: in the spectacle of kings and princes, which is what tragedy is supposed to be, a crowd of people has to know its place. The chorus is thus more an echo than an actual voice in the play.

Voltaire's choices both in his aesthetic and social representation of the chorus were lampooned in a one-act parody by the Italian author and actor 'Dominique' (Domenico Giuseppe Biancolelli), performed at the Théâtre Italien: *Oedipe Travesti*. Hierarchy disappears since Trivelin, the Oedipus

---

[37] Voltaire (2001: 374): 'J'en ai fait un personnage qui paraît à son rang comme les autres acteurs et qui se montre quelques fois sans parler, seulement pour jeter plus d'intérêt dans la scène et pour ajouter plus de pompe au spectacle.'

[38] Voltaire (1998: 176): 'Le parterre . . . ne sentit d'abord que le prétendu ridicule d'avoir mis ces vers dans la bouche d'acteurs peu accoutumés, et il fit un éclat de rire.'

character, is an innkeeper rather than a king. In Voltaire's play, the dying people of Thebes are entirely loyal to their king, to the extent that they regret saving themselves at the cost of their king's downfall. In stark contrast, the chorus of village people in Dominique's play makes it very clear that Trivelin is to be executed if he really is the cause of the plague. In a parody of Voltaire's Act III, scene 4, Lucas, the one and only speaking chorus member, says in scene 6: 'I will die of the plague if you don't name him', 'when he is executed, we will be saved'.[39] The peasant Lucas voices the concern of all the villagers using, like the bumpkin that he is, the French 'je nous sauverons', the first person of the singular ('je') followed by the verb in the first person plural ('sauverons'). The obvious aim here is to make fun of the social status of Voltaire's chorus of ordinary Thebans in a tragedy. It could also target the uneducated declamation of the original chorus of Voltaire's play, since the regionalism strongly indicates that the actor playing Lucas delivered his lines with a strong rural accent. But the collision between 'I' and 'we' is very apt indeed, in as much as it echoes and ridicules at the same time the problematic collective voice of Voltaire's chorus.

Voltaire's members of the chorus were hampered in their speech—how did they occupy the performing space? As the dying people of Thebes, they could not with much similitude move together in a beautifully ordered way. According to the stage directions in the published text, at the beginning of Act I, scene 2, they are meant to stand together in a group: 'The gates of the temple open to reveal the High Priest surrounded by chorus members.'[40] They first appear in the second scene of Act I (which corresponds to the parodos or chorus entrance in Sophocles' play) through the door of the temple at the back of the stage. This chorus entrance recalls what Racine had done in *Athalie*, where a door opens and spectators are made to see, beyond it, guards approaching from every quarter. Similarly, Voltaire's chorus probably stood on each side of the great priest.

THE SILENT CHORUS

Voltaire tried and failed to integrate a chorus in a later tragedy with a similar plot, *Eriphyle* (1732). The play was never published or performed a second time after its unsuccessful premiere, but was adapted, without the chorus, into another tragedy, *Sémiramis*, so that he never actually wrote another play with a chorus. Besides the cold reception of his first chorus in *Oedipe*, another

---

[39] 'Quand il sera branché, je nous sauverons tous' (Degauque 2002: 114).
[40] Voltaire (2001: 178): 'La porte du temple s'ouvre, et le grand-prêtre paraît au milieu du chœur.'

concern might have checked Voltaire's further experiments with choruses: sheer lack of space. Voltaire's *Oedipe* was performed by the *Comédiens du Roi* in the theatre of the Rue des Fossés Saint-Germain des Près, on a stage occupied on both sides by benches for aristocratic members of the audience. The presence of spectators on stage allowed for very lively interactions between the audience and the performance, but was frequently denounced by authors and actors alike and was held responsible for the failure of more than one play. This setting allowed very little room for a chorus of around ten to evolve on stage. When the performing space was freed of spectators in 1759, Voltaire immediately wrote a play to exploit the potential of the new arena open to him. In *Tancrède* he had no less than eighty supernumeraries present on stage. Forty years after *Oedipe*, the hampered chorus had become a silent troop of soldiers impersonated by stage extras.

In 'Oedipe à Vicence et à Paris: Deux moments d'une histoire', Pierre Vidal-Naquet wrote that *Oedipus Tyrannus* required a threefold dimension: 'the tyrant, the civic presence of the chorus and Tiresias, embodying the access to the sacred'.[41] Voltaire is the first to translate this threefold dimension on stage. His *Oedipe* involves a temple, just as in Racine's *Athalie*. But, whereas *Athalie* takes place within the temple in typical Racinian dramaturgy, where the stage is an inbetween space between both the inner sanctum and the outside, Voltaire sets it just outside, in the public space in view of both the palace and the temple. This threefold dimension is present not only in Voltaire's *Oedipe* but in a sequence of tragedies that span his career, which could be called, because of this essentially Greek inspired choice of setting, his 'Sophoclean plays'. The plots of these plays present variations on both the Oedipian and the Oresteian storyline: an old king is killed by the queen or by the queen's lover, and a son is confronted with the task of avenging his father's death. These include *Oedipe* (1719) and *Oreste* (1750), of course, but also *Mérope* (1743), *Sémiramis* (1748), and its earlier version, *Eriphyle* (1732); this plot type can also be found with variations even in the later plays such as *Olympie* (1762) or *Les Lois de Minos* (1774). Voltaire chose for these plays a public space framed by the monuments of temporal and spiritual power: a temple and a palace, with, in many cases, the tomb (or the actual body) of the dead king. Voltaire thus draws the tragic action outside, and effectively puts it under the public eye (as well as under the eye of his audience) after decades of tragic vestibules and anterooms. Choosing as he did to set his plays in public places, he thus created a void calling for the presence of the citizens or the subjects ruled by the political and religious powers at play in the drama.

Voltaire's attempts to come to terms with the chorus go beyond Brumoy's idea that in some situations it is only too *vraisemblable* that a great number of

---

[41] Vidal-Naquet (1981: 17): 'Le tyran, le chœur, organe civique, et le détenteur de l'accès au sacré Tirésias.'

people be present. There is in Voltaire's vision of tragedy the idea that a representation of power fails if one merely sees the few who wield it. A multitude of stage extras silently find their way into plays like *Sémiramis*, *Tancrède*, and *Olympie*, after the failure of the collective voice of the chorus in *Oedipe*. Their theatrical importance lies not only in the pomposity of show or in increased verisimilitude but in a political vision that the representation of kings is trivial if it is not for the representation of the subjects. In the setting he creates for his Sophoclean plays (much more than in the actual plot of *Oedipe* and *Oreste*), Voltaire links the fates of the ruler and his subjects in a public performing space, which calls out for a collective presence. The Voltairean tragic day, to quote *Oedipe*, 'va du peuple et du roi changer la destinée', and sets the scene for a change in the joint destinies of both people and king.[42]

---

[42] Act I, scene 3; Voltaire (2001: 179).

13

Sunk in the 'Mystic Abyss': The 'Choral' Orchestra in Wagner's Music Dramas

Laurence Dreyfus

Richard Wagner's debt to classical Greek theatre has enjoyed a sporadic, if also chequered, reception within Wagner studies. The first writer to treat the matter was Friedrich Nietzsche, whose *Birth of Tragedy out of the Spirit of Music* (1872) is dedicated to Wagner. Though indifferent to any Greek 'influence' on Wagner, Nietzsche saw in Wagner's works a reincarnation of the Attic spirit that joined Apollonian dreams and Dionysian intoxication in an ecstatic amalgam, cementing 'the fraternal bond of both deities of art in tragedy'.[1] So pronounced was this fusion that Wagner's *Tristan* sired a 'truly aesthetic listener'—*alias* Friedrich Nietzsche—for whom, just like the ancient Greek audience, art defeated pessimism by acting as 'as a rescuing, expertly healing enchantress'.[2] Astonishingly, Wagner's *Tristan und Isolde* was the only piece of music described in the entire text.[3] Wagner's dramas served not so much as a recipient of classical values but rather as an exemplar that explained Greek tragedy by clothing its spirit in a contemporary guise. Schopenhauer's elevation of music above the other art forms also pulled Nietzsche's strings, so that the life force (*der Wille*) embodied in music inspired Dionysian ecstasy within Aeschylean tragedy before the form's later decline under Euripides and Athenian rationalism.

Nietzsche's fantasies resulted in a famous attack by the young philologist Ulrich von Wilamowitz-Moellendorff, who reproved Nietzsche for his

[1] Nietzsche (1984 [1895]: 144–5). Translations are mine unless otherwise noted.

[2] Nietzsche (1984 [1895]: 148).

[3] Nietzsche refers to a performance of Wagner's *Lohengrin* and, obliquely, to the text of the *Ring des Nibelungen*. He also cites Hans Sachs's text on poem as dream from *Die Meistersinger*. The only other composers named are Palestrina, J. S. Bach, and Beethoven, the last in two passing references to the 'Pastoral' Symphony and the 'Ode to Joy' from the Ninth Symphony, respectively.

unscholarly approach and—coincidentally—for serving as Wagner's apologist.[4] Years later, embarrassed by his early work, Nietzsche admitted his disregard for coherent argument and neglect of evidence in the *Birth of Tragedy*.[5] He had certainly produced some stirring propaganda for Wagner, but revealed little about the birth of Wagner's theories out of the spirit of the Greeks.

Why anyone in the nineteenth century bothered to ask about Wagner and the Greeks is not entirely obvious. Despite Wagner's documented enthusiasm for Attic tragedy in his Dresden period in the 1840s and in the Zurich writings just thereafter—when he was theorizing a synthesis of the arts in his music dramas—the composer made a point of devising texts that avoided classical subjects and references. His sources drew rather on Norse and Germanic sagas for the *Ring* and on later medieval romances by Gottfried von Strassburg and Wolfram von Eschenbach for *Tristan* and *Parsifal*.[6] Only when the twentieth-century classicist Wolfgang Schadewaldt (1900–74)—a pupil of Wilamowitz-Moellendorff—finally began peering behind Wagner's medievalist façade did he notice not only the composer's enthusiastic Hellenism, but also his wide, if amateurish, reading of nineteenth-century scholarship on the Greeks. It became easy to propose a host of classical models lurking behind the scenes, models whose formative hand could be detected in a plethora of dramatic contexts.[7] Within Wagner's voluminous theoretical writings, moreover, an idealized view of Greek culture popped off the page, and, in more recent studies, writers have stressed how Wagner valued the Greeks as an antipode to a debased German and European culture laid low by crass materialism, Latinate lethargy, and what he targeted as a pernicious 'Judaism'. John Deathridge and Simon Goldhill have rightly drawn attention to the insidious political dimensions of these connections, and it is fair, from an ideological

---

[4] Wilamowitz-Moellendorff (1969 [1872]). The attempted rebuttals by Erwin Rohde and Wagner himself are detailed in Silk and Stern (1981: 95–107) and encapsulated in the sentence: 'It is not easy to summarize what Wilamowitz objected to in *The Birth of Tragedy* except with the one word, *everything*' (Silk and Stern 1981: 96). Wilamowitz later claimed that he had been incensed by Nietzsche's slight of his mentor at Bonn, Otto Jahn. Jahn, Mozart's first serious biographer, had written negative reviews of *Tannhäuser* and *Lohengrin* in 1853–4. Nietzsche encountered them in Jahn (1866). See Silk and Stern (1981: 383).

[5] Nietzsche's subsequent embarrassment over the *Birth of Tragedy* concedes its absence of 'logical tidiness . . . thus overreaching with evidence, even distrustful of the propriety of evidence'. The new opening section is entitled 'An attempt at self-criticism'. Nietzsche (1984 [1895]: 10).

[6] The sources for the *Mastersingers of Nuremberg* are nineteenth-century literary and historical works, including also the libretto for an opera on Hans Sachs by Lortzing.

[7] Schadewaldt was invited by Wieland Wagner in 1962 to deliver a series of lectures on Wagner and the Greeks at the Bayreuth Festival. These are published in Schadewaldt (1970) and translated in Schadewaldt (2000). Subsequent works of criticism, such as by Michael Ewans (1982), pursue similar dramatic and structural parallels.

perspective, to treat Wagner's reception of the Greeks as far from innocent or naive.[8]

At the same time, it is misleading to claim that Wagner's Hellenism is directed primarily to serve a nationalist political agenda. Daniel Foster, for example, intimates this kind of connection in claiming that, in Wagner's translation of aesthetic function, 'the chorus handed down to the orchestra the duty of conveying commentary and narrative wisdom both from and to *das Volk*'.[9] However, it is Foster, not Wagner, who links the Attic Chorus with the idealized German *Volk*, which Wagner nowhere identifies as such. By placing 'das Volk' in German 'scare' italics, Foster also evokes a presumed nationalist trajectory from Herder to Hitler. Wagner, on the other hand, is constructing a potted history of the Greek chorus in later tragedy, so that, when he speaks of the 'chorus stepping down from the stage into the people'—quoted by Foster—he is actually characterizing the superiority of Shakespearian tragedy, whose 'artistic technique had completely overcome the necessity of the chorus'.[10] English audiences at the Globe, needless to say, are unlikely participants at Nazi rallies.

Wagner's appreciation of the Hellenist chorus proves an interesting case, precisely because it has nothing to do with German *völkisch* superiority, but everything to do with the composer's mature theories of music and drama. The Greek choral ideal in Wagner's writings, as I shall try to show, has been less than precisely understood, and gave rise to one of the most exciting developments in the history of opera. For, in enthusing over the Aeschylean chorus, Wagner was able to change the face of opera, thereby reconfiguring fundamental issues relating to music and drama.

The stage chorus had featured in opera from its beginnings in the seventeenth century, and Wagner was prolific in deploying large choral forces in early works such as *Das Liebesverbot* and *Rienzi* in which he aped all the conventions of contemporary Franco-Italian works. By the end of the 1840s, though, he became increasingly scathing about opera's inadequacies and started to work out a more unified poetic conception of a staged and sung drama indebted to a choral ideal invoking Antiquity. From his new critical perspective, the stage chorus was an index of opera's dramatic inadequacy. How to rethink the Greek chorus was a theme on which he expended considerable effort, though the solution was not immediately clear.

Wagner was, of course, not the first German dramatist to call for a revival of the Greek chorus, and he certainly knew the celebrated preface to Friedrich Schiller's *Bride of Messina* (1803), which had defended a choral renewal in modern tragedy. Schiller suggested the chorus would 'be its own advocate if it had ever been presented in a proper manner':[11] 'The abolition of the chorus

[8] Deathridge (2008) and Goldhill (2008).   [9] Foster (2010: 223).
[10] Wagner (1983 [1850]: 61–2).   [11] Schiller (1986 [1803]: 3).

and the collapse of this sensibly powerful device into the characterless substitute of a dull confidant had by no means improved tragedy as much as the French and their imitators imagined.'[12] For Schiller, the chorus enables the modern dramatist 'to dispense with all that is antagonistic to poetry, and leads him back to the most simple, original, and natural motives [*naivesten Motive*] of action'.[13] It does this by bringing out the poetry of the play, thereby converting the modern world into a poetic one: 'The chorus thus purifies tragic poetry, insomuch as it separates reflection from the action, and by this separation arms tragedy with a poetic power, as the visual artist, by means of a rich backdrop, transforms the ordinary poverty of costume into charm and beauty.'[14] As a representative of an ideal person, Schiller's chorus is split into two, and is represented 'in contest with itself'.[15] In the *Bride of Messina*, two semi-choruses are attached to the two 'enemy brothers', so that, dramatically, the chorus represents both an ideal person and a real character.

Wagner's view of the Greek chorus was even more idealized and abstract than Schiller's, and it was this ability to engage with a distant apparition that helped him diagnose what was wrong with modern opera. His Romanticised vision of the chorus in Attic tragedy, drawn particularly from his reading of Gustav Droysen's translation of the *Oresteia* (1832), prompted him to address the dramaturgical foundations of lyric theatre *tout court*. While there could be no question of reviving the Greek chorus in an unmediated form, Wagner's new dramatic theory cast the modern Beethovenian orchestra in the role of the chorus. With the chorus transposed into the orchestra pit and its voice admirably suited to expressing a collective sentiment, there was not much need for an actual chorus of persons on stage. While conceiving of the *Ring* in 1850—the complete poem was already published in 1853, the same year that he began composing the music for *Das Rheingold*—Wagner even toyed with banning a singing chorus outright, so extreme was his antipathy to the conventions of modern opera. Instead, he theorized that the new 'choral' orchestra would speak more directly to the spectator precisely when it was *hidden* from view. So, in Wagner's subsequent plans for a festival theatre designed for performances of his *Ring*, he ensured that instrumentalists and conductor were enclosed in a deep subterranean pit covered in part by a shell-like lip so that the orchestra was partially visible to the singers but not at all to the audience.

Sunk in this invisible space—which Wagner called the *mystischer Abgrund* or 'mystic abyss'—the new choral orchestra foreshadowed action on the stage as much as reflected on it by way of repeated musical gestures, which later came to be called musical leitmotifs or leading motives. A ban on the stage chorus is upheld in the first three *Ring* operas, and it appears only in

---

[12] Schiller (1986 [1803]: 7–8).   [13] Schiller (1986 [1803]: 8).
[14] Schiller (1986 [1803]: 10).   [15] Schiller (1986 [1803]: 12).

Götterdämmerung, Act II, where Wagner retained the structure of the libretto he had written for *Siegfrieds Tod* (1848), a successor to the Romantic opera *Lohengrin* with a new genre dubbed a Grand Heroic Opera (*eine große Heldenoper*). By the time the composer reached the composition of the music for his newly titled finale to the *Ring*, *Götterdämmerung* (*Twilight of the Gods*), he was able to achieve something he could never have imagined in 1850: an amassed stage chorus of Gibichung vassels sing a horrifyingly ironic inversion of a Meyerbeerian choral *unisono*.[16]

The stage chorus makes limited if important appearances in each of Wagner's other mature operas, *Tristan und Isolde* (1857), *Die Meistersinger von Nürnberg* (1868), and *Parsifal* (1882), but in each case its use is subordinated to the by now well-entrenched choral orchestra in the pit. It is fair to say that in none of these works is the choral function either neo-Hellenist or an echo of the static mob calling 'Hail to the Prince'. In *Tristan*, the Cornish sailors are completely ignorant of the Love–Death that preoccupies the protagonists who have declared their hopeless passion at just the wrong moment. While the sailors hail King Marke in the blameless key of C major as they prepare for landfall, it is the choral orchestra that experiences the cognitive dissonance between the diatonic realm and the eroticism of the chromatic *Tristan* harmonies of Desire. In *Die Meistersinger*, the stage chorus runs riot in the second act as a foil for Hans Sachs's Schopenhauerian ruminations on delusion (*Wahn*) and renunciation: they certainly react impulsively as the People to Beckmesser's mangling of the Prize Song but end by praising—not the German people—but German art composed by individual master singers. And in *Parsifal*, the chorus acts out the ritual of the Grail ceremony in Act I, reacts angrily in Act III to Amfortas's failure to celebrate it, and finally sings an extraordinary apotheosis of Amens, an operatic oxymoron if ever there was one. The point is that Wagner allows a return to the stage chorus only after he is able to transmute its ideal Greek function into the instrumental orchestra. One could equally assert that the stage chorus no longer posed an aesthetic threat but became a place to experiment further with new dramaturgical impulses.

Based on a design initially drafted together with the architect Gustav Semper, the Festival Theatre in Bayreuth was built in the early 1870s to put

---

[16] Foster (2010: 221) insightfully treats this use of the chorus as a parody of Meyerbeer, calling it 'the joke behind *Götterdämmerung*', but, like the old line about German humour, it is no laughing matter. Foster's idea of Hagen as a Franco-Jewish choir master is not based on historical evidence, but rather a tissue of associations that reduces all negative characters in Wagner's operas into anti-Semitic or anti-Gallic stereotypes (Foster 2010: 224–8). What Foster fails to cite is that Wagner's polemic against Meyerbeer's unison chorus is actually a left-wing critique of mass uniformity associated with Germans rather than with Jews: 'when Meyerbeer's Huguenots soar to the highest pitch, we *hear* in them what we *see* in a Prussian battalion of Guards, what German critics call . . . the emancipation of the masses' (Wagner 1983 [1850]: 64).

Wagner's choral ideal into practice. The striking construction of the *Orchestergraben* occasioned widespread critical comment at the premiere of the four *Ring* operas in 1876—*Das Rheingold, Die Walküre, Siegfried,* and *Götterdämmerung*—and with one fell swoop breathed into life a novel theatrical experience. In Wagner's dramas—as he preferred to call his operas after 1850—there was to be no customary entry of the conductor through the orchestra pit accompanied by the applause of the audience. Rather, the hall was darkened, with only the faint glow of light emanating from just below the stage. There the conductor could sit or stand at his podium in full view of the singers and orchestral players, who might decipher their parts in shirt sleeves, since no one ever saw them. Even today, the first low E flat octaves sounded by the contrabasses at the opening of *Das Rheingold* are shrouded in mystery because no one in the audience sees the conductor's upbeat that ushers in the opening tones. (Figures 13.1 and 13.2 show the Bayreuth Festspielhaus in 2008.)

From a musical point of view, the move away from traditional opera—with its recitatives, arias, choruses, finales, and dance numbers—towards sung drama stocked with a lexicon of leitmotifs played by a 'choral orchestra' sparked a revolution in musico-dramatic thinking. Not only have later opera composers—such as Richard Strauss, Claude Debussy, Alban Berg, even Giacomo Puccini—adopted this method, but since the 1930s film scores have been routinely composed in a pseudo-Wagnerian vein. And though within the field

Fig. 13.1. The hall from the royal loge of the Bayreuth Festspielhaus, 2008. Photographer: Enrico Nawrath

Fig. 13.2. The orchestra pit or *Orchestergraben* of Bayreuth Festspielhaus as occupied by instrumentalists and conductor, 2008. Photographer: Enrico Nawrath

of musicology we think we know pretty much what a Wagnerian leitmotif is and how it works, it is actually Wagner's classical references and his notion of the Greek chorus that shed new light on the technique and its developed forms.

On first acquaintance, Wagner's term, the 'mystic abyss' or *mystischer Abgrund*, seems to have been coined half in jest, whereas, in fact, it depends on a telling classical reference. The phrase, Wagner says, arose out of his discussions with the architect Gottfried Semper for the Festival Hall in Bayreuth in which the 'empty space between the proscenium and the front row of seats had to separate reality from ideality'.[17] That is fine as far as it goes, but this first definition omits the reason why this abyss or gulf was in any way mystical. In a subsequent long-winded paragraph, Wagner clarifies how he intended the music emanating from the hidden pit to function as a vehicle of prophecy and oracle. What he describes is

a transported picture of the inapproachability of a dream-like phenomenon: the phantasmal music resounding from out of the 'mystic abyss'—just like the rising vapours from Gaia's holy womb beneath the seat of the Pythia—[which] transpose [the spectator] into that enthralled state of clairvoyance in which the scenic picture now becomes the most truthful copy of life itself.[18]

---

[17] Wagner (1911–14 [1873]: 337).   [18] Wagner (1911–14 [1873]: 338).

Fig. 13.3. *Priestess of Delphi* (1891) (oil on canvas), John Collier (1850–1934). Art Gallery of South Australia, Adelaide, Australia; Gift of the Rt Honourable, the Earl of Kintore 1893; The Bridgeman Art Library

The music is therefore compared to the mist rising from a chasm in the rock, which induced the Pythia to deliver her cryptic oracles in a heightened, frenzied state. The image of the Pythia shown in Figure 13.3, a Pre-Raphaelite depiction (1891) by the English painter John Collier (1850–1934), shows the rising vapours emerging from the earth's chasm, which Wagner heard as analogous to his mysterious orchestral music inducing a kind of second sight or clairvoyance. The tripos on which the Pythia sits is, perhaps not by accident, a kind of high conductor's stool such as would have been placed in the mystical abyss. This directorial seat of power recalls Wagner's notion of the conductor of his works as the composer's *alter ego*, an appellation he offered to Franz Liszt and Hermann Levi when they conducted *Lohengrin* and *Parsifal*, respectively. The clairvoyant aspect also recalls Wagner's views on conducting expressed in his eponymous essay in which he envisaged a parallel transmutation of personae: the conductor (Wagner) imagines the voice of Beethoven calling from the grave, instructing him how to play the fateful opening of the Fifth Symphony.[19] In all these cases, the rendition of a musical work entails some imagined or mystic substitution of one personage for another, evoking some ideal agency imbued with authority. As for the status of his own musical scores—following from this reference to the Pythia—what Wagner has mind is far from a simple commentary on stage action but rather a vision of music that transfixes the listener by an oracular communication.

By the time of his 1873 essay on the Festival Hall, Wagner had already composed virtually all the music to his tetralogy *Der Ring des Nibelungen*, but even much earlier, while in Swiss exile when he was first drafting its initial ideas during the period 1849–51, he was obsessed with the Greek theatre in which the ancient chorus played such a crucial role. In his essay 'Art and Revolution' of 1849, for example, Wagner writes of

all the urges of [the Athenian's] handsome body, of his restless spirit [which] propelled him toward the rebirth of his essential being through ideal expression of art; when the fully resounding voice was raised into choral song to sing of Apollo's deeds and at the same time give the rousing beat to the dancers for the dance which pictured those very deeds in elegant and dashing movements.[20]

Choral song, according to this account, (1) was full and sonorous, (2) recounts noble actions, and (3) triggers a dance impulse that gives gestural shape to the action, a description that resembles Wagner's praise of Beethoven's instrumental music, with its 'boundless inner capacity', which expresses 'specific, characteristically individual impressions ... in an ever more compulsive force'.[21] (From a dramaturgical point of view, Beethoven lacks only the recounting of precise deeds.) Indeed, Wagner evokes the Pythia also in connection with Beethoven, writing that 'these mighty convulsions and the painfully blissful stammerings of Pythian ecstasy ... could only create the impression of a genial madman'.[22]

Given Wagner's idealization of choral song, one might have thought that the reform of opera demanded an imaginative reconstitution of the Greek chorus in modern form. Having experienced just such an attempt in Dresden in 1841, however, Wagner was sure that historical posturing was doomed to fail. Not only was the conventional baggage of the bourgeois opera house in no way equipped for oracular and mystic utterances, but historic reconstructions

---

[19] See Dreyfus (2007: 263–5).
[20] Wagner (1983 [1849]: 275).
[21] Wagner (1983 [1850]: 72, 73).
[22] Wagner (1983 [1850]: 73).

were themselves lame and by definition anti-dramatic. Wagner was sweep-
ingly dismissive of Felix Mendelssohn's hugely successful incidental music for
Sophocles's *Antigone* (op. 55), for example, which had been rendered in a
metric translation by Johann Jakob Christian Donner (1839) and staged in
Berlin by Ludwig Tieck in 1841.[23] The Donner translation substituted
accented and unaccented stresses in the German for the quantitative patterns
in the Greek, and Mendelssohn introduced this formal distinction into a
highly artificial music that saw performances all across Europe.

Wagner was less than impressed. In *Opera and Drama*, he belittled the
'antiquarian fidelity' that resulted in a 'coarse and arty white lie . . . spawned by
a poverty of artistry so as to gloss over the sham of our entire art-world'.[24] Yet
this travesty revealed a useful 'truth': that an authenticist revival could never
equal true drama. In a private joke—years later in 1880—Wagner sang to his
family the choral setting of the first stasimon (the Ode to Man), alluding to
Mendelssohn's stylized music while miming Tieck's stilted stage action of
the chorus, which consisted, he said, of 'two steps forward, one back'.[25] This
was music that could please only scholars, not theatre folk, as when the
eminent Leipzig philologist Gottfried Hermann, after hearing *Antigone* with
Mendelssohn's music, reportedly told the composer: 'You even observed the
metre in the choruses!'[26]

Wagner's critique of *Antigone*'s awkward declamation and sentimental
musical style betrays an aesthetic incompatible with Mendelssohn's intentions.
One can see what Wagner was reacting against by examining the choral setting
of 'Numberless are the world's wonders, but none more wondrous than man'.
Mendelssohn conjures his vision of the antique world by intentionally muti-
lating the pastoral musical genre of the *siciliano*: instead of gentle dotted lilts in
the music, false accents and a thwarting of conventional phrase lengths mimic
artificial accents in the translated poetry. Combined with tuneful but banal
harmonies, the effect is distancing and falsely historicized: the musical setting
hinges on the depiction of a radically foreign 'other' to be espied from afar by a
contemporary listener. Married to the rather silly choreography Wagner
described, one can see how this attempt at an 'authentick' Hellenic chorus
fell flat. John Deathridge presumes there was a 'strong anti-Semitic sentiment'
motivating 'Wagner's belief in the fundamental untruth of [Mendelssohn's]
revival',[27] but, if anything, Wagner was intimidated by Mendelssohn's classical
learning, and was certainly not one to muzzle himself when fired up about a
supposedly baleful influence of *Judentum*, should he have chosen to do so.

---

[23] See Geary (2006).   [24] Wagner (1983 [1850]: 149).
[25] Gregor-Dellin and Mack (1978: ii. 495).
[26] Geary (2006: 191).   [27] Deathridge (2008: 103).

As vital as he found the literary spirit of the Greek chorus, Wagner was convinced that theatrical and operatic developments made it obsolete. Instead, he argues in *Opera and Drama* (1850):

The Chorus of Greek Tragedy has lent its affective significance for the drama to the modern orchestra alone, which is allowed to develop a limitless and diverse form of enunciation, free from every restriction. Its actual human aspect is relocated *from the orchestra onto the stage* [emphasis added] so as to expose the core of its human individuality found in the Greek chorus to the highest and most self-conscious flowering as the visible actor or sufferer participates in the drama itself.[28]

Like the ancient chorus, the modern orchestra was uniquely placed to voice the 'unutterable', both by 'instrumental motives' or 'melodic moments' in their foreshadowing and recollection of the experience underlying events, but also in the embodiment of choral gesture, which disclosed the sense and emotive framework behind actions. Interestingly, Wagner's view of music, though indebted to garden-variety Romantic philosophy, was not yet nuanced by Schopenhauer's empowering musical metaphysics. Wagner was introduced to Schopenhauer's writings by Georg Herwegh only in 1854, and thereafter he abandoned his explicit attacks on the outrageous supremacy of the 'feminine' spirit of music in opera—compared to the outrage of a woman at the helm— since Schopenhauer had made clear that music was indeed for ever in charge, and that was a very good thing. Wagner, on the other hand, would at least have been able to console himself that his choral orchestra, in voicing the 'unutterable', anticipated Schopenhauer in embodying and enacting the secret life of the Will.

Like Schiller, Wagner splits the ancient chorus into two, though with a radically different division of labour. The chorus's dramatic agency is invested in individual protagonists seen onstage, while its signifying affects and danced gestures are hidden from view in the mystic abyss. The singing actors maintain their relationship with the new orchestral chorus, but no longer turn their back to the chorus to put into practice the oracular pronouncements now heard in the orchestra.

As much as Wagner sought to transform one side of the spirit of the ancient tragic chorus into an orchestral evocation, he also distanced his new choral orchestra from the modern opera chorus. As against the Greek models in all respects, the modern chorus was opera's greatest contemporary abomination, devoid of dramatic function. By contrast, in his favourite scenes from the *Oresteia*—such as Cassandra and the chorus in *Agamemnon*, which in 1874 he called 'the most perfect thing mortal art has ever produced'[29]—the chorus engaged in subtle dialogue with the protagonist. He was also wildly attached to 'the profoundly mystical feature' of the opening allegorical chorus about eagles

---

[28] Wagner (1983 [1850]: 328).   [29] Gregor-Dellin and Mack (1978: i. 805).

and hares in *Agamemnon*,[30] in which Aeschylus was able to speak 'like a priest in the midst of a community'.[31] Here was a clear case where 'art works in metaphors and allegories as such but at the same time conveys to the emotions the truth behind the dogmas'.[32] Speaking true is a matter not merely of revealing a plotline unknown to a protagonist, but of conveying an emotional reality via a powerful use of metaphor.

There was a musicality, moreover, which Wagner detected in the rhythm of these choruses. In the first scene in *Choephoroi*, Wagner described to Cosima 'its surgings and its constantly returning flow'. Moreover, he continues: 'I know something else like this: *Tristan and Isolde* in the 2nd act.'[33] Both the literary content of Aeschylus's great choruses as well as their large-scale formal patterns were, therefore, to be imagined and reconstructed within a musical sphere. According to Cosima's diaries from 1879, Wagner expounded one day 'about Aeschylus's chorus', saying 'one could write a whole book about it'.[34] Though it is difficult to know exactly what Wagner perceived in the *Choephoroi*, it was probably the sequence of strophes and antistrophes with the imagined movement of the chorus from west to east and then east to west that he heard as parallel to the ebb and flow of contrasting musical material in *Tristan*, which delineates in striking detail successive stages of the lovers' desire: from increased yearning and passionate impatience through to sudden rapture and somnolent caresses.[35]

The opera chorus, on the other hand, lacked both dramatic motivation and rhythmic impulse. 'The massive chorus of our modern opera'—Wagner writes—'is nothing other than the theatre scenery and curtains made to move around and sing, the mute grandeur of the backdrops transformed into mobile noise'.[36] These choruses not only lack dramatic function but can do no more than cry out 'Prince and Princess' and repeat in thunderous unison the melody just sung in the aria by the protagonists:[37]

The individual personalities to whom the chorus had once sung their poetry [*gedichtet*] dissolved into a colourful massed milieu [*Umgebung*] without a centre point. As this milieu in the opera acts as a kind of tremendous stage apparatus, with its machines, painted backdrops and colourful costumes, the voice of the chorus calls out to us: 'I am I, and there is no other opera beyond me.'[38]

---

[30] Gregor-Dellin and Mack (1978: ii. 378).   [31] Gregor-Dellin and Mack (1978: ii. 637).
[32] Gregor-Dellin and Mack (1978: ii. 475).   [33] Gregor-Dellin and Mack (1978: ii. 496).
[34] Gregor-Dellin and Mack (1978: ii. 402–3).   [35] See Dreyfus (2010: 108–10).
[36] Wagner (1983 [1850]: 63–4).

[37] In *Opera and Drama*, there is still a leftist slant to Wagner's critique in which he hears the complete suppression of individual liberty congealed in the choral *unisono*: 'Thus too has our state nowadays emancipated the masses, when it makes them march battalion-wise in military uniform, wheel left and right, present and shoulder arms: when Meyerbeer's "Huguenots" [in the opera by the same name] reach their highest pitch, we *hear* in them the same thing we *see* in a Prussian guard battalion' (Wagner 1983 [1850]: 64).

[38] Wagner (1983 [1850]: 63). The reference to what Wagner would have taken as the God of the Old Testament in the first of the Ten Commandments (Exod. 20:2–3 and Deut. 5:6–7) is

The new Wagnerian choral orchestra shuns extraneous spectacle and super-fluous 'interludes', but is a vehicle for striking metaphors, tragic allegories, and deciphering gestures expressed in surging flows and hyper-rhythmic swirls. The orchestra's 'melodic moments' are fundamentally 'guides to feeling' (*Gefühlswegweiser*), music that also supports words sung onstage 'according to its illustrative capacity' (*nach seinem verdeutlichenden Vermögen*).[39] At least that was the plan. A tall order to be sure.

Wagner was imprudent enough to outline his new compositional practice long before he wrote a note of music for the *Ring*, and it has become customary to call him harshly to account, showing how his subsequent practice departs dramatically from his theory. But how could the composer know, after all, in 1850 how he would be able to handle the constitution of musical leitmotifs and larger issues of musical form in a work like the *Ring*, which he would complete only a quarter of a century later? What Wagner subsequently (in 1879) described as motivic 'fabric of basic themes embroidered throughout the entire art work' (*in einem das ganze Kunstwerk durchziehenden Gewebe von Grundthemen*),[40] in particular, has come under special attack. This has oc-curred in part because of the banal reception of the motives in the hands of Wagner's acolytes, chief among them, Hans von Wolzogen. Wolzogen was only the first of many who issued simplified leitmotivic guides in the form of popular brochures and tables attached to piano–vocal scores. In these guides and tables each leitmotif is given a pithy name and a melodic identity in musical notation so clear that everyone can brush up in advance for a Wagner performance and mentally congratulate themselves whenever they hear the SWORD or VALHALLA in the smug assurance that they understand exactly what is going on. The ease with which even musically unlettered listeners can learn to tag the leitmotifs led Thomas Mann to call Wagner 'a musician who can persuade even the unmusical to be musical'.[41] The ease of hearing the leitmotifs also prompted Theodor Adorno to stress their regressive nature, a gesture, he wrote, 'never able to express an emotional content directly', 'an allegorical picture . . . whose supposed psychological variations involve only a change of lighting'.[42]

For some years now Wagner scholars have been leading a retreat away from a serious consideration of leitmotifs, in part reacting against the leitmotif's appeal to amateur Wagnerians. Carolyn Abbate goes so far as to suggest that 'that Wagner's motifs have no referential meaning', arguing that Wagner

---

probably a crude anti-Judaic jibe linked also to his favourite Jewish whipping boy, Giacomo Meyerbeer, whose choruses Wagner is criticizing.

[39] Wagner (1983 [1850]: 338–9).

[40] Wagner (1983 [1879]: 334).

[41] Mann (1937: 134).

[42] Adorno (2005: 34–5). Adorno's assessment is contradicted by his own extensive critical practice devoted to Wagner's works.

writes music that 'projects poetry and stage action in ways far beyond motivic signs'.[43] What is remarkable in this scholarly development is that the debate has not actually been conducted between Wagner's music and his theoretical writings but rather between the music and the popular post-Wagnerian reception of the leitmotif. Strikingly, none of Wagner's own rhapsodies on its oracular function and gestural properties come into commonly encountered definitions of the leitmotif. For Arnold Whittall, writing in the authoritative *New Grove Dictionary* (1980), 'the leitmotif is a theme, or other coherent musical idea, clearly defined so as to retain its identity if modified on subsequent appearances, whose purpose is to represent or symbolize a person, object, place, idea, state of mind, supernatural force, or any other ingredient in a dramatic work.'[44] Not much room here for the unutterable or for music embodying gesture. So it is easy to see that the 'choral' orchestra in general and leitmotifs in particular have a tendency to look either blindingly redundant, repetitive, or inscrutable in cases where their associated names fail to live up to their pre-assigned function, names that were nowhere publicly labelled by Wagner.

To match Wagner's theory of the gestural choral orchestra to his leitmotivic practice opens up some interesting avenues, not least prompting one to ask how exactly the music aspires to express the 'unutterable'. In the remaining section of this chapter, I consider how a 'choral' reading of one of Wagner's leitmotifs exceeds the usual hermeneutic parameters and suggests how Wagner's theories had more predictive power than one commonly grants them.

A motive that occurs in all four operas of the *Ring* is the unambiguous CURSE (*der Fluch*), which first sounds in *Das Rheingold* after Wotan, chief among the gods, has wrested the all-powerful ring from Alberich, the dwarf who forged it—in effect, stealing it from him. Forging the ring had come at great cost to Alberich, who was forced to forswear love in order to steal the gold from the Rhine. Now outsmarted by Wotan, Alberich curses the ring, singing:

> Wie durch Fluch er mir geriet,
> verflucht sei dieser Ring!'
>
> (Just as [the ring] came to me through a curse
> Accursed be this ring!')

Wagner had predicted that 'melodic moments' such as these would derive from the verse melody and hence the declamation of the poetic text. However, it is clear here that the composer fitted the words to the music rather than the other way around. As can be seen in Figure 13.4, there are too many words for the notes of the actual motive, and Alberich has to repeat pitches to fit the

---

[43] Abbate (1989: 45).   [44] Whittall (1980).

Fig. 13.4. The CURSE motive from *Das Rheingold* in its initial and then 'ideal' form

music. In fact, Wagner sounds the ideal form of the CURSE for the first time when it takes effect—that is, when in the struggle for the ring between the two giants, Fafner murders his brother Fasolt in cold blood (see the lower system in Figure 13.4). As the gods stand in horror observing this act of barbarism, the choral orchestra sounds the CURSE, followed by Wotan's verbal commentary, 'Furchtbar nun erfind' ich des Fluches Kraft', the god's terrible discovery of the curse's power. Wotan's verbal interpolation is followed by another statement of the CURSE heard a step lower. This confirmatory consequent phrase answers the initial antecedent one. Taken together, the two musical statements form a dual unit that Wagner will use frequently throughout the *Ring*. Note the verbal redundancy if all the music does is refer back to Alberich's words at the first pronouncement of this evil oath as a reminiscence or as a hortatory choral commentary spouting the words, 'Curse—Curse'! Or even 'Remember the Curse, remember the Curse!'

The CURSE offers little in the way of hermeneutic commentary and is only in a limited sense an 'arbitrary and associative sign'. The motive is better grasped as a choral incantation that functions as a metaphor in which the music is 'heard-as' a curse to generate some new metaphorical content. The notion of 'hearing-as', developed by Christopher Peacocke, is an attractive way to think of musical representation,[45] but, interestingly, it is hard to tell the tenor from the vehicle in the metaphorical pairing.[46] That is, we both hear the music as the CURSE (because Alberich has named it) as much as we hear Alberich's curse as *this* music. Although we might like only to transfer the threatening qualities of curses to this passage of music, we also transfer perceived qualities of the passage of music to curses—here the obscene

---

[45] Peacocke (2009).   [46] See Dreyfus (2009: 294).

ugliness of a horizontalized half-diminished chord on F sharp over the timpani pedal tone followed by a rude interruption of a C major triad with an additional tuba, all blaring a demonic fanfare of hopelessness. Indeed, at the end of the first phrase of the CURSE, the ninth chord stifles any thought of resolution, which is felt only in the second phrase, which implies a dominant resolution though without ever stating the resolving tonic chord.

There is also a telling choice of orchestration in Wagner's use of three trombones, a traditional sign in opera for the spirit-underworld and for images of darkness and death. It is trombones that play at stately funerals and accompany otherworldly figures such as in the oracle scene in Gluck's *Alceste* (Act II, scene iii) or the appearance of the ghostly Commendatore in the Finale to Mozart's *Don Giovanni*. The formality of the two halting patterns of dotted figures—and especially the ominous descent in the musical register mid-stream—fuels the pure nastiness of a phrase that had never before been composed with such brazen dissonances. The rising and precipitous falling gesture seems to mime the movement of turning one's lip up and down to signal sneering disgust. The sneer nearly borders on an olfactory reaction—as if the ugly harmony gives off a malodorous scent and prompts an involuntary gestural reaction. Perhaps this goes too far, but, if we try imaginatively to embody the gesture of the music, alert to all its musical parameters—metre, tempo, melody, dynamics, texture, orchestration, and so on—we arrive at a cipher of its musical sense. It is in fact these gestures that show up in sanitized form on the faces of performers or conductors, or in the miniaturized choreographies they trace while playing or conducting. And it is these bodily signals and movements, one can argue, that Wagner has embedded into his leitmotifs.

With a reciprocity between the motive and its signified curse, Wagner creates a theatrical tool not just for recalling Alberich's imprecation but a clairvoyant choral pronouncement that structures and transforms the affective experience of an ugly dwarf cursing love. From the ludicrous, chattering caricature of a love-struck fool who accosts the Rhinemaidens in the first scene of the opera and is mercilessly teased by them, the choral rendition of his CURSE boasts an apodictic authority and threatening power, even as it dispenses with a narrative voice: the music imparts the ever-changing experience of the CURSE/curse rather than relate its story or impersonate Alberich's voice. The new dramatic situations in which the CURSE resurfaces colour this experience, but so too will subtle changes in its musical structure and presentation later in the *Ring*.

Traditional critics have made much of the dramatic recall that the leitmotifs enable, but precious little of their lyrical content and bodily gesture. Consider, for example, the moment (*Das Rheingold*, scene iv) when Wotan halts before his newly completed Valhalla founded on his corrupt and deceitful machinations. He has paid for the building at a 'wicked expense': 'Mit bösem Zoll zahlt' ich den Bau.' Wagner girds his despair with a remarkable choral 'elucidation',

Fig. 13.5. Leitmotivic mélange from *Das Rheingold*, sc. iv

which overlays snippets of three leitmotifs in quick succession: the grandiose vision of his shining fortress VALHALLA, the sinister might of the RING itself, and the end of Alberich's CURSE (see Figure 13.5). Especially striking is that VALHALLA 'morphs' into the Ring—Wagner had followed the reverse procedure in the transition from scene i to scene ii—and that we can hear the RING and the CURSE (which starts a bar later) at the same time, a musical pronouncement that overlays the associations and gestures in a way that verbal language cannot manage.

The hermeneutic gain is slight, but the affective grasp is enormous. For this kind of experience is rather unlike Jastrow's ambiguous drawing (1899) of a rabbit and/or a duck (discussed by Wittgenstein), where the brain can see only one image at a time, even if one is conscious of the ambiguity.[47] In the leitmotivic technique that Wagner began to develop, the vapours of the choral orchestra rising up from the chasm below the Pythian tripod project oracular properties, and condense into a phantasmagoria whose imagery keeps mutating to draw one into the ideality of the experience. In the case of the CURSE, the leitmotif offers subtle changes over the next twenty or so hours of music, responding affectively to Wotan's dilemma in his treatment of Siegmund and Brünnhilde, to Siegfried and Fafner the dragon, to Hagen and Siegfried's death, even to the last moments of *Götterdämmerung*. Here, in the Immolation Scene, Wagner sounds the confirming second phrase of CURSE as a memory of an evil deed that can now be expunged. And, in a final curtailed statement, he offers just an incomplete opening of the CURSE's first phrase as Hagen plunges into the Rhine in a fruitless attempt to act out his father's rage one last time: rather than complete the motif, the choral orchestra effaces its harmonic sneer and softens it with a peaceful harmonic resolution into the innocent RHEINMAIDENS. Adorno's judgement that these both vatic and expressive phenomena are mere 'changes of lighting' could not be more wrong, for the pleasure in hearing Wagner consists not so much in recognizing the tag, but in confronting an ever-changing oracular announcement, miming along with its gesture and affect.

---

[47] Wittgenstein (1958 [1953]: 165–7).

Wagner aims to speak, as does Aeschylus, 'like a priest in the midst of a community', and he marshals his orchestral forces as Aeschylus deployed his chorus. One may disparage Wagner's temple and dismiss the devotion of the assembled congregants, but what is undeniable is a reclamation of Athenian tragedy in a remarkably original form.

14

'How do you solve a problem like the chorus?': Hammerstein's *Allegro* and the Reception of the Greek Chorus on Broadway

Zachary Dunbar

As an offspring of opera, ballet, and popular entertainment, musical theatre not surprisingly inherited and developed a wide variety of choruses. During the early twentieth century alone, the popular Gaiety and Florodora Girls, glamourized versions of the *fin-de-siècle* female chorus line, featured in the opulent Ziegfield's Follies, while the iconic precision choruses represented in Busby Berkeley films and in the Radio City Music Hall Rockettes spun off the commodification of the female form. The mid-century 'book-based' form of the Richard Rodgers and Oscar Hammerstein musical turned the homogenized chorus into psychologically believable characters. Since the mid-twentieth century, choruses have continued to appear on stage in an assortment of forms: *Jerry Springer, The Opera!* (2003) has a chorus in the style of an Oratorio Ballad opera chorus; *Les Misérables* (1980, French version; 1985, English version) and *The Phantom of the Opera* (1986) both contain a French grand opera chorus; *Hair* (1967) an idiomatically 'Hippy' chorus; *Cats* (1981) an anthropomorphic dance chorus; and both *West Side Story* (1957) and *A Chorus Line* (1975) contain the 'synthesizing' chorus that dances, sings, and acts.[1]

Of all the reimagined ancient choruses, it is perhaps the descendants of the Aristophanic chorus that have found Broadway most congenial. Most recently, the 'Greek' sorority sisters of *Legally Blonde* (2010) at London's Savoy Theatre and Broadway's Palace Theatre jettisoned the former stiff

---

[1] The various styles, images, and formations of the choruses also reflect the hybrid, collaborative, and totalizing nature of music theatre. See Dunbar (2012).

tunic-clad choruses with the sass and swish of West Coast girl power, while, in Broadway's Walter Kerr Theatre, the chorus of high-school cheerleaders in *Lysistrata Jones* (2011) high-legged Aristophanes' sexual politics on the bas-ketball court. In 1947, a prototypical 'Greek chorus' made its one and only appearance in a new Rodgers and Hammerstein musical called *Allegro*. Unlike the hallmark foot-stomping folksy choruses in such hits as *Oklahoma!* (1943) and *Carousel* (1945), the solemn commentators of *Allegro* observed and explained dramatic events that unfolded in the life of a small-town doctor. This newfangled chorus empathized emotionally and visually with the life of the hero, thus creating a form of onstage spectatorship and surrogacy for the Broadway audiences. In other words, Hammerstein (as the lyricist and book writer) had turned the chorus into 'idealized spectators' of the kind August Schlegel in the nineteenth century would have recognized in the Hoftheater of Schiller and Goethe.[2] Why such an idiosyncratic choice by this trusted stalwart of Broadway—why this experimental turn, which resulted in Hammerstein's only major failure during the Golden Era of 1940s and 1950s Broadway musicals?

This chapter seeks to examine the reasons behind Hammerstein's choice with reference to the general theatrical context, in which Thornton Wilder and T. S. Eliot were experimenting with the chorus of ancient Greek tragedy, and Arthur Miller was exploring the tragic 'Everyman' in relation to modern American society. Less immediate, but no less influential, were the theatrically effective choruses in acclaimed productions of Greek tragedy on Broadway, including Laurence Olivier's 1946 landmark Old Vic production tour to Broadway to enormous acclaim, which was to remain in the American popular imagination for at least the next decade when it re-emerged in Vicente Minelli's 1953 film *The Band Wagon*, with Jack Buchanan in the role of Oedipus in declamatory, portentous style.[3] Post-Depression musical theatre itself was undergoing substantive change in form and content, and part of the new musical realism, which expressed itself most notably in Kurt Weill/Ira Gershwin/Moss Hart's psychoanalytically themed *Lady in the Dark* (1941), featured a stylized chorus.

If these forays into the realms of Greek tragedy worked, why did *Allegro* fail? This is not simply an academic question: it has, as we will see, serious implications for the writing of musical theatre history, which needs to be seen to be much more in dialogue with a broader theatre history than has often been the case.

---

[2] A. W. Schlegel (1894: 70). For history, see Carlson (1978: 243), Schadewaldt (1996: 286), and Macintosh (1997: 286). For comment, see Goldhill, Chapter 2, this volume.

[3] Macintosh (2009*a*: 152–3).

ALLEGRO AND MUSICAL THEATRE

As part of serious or popular drama, the chorus was simply part of American intellectual and cultural history for the likes of Hammerstein. In his youth, he had seen vaudevillian-style and also the operetta choruses in the shows produced by his grandfather, the impresario Oscar Hammerstein I.[4] Ancient Greek and Latin literature was part of the 'classically saturated curricula' of American higher education,[5] and possibly the middle-class Manhattan up-bringing and education that Hammerstein received. Hammerstein would have come across staged Greek choruses, parodied or otherwise, at New York City's Columbia University, where he enrolled to study law and dabbled in 'Varsity Show' amateur dramatics.[6] Ethan Mordden refers to Hammerstein's easy appropriation of *Allegro*'s 'Greek chorus', which addresses the protagonist and 'elaborates poetically on the events of the play'.[7] For Stephen Sondheim, a protégé of Hammerstein who assisted his mentor in the making of *Allegro*, the experimentalism of *Allegro* springs from 'an attempt to use epic theatre in contemporary musical theatre', analogous to the Greek chorus that seeks 'to tell the story of a life, not through events but through generalities. This is now what would be called a Brechtian approach.'[8]

Allegro depicts the life and times of a small-town doctor named Joseph Taylor Jr, who goes to the city and discovers that home sweet home, and its simple values, is where the heart of his career and ultimately his happiness lie. This Everyman allegory, which Hammerstein thought up and suggested to Rodgers, represented a radical departure for the pair who two years previously had created the hugely successful landmark 'book-based' musicals—namely, *Oklahoma!* and *Carousel*. That Hammerstein should stray from a successful working model represents an experimental impulse in search of a new theat-ricality. In step with that process, Hammerstein envisioned a stage *sans* scenery, so that his Everyman allegory could flow quasi-cinematically from one episode to the next. The legendary scenographer Jo Mielziner actualized Hammerstein's concept by using a semi-circular treadmill, three tiers of moving platforms, loudspeakers, and large stereopticon projections.[9] Lifting imagery into the air undoubtedly created visual and physical breathing space

---

[4] Nolan (1979: 35).   [5] Winterer (2002: 16).
[6] Winterer (2002: 35, 37).   [7] Mordden (1992: 97); cf. Van Aken (2006: 231).
[8] Nolan (2002: 173). Sondheim perceives Hammerstein's experimentalism to be on a Brook-ian level: 'What few people understand is that Oscar's big contribution to the theatre was as a theoretician, as a Peter Brook, as an innovator.' See 'Conversations with Sondheim', by Frank Rich, *NYT Magazine,* 12 March 2000 <http://www.nytimes.com/library/magazine/home/20000312mag-sondheim.html> (accessed 2 June 2012). Further readings: Bryer and Davison (2005: 193–4), and 'Stephen Sondheim Recalls Allegro', in the CD notes for Rodgers and Hammerstein's *Allegro* (Rodgers and Hammerstien 2009: 15–17).
[9] Henderson (2001); cf. Fordin (1995: 253); Long (2003: 46).

onstage for a large cast, which included twenty-two dancers, thirty-eight singers, and eighteen principal actors who were supported by a veritable army of forty stagehands.[10] The stage traffic and overall direction were left to Agnes de Mille, who, uniquely for a Broadway production, was entrusted with the joint role of director and choreographer. The experimental drive behind the musical allowed de Mille to put into good use the effective representational dancing and acting she brought to *Oklahoma!* and *Carousel.*[11]

In that reimagined theatre space, Hammerstein envisioned a chorus—three in fact: a balletic *dancing* chorus, an operetta-style *singing* chorus, and a dramatic *speaking* chorus (or Greek chorus). During the two-act musical, the Greek chorus functioned interchangeably with its dancing and singing counterparts, addressed the audience, and offered commentary or reflection on the formative years of its main protagonist (that is, Joseph Taylor Jr's birth, his first baby steps, college years, and marriage). They dressed variously as a collegiate choir with mortar boards, as high-school friends, and as a college fraternity, and they formed in rank and file, configured on slightly raised terraced platforms, as solemn witnesses and lifelong companions.[12] The chorus could thus function as the eyes and ears of characters onstage as well as for the audience, which is evidenced, for instance, in this excerpt, when Joe Jr takes his first steps and the chorus collectivizes a grandmother's thoughts:

> You felt yourself falling
> And you put one foot out to save yourself,
> And you didn't fall!
> Say! Maybe if you keep taking steps,
> One after the other,
> One after the other—
> Maybe going forward is easier than standing still![13]

The decision to use a Greek chorus was pragmatic both from a dramaturgical and aesthetic point of view; simple town folk vocally signpost narratives and can also collectively function as demarcation for scene changes:

I think I got the idea because I was trying to write a play without much scenery. I was thinking not only of Broadway, but the colleges . . . I evolved a play with just props, chairs and tables and so forth . . . I borrowed the chorus idea from the Greeks, and then

---

[10] Fink (2009: 12).

[11] Easton (1996: 208, 265–71); Stempel (2010: 564–7); John Martin's *New York Times* review, 'The Dance: De Mille's Oklahoma', 9 May 1943.

[12] *Allegro* publicity photos, Billy Rose Theatre Division, New York Public Library.

[13] From the song 'One Foot, Other Foot', in *Allegro*, 16–17. In this chapter, all citations of Hammerstein's *Allegro* are taken from the online perusal libretto <https://www.rnh.com> (accessed 30 June 2012).

found that I could do other things with the chorus to provide the audience with insight into the characters.[14]

Rodgers too understood the multi-dramaturgical function of the chorus in the Everyman allegory proposed for *Allegro*:

We also realized that such an episodic story would need something like a Greek chorus to bridge the scenes, comment on the action, and talk and sing directly to the actors and audience.[15]

It is unlikely that such pragmatic decisions were borne of German Romantic philosophical reflection; if Hammerstein kept a well-thumbed copy of Schlegel's *Lectures* on Greek drama or of Schiller's *Bride of Messina*[16] on his piano, biographers make no mention of it, and neither does Hammerstein. Yet all Greek choruses interpreted on stage as 'idealized spectators', musical or otherwise, lead one way or another to German Romantic thinking. Whether there was some cultural transfusion of a hundred years via mid-nineteenth-century German immigration to New York, Hammerstein's *Allegro* chorus and Schiller's *Messina* chorus both reimagine the Greek chorus as a 'reflecting spectator', a dramatic persona that 'contemplates and weighs the circumstances, pacifies those who are in conflict, supports the understanding, calls the deluded to their senses, [and] draws a lesson from what happened'.[17] A brief example of this is in scene two of *Messina*, where a double chorus reflect back to the audience the polarity experienced in tragic conflict; they inhabit a state of calm reflection (objectivity) and also, in passionate moments, embody 'a stage character itself'.[18] This tension is captured in Don Caesar's guilty outburst, which is followed by a chorus represented as a 'stage character' by Bohemund:

DON CAESAR. Accursed
 The womb that bore me; cursed the secret arts,
 The spring of all this woe; instant to crush thee,
 Though the dread thunder swept—ne'er should this arm
 Refrain the bolts of death: I slew my brother!

  . . . . .

CHORUS (AS BOHEMUND). The tidings on thy heart dismayed
 Have burst, and naught remains; behold!
 'Tis come, nor long delayed,
 Whate'er the warning seers foretold:
 They spoke the message from on high,
 Their lips proclaimed resistless destiny!

---

[14] Cited in Citron (1996: 181).   [15] Rodgers (2002: 251).

[16] Schiller (1841). A modernized version of Sophocles' *Oedipus* which Schiller turned into a story of two warring brothers. See further Goldhill, Chapter 2, Billings, and Chapter 8, this volume.

[17] Prader (1996: 150).   [18] Prader (1996: 152).

In the opening of *Allegro*, the chorus bears witness to Joe's birth. Having the chorus members directly address the audience as fellow witnesses presents the 'folks' of small-town Illinois as the idealized spectator: like them, powerless to influence the actions of the protagonist or the story, yet, in a sense, one foot ahead of Life's game and therefore wise enough to universalize the conflicts and tensions along the way. In the 'One-foot, Other foot' number, the chorus enact the wonderment of a grandmother at the sight of her baby grandson's tentative steps. When the grandmother dies during a dance in which they play-act scenes of childhood, the chorus, nanny-like, offer sympathy and instruction:

> 'These things are nothing for kids...'
> But it *did* happen to you.
> You're a kid,
> And yet here you are,
> And suddenly you have no Grandma.

In another instance, a wedding scene (at the end of Act One of *Allegro*) depicts Joe marrying Jennie. Hammerstein's Greek chorus is ever-knowledgeable of internal as well as external conflicts in a relationship that points to uncertain outcomes. Like Schiller's *Messina* chorus, the bride and groom's entourage is represented by a kind of double chorus—the Brinker and the Taylor group. A hymn-like church choir accompanies a narrator who speaks 'softly and earnestly' to the audience about what they should be feeling when the vows are read ('a change has come over us') and what they should be wishing for the newlyweds as the curtain goes down ('these children desperately need our hope'). The scene ends with a rousing chorus finale about 'hope'.

On the whole, the *Allegro* chorus is like a character in a Norman Rockwell painting, a collective of wise diagnosing doctors who mark Joe's progress, say what's gone wrong, offer cure-alls, and dispense universal prescriptions, as captured in the lyrics of the penultimate song, 'Allegro':

> Our world is for the forceful
> And not for sentimental folk
> But brilliant and resourceful
> And paranoic folk...
> 'Allegro' a musician would so describe the speed of it
> The clash and competition of counterpoint—
> ...we know no other way
> Of living out a day.

The reviews for *Allegro*, when it premiered at Broadway's Majestic Theatre on the 10 October, oscillated between dutiful reverence and outright rejection. Brooks Atkinson, a stalwart supporter of Rodgers and Hammerstein, wrote in the *New York Times* about 'the lyric rapture of a musical masterpiece' and the staging, which demonstrated 'the eloquent simplicity of genuine art'.[19] Detractors such as George Jean Nathan, in the *New York Journal-American*, found it 'as pretentious as artificial jewelry and just about as valuable',[20] and Louis Kronenberger, in the New York newspaper *PM*, 'an out-right failure'.[21] The reaction to the Greek-style chorus was caught up in similar jousting. Atkinson in the same review congratulated the show's creators for 'abandoning the routine of musical comedy choruses', and for returning the chorus to its 'original function as comment and interpretation'. Others found the chorus heavily didactic in an already belaboured drama. John Gassner, remarking that 'Largo' rather than 'Allegro' suited the title of this cumbersome show, cavilled further that the 'use of the chorus is unquestionably the most original and the boldest innovation in the field, even if their craftsmanship is defeated by their matter',[22] a sentiment echoed by Cecil Smith, who called Hammerstein's chorus the 'most verbose speaking chorus in all history'.[23] The reception of out-of-town try-outs in Boston should have already warned Hammerstein that the chorus had outstayed its welcome: '"Allegro" puts so much time and effort into the massive speaking and singing choruses and devotes so much space to ballet . . . Individual lives do not develop well enough to sustain interest in a story.'[24]

By July 1948, ten months after its premiere in New York, this most anticipated musical in the history of Broadway (it was given cover stories in both *Life* and *Time* magazine), with record-setting advance ticket sales of $750,000,[25] closed. Following *Oklahoma!* and *Carousel*, expectations were indeed high for Broadway's dynamic duo, if not the unfailing creative trio that included Agnes de Mille. De Mille, having to accommodate Hammerstein's last-minute rewrites while coping with a Leviathan production, was redeemed at least by parts of the press for having 'absorbed these apparently indigestible lumps of massed humanity without calling attention to her own mechanisms or shortcomings of the script'.[26]

---

[19] *New York Times*, 11 October 1947.

[20] Cited by Fink (2009: 10).

[21] *PM*, 13 October 1947. Hammerstein cites this critic in 'Note from the Author', in his preface to the *Allegro* libretto.

[22] Gassner, 'The Theatre Arts', rev. of *Allegro*, in *Forum*, Jan. 1948: 23–4, cited by Van Aken (2006: 240).

[23] Smith, 'Three New Musicals', rev. of *Allegro*, in *Theatre Arts Monthly*, November 1947: 13–15, cited by Van Aken (2006: 239).

[24] Elinor Williams, *Boston Herald*, 14 September 1947.

[25] In today's value, $75 million <http://www.bls.gov/data/inflation_calculator.htm> (accessed 2 February 2012).

[26] Easton (1996: 265–71). In *CUE* entertainment magazine (16 August 1947) (no author indicated), a review states how 'the dances are devised so as to be integrated with the action, instead of against it, as happens in musical stock comedy'.

Rodgers and Hammerstein, mulling over their first defeat at the box office, conceded that the story of *Allegro* just did not get through to their audience. Hammerstein stood by an old dictum: 'If the writer's aim is misread, it can only be because he hasn't written it clearly enough.'[27] Part of that misreading had much to do, as the historian Ann Sears points out, with 'the commentary of the "Greek chorus" [which] seemed too moralistic' and outweighed the importance of the main characters.[28] The revelatory role of the chorus often meant that subtext was overexposed at the expense of dramatic tension. For instance, in Act Two, Joe and his wife Jennie have a row over Joe's career. The characters' actions and emotional journey are blatantly clear, yet the ever-present chorus weigh in:

> ENSEMBLE (OF WOMEN). Go easy, Jenny!
> When a man slams a bathroom door like that,
> You're in trouble!
> Use your head!
> This is the biggest chance you'll ever have—
> Maybe the *only* chance—
> To get the kind of life you want.
> Don't throw it away with a few angry words.
> Use your head.

And, while the chorus dominated in the first act, it became less important in the second as the life of the hero–protagonist belatedly asserted its importance. Joe Jr may have seen the error of his ways and returned home, but for the chorus there was no *peripeteia*.

We might now take stock of the problems of the Greek chorus in *Allegro*, and note in its Broadway reception those same conceptual and staging issues—the visual cumbersomeness, stilted characterization, stuck-in-the-mud moralizing, and confusing polymorphic role—that have dominated modern criticism of the chorus since the Renaissance and French neoclassical theatre. It is, however, Hammerstein's idealization of the chorus that situates the analysis nearer to the framework of German Romantic Idealism, in which the Greek tragic chorus was given a privileged, albeit brief, reception in the writings of the post-Kantian philosophers, including Schiller, Schlegel, Hegel, and Nietzsche. By evoking such a chorus, Hammerstein strayed close to Schiller's perception of that role of the chorus as an embodiment of 'first the common mind of the nation, then the general sympathy of all mankind'.[29] But how do *nationhood* and *human sympathy* translate into the terms of musical theatre?

Musical theatre choruses are special because they can accomplish theatrical feats that individual characters on their own cannot. The choral aggregation,

---

[27] Fink (2009: 13).   [28] Sears (2008: 157).   [29] Schlegel (1894: 71–2).

or 'ensemble effect',[30] of singing and acting, as in opera, potentially induces high-octane moments, or a hyper-theatrical sense of the drama. Such an effect of course necessitates a 'co-presence' of the spectator to be able to *co*-manifest such a transformative event.[31] Utopian (or dystopian) feelings of nation-hood[32] may arise because the sight and sound of geometrically perfect assembly-line parades of humans, decked out in finest apparel, or town folk harmonized in thought and action, combine with the principles of physical and ethical excellence; America, emerging as a global power in the twentieth century, sounds and looks best through the musical chorus doing what it, and no one else, can do.[33]

Allegro's chorus may have 'sounded' and 'acted' apple pie, but it ended up alienating Broadway audiences and critics, who expected their choruses to entertain them, not to educate them overtly. Near the close of the nineteenth century the director of the Vienna Burgtheater, Adolf Wilbrandt, declared the chorus an impenetrable 'enchanted castle';[34] earlier, the young firebrands Clemens Brentano and August Schlegel found the Schiller chorus 'a wretched hotch-potch, tedious, weird, and ridiculous throughout'.[35] However the principles of German Romantic Idealism found their way into Hammerstein's creativity, there still remain unanswered: why the experimental turn?; and why in 1947? Hammerstein was in serious pursuit of capturing in musical theatre a transcendent element (what Goethe might have called the 'Urphenomenon'); and it was no doubt recent developments in the American theatre, both in its interest in Greek tragedy and its preoccupation with the chorus, that led to his experimental turn.

NEW THEATRE AND THE EXPERIMENTAL TURN OF THE 'THE CHORUS'

In 1922, the third annual meeting leaflet of the American Classical League records Nicholas Murray Butler, then President of Columbia University, as having endorsed classical studies: 'The classical past might be culturally and

---

[30] McMillin (2006: 78–101).

[31] Fischer-Lichte (2008) argues the case for the 'transformative' and the necessary 'co-presence' of spectator and performer.

[32] For musical theatre and its relation to American national identity, see Knapp (2006); for discussion of Utopia and political theatre, see Dolan (2005).

[33] Schneider (1998) offers an overview of dance and physical education in America and the development of musical theatre dance forms. Cf. Dunbar (2011) for cultural resonances of Apollonian and Dionysian in the musical theatre chorus.

[34] Wilbrandt, cited by Schadewaldt (1996: 292).

[35] Boyle (2000: 742).

chronologically remote, but it informed the present age by showing how "they" had become "us".[36] Butler's view chimed with the educators in the previous century who wanted to advance moral and educational instruction by combining the lessons of ancient tragic heroes and heroines with Anglo-Christian ethics. Such purveyors of ennobling instruction were keen to mould the mind and spirit of American men (and increasing numbers of women) who enrolled in undergraduate humanities curricula in the early twentieth century. Hammerstein would have been one of the 'moulded', having pursued his education privately first at a school in Central Park West, and then as an undergraduate enrolled in Columbia in 1912–15, which was followed by Law School.[37]

Butler's Anglo-centric antiquarianism found a synchronicity with early twentieth-century Broadway reception of Greek tragedy, which led to a new critical consensus that 'Greek drama is worth seeing'.[38] Barker's staging of Euripides' *Trojan Women* in 1915 and M. Vladimir Nemirovitch-Dantchen-ko's 1925 *Lysistrata* (as part of the Moscow Art Theatre Musical Studio) demonstrated that Greek drama and choruses could hold their own on Broadway. The reviews of Greek tragedy productions resonate with the sentiments of Butler, or at least appeal to cultural pragmatism. Atkinson, reviewing the 1932 New York production of Sophocles' *Electra,* states: 'To understand the history of the [ancient] drama it is good to have Greek tragedies staged occasionally. If it does nothing else it reminds us of the theatre's heritage.'[39] Of the productions that featured choruses, it was perhaps the Federal Theatre Project's militantly anti-war *Trojan Incident* (1938), with its double chorus of twenty-three—a singing chorus representing the 'voice' of the people and a dancing chorus its communal 'body'—that most prefigures the use of a multiple chorus in *Allegro.*[40]

When, or in what manner, artists choose to move away from convention may tie in with any number of circumstances. In Hammerstein's case, being part of a progressive theatrical environment that emboldened new creative and career directions, and having a hand in the development of an integrated form of musical theatre (one necessarily evolving the function of the chorus ensemble in storytelling), set up conditions for his own experimental turn.

As a college graduate fresh out of Columbia University, Hammerstein started his career on Broadway relatively successfully, penning operettas and musical comedies. *Showboat* (1927), which he wrote with the composer Jerome Kern, marked Hammerstein's legitimate entry into the A-list of musical theatre writers. The Depression-era 1930s proved to be wilderness years,

---

[36] Winterer (2002: 135).

[37] Nolan (1979: 37). Hammerstein attended Columbia University Law School from 1915 to 1917 but did not complete his degree.

[38] Hartigan (1995: 20).   [39] Hartigan (1995: 29).   [40] Davis (2010/11: 463–4).

until his career revived when his collaboration with Richard Rodgers, through the Theater Guild, resulted in the Guild's productions of *Oklahoma!* and *Carousel*. The Guild, after 1919, was credited in New York City with having fostered and produced several landmark plays and musicals in the 1920s and 1930s, including those by O'Neill, Ference Molnár, George Bernard Shaw, and George Gershwin. The Guild's non-commercial ethos helped sustain an environment in which new writing and writers could flourish, and it was not mere happenstance that *Allegro* was backed by Guild associates, Lawrence Langer and Theresa Helburn. Buoyant from their two major musical hits, Rodgers and Hammerstein also dabbled as theatre producers themselves, and backed two successful comedy shows in 1946—Irving Berlin's *Annie get your Gun* and Anita Loos's *Happy Birthday*. In the same year, Hammerstein may have seen the Old Vic Company tour in New York of Laurence Olivier in Sophocles' *Oedipus*, or at least read the reviews that highlighted again the popularity among critics of Greek tragedy: 'If all productions were like this [*Oedipus*], the public would be clamouring for more.'[41]

American musical theatre with its bricolage of loosely drawn characters, revue-style entertainment, and light drama developed, during the 1940s, into a dramaturgically integrated form: songs furthered plot, character development mattered, and the music and plot worked together to achieve a coherent narrative. The chorus also emerged as an actively storytelling ensemble, no doubt encouraged by developments in dance. George Balanchine, soon after arriving in New York, started the School of American Ballet in 1934. The principles of the *corps de ballet*, its ability to communicate plot and character's emotions, combined with the melting pot of jazz and modern-dance idioms on Broadway, gave future choreographer–directors such as Agnes de Mille, Jerome Robbins, and Hanya Holm a means to evolve the chorus from the iconic drill team and girl revue follies of yesteryear to a psychologically expressive ensemble.

At the same time, the theatre of realism fostered both by the Guild and by the Federal Theatre Projects in the post-Depression America sustained an increasing trend in Broadway for the darker workings of the mind and themes that explored a bifurcated sense of self and society. Following the 1930s' revue-style spoofs on American-brand politics created by George Kaufman, Morrie Ryskind, and Ira and George Gershwin, in the 1940s the chorus moved into a mediating role as commentator on action and character. In the psychoanalytical drama of Weill and Gershwin's *Lady in the Dark* (1941), with book by Moss Hart (one of the few legitimate theatre playwrights to cross into writing for musical theatre), a stylized chorus materialized as though recalled in a therapeutic trance. The dream scenes, which included a 'glamour dream',

---

[41] Herrick Brown, *New York Sun*, 21 May 1946, cited by Hartigan (1995: 40). Hartigan's brackets.

'wedding dream', and 'circus dream', are startlingly similar to the episodic structure that Hammerstein used in *Allegro*: a penultimate wedding scene in *Lady*, for instance, depicts a mood of ambiguity and moral uncertainty wherein the chorus in counterpoint and in unison interjects matter-of-factly of the couple's situation: 'This is no part of heaven's plan. This woman knows she does not love this man.'[42]

In the era of theatre that produced plays such as *Our Town* (1938), *The Iceman Cometh* (1939), *The Glass Menagerie* (1944), and *A Street Car Named Desire* (1947), and dark-hued musicals such as *The Cradle will Rock* (1937), and *Pal Joey* (1940), 'melodramatic heroes were replaced by so-called anti-heroes, action was replaced by introspection, clear-cut morality was replaced by ambiguity, and the traditional dramatic model was replaced by free-form structures or structure devoid of meaningful content'.[43] In view of an American theatre that was retreating from normative, lyrical *mimesis* and heroic Aristotelian narratives to coarser diegetic or Brechtian models, it made sense for playwrights to have perceived the chorus as the necessary eyes and ears of the audience; or, if you will, the chorus was situated in the role of spectator's therapist who gazed at the deeper disturbing psyche beneath archetypal stories. Yet, prior to the 1940s, the chorus, in serious theatre, was already being put through its experimental paces: as the multiple chorus in Eugene O'Neill's *Lazarus Laughed* (1925) and *The Great God Brown* (1926); a chorus-like compère (in the guise of a stage manager) and the spectral faces in the graveyard scene of Thornton Wilder's *Our Town*; and the discursive commentators in Wilder's absurdist play, *The Skin of Our Teeth* (1942).

When *Allegro* arrived on the scene in 1947, given Hammerstein's wave of successes, his exposure to new theatre, and his part in the development of the integrated form of musical, he could feel himself an experimentalist in line with the great playwrights of his day. Yet the Greek-like chorus, as conceptualized in new playwriting, does not in itself explain its theatrical appeal to Hammerstein in the manner it presented itself either as a pragmatic tool in connecting episodic scenes, or as a dramatic device that Broadway critics and audiences seemed to accept in serious straight theatre. The Greek chorus spoke directly to Hammerstein's personal experience and his relationship to the allegorical Everyman story.

According to Francis Fergusson, modernists such as Brecht, Wilder, and Eliot rejected realism and sought 'to use theater in the service of their consciously worked-out moral and philosophical ideas'.[44] Part of that plan was to emphasize the artifice of theatre, its make-believe qualities. In pursuit of those aims, such playwrights used the chorus to provoke 'the collaborative activity of the spectator's imagination' and raise the play's action 'from the

---

[42] McClung (2007: 11–14).   [43] Aronson (2000: 88). Cf. Adler (2005: 159–74).
[44] Fergusson (1996: 61).

specific' to the universal.[45] The universal principles, *consciously* worked-out in Hammerstein's imagination, are embodied in the American Everyman, who finds himself trapped between the bygone years of isolationist small-town values and the alluring materialism following America's post-Second World War success. There is a deep vein of morality and personal history that taps into the conflicted nature of Hammerstein's Everyman doctor (and possibly alter ego), Joseph Taylor Jr:

> I was concerned when I wrote *Allegro* about men who are good at anything and are diverted from the field of their expertise by a kind of strange informal conspiracy that goes on... People start asking them to join committees... and the first thing you know they are no longer writing or practising medicine or law.[46]

Hammerstein's increasing fame and influence were accompanied by a demanding schedule, which meant presiding over committees and championing causes, including those of the Anti-Nazi league, War Writer's Board, and the Author's League.[47] If the Everyman allegory appealed to Hammerstein in his conflicted state, the artistic bridge was offered through two significant plays that used choruses: T. S. Eliot's *Murder in the Cathedral* (1935) and Wilder's *Our Town*.

Eliot's *Murder in the Cathedral*, the story of the martyrdom of Thomas Becket, premiered in England in 1935, and a year later on Broadway's Manhattan Theatre. Eliot progressively experimented with the chorus, farcically as music hall-style chorus characters in *Sweeney Agonistes* (performed in 1934), and as a chorus communicating the meaning of significant biblically themed events in his pageant play *The Rock* (1934). By the time he wrote his famous Everyman play, the chorus assumed almost Aeschylean proportions, which, in accordance with David Jones's critique of Eliot's choruses, uttered wisdom as part of a 'spiritual community' and also from the unique perspective of 'individual [Christian] sacrifice'.[48] As in *Allegro*, in which the chorus comments on the conflicts facing the protagonist in a seemingly materialistic world, in *Murder in the Cathedral* the chorus aids in setting forth 'the eternal and universal moral struggle in which any man is obliged by circumstances to choose between life and integrity'.[49] The experimental turns that Eliot continuously makes with the chorus represent a theatrical response to a deep personal belief in the Anglican–Christian faith, which assumes that personal sacrifice is a means to achieve salvation and yet has to coexist with the secular values of the sensual Everyman. Hammerstein's Everyman doctor grows up in a world of Judeo-Christian values, and, when the chorus call Joe 'home' at the end of the musical, like Eliot's *Cathedral* chorus, it is to remind the audience of the Christian home ground in which personal idealism and sacrifice are rooted.

---

[45] Fergusson (1996: 64).   [46] Citron (1996: 181–2). No citation given by Citron.
[47] Citron (1996: 181–2).   [48] Jones (1971: 80).   [49] D. Clark (1971: 7).

If we take Wilder's *Our Town* as our second example, the playwright's comments in the preface to his play seem to mirror Hammerstein's creative impulses in having 'wished to record a village's life on stage, with realism and with generality'.[50] The setting of a small-town America and its simply sketched characters constitute natural tropes in an allegorical story, one that starkly juxtaposes, on the one hand, the triviality of daily life and, on the other, significant themes about death, geological time, and the ephemeral human condition. The licence to unite seemingly opposing worlds on stage may have been the influence of Pirandello's meta-theatre. We observe the legacy of *Six Characters in Search of an Author* particularly in *Our Town* in the use of a stage manager who stands outside the drama, a disintegration of theatre's illusory fourth wall, and a simple, direct style of dialogue. The stage manager in *Our Town*, functioning almost as a chorus, bridges the trivial and the universal as he addresses the audience. A 'chorus' is also implied in the spectral ensemble of the Grover's Corner departed, who appear in Act III. Like memorial folk painting, the chorus of the dead stare off into infinite space (past the fourth wall), and they mouth and perceive what the audience is possibly thinking and feeling as they, too, stare into the moral and dramaturgical vacuum imagined in Wilder's play.

Wilder's innovations are also part of the experimentalism connected to his earlier plays such as the collection *The Angel that Troubled the Waters and Other Plays* (1928) and *Pullman Car Hiawatha* (1931). The playwright dissolved the Aristotelian logic imposed on modern drama, and instead followed a decidedly anti-naturalistic (or realistic) style. David Castronovo makes the point that Wilder's plays broke down the 'illusions of real events that take place on stage' so that an audience can directly apprehend as their own the 'established patterns of action' in people's lives as they confront forces beyond their control.[51]

Whether or not Hammerstein felt a Eureka moment deep in his psyche when he encountered Wilder's theatre, such innovative plays (and their successful reception by the Broadway public) provided a paradigm that encouraged the American innovator of musical theatre to move in a direction that, like Goethe in Weimar, was meant to raise the Broadway theatre experience to a more exalted level, and, like Wilder, tap more deeply into the elemental need to perceive the people onstage as truly and vividly 'us'. It was a very short leap of imagination from Hammerstein's previous musicals to come up with a chorus of life-like town folk who chummily and effortlessly compère everyday realities and larger-than-life emotions. That Hammerstein labelled his chorus 'Greek' was in some ways a mediation between its current musical incarnations and Broadway's classical heritage.

---

[50] Wilder (2007: 657).   [51] Castronovo (1986: 61–2, 72).

CODA

Two years after *Allegro*, Rodgers and Hammerstein quickly returned to conventional form in their highly successful musical adaptation of James Michener's semi-autobiographical novel *South Pacific* (1949). *Allegro*, however, continued to weigh on Hammerstein's mind. Many years later, in a taped interview at his college alma mater, Hammerstein recalls the use of the chorus and infers a sense of having bitten off more than he could conceptually chew:

> I intended Dick [Rodgers] to write music for it [the chorus] but we wound up reciting the chorus instead; we also wound up with a great deal of scenery . . . without this device, it was much better I thought . . . I'm not blaming anyone, because we all accepted it, we all collaborated . . . but it was a mistake.[52]

And revising *Allegro* for television thirteen years later, a terminally ill Hammerstein, ever experimental, reimagined the cumbersome chorus as Beckett-like 'unseen voices', and 'not [as] a lot of people [who] march up and down the stage aimlessly'.[53] Schlegel remarked of Greek tragedy that it remained 'an exotic plant, which we can hardly hope to cultivate with any success, even in the hot-house of learned art and criticism'.[54] Hammerstein should have heeded his advice. But caught up in an experimental mood, he could already hear a Greek chorus urging his alter ego, Joe Jr: 'Maybe going forward is easier than standing still!'

Yet, Hammerstein did not 'go forward', and the problem of the Greek chorus remained unresolved. And his view of himself as the tragic poet–dramatist of musical theatre failed. Cogitating on the 'unmitigatedly commercialized system' of New York theatre in the 1990s, Arthur Miller harked back to the days of Broadway's betting men, producers in the late 1940s and early 1950s, who took him on and also the 'theatre's ancient burden . . . the moral illumination of society and the human condition'.[55] Miller's seminal tragic illuminations, *All My Sons* (1947) and *Death of a Salesman* (1949), situate Hammerstein's *Allegro* in that culture of creative gambling and of shouldering the 'ancient burden'. *Allegro* was Hammerstein *agonistes*, the musical Greek chorus his interlocutors whom he gifted with homespun platitudes in an attempt to educate his public in the 'ethical self-positioning' (or German Romantic *Sittlichkeit*[56]), which he himself was undergoing in his professional life. Hammerstein was sailing close to the Parnassus of the tragic Everyman in American society, Miller's territory, and a subject the celebrated playwright explored in his landmark essay 'Tragedy and the Common Man' (1949). From

---

[52] Fordin (1995: 257). My brackets.
[54] Schlegel (1894: 71).
[56] Goldhill, Chapter 2, this volume.

[53] Fordin (1995: 256).
[55] Miller (1994: p. xv).

a Wilderian perspective, Hammerstein's Joe Taylor was Oedipus, a 'man setting out on the journey of self-knowledge and inquiry'.[57]

Allegro's chorus gestured academically towards the 'experimental' Greek chorus because that choice synchronized with 1940s-style experimentalism and a modernized 'tragic' Everyman. In the context of commercial musical theatre, where boy meets girl is much preferred over boy meets chorus, *Allegro's* chorus could offer only an empty Utopia, a nostalgic salvaging of Americana, which the audiences and the critics did not entirely take to heart. Twenty-three years later, George Furth and Stephen Sondheim solved the problem of the chorus in *Company* (1970). With rocketing divorce rates and impending stagflation, theirs was a decisively dystopian ensemble.

[57] Wilder (2007: 716).

Part IV

Community

15

The Politics of the Mystic Chorus

Richard Seaford

The political significance of the ancient Greek χορός (a group that sings and dances) is based in part on its implicit claim to public *space*. My chapter centres on this general proposition, but has two specific focuses. One is on the special kind of solidarity in the chorus of *mystery cult*, and on the political significance of this solidarity. The other is on *Athens* of the *classical period*, about whose space and choruses we have especially good knowledge. But these focuses are not exclusive, for I also discuss (Section 6) a non-mystic choral performance in Sparta.

1. CAPITALIST SPACE

I start by sketching some features of space in advanced capitalist countries that contrast with the space of the classical polis, and that—however natural they may seem—we must think away if we are to understand the politics of the ancient Greek chorus. Most of our built environment consists of private space, and an aspect of this predominance of private space is the public invisibility of (real) political *power*. We also lack visible *communal actions* (as opposed to mere mass spectatorship), and of those that do occur almost none is transformative. Our public space is almost entirely given over to private purposes and commercial interests.[1]

By contrast, ancient Athenian private buildings were—at least in the classical period—relatively small,[2] and dwarfed by imposing communal buildings.

---

[1] Indeed, our advanced process of capital accumulation includes an incessant tendency to encroach—if unresisted—on all available space (and time). The result is the pervasive *fragmentation* and incessant *mutability* that are at the heart of 'postmodern' experience.

[2] See, e.g., Michael Jameson in *Oxford Classical Dictionary*, s.v. houses (Greek): 'The modesty of the Classical houses of all classes is striking'; Dem. *Olynth.* 3.25–6; Aristocr. 207.

The Athenian assembly (in contrast to parliament) visibly embodied genuine political power. And, as an example of transformative communal action, spectacular processions not only displayed the purposive cohesion of the polis to itself and to others but were also imagined to maintain or transform the relationship between polis and deity.

Our power of abstraction has furnished us not only with maps but also with the idea of an abstract spatial framework in which all else is somehow contained, and which may even seem ontologically superior to any concrete marker of space. This superiority of abstraction may have particular applications. For instance, any concern I may have about the visible manifestations of the boundary between my land and my neighbour's is reduced by my knowledge that I possess a legal document containing a map. But in classical Athens there were few maps and no public register of land,[3] with the result that publicly visible markers (*horoi*) and publicly visible *actions* were all the more important. For instance, in a law preserved by Theophrastus we hear of the requirement that purchase be accompanied by a public sacrifice.[4]

2. ANCIENT GREEK PROCESSIONS

The *public procession* was transformative communal *action* (πομπή means 'escorting'). It often included the politically excluded: women, young people, metics (resident aliens), and perhaps sometimes even slaves.[5] Conversely, a procession expressing the solidarity of a *clan* might seem politically disintegrative: there were accordingly legal restrictions on funeral processions at Athens and elsewhere.[6]

The procession might express the communal occupation of space, whether urban space or—in the case of processions between urban and peripheral sanctuaries—the territory of the polis.[7] It might even, in the general absence of maps, serve to shape the conception of space outside the borders of the polis. A nice example is in Aeschylus' *Eumenides* (ll. 12–14): 'The path-making sons of Hephaestus escort him [Apollo from Athens to Delphi] and greatly revere him, making the untamed land tame.' The scholia (ancient marginalia) on this passage reveal that, when an Athenian *theoria* (sacred delegation) went to Delphi, it was preceded on the road by men carrying axes as intending to tame the land. A fourth-century *horos* (boundary stone) in the Athenian *agora*

---

[3] Finley (1952: 13–15); A. R. W. Harrison (1968: 305–7).
[4] F97 (3), Wimmer = F21 Szegedy-Maszak (1981). For the role of ritual in early contract, see Gernet (1981: 143–215).
[5] Kavoulaki (1999: 300); see also Graf (1996).
[6] Seaford (1994: 74–86).
[7] Kavoulaki (1999: 297–9); De Polignac (1995: 24, 37, 40–3, 52–3).

marked out 'the sacred road through which the *Pythaïs* [i.e. the delegation] journeys to Delphi'.[8] The Athenians' conception of the route is shaped by the procession.

Ancient processions bring offerings (sacrificial animals, a robe, and so on), and sometimes the deity himself, to a sanctuary. They are—unlike 'parades'—*preliminaries*.[9] They gather the community for focus on a temple, enhancing the power of such buildings to articulate public space. And they may be as pleasing to the deity as are the offerings and choral performances at its destination. For instance, according to Xenophon (*Hipparchicus* 3.2)

I would think processions most pleasing to the gods and to the spectators if beginning from the Herms they move in a circle round all the shrines and images in the *agora* honouring the gods, and at the Dionysia the choruses give extra pleasure to the gods, especially the twelve gods [i.e. at their altar in the *agora*].

This reveals much. Processions have 'spectators', please the gods, and may stop and give choral performances. These features reappear in other texts.[10]

The procession may also sing as it proceeds.[11] Choral performance re-inforces processional occupation of space. Herodotus[12] reports that, when the Persians were ravaging an Attica empty of its inhabitants (in 480 BC), there was seen 'a cloud of dust moving from Eleusis, as of about 30,000 men', and the 'mystic Iacchus [song]' was heard. This was interpreted as a divine voice that would ensure victory for the Athenians. The purposive unison of the song of the vast[13] mystic procession that traversed the territory of the polis was of a kind to strengthen the will of the Athenians to survive, to reoccupy their land.

The procession of Eleusinian mystic initiates is represented in Aristophanes' *Frogs* as taking place in the underworld. They enter singing and dancing as they move in procession, and their repeated references to this combination[14] indicate that it occurred in the actual Eleusinian procession on the 'sacred road' between Athens and Eleusis.[15]

The procession escorted Iacchus, the Eleusinian Dionysus, and so the song sung in it is comparable to the dithyramb. For in its earliest detectable phase the dithyramb was sung in the Dionysiac procession, which sometimes had the function of escorting Dionysus. At Athens the dithyrambic performance at

---

[8] *Agora* XIX, H 34; Parker (2005: 86).

[9] Kavoulaki (1999: 302).

[10] The Milesian Molpoi: *Syll.*[3] 57 = Sokolowski (1955), 50; Eleusis: *IG* II[2] 1078, Plut. *Vit. Alc.* 34.4; for 'spectators' see texts cited by Kavoulaki (1999: 294).

[11] On the various uses of the term *prosodion*, 'processional song', see Rutherford (2003).

[12] 8.65; see also Ael. Aristid. *Or.* 22.6.

[13] Parker (2005: 348).

[14] 326, 336, 351–2, 372–5, 377–9, 396, 403, 440–1, 447–51.

[15] The building of bridges on this road is attested by inscriptions that express concern for the safety of the sacred objects: Parker (2005: 346–7).

the destination of the procession grew in importance, and developed into tragedy at the Dionysiac festival, in which stationary dithyrambs were also performed.[16]

3. THE MYSTIC CHORUS

Robert Parker notes that 'hymning the god and dancing for the god are fundamental forms of Greek worship, and yet it is remarkably hard to find Athenian men engaging in them in their simple form in the classical period'. From the simple form he excludes the dramatic choruses as well as the (stationary) dithyrambs, and concludes that there was 'a transformation undergone [in Athens] by a traditional religious element, choral song, which lived on in Sparta in more or less its old form'.[17] I will return to this problem in Section 6.

Mystic ritual was secret, but the singing and dancing Iacchus procession of mystic initiates was in full public view, as was also presumably the dancing at Eleusis around the *Kallichoron* well.[18] Mystery cult could include the movement of the initiates through the streets.[19] Similarly, the early dithyramb was sung in a public procession, even though the earliest remains of the dithyramb are closely associated with the Dionysiac mysteries.[20] In Aristophanes' *Frogs* an aspect of the mystic experience, the exhilarated solidarity of the processional singing and dancing initiates, can be publicly displayed (Section 5) without revealing what was revealed only in the rite of passage. Much the same can probably be said of the early dithyramb. Besides public choruses associated with mystery cult, it seems that there were also choruses of which only the initiated had knowledge, and it is not always clear which type a chorus of initiates (what I will call the 'mystic chorus') belongs to. That the chorus might be a bridge between mystic secrecy and public display is suggested by the phrase 'to dance out the mysteries', frequent in many late texts.[21]

The major public choruses at Athens, dithyrambic and tragic, developed out of the mystic chorus. What was it about the mystic chorus, whether Eleusinian

---

[16] Seaford (1994: 241–3, 267–8); D'Angour (1997).

[17] Parker (2005: 181–2). He excludes the dithryambs because they were performed for competition and 'not necessarily very religious in theme'.

[18] Pausan. 1.38.6.

[19] Demosthenes (18.260): Sabazios.

[20] Seaford (1994: 268); Lavecchia (2000: 11–12, 136); Kowalzig (2007*b*).

[21] ἐξορχεῖσθαι τὰ μυστήρια: e.g. Lucian, *Salt.* 15; Alciphron 3.72; Achilles Tatius 4.8; *P.Oxy.* 411.25.

or Dionysiac, that gave it, paradoxically, such an important *public* role in Attica?

An answer to this question will emerge in due course. But let us first note that mentions of the mystic chorus are plentiful, of various kinds, and from different periods.[22] Categorical is the statement of Lucian that 'no ancient mystic initiation [τελετή] can be found that is without dance' (*Salt.* 15).

According to Plato in *Phaedrus* we are sometimes reminded of a vision (of reality and beauty) that all human souls had in a previous existence. It is presented as a mystic vision ('the most blessed of mysteries') that we had while following gods, 'with a blessed χορός' (250b). Now χορός here is generally translated 'company' or 'band', but in fact means—as elsewhere[23]—*chorus*. The mystic chorus is impressive enough for Plato to associate it with our defining vision of reality and beauty. There is a hint—albeit no more than a hint—of this mystic vision as dependent on choral participation.

Moreover, the unison of the chorus was connected with a fundamental vision, six centuries later, by Plato's follower Plotinus—but merely as a *metaphor* for the vision of the *individual soul*. The χορός stays around its leader (*koruphaios*), sometimes turns away and loses sight of him, and when it turns back to him sings beautifully and is truly around him. 'So too we are always around him (i.e the One), but not always turned to him. When we do look to him, then we have our goal and repose and do not mis-sing [ἀπᾴδειν] as we truly dance our god-inspired dance around him.'[24] Plato wrote of 'sharing in philosophical madness and *bakcheia*' (*Symp.* 218b3), where sharing in *bakcheia* is a metaphor referring to the ecstatic, music-driven movement of the group in Dionysiac (bacchic) cult. Here again, Plotinus takes a Platonic image and applies it to the *inward vision of the individual*: the ecstasy of the bacchic movement (*anabakcheuesthe*) is associated with the 'longing to be with yourselves, in gathering yourselves together apart from the body' (*Enneads* 1.6.5). In Plotinus, choral unison and Dionysiac movement unify—if only as metaphors—the individual, but in an earlier era they actually unified the mystic chorus (Section 5), and moreover this unity or unison could be a politically significant paradigm for the right relationship *between* individuals.

---

[22] E.g. an inscription of 92BC provides evidence for choral dancing in the mysteries at Andania (Sokolowski (1969) = *LSCG* 67. 73, 98). See also, e.g., Eur. *Bacch.* 21–2; Pl. *Leg.* 815cd, *Euthyd.* 277de; Schol. Lycoph. *Alex.* 212; further passages in Burkert (1983: 288) and Hardie (2004: 14–20).

[23] It can be used metaphorically, which is clearly not the case here. It never means just 'company' or 'band'.

[24] *Enn.* 6.9.8; cf. 3.6.2.

4. MYSTIC CHORUS, COSMOS, AND ETERNITY

The defining mystic vision in Plato's *Phaedrus* is of what is above the sky.[25] Mystic ritual may provide for the initiates not only *doctrine* about the nature of the cosmos but also an *experience* of transcending cosmic divisions—for instance, of the sun shining in the underworld.[26] Experience of this kind, even a feeling of coextensiveness with the cosmos, may be aroused in the chorus of initiates by their song and dance. It is this that may be hinted at by the souls in *Phaedrus* having their mystic super-celestial vision 'with a blessed chorus'.

Ancient Greek choruses are sometimes imagined as embodying heavenly bodies, in particular the stars. Such choruses are, in various texts and periods, especially—though not always (Section 6)—associated with mystery cult, not least in Attic tragedy. These texts have been assembled and discussed by Csapo.[27] My concern is with the relationship between this cosmic reach and the internal dynamic of the mystic chorus, as well as with the political significance of this relationship.

In a choral song of Sophocles' *Antigone* the Eleusinian (l. 1120) Dionysus is called Iacchus (l. 1152) and 'chorus-leader of the stars' (l. 1147), on which the scholiast (ancient commentator) comments that 'it is according to a mystic *logos* that he is called chorus-leader of the stars'. In *Frogs* the chorus of initiates invoke Iacchus as brandishing torches, and then immediately call him 'light-bearing star of the nocturnal mystic ritual [τελετή]'. Torches in the darkness can easily be imagined as stars. A fragment of Aeschylus' *Bassarae* implies that the torches carried in Dionysiac cult could be imagined as *lightning*.[28]

Other instruments carried by the Dionysiac chorus of initiates could make a sound as of *thunder*. The dithyrambic fragment 70b of Pindar describes, as belonging to the Dionysiac mystic ritual (τελετά)[29] of the gods, the 'ῥόμβοι of drums' and a fire-breathing thunderbolt. Shortly afterwards the papyrus breaks off as it begins to narrate the birth of Dionysus. The ῥόμβος (*rhombos*) was an instrument, used in mystery cult, that made a roaring sound by being whirled, and ῥόμβοι is here generally translated 'whirlings'. The conflation of ῥόμβοι with drums implies a confusion of roaring sounds, easily imagined as thunderbolt or earthquake. A fragment (57) of Aeschylus describes, in the cult of Dionysus, 'the deep frightening sound of the drum, as of thunder beneath the earth'. The thunderbolt is brought down from heaven to earth, or even under the earth (like the roar of an earthquake), by the sound of *rhombos* and

---

[25] *Phdr.* 247c2; 248b (quoted in Section 5).
[26] Seaford (2005).
[27] Csapo (2008); see also Ferrari (2008).
[28] 23a: τὸ τῆς ἀστραπῆς πευκᾶεν σέλας.
[29] *Teletā* here means mystic ritual, as the object of the chorus's 'knowing' (εἰδότες): cf. Eur. *Bacch.* 73–4 with Seaford (1996: 157–8); Lavecchia (2000: 135–6, and 106) (on the assignment to this poem of *fr.* 346 with its mention of the Eleusinian mysteries).

drum in choral performance. The thunderbolt that was in mystic ritual[30] enacted here on earth was in all likelihood imagined as the thunderbolt that came down to earth at the birth of Dionysus. And the birth of Dionysus was strongly associated with the dithyramb.[31]

A similar experience of cosmic interconnection is indicated by the 'whirling circular aetherial shaking [*enosis*] of the *rhombos*' in a mystic context in Euripides' *Helen* (ll. 1362–3): *enosis* connotes earthquake,[32] and so to call it *aetherial* implies a confusion of the roar of thunder with the subterranean roar of earthquake.[33] In the lost drama *Peirithous*, set in the underworld, the chorus—almost certainly of mystic initiates—refer to an aetherial *rhombos* around which dance night and the stars.[34] The most detailed reflection of the mystic re-enactment of the Dionysiac thunderbolt-with-earthquake is, we shall see (Section 7), in Euripides' *Bacchae*. Choral song and dance may create a sense of the earth moving. When the maenads dance and call on Dionysus 'in unison' (ἀθρόωι στόματι), the 'whole mountain was joining in the bacchanal . . .' (Eur. *Bacch.* 724–7). When the chorus of Sophocles' *Antigone* sing 'Let us go to all the temples of the gods with all-night choruses, and let Dionysus earth-shaker of Thebes lead us!' (ll. 152–4), it is the *dance* by which the earth is shaken. And we have seen that the mystic chorus may also, in imagining themselves as transcending cosmic boundaries, use their equipment—torches, *rhomboi*, drums—to *make present* phenomena that belong above or beneath the earth: stars, thunder, lightning, and earthquake.

Why does a chorus imagine itself as having cosmic reach? The Andaman dance, as described by Radcliffe-Brown in 1922, has the following features:

1. It is an activity of the whole community: every able-bodied adult takes part.
2. The whole personality of each dancer is involved.
3. Each dancer is constrained by rhythm and custom to conform in his movements to the communal action.
4. This loss of self creates in the dance unusual energy and ecstatic harmony with the fellow-members of the community.[35]

---

[30] Texts cited by Seaford (1996: 195–7).

[31] Plato *Leg.* 700b; Eur. *Bacch.* 526–7; Seaford (1996: 156).

[32] It means earthquake in the mystic passage of *Bacchae* (587), and in its only other fifth-century occurrence (Eur. *Tro.* 1326) is of the *earth*, as also in the common compound adjectives for Poseidon.

[33] Compare the earthquake and underground thunder in the mystic pattern in *Prometheus* (Seaford 1986), and in Soph. *OC* (Seaford 2012: 335).

[34] Critias *fr.4 TGF*, discussed by Csapo (2008: 273).

[35] Radcliffe-Brown (1922: 251–2).

That synchronized movement increases rapport, liking, and prosocial behaviour has been demonstrated by recent experimental psychology.[36] Rappaport, who cites Radcliffe Brown, goes further in generalizing about certain circumstances in which

the boundary between individuals and their surroundings, especially others participating in ritual with them, may seem to dissolve.... such a sense of union is encouraged by the coordination of utterance and movement demanded of congregations in many rituals. To sing with others, to move as they move in the performance of a ritual, is not merely to symbolize union. It is *in and of itself* to reunite in the reproduction of a larger order. Unison does not merely symbolize that order but indicates it and its acceptance. The participants do not simply *communicate* to each other *about* that order but *commune* with each other *within* it. In sum, the state of communitas experienced in ritual is at once social and experiential. Indeed, the distinction between the social and the experiential is surrendered, or even erased, in a general feeling of oneness with oneself, with the congregation, or with the cosmos.[37]

The dissolution of the boundaries around the self may create a sense of boundlessness, of the group extending into the cosmos. And the coordination may be enhanced by *tempo*:

The tempos typical of such coordination, and perhaps requisite to it, are quicker than those characteristic of ordinary social interaction and the coordination itself is tighter. The rhythm of the drum may approximate to the rhythm of the heartbeats, and, as it synchronizes the movements of the dancers' limbs and unifies their voices into the unisons of chant or song, it may entrain their breaths and pulses, or at least be experienced as if it does.[38]

Not only may such regular repetition occur within ritual, but the ritual itself may be repeated at precise intervals. 'That which is performed at rapid tempo and in tight coordination, and which through that tempo and coordination united participants more tightly than they are under normal circumstances, is, *in being punctiliously repeated from one performance to the next, experienced as never-changing.*'[39] Moreover if, say, the dithyramb sung in the annual processional escort of Dionysus was experienced as never-changing, then the experience would have been amplified by the conviction that an ancient event is being re-enacted (the birth or original arrival of the god), and that it will continue to be re-enacted for ever. The solidarity of choral performance seems to extend indefinitely not only over space (as we have seen), but also over time.

---

[36] Miles et al. (2009); Wiltermuthet and Heath (2009); Valdesolo and DeSteno (2011).
[37] Rappaport (1999: 220).
[38] Rappaport (1999: 221).
[39] Rappaport (1999: 221–2) (emphasis in original).

This may have political significance: the spatial claim of the dithyrambic procession is—by means of myth—for all time.[40]

Myth may be re-enacted also by the secret mystic chorus. Plutarch's account of the initiands' wanderings in the dark (Section 5) may derive from the Eleusinian initiands' enactment of Demeter's search for Persephone.[41] But Eleusinian initiation is for the individual not regularly repeated, it occurs once in a lifetime. Its embodiment of permanence consists rather in pre-enactment of post-mortem participation in the eternal unison of the mystic chorus. The pre-enactment is, of course, temporary, but is united with post-mortem eternity by means of *memory*, which was of great importance for mystic initiates.[42]

5. THE SOLIDARITY OF THE MYSTIC CHORUS

This group solidarity, expressed in the dissolution of the normal articulation of space (and of time), is a potential effect of choruses in general. There are three reasons why it may be found in the mystic chorus in particular.

One reason is that mystic ritual, as a rehearsal of death and of post-mortem bliss, transcends cosmic divisions and aspires to eternity. Secondly, whereas on many occasions choral performance has a function external to itself (funeral, wedding, praise or escort of god or human victor, delighting audience and deity, and so on), the only function of the *secret* mystic chorus is—we shall see—to enact (or pre-enact) its own blessed solidarity and eternal well-being: the sense of unlimited space and time, which in many contexts may be merely a by-product of intense unison, is in the mystic chorus closely associated with its function.

Thirdly, the ritual as a whole enacts the *transition* from individual suffering to choral happiness, and this surely intensified the solidarity of the chorus by a sense of contrast with its opposite.[43]

The contrast deserves our attention. Every Eleusinian initiand was required to sacrifice a pig 'on his own behalf'. Parker notes that this unusual individualism[44] reflects the character of mystic initiation as preparation for

---

[40] For the 'timeless continuity' that mythical aetiology seems to establish, see Kowalzig (2007a: 26–32); for time and performance, see D'Alessio (2004: 292–4).

[41] Seaford (2012: 28 n. 27).

[42] Especially on the gold leaves: Graf and Iles Johnston (2007: nos 1, 2, 8, 25); *Orphic Hymn* 77 9–10 (Quandt).

[43] In one form of mystic initiation a group danced around a seated initiand or initiands (*thronosis*): Pl. *Euthyd.* 277de; Dio Chrys. 12.33; Lada-Richards (1999: 101).

[44] 'At collective rituals one animal or group of animals was commonly brought "on behalf of all"' (Parker 2005: 342).

the individual experience of death. But mystic ritual pre-enacts not only the isolation of death but also the subsequent blissful cohesion of the initiates in the underworld, which was accordingly imagined as containing choral dancing that is joined by the dead individual.[45] Mystic ritual dramatizes individual isolation so as to transform it into its opposite—choral solidarity.

A famous fragment of Plutarch (178) compares the soul on the point of death to the transition in mystic ritual from ignorant fear in darkness to pure places and meadows in which there are a wonderful light, voices, choral dances (*choreiai*), sacred sounds, and holy visions: here the initiate 'is with [*sunestin*] holy [*hosiois*] and pure men'. Entry into this happy state is the consummation, *telos*, of a terrifying process of wearisome runnings around and movements through the darkness that are 'without *telos*' (*atelestoi*) and 'viewed with suspicion': they seem endless, pointless, and directionless. This preliminary stage dramatizes the spatio-temporal boundlessness of the isolated individual: in the darkness he can discern neither spatial nor temporal end (*telos*) to his movements. Random movements in the darkness deprive the individual of all sense of social space: this is an apt expression of extreme isolation, for it is space on which social being primarily depends. Being *atelestoi*, the movements also deprive the individual of social temporality. But eventually there is temporal completion (*telos*) that consists of entry into an eternal social space of purity and choral cohesion.[46]

The other initiates whom the initiate joins are 'pure', and he has himself been purified by initiation. This mystic transition is alluded to by Plato in the *Republic* (560e) in his description of the degeneration of the democratic man: 'having emptied and purified of these things (virtues) the soul of the man who is . . . being initiated with great initiation rituals, after this they bring in insolence and anarchy and profligacy and shamelessness, resplendent with a great chorus, crowned . . .'. Plato here describes degeneration, perversely, in terms of the positive psychic transition of mystic initiation that we have seen in Plutarch. The emptying or purification of the soul by individualizing disorientation is followed by the impressive arrival of a chorus.[47] In Plato the chorus with its resplendent accompaniment is *brought in*. This corresponds to (in Plutarch) the wonderful light 'meeting' (*apantan*) the initiand: the light is brought into the darkness (as in the Orthodox Easter ceremony), and in the light there are *choreiai*. And, just as the initiates in Plutarch are pure, so in the Plato passage the initiate is purified. So too in Plato's *Phaedrus* choral initiates

---

[45] Plut. *Mor.* 1105b; epitaphs: Jaccottet (2003: nos 112, 180, 29).

[46] In an epitaph from Philippi (3rd cent. AD), Dionysiac initiates in the hereafter claim the dead man as *congrex*, to lead with torches the festal corteges: Jaccottet (2003: no. 29, ll. 19–21).

[47] What follows, 'calling insolence good education, anarchy freedom, etc.', may be designed to evoke the mystic formulae expressing the unity of opposites: cf. Seaford (2003*b*: 143–9).

are pure (250c). The homogeneous purity of the mystic chorus expresses its cohesion.

Any sense of purity and cohesion was surely enhanced by the contrast with the terrified isolation that preceded it. Mystic ritual rehearses the individual isolation of death so as to transform it into choral communality. Moreover, in the Plutarch passage the initiate, even as he consorts with pure men, looks down on the 'uninitiated and unpurified mob of those here on earth, in much mud and mist driven together and trampling on each other'.[48]

Solidarity may be enhanced by exclusion.[49] But in this context the exclusion may seem paradoxical, for the Eleusinian mysteries, which Plutarch probably has in mind, were open to all.[50] The same contradiction, between universal access to mystic initiation and conflict between impure uninitiated individuals, reappears in a different form (adapted to his philosophical purpose) in Plato's *Phaedrus*: all human souls had pre-natal access to the mystic vision of reality (249e5), and indeed it is in the nature of immortal souls to fly upwards like winged chariots to the region where the gods reside, and anyone who is willing and able follows their celestial movement, 'for resentment is excluded from the divine chorus' (247a). However, some souls form a mass of chariots, 'trampling and jostling each other, each trying to get ahead of the other', and so depart 'uninitiated in the sight of reality' (248b). As a result, not every soul can recollect its earlier (brief or partial) vision (250a). Here the cohesion and general accessibility of the mystic chorus are projected onto heaven, and it is only non-philosophical human weakness that prevents their universality.

The mystic solidarity that is enhanced by exclusion may have a political function, which is seen in fifth-century drama, most clearly in Aristophanes' *Frogs*. The initiated chorus of the dead in their underworld meadow are *hosioi* (ll. 327, 336), a model of joyful and egalitarian cohesion, with the unusual energy (ll. 345–50, 402–4) observed among the Andaman islanders by Radcliffe-Brown. We noted that the chorus might be a bridge between mystic secrecy and public display, and that the dithyramb, despite its association with mystic ritual, became a very public performance (giving rise to tragedy).[51] Similarly here the leader of the mystic chorus makes a public proclamation, excluding from the 'initiated choruses' (l. 370) the impure and the uninitiated (ll. 354–7)[52]—as well as a wide range of *political* undesirables—for instance, 'anyone who does not dissolve hostile civil conflict [*stasis*] and is not at ease with citizens' (l. 359).

---

[48] Cf. also Plut. *Mor.* 81de.

[49] Kowalzig (2007*a*: 169) suggests that mystic exclusivity could be a basis for creating civic identities.

[50] Provided that they knew Greek and were not polluted by murder.

[51] Seaford (1994: 241–3, 267–8).

[52] Hardie (2004: 20) notes the verbal parallels in Clement of Alexandria (*Strom.* 5.19.2), comparing the non-Christian to the uninitiated: he must 'stand outside the divine chorus'.

In Euripides' *Bacchae* Dionysus has come to initiate the whole polis (ll. 39, 208). The chorus states that mystic initiation means to 'join the soul to the *thiasos*' in the purifying dance. As for the maenads outside the city, even the mountain and its animals join in their dance (ll. 726–7), and they exhibit the cohesion of a flock of birds flying upwards (l. 748). By contrast, the uninitiated *turannos* Pentheus displays a disastrously obstinate individualism. The members of the chorus are isolated from each other by the temporary loss of their god, and restored to joy by his epiphany (l. 609), in a scene in which the impervious isolation of Pentheus is expressed in terms of the experience of the preliminary stage of initiation (the detailed similarity with Plutarch *fr.* 178 is astonishing). We will develop the political significance of this passage in Section 7.

In Sophocles' *Antigone* the Eleusinian Dionysus, mystic 'chorus-leader of the stars' (Section 4), is invoked to come to purify with dancing the polis from a disease (l. 1141) that has arisen from the mind (l. 1015) of the isolated *turannos* Creon.

In these three passages there is a contrast between the cohesion and purity of the mystic chorus and the individualism of one or more individuals outside the chorus. This contrast originates, I suggest, in the memorable and widely experienced transition, in mystic ritual, from competitive individual isolation to the cohesion and purity of the chorus. In our three passages, all from the dramatic performances of the democratic polis, the contrast has been adapted by the drama and has therein acquired a *political* significance (of various kinds). But how did this happen?

The chorus in general could be an image or agent of ordered political unity.[53] Especially significant in this respect was, I suggest, the mystic chorus. It is not just that—as we have seen—the mystic chorus both embodies and *celebrates* egalitarian unity imagined as *all-pervasive* (cosmic) and *permanent*. It is also that the Eleusinian cult involved mass participation, was a ritual of the polis,[54] and in the anecdote told by Herodotus (8.65) embodied victory for Athens over the invading Persians. The Athenians had a 'passionate sense . . . that their welfare was tied up with' the mysteries.[55]

Secret mystic ritual was sometimes celebrated in public festivals.[56] It was the *public* (processional) mystic chorus that in Herodotus' anecdote embodied victory. Whereas the only purpose of the *secret* mystic chorus is its own well-being, the *processional* form of the mystic chorus—whether Iacchus song or dithyramb—may acquire other functions, notably escorting the god (Iacchus,

---

[53] E.g. Xen. *Oec.* 8.3; Polyb. 4.20–21; Paus. 5.16.5; *PMG* 713 (iii); Plut. *Vit. Lyc.* 4.1–2; Nagy (1990: 368); Wilson (2003); Kowalzig (2004).

[54] Sourvinou-Inwood (1997: 144–6).

[55] Parker (2005: 343, 348).

[56] For several Dionysiac instances see Seaford (2006: 71–2).

Dionysus) or symbolically occupying territory. I suggest that the public form of the mystic chorus emerged—at least in part—from the tendency to extend the egalitarian solidarity of the mystic chorus to the whole community. This is manifest in the stationary dithyramb (Section 7), and even more so in drama. In *Frogs* the chorus of initiates embodies the unity of the polis. In *Bacchae* mystic initiation is secret, but the whole polis is to be initiated and Dionysus requires honour from all (ll. 36–40, 114, 208, 472–4). In *Antigone* it is 'the polis with all its people [*pandamos*]' that is to be purified by the mystic chorus-leader of the stars.

In both *Bacchae* and *Antigone* the solidarity of the chorus contrasts with the impervious isolation of a *turannos* (Pentheus, Creon) who at certain key moments of the drama is preoccupied with *money*. The significance of this will emerge in the next section.

6. CHORUS AND POWERFUL INDIVIDUAL

Kosmos can mean the political order, as well the cosmic order, and we have seen that the chorus can seem to embody both polis (social totality) and cosmos (physical totality). But the Olympian deities did not on the whole personify heavenly bodies, and the grounding of political practice in cosmic order was not a feature of Greek society to the extent that it was in, say, Egypt or Babylon.[57] In Greece the most striking conjunction of cosmos and polis was in the chorus.

An instance of this conjunction is provided by a song written in the seventh century BC for performance in Sparta, Alcman's *Partheneion*, as interpreted by Ferrari.[58] Although I am largely persuaded by it, this interpretation is far from generally accepted. I mention it here because it gives us a chorus that embodies both cosmos and (in a sense) polis and yet—in contrast to the solidarity of the mystic chorus—expresses rivalries. There is tension between two choruses, and between individual chorus members, expressed hyperbolically as combat: a rival chorus 'fights' with us, and Hagesichora με τείρει (l. 77), 'wears me down'.[59] Similar is the competition in beauty referred to by Euripides: 'May I take my place in the choruses . . . the ἁμίλλαι [conflicts, contests] in loveliness, with strife of delicately luxuriant hair.'[60] Hagesichora ('Leader of the Chorus') defeats me, effaces me, in the way that in other texts Artemis

---

[57] The heavenly bodies influenced the timing of agricultural activity, of festivals, and of military activity. And cosmic order might be used to justify a political principle, e.g. at Soph. *Aj.* 668–75; Eur. *Phoen.* 541–7.

[58] Ferrari (2008: 17).

[59] τείρει is more often taken as 'erotic', but I follow Ferrari (2008: 80).

[60] *IT* 1143–8; Burnett (1985: 10, 160).

outshines the nymphs, Aphrodite the Graces, Thetis her sisters, and Helen her companions. 'Like the rising dawn...Helen shone among us', sing the dancing chorus at her wedding.[61] And Sappho writes of a girl who is now conspicuous among Lydian women as the moon surpasses all the stars.[62] These passages are adduced by Ferrari, who argues that the singing chorus is impersonating the Hyades, that the Pleiades are a rival chorus, and that Hagesichora is the moon.[63] Here coextensiveness with the cosmos expresses not unison but rivalry.

In the *Partheneion* the *choragos* (chorus-leader) exercises authority within the chorus, and elsewhere Alcman applies the word to Agesidamos, 'leader of the people'.[64] The chorus may seem to embody the social totality, and accordingly the word *koruphaios* could refer both to chorus-leader and to political leader (e.g. Hdt. 3.82.3). In Sparta a central public space was called χορός.[65]

This brings us back to the 'transformation undergone [in Athens] by a traditional religious element, choral song, which lived on in Sparta in more or less its old form'.[66] We may add here that a factor in this transformation was the institution of the tragic and dithyrambic competitions at Athens at the City Dionysia[67] in the last decade of the sixth century BC, a time of democratic transformation.[68]

A crucial factor in this distinctively Athenian development was, I believe, the *monetization* of festivals in the latter part of the sixth century, which resulted in choruses at the Dionysia being financed and controlled by powerful individuals. In democratic Athens the word *chorēgos*, 'chorus-leader', referred to a wealthy individual who did not belong to the chorus but provided the money to equip and train it.[69] The kind of tension exemplified by the *Partheneion* may have developed into tension between the dithyrambic chorus and the centralized monetary power of the tyranny. If so, then after the overthrow of the Athenian tyranny this tension was remembered in tragedy, as it emerged from dithyramb, and was assimilated to the ancient myth of the

---

[61] Theoc. *Id.* 18.7–8, 26–8.   [62] Sappho *fr.* 96; cf. *fr.* 34.

[63] Ferrari (2008: 83–105).

[64] *PMG* 1.43–5; 10(b).11. For the connection between choral leadership and kingship in Sparta, see Nagy (1990: 347–9).

[65] Paus. 3.11.9. An account of the forging of 'religious space' by choral performance (on Delos) is by Kowalzig (2007a: 69–80).

[66] Parker (2005: 181–2).

[67] There is no good reason to suppose that the choruses at the Thargelia were dithyrambs: Wilson (2000: 314 n. 22; 322 n. 115).

[68] Perhaps these splendid new public choruses in a developing polis festival were thought to outshine the more private choruses that were an essential element of aristocratic education (Ar. *Ran.* 729).

[69] 'Athenian choral forms (dithyramb, tragedy, and comedy) strikingly plucked the *chorēgos* out of the chorus' (Kurke 2007: 100).

rejection of Dionysiac cult by the king (as well as to the contrast between isolated initiand and initiated chorus).[70]

The tension between Dionysus and the *turannos* Pentheus in *Bacchae* includes the fact that they both want to be the focus of the pandemic festival. Pentheus rejoices 'when many stand at the gates, and the polis magnifies the name of Pentheus. He too (Dionysus)...enjoys being honoured.'[71] In *Frogs*, and in the anecdote recorded by Herodotus, the mystic chorus seems to embody the whole polis, and in *Bacchae* the celebrations of the mystic chorus prefigure the initiation of the whole polis. The focus of the mystic chorus (on Iacchus or Dionysus) may become the focus of pandemic celebration. But Iacchus or Dionysus may be replaced there by the mortal potentate.

After Athens had lost its democratic autonomy, Demetrius Poliorcetes was on one occasion welcomed as a god with processional choruses and with an *ithuphallos* (a hymn sung in festivals of Dionysus) that contained the verses

> Here the time has brought together Demeter and Demetrios.
> She comes to celebrate the solemn [σεμνά] mysteries of Kore,
> And he glad, as the god should be, and beautiful and smiling [γελῶν] is present.
> Something solemn [σεμνόν τι] he seems, his friends all in a circle and in the
>   middle of them he himself.
> Similarly as if his friends are the stars, and he the sun.[72]

Demetrius has arrived at the time of Demeter's mysteries at Eleusis, in which Dionysus–Iacchus is celebrated in a choral procession. It has been argued that the ancient accounts of Demetrius have numerous details based on his assimilation to Dionysus.[73] Moreover, Plutarch tells us that the god Demetrius most emulated was Dionysus (*Dem.* 2.3), that it was proposed that whenever he came to Athens he should be 'received with the ξενισμοί [welcoming entertainments] accorded to Demeter and Dionysus' (12.1), and that the Athenians renamed the Dionysia after him 'Demetria' (12.2). In the hymn, 'as *the* [τόν] god should be' (not '*a* god') probably refers to Dionysus,[74] who is elsewhere beautiful and γελῶν.[75] The repetition of σεμνός indicates, I suggest, that his identification with the sun is based on the identification of Dionysus with the sun in the mysteries. The Eleusinian Dionysus–Iacchus is in the fifth century 'light-bearing star of the nocturnal mystic ritual' and 'chorus-leader of the stars'. The Stoic Cleanthes, a contemporary of Demetrius and resident of

---

[70] This paragraph states conclusions for which I have argued in detail in Seaford (2012: chs 4–6).

[71] *Bacch.* 319–20; the *turannos* of *Antigone* thinks that he owns the polis (l. 738).

[72] Demochares *FGrH* 75F2, Douris *FGrH* 76F13, both ap. Athenaeus 253.

[73] Scott (1928: 226–39).

[74] Perhaps Demetrius was associated or identified with Dionysus in the lost beginning of the hymn.

[75] E.g. *Bacch.* 454, 439 (with Seaford 1996: ad loc.). Similarly, Mark Antony was celebrated as Dionysus as he entered Ephesus and Athens: Plut. *Ant.* 24; Seneca *Suas.* 1.6.

Athens, identified the sun with mystic torchlight[76] as well as with Apollo and with Dionysus.[77] There are also later texts indicating the mystic identification of Dionysus with the sun.[78] The hymn states that of the gods only Demetrius can save them in the war: the Athenian polis is asserting its survival with a mystic chorus addressed not to Iacchus (as in Herodotus' anecdote) but to a more effective, human potentate.

In democratic Athens, on the other hand, the mystic chorus had been saved by their divine master from subjection to a human one. In Euripides' *Bacchae*, just as in his satyric *Cyclops* and indeed in many other satyr plays, it is in the anomalous absence of Dionysus from its dancing that the thiasos falls under the power of the man of money[79]—and is eventually liberated, just as in general the tragic chorus survives the downfall of powerful individuals.

The mystic chorus may embody the cosmos, but—in contrast to Alcman's *Partheneion*—is characterized by the cohesive anonymity of its members. Moreover, its allegiance is to deity rather than to any mortal: to Dionysus in *Bacchae* and (as 'chorus-leader of the stars') in *Antigone* (l. 1147), to Iacchus in *Frogs*.[80] I suggest that the fifth-century tragic chorus—diverging from the aristocratic choruses of, for example, Sparta—retains the internal anonymity and egalitarian solidarity[81] of the mystic chorus from which it is in part ultimately derived.

7. THE POLITICIZATION OF THE DITHYRAMB

Why was such a large proportion[82] of the public *choroi* in democratic Athens constituted by the dithyrambic and tragic *choroi* at the polis festivals of Dionysus? Any answer cannot ignore the combination in the dithyramb of various features tending to promote a sense of community: its association with mystery cult (Section 3), its internal unity, its escorting into the city of a *god* who comes *from outside*[83] at a pandemic festival. In this combination of the mystic, the processional, and the pandemic, it resembled the Iacchus song. Pindar's dithyrambic fr. 70c contains what seems to have been a wish that

---

[76] *SVF* 1.538.   [77] *SVF* 1. 540, 541, 546.

[78] Seaford (2005). Cf. the mystic saviour Dionysus as 'greatest light' at Eur. *Bacch.* 608.

[79] Eur. *Bacch.* 547–59; *Cyc.* 73–81. Pentheus and Polyphemus and other captors of the thiasos as men of money: Seaford (2003a).

[80] Cf. also Eur. *Bacch.* 141.

[81] Tension is rather with the *turannos*. The closest to internal tension is the spoken passage at Aesch. *Ag.* 1348–71, even though the variety of views does not in fact produce contradiction. Aesch. *Sept.* 1066–77 is a post-classical interpolation.

[82] Parker (2005: 181–2).   [83] Seaford (2012: 44).

stasis (internal conflict) should be resolved, together with an invocation of Dionysus.[84]

The sense of community surely persisted even after the dithyramb became a stationary (rather than escorting) song as part of its development into tragedy. 'The characteristic circular dance of the dithyrambic chorus meant that it was endless and boundless—it had no head or leader.'[85] But it was tragedy that acquired, in connection with the developments described in Section 6, a new kind of political significance.

Another dithyrambic fragment of Pindar (70b) contains mention of the transition from processional to static dithyramb,[86] as well as mystic ritual in an (Olympian) μέλαθρα (palace) with 'ῥόμβοι of drums' and a 'fire-breathing thunderbolt', and the birth of Dionysus (Section 4). The dithyrambs in *Bacchae* also embody the transition from processional to stationary dithyramb,[87] as well as—also in μέλαθρα (ll. 587–9)—mystic ritual containing a thunderbolt associated with the birth of Dionysus.[88] But they are also significantly different from the Pindaric dithyramb.

The entry-song of *Bacchae* exemplifies precisely the transition from processional to stationary dithyramb that was a crucial step in the development of tragedy. Dionysus tells his entering choral escort to go around the royal house and beat their drums, 'so that the polis of Cadmus sees' (l. 61). Having called on anyone inside the *melathra* to come out, they pronounce the mystic *makarismos* and narrate the birth of Dionysus by the thunderbolt that killed his mother Semele. Whereas this is a *public* dithyramb, the second *stasimon* ('stationary song') has more affinity to the *secret* mystic chorus. First the chorus narrate, or rather dramatize, the birth of Dionysus, who is called 'Dithyrambos'. He was, they say, as a baby washed in the streams of Dirke. 'But you, o blessed Dirke, are thrusting me away when I have crown-wearing *thiasoi* in you [i.e. on your banks]. Why do you reject me? Why do you flee from me? In the future . . . Bromios will be of concern to you' (ll. 530–6). Here the performance of the dithyrambic myth of birth embodies a claim to both time (past, present, and future) and space. The dual claim is then implicitly repeated when, after their invocation of Dionysus to come from afar, he appears along with earthquake and with the reactivation, at the tomb of Semele, of the flame that Zeus' thunderbolt once left when it killed Semele at Dionysus' birth (ll. 585–99, 6–9). The sounds as of thunder and earthquake were surely created here by drums, just as they were perhaps evoked earlier by the drumming 'around the royal house' in the first dithyramb.[89]

---

[84] Wilson (2003: 179) suggests that this 'represents a politicization of the mystic, choral powers of Dionysos'.

[85] Kurke (2007: 100), based on Martin (2007).

[86] D'Angour (1997: 340–3).

[87] *Bacch.* 55–61; Seaford (1996: 156).   [88] Seaford (1996: 195–203).

[89] *barubromos* ('heavy-roaring'), of their drums (l. 156), occurs also of thunder (Eur. *Phoen.* 182; cf. Eur. *Hipp.* 1201–2). And cf. Section 4.

Whereas in the Pindaric dithyramb it seems that the μέλαθρα contain the mystic ritual as a context for the drumming enactment of the thunderbolt at the birth of Dionysus, in *Bacchae* this is directed *against* the μέλαθρα, which consequently collapses.[90] The cosmological power of the dithyramb, with drums making present the thunderbolt of Zeus, is—in the aetiological myth of resistance to the new cult—deployed on behalf of the polis against the resistant royal household. As the house collapses, Dionysus is greeted by the chorus as 'greatest light' and urges them to rise from the ground, where they have just fallen in terrified individually isolated (μονάδα) desolation. The cosmological demolition of the royal house combines with the mystic transition from frightened isolation to (restored) choral solidarity. The cosmic reach that emerges from mystic choral solidarity acquires *political* power, by which mystery cult is established for the whole polis.[91]

8. PUBLIC AND PRIVATE SPACE

This power of the dithyramb to extend cosmic–communal space into the household has to be seen in the context of our earlier account of the power of the performers of ritual—unknown in our society—to create and possess communal space. The extensive communal space of the polis contains places for numerous superhuman powers (deities, heroes). It was—in the imagination of the citizens—defined and maintained as public space not only by boundary stones but also by communal rituals associated with constructions such as sanctuaries, temples, altars, and statues. Participation in ritual, and especially in choruses, creates—for both participants and onlookers—a memorable paradigm of the cohesive energy and consensual power needed to control and defend space. Εὐρύχορος, literally 'with broad choruses', is regularly translated 'with broad places'. The choral dance was a vital instrument of military training,[92] and soldiers would march singing into battle.[93]

The space of the household too was a place of ritual and of gods. For instance, it is as protector of house and property that Zeus is called *ktēsios*. But his general presence in households qualifies the absolute possession of each household by its owner. In the polis all space is in a sense one space. 'Public ill goes into everybody's house, and the courtyard walls are no longer disposed to hold, but it leaps over the high wall, and finds him for sure, even if

---

[90] On the democratic polis physically demolishing the houses of its internal enemies, see Connor (1985).

[91] Eur. *Bacch.* 39–40, 49; Seaford (1996: ad 1329–30).

[92] Pritchett (1974: 216–17); on the choral *purriche*, with some affinities to the dithyramb, see Ceccarelli (1998).

[93] Rutherford (2001: 42–7).

he takes refuge in the inmost room.'[94] In Aeschylus' *Agamemnon* the whole household participates in sacrifice at the altar of Zeus *ktēsios* (ll. 1036–8), but at the end of the *Oresteia* it is Zeus *agoraios* (of the *agora*) who 'obtained power' (*Eumenides* 973). *Agora* could mean both assembly and a central public space. Zeus *agoraios* had an altar not only in the *agora* (in Athens and elsewhere) but also on the Athenian Pnyx, where the Athenian assembly met.[95] In the same Oresteian movement from household to polis, the Furies in Argos are 'hard to send out' from the royal house (*Ag.* 1190), in Delphi beset Orestes inside the temple of Apollo, and in Athens obtain a place of public cult, without which no household will flourish (*Eum.* 895), and proceed to invoke in their choral song and dance blessings on the polis. Tragedy is frequently set at the point of confrontation between the private space of the household and the public space of choral dance. And it is above all the god of tragedy, Dionysus, who in both public ritual and myth irrupts into the private household.[96]

Finally, just as the inclusiveness of ritual solidarity may seem to extend itself outwards to include the cosmos, so conversely the exclusiveness of the ruling family is expressed by the inward movement of confinement in a small space. The endogamy that embodies this exclusiveness is often accompanied, especially in tragedy, by the *spatial confinement* of the isolated female by the male(s) of the household.[97] In *Antigone*, for instance, the spatial confinement of Antigone in her bridal tomb is associated with the reproductive introversion of the Theban royal family,[98] whereas—at the other extreme, just after it is decided to release Antigone—it is as chorus-leader of the stars that the mystic Dionysus is invoked by the chorus to come from afar to purify the polis with dancing.

To conclude, the singing and dancing group had in the classical polis an importance that is entirely unknown in mainstream monotheism. This importance was both religious and political, and was based on the implicit claim of the group to space (and time). In particular, the chorus of mystic initiates, in imagining themselves as coexistent with the cosmos as they prefigured their eternal solidarity, provided both for Platonic philosophy and (differently) for the polis a transcendent model of happy cohesion. It is as a result of this political significance that the mystic chorus developed at Athens into the public performance of dithyramb and tragedy, in both of which the chorus is marked by solidarity and anonymity. Rivalry and the naming of individuals, which in Alcman's *Partheneion* occur *within* the cosmic chorus, in tragedy serve to *contrast* the (autocratic) individuals with the chorus.

---

[94] Solon 4.26–9.   [95] He was also a patron of politicians: Sommerstein (1989: 269).
[96] Seaford (2012: ch. 4).   [97] Seaford (1990).   [98] Seaford (1990).

16

Mob, Cabal, or Utopian Commune? The Political Contestation of the Ancient Chorus, 1789–1917

Edith Hall

In 1901, the Russian revolutionary intellectual Anatoly Lunacharsky had returned from Germany and his period of direct association with Rosa Luxemburg and the German Spartacists. Now in political exile in Kaluga, an industrial town ninety miles south-west of Moscow, he turned to creative writing, and in a linen mill organized a workers' theatre, which he called 'a miniature Athens'.[1] One of his works was a revolutionary epic poem, *Music: A Dithyramb to Dionysos* (1901), which builds to an excited climax in which the plural lyric voice of the Dionysiac brotherhood calls for unification as an ecstatic, unindividuated 'we':

> Let us intoxicate ourselves
> > with the juice of the grape
> Let our dithyramb ring out
> > Loud and strong
> Let us in our ecstasy break
> > Down all barriers
> And steal a kiss from the lips
> > Of Bacchus.
> Be welcome, Death: A just
> > Reward awaits us
> In our hearts we all shall
> > Live again.
> Evoe! Give me your hands, my
> > Brothers
> And forget that you are only
> > You—

[1] Tait (1984: 46, 60).

> Let us be We: and in a sea of
> Misery
> *Create great beauty for an instant too.*[2]

The indivisible *thiasos* of Nietzsche's *Birth of Tragedy out of the Spirit of Music* meets the idiom of the choruses of Euripides' *Bacchae* in a strikingly Modernist call to aesthetic as well as political revolution: 'Let us be We: and in a sea of Misery | Create great beauty for an instant too.'

Lunacharsky was to become one of the chief architects of the ideology of both Russian revolutions, and in 1917 Lenin appointed him Commissar of Enlightenment. In *Music*, he expressed his deep-felt intuition that the dithyramb provided the perfect form for the expression of the collective yearning for socialist utopia shared by the international working class. When 'you' and 'I' become merged into 'We' in the Dionysiac thiasos, we can 'break | Down all barriers'. In a new development, the specific Greek chorus to which the political revolutionaries now began to look, along with the anthropological 'ritualists' such as Jane Ellen Harrison and Gilbert Murray,[3] was the chorus of Euripides' *Bacchae*. In the nineteenth century, on the other hand, as we shall see, the choral archetypes that dominated the cultural imagination were rather different. They were usually those of the Aeschylean *Prometheus* or *Oresteia* and Sophocles' *Antigone*, especially after the international impact made in the 1840s by 'Mendelssohn's *Antigone*'.[4] There was also a pervasive stereotype, used in negative characterizations of groups, of a chorus of emotionally effusive young women, a type broadly associated with Euripides' *Hippolytus* or *Medea*. But by the turn of the twentieth century, when Lunacharsky discovered Euripides' maenads, the Russian theatre was also moving on from the more traditional apprehension of Greek chorality into something much more avant-garde: Stanislavsky's *Antigone* of 1899 still used Mendelssohn's Romantic musical setting. But he experimented with quite different, mass choruses in his subsequent productions of classic drama, notably *Julius Caesar*, which he conceived as 'bright, burning, and revolutionary', at the Moscow Art Theatre in the 1903–4 season. The chief role was played by the People, and Stanislavsky used a cast of more than 200 Romans, played by workers and university students,[5] in an experiment in mass chorality of the type that was made more familiar in Western Europe a few years later in the *Oedipus Rex* directed by Max Reinhardt.[6]

The revolutionary potential of Greek theatrical chorality was more clearly realized than ever before in revolutionary Russia, but it was of course built into

---

[2] Tait (1984: 48).
[3] See Hall and Macintosh (2005: 492–508); Hall (2012a: ch.11).
[4] Macintosh (1997: 286–8); Hall and Macintosh (2005: 318–32); Fischer-Lichte (2010).
[5] Nemirovitch-Dantchenko (1937: 245, 248–52).
[6] Macintosh (1997, 2009a); and Fischer-Lichte, Chapter 19, this volume.

the medium from the moment of its genesis. The Greek tragic choruses that have survived are the products of democratic Athens, a society that had recently given more political power to more—and poorer—people than any previously. The complex generic form and fluctuating metrical components of our extant fifth-century dramas reflect at a mediated aesthetic level the social tensions and radical newness of the Athenian revolution.[7] Since as early as the seventeenth century, the more astute commentators on the ancient genre saw that the chorus had a subversive and radical political potential that, in at least some of the surviving Greek tragedies, created a tension in the monarchical constitutional worlds they re-created. Corneille and Dacier, for example, had objected to the lack of loyalty—even treasonable insubordination—that the chorus in Euripides' *Medea* shows towards their king by taking Medea's side.[8] Brumoy's *Le Théâtre des Grecs* (1730), read widely in Britain, sees the political culture of democratic Athens as explaining the chorus: they are a reflection of the Athenian spectators, who were 'accustomed to be involved in public affairs' and therefore had 'a quite different taste from the French spectators, who meddle not with anything in their own happy and tranquil monarchy'.[9] In England, on the other hand, Ralph suggests that the chorus was a result of the *decline* of Athenian freedom, added as an ornament after Pericles established the theoric fund, to mask the decreasing political freedom of the playwrights.[10] Richard Hurd was one of the few to see the political complexity of the relationship between democratic Athens and her tragic choruses. The chorus can speak the *truth* only if it consists 'of citizens, whether of a republic, or the milder and more equal roialties'. Yet Hurd sees that a good playwright can use the chorus even of a play set in a tyranny to imply political truths. His subtle reading of *Antigone* points out the chorus's reluctance to protest against Creon's edict, and the way its members 'obsequiously go along with him in the projects of his cruelty'. But Sophocles, he argues, was still using the chorus in a morally effective way. He is deliberately showing how men become incapable of moral protest under despotism. Sophocles 'hath surely represented, in the most striking colours, the pernicious character, which a chorus, under such circumstances, would naturally sustain'.[11]

Discussion of the ancient tragic chorus, in the era sometimes known as 'Modernity' between the later Enlightenment and the Modernist moment just before the First World War—that is, between the French and Russian revolutions of 1789 and 1917—provides a particularly accurate aesthetic and intellectual thermometer with which we can test the temperature of the political arguments of the times. The ancient chorus represents the plural voice of a community consisting of people of identical status. As such, it is an

---

[7] Hall (2012*b*).   [8] See the discussion in Hurd (1749: 76–80).
[9] Cited from Lennox's translation, in Lennox (1759: i, p. cix).
[10] Ralph (1743: 16).   [11] Hurd (1749: 76–7).

inherently radical or subversive entity if viewed from the perspective of a society that endorses anything other than absolute equality. For the hierarchical world of pre-revolutionary Europe, there was no contemporary equivalent, in terms of political bodies or groups, which was not problematic.

It is not just that the shift from feudalism to early capitalism and subsequently industrialization delivered the death blows to any ancestral traditions of collective dance or song in northern Europe, alongside the triumph of bourgeois individual subjectivity in most media and genres of art. More importantly, and more directly, in the Greek chorus a substantial group of absolute equals is seen and heard operating in unison. Moreover, as ancient critics were aware, the chorus members are not of high social status, like the principal characters of tragedy: in the old days, says an author in the Peripatetic tradition whose works have come down to us under Aristotle's name, in tragedy only 'the rulers [*hēgemones*] were heroes, while the rest of the people [*hoi de laoi*], to whom the chorus belong, were ordinary human beings' (*anthrōpoi*, [Aristotle], *Problems* 19.48).[12] In the eighteenth and nineteenth centuries, the 'problem' of the Greek tragic chorus was usually articulated in aesthetic terms: it seemed incongruous, or absurd, or superfluous to the world created in theatre. But these aesthetic reactions were related to, and functioned to obscure, the underlying political issue. How could the tragic chorus not seem absurd, when there was no social or political equivalent to the chorus as a group of equal, ordinary human beings whose interests only partially coincided with those of their rulers but whose opinion actually mattered?

THE CHORUS BETWEEN NATION AND CLASS

Greek tragedy is conventionally acknowledged to have chimed in tune with some of the central concepts of Modernity—scientific rationalism, Kantian Idealism, Darwinian anti-providentialism, and above all European nationalism. Goldhill has recently emphasized the connections between German Idealism, tragic theory, and nationalism, especially as focused in discourse on the tragic chorus.[13] He has gone so far as to argue that the supreme manifestation of Greek tragic chorality for Modernity is in the foundational works of the nineteenth-century German national operatic repertoire, basing his argument on a claim that the master episteme for understanding the chorus in the nineteenth century was a fusion of the emergent idea of a unified Germany, Kantian Idealism, and the promotion of the 'idealized spectator' (*idealisierte Zuschauer*) by Schlegel, who of course found this concept in

---

[12] Hall (2006: 319).   [13] Goldhill (2012) and Goldhill, Chapter 2, this volume.

another part of the same Aristotelian text as the class distinction between the individual characters and the chorus to which I have referred above (*Problems* 19). In this volume, Goldhill claims that 'when we look at the chorus of Greek tragedy, then and now, we are always viewing through German-tinted spectacles'. But there is a conundrum here. It would be silly to dispute Goldhill's demonstration of the triangular connections between the theorization of tragedy, German nationalism, and German Idealist aesthetics. It would be even sillier to disagree with his claim for the prominence and centrality of Wagnerian opera to the nineteenth-century cultural scene as a whole. Yet I begin to part company with him when he makes the grander claim that it is in these foundational works of a particular medium in a particular culture—the German operatic repertoire—that we find the definitive manifestation of Greek tragic chorality in this era (and his enthusiasm for Wagner's magnificent music implicitly suggests, perhaps in all eras).

An equally good case could be made that the definitive manifestation of chorality in this period is to be found in the much more status-and-wealth-conscious delineation of the tension between individual self-determination and the demands of society and community in the repeated use of the Greek chorus as model in the English-language novel from George Eliot to Thomas Hardy, George Meredith, and Virginia Woolf.[14] In this article, however, I look at two other fields in which the cultural presence of the ancient chorus was often felt outside Germany. First, it is a regular image conjured up in British journalism, and, secondly, it is an important constitutive idea in the development of radical lyric poetry, an advanced stage of which is exemplified in the verses by Lunacharsky that opened this chapter. In the English-speaking tradition, the most influential contribution was made by Shelley's great lyric poems inspired by Aeschylean drama, *Prometheus Unbound* and *Hellas*. Shelley's admirers and imitators were, however, by no means confined to English speakers, and his radical use of the chorus found parallels in the work of poets in every European land, from Pushkin to Rimbaud. When Rimbaud briefly joined the 1871 Paris commune, for example, he experimented with new collective verse forms to suit the revolutionary future to which he and his associates aspired—for example, in the oscillation between 'We' and 'I' in 'Chant de guerre parisien' and 'Qu'est-ce pour nous, mon cœur . . .'.[15]

The manifestations of chorality in the genres of journalistic prose and poetic lyric were interrelated, and mutually affirmed one another. In the later nineteenth century, an admirer of Byron compares him with a Greek chorus, inspiring and admonishing struggles for freedom and revolutions against tyranny across the European continent:

[14] See Deen (1960); Reader (1972); Fowler (1999).
[15] On such experiments in poetry by Rimbaud and others, see Brecy (1991).

Contemporaneously with discussions in the press and debates in Parliament, with the chronicle of foreign risings or the struggles of native parties, the strains of the self-exiled bard rose, year after year, like the monitory warnings of an old Greek chorus, giving forth to the audience of assembled nations the pregnant comment on unmerited suffering, and successful crime.[16]

The chorus as understood by journalists and lyric poets also, as we shall see, shared an aetiology extending back to eighteenth-century Celtic revivalism. More importantly, the chorus had a past very specifically in the landmark mass choruses of the French Revolution, the 'voice of the cities'.[17] Not only did newly composed popular songs help spread the revolutionary identity across France, but, in Republican spectacles and especially festivals, there was 'an unparalleled development in music, open air music made for all the people, simple and comprehensible in form, sonorous and grandiose in its effect, with massed hundreds of thousands of performers'.[18] The illiterate could learn catchy songs in which to 'express their longing for bread and security, their will to build a better social order'.[19] At the great festivals, the collective became the protagonist in its own mass choruses as it was in the history of the times, in accordance with Rousseau's admonitions concerning outdoor spectacles in his *Lettre à M. d'Alembert sur les Spectacles* (1758): 'present the spectators as a spectacle; make them the actors themselves; let each one see himself in the others that all may be better united.'[20] But the main point I would like to press in this chapter is that both journalism and lyric poetry throughout the long nineteenth century reveal that one reason why the chorus was so often and so prominently evoked was that it offered a place for thinking about the other urgent political issue of the day, besides nationalism—democratic revolution. The chorus did without question offer a promising paradigm in imagining a univocal *Volk* or compatriots within the emergent ideal of the unified nation state. But surely it is of equivalent significance that it could also look like a threatening rabble or a utopian projection of an egalitarian commune, depending on your *class*-political perspective?

Two contrasting examples from the British press of the 1860s will demonstrate this beyond any question. First, the author of an article in a conservative newspaper in Cheltenham writes in 1866 to defend a Tory Member of Parliament who has been accused of financial corruption. The central strategy is to denigrate the MP's accusers: 'working-men's clubs, missionary societies, broken-down tradesmen, unemployed labourers, political hangers-on, and the members of that Greek chorus of applause who believe it to be their duty to howl themselves hoarse at election times.'[21] Organized labour activists,

---

[16] Leader in the London *Morning Post*, Wednesday, 17 October 1866 (issue 28970), 4.
[17] Hughes (1940: 193). Cf. Biet (1994).
[18] Hughes (1940: 194).   [19] Hughes (1940: 194).   [20] Rousseau (1987).
[21] Quoted in the *Bristol Mercury*, Saturday, 1 September 1866 (issue 3987).

philanthropic Christians, and the unemployed are here seamlessly fused with 'political hangers-on' and a cabal of noisy demonstrators—a Victorian rent-a-mob. This rhetorical procedure allows the author to insinuate a comparison with a Greek chorus, conceived as a group who like to shout for the sake of it rather than because they are committed to any particular cause or have any valid point to make. Here is the Greek chorus as terrifying crowd, the *ochlocracy* into which ancient political theorists always feared any democracy could descend, explicitly connected with organized labour, social-reformist Christianity, and the unemployed underclass.

Yet the use of the stereotype of the Greek chorus in an insult can also be found frequently in writers of quite the opposite political persuasion. Three years later, a storm of controversy broke out when Frederick Temple was appointed Bishop of Exeter. He was regarded as dangerously avant-garde, since he was a vocal opponent of doctrinal conservatives and an ardent campaigner on behalf of the working class, especially for improvements in the state education system. But other reformist Christians could not praise his appointment too highly, one of them complaining vociferously about the stranglehold of respectable mediocrity on the Church of England, where

the workers and thinkers in the clerical ranks are passed over in favour of elderly gentlemen of good connections and unexceptionable manners, who have never thought far enough to have their doctrinal soundness questioned nor acted with sufficient energy to make enemies, who are great on a Greek chorus and infallible judges of old port?[22]

So a Greek chorus, in political invective, could denigrate *both* an unthinking revolutionary rabble—an out-of-control *ochlos*—*and* the preferred reading of the conservative faction in the Anglican establishment, depending entirely on whose side the rhetorician was supporting. In the factional politics of Ireland, the allegation that the opponents are using corrupt witnesses and pleaders in a court of law typically produced the comparison of their evidence to the effusions of a Greek choral rabble.[23] The cultural history of the relationship between the Greek tragic chorus and Modernity is not only more political in the sense of its relationship with agitation for democracy and widening of the franchise, but more nuanced, dialectical, and conflicted than the model focused on the nation state and Wagnerian opera has allowed us to appreciate. The tension between the German Idealist model of chorality and the increasing political contestation of the plural lyric voice underpins an intelligent review of A. Lodge's English translation of Schiller's *The Bride of Messina: A Tragedy with Choruses*, published by Bohn in 1841:

[22] 'Archdeacon Denison and Dr. Temple', *Bradford Observer*, Wednesday, 20 October 1869 (issue 2130), 2.
[23] 'Altar Denunciations in Kerry', *Belfast News-Letter*, Thursday, 6 November 1862 (issue 15428).

The chorus of old was a voice of sympathy and contemplation elevated far above anything personal: to use Schiller's own words, it 'forsook the contracted sphere of the incidents to dilate itself over the past and future, over distant things and nations and general humanity, in order to deduce the grand results of life and pronounced the lessons of wisdom': but in the *Bride of Messina*, it professedly contracts or enlarges its sphere with every new necessity of the scene; each contending party has his peculiar and rival chorus; and we cease to consider it in any loftier light than as an actor in the piece.[24]

In 1841, as the Chartists in Britain were making rapid progress, this literary journalist asks whether the Greek chorus could and should be the ideal disinterested spectator, or the voice of an *engaged* collective demanding to be a *participatory* agent with claims that rival those of other parties.

The political dimension of the Greek dramatic chorus was even contested in the discussions surrounding the most popular forms of British musical theatre. The most politically radical of the burlesque dramatists, William Brough, insisted that his chosen medium descended directly from the tradition of the working-class heroes and heroines and their choral as well as solo songs in John Gay's *Beggar's Opera*.[25] He raised eyebrows when he intermingled 'popular negro melodies' with Italian choruses and arias in his extravaganza adaptation of Bellini's *La Sonambula*, and especially by the 'liberty' he was accused of taking 'in introducing two characters who act at the beginning as a kind of negro "Greek chorus" to introduce the leading persons'.[26] On the other hand, James Robertson Planché, by far the most conservative writer of burlesque, used the Greek chorus to deride advocates of social reform and universal suffrage in his adaptation of Aristophanes' *Birds* (1846),[27] and offered a quite different model of the chorus from Brough's in introducing the arch, knowing, cynical, reactionary, and ultimately 'safe' character of Public Opinion into his new libretto to the music of Offenbach for *Orpheus at the Haymarket* (1865); she reappeared 'intermittently throughout the piece' to comment, like the 'old Greek chorus'.[28]

I am not denying that British national identity could draw on the Peripatetic/Schlegelian model of the idealized spectator quite as much as Wagnerian opera did; indeed, the idealized British spectator was often invoked in the British press to imply that the dispassionate Anglo-Saxon was watching with sad gravity the 'Greek tragedy' of violent politics on the international scene. British statesmen can be said quietly to reflect on the 'sad drama' of the deteriorating international relationship between the Tsar of Russia and

---

[24] 'The Literary Examiner', in *Examiner* (London), Saturday, 23 October 1841 (issue 1760).
[25] 'Mr William Brough's Lecture on Burlesque', *Morning Chronicle*, Tuesday, 20 January 1857 (issue 28105).
[26] 'Public Amusements', *Liverpool Mercury*, Tuesday, 4 February 1868 (issue 6247).
[27] Hall (2007: 79–81).
[28] 'The Pantomimes', *Morning Post* (London), Wednesday, 27 December 1865 (issue 28718), 5.

America, like the Greek chorus, but without intervening. A British MP addressing electors in 1860 praises the conduct of the British parliament in relation to the wheeling and dealing over France's annexation of Savoy on the continent: 'In the momentous drama which has been acted in Europe during the last few months, it has supplied the place of the Greek chorus, and its sentiments have ever been in accordance with justice, virtue and truth.'[29] But often there is far more to this clichéd formulation than national self-definition. Indeed, it provides us with a handle with which to grasp the connection between chorality and discourse on revolution.

Take the different conceptions of the chorus underlying two articles in British newspapers from the years 1848 and 1849, at the time of the wave of revolutions that began in France but swept across Europe and even to South America. These show that even the *nature* of the Greek chorus and its performances was not as settled a matter as Goldhill's emphasis on the Peripatetic/Schlegelian 'idealized spectator' implies. This idealized figure does indeed lurk beneath the smug observation in a London newspaper discussing the 1848 revolution in France: the foreign perspective of the author, he claims, 'involves some advantages. It sees, for the most, impartially and broadly, without prejudice or prepossession; it looks on, at a certain distance, like a Greek chorus, and appreciates motives, incentives, conditions of action, far better than the actors themselves engaged'.[30] The patronizingly calm Briton can see far better than the frantic Frenchman what is really going on in the country: the implication is that the relationship of the British (who have managed to avoid outright revolution despite the best attempts of the Chartists) to the French is something like that of a Sophoclean chorus (and, because of the gender of the journalist, a male Sophoclean chorus in one of the 'Theban plays' at that) to the violent, criminal, and frenetic principal characters battling it out within the royal house of Labdacus. Here we see, I think, the enduring legacy of the Mendelssohn *Antigone*, the contemplative choral music of which was contrasted very positively with the 'mob' to which the continental operas of the excitable inhabitants of France and Italy subjected their audiences: as one English reviewer of Mendelssohn's score wrote in the revolutionary year of 1848, 'how wonderfully he has sustained and interpreted the antique grandeur, and breathed into it the living principle! It must be kept in mind that the Greek chorus was not the mere mob of the modern opera. In the ancient drama the chorus was the grand exponent, not a mere accompaniment.'[31]

[29] 'R. Grant Duff, M.P., at Elgin', *Morning Chronicle* (London), Friday, 5 October 1860 (issue 29247).
[30] 'September 19, 1848', *Morning Chronicle* (London), Tuesday, 19 September 1848 (issue 24621), 4.
[31] 'French Plays', *Morning Post* (London), Thursday, 6 January 1848 (issue 23114), 6.

In another article observing French radicalism published in a London newspaper just a few months later, however, the rhetorical effect depends on the invocation of a very different stereotype of the Greek tragic chorus: the idea that it was inherently a superfluous ornament, which could all too easily become absurdly comical and probably constituted by young women rather than sagacious old men. The article, entitled 'A Scene amongst the French Socialists',[32] adopts a rather snide tone as it describes the electoral visit of the notorious populist politician, the 'tribune' Alexandre Auguste Ledru-Rollin, to Chateauroux in central France. He had been invited there 'to preside at a socialist banquet' for 700 people held in the capacious storeroom of a timber merchant. In a theatrical civic display, four stewards escorted M. Rollin to the feast, along with a Greek tragic chorus:

twelve young damsels, clothed in white, and adorned with red sashes, accompanied him the whole of the way. The young girls were stationed at his side in the tribune, and very innocently passed their time in eating gingerbread and apples. The maidens were intended to represent the chorus of the ancient drama, and to cough, or stamp with their feet by way of giving the signal when the guests were to applaud!

In a throwback to the ancient Greek female costumes and festival choruses clad in white so popular in France during and after the 1789 revolution,[33] the socialists of this provincial town have furnished their hero with a full chorus of triumphal maidens. They are the figures of by far the greatest absurdity in this British deflation of French ostentation. The journalist insists that the French politician himself found them comical: 'It was with difficulty that M. Ledru Rollin himself could keep his gravity at the sight of the virgins in white by his side.' He himself becomes the butt of the humour subsequently:

As a matter of course, he delivered a few of his sonorous phrases about liberty, equality, and fraternity, and other such branches. The part of the speech which produced the greatest effect on his guests was when he made a fierce attack on the inhumanity, and the injustice of the government in keeping up the tax on spirituous liquors, and which was applauded with phrenzy.

But the maidens of the chorus upstage even Rollin when it comes to ludicrous effect.

What these newspaper articles reveal is that the Greek tragic chorus is indeed a useful tool in the creation of national identity and the disparagement of the identity of other nations, but that such rhetoric is also expressing fundamentally *class-political* positions related to the electoral and economic organization of society. The first British journalist can identify himself as a

---

[32] 'News for Emigrant's Friends', *Lloyd's Weekly Newspaper*, Sunday, 6 May 1849 (issue 337).
[33] See Macintosh, Chapter 17, this volume.

spokesperson of an ancient chorus if that chorus is understood as serious, male, and dispassionate, perhaps the citizens of *Agamemnon* but more especially those of *Antigone*. The second journalist, setting out to disparage French radicalism, can extract good mileage out of the idea of a young, female, rather hysterical Greek chorus of white-robed local virgins of a Euripidean type, working an audience into an emotional (alcoholic) frenzy. The patronizing British national stereotype of the passionate and political Frenchman, indeed, found a long-standing resonance during the Victorian period in the idea of the near-hysterical Greek chorus, as is evident from an account from the 1860s of a Frenchman at the London Adelphi Theatre, who was arrested after watching a performance of Watts Phillips's *The Dead Heart: A Story of the French Revolution in a Prologue and Three Acts*: 'So much did the sufferings of his compatriots affect him that he exercised himself in crying, shouting, and screaming, taking the part of a voluntary Greek chorus.'[34]

In Britain, one of the most frequent contexts in which reference is made to the Greek tragic chorus is education, where it becomes a symbol of the elitist class connotations of the classical curriculum. Reading choruses in the school or university classroom was regarded as mentally strenuous. The Greek tragic chorus often functions as a symbol of extremely advanced esoteric intellectual matters or educational achievement, as people today talk about 'rocket science' or 'brain surgery'. One newsman argues that the popularity of comedy in British theatres is a result of a general lack of serious education: audiences want light theatre because they have no acquaintance 'with atomic theory, the Greek chorus, the polarisation of light, the Lockian [*sic*] and Kantian metaphysics', or other 'heavy matters' of that kind.[35] But in the polemics of educational reformers, the Greek chorus—or at least the advanced matter of the scansion of its recalcitrant lyrics—becomes the emblem of 'useless' education for its own sake. In 1871 a Yorkshire advocate of reformed, utilitarian, and science-based education wrote an article entitled 'Useful versus Ornamental Learning':

Many men brought up in the strict traditions of academical learning will look with eyes of scorn upon the new College of Physical Science, just opened in Newcastle-upon-Tyne . . . How can a nation prosper, will old college Dons think, whose sons let their wits go wool-gathering after chemistry and natural philosophy, when they ought to be hard at work unravelling the intricacies of a Greek chorus, which sounds remarkably well in the sonorous rhythms of Eurypides [*sic*], but which is found to be a trifle vague, not to say idiotic, when translated: to be, in fact, a series of platitudes worthy of Mr TUPPER himself.[36] Verily will our Don think the old

---

[34] 'Ulster Railway Company', *Belfast News-Letter*, Thursday, 25 February 1869 (issue 44390).
[35] 'Modern Comic Writers', *Manchester Times*, Saturday, 8 February 1851 (issue 237), 3.
[36] Martin Farquhar Tupper (1810–89) was the author of a collection of notoriously sententious and archaizing verse *Proverbial Philosophy* (1837).

order changeth when hydraulics and hydrostatics are prized above choriambics and catalectic tetrameters...[37]

In many other, similar polemics, the very names of the lyric metres of the choral sections of Greek drama come to stand metaphorically for the entire reactionary curriculum of the public schools: 'it is a sad waste of a life destined to activity, to learn little or nothing else—to be taught, as the summit of achievement, the knack of putting together ordinary Alcaics, or to scan the antispastick acatalectic tetrameters of a Greek chorus.'[38]

Yet while some educational reformers thought that the Greek tragic chorus should be consigned to the dustbin of educational history, others apparently argued that education in the nicer points of the Greek chorus could and should be made available to all social classes. At least, that is what is implied by the professional man who sneers at the kind of earnest do-gooders who have cranky views on education, the sort of 'educated man who believes that an ignorant servant, who cannot with both her eyes read "slut" visibly written on a dusty table, can...read a Greek *chorus* with her elbows'.[39] The rhetorical effect here comes from the manifest absurdity of imagining that a working-class female could achieve the high educational standard symbolized by reading a chorus in Greek. The major point is dependent on extreme class snobbery as well as misogyny: the serving girl, whose brain can never be developed (note that the only body part mentioned is her elbows, symbol of manual labour), is only by a syntactical hairsbreadth not dismissed as sexually depraved as well as educationally retarded. In a short story published twenty years later, the responses to an educated person made by a repetitive old lower-class woman are said to be 'as bad as a Greek chorus'.[40] Lurking beneath these tropes is the standard joke of the classically educated English gentlemen at the expense of the Euripidean chorus of lower-class females, especially the Troezenian laundresses of *Hippolytus*. At one point in negotiations about the 1772 staging of William Mason's *Elfrida*, a musical drama 'on the Grecian model' featuring a lyrical chorus of twenty Anglo-Saxon virgins, the Covent Garden manager George Colman wittily threatened Mason with a chorus of Grecian washerwomen.[41]

---

[37] 'Useful versus Ornamental Learning', *Huddersfield Chronicle and West Yorkshire Advertiser*, Saturday, 28 October 1871 (issue 1319), 8.

[38] 'Spirit of the Press', *Leicester Chronicle: or, Commercial and Agricultural Advertiser*, Saturday, 14 March 1840 (issue 1530). See also the wry reference in a polemic against the temperance movement to the numerous people who cannot function without alcohol, including 'scholars who cannot unravel a Greek chorus' without it ('Mr Lawrence Heyworth on the Temperance Movement', *Derby Mercury*, Wednesday, 22 October 1856 (issue 3391)).

[39] 'Provincial Medical and Surgical Association', *Trewman's Exeter Flying Post or Plymouth and Cornish Advertiser*, Thursday, 26 August 1852 (issue 4522).

[40] 'Clumsy Players', *Manchester Times*, Saturday, 19 October 1872.

[41] Hall and Macintosh (2005: 194).

THE POLITICS OF AESCHYLEAN CHORALITY

If the 'Euripidean' chorus of lower-class women was useful, as a point of negative comparison, to witty gentlemen or reactionary polemicists, the sympathetic chorus of the Aeschylean *Prometheus Bound* was, from the late eighteenth century onwards, adopted as the 'idealized spectator' of the suffering of slaves and the poor by abolitionists and other social reformers. Aeschylus had not become available in any modern language, including English, until the 1770s. The possibility that Aeschylus might profitably be translated was entertained after the appearance of the Marquis J. J. Lefranc de Pompignan's French version of 1770,[42] and the first English rendering of *Prometheus Bound*, by Handel's erstwhile librettist Thomas Morell (1773). These were followed by the complete 1777 translation of Aeschylus by the Norfolk abolitionist Robert Potter. Shortly afterwards, in 1774, J. G. Schlosser published his German translation *Prometheus in Fesseln* in Basel, soon followed by versions in other European languages, including Ferenc Verseghy's Hungarian translation of 1792 and Melchiorre Cesarotti's Italian of 1794. The sudden accessibility of Aeschylus' play certainly lies behind the ease with which Prometheus became such a pervasive political icon on an international level for the Romantic period, representing, as Curran has shown, the ultimate triumph of liberty through steadfast courage against a tyrannical regime.[43]

At a time when slavery was climbing ever higher on the political agenda, however, any image of the chaining and fettering of a naked body—the ghastly sight that confronts Aeschylus' chorus of Oceanids—inevitably triggered a connection with the terrible descriptions and images of punishments of slaves in the contemporary world that abolitionists were ensuring achieved widespread circulation. The edition of the Greek text of Aeschylus by the renowned English classicist Richard Porson was published in 1795, interleaved with engravings by Tommaso Piroli of illustrations by John Flaxman, the artist so closely associated with Josiah Wedgwood (who also produced the famous 'Am I not a man and a brother' cameo for the abolitionist campaign). These engravings were published separately during the same year. *Prometheus Bound* could now be easily read in English, and its effect in performance, with the chorus of sympathetic, anti-tyrannical witnesses, helpfully visualized, for example in an image of the Oceanids clustering around Prometheus in Flaxman's *The Storm* (Figure 16.1).[44]

I have written elsewhere about the popularity of *Prometheus Bound* in British and North American abolitionist poetry and iconography in the decades following Goethe's unfinished *Prometheus* (*c*.1773),[45] which (although no chorus) is a visionary lyric in which Prometheus finds a new role

---

[42] Macintosh (2009*b*).   [43] Curran (1986).
[44] Hall (2011: 214–18).   [45] Hall (2011).

Fig. 16.1. Flaxman's *The Storm*: the Oceanids clustering around Prometheus in Aeschylus' *Prometheus Bound*. Courtesy of APGRD

as spokesman of *Sturm und Drang*, calling for cosmic *Freiheit*. The centrality of this particular ancient Greek play to the discourse on slavery is underlined when it even becomes appropriated by individuals *opposing* precipitate action to abolish it. The secretary of the American Colonization Society and pamphleteer, the Revd Ralph Gurley, argued in an 1839 speech in Pennsylvania against any abolitionist action that might instigate a civil war in the USA, fearing that the new republic of the Union, in this interpretation the Promethean symbol of world liberty, will be torn apart:

All nations will gather in grief around the agonies of our dissolution as, old Ocean and his daughters gathered with sympathising hearts around the tortured Prometheus, chain-bound inexorably by Force and Fate to the Caucasian rock. At the horror of the scene they might be tempted to cry out, with upbraidings of destiny, the words of the ancient tragic chorus:—

> 'I see, I see—and o'er my eyes,
> Surcharged with sorrow's tearful rain.
> Darkly the misty clouds arise—

I see thine adamantine chain:
In its strong grasp thy limbs confined,
And withering in the parching wind,

Is there a god whose sullen soul
Feels a stern joy in thy despair?
Owns he not pity's soft control,
And drops with sympathy the tear?'

Oh! in case of so dreadful a catastrophe, where will be found a heaven-born Prometheus, to reanimate, with a Divine spark, the lifeless form of Liberty?[46]

This speaker tries to reclaim Promethean 'liberty' from the abolitionists and bestow it on the now creaky ideal of the (slave-owning) American independent republic, the unity of which, in his view, must take priority over bestowing liberty on the slaves in its citizens' possession. Yet, by the 1840s, the Aeschylean *Prometheus Bound* and its chorus were actually associated with revolutionary politics that went far beyond the abolition of slavery. Karl Marx represented the censorship imposed on his revolutionary newspaper *Die rheinische Zeitung* as a scene from the play: Marx is chained to his printing press, tortured by the eagle of Prussian censorship, and comforted by a chorus of equally persecuted Oceanids, who have become fused, as Rhine maidens, with the impoverished farming, vine-growing, and fishing families of the Rhineland on whose behalf Marx's newspaper was protesting (Figure 16.2). For between the early abolition debates and the 1840s there lay one of the most influential poems in the history of the Greek chorus in modernity, the *Prometheus Unbound* of Percy Bysshe Shelley (1820), written, as he states in his preface, to indulge his 'passion for reforming the world'.

There is a sense in which the many different choruses of *Prometheus Unbound* are 'largely mystic and lyric embodiments of ideas' and they 'lead the drama toward song'.[47] In the Greek tragedy, as Shelley seems to have intuitively grasped, the chorus is used far more extensively than in many plays, and in a very specific way later described with his usual acuity by H. D. F. Kitto: this chorus, he writes,

does not tell a plain tale plainly; it is not interested in the telling of a tale. It allows memory to hover and to pounce on the memorable scenes and to omit the rest. Logical and chronological order are nothing to them; these are lyrics and this is the lyrical method. The chorus does not narrate, putting itself at our disposal and arranging its material for presentation to us; it follows the wheeling flight of its own thought and we are to accommodate ourselves to it.[48]

Yet it is quite as important that there is more than one chorus using 'the lyrical method' as it 'follows the wheeling flight of its own thought': the

---

[46] Gurley (1841: 40).   [47] Weaver (1949: 132).   [48] Kitto (1950: 70).

Fig. 16.2. Karl Marx, as Prometheus, chained to the printing press. Lithograph by Wilhelm Kleinenbroich, *Der neue Prometheus* (Düsseldorf, 1842). Courtesy APGRD

claim to the authority of the collective consciousness is contested from beginning to end. Shelley pits the sympathetic and progressive spirits against the chorus of reactionary Furies, the chorus of *Prometheus Bound* against that of *Eumenides*. The function of his chorus of Furies is to reveal the full horror of all regimes based on terror and revenge, and in particular the terror that followed the 1789 revolution in France.

In fact, Shelley is responding to a pre-existing tradition. In the poetry created by the original French revolutionaries, the Furies had been identified with the old despotic order that the events of 1789 were intended to eradicate for ever. One of the *Republican Odes to the French People* published by 'Lebrun-Pindare' (that is, Ponce-Denis Écouchard Lebrun), the 'Hymn of the 21st of January', celebrates the execution of Louis XVI:

> Les flammes d'Etna sur ses laves antiques
> Ne cessent de verser des flots plus dévorants.
> Des monstres couronnés, les fureurs despotiques.
> Ne cessent d'ajouter aux forfaits des tyrans.
> S'il en est qui veulent un maître,
> De rois en rois dans l'univers
> Qu'ils aillent mendier des fers,
> Ces français indignes de l'être,
> Ces français indignes de l'être!

> Etna's flames of ancient lava
> Ceaselessly flow, ever more devouring.
> Crowned monsters, despotic furies.
> Ceaselessly add to tyrants' hideous crimes.
> If some want a master,
> In a world from king to king
> Let them beg for shackles
> Unworthy to be called Frenchmen,
> Unworthy to be called Frenchmen!

The very form of the song, as a choral ode with strong Pindaric resonances (especially the lava of Etna so intimately associated with *Pythian* 1), is locked in struggle with the images it conjures up of the monstrous monarchs, and despotic furies, 'les fureurs despotiques'. This hymn was indeed sung by choruses, to specially commissioned music, at the festivals organized to celebrate the revolution.

Yet the bloodletting into which the revolution soon descended invited parallels with bloodthirsty and vindictive furies in its turn. By January 1795, a new choral song had been adopted by the Thermidorean reaction, the 'Réveil du Peuple' ('Awakening of the People'). To a tune by Gaveaux of the Opéra Comique, the text adjures the people of France to resist the horror and carnage around them:

> Peuple français,
> peuple de frères,
> Peux tu voir, sans frémir d'horreur,
> Le crime arborer les bannières
> Du carnage et du terreur?

It is the republicans who have now dialectically turned into the opposite of the emancipatory chorus and are now the drinkers of human gore, the 'buveurs de sang humain'.[49]

The possibility of the *counterposed* choruses was built into the French Revolution from the start, when Louis XVI had responded to the early republican adoption of collective song as an instrument of mass mobilization by commissioning market women to emulate an ancient chorus, dressing in white and greeting him with laurel branches.[50] It became confirmed when the revolution started to devour its own children, and to persecute disappointed interest groups such as the proletarian Babouvists: they had their own 'counter-choruses', the words of which have survived only because they appeared in the court records of the evidence used to prosecute the singers. The 'Chanson Nouvelle à l'usage des Faubourgs' sings of the people 'dying of hunger, ruined, naked, degraded, troubled', who are contrasted with both the rich and the corrupt heads of the government.[51] But the opposition of bloodthirsty Furies and Promethean liberators in Shelley's poem may, however, have been more directly influenced by verses written by the radical abolitionist James Grahame, and entitled 'Prometheus Delivered'. Although long forgotten, this poem was well known in Shelley's youth, since it opened a widely disseminated collection published in order to celebrate the passing of the 1807 Slave Trade bill. The poem uses the liberation of Prometheus by Hercules to symbolize British legislators aiding slaves, but opens with Prometheus being nailed to his rock in the presence of a vindictive chorus of Furies who revel in his suffering:

> Come, Outcast of the human race,
> Prometheus, hail thy destined place!
> Death shall not sap thy wall of clay,
> That penal being mocks decay;
> Live, conscious inmate of the grave,
> Live, outcast, captive, victim, slave![52]

But in Shelley's near-cosmic Caucasian landscape, the chorus of benign Spirits in the fourth and final act do eventually drown out the bloodthirsty voice of terror in which the Furies of Act I had expressed themselves.[53] It is still difficult not to be moved by the utopian ardour and energy of the Spirits' evocation of a human race that can transcend its bloody history and aspire to living in a paradise ruled not by hatred but by love:

> Years after years,
> Through blood, and tears,

---

[49] Hughes (1940: 199).   [50] Hughes (1940: 195).   [51] Hughes (1940).
[52] James Grahame, 'Prometheus Delivered', in Montgomery, Benger, and Grahame (1807).
[53] Cameron (1943).

And a thick hell of hatreds, and hopes, and fears,
    We waded and flew,
    And the islets were few
Where the bud-blighted flowers of happiness grew.

    Our feet now, every palm,
    Are sandalled with calm,
And the dew of our wings is a rain of balm;
    And, beyond our eyes,
    The human love lies,
Which makes all it gazes on Paradise

.   .   .   .   .

    And our singing shall build
    In the void's loose field
A world for the Spirit of Wisdom to wield;
    We will take our plan
    From the new world of man,
And our work shall be called the Promethean.

CHORALITY AND THE ANTHROPOLOGY OF EMPIRE

The chorus as vehicle for emancipatory sentiments is also a central feature of the poetic drama Shelley completed the year after *Prometheus Unbound*, his similarly Aeschylean *Hellas* (1821), inspired by the Greek tragedy *Persians* and the uprising against Ottoman rule in Greece. Shelley was drawing on a tradition already inaugurated by the time of Thomas Maurice's *The Fall of the Mogul* (1806), a tragedy 'attempted partly on the Grecian model', which borrows from the Sophoclean Oedipus, but also from Aeschylus' *Persians*. The latter play is especially apparent in Maurice's battle narrative and the laments of his mutinous choruses of Brahmin and Zoroastrian priests, who predict that the persecution their religions have suffered will become worse under their newest Islamic ruler, Nadir Shah, before the subject Hindu and Parsee peoples will one day be liberated from imperial oppression.[54] The political thrust, Islamic principal characters, Indian slaves, eastern palace setting, and trans-historical vision of Maurice's choruses directly anticipated those of Shelley's *Hellas*. Shelley also synthesized contemporary Turk with ancient Achaemenid Persian. His scene is set at Constantinople, in the seraglio of Mahmud II, who was the Ottoman sultan between 1808 and 1839.

Shelley replaces Aeschylus' chorus of male Persian elders in the Greek tragedy with a chorus of Greek captive maidens. The shift from masculine

---

[54] Maurice (1806: 30).

to feminine seems to allow him to write much less warlike sentiments, thus creating an opportunity for more spiritual expansiveness; this chorus's fundamental role is to translate the specific events unfolding in 1821 into events of diachronic and cosmic significance, in which the current struggle is emblematic of, and an important step in, the march of history towards a transcendental notion of human Freedom. In the fifth stanza of their first ode, while Mahmud sleeps on his couch surrounded by opium petals, they invoke the idea of Freedom, the mighty mistress; by stanza nine they are warming to the theme.

> In the great morning of the world,
> The spirit of God with might unfurl'd
> The flag of Freedom over Chaos

It turns out that Freedom's splendour first 'burst and shone' from 'Thermopylae and Marathon'. With this move, the ancient Greek resistance against Persia and the contemporary struggle are explicitly associated. In a truly memorable image, maternal Greece is figured as mourning at the funeral of the infant Freedom, whose bier she follows through Time.[55]

There is a contradiction in this chorus, created by Shelley's ambivalent stance on Christianity. Himself an agnostic moral Idealist, with leanings towards the epistemological and metaphysical theories of George Berkeley, in this poem he had the chance to divorce the question of the political domination of Greece from the religious conflict between Islam and Christianity. But, faced with the history of monotheisms, he stepped back from such a radical step on its very brink. In the second long choral lyric, the famous 'Worlds on worlds are rolling over', the universe is run by the mysterious cosmic figure of 'the unknown God'. But this unknown deity, in Shelley's conception of the history of religion, has from time to time sent forth to humanity individual figures, including the 'Promethean conqueror', who trod the 'thorns of death and shame'. This chorus argues that Olympian polytheism died in the face of the star of Bethlehem:

> Apollo, Pan, and Love,
> And even Olympian Jove
> Grew weak, for killing Truth had glared on them.

Islam subsequently arose, but will be short-lived:

> The moon of Mahomet
> Arose, and it shall set:
> While blazon'd as on heaven's immortal noon
> The cross leads generations on.[56]

---

[55] Shelley (1822: 4–8).   [56] Shelley (2003: 13).

All this is in the mouth of the Greek chorus. They are presumably Orthodox Christians, although they are endowed, like the chorus of *Prometheus Unbound*, with a vision that transcends their specific identity and place in space and time. Yet their own religious stance can never offer a parallel to the eclectic, mystical, and global spirituality of *Prometheus Unbound*, which was profoundly affected by Shelley's interest in both Platonism and—in a response to the early works on comparative religion by the Indo-Europeanist William Jones and other British imperial scholars in India—Hinduism. Shelley was well aware that in the issue of religion he faced a real problem in *Hellas*, for he appends an extensive note to this chorus, in which he attempts to explain what exactly it is that he means. Here he tries to have his agnostic cake and eat it; Christianity is, on the one hand, just another temporary and contingent manifestation of humanity's relationship to the Supreme Being; but, on the other hand, it was in the past superior to, and more truthful than, pagan polytheism; it is now superior to the Islamic religion, and will undoubtedly outlast it. He writes: 'The popular notions of Christianity are represented in this chorus as true in their relation to the worship they superseded, and that which in all probability they will supersede, without considering their merits in a relation more universal.'[57] He continues in this note to argue coherently and precisely for the necessity for agnosticism: that 'there is a true solution of the riddle [of the universe], and that in our present state that solution is unattainable by us, are propositions which may be regarded as equally certain'.[58]

In *Hellas*, however, Shelley has found it impossible to configure the Greek War of Independence in terms solely of the human need for ethnic self-determination and political self-government. The true extent of Shelley's absorption of the Christian imagery of the infidel emerges in the interchange between Mahmud and his henchman Daood. The poet has been unable to liberate his verse sufficiently from the contemporary stereotypes of Islam, and the Christian rhetoric of the crusade, in order to leave the notion of a religious war back in the medieval period where it surely belongs. The still stirring politics and utopian Idealism of *Hellas* are thus compromised by its complicity in the ideology of the Christian crusade. It was certainly in imitation of Shelley's work that a whole tradition of patriotic Salamis choruses was established in proudly imperial crypto-Christian Victorian literature, including William Bennett's 'The Triumph for Salamis', a 'lyrical ballad' for twin choirs of young men and female virgins. The imaginary setting is a circle on an Attic beach around the victory trophy. These young Athenians, transparent avatars of the staff of the British Empire, sometimes even forget that they are pre-Christian pagans, as when they execrate 'the fell barbarian', who was 'accursed of God', and lusted 'to crush the guiltless and the free'.[59]

---

[57] Shelley (2003: 55).   [58] Shelley (2003: 56).   [59] Bennett (1850: 29, 39).

But it was probably the quasi-Aeschylean Furies of Shelley's *Prometheus Unbound* rather than his Greek maidens in *Hellas* who underlay the frequent association in the nineteenth century of Aeschylean ancient Greek chorality with a vindictive press. A politician who has fallen from favour then suffers further public humiliation when 'the newspapers burst out upon him like a Greek chorus'.[60] In an example that is striking because abject terror and calls for vindictive reprisals were the almost universal response in Britain to the 1857 uprising or 'mutiny' in India, an article in *Reynolds's Newspaper* took a critical and humane line on the British attitude to the rebel 'sepoys', and in particular the plans for mass executions as advocated in *The Times*:

The *Times* preaches the horrible doctrine of indiscriminate slaughter and incendiarism . . . we cannot yield India, in the sight of the world. Such is the dilemma in which our rulers have placed us. And now they own nothing, amend nothing, promise nothing. They seek only to rouse the fierce passions of the thoughtless. The *Times* raves, like a Greek chorus in some old tragedy scenting blood, and crying for victims to the ruthless Nemesis, whom it invokes, inebriated with the horrid fumes of vengeance.[61]

This rhetorical move is remarkable because, in British imperial discourse on India, the primitive chorus had almost always been identified with the colonized natives of that subcontinent rather than the British colonizing power. Writers on India conventionally construed its inhabitants—Hindu, Muslim, and Sikh—as akin to ancient Greeks themselves.[62] Manifestations of group song and dance performances were identified in Hindu artworks that reached a wide audience in Britain through the circulation of engraved reproductions. Vasunia has shown how, in the *Lakshmi* of Dalpatram Dahyabbai, this Gujarati adaptation of Aristophanes' *Plutus*, published in 1850, synthesizes Gujarati folk culture and performance styles with the Athens of Aristophanes.[63]

It is significant that Dalpatram had been encouraged in this project by Alexander Kinloch Forbes, his associate and the Assistant Judge of Ahmedabad. Indeed, Forbes's own perception of India as retaining some cultural elements from the archaic Indo-European past reflected in ancient Greek literature can be seen in his own description of women engaged in a ritual lament, first published, like *Lakshmi*, before the uprising (in 1856):

the relations and neighbours assemble at the house of the deceased; and, like an *entre acte* to the tragic drama, commences the humming moan of lamentation. The nearer relatives enter the habitation, exclaiming, 'O, father! O, Brother!'. The women, standing in a circle near the door, bewail the deceased, and sing a funeral dirge, beating their breasts to the sad accompaniment of the measure . . . The dirge, which usually consists

---

[60] 'Mr Edwin James', *Nottinghamshire Guardian*, Thursday, 18 April 1861 (issue 786), 4.
[61] Leader in *Reynolds's Newspaper*, Sunday, 25 October 1857 (issue 376).
[62] Hall (2010).   [63] Vasunia (2007).

of unconnected exclamations of grief, is sung by one or two women, while the remainder join in chorus ...[64]

As Parita Mukta has observed, by setting this display of grief in a public space and comparing it with the performance of a Greek tragedy, Forbes is both familiarizing the Indian women to his classically trained readership, and rendering them archaic and alien—twin strategies typical of the colonizer's vision of the colonized.[65]

Examples could be multiplied of the Greek chorus being invoked in descriptions of the recreational activities of pre-industrial societies,[66] especially India. A reporter in Lucknow, trying to describe a native musical entertainment in which young women danced, says that the effect is profoundly confusing, reminding him simultaneously of Roman triumphs, Druidic rituals, the 'Greek chorus', the dancers around David as he introduced the ark of the covenant, and indeed ancient Nineveh.[67] The elision here of Druidic rituals and the Greek chorus with the biblical dances of ancient Hebrews and Babylonians is, however, very significant. The cultural background to this kind of colonial–ethnographic trope will underline just how radical was the sudden transference of the idea of a primitive Greek chorus—and a furious, vindictive one at that—to the implementers of British rule in India in *Reynolds's Newspaper* at the time of the mutiny. For the chorus had been an important presence in the eighteenth-century colonial thinking of, for example, the musicologist John Brown, about non-Western peoples. John Brown drew parallels with the Iroquois in North America. He argued that a form of drama similar to Greek tragedy is practised by all primitive tribes: a chief sings some great action of a god or hero, and 'the surrounding Choir answer him at Intervals, by Shouts of Sympathy or concurrent Approbation'.[68] The eighteenth century had adopted the ancient Greek chorus in its anthropological version of primitivism as the 'other' or the anterior, like Thucydides' vision of backward barbarians still doing things, such as participating in athletics fully clothed, which the Greeks used to do in the past (I.7). From this perspective the chorus was not an inspiration for a more civilized future, like Shelley's benevolent time-transcendent Spirits of revolutionary utopianism, but a marker of Modernity's colonized other, of ethnographically defined anti-Modernity.

---

[64] Forbes (1878 [1856]: 635–6).

[65] Mukta (1999: 34).

[66] A typical example occurs in an 1860 description, during an account of travels in Georgia, of 'the favourite dance of the Georgians, which is exactly like the Greek chorus. A number of men form a large circle, each lays his hands on the shoulders of his neighbours, and off they go, round and round, singing in a circle, and the loud acclamations of the bystanders, who beat time by clapping their hands. The songs ... are mostly descended from olden times'. See 'Street Life in Tiflis', *Liverpool Mercury*, Friday, 5 September 1851 (issue 2325).

[67] 'R. Grant Duff, M.P. at Elgin', *Morning Chronicle*, Friday, 5 October 1860 (issue 29247).

[68] Brown (1763: 41–2).

Yet the politics of this identification of the chorus with a less advanced level of civilization had become complicated decades before Shelley at the moment when progressive thinkers began to sense that some models of ideally free-dom-loving and egalitarian communities might be discovered in their own national pre-capitalist pasts. Fiona Macintosh and I have written elsewhere about William Mason's *Caractactus*, a successful play performed at Covent Garden in 1776–8. *Caractacus* stages a conflation of Tacitus' description of the indomitable Briton captured during the reign of Claudius (*Annals* 12. 33–7) with the same historian's account of the last stand of the druids of Mona (Anglesey) against Suetonius Paulinus (*Annals* 14. 29–30). Mason's tragedy is modelled, however on Greek tragedy, not only in content (the plot imitates Sophocles' *Oedipus at Colonus*), but in its form. 'Written on the model of the ancient Greek tragedy', *Caractacus* presented its audience with a singing, dancing, involved and interactive tragic chorus. Mason's choice of identity for the chorus (druids and bards) demonstrates the extent to which Hellenic and ancient British revivalisms were conflated. But it also demonstrates the impossibility of separating the aesthetic from the political: Mason's druids, by singing of ancient Celtic resistance to Roman tyranny in the ancient Greek plural lyric voice, are a dramatic analogue of Collins' Druidic temple of Freedom in the British woodland, allegorically also representing the renewal of English poetry (*Ode to Liberty*, 1746):

> In Gothic pride it seems to rise,
> Yet Graecia's graceful orders join
> Majestic through the mixed design.

Making connections between ancient Britons and ancient Greeks seemed appropriate at a time of British opposition to Rome's descendants in the 'ancient regimes' of Europe. *Caractacus* encouraged identification with the Greeks and the drawing of parallels between the culture of Athens, where tragedies were performed, and that of early Britain. During this period, classical and 'Gothic' political revivalism were not so very different. Whigs like Mason believed that early British culture, until the Norman invasions, had enjoyed a democratic assembly—the Anglo-Saxon *myclegemot*—equivalent to that of classical Athens.

The play's rituals blatantly conflate the British druids with ancient Greek choruses. The druids enter with a circular dance in the 'sacred space' of the grove on Mona. Later, they perform rites to the sound of the harp: the chorus leader Mador sings antiphonally to them, 'Rustling vestments brush the ground, | Round, and round, and round they go.' The druids share the grove with bards, who play 'immortal strains' on their harps: 'In visible shapes dance they a magic round | To the high minstrelsy.' The choral odes are sometimes sung by the druids, sometimes by bards, and evince diverse metrical patterns, antiphony, solo and *kommos*, refrain, and dyadic or triadic systems with strophe, antistrophe, and epode. It is impossible, moreover, that Shelley was not aware of Mason's freedom-loving rebel chorus. Both Byron and Words-worth show traces of Mason, and his type of Hellenism lay behind the self-styled 'Greek school' of minor Romantic poets. These included Frank Sayers, who in 1790 published two tragedies using 'the Greek form' with choruses of bards or druids, and William Sotheby.[69] In 1808 a balletic version of *Caract-acus* was performed at Drury Lane. It opens on Mona with a chorus of harp-strumming bards, and concludes with another bardic chorus singing defiantly in the Roman forum.[70]

THE BOLSHEVIK CHORUS

This chapter sprang from my conviction that there was much more to the story of Greek tragic chorality in the long nineteench century than German Idealism, German nationalism, and Wagnerian opera. The collective of equals, not of high status, who express themselves in the first-person plural, moving as one, had resonances that were often connected with groups defined by status or class rather than nationality (although the ideas of the nation and the political collective often overlapped or coincided, as when British writers who criticized the French were actually criticizing political movements). We have seen how the idea of the Greek chorus could be used both to denigrate and to promote egalitarian reform and democratic agitation. But perhaps the most important point is that Greek chorality was indeed a 'supreme' cultural touchstone of Modernity because the way it was conceived oscillated so frequently and perceptibly between the two great collectives of nineteenth and early twentieth-century thought: the collective as an ethnic/national entity, and the collective as the working class, which could and should transcend all national barriers and define itself not against other nations but against the interests of the international plutocratic ruling class.

The pageant Jack Reed organized for the Paterson silk-workers' strike in Madison Square Garden on 7 June 1913 featured choral singing of socialist anthems as a central strategy of the Industrial Workers of the World, who were sponsoring the strikers.[71] But the chorus as the revolutionary workers' collective perhaps attained its own 'supreme manifestation' in the great public performances held in Russia in the years immediately after the 1917 revolu-tion, which were enacted by large groups of ordinary people. One of the largest, most famous, and certainly the best documented was the mass

[69] Hall and Macintosh (2005: 211–13).
[70] Hall and Macintosh (2005: 214).
[71] Hall (forthcoming).

spectacle of 1 May 1920, *The Mystery of Freed Labour* directed by Yuri Annenkov and Alexander Kugel, one of many such events all round Moscow streets and parks and public areas. But this was huge. It was performed between the portals and on the step of the former Stock Exchange. The class struggle was conceived on three levels of space—top platform, stairs, and approach area. The Kingdom of Freedom was inside and the class struggle took place on the stairs. There were no fewer than 35,000 spectators in the square! The idea was to create a new revolutionary mythology, and the first stage in the *Mystery* was Spartacus' uprising, followed by the 1670 revolt of the Cossack leader Strenka Razin, and then the October Revolution. Slaves and serfs were acted by men from the Red Army Theatre workshops.

The first scene depicted a life of leisure, with ancient Romans eating and drinking and pantomime dancers entertaining the rich. Then, to the tune of Chopin's 'Funeral March', a crowd of slaves filled the space in front of the stairs. A mime of the work of slaves was performed while the rich ate and were entertained. Gradually, more attention became focused on the slaves and the hardships they were facing (brutal whippings). At different moments the slaves stopped working to listen to the summons from the Kingdom of Freedom (in a reminder that the appeal of Wagner was not exclusive to German nationalism), a tune from *Lohengrin* sounding from backstage. They revolted, with Spartacus leading them, a red flag in his hand, but were beaten back by Roman soldiers from the steps: their storming of the Kingdom of Freedom was delayed until the end of the spectacle.[72]

In *The Mystery of Freed Labour*, the mass chorus supplied by the Red Army performers erased completely the distinction between mimetic spectacle and history, as the chorus members re-created the very same Kingdom of Freedom they believed they had in reality wrested from the hands of the ruling class during the 1917 revolution. But instead of any tunes from Chopin or Wagner, the rather traditional choice of composers used in the spectacle, the piece that became the semi-official anthem of the Russian Revolution harked back to earlier Promethean choruses—it was Alexander Scriabin's *Prometheus: The Poem of Fire* (1910). Scriabin had studied at the Moscow Conservatory with Sergei Taneyev, the composer of the *Oresteia* first performed at the Mariinsky in 1895 and much admired by the Commissar of Enlightenment Lunacharsky, with whose revolutionary dithyramb this chapter began.[73] But, in *Prometheus*, Scriabin created an artwork, complete with chorus, so aesthetically and technologically revolutionary that, on the rare occasions when it finds a full performance, it still amazes today. Scriabin wanted to create a synaesthetic performance where colour and light interacted with sound, both instrumental and vocal, in the creation of a world of sensory experience more total and

---

[72] The source for most of this is the eye-witness account by Fülöp-Miller (1927).
[73] Trubotchkin (2005: 255–73).

more radical than anything that had gone before. It includes a solo piano part and one for a machine known as a *Luce* or *Clavier des Lumières* or 'colour organ', designed especially for *Prometheus*. Scriabin's own machine can still be seen in the museum situated in his apartment in Moscow. Although played via a keyboard like a piano, the machine generates light of different colours, which is projected onto a screen in the concert hall.

But the choral part is as revolutionary as the beams of multi-coloured light. There is no 'libretto', and the 'text' is usually said to be the first important instance in musical history of the completely 'wordless' chorus, where the massed human voice becomes the instrument of emotion and meaning beyond any specific time, place, language, or culture. In the final section, the full choir of mixed male and female voices sings in succession 'Ah, oh, o, é, a', 'raising the music to a prodigious climax of sound'.[74] This chorus is pre-linguistic, but also post-linguistic. In a world where the revolutionary immersion of self and other will not only erase all hierarchies and class distinctions, but extend to all nationalities and all languages, why would the choral collective need to close off its open vowels with the consonants that demarcate one language from another? It is scarcely surprising that the fire-poem chorale became the Bolshevik theme song in a futuristic novel by Alexander Chayanov called *Journey of my Brother Alexei to the Peasant Utopia* (1920). This imaginatively describes the rural economy of the blissful post-revolutionary world of smallholdings that will have been established by 1984; it is predicted that the churches of Moscow will still be open, but pealing out Scriabin's *Prometheus* instead of any national anthem.[75] Neither the terror following the 1789 revolution in France, nor the painful failure of the historical Soviet Union, which we now know was in 1984 headed for dissolution, should be allowed to blind us to the extraordinary experiments in egalitarian chorality that the revolutionary moments in these two countries produced.[76]

---

[74] Hull (1927: 344).

[75] See Stites (1989: 186) and the English translation of Chayanov's story in R. E. F. Smith (1977: 67–113).

[76] This paper developed out of my response to a paper delivered by Simon Goldhill at a UCL conference, 'Tragedy and the Idea of Modernity', held on 22 July 2011. The convenors were Joshua Billings and Miriam Leonard. I am very grateful to both of them, and to Simon, for helpful comments, as am I to Fiona Macintosh.

17

Choruses, Community, and the
Corps de Ballet

Fiona Macintosh

The early interconnections between traditional ballet and the *ballet de cour* have proved hard to sever. Modern Dance was predicated upon the belief that, by breaking with the strictures of traditional ballet, the dancer would be liberated and dance itself democratized. These long-standing associations with the monarchy and aristocratic *noblesse oblige* have cast traditional ballet as profoundly antithetical to ancient Greek culture, and the *corps de ballet* in particular as completely other than the ancient chorus.

In the *Querelle des anciens et les modernes*, ballet (like opera) was on the side of the moderns, whose taste in baroque extravagance and bombast was amply satisfied by the virtuosic display and elaborate scenic effects of contemporary ballets. Invocations of the ancient Greeks in the history of dance in the modern world have tended to come to the fore at moments of transformation—precisely at times when the formality, refinement, and rigidity of form trad-itionally associated with ballet have been rejected. These notable classically inspired turning points include Noverre's eighteenth-century dance reforms, which sought ancient pantomime as source for the new *ballets d'action*; and they encompass, in the early twentieth century, the Greek-inspired bare-foot dances performed by the pioneers of Modern Dance and the Ballets Russes' adoption of folk tradition and archaic Greek inconography, both of which energized and resisted the ossifying conventions of contemporary ballet.[1]

Whilst the collaboration between Noverre and Gluck in the second part of the eighteenth century is the first serious modern attempt to re-create the singing *and* dancing chorus of antiquity, it is generally averred that the ancient model was not successfully adopted systematically on the modern stage before

---

[1] For eighteenth century, see Hall (2008) and Lada-Richards (2010); for modernism, see Macintosh (2010) and generally Naerebout (1997, 2010).

the twentieth century.[2] The large-scale productions of Greek tragedies directed by Max Reinhardt adopted choruses choreographed in accordance with developments in Modern Dance. These may well be considered the first successful attempts to revive the ancient tragic chorus (see Goldhill, Chapter 2, and Fischer-Lichte, Chapter 19, this volume). But these choruses did not appear *ex vacuo*.

This chapter seeks to reinsert the nineteenth-century *corps de ballet* into an account of the reception of the ancient chorus and to probe the reasons for its earlier omission. If the *corps de ballet* today summons up sanitized images of white gauze tulle tutus, the skirts were not always so short nor the dancers' image always so saccharine or sentimental. As Matthew Bourne's all-male version of *Swan Lake* (1995) reminded audiences, the *corps de ballet* embodies power, especially power of the collective; and, in the early nineteenth century, it embodied the power of female collectivities at a time when the principal ballerina was literally bathed in the newly invented stage gas lighting.

Romantic ballet was no different from other Romantic art forms in proclaiming its differences from neoclassicism in terms of its new, non-classical content. But dance historians' ready adoption of a narrative of rupture has obscured the ways in which the nineteenth-century hallmark of traditional ballet aesthetically resembled particular ancient tragic choruses in terms of both its method and its affect. Furthermore, this narrative also occludes the *corps de ballet*'s significant genealogical links with the French revolutionary festivities and their ancient models (see Hall, Chapter 16, this volume).[3]

It addition to the changes in content, there is a second and more significant reason for the neglect of the *corps de ballet*. During the course of the nineteenth century, ballet became increasingly associated with lowbrow culture, and the roles of dancer and prostitute hard to disentangle. Ballet as an art form was sullied as a consequence, especially for those who sought to dissociate it from the alleged purity of Graeco-Roman antiquity. As Marian Smith has demonstrated, there are considerable links between opera and dance in Paris at this time, but prejudices on the part of musicologists towards dance have meant that, until very recently, these interconnections have been overlooked.[4] Indeed, the *corps de ballet*, one of the staples of the Romantic ballet repertoire, is no less important to discussions of the reception of the ancient chorus than the grand operatic choruses that it regularly accompanied.

---

[2] See Hall and Macintosh (2005) for other eighteenth- and nineteenth-century British experiments with performing choruses by Mason and the writers of burlesques.

[3] Homans (2010: 112).

[4] M. Smith (2000: 19–58).

CHORUS VERSUS THE *CORPS DE BALLET*

Before the end of the eighteenth century, the ballet chorus was regularly referred to as a 'chorus' ('chœur de danse') to distinguish it from a singing chorus. So Noverre speaks of a 'Dame des chœurs, celle qui danse dans les chœurs et qui ne danse pas seule'.[5] By the early nineteenth century, however, the dancing 'chorus' is replaced by the *corps de ballet*, which originally refers in France (at least) to the whole company of dancers, but increasingly, and especially in English usage, refers to the chorus members who are neither the principals nor the character parts.[6] This new coinage reflects, on the one hand, institutional changes, which were the result of post-revolutionary reforms in the Académie de Danse at the Opéra designed to improve the status of the company (hence it was now a 'corps de ballet').[7] The move to larger venues, and, from 1822, the use of gas lighting, which enabled large groups to be illuminated as they moved across the stage, may also be reflected in this new designation. On the other hand, the English usage also reflects a concomitant decline in the skill and status of the dancers, who are now confined to the 'corps' (the 'body') and never permitted to aspire to the status of principals ('the head'), who are routinely brought in from abroad (usually Italy or increasingly Denmark). The *corps de ballet* in this sense begins to acquire additional class connotations, which become increasingly patent during the course of the century.

From the 1850s there is no home for British ballet at either Covent Garden or Her Majesty's Theatre and it is forced to migrate to two venues of dubious repute, the Alhambra (formerly known as the Royal Panopticon, from 1854) and the Empire (from the 1880s), where it sits slightly uneasily within a bill alongside music hall acts.[8] Paris was quick to learn from London's new risqué dance forms: the Folies Bergère, modelled on the Alhambra, opened in the 1860s, and dancers in the *corps de ballet* at the Paris Opéra were subject equally to adoration and censure. The young trainee dancers who often filled the lower ranks of the *corps* were fondly, but deeply pejoratively, dubbed 'les petits rats': living in dilapidated dormitories at the Opéra, they shared spaces with the vermin, and, like them, were plentiful in number and pace, both on and offstage (see Figure 17.1). From 1831 these young (often very young, from 12–13 years old) dancers were subjected to the questionable gaze (and advances) of aristocratic patrons and members of the so-called Jockey Club

---

[5] Noverre (1807: lettre XXV), 'Sur les arts imitateurs': 'Lady of the chorus, who dances in choruses rather than solo'.

[6] *OED*, s.v. 'corps de ballet', first recorded use 1826; *Le Grand Robert*, s.v. 'corps de ballet', first recorded use 1835.

[7] Chapman (1989) on dance school reforms.

[8] A. Carter (2005).

Fig. 17.1. 'Les Petits Rats' at Paris Opéra, *c*.1841. Caricature by Benjamin, part of sequence entitled 'Chemin de la Posterité'

through the system of *abonnements* (subscriptions), which granted male aristocrats access to the *foyer de la danse* (the warm-up studio) for their own delectation. Degas was one such voyeuristic patron, and his paintings amply capture the ambiguity of the patron's gaze of the vulnerable dancers, whose lowly socio-economic position meant that dependency was the sole means of survival. Even the highly distinguished poet, critic, and balletomane, Théophile Gautier, who praised ballet above all for its transformative, hyper-real potential, reduced the dancer in his criticism to a collection of body parts.[9] The dancer was reducible to a commodity no less than the woman on the street.

Dance, then, was charged with such low status and moral ambiguity by the mid-nineteenth century that it could be deemed altogether incompatible with tragedy. When Mendelssohn's *Antigone* transferred from Paris to London in 1845, the inclusion of a ballet to accompany the ode to Dionysus prompted much mirth and derision. Mendelssohn himself commented to his sister, Fanny, on what he saw as the hilarious and gratuitous ballet at Covent Garden, which had presumably been inserted on the ground that the sixty-strong, static, male singing chorus was unlikely to be able to convey the full force of the invocation to the 'lord of the dancing'.[10] The *divertissement*, normally

---

[9] Guest (1986) reproduces Gautier's ballet criticism.   [10] Wyndham (1906: ii. 177).

inserted into grand opera, was clearly incongruous on this occasion for the simple reason that the *corps* by this time consisted solely of female dancers, who were now being charged with the impossible task of embodying the words of the Theban elders.

The production as a whole led to further reflection on the role of dance in ancient tragic choruses. J. W. Donaldson's earlier comments on dancing in tragedy in *The Theatre of the Greeks* (1830), which was widely published throughout the century, significantly includes a comparison with dance in the modern world: 'There perhaps is nothing in which ancients more surpassed the moderns than in the perfection of their dancing.'[11] The perceived failure of the *divertissement* in the 1845 production prompted the well-known theatre critic, George Henry Lewes, to undertake 'some months of very careful research' for an article in *The Classical Museum* in order 'to prove that there was no dancing whatever in the Greek tragic chorus'.[12] In his view, dancing is 'so contrary to all notions of tragedy', and he maintains that the development from the dithyramb to drama and its consequent loss of the satyric entailed a loss of dance, which is preserved only in the satyr play.[13] Although he was by no means the first to reach this conclusion—Du Bos's neoclassical treatise made similar inferences—his claim that the ancient chorus merely gesticulated was founded upon his own observations of 'the effective and artistic attitudes' struck by the choruses drilled by the actor–manager, Charles Macready.[14] Lewes examines the choral references in tragedy to dance and concludes that here, at *Antigone* line 1277 the chorus is not (*pace* the scholar and academic adviser in Potsdam, August Boeckh, or the London production) dancing at all, but is merely speaking *about* dancing.[15] How, indeed, could a morally compromised group of female dancers begin to replicate Schlegel's 'idealized spectators'?

The subsequent issue of the journal carried a response from the historian Henry Thomas Dyer, who had recently completed a study of Aeschylus and who robustly argued for the inclusion of dance both in ancient tragedy and the epinician ode.[16] Dyer aptly concludes: 'We should form a wrong estimate, then, of the notion which the Greeks attached to dancing, if we viewed it through the light of our own prejudices.'[17] But prejudice towards ballet, and towards the dancer in particular, was hard to shake off at this time. This related in part, as Donaldson's comment implies, to the quality of the dancing on display: the serried ranks were determined as much by looks as by skill, with the third row compromising beginnners, the ageing, and the unskilled.[18]

---

[11] Donaldson (1830: 125 n. 4). Although the text is based on Karl Otfried Müller's manuscript, the comment appears in an editorial note.

[12] Lewes (1845: 366, 344).   [13] Lewes (1845: 346).

[14] Lewes (1845: 349).   [15] Lewes (1845: 366).   [16] Dyer (1846: 229).

[17] Dyer (1846: 236).   [18] A. Carter (2005: 37–8).

The official function, moreover, of the exclusively female *corps de ballet* was alternately to give the soloist a rest and to echo or throw into relief the virtuosity of the star, whose skills far surpassed those on display in the *corps de ballet*.[19] But the prejudice demonstrated by Lewes and others also stems from that further unofficial 'function' of the dancers, which was to signal their availability during their performances. During a visit to the ballet, Thackeray's Arthur Pendennis excitedly notes 'the glances which all the corps-de-ballet . . . casts towards his box'; and the 'glances . . . towards his box' came from desperately low-paid full-time workers in search of a patron to enable them to survive.[20]

Later in the century, in Act II of Gilbert and Sullivan's *Patience* (1881), the Chorus of (lovesick) Maidens retaliate after some fifty years of being subject to the male gaze. They enter 'two and two, each playing on an archaic instrument', singing in an effort to attract the distracted Archibald Grosvenor, who leads them, head in a book:

> Turn, oh, turn in this direction,
> Shed, oh, shed a gentle smile,
> With a glance of sad perfection
> Our poor fainting hearts beguile!
> On such eyes as maidens cherish
> Let thy fond adorers gaze,
> Or incontinently perish
> In their all-consuming rays!

Now it is the would-be patron who is urged to 'turn . . . turn'—the standard movement of the *corps de ballet*[21]—for the female onlookers. Eventually the chorus persuades Grosvenor to read out his excruciatingly bad poems, one of which is about Teasing Tom, whose thoroughly ignoble life is met with what is clearly understood by Grosvenor and his peers as a fittingly shaming and chastening conclusion:

> The consequence was he was lost tot*ally*,
> And married a girl in the *corps de bally*![22]

Modest and amateur dancing in 'chorus', with its echoes of Greco-Roman antiquity, brought with it some degree of respectability by the 1880s, and the fashionable philhellenism that captivated London's high society and prompted numerous stagings of Greek drama at this time is Gilbert's principal target here.[23] Dancing in the *corps de ballet*, by contrast, remained a lower-class and morally compromising profession.

---

[19] A. Carter (2005: 30, 56).   [20] Thackeray (1888: 125).
[21] Cf. Bell (1919: 415), who compares the excitement of the Ballets Russes with the earlier 'turn-turn chorus giving the soloist a rest'. See S. Jones (2013).
[22] Gilbert (1994: 180–2).   [23] Hall and Macintosh (2005: 462–87).

REVOLUTIONARY DANCES

The origins of the modern *corps de ballet*, however, were far from tainted but began with the unblemished citizen women, dressed in white, Greek-style tunics, who appeared in the revolutionary festivals, under the direction of Jacques-Louis David. According to David some years later, they were 'superb women... the Greek line in all its purity, beautiful young girls in chlamays throwing flowers; and then, throughout anthems by Lebrun, Méhul, Rouget de Lisle'.[24] What links the *corps de ballet* to these citizen women is not only their costume—which was increasingly adopted on the stage by dancers, whose white skirts replaced eighteenth-century panniers and whose earlier high-heeled shoes were jettisoned in favour of Greek-style sandals tied with ribbon at the ankle or, occasionally at this time, bare feet. It was also, as we have heard, the dancers' social status that related them to these citizen women with whom they were to become increasingly associated. In the 1770s and 1780s artists at the Opéra began to assert their rights and demand a say in the running of the theatre, and temporarily, at least, they acquired a modicum of autonomy and influence.[25]

The festivals of the Revolution were designed to make citizens active participants rather than spectators; but, given their careful choreography, they in fact succeeded in bringing theatrical spectacles into France's public spaces. The Revolution, as one commentator has suggested, was one 'gratuitous, choreographed ballet'.[26] The inaugurating festival, *Fête de la Fédération* (14 July 1790), held to mark the first anniversary of the Fall of the Bastille, began at Notre Dame with professional singers and dancers from the Opéra and the Théâtre Italienne. A vast dance pavilion was constructed at the Bastille, and the festival culminated in a gathering of 400,000 spectators at the Champ de Mars. This was promenade theatre on an epic scale, and many of its tableaux, as in other revolutionary festivals, were shaped by and in turn shaped theatrical performances at this time. The festivals turned to ancient Greece as model, not to reclaim antiquity but to replicate its perceived communality, simplicity, and unaffected beauty.[27]

Earlier in the year the choreographer of numerous subsequent festivals and *maître de ballet* at the Opéra, Pierre Gardel, staged one of the most successful ballet pantomimes in the pre-Romantic period, *Télémaque dans l'île de Calypso* (1790).[28] Even though Gardel borrows much from popular vaudeville pantomime traditions for this ballet pantomime, his chorus of Greek nymphs

---

[24] Cited in Ozouf (1998: 172).   [25] Homans (2010: 105).
[26] Ozouf (1998: 172).   [27] Ozouf (1998: 275).
[28] M. Smith (2000: p. xxi) for the designation 'ballet pantomime' for stand-alone dramatic ballets in the early nineteenth century, in contrast to 'ballets', which were danced sections in opera, also known as *divertissements*.

served, in many ways, as prototype for the role of the Romantic *corps de ballet*. Homans sees the nymphs' eroticism as a mark of distinction from their more ethereal successors,[29] but their dual nature in many ways anticipates the morally ambivalent *corps* of the so-called *ballets blancs* to come. As a pupil of Jean-Georges Noverre, the dancer reformer and collaborator of Gluck, Gardel heeded in this ballet, in particular, his master's exhortation to give the chorus members a significant role in the action, so that they display 'a lively and animated expression which keeps the spectator always attentive to the theme which the preceding actors have explained'.[30] At a time when interrogatory Greek choruses had been increasingly reinstated in versions of ancient tragedy for decidedly republican reasons,[31] Gardel's female chorus acquires agency that parallels, and perhaps even mirrors, the role played by women during the Revolution.

Based on Fénelon's didactic tale *Les Aventures de Télémaque* (1699), written to instruct the grandson of Louis XIV in the principles of government, Gardel's ballet becomes a cautionary tale of the perils of seductive pleasure. The chorus of nymphs is present throughout the action as active participants (albeit temporarily absent from the stage during scenes of intimacy, as in Eucharis' grotto in Act III), supporting not the duplicitous and vengeful lover of Telemachus' father, Calypso (a mime role), but the nymph, Eucharis (a dancing role taken by Marie Miller, soon to be Mrs Gardel), with whom Telemachus (the only male danced role taken by Gardel himself) falls madly in love following her intoxicating dance to the violin in Act I.[32]

It is the lithe and beguiling chorus, above all, that enhance the island's all-pervasive atmosphere of sensuality and natural beauty, which Telemachus finds impossible to resist. These nymphs constitute the core grouping in this thirty-two-cast ballet (of which only two were male roles) and themselves number twenty-four in total. They not only pick flowers, they also take a leading role in the games staged in Telemachus' honour in Act I; and, smitten by Cupid's darts, they exhort him to join them in a voluptuously beguiling dance, which acts as prelude to the intimate duet between Telemachus and Eucharis that follows their departure from the stage in Act II. The critic Geoffroy, in a review of a revival in 1813, reports that 'Calypso's nymphs dance so beautifully and with movements so graceful that the audience envies Telemachus his lot and finds Mentor's action excessive in exposing his charge to a watery grave to remove him from such delightful company'.[33] However, in the final act this 'graceful' chorus acquires, under the influence of Cupid, a

---

[29] Homans (2010: 113).   [30] Noverre (1930: lettre III, 23).   [31] Biet (1994).

[32] Guest (1996: 307) reports that the violin solo, from Giornovichi's first violin concerto, was performed at the premiere by the virtuoso Rodolphe Kreutzer, to whom Beethoven dedicated his famous sonata.

[33] *Journal de L'Empire*, 12 January 1813, cited in Guest (1996: 310).

new, terrifying power as it seeks to foil Mentor's plot to make Telemachus flee the island. Armed with torches, and now dressed and twisting and turning like bacchantes,[34] the nymphs proceed to set fire to Telemachus' boat. Only the intervention of Venus can return the nymphs to their former dignified selves. Gardel's female chorus has been transmogrified from Greek idyllic woman-hood to wild, vengeful maenads during the course of the action; and it is this fascination with both ideal and demonic womanhood that will constantly be replayed in ballets of the Romantic period.

Gardel went on to choreograph the movement for a *divertissement lyrique* at the Opéra entitled *L'Offrande à la Liberté* (30 September 1792 and regularly revived throughout Europe until 1797; and then again in the revolutionary year of 1848). Here, to the accompaniment of a stirring rendering of the 'Marseillaise', women and children dressed in white rushed onto the stage from all directions to dance in front of the Temple of Liberty and take up arms in the goddess's honour.[35] As with events outside the theatre, women and children are shown publicly to be capable of acts of altruism as well as defiance. In the second act of Gardel's choral dance drama *La Réunion du Dix Août*, which was performed both indoors and outdoors in 1794, the chorus of women assume an increasingly important role in the action, cul-minating in a ferocious and triumphant balletic sequence.[36]

In another *divertissement* staged six days after the execution of the king at the Opéra, *Le Triomphe de la République, ou le Camp de Grand Pré* (27 January 1793, lyrics by Marie-Joseph Chénier and music by François-Joseph Gossec), Liberty herself appeared to announce: 'Do not envy Greece any longer, the French nation has better known her freedom; banishing her kings, she knew how to proclaim the unity of a republic.'[37] Set at a French army camp on the Prussian border, Gardel's *divertissement* included both men and women dancing round the Tree of Liberty. Although Gardel clearly did not represent the full fervour and frenzied potential of the *carmagnole* in his *divertissement*, it is this revolutionary ring dance, danced round the Tree of Liberty as well as round the guillotine, that serves as a reminder of the power of dance both to unite and to unleash demonic energy.

Dickens gives a chillingly graphic evocation of the brute forces at play in the *carmagnole* some years later in book III, chapter 5, of *A Tale of Two Cities* (1859):

A moment afterwards, and a throng of people came pouring round the corner by the prison wall, in the midst of whom was the wood-sawyer hand-in-hand with The Vengeance. There could not be fewer than five hundred people, and they were dancing like five thousand demons. There was no other music than their own singing. They

---

[34] Gardel (1790: 15).   [35] Chazin-Bennahum (1988: 98).
[36] Chazin-Bennahum (1988: 173).   [37] Chazin-Bennahum (1988: 103).

danced to the popular Revolution song, keeping a ferocious time that was like a gnashing of teeth in unison. Men and women danced together, women danced together, men danced together, as hazard had brought them together. At first, they were a mere storm of coarse red caps and coarse woollen rags; but, as they filled the place, and stopped to dance about Lucie, some ghastly apparition of a dance-figure gone raving mad arose among them. They advanced, retreated, struck at one another's hands, clutched at one another's heads, spun round alone, caught one another and spun round in pairs, until many of them dropped. While those were down, the rest linked hand-in-hand, and all spun round together: then the ring broke, and in separate rings of two and four they turned and turned until they all stopped at once, began again, struck, clutched, and tore, and then reversed the spin, and all spun round another way. Suddenly they stopped again, paused, struck out the time afresh, formed into lines the width of the public way, and, with their heads low down and their hands high up, swooped screaming off. No fight could have been half so terrible as this dance. It was so emphatically a fallen sport—a something, once innocent, delivered over to all devilry—a healthy pastime changed into a means of angering the blood, bewildering the senses, and steeling the heart. Such grace as was visible in it, made it the uglier, showing how warped and perverted all things good by nature were become. The maidenly bosom bared to this, the pretty almost-child's head thus distracted, the delicate foot mincing in this slough of blood and dirt, were types of the disjointed time.

This was the Carmagnole.[38]

Here the protagonist Lucy Manette, on her way to visit her husband in prison, is encircled by a dance that is more terrifying in its ferocity than battle; and what is most horrifying, according to the narrator, is that Lucy is witnessing a 'fallen sport . . .'. Dance has become devilry, the maiden a demon, and 'the delicate mincing foot' of the dancer now wades in a 'slough of blood and dirt'. This was dance at its rawest; and the Revolution left its mark upon theatrical dance no less than it did on other aspects of French cultural life.

ROMANTIC BALLET AND THE FURIES

Gardel's ballet remained in the repertoire until 1826, receiving, after its 1790 premiere, a remarkable 413 performances during the Revolution, the Napoleonic period, and under the Bourbons. The durability both of the ballet and of Gardel himself can be explained with reference to the ways in which he extended Noverre's *ballet d'action* by including more dance sequences within mimed sections, and also to the fact that he foreshadowed the themes that were to preoccupy ballet in the next generation, for whom ballet came to 'represent a new matriarchy'.[39] At a time when the operatic chorus at the Paris

---

[38] Dickens (1998: 267–8).   [39] M. Clark (2001: 243).

Opéra was overwhelmingly male,[40] ballet became an increasingly female preserve once the *danse noble* style with its aristocratic associations disappeared in the aftermath of the Revolution and even male roles were increasingly played *en travestie*.[41] But, if ballet came to represent a new matriarchy, it did so only in terms of what was presented on stage. The emergent stars, in the wake of the commercial changes brought about after the 1830 July Revolution, were now in the hands of the Opéra's new entrepreneurial director and instigator of the practice of paying for the privilege of gaining access to the *foyer de la danse*, Louis Véron. Marie Taglioni was the first star fashioned by him; and her reluctant appearance in what has been seen as the first of the *ballets blancs*—the *divertissement* referred to as 'The Ballet of the Nuns' in Act III of Meyerbeer's 1831 grand opera, *Robert Le Diable*—is testimony to the patriarchal power structures at the Opéra.

Taglioni had every excuse to feel uncomfortable about her role as Héléna, Reverend Mother and leader of the chorus of ghostly and fallen nuns, called up from the grave by the Devil himself (Bertram) in order to seduce and damn the hero (Robert) to perdition. For Taglioni's role, and indeed that of the other sixteen nuns, involved not just thraldom to the Devil but also seduction through disrobing. Taglioni, whose signature role was to become the delicate, capricious heroine, 'la sylphide', in the eponymous ballet the following year, was famously called upon here to emerge from the depths and breadths of the gloomy cloisters with her fellow sisters, dressed in pale blue and white habits, only to discard them shortly after and spectacularly to reveal the translucent white tulle underskirts (now illuminated by the newly installed gas light) that were to characterize and give the name to the costumes of all subsequent *ballets blancs*.[42] Despite Taglioni's discomfort in the role, Véron held her to the terms of her contract, and it has been suggested that the picquancy afforded by her ambivalence considerably enhanced her reluctant performance in the role of nun/whore.[43]

The power of this transmutational scene to shock, amaze, and haunt the public imaginary continued throughout the century. Mendelssohn, who will laugh at the *Antigone* ballet in London in 1845, considers the nuns' ballet 'vulgar'; others find it 'revolting'.[44] Indeed, the 'vulgar' was not only related to lapses in moral probity; it was also due to the shameless borrowing of technical innovations from popular entertainment. The use of gas lighting, as we have already heard, rendered the tulle underskirts translucent; and Pierre Cicéris's designs for Act III replicated the effects created by Daguerre's 'dioramas', which by subtle changes of light gave the impression that the spectator was

---

[40] Parakilas (2003).   [41] Leigh Foster (1996).
[42] Beaumont (1944: 66) on the links between the *ballet blanc*'s costume and the 'classic peplum drawn in at the waist'.
[43] Homans (2010: 151).   [44] Homans (2010: 151) on the reception of the ballet.

Fig. 17.2. Edgar Degas, *The Ballet Scene from Meyerbeer's 'Robert Le Diable'* (1876). © Victoria and Albert Museum, London

watching a real-life scene. The most significant innovation in the production, however, related to dancing technique, whereby the nuns, and Taglioni in particular, gave the impression of gliding through space as they danced on pointes. Dancing on pointe, as is regularly observed, involves both a rooted-ness to the ground as well as the illusion of not touching the ground at one and the same time.[45] For the fallen nuns, the image was perfect: they were spectral but also tangibly and shockingly real.

The impact of the act on the audience is vividly and almost palpably captured in Degas's 1876 painting of a revival in the early 1870s, in which the contorted (and almost cavorting), swirling figures of the nuns loom out of the lugubrious gothic convent in the background (Figure 17.2).[46] They are

[45] On pointe work, see M. Kant (2007).

[46] Degas's earlier painting, dated 1872 though completed in 1871, which hangs in the Metropolitan Museum of Art in New York, shows the same view of the stage, albeit slightly to

balanced in the foreground by the jumble of enrapt male spectators (one of whom clutches his binoculars in search of another offstage attraction), who sit claustrophobically close to the bassoonists in the orchestral pit, whose middle register notes (which the viewer almost hears) eerily conjure the spirit world before their eyes. What is interesting about Degas's painting is the impression it gives of movement by dancers and landscape: both seem equally organic, mutable, and insubstantial. It was scenes like this that led to Gautier's observation that ballet provided a kind of hyperspace for the Romantic imagination; and the membrane that separated audience from the viewing space, good from evil, male from female, was so porous that it heightened and prolonged its erotic and teasing potential.

A contemporary artist depicted the nuns as half-naked bacchantes with tousled hair, bare legs, and wild ecstatic movements.[47] As with Gardel's *Télémaque*, these bacchantes also resemble the Furies as they serve as objective correlatives of the troubled male soul torn between a strong moral inheritance and the lures of the flesh. Once Robert falters, he unleashes the demonic in the nuns, who, maenad-like, ply him with drink, before blocking his path menacingly, encircling him with erotic moves, and eventually overwhelming him with their voluptuousness. Héléna, by contrast, pursues seduction by slow degrees and succeeds in entrapping Robert completely as he finally succumbs and reaches for the branch. At that point, thunder claps, the nuns recede, and spectres and demons swarm to make 'an infernal chorus' that marks the end of the act.[48]

Contemporary, political readings of the opera were divergent: Robert was France torn between revolutionary hell (Bertram) and venerable monarchy (his mother), with the nuns emblematizing the deception of 'white' revolutionary womanhood; or the opera was said to urge reconciliation after forty years of turmoil and carnage, especially in the wake of the most recent bloody riots at Lyons.[49] For the German poet Heinrich Heine, Robert is Louis-Philippe, the new 'bourgeois king', the product of a revolutionary father and an *ancien régime* mother, but too weak to embrace his revolutionary inheritance, remaining liberal only in name not in substance.[50]

It may well be significant to note that Act III was not originally planned by the librettists, Eugène Scribe and Germain Delavigne, to take place in a medieval convent at all. Instead, Robert was to find the fatal cypress branch, which Bertram falsely promises will grant him access to his beloved Isabella,

---

the left, but has a closer and sharper perspective on members of the audience and different players in the orchestra.

[47] Homans (2010: 189).   [48] Meyerbeer (2008).

[49] Homans (2010), on reviews in *Gazette de France*, 4 December 1831; *Le Globe*, 23 November 1831, 27 November 1831.

[50] Petrey (2001: 137–54).

on Mount Olympus.[51] Commentators have remarked upon the links between
the opera and Shakespeare's *Hamlet* (with the claims of good and evil here
being represented by mother and father respectively), but perhaps no less
detectable are those with that other nexus of plays that has often been detected
behind Shakespeare's tragedy, Aeschylus' *Oresteia*. Robert, like Orestes, is
acting at his father's prompting to reject and destroy his maternal inheritance;
and, at the point of fulfilling Bertram's command, when Robert sees the
branch, he is similarly confronted by (the ghost of) his mother and her
reproachful warning.

The *Oresteia* was routinely invoked by both republicans and royalists to
illuminate the Revolution (see Hall, Chapter 16, this volume); and in opera
and ballet the Orestes myth had been central to the repertoire since Noverre's
Agamemnon Vengé of 1771. It would be churlish, of course, to claim that
Scribe/Delavigne were attempting a version of the *Oresteia* in *Robert Le
Diable*, but it would not be wide of the mark to probe the interconnections a
little further. Since the rediscovery of Aeschylus in both France and in Britain
towards the end of the eighteenth century, the power of the chorus of Erinyes
had always proved to be the most striking for commentators. Aeschylus' first
translator, the counter-revolutionary Lefranc de Pompignan, had singled out
the trilogy for particular praise because here 'la plume d'Eschyle est trempée
dans le sang. On entend dans ses vers le bruit de la foudre, le cri des Furies, le
hurlement des enfers.'[52] Given that Scribe/Delavigne's original scenario had a
classical, rather than the more 'popular' gothic setting, does Orestes' parallel
experience in the opening scene of the *Eumenides* in Apollo's temple at
Delphi, where his mother's ghost appears to invoke the Erinyes, lurk somewhere behind Act III of Meyerbeer's opera?

COMMUNITY AND POWER

The predominantly male chorus of grand opera has been said to represent
the power of the crowd to determine political affairs and to have 'allowed
nineteenth-century audiences to recognize the irresolvable dissonance of their
own political order'.[53] The *corps de ballet* at this time also represents communities but, as we have seen, marginal, unassimilable groups who lure, delight,

---

[51] Williams (2003: 71).
[52] Lefranc de Pompignan (1770: 495): 'Aeschylus' pen is soaked in blood. One hears in his
verses the sound of thunder, the cry of the Furies, the howls of hell.'
[53] Williams (2003: 83, 92).

but also destroy.[54] This is true of the ballet chorus of nuns in Meyerbeer's opera and it is especially true of the famous chorus of Wilis in Act II of *Giselle ou les Wilis* (1841), whose spectral state, in marked contrast to the nuns, becomes even more terrifying because they work not for the Devil, but for themselves. As ghosts of virgin women, they appear by night in the forest and 'feed' on young men, whom they dance to death. The latent connections between dance and sexual gratification at this time—dancing too much is code for nymphomania; viewing dancers, as we have seen, a form of surrogate sex—are extended in *Giselle*'s narrative of social class and female desire.[55] Giselle's discovery that the man she loves is a member of the nobility leads her to taking her own life with his sword—a symbolic enactment of the union denied in life and, one might add, the real-life relationship between the dancer and her patron. In Act II Giselle is poised to join the company of women who have died for similar reasons, but along with her lover Albrecht is pitted against the avenging collective in her struggle to save him and remain true to her own desires.[56]

Heinrich Heine, whose *De l'Allemagne* (1835) served as one of the sources for the Gautier/Saint-Georges libretto, described the chorus of Wilis in Act II as 'dead bacchantes', who 'laugh with a joy so hideous...they call you so seductively...[and] have an air of such sweet promise', which is 'irresistible'.[57] Even though the original choreography is lost, it is clear that it is the movement patterns of the dancers that signal their maenadic power and its deadliness. If pointe work enhances the dancer's sense of liminality, in the first production the Wilis were granted command of both the air (wires were used, despite technical difficulties, to bring some of them down from the trees) and the earth (as they emerged from the tangled vegetation of the forest).[58] Before Albrecht is forced to dance, it is Hilarion (who had shattered Giselle's illusions by revealing Albrecht's noble status) who meets with the Wilis' blocking power as they surround him 'in a vast circle which contracts, little by little, closing in on him little by little', forming a 'graceful and deadly web'.[59]

---

[54] Cf. *La Sylphide*'s ethereal *corps*. Although the threat here is from the witch and not them, there are striking similarities between Bournonville's choreography of 1836 and *Giselle*. I am grateful for Sue Jones's help with this point.

[55] See the contemporary review by Janin in *Journal des Débats* in Leigh Foster (1996: 198).

[56] The libretto/scenario, which was on sale in the Opéra lobby, is reproduced in Beaumont (1944: 39–52) (in English) and M. Smith (2000: 213–38) (in French and English). There is no systematic notation at this time, only staging manuals, the musical score, and reviews and testimonies to re-create the original choreography. The most widely used version today is by Marius Petipa (1884, 1899, 1903).

[57] M. Smith (2000: 213–38) (for original libretto), which cites the relevant passage from Heine (1835: 215–16).

[58] Beaumont (1944); M. Smith (2000: 234).

[59] M. Smith (2000: 236); cf. Gautier (1841), cited in Guest (1986: 100): 'A wall of dancers bars his way.'

Compelled to turn and turn 'in a chain of waltzes' with each member of the *corps*, Hilarion 'arrives at the water's edge, opens his arms, expecting to find the next waltzer, and goes tumbling into the abyss'.[60] Gautier/Saint-Georges's libretto continues: 'The Wilis commence a joyous bacchanale.'[61]

This white group of women is so far removed in many ways from the citizen women who processed during the revolutionary festivals; but in others, it is acting out energies and feelings that were unleashed during those years. As Marion Kant has rightly asked: 'Do . . . audiences of a modern performance of *Giselle* know that they are about to confront an existential conflict about the place of women in society?'[62] The cuts to the original choreography in modern versions of *Giselle* have reduced the power of the *corps* in Act II and shifted attention to the lead couple and their *pas de deux*. Notable is the omission of scene xii, when Albrecht (like Orestes at the *omphalos* at the start of the *Eumenides*) clutches at the cross as he is besieged by the swarming Wilis, whose frequent, predatory advances are each time rhythmically repelled by 'a power greater than their own'.[63] But, even if considerably more of these energies have today been dissipated in a confectionery of colour and glitter, it is hard not to overlook the *furor* of the collective that is released during the Wilis' defiant and apparently all-powerful dances. The heat engendered here may be some way from the *carmagnole*, but it is not entirely unrelated to it. By the 1830s, with the 'bourgeois king' on the throne, women's feelings, unlike those of the men in the stalls at the Opéra, needed to be held in check. The Wilis in the *corps de ballet* serve, therefore, as a *locus* of both power and desire, which is conveniently sited deep in the past or resited within the realms of the imagination alone. Significantly, in the original libretto the dying Giselle bequeaths Albrecht to his social equal and blesses their future union. Gautier could write in the 1840s: 'Nothing resembles a dream more than a ballet and it is this which explains the singular pleasure that one receives from these apparently frivolous representations. One enjoys, while awake, the phenomenon that nocturnal fantasy traces on the canvas of sleep: an entire world of chimeras moves before you.'[64] But, with the advent of Realism from the 1850s onwards, Gautier's nocturnal fantasies seemed nothing but fantasies, and ballet was increasingly confined in both Paris and London either to the realm of fairy tales and/or to bawdy banality.

---

[60] Cf. Gautier (1841), cited in Guest (1986: 100): 'bemused, he is buffeted hither and thither, and letting go the cold hand of the last dancer, he staggers and falls into the water.'

[61] M. Smith (2000: 236–7). Kirstein (1970: 15) notes that the *corps de ballet* here is especially powerful, regardless of whose choreography (revivals of Coralli/Perrot's 1841 or Petipa's 1880s version).

[62] M. Kant (2007: 196).   [63] M. Smith (2000: 237).

[64] Gautier, *La Presse*, 23 November 1849, cited in Chapman (1988: 375).

CONCLUSION

From Gluck/Noverre's attempts to revive the ancient chorus to Diaghilev's desire to realize the *Gesamtkunstwerk* with the Ballets Russes, there are animated choruses, which stem directly from attempts to re-create ancient choruses, and which operate in many ways like Greek tragic oppositional female choruses. The women citizens who processed in Greek-style white tunics in David/Gardel's festivals did not only provide the costumes for the *ballets blancs*; they also furnished Romantic ballet with its subjects and, in turn, much of its technique. After the ring-dance of the *carmagnole*, dancing could no longer be courtly pure and simple: new energies had been released from collective physical movement as much as they were by rousing political discourse. At a time when the operatic chorus at the Opéra was overwhelmingly male, the ballet chorus or *corps de ballet* provided one of the few public explorations of female subjectivity and power. That these choruses have been ignored by classicists is clearly related to Romantic ballet's complex history of repression, regression, and reinvention in the second half of the nineteenth century. Classical scholars would do well to recall that not only was the chorus originally a dancing chorus in antiquity (see Peponi, Chapter 1, this volume); they should also take heed of the early nineteenth-century *corps de ballet* as an example of just how effectively a dancing chorus can provide the spinal column, and thus the nerve centre, of the action.

18

Chorus and the *Vaterland:* Greek Tragedy and the Ideology of Choral Performance in Inter-War Germany

Eleftheria Ioannidou

On 22 February 1925 a theatre group of students at the University of Berlin under the name *Sprechchor* gave a matinée performance drawing on Goethe's plays and poems at the Theater am Kurfürstendamm. The performance featured large speaking choruses, and it was directed by Wilhelm Leyhausen, a teacher of rhetoric and poetics at the university. The technique of *Sprechchor* employed by the students in the performance went back to a long German tradition of poetry declamation, but by the 1920s the practice of choral speaking had become popular within emerging social and political collectives.[1] The organized labour movement in the Weimar Republic employed choral performance as part of its public events and festivities; the massive choruses in the celebrations of the Socialist Party (SPD) and, to a lesser extent, in the agitprop theatre of the communist party (KDP) enacted in various ways an imagined classless community.[2] The associations of *Sprechchor* generally,

The present article is part of a larger research project on the appropriations of Greek tragedy under Nazi and Fascist regimes in inter-war Europe undertaken at the Freie Universität of Berlin in 2010–12 under a Research Fellowship of the Humboldt Foundation. I would like to thank the editors of the volume and especially Fiona Macintosh for invitations to present aspects of this research at conferences.

[1] See dictionary entry in Krieger (1986: 802); and Revermann, Chapter 9, and Fischer-Lichte, Chapter 19, this volume. The term *Sprechchor* in the present article is used to refer to the speaking chorus or the practice of choral speaking, except in cases where it denotes the name of the theatre group, where it is referred to as Berlin Sprechchor.

[2] On this matter, see Warstat (2004: 313–67). Warstat proposes two models to differentiate between the communal concepts promoted by the SPD and KPD: while socialist choruses mirrored an all-embracing festive community (*Gemeinschaft im Spiegel*), agitprop choruses were explicitly oriented towards mass mobilization of their audiences (*Gemeinschaft in Front*). Part of Warstat's discussion of proletarian mass theatre is available in English in Warstat (2005).

then, with its political contexts were clearly strong enough to recur in the case of Leyhausen's students' performance of Goethe's extracts. Yet, it was also clear that the Berlin Sprechchor was a far cry from a proletarian chorus.

In the years to come *Sprechchor* became no less appealing to the National Socialists as an effective medium of forging the sense of *Volk* community. Nazi public rituals appropriated massive choruses, adjusting them to their own ideological and political orientations. Speaking choruses were also a key element in the performances of the short-lived theatrical genre of *Thingspiel*, which was promoted by the Nazi regime between 1933 and 1937.[3] While proletarian *Sprechchor* performances were silenced after Hitler's seizure of power, the Nazis themselves eliminated and finally banned the choral element from *Thingspiel* in 1936, being unable to combat its former connection with the labour movement.[4] At the same time, there had been some circumspection in Nazi circles about choral singing as a petty bourgeois expression that did not suit the ideals of National Socialism.[5] From 1937 the regime showed a predilection for heroic tragedy, which towards the end of the war incrementally gave its place to the European classics and commercial repertoire.[6] It is, thus, notable that Leyhausen was able to direct speaking choruses even after the Nazi ban of *Sprechchor* from *Thingspiel* and down to 1942, most probably because of the commitment of the Berlin Sprechchor to classical tragedy.

It is most likely because of their semi-amateur character and the marginal position they were allotted within offical Nazi theatre that Leyhausen's productions have so far been overlooked within studies on fascist theatre and culture. However, his stagings of Aeschylus have received some limited attention within scholarly discussions on the performance reception of Greek drama. These discussions touch upon the ideology underlying this particular use of *Sprechchor*, but they still consider it as amateur without scrutinizing its affiliations with the totalitarian imagination.[7] Leyhausen's controversial relationship with the Nazis seems to complicate this matter further. Not a member of the National Socialist Party himself, he maintained contacts among Nazi officials and backers; although he was never offered a full professorship, these contacts contributed to his nomination as Honorary Professor in 1934 and non-tenured Professor in Diction and Delivery (*Sprecherziehung und Vortragskunst*) at the Friedrich-Wilhelm University of Berlin in 1939. His

---

[3] Fischer-Lichte (2005: 122–58) discusses the development and the decay of the *Thingspiel* movement. See also Fischer-Lichte, Chapter 19, this volume.

[4] On the Nazi ban on *Sprechchor*, see Menz (1976).

[5] See the critique of the *Thingspiel* expert Wolf Braumüller, quoted in Fischer-Lichte (2005: 135).

[6] On repertoire choices during the war, see also Rühle (2007: 872 ff.).

[7] Flashar (2009: 155–6) underscores the dilettantism of Leyhausen's work and quotes from reviews that dismissed the chorus's rhythmic delivery as symptomatic of false idealism or even barbarity. See also Mavromoustakos (2004).

correspondence provides evidence that the *Persians* was performed on the occasion of Hitler's birthday at the then Berlin Volksbühne in Horst-Wessel-Platz in 1935.[8] In 1934 and 1935 the Berlin Sprechchor toured to Greece and Scandinavia respectively, under the auspices of the Ministry of Public Enlightenment and Propaganda of the Third Reich.[9] In a letter Leyhausen stresses that the tour of the Berlin Sprechchor abroad fulfilled a 'cultural–political task'.[10] Yet, within Nazi circles there was some scepticism over the contribution of Leyhausen's *Sprechchor* to a folk-minded communal experience;[11] and a 1940 letter to the Reich's Ministry of Science, Education, and National Culture describes him as politically unreliable or even whimsical and deems his activities abroad as of little avail to the reputation of the German people.[12]

In a full-length article on Leyhausen, Ulf Heuner acknowledges the resemblances between his use of *Sprechchor* and the common Nazi rhetorical style, drawing a sharp distinction between structural analogy (*Strukturanalogie*) and ideological homology (*Ideologiehomologie*), which disregards any correspondences with Nazi ideology.[13] To elaborate on the Nazi associations that Leyhausen's choruses evoke, Heuner takes recourse to the idea of shared experience (*Mit-teilung*) in performance. Although it is far from axiomatic that structural analogies constitute ideological homologies, I would like to suggest that Leyhausen's so-called romanticism was adjacent to the Nazi imagination. To this end I undertake a cross-examination of Leyhausen's writings with the available documentation of his productions.[14] I understand

---

[8] Letter dated 14 April 1935. Source: Stiftung Stadtmuseum Berlin, Theatersammlung. See also Heuner (2002: 116).

[9] Letter from the Ministry dated 26 April 1934. Source: Stiftung Stadtmuseum Berlin, Theatersammlung. The invitation to perform *Persians* in Athens followed Leyhausen's talk on Greek theatre at the German School at Athens the previous year. Wulf (1989: 47) mentions that Leyhausen was delegated to give this talk by Joseph Goebbels. For information on the state support to Leyhausen's productions, see also Schirmer (2002).

[10] Letter dated 18 September 1935. Source: Stiftung Stadtmuseum Berlin, Theatersammlung.

[11] This information is derived from data published by a research project on the art of rhetoric in the Third Reich carried out at the University of Tübingen. See Simon (2005).

[12] Simon (2005: 41): 'Das Promi beurteile Leyhausen "in gleicher Weise", Leyhausen sei politisch unzuverlässig, "sein Verhalten im Auslande dem Ansehen des Deutschtums wenig förderlich gewesen", die Deutsche Gesandtschaft beurteile Leyhausen als "Romantiker, dessen Pläne manchmal zu fantastisch seien".'

[13] Heuner (2002: 121–2).

[14] The archive deposited at the Archive of Performances of Greek and Roman Drama (APGRD) at the University of Oxford under the name Leyhausen–Spiess Collection documents Leyhausen's productions before the Second World War as well as the activities of the Delphic Institute he founded in the post-war period. Its wide display of photos from rehearsals and performances, publicity leaflets, programmes, prompt books, as well as audio excerpts from poetry recitations and live choral performances allows us to draw some more confident conclusions on the performance style. The collection is named after Eberhardt Spiess, a former secretary of the Institute who curated the archive after the Institute's closure in the late 1960s. Further materials on Leyhausen's productions can be found in the Stiftung Stadtmuseum Berlin,

instead the adjacency not just as determined by the political context, as argued by Heuner, but as a case of intricate entanglement between aesthetics and ideology that is conditioned, implemented, and mediated by the performance medium.

Leyhausen's work on *Sprechchor* was a lifelong project. He read for a doctorate in History and Philosophy at the Friedrich-Wilhelm University in Bonn[15] and he founded the first student *Sprechchor* in Cologne in 1920, while working as a lecturer in Aesthetics and Psychology at the Music Conservatory there. In 1923 he moved to Berlin at the invitation of the philologist Wilamowitz-Moellendorff and the German medievalist Gustav Roethe to take up a teaching position in Aesthetics and Rhetoric at the University of Berlin. He founded the Berlin Sprechchor in the same year. Between 1920 and 1942 Leyhausen staged, with the Cologne and Berlin Sprechchor groups, Aeschylus' *The Persians*, *Agamemnon*, and *Prometheus Bound* in his own translations, as well as Goethe's *Faust*, *Prometheus*, and *Pandora*, while he also translated and most probably mounted Lord Byron's verse drama *Sardanapal*.[16] In these performances the students participated in the choruses, while individual roles were played by professional actors.

The newspaper *Die Welt am Montag* praised the powerful delivery of the text in the 1925 performance at the Theater am Kurfürstendamm, pointing out that the function of choral speaking was here 'fundamentally different from that of proletarian Sprechchor groups'. In this instance, continues the critic, *Sprechchor* was 'to be *nothing other than* an artistic instrument, through which great choric effect is produced'.[17] Although the choruses in the performance neither addressed nor represented a socially or politically defined community, they were nonetheless capable of stirring national imagination. Another critic spoke of the resurgence of monumental drama, concluding that such an endeavour should 'awaken an echo in the remotest corner of our German *Vaterland*'.[18]

Theatersammlung, and the Walther Unruh Sammlung of the Institut für Theaterwissenschaft, Freie Universität Berlin.

[15] Leyhausen worked on education in Cologne during the period of French occupation. The original title of his doctoral dissertation was 'Zur Geschichte des höheren, öffentlichen Unterrichts in der Stadt Köln zur französischen Zeit'.

[16] He had also translated Byron's mystery play *Heaven and Earth* into German. Manuscripts of both *Sardanapal* and *Heaven and Earth* (*Himmel und Erde*) are deposited at the Leyhausen–Spiess Collection, APGRD.

[17] *Die Welt am Montag*: 'Zielsetzung ist eine grundsätzlich andere, als die des proletarischen Sprechchors . . . er will nichts sein als ein künstlerisches Instrument schlechthin, durch das sich grosse chorische Wirkungen hervorbringen lassen.' Most interestingly, the excerpt was reproduced in the publicity leaflet of the performance. Source: Leyhausen–Spiess Collection, APGRD (emphasis added). (Translations from the German are mine throughout. Original passages are also quoted.)

[18] *Tägliche Rundschau*: 'Der Erweckung des Monumentaldramas, all dem, was nach Grösse strebt, sind diese Bemühungen geweiht, deren Ziel und Leistung bis in die fernsten Ecken unseres

Unlike political speaking choruses, the choral performance of the Berlin students claimed to be an exclusively aesthetic pursuit. Leyhausen's systematic employment of *Sprechchor* was inextricable from his consistent efforts to provide a method of speech delivery for poetic drama, most prominently of Aeschylus and Goethe. In the context of Weimar culture, similar claims could be viewed as a manifestation of the tense relationship between aesthetics and politics, affirmed later in Walter Benjamin's famous pronouncement on fascism's aestheticization of politics to which communism responded by politicizing art.[19] To understand Leyhausen's *Sprechchor* within this framework by no means implies reducing Benjamin's analysis to a polarizing schema; on the contrary, it provides an attempt to grasp similar phenomena in their complexity. It could be argued that the turn to older forms of choric theatre in Leyhausen's case contested contemporary political uses of *Sprechchor*. In this way, Leyhausen's work exemplifies the tensions, interfaces, and osmoses between politics and aesthetics involved in the dialectics established by Benjamin.

My analysis is aligned with the cultural turn taken by recent fascist studies, which tend to get a grip on the wider diffusion of fascist ideology beyond official fascist culture and its avowed artists and intellectuals.[20] Notwithstanding Leyhausen's connections with Hitler's regime as well as the similarities of his method to Nazi rhetorical style, it is precisely due to the noncommittal relationship with the regime that his productions can be used to disentangle the cultural and aesthetic strains that partook to a lesser or greater extent in the making of Nazism. From a method of delivering poetic drama, *Sprechchor* was developed into a means of organizing voice and body as well as synchronizing the chorus in performance. In a less explicit manner than in contemporary political performances, the choruses in Leyhausen's productions nonetheless invoked a community that, similarly to those embodied and represented by the *Thingspiel* choruses, appeared to be self-organized as much as self-organizing.[21] Rather than viewing the development of Leyhausen's choruses *vis-à-vis* rising fascism, I would propose scrutinizing *Sprechchor* as a poetological mode that concurred with totalitarian aesthetic ideology. The revival of older forms of choric drama that lies at the heart of Leyhausen's work was a reactionary move that would even seem to contradict Nazi aspirations to create radically new forms of art. Yet, *Sprechchor* as a means to reach back to older dramatic forms signified an attempt to retrieve the essence of great

deutschen Vaterlandes Echo wecken müssten' (quoted in the publicity leaflet of the performance). Source: Leyhausen–Spiess Collection, APGRD.

[19] Benjamin (1968 [1936]: 242).

[20] For a discussion of methodological difficulties and a critique of different strands within fascist studies, see Griffin and Matthew (2004).

[21] Fischer-Lichte (2005: 139).

poetry for the sake of cultural renewal. It is then the embodiment of the poetic essence by an organized chorus that gives *Sprechchor* a decisive turn towards fascist communal imaginings. Against the backdrop of these co-articulations, the performance of Aeschylus' tragedy occupies centre stage.

SPRECHCHOR VERSUS HISTORY

The critics promptly differentiated Leyhausen's work from the politicized theatre of left avant-garde directors such as Erwin Piscator or Leopold Jeßner.[22] Similar verdicts would, in fact, seem to vindicate the director's struggle to dissociate *Sprechchor* both from contemporary theatrical experimentations as well as from political choral performances. Leyhausen's persistent claim was that he treated *Sprechchor* as a purely artistic medium to serve a high aesthetic purpose. In an article published in the *Kölnische Zeitung* in 1929 he made it clear that, ever since his first *Sprechchor* group in Cologne, his students' task had been to put 'monumental poetry' back onto the stage.[23] This task was, he explained, by no means tantamount to a modern reconstruction of ancient drama; by contrast, it was an attempt to celebrate what was perceived eternal about it. Furthermore, Leyhausen took issue with contemporary uses of *Sprechchor* in both political and theatrical contexts, which, he alleged, misled the younger generation by distorting their experience of both their mother tongue and poetry. His own work was argued to provide the counter to those earlier performances:

Work in this area of our culture seems to me nowadays particulalrly necessary, after about 50 years of most different tendencies—*their names usually ended in ...ism*—which have caused a worrying confusion. Yet, I daresay that nowadays people work very seriously, especially so the youngest generation.

(*Die Arbeit in diesem Bezirk unser Kultur scheint mir heute besonders notwendig, nachdem seit etwa 50 Jahren die verschiedensten Richtungen*—ihre Namen enden meistens auf . . . ismus—*eine bedenkliche Verwirrung geschafft haben. Aber ich kann wohl sagen, daß heute sehr ernstlich, und vor allen Dingen von der jüngsten Generation, gearbeitet wird.*)[24]

The attack on political uses of *Sprechchor* does not entail a rapprochement with Nazi aesthetics *per se*. It could well signify an adherence to the bourgeois tradition of choral recitation of classical or religious texts, which was popular

---

[22] Excerpt from the newspaper *Der Montag*, undated [damaged typed text]. Source: Leyhausen–Spiess Collection, APGRD. See also the review by the well-known critic Herbert Ihering, 'Staatstheater: *Agamemnon*', *Berliner Börsen-Courier* (1931) [exact date illegible]. Source: Walter Unruh Sammlung.

[23] Leyhausen, *Kölnische Zeitung*, 23 November 1929.

[24] Leyhausen, *Kölnische Zeitung*, 23 November 1929 (emphasis added).

in educational circles until the inter-war period.[25] Leyhausen's apprehension about the degeneration of *Sprechchor* within political groups occurs in these circles as well, identified as a 'crisis of Sprechchor'.[26] However, Leyhausen was generally critical of the humanistic classical tradition as well as of the bourgeois use of language, both of which he considered to be impervious to great poetic forms.[27] The practice of choral speaking was employed in his own work as a performance medium that could retrieve forms of choric drama for the contemporary era.[28]

Sprechchor in Leyhausen's stagings of Greek drama refers to the simultaneous rhythmic recitation of the chorus as much as to the musical rendering of the text by the actors, in general. Leyhausen had a background in music and he had intended to become a conductor.[29] The preface to his translations of *Persians, Prometheus Bound*, and *Agamemnon*, published together in 1948,[30] makes no secret of his musical perception of Greek tragedy. Leyhausen underscores the significance of the rhythm and melody of the spoken word, comparing the artistic necessity of poetic metre to that of metre in music.[31] Following this approach, his method of work treated the tragic texts as musical scores, trying to render the original rhythm in translation as well as in performance. Moreover, his commentaries on the individual plays extensively apply musical terminology (*andante, presto*, and so on) and references to analyse the function of certain passages or scenes. In this spirit, the choruses of the Oceanids are compared to the side theme of a symphonic sentence in the form of a soft Mozartean serenade that is contrasted to the power represented by Prometheus.[32] The treatment of poetic drama as a musical composition also provided the basis for the development of the acting style: musical terms and, occasionally, punctuation are also used in his prompt books to indicate the vocal modulations, crescendo and diminuendo in tone

[25] J. Clark (1984: 148 ff.), firmly places Leyhausen's work within the bourgeois *Sprechchor* tradition.

[26] Gentges (1931: 4–8) observed that the *Sprechchor* movement stood at a critical point because of its wide appropriations among various groups, most probably by the labour movement. Gentges presented a series of religious texts intended to help overcome this crisis, which, in his view, indicated a crisis of community-building as well.

[27] Leyhausen (1948: 5–24, esp. 10–11, 18).

[28] The spokesman of folkish ideology in theatre Heinz Kindermann referred to contemporary choric forms of poetry as organic expressions of the communal will of the German people, emphasizing the development of *Sprechchor* into a high artistic genre. See Kindermann (1935).

[29] This information comes from the account of the theatre critic Paul Fechter of his personal acquaintance with Leyhausen. Fechter (1955: 281–91, esp. 288).

[30] The translations had appeared in earlier individual editions and they had been staged by different student groups in the previous decades.

[31] Leyhausen (1948: 20): 'Wie man in der Musik des Taktes bedarf, so braucht der Dichter das Versmaß, um das aufzuzeichnen, was er endlich meint, nämlich die künstlerischen Formen der tönenden Musiknote sowie des tönenden Wortes, und das sind einzig und allein Rhythmus und Melodie.'

[32] Leyhausen (1948: 96).

and volume, and the rhythm of speech delivery. The later prompt book for the *Persians* owned by Leyhausen's wife and actress Anne-Marie Loose, who seems to have followed his method of directing closely, goes as far as to divide the cast into basses, tenors, and sopranos. Most importantly, the musical reading of the tragic plays establishes cultural analogies between Greek drama and German classical music. The plays of the Greek tragedians are deemed 'great symphonies', Aeschylus 'the Mediterranean Beethoven', while *Agamemnon* is compared to 'the Ninth'.[33]

Leyhausen recast the old principle of fidelity to the original, but he conceded that it was necessary to redefine it in relation to the nature of poetry. Interestingly enough, he introduces a hierarchy of fidelity: while reverence to the ideas articulated in the text is compared to the respect due to a testament, the translator should also remain true to the 'rhetorical particles' (*rhetorische Dinge*) of the literary work,[34] which for him relate to the power of poetic imagination. However, the foremost imperative of the translator is, in Leyhausen's view, to recapture the inner musical qualities of the poetic text.

In 1934 Leyhausen published a concise textbook consisting of two parts under the common title *Wir sprechen im Chor*: the first part provides a discussion on choral poetry, while the second presents an anthology of poems to assist the practice of recitation. In the first part Leyhausen eloquently describes the function of *Sprechchor*. The passage deserves to be quoted at length:

that the poetry of Sprechchor itself uses a great artistic form, which consciously distances itself from the reality of everyday functional language . . . The sound of the word spoken to us by the chorus rises to the extreme compared to any word of a single speaker. The music of the language rises to greatness, and at especially great and beautiful points the musical power and beauty then bring themselves to prominence. The rhythm and melody of the words are then able to make such a great impression on the sensitive listener *that the meaning*, the actual *content*, *recedes into the background*. In fact more often than we are aware, *meaning and content in great choral poetry are only little or even hardly noticed*. The listener then gives himself over to the beauty of the language to such a degree that he makes hardly any effort to gain an intellectual grip of the content.

(daß die Poesie des Sprechchors sich einer großen künstlerischen Form bedient, die sich bewußt von der Wirklichkeit unserer alltäglichen Gebrauchsprache fernhält . . . *Der Klang des Wortes, der von einem Sprechchor zu uns herklingt, ist jedem Wort eines einzelnen Sprechers gegenüber ins Gewaltige gesteigert. Die Musik der Sprache ist ins Großartige gehoben, und an besonders großen und schönen Stellen kann sich dann die Sprachmusikalische Kraft und Schönheit vordrängen. Rhythmus und Melodie der Wörter vermögen dann auf den empfindsamen Zuhörer einen so großen Eindrunk zu machen, daß der Sinn, der eigentliche Inhalt in den Hintergrund*

---

[33] Leyhausen (1948: 8–9, 160).   [34] Leyhausen (1948: 16).

tritt. *Ja, es geschieht sogar öfter, als wir uns dessen bewußt sind,* daß Sinn und Inhalt bei der großen chorischen Poesie wenig oder nur kaum beachtet werden. *Der Zuhörer gibt sich dann der Schönheit der Sprache so fern hin, daß er sich um das gedankliche Verstehen des Inhalts kaum bemüht.*)[35]

The emphasis on musical delivery here establishes a poetics of *Sprechchor* that treats musicality as the quintessence of poetry, while also regarding the intellectual element as superfluous to the experience of the poetic text altogether. This view of poetry has certain implications for the particular relationship between stage and auditorium. In another passage from the same book, Leyhausen concedes that the beauty of poetry cannot be proved. It is still possible, he goes on, to reveal it to the listener as follows:

One can make it explicit to someone, who has a sensitive disposition for the beauty and the form of language; namely, by standing before him and reciting this or that verse.

(*Mann kann es aber wohl jemandem, der für die Schönheiten und die Formen der Sprache ein empfängliches Gemüt hat, klar verständlich machen; nämlich dann, wenn man vor ihm steht und ihm diese oder jene Verse laut vorspricht.*)[36]

The revelation of poetic beauty is envisaged in terms of performance inasmuch as it presupposes that somebody *stands before* somebody else. Unlike the frontal speaking choruses of agitprop, which passed on clear political statements in order to mobilize their audiences, the effect of *Sprechchor* here is grounded on the sensuous communication of the musical qualities of the text. The performance does not break with textual authority, but it actually re-establishes it through the powerful acoustic impression, which imposes on the spectator a poetic beauty that lies beyond intellectual reach. In this respect, Leyhausen proffers an anti-intellectual form of theatre that would seem to be consonant with the irrational strains in fascist ideology; textual logos reinforces a performance aesthetics that, it is implied, operates outside the legitimacy of reason.

The dominance of rhythm and melody has implications that run deeper than the performance impact, entailing a rupture with the notion of historicity. The function of *Sprechchor* can be compared to that of the Wagnerian leitmotif as analysed in Theodor Adorno's polemic on Wagner. Adorno offers an insightful view of the leitmotif in Wagner as a reactionary force that denies musical progression; according to Adorno, the leitmotif can be described as an endless gesture that expands only to return indefinitely to itself, concluding that: 'The eternity of Wagnerian music . . . is one which proclaims that nothing has happened; it is a state of immutability that refutes all history by confronting it

---

[35] Leyhausen (1934: 23) (emphasis in original).   [36] Leyhausen (1934: 4).

with the silence of nature.'[37] In a similar manner, the rhythmic delivery of *Sprechchor* consists in alternating rises and falls of the voice and changes in volume; although the vehemence of choral speaking creates the constant sense of a radical shift, its repetitive character eventually commits the spectator to the state of an atemporal present. Furthermore, the practice of *Sprechchor* would seem to defy the play's historicity in a twofold way: the extreme attention to the poetic metre privileges formal characteristics over the historical foregrounding of the play, while the musicalization of the text resists the idea of progression by means of undermining the dramatic economy. Leyhausen's *Sprechchor* participated in and anticipated the dehistoricizing move, which by sublimating history into aesthetics proclaimed the totalitarian present as eternal.[38]

Classical antiquity became instrumental in coalescing past and present time, while also being subjected to an unhistorical reading itself. Leyhausen accused both Plato and Aristotle of overemphasizing the ethical and historical aspects of Greek tragedy at the expense of what is 'essentially artistic' about it.[39] In stark contrast, *Sprechchor* as a means to retrieve artistic essence in performance complements the appeal to the timelessness of Greek tragedy. In the programme for the production of *Persians* at the Berlin Städtische Oper in 1927, the timelessness of Aeschylus' play is contemplated as a source of youth, power, and natural force:

A staging of the *Persians* does not go back 2,000 years, but a genius extends over many thousand years. With the natural power of a vivid pulse his eternal youth constantly points forward to infinity. And the infinity is the homeland of youth, in its power lies life eternal.

(*Eine Aufführung der* Perser *greift nicht 2000 Jahre zurück, sondern ein Genie ragt über viele tausend Jahre hinaus. Seine ewige Jugend weist mit der Naturkraft eines lebendigen Pulses immer ins Unendliche vorwärts. Und das Unendliche ist die Heimat der Jugend, in ihrer Kraft ist das ewige Leben.*)[40]

The impact of *Sprechchor* performances on the audiences must have fulfilled Leyhausen's aspirations. The reviews often speak of spectators watching spellbound and responding with enthusiasm, as in the case of the 1927 *Persians*, which is described by the well-known critic Alfred Klaar as follows:

---

[37] Adorno (2005: 30).

[38] Pois (1995: 25–6) identifies in Nazi rallies an experience that overrides historical time: 'What is being described is an "eternal present" within which past and future (however ill-defined) are somehow brought together in the solvent of immanency. The dead of the Great War have not died in vain, a new yet old Reich has been founded, and a "healing spirit" beckons seductively toward a glorious future . . . The Volksgemeinschaft would find spiritual articulation in numberless, history-defying "eternal presents", embodiments of the "laws of life".'

[39] See Leyhausen's remarks on Aristotle and Plato in Leyhausen (1948: 184–5).

[40] Theatre programme. Source: Walter Unruh Sammlung. The play was performed on 23 January 1927 and 27 March 1927.

The listeners and spectators stood under a power which has transcended all times and expands to an eternally present greatness, and they thanked the contributors with enthusiastic applause.

(*Die Hörer und Schauer standen unter dem Eindrucke des Mächtigen, das die Zeiten überwunden hat und zu ewig aktueller Größe anschwillt und dankten den Veranstaltern durch enthusiastischen Beifall.*)[41]

Leyhausen's *Sprechchor* can be understood as an attempt to embody the alleged every-youth of the text by providing a physical equivalent to its 'vivid pulse'. For Leyhausen, the rhythm of poetic drama is inseparable from its performance. In his edition of Aeschylus' tragedies he gives an account of his translational approach to the Greek text: as long as poetic metre preserves elements of the original performance, the performance itself is treated as the organic medium, which can unleash the poetry of the text. Leyhausen argues that the rhythm of Greek tragedy is the national, natural property of Greek culture, which cannot be delivered in any other language. The choral parts, in particular, confront the translator with a far more intricate task, since the metre corresponded to certain movements of the chorus. The reproduction of the original rhythm is, thus, linguistic as much as corporeal. To overcome the translational difficulties posed by Greek tragedy Leyhausen relied on what he called the 'nationally specific, physical capacities' (*nationalbedingte körperliche Vermögen*) of the German language.[42] His method consisted of reading aloud the original text and then trying to reproduce the sounds as closely as possible in German. The translation was finalized only after it had been rehearsed by the group, a process that entails, according to Leyhausen, the materialization of the form through speaking bodies.[43] The *Sprechchor* performance is described as an act of appropriation during which the classical text, filtered through the natural qualities of the national language, is consummated in the resonating bodies of the chorus participants.

AN ETERNAL ANTIQUITY

Both proletarian performances and the Nazi *Thingspiel* invoked Greek theatre, yet in search of distinctively different features and qualities. While socialist intellectuals were principally interested in the festive and communal character of the ancient performance,[44] it was the element of mass spectacle in a monumental space that mostly appealed to the Nazis. In the latter case,

---

[41] Alfred Klaar, 'Die Perser des Aischylos', 25 June 1927.
[42] Leyhausen (1948: 22–3).
[43] Leyhausen (1948: 23): 'jene Formen mit ihrem sprechenden Körper zu realisieren'.
[44] Warstat (2004: 291–8) discusses contemplations of Greek theatre within socialist communuties.

Greek theatre was used to sustain the idea of an ancient past envisioned as inherent in the *Volk* community, albeit created and enforced through specific cultural policies of the Third Reich. From its initial conception the *Thingspiel* movement promoted the construction of the open-air stages (*Thingstätte*) designed for the performance of the new dramaturgy across Germany. These were modelled on Greek amphitheatres, while the locations that were chosen for their construction were related to an old Germanic cultic tradition of communal gatherings. On no occasion was the coalescence between Greek antiquity, Germanic past, and the Nazi state acted out more overtly than during the 1936 Berlin Olympic Games. The official celebrations for the international audiences included the *Thingspiel* performance of the *Franken-burger Würfelspiel* (*Frankenburg Dice Game*) by Eberhard Wolfgang Möller as well as a staging of Aeschylus' *Oresteia* directed by Lothar Müthel. While Möller's play was staged at the newly built Dietrich-Eckart-Bühne, the *Oresteia* took place at the Berlin Staattheater. Nonetheless, in the theatrical programme of the *Oresteia* an image of the Dietrich-Eckart-Bühne was put on display next to a reconstructed version of the Theatre of Dionysus in Athens.[45] It was not the first time Greek theatre found itself at the centre of modern renegotiation with antiquity. But, in this historical instance, reactionary modernity assimilated classical models into new theatrical forms, which claimed victory in the long-fought-out struggle with the ancients.

Leyhausen kept a copy of the programme of the 1936 *Oresteia* in his personal archive.[46] In the previous years he had diligently documented performances of Greek drama in Europe, showing a special interest in the use of open-air spaces, ancient theatres, and monuments. His archive holds numerous pictures and various materials of productions of the Istituto Nazionale del Dramma Antico at the Ancient Theatre of Syracuse in the 1920s and the 1930s as well as the First Delphic Festival organized by Eva Palmer and Angelos Sikelianos in 1927. Leyhausen was invited to attend the 1927 Festival and he most probably attended the Second Delphic Festival in 1930. He shared Sikelianos' vision to create an international spiritual centre in Delphi, and in the early 1930s they co-founded the Delphic Organism to promote theatrical and cultural activity at the site. This contact must have played a role in the invitation of the Greek government to the Berlin Sprechchor to perform *The Persians* at the Roman Odeon of Herodes Atticus in Athens in 1934.[47]

---

[45] The theatre is mentioned as the theatre of Lycurgus.

[46] The copy is deposited at the Stiftung Stadtmuseum Berlin, Theatersammlung.

[47] In the short video extract of the Athenian performance, Leyhausen appears together with Sikelianos. On the Greek reception of Leyhausen's *Persians*, see Mavromoustakos (2004) and Iliadis (2011). See also the documentary 'Classical Greece in the Inter-War: Delphic Festivals and Productions of Greek Drama', Historical Archives of the Greek National Television (ERT) <http://www.ert-archives.gr/V3/public/main/page-assetview.aspx?tid=27863&autostart=0> (accessed 14 January 2013).

The representation of Greek antiquity in Leyhausen's stagings demonstrates a broader shift in the performance of Greek tragedy in the inter-war period. Both Sikelianos and Leyhausen stayed exclusively with Aeschylus, while their stagings drew on archaic art and iconography. The lion gate of Mycenae appeared in various versions of Leyhausen's *Agamemnon*, while a voluminous oriental mausoleum provided Friedrich Winkler-Tannenberg's set design for his *Persians*. Leyhausen's Egyptian-inspired costume sketches for the production of *Agamemnon* were reminiscent of Eva Palmer's costumes of the *Suppliants* in the Second Delphic Festival. Yet, like most of the artists and intellectuals involved in the productions in Delphi and Syracuse, Leyhausen came to Greek tragedy less out of philological or archaeological interest, rather to provide a theatrical experience outside the conventions of bourgeois culture. The turn towards pre-classical antiquity that these performances visualized was in line with the fascination with the primordial, the Dionysiac, and the irrational from the end of the nineteenth century, which the inter-war period transformed into a plea for a pre-modern order.

The use of archaic imagery complemented the use of *Sprechchor* in sustaining the idea of an eternal antiquity. The siting of Greek tragedy within an unhistorical mythical setting that displaced it from the civic context of the ancient polis would seem to affirm the permutation of history to myth. Not surprisingly, the eternal provided an apt way of validating the organic connection between ancient Greece and contemporary Germany. The symbiosis of Goethe and Aeschylus in the repertoire of Leyhausen's *Sprechchor* groups testifies to the attempt to forge links between the tradition of German classics and Greek antiquity.

Leyhausen did not succeed in having his *Persians* included in the official celebrations of the 1936 Olympics, as he had hoped.[48] Yet, in August of 1936 the Berlin Sprechchor played *Prometheus Bound* in the ruins of the Romanesque abbey in the town of Bad Hersfeld. The performance was part of an eight-day *Festspiele* that also included extracts from both parts of Goethe's *Faust*, scenes from *Pandora* as well as musical parts from Schubert, Hebbel, and Beethoven. The choice of the Romanesque church should be related to the use of ancient monuments and temples as performance spaces of ancient drama in Italy and Greece. There must have been more than a glaring coincidence between this event and the Olympic Games as well as with the climax of the *Thingspiel* movement. The publicity leaflet of the *Festspiele* stated that Berlin Sprechchor chose the ruin as its 'national theatre'.[49] The student groups from Germany

---

[48] Lothar Müthel, who directed the *Oresteia* in 1936, had played the Herald in *Agamemnon* and the Messenger in *Persians* of the Berlin Sprechchor. He had also directed for the *Thingspiel* movement, and, interestingly enough, he had taken part in proletarian speaking choruses as well as in Max Reinhardt's productions at an earlier stage.

[49] Source: Leyhausen–Spiess Collection, APGRD.

and abroad were promised a wide-ranging programme, which, apart from the performances, offered various team activities from hiking and visits to a labour camp (*Arbeitslager*), to camp fires and participation in a local community picnic. Similar events were organized within the Nazi youth movement. Indeed, the local press greeted the avowal of Germany's university youth in accordance with the Führer principle.[50] The festive character surrounding the performances raised quests for a festival that could make Hersfeld a new Bayreuth or Oberammergau.[51] The performance of *Faust* was attended by the Reich's Minister of Education Bernhard Rust; and his enthusiastic response attested to the convergence of past and present: Rust assured Leyhausen that Hersfeld was not a ruin, but 'the future' ('*Hersfeld ist keine Ruine, Hersfeld ist Zukunft!*').[52] Despite Leyhausen's claims that, unlike the political choruses, his *Sprehchor* would serve exclusively as an artistic medium, the performances of his students were enmeshed in contemporary German politics. Paradoxically, the alleged timelessness of Greek tragedy became an indispensable component in creating this historically specific enmeshment.

A CHARISMATIC COMMUNITY

Leyhausen disputed the image of the classical world produced by the nineteenth-century philological tradition. In his view, Aeschylus' plays were not addressed to the critical eye of the armchair reader,[53] but they should be treated as works of choric poetry made for those who possess the *organ* by which poetry is perceived. In his writings he also stressed the need to dispense with both Plato and Aristotle, while promulgating the idea that it is the 'task of the students, the new generation', to create a novel rhetoric and poetics.[54] His fervour was evidently shared among the students of the Berlin Sprechchor. In the calls for participants, the student Georg Pohl concedes that the group's aim was the revival of monumental dramatic poetry of the Greek dramatists as well as of modern poetic geniuses such as Goethe, Schiller, and Byron. In the student's words, the absence of great works from the contemporary theatre and the urge for older values and poetic forms created an imperative for the younger generation. The call invites new members to join the Berlin Sprechchor to celebrate the active idealism of youth, which alone can fulfil this task ('*Nur der tätig Idealismus unserer Jugend kann diese Aufgaben erfüllen*').[55] The

---

[50] Heuner (2005: 116).
[51] Newspaper cutting. Source: Stiftung Stadtmuseum Berlin, Theatersammlung.
[52] Newspaper cutting. Source: Stiftung Stadtmuseum Berlin, Theatersammlung.
[53] Leyhausen (1948: 20).
[54] Leyhausen (1948: 185).
[55] Leaflet. Source: Leyhausen–Spiess Collection, APGRD.

erudite elite gives place to an elect community that tunes itself to great poetic artworks and comes onto the theatrical stage to convey its impact to its contemporaries. The conviction that student groups will restore *Sprechchor* to its higher end of serving poetic drama, resisting the degeneration of modern culture, gives Leyhausen's appropriations of antiquity a decidedly totalitarian leaning.

The reviews compared Leyhausen's performances with those of Max Reinhardt in the previous decades.[56] Indeed, Leyhausen's earlier *Sprechchor* groups in Cologne, in particular, bore clearer similarities with Reinhardt's massive choruses. The photographic evidence shows a gradual decrease in the number of the chorus members as well as a stronger tendency towards synchronized movement and organization of bodies within space (see Figures 18.1 and 18.2). While in Reinhardt's productions both choral speaking and movement tended to be excessive and uncontrolled, Leyhausen's choruses were characterized by extreme orchestration of voices and bodies.[57] The images from the rehearsals of the *Persians* depict Leyhausen's intensive work with the students, who are asked to reproduce the postures he shows.

Fig. 18.1. Performance of *Persians* by the first Sprechchor group in Cologne, 1920. Courtesy of APGRD

[56] See Baur (1999) for a full discussion of the various transformations of the chorus from Reinhardt's theatre to the *Thingspiel* movement.

[57] Schirmer (2002: 37) contrasts Reinhardt's continuous search for new theatrical spaces with Leyhausen's conservative use of the proscenium stage with the addition of stairs and different levels.

Fig. 18.2. The Berlin Sprechchor rehearses the *Persians* at the Herodes Atticus Theatre in Athens, 1934. Courtesy of Stiftung Stadtmuseum Berlin, Theatersammlungen

According to Matthias Warstat, strategies to homogenize human bodies in performance were also developed within the labour movement.[58] Yet, as we have heard, the organization of the chorus in Leyhausen was bared of its political stakes, aiming instead to reproduce an aesthetic order alone. The relationship of Leyhausen's staging techniques to earlier theatrical pursuits is reminiscent of *Thingspiel*'s ability to 'drive all earlier tendencies towards the statuary, towards massive and content-free pure existence'.[59]

From Leyhausen's prompt book for the *Prometheus Bound* it can be de-duced that the chorus was directed to accentuate emotions with large move-ments and rhythmic paces. Its members took various formations and united into a whole following the climaxes of the dramatic action. In the second *stasimon* before the entrance of Io, the Oceanids express their sympathy for Prometheus with loud cries and intense bodily movements. Yet, Leyhausen's pencil-note direction to the chorus corresponding to the line in which Io comes on stage reads: 'stand still when Io appears' (*stehen bleiben wenn Io erscheint*). Similar guidelines are given in Anne-Marie Loose's prompt book for *Persians*. At the end of the play the chorus of Elders join the defeated Xerxes in mourning. The instruction given to the chorus members once again defines their relationship to the protagonist: 'Always stand still when the protagonist speaks' (*Aber immer stehen bleiben, wenn der Protagonist spricht*).

---

[58] Warstat (2004: 382).
[59] Menz (1976:, 337): 'treibt die früheren Tendenzen alle in die eine Richtung des "Statuar-ischen", des massenhaften und inhaltsleeren bloßen Daseins'.

The chorus in these productions is a community characterized by vocal and physical intensity, but its power and energy eventually succumb to the unquestionable supremacy of the individual hero.[60]

The relationship between the chorus members and the individual roles in the Berlin Sprechchor performances recalls the attempts of the Nazis to restrain the excessiveness of the chorus in *Thingspiel*. In 1935 the Reich Dramaturge and President of the Theatre Chamber Rainer Schlösser published a treatise entitled the *Das Volk und seine Bühne* (The People and its Stage). Schlösser expressed his concern about the presence of large numbers of choruses in *Thingspiel*, arguing instead for interaction between choruses and heroes. For Schlösser, the rejection of the individual and the emphasis on the masses should be opposed as 'collectivist-minded'. The model he proposes instead justifies the individual character as a figure commited to the communities represented on the stage.[61]

Sprechchor in Leyhausen's performances is made into an organizing principle that regulates the actor in rehearsal, the chorus in performance, and, finally, the spectator's response to the spectacle. The homogenized choruses were not without allusions to a burgeoning community, even though they did not aspire to establish equivalents beyond the stage, as was the case with the political *Sprechchor* that Leyhausen discredited. The community they envisaged was constituted on the basis of its special relationship with antiquity as well. It is a charismatic community that organizes itself around a higher spiritual mission, which warrants cultural regeneration. While touring their *Persians* to Athens, the Berlin Sprechchor students rehearsed in the Theatre of Dionysus and visited ancient monuments. A photo taken on one of those visits offers clear testimony to the subjection of the group to Hitler: the students are shown in distinctive arrays and with raised hands in Nazi salute (see Figure 18.3). Speaking in Leyhausen's fond musical terms, the choruses in his productions of ancient tragedy were only a prelude to the community that was looming large.

EPILOGUE

Engagements of the totalitarian imagination with Greek antiquity might have been bolstered by official Nazi culture, but they certainly did not originate in Hitler's seizure of power. Totalitarian imaginings of antiquity did not provide

---

[60] Heuner (2002: 120) discusses the hierarhical arrangement between chorus and protagonist on the stage, while also arguing that the chorus leader emerges as a dominant presence that organizes the chorus.

[61] Schlösser (1935: 59).

Fig. 18.3. The Berlin Sprechchor during its visit to Athens in 1934; damaged news-paper cutting, most probably due to later self-censorship. Courtesy of Stiftung Stadt-museum Berlin, Theatersammlungen

a radical break with previous cultural discourses; rather they assimilated ideas that were well under way within bourgeois culture. Leyhausen's claims to revive Greek tragedy extended far beyond fidelity to the text or an interest in ancient spaces. His stagings of Aeschylus treated the ancient text as a musical composition aspiring to recapture its inner poetic essence. *Sprechchor* was made the cornerstone of a sublime poetics, but, similar to its previous uses in political contexts, it alluded to an organized community. Leyhausen's students identified themselves as a new generation that set itself the task of leading their audiences to the eternal realm of poetry. Their choruses performed a cele-brated exodus from history, heralding a community that was envisioned to embody eternal values.

After the end of the war, Leyhausen had to leave his position at the Univer-sity of Berlin, and he moved to Mainz in 1949. He maintained contacts with student theatre groups as well as with some of the artists with whom he had been in touch in the pre-war years.[62] In 1950 he founded the Delphic Institute, an organization aiming to bring together European and international theatre groups, which met at biennial Delphiads held in different cities. The German group of the institute named as Collegium Delphicum produced new versions of Aeschylus and Goethe until Leyhausen's death in 1953 and remained active

---

[62] The choreographer Koula Pratsika from Sikelianos's circle participated in the Delphic Institute.

afterwards under the guidance of Anne-Marie Loose. The Collegium continued practising choral speaking, even though the term *Sprechchor* was dropped from their official name. Moreover, their choruses were limited to fewer members, while the stagings adopted means, such as masks, that gave them a classical-looking twist.

While the production of official Nazi culture ended in the defeat of the regime, fascist art was generally dismissed and passed into oblivion in post-war Europe. Leyhausen's staging practices, by constrast, outlived the perform-ances of the Berlin Sprechchor and escaped immediate associations with fascism. The ideology of *Sprechchor* transformed performatively the convic-tions of classical Idealism into a dehistoricizing apparatus that corresponded to certain structural principles of fascism. By praising tragedy's atemporal poetic essence, it could also resist its own historical ties and readily accommo-date itself within post-war artistic and cultural practices anew.

19

Revivals of Choric Theatre as Utopian Visions

Erika Fischer-Lichte

Choruses never posed a problem for opera. Invented by the Florentine camerata as a supposed revival of ancient Greek theatre, choruses always featured prominently in operatic performances. Modern performances of Greek tragedies, however, were a completely different story. Here, the inclusion of choruses seemed to present almost insurmontable difficulties. Usually, the tragedies were simply rewritten in order to adapt them to the dominant staging conventions that did not include choruses. With the beginning of historicism, this changed. The Potsdam *Antigone* (1841), commissioned by the Prussian King Friedrich Wilhelm IV in the second year of his reign, did feature choruses. In fact, it was none other than Felix Mendelssohn-Bartholdy who composed the music for it.[1] Overall, the production was a success. After that point, productions of Greek tragedies often included singing choruses.

Over the course of the twentieth century, the chorus was granted a new status. Two different periods during the twentieth century proved particularly fruitful for the formation of new forms of choric theatre as a result of productions of Greek tragedies with speaking choruses: the first decades of the twentieth century, as well as the late 1980s and the 1990s. A third revival, as a kind of continuation of the second, happened in the first decade of the twenty-first century.

At the beginning of the twentieth century, anthropologists, sociologists, and theatre artists from all over Europe entered into a heated discussion on how individuals and communities relate to each other in a society slowly disintegrating as a result of the growing division of labour. The by then ubiquitous and growing dichotomy between individuals nurturing cults of personality and the anonymous 'masses' threatened to undermine—even shatter—society. In this

---

[1] For the Potsdam *Antigone*, see Fischer-Lichte (2010: 329–52).

moment of crisis, these scholars and artists set out to find new forms of integration and social bonding. Theatre artists in particular felt that a new popular theatre would be able to achieve such a reconsolidation of society. The express purpose of these new forms of theatre was the creation of communities—not merely the representation of a community on stage, but the coming into being of a community involving actors and spectators alike.

In the late 1980s, the question of the relationship between the individual and the community in late industrial, partly even post-industrial, societies came up again. In the 1990s, it merged with more abstract concerns that had become increasingly pressing issues, such as the financial crisis or the doping practices of professional athletes, resulting from certain pressures exerted by post-industrial capitalist societies. The millennium began with a discussion of new forms of participatory democracy. This issue was to be dealt with most appropriately through forms of choric theatre.

This chapter discusses in detail four productions of Greek tragedies that can be regarded as representative of each stage in this choric revival: Max Reinhardt's productions of *Oedipus Rex* (1910) and the *Oresteia* (1911) at the Circus Schumann Berlin with which he established his Theatre of the Five Thousand as a revival of choric theatre; Einar Schleef's *The Mothers* (1986, Schauspielhaus Frankfurt), a combination of Euripides' *Suppliant Women* and Aeschylus' *Seven against Thebes*; and *The Persians*, staged by Theatercombinat in Geneva in 2006.

PEOPLE'S THEATRE

Reinhardt conceived of his Theatre of the Five Thousand as a choric theatre in order to induce the production of community not only onstage but also *between* actors and spectators during the performance. It was meant as a festive event bringing together people from different social classes, strata, and milieux. Reinhardt proceeded from the assumption that theatre as festival could come into being only when both parties joined forces—actors and spectators alike. For he was convinced that

the best theatre is not only performed on stage. Actually, the most important actors are sitting in the auditorium ... One day, the two-way flow which passes from stage to auditorium and from auditorium to the stage will be scientifically researched. When he who creates receives at the same time and the receiver becomes the one who creates, the precious and incomparable secret of theatre is born.[2]

---

[2] Cited in Fetting (1973: 61).

One of Reinhardt's strategies to create such moments was the invention of a new choric theatre. He realized his vision at the Circus Schumann in Berlin with his two productions, *Oedipus Rex* (1910) and *The Oresteia* (1911). The Theatre of the Five Thousand sought to attract 'large sections of the population as visitors, the many people who today, for economic reasons, are unable to attend'. Reinhardt declared that 'if thousands upon thousands were to unlock the sealed doors, theatre would again become a social factor in this day and age'.[3]

Yet Reinhardt's work, at the forefront of social change, was not welcomed everywhere. Partly confused and irritated, even disgusted, all critics of *Oedipus* remarked on the fact that the chorus consisted not of a mere fifteen members but of hundreds. The chorus members not only moved, acted in, and thus overcrowded the orchestra—that is, the ring; they also occupied the space otherwise 'reserved' for the spectators. They had entrances that led them right past and also into the midst of the spectators. They were everywhere; they occupied the whole space. In the *Oresteia*, in which Reinhardt also used this device, the critic Alfred Klaar felt most uncomfortable because of

the distribution of the acting into the space in front of, beneath, behind, and among us; the never-ending demand to shift our points of view; the actors flooding into the auditorium with their fluttering costumes, wigs, and make-up, jostling against our bodies; the dialogues held across great distances; the sudden shouts from all corners of the theatre, which startle and misguide us—all this is confusing: It does not reinforce the illusion but destroys it.[4]

The critic not only felt uncomfortable because as a spectator he had to keep changing his position if he wanted to see and hear what was going on in the space, but also because the performers moved among the spectators, occupied the space of the auditorium, 'jostling against' the spectators' bodies and thus failing to respect the boundaries separating one individual from another. The occupation of the whole space by the performers, on the other hand, erased the difference between performers and spectators. The performers moved among the spectators; they seemed to be one with them. They drew the spectators into the action and made it difficult to distinguish between actors and spectators. All together they formed one mass.

This point is made by another critic, who first mentions the presence of Prince August Wilhelm and Prince Oskar. He continues:

But the individual has no impact here. In this half light, only the crowd has an impact. One begins to understand what 'the public' means. This is what Reinhardt needs . . . He believes the crowd is everything, subject and object. He rewards five thousand

---

[3] Reinhardt in *Das Literarische Echo*, 13, cited in Fetting (1974: 331).
[4] Alfred Klaar, *Vossische Zeitung*, 4 October 1911, n.p.

spectators by presenting a company of seemingly ten thousand. He presents the masses to the masses. He shows them themselves in the exaggerated form of passion and costume.[5]

It seems significant that the critics who adhered to bourgeois individualism did not use the term community but 'the masses', which has a distinctly negative connotation. What we can gather from their remarks, however, is that Reinhardt's special devices not only presented and represented a community of hundreds to the spectators in the *orchestra*, but also brought forth a community in the course of the performance, a community of thousands, comprising both performers and spectators.

Since the sense of community did not arise through a common symbolism that explicitly referred to beliefs, ideologies, and so on shared by all spectators—or at least by a majority of them—but was due to very special physical effects brought about by the presence of the masses in the space and by the frequently changing atmosphere, it cannot be regarded as a political, national, religious, or ideological community. It came into being mainly, if not exclusively, through performative means developed and refined by Reinhardt in his theatre begun at the turn of the last century. Therefore, I shall call it a theatrical community.[6] A theatrical community is a temporary community, as transitory and ephemeral as the performance itself. The longest it can last for is the length of the entire performance, as it must dissolve when the performance comes to an end. As long as the performance lasts, it is capable of establishing a bond between individuals with the most diverse biographical, social, ideological, religious, and political backgrounds. They remain individuals with associations of their own that can generate vastly different meanings. The performance does not force anyone into a common confession; instead, it allows for shared experiences enabled solely through performative processes.

These experiences do not necessarily dissolve the selves of the people who undergo them, but they certainly cannot be conceived of as something stable, fixed, or rigid. Rather, they must be thought of as fluid and transformative. It seems that the community presented and represented on Reinhardt's stage was conceived of and displayed in this way. At no time did individuals vanish or dissolve into the chorus; they remained individuals even as members of this community:

The people push and shove each other, they crowd together, separate. They move as a unit and yet at the same time stand out from one another; each individual remains himself—one in red, one in green, one with a bare chest, and yet he is also one piece of the whole. He belongs to the 'people'. I have never seen such a thing happen in a scene before.[7]

---

[5] Fritz Engel, *Berliner Tageblatt*, 8 November 1910, n.p.
[6] The term 'theatrical community' was coined by Warstat (2004).
[7] Fritz Engel, *Berliner Tageblatt*, 8 November 1910, n.p.

Following this description, other critics emphasized that individual voices could be clearly distinguished within the chorus, one whispering, another mumbling, and a third one screaming.

With these two productions of Greek tragedies, Reinhardt realized his idea of a choric theatre by allowing for a community to emerge during the performance that consisted of individuals who remained individuals without ever merging into an anonymous 'mass'; a community that never claimed a long-lasting existence—a kind of community that seems a viable concept even in today's late capitalist, post-industrial societies.

After the war, in 1919, the architect Hans Poelzig rebuilt the Circus Schumann as Reinhardt's Grosses Schauspielhaus. The new theatre opened with a new production of the *Oresteia*, this time with the addition of *The Eumenides*, which had been left out in 1911. On the occasion of its opening, the Deutsches Theater published a booklet in which playwrights, set designers, and dramaturgs who had cooperated with Reinhardt summarized the most important arguments in the debate on a new choric theatre as a people's theatre. Heinz Herald, Reinhardt's dramaturg, emphasized that, in the circus arena, theatre will 'from a matter of the few once again turn into a matter of the masses', for an audience 'which derives from all classes' was to be assembled here and would 'comprise the masses who, up to now, have been strangers to the theatre'.[8] Carl Vollmoeller, who adapted the *Oresteia* for Reinhardt's purposes, praised the arena theatre as

an assembly for the people of today . . . What the de-politicization of our people during fifty years of imperial reign prevented is possible today: a gathering of thousands in a theatre space to build a community of active, enthusiastic, and emphatic citizens.[9]

Clearly, the choric theatre, for which the circus had been rebuilt, aimed at realizing a social and political utopia. The fact that this utopian vision could not be achieved under the conditions of the early years of the Weimar Republic is clearly expressed in the review by the critic Stefan Grossmann of the opening performance:

The image of a community of thousands was wonderful and heartening. Perhaps all the more so for the German intellectual citizen because the spatial unity of the masses reawakened his yearning for an inner sense of belonging. Can we be one people? Here sits Herr Scheidemann, over there privy councillor Herr Roethe, there is Hauptmann's Goethe-like head, over there Dr Cohn waves to a comrade. But Scheidemann looks past Roethe and Cohn, passes Hauptmann with only a shrug of the shoulders. Even outside the work environment there is no feeling of unity. There is no nation on earth

---

[8] Cited in *Das Deutsche Theater* (1920: 11).
[9] Cited in *Das Deutsche Theater* (1920: 21).

which so lacks a feeling of community and the war has consumed us even more . . . So we have the greatest people's theatre, but no people.[10]

Even if Reinhardt's choric theatre failed to unfold its utopian potential fully, its devices—such as the occupation of the space by the masses, the importance of atmosphere, the dynamic and energetic bodies moving through the space—served as a model for new forms of choric theatre to be established in the 1920s and 1930s. However, these new forms claimed to bring about communities that lasted longer, based on common convictions and ideologies such as communism, national socialism, and Zionism.

The beginnings of the mass spectacles held from the spring of 1918 onwards in the newly founded Soviet Union can be traced to a revival of Reinhardt's *Oedipus Rex* in the Chiniselli Circus in the renamed city of Petrograd. It had been performed here previously during Reinhardt's guest tour of 1911. The restaging was initiated by Yuri Yurev, the leading actor of the Aleksandrinsky Theatre. The original set of the 1911 performance was still intact, so that an 'authentic' space was available. Yurev asked Aleksander Granovsky, a disciple of Reinhardt who had just returned from Berlin, to direct the revival. Yurev played the part of Oedipus and Granovsky directed the chorus, following Reinhardt's principle of using it to draw in the spectators while maintaining the individualism of each member. The revival turned out to be as great a success as the original, attracting spectators from all social classes, strata, and milieux in its week-long run. In the spring of 1919, *The Overthrow of the Autocracy* was performed, the first in a series of mass spectacles, which culminated in Nikolaj Evreinov's production of *The Storming of the Winter Palace* on 7 November 1920.[11]

Another form of choric theatre inspired by Reinhardt was the Nazi *Thingspiel* movement.[12] It drew heavily on the devices Reinhardt had developed for enabling the creation of a community. However, the aspect of individualism of the chorus members, so prominent in Reinhardt's productions, was missing here. What the Nazis aimed to create was the so-called *Volk* community.

Early *Thingspiel* plays and their concepts of community, however, did not strictly adhere to the National Socialist concept of the *Volk* community. The underlying idea of this concept was the unity of all people in a social order that would allegedly be free of class conflicts on a national and racial basis. The democratic principle of equality and majority was replaced by that of a *Führer*. The social rank of the individual was no longer to be determined by one's job, education, fortune, ownership of property, or means of production but by accepting a 'natural' inequality between men necessitating a 'natural' division of society into a *Führer* and a *Gefolgschaft* (followers), the leader and the led.

---

[10] Grossmann (1919: n.p.).   [11] Cf. Fischer-Lichte (2005: 97–121).
[12] See Ioannidou, Chapter 18, this volume.

The relationship between them was to be defined by consanguinity and moral responsibility—which meant that the followers owed allegiance to the *Führer* and found comradeship among themselves as his followers. From the very beginning, this concept radically excluded all so-called non-Germans and un-Germans, in particular Jews and political enemies.

It cannot be overlooked that the idea of community underlying the *Thingspiel* plays strikingly deviated from the official concept of *Volk* community in one aspect. The *Thingspiel* plays operated on the assumption that the community was self-organizing and self-organized, obviating the need for a leader. The Führer principle was ignored. Moreover, the early *Thingspiel* plays lacked the necessary criteria for exclusion from the *Volk* community. This might be one of the reasons for the rather short life of the *Thingspiel* movement: in May 1936, for example, just before the Olympic Games, Goebbels decreed a prohibition of the *Sprechchor* (speaking chorus), the main artistic means of the *Thingspiele*; and, after the Games, in 1937, Goebbels withdrew the so-called *Reichswichtigkeit* (importance to the Reich). This meant the loss of state subsidies, leading to the demise of the movement.

The 'ideal' *Volk* community, by contrast, was represented in Leni Riefenstahl's film on the *Reichsparteitag* of 1934, entitled *Triumph of the Will* (*Triumph des Willens*). Here, Hitler as the leader is shown as distinct from the masses of labourers and the youth. They respond to each other—the masses clearly accepting the leader's superiority: he is the one who organizes their community and their interactions.

The *Thingspiel* movement never even attempted to create a community of actors and spectators. The performance of Kurt Heynecke's *Thingspiel, Neurode: Ein Spiel von deutscher Arbeit* (*Neurode: A Play on German Labour*), for instance, brought forth a self-organizing community on stage. It was presented as an ideal community with which all spectators, representing the entire social spectrum, were called upon to identify. It was claimed that the performance allowed for and gave rise to an ideal community of performers and spectators. Whether this actually happened is doubtful. The reviews, while praising the overall impression of the play, nonetheless criticized the lack of dynamism and demanded that the 'tempo . . . must be increased . . . the people must be moved faster'.[13] They complained that the choruses did not move in the space after they had taken up their positions on the stage area—which marked an important difference not only from Reinhardt's choruses but also from those of the Social Democrats in their performances. We may thus conclude that, since the occupation of the space was static and the movements of the individual performers' bodies were neither dynamic nor energetic, any energy circulating in the space was not transferred to the spectators. Neither a living

---

[13] *Deutsche Bühnenkorrespondenz* (1934), cited in Stommer (1985: 73).

experience of a community nor the experience of a living community emerged. It might be true that an ideal, classless community was shown onstage. However, a corresponding community of performers and spectators failed to come into being.[14]

Another form of choric theatre that sprang up in the 1930s and was inspired by Reinhardt's productions was the American Zionist pageant movement, initiated by Meyer W. Weisgal, a committed Zionist who worked in the Chicago office of the Zionist Organization of America (ZOA). The first pageant, *Israel Reborn*, took place during Hanukkah in 1932. Isaac van Grove, the former Director of the Chicago Civic Opera and Chief Manager of the Cincinnati Summer Opera, served as Master of the Pageant. He wrote the play, composed the music, and conducted the performance. When asked about the model he was following, he explained that he had in mind something along the lines of Max Reinhardt's spectacular productions of choric theatre, such as *The Miracle*, which toured the United States in 1924. Van Grove again served as Master of the Pageant for the next one, the *Romance of a People*, performed in the Soldier Field Stadium in front of 150,000 spectators on the occasion of 'Jewish Day' at the World Fair on 3 July 1933. It was a choric form of theatre of gigantic proportions, celebrating Jewish history as a national history bound to a particular land—Zion, as well as the Yishuv, the Jewish community in Zion. The third pageant, the *Eternal Road*, was directed by Reinhardt himself and premiered in January 1937 in New York. Two other pageants followed—*We Will Never Die: A Memorial. Dedicated to the Two Million Jewish Dead of Europe*, initiated by Ben Hecht, famous for his Broadway plays and Hollywood scripts, while the songs were composed by Kurt Weill. The pageant premiered on 9 March 1943. It was followed by *A Flag is Born*, again staged by Hecht and Weill, premiering at the Alvi Theater on Broadway on 5 September 1946—that is, fifty years after the appearance of Theodor Herzl's book *The Jewish State*.[15] All these different versions of choric theatre, inspired by Reinhardt's *Oedipus Rex* and the *Oresteia* and also by *The Miracle*, were forms of political theatre, aiming at establishing new kinds of ideological or national communities.

INDIVIDUAL AND COMMUNITY

After the Second World War, the idea of a community, in fact the very word itself, became anathema in West Germany. Performances of Greek tragedies in the 1950s often turned the chorus into an abstract element—as abstract as the

---

[14] Fischer-Lichte (2005: 122–58).   [15] Fischer-Lichte (2005: 159–97).

stage space. Gustav Rudolf Sellner's various productions of Greek tragedies were guided by stylization and abstraction. The chorus appeared and moved according to geometric patterns. Paralysis and ceremoniousness became characteristic features. The chorus steered clear of representing anything close to a community. In a different sense, this still holds true for later productions of Greek tragedies. No longer static and ceremonious, Grüber's *Bacchae* and Stein's *Oresteia*, for example, referred back to Reinhardt's choruses insofar as they individualized their own choruses to a high degree, albeit preventing any sort of community from emerging.[16]

This changed with Einar Schleef's 1986 production of *The Mothers* at the Frankfurt Schauspielhaus. Here, the subject of community was taken up again, despite a telling variation: the focus now lay on the relationship between the individual and the community. The production rooted itself in the belief that individuals, communities, and the tensions between them are an anthropological given. There could be no viable society that could avoid it, the production seemed to say: there is no healthy society without individuals and communities.

Schleef started his career in the early 1970s as a stage director and set designer at the Berlin Ensemble in the German Democratic Republic (East Germany). In 1976, he left for the West. He pursued projects in Düsseldorf and Vienna without ever completing them. After ten years of searching, he staged Euripides' *Suppliant Women* and Aeschylus' *Seven against Thebes* at the Frankfurt Schauspielhaus (1986). The production, which lasted for almost four hours, was entitled *The Mothers*. In this, his first production in the West, Schleef created a new form of theatre, which he developed in all of his later productions until his untimely death in July 2001. In *The Mothers* he experimented for the first time with what from now on would become the trademark of his theatre: the chorus.

Schleef created a unique space for his *mise en scène*. Except for the three back rows (for elderly or disabled people), all the seats in the auditorium were removed. The floor gradually sloped up to the back rows in flat steps on which the spectators sat. From the stage, a broad runway, also sloping upwards with the steps, cut through the middle of the auditorium to the back wall where it connected with a second, narrow stage behind and above the remaining seats. In this way, the acting space was spread out in front of, behind, and among the spectators, so that they were often more or less surrounded by the performers.

There were three different choruses in the performance, all consisting of women: the chorus of widows, dressed in black and meeting Theseus (Martin Wuttke) with axes in their hands; the chorus of virgins, dressed in white tulle in the first part, red in the second; and the chorus of women dressed in black overalls and resembling workers in a munitions factory. They occupied and

---

[16] Fischer-Lichte (2004: 329–60).

ruled over the space: the stage in front of the spectators, the runway on which, particularly in the second part, they ran and stomped up and down wearing black, steel-capped shoes, as well as the stage behind the spectators—recalling, to a certain extent, Reinhardt's dynamic and energetic choruses, which also occupied the whole space. But, in *The Mothers*, the members of each chorus not only wore identical clothes. They seemed to move their bodies in the same rhythm, perform the same movements, and speak, whisper, shout, roar, howl, scream, whimper, and whine the same words in what appeared to be unison.

Nevertheless, this did not mean that the chorus acted as a collective body, in which the individuality of the different chorus members dissolved and merged with the others. Rather, the chorus appeared to constitute a permanent battleground between individuals who wanted to join the community while maintaining their individuality and the community, which strove for the complete assimilation of all of its members and threatened individuals with exclusion. Thus, a permanent tension existed in the chorus between the individual members and the community which they formed—a tension that caused a constant flow within the chorus and established a transformative dynamic with regard to the individual's position in and relationship to the community. This tension never vanished; the chorus never transformed itself into a harmonious collective. Instead, the tension intensified. It repeatedly made itself felt as acts of violence were committed on the individual by the community and on the community by the individual.

In some respects, Schleef's treatment of the chorus referred back to Nietzsche. Nietzsche claimed that the chorus was the origin of theatre and that tragedy was constituted by the incessant battle between two conflicting principles: that of individualization and that of its destruction or dismemberment. This could, in fact, be observed in the choruses of *The Mothers*. On the other hand, it also recalled the ur-scene of sacrifice as described by René Girard in his seminal study *Violence and the Sacred*.[17] Schleef was clearly inspired by it, as a passage on the chorus in his book *Droge Faust Parzifal* (*Drug Faust Parsifal*) suggests:

The ancient chorus is a terrifying image: crowds of figures, huddling close together, seeking shelter, yet energetically rejecting each other, as if the proximity of the other poisoned the air. This threatens the group, which would easily collapse on attack. Prematurely frightened, it finds and expels a victim to buy itself out. Although the chorus is aware of its betrayal, it does not rectify the situation. Instead, it clearly presents the victim as guilty. That is not just an aspect of the ancient chorus but a process repeated every day. The enemy-chorus does not primarily represent the millions of non-whites, the dying, war pillagers, and asylum seekers, but the dissenters, especially those speaking our own language; they are to be eliminated first and using all means available.

---

[17] Girard (1977).

Until that moment of elimination, the ancient constellation remains in place; the chorus and the individual will continue their struggle. Haunted by its relationship with the others, that is, the formerly isolated, and by their relationship amongst themselves and as a whole against the chorus, the latter successfully hopes to fend them off.[18]

Although Schleef's description of the situation at first glance appears to follow the model of Girard's ur-scene, he deviates from it in one important aspect: he does not legitimize or even judge the violence of the chorus/community on the victim as a form of cathartic violence that would save the community from its total destruction through mutual violence. Rather, he regards such violence as a permanently impending threat which the community must always evade, because it destroys an innocent victim and, at the same time, does not save the community from mutual violence among its members. The battle between individual and community is an ongoing, never-ending process. The tension that determines the relationship between individual and community cannot be eliminated by acts of joint violence on one individual.

In Schleef's view, the situation described in the passage above is characteristic not only of the ancient chorus but also of modern societies—that is, of the post-industrial society of his times. As such, it is not surprising that the permanent tension in *The Mothers*, which defined the relationship between individual and community, extended into the auditorium and also determined the relationship between actors and spectators. In this respect, the spatial arrangement had a dual effect.

On the one hand, it allowed the actors to surround or be among the spectators, suggesting a fundamental unity, a single—perhaps even harmonious—community formed out of these two groups. On the other hand, this unity was constantly under threat. Whenever it came into being, the community was immediately broken up again. Unity was trumped by conflicting forces. This was partly also due to the fragmented spatial arrangement, because the runway, while enabling the actors to mingle with the audience, also dissected and thus permanently threatened the dismemberment of the audience's collective body. Moreover, it exposed the spectators to the violence done to them by the chorus when the latter trampled up and down the steps and shouted them down. The audience responded to these physical attacks either by retreating or by aggressively defending themselves—for instance, by stamping their feet, rhythmically clapping their hands or shouting comments. Here, too, a power struggle was fought out between the chorus and the audience. The ecstatic chorus aimed to overwhelm the audience in order to bring about a state of ecstasy. Individual members of the audience resisted this, either verbally or by leaving the auditorium. Others, however, seemed to succumb to the union with the chorus either out of fear or with pleasure.

---

[18] Schleef (1997: 14).

There were only rare moments when chorus and auditorium formed a harmonious community—moments of transition before the next outbreak of conflict between the two groups that turned the house into an inferno.

With *The Mothers*, Einar Schleef laid the foundation for his tragic theatre based on the chorus. He continued to develop this concept, but never again returned to Greek tragedy. In his very last production *Verratenes Volk* (*Betrayed People*, performed at the Deutsches Theater Berlin, in 2001), however, he appeared on stage as Nietzsche, reciting from *Ecce Homo* for forty-five minutes. In his once scandalous book, *The Birth of Tragedy* (1872), Nietzsche had developed the theory that sacrificial rituals constituted the origin of Greek theatre. He did so in order to lay the foundations for a new theatre, a theatre of the future, which he saw partly realized in Richard Wagner's music theatre. Schleef, in turn, turned to ancient Greek theatre and, in particular, to the chorus in order to establish a contemporary form of tragic theatre, a theatre that featured the complicated and ever-changing relationship between individual and community, a relationship that can only momentarily achieve a state of harmony or balance. His form of tragic theatre was a theatre of violence, a theatre that could inflict physical and spiritual injuries and yet fiercely opposed the idea of sacrifice. Schleef did not resort to ancient Greek theatre in order to construct and convey a new image of Greek culture or theatre, nor to emphasize its fundamental strangeness and inaccessibility. He did not attempt to topicalize it by making references to current social and political problems. For Schleef, the chorus was the indispensable condition of tragic theatre. This was what he strove for—in times that, unfortunately, had completely lost any sense of the tragic.

COMMUNITY CHORUS

While Schleef conceived his choric vision as a revival of tragic theatre in post-industrial societies, other directors and ensembles since the 1990s have been following in his footsteps to tackle more abstract subjects that reach far beyond the scope of individuals while still affecting them strongly, such as the financial crisis or the doping practices of professional athletes. In these cases, the language used mostly consists of ready-made, stereotypical formulations from the world of economics, finance, or sports management. Examples include Jossi Wieler's production of Elfriede Jelinek's *Wolken Heim* (*Home in the Clouds*, Deutsches Schauspielhaus Hamburg 1993), Christoph Marthaler's *Murx den Europäer! Murx ihn! Murx ihn ab!* (*Snuff the European!*, Volksbühne am Rosa-Luxemburg-Platz Berlin 1993), Volker Hesse's and Urs Widmer's *TOP DOGS* (Theater am Neumarkt, Zurich 1997), or Nicolas Stemann's production of Elfriede Jelinek's *Die Kontrakte des Kaufmanns* (*The Merchant's Contracts,* Thalia Theater Hamburg 2009).

These, in addition to many other productions since the 1990s, constitute a form of choric theatre that is far removed from the tragic. Instead, they are meant as searing critiques of late capitalist, post-industrial societies. The market and the Internet are condemned for having no need for individuals—of any particular identity—for wanting to create only consumers and surfers. Their purposes were best served by isolated conformists, people who unquestioningly complied with all rules and demands. Post-industrial societies, as presented and analysed in the choric theatre of the 1990s, seem to want to transform individuals who have proved resistant to new trends into conforming consumers and net users. Those who, for whatever reason, drop out of society are not regarded as victims, sacrificed on the altar of capitalism, globalization, and worldwide communication networks, but as faceless losers who could have performed better but did not want to. If they were unable to perform better, it was their fault alone. Performances of choric theatre in the 1990s deplored the fact that the utopian vision embodied in theatrical communities seemed to have disappeared from the agenda of modern Western societies in the same way as the idea of a tragic theatre.

In *The Mothers* Schleef had worked with choruses consisting of amateurs, migrant women from different cultures in which traditions of mourning and wailing are still alive. Thus, the spectators, mostly from the educated middle classes, were confronted with a particular marginalized group of society. In the first decade of the new millennium a new discourse on participatory democracy was launched, in which choric theatre reappeared in new forms and, once again, first through performances of Greek tragedies. The chorus served to place the marginalized at the centre and to give a voice to the voiceless, as Schleef had done in *The Mothers*. Volker Lösch in his production of the *Oresteia* (Staatsschauspiel Dresden 2003) invited unemployed people from Dresden to act as the chorus and Peter Sellars, in his *Children of Heracles* (Vienna Festival 2003), cast asylum-seekers as chorus members. In both cases, a certain ambiguity could not be avoided as the marginalized took their place centre stage. Yet, by being exposed to the gaze of the spectators, they were also exoticized at the same time.

This form of choric theatre was further developed and radicalized by the Viennese group Theatercombinat. In 2006, they staged *The Persians* in Geneva (Figure 19.1), which was redone with slight variations in Vienna the same year and in Braunschweig in 2008. It was no coincidence that the premiere took place in Geneva. In his *Letter to Monsieur d'Alembert* (1758), Jean-Jacques Rousseau passionately disputed d'Alembert's suggestion[19] that Geneva

---

[19] In d'Alembert (1757).

Erika Fischer-Lichte

Fig. 19.1. Claudia Bosse's *Persians*, Geneva, 2006. Courtesy Theatercombinat

required a theatre in order to keep up with other European cities. Rousseau's main argument was that a theatre would threaten, perhaps even destroy, the identity of Geneva's inhabitants. He placed theatre in opposition to the festival, in which the citizens turn themselves and their customs into a spectacle for their own enjoyment.[20] Referring indirectly to this argument, Theatercombinat aimed at staging the chorus songs of *The Persians* with 500 citizens of Geneva. Since representative democracy with its bureaucracy and non-transparent decision-making processes increasingly marginalizes all citizens, the question arose as to how to regain agency and to transform representative democracy into a participatory one.

In *The Persians* there were no seats in the auditorium, so that everybody could move through it freely. No separation occurred between the citizens who acted as chorus members and those who were spectators. The spectators moved among the chorus members without any resistance but also without the possibility of taking in the chorus as a single entity through a 'superior' perspective. In the final passage, the members of the wailing chorus held the text in their hands. The spectators could also take a copy or look over the shoulder of a chorus member to join the lament. It was up to each individual to participate in whatever way he or she liked—to join the speaking or singing chorus or to move through the space, listening and looking around. In this manner, the citizens together became the spectacle they themselves constituted. The community that came into being here could be regarded as a kind of swarm, a self-organizing collective that did not exert any pressure on its members and enabled everybody to include or exclude themselves.[21]

In recent years, other groups, such as Ligna in their so-called *Radio Ballets*, have been working with similar models without explicitly referring to Greek tragedy. This form of choric theatre allows for a kind of participation that, in stark contrast to the forms of audience participation prevalent in the 1960s and 1970s, does not manipulate or exert any power on the spectators but leaves it entirely up to them whether and in what way to participate. No rules determine anyone's inclusion or exclusion, allowing us to conclude that, even today, choric forms of theatre have the potential to realize utopian visions.

---

[20] Rousseau (1987).

[21] Regarding the phenomenon of swarms, see Granover (1973); Kelly (1994); also Rheingold (2003).

20

Chorus in Contemporary British Theatre

Helen Eastman

Britain's theatrical landscape has shifted radically in the late twentieth and early twenty-first centuries: British theatre, for centuries dominated by a textual tradition, has embraced new styles and methodologies of theatre-making, variously labelled 'physical theatre', 'ensemble theatre', or 'devised work'. Chorus, as a process and methodology, as well as a form, is at the heart of much of this work and its germination. For centuries British theatre has referred to the 'problem' of the chorus in staging Greek drama,[1] conjuring up images of static attitudinizing choruses, standing and chanting. Yet, never has chorus been less of a 'problem' for British theatre practitioners than now.

Chorus is the key theatrical component in a wide range of contemporary theatre works, extending far beyond versions of Greek drama. Some practitioners we will consider here have gone on to apply their own chorus techniques to tackling a Greek drama within their career; conversely, others have gone on to expand the choral elements of their work outside Greek drama after working on Greek choruses. Both of these narratives constitute a creative dialogue between classical reception and the broader theatrical landscape (and indeed wider communities, when we come to consider community choruses). This choral practice has largely been director-led and needs to be compared with contemporary British writers' responses to Greek tragedy in order to consider where 'physical theatre' and the textual tradition start to become more profoundly integrated.

The rise of physical theatre in Britain can be ascribed to a number of factors.[2] Many of today's key practitioners left the UK for Europe to train, either at the École Internationale de Théâtre Jacques Lecoq in Paris (innumerable examples would include Complicité's Simon McBurney, Theatre O's

---

[1] Goldhill (2007: 45) still describes it as an 'acute problem'.
[2] Struan Leslie, Head of Movement at the RSC from January 2009, provides an interesting insight into this shift: Leslie (2010: 411).

Joseph Alford, Told by an Idiot and Trestle's John Wright, Steven Berkoff, Toby Jones, Toby Sedgwick, The Clod Ensemble's Suzy Willson) or to spend time with East European ensembles (both Kneehigh's Emma Rice and Katie Mitchell spent time at Włodzimierz Staniewski's Gardzienice Centre for Theatre Practices in Poland[3]). They brought back to the UK new working practices, which have pervaded British theatre-making.

In the unique two-year physical training for actors that Lecoq developed for his school,[4] 'chorus' is a key component. The chorus work is not specific to Greek tragedy, though he acknowledges that he learnt and developed his pedagogy of chorus while working on the Greek chorus at Syracuse in Sicily;[5] exercises (many of which, such as 'balancing the space',[6] are now common-place in drama teaching) develop a group who can move as one body, like a flock of birds or shoal of fish, without one defined leader. These techniques have come to be used not just to create choruses but to underpin the way ensembles devise together: Simon McBurney, for example, uses these exercises extensively in morning warm-ups with Complicité. As important is the positive emphasis the Lecoq school puts on chorus work: 'The chorus is one of the most important components of my teaching method and, for those who have taken part in one, it is the most beautiful and the most moving dramatic experience.'[7] This attitude has contributed in Britain to a generation of theatre-makers who aspire to excellent chorus work, and use it as a creative process, as well as as an end.

It is important to make the distinction between chorus work, which is rooted in Lecoq's practice, and the choreographed chorus, which draws on the contemporary dance tradition. While many choreographers use improvisation in their process, the choreographed chorus predominantly arrives at a fixed performance, choreographed by an external individual, with aesthetic priorities, and a dance movement vocabulary. Lecoq's chorus trains to be able to work as one without an identified leader.[8] This means they can improvise within a scene (and indeed within a performance, essential for audience-interactive or site-specific work, as we will go on to discuss). This is not only empowering to the performers and their role in creating the piece of theatre; it can allow them to be continually responsive throughout performance. Though a decision may be taken to 'fix' the performance after a period of experimentation, equally the decision can be taken to leave space for ongoing improvisation. While the choreographed chorus is bound by its choreography and can

---

[3] For an introduction to Staniewski's chorus practice, see Zarifi (2010: 389 ff.).

[4] His pedagogic practice is recorded in his book *Le Corps poétique*, written with Jean-Gabriel Carasso and Jean-Claude Lallias (1997). It was translated into English by David Bradby in 2000, who titled the volume *The Moving Body*, though many of Lecoq's students use the phrase 'the poetic body' in English—for example, Willson and Fusetti (2002).

[5] Lecoq (2000: 139).   [6] Lecoq (2000: 141).

[7] Lecoq (2000: 139).   [8] Lecoq (2000: 140).

offer only a rehearsed response, the improvising chorus can continue to make active, group choices.[9] Moreover, chorus as a rehearsal technique can become invaluable to experimentation and devising, whether or not it manifests in the final performance, both to allow a group to play together in the rehearsal room within a scene without external instruction, or just to develop a company's ability to work together and be highly responsive to one another.

The influence of Lecoq's poetics of the body on British theatre cannot be underestimated;[10] the basic concepts of his pedagogy have now become part of the curriculum for most British drama training. Twenty years ago 'acting' classes at the key institutions (for example, the London Academy of Music and Dramatic Art[11]) were almost entirely based on the principles of Stanislawski (filtered through Drama Centre in the 1960s), taking an essentially psychological approach; now 'physical theatre' techniques, based on Lecoq's principles, are taught alongside. Different schools give them vastly different weight in the syllabus, but all graduating actors would be expected to have some physical theatre training. Schools entirely devoted to his teaching practice have now been established in London (for example, the London International School of Performing Arts), as have graduate courses that explore group-devising techniques that draw on his practice.[12] Even within secondary education in the British school system, teachers are using these methodologies to engage classes of young people and empower them to create theatre. Many warm-ups for actors across all kinds of productions use Lecoq's choral techniques to get a company of actors ready for the working day, without any reference to Greek drama.

In 2010 when asked to work on a Greek tragedy with second-year students at the Royal Academy of Dramatic Art (RADA) across the course of a term, I was aware that the principal's intention in putting this back into the syllabus (Greek tragedy had been absent for some time, in favour of studying the Jacobeans at this point in training) was only partly about teaching students about Greek tragedy; the more important goal was getting them to develop their skills in chorus and ensemble work. I was effectively showing them how to apply skills they had been developing in movement classes to an actual play. British actors now graduate with the skill-set for working on choruses, though it may not have been linked with Greek drama in their training.

---

[9] This polarization of choreographed and improvising chorus is obviously blurred by the work of some practitioners who are now blending these traditions in their process.

[10] For an interesting discussion on this topic, see Willson and Fusetti (2002: 93 ff.).

[11] For an overview of Higher Education vocational drama training in the UK, start with the Conference of Drama Schools website www.drama.ac.uk (accessed 14 January 2013).

[12] The most established of these is probably the Advanced Theatre Practice MA at the Central School of Speech and Drama, from which many practitioners have gone on to form their own devising companies.

Certain artistic directors have had key roles to play in the paradigm shift in British theatre towards devised physical theatre. A notable example is Tom Morris, who, as artistic director of Battersea Arts Centre from 1995 to 2004, established, with creative producer David Jubb, the 'scratch' process of developing new work (the term is now used industry-wide);[13] and has taken many of its principles with him through his moves to the National Theatre (as Associate Director) and on to the Bristol Old Vic (where he is currently Artistic Director). Battersea Arts Centre, in this period, developed the work of many devising companies (for example, the Gecko Theatre Company, led by Amit Lahav, who cites Lecoq as a major influence; the David Glass Ensemble; Told by an Idiot). Venues such as the Lyric Hammersmith and the Barbican have championed the programming of work by devising physical theatre ensembles, such as Frantic Assembly and Complicité, and, outside London, venues such as the Unity (Liverpool), the Met (Bury), the Centre for Performance Research (Cardiff), the Unity (Glasgow), and the Lowry and Contact (Manchester) have nurtured such work. Fuel Theatre became the first company of creative producers to be funded by the Arts Council in 2004 to provide production support to emerging ensembles and collectives.

In emphasizing the European training influence, we would be wrong to neglect the influence of left-wing, political companies in Britain in the 1960s and 1970s (for example, Welfare State International, 7:84[14]), which drew on traditional British, populist theatre techniques and saw the company ensemble, non-hierarchical structure as politically important. These companies paved the way for artists to form collaborative ensembles outside the mainstream and make work in unusual spaces, particularly bringing work closer to communities (performances in village halls and reclamation of public spaces) and celebrating non-naturalistic form and total theatre.

This combination of factors has produced a generation of physical theatre ensembles throughout the UK at every scale and stage of the industry. Most of these companies are using chorus techniques within their devising process, whether or not it is manifest in the end performances. Where it is manifest, there are examples where a defined chorus is created and maintained throughout a piece, and examples where moments of chorality are fleetingly seen within the overall dynamics of the performance. It is worth pausing to clarify the use of the terms 'ensemble', 'chorus', and also 'chorality' and 'choral'. I use

---

[13] 'Scratch' performances are where work in progress is shown to an audience, for feedback. Many projects were developed in this way at Battersea Arts Centre: a devising process would take place in the rehearsal room, a section of work would be shown to an audience, then the piece would be reworked and further developed. The idea was to integrate audiences into the developmental process of theatre. It is a practice that has proliferated and this term is now widely used.

[14] Kneehigh cites Footsbarn and Welfare State International as important influences on their early site-specific work (Wildworks has now broken away from Kneehigh to continue this).

'ensemble' to refer to the entire company that is performing in a show where there is a focus on group movement and absence of company hierarchy (and to refer to certain theatre companies that work in this way, many of whom, like The Clod Ensemble, use the word in their name). I use 'chorus' to refer to a group on stage working as one unit, bound by either shared movement, voice, characterization, or text, where they represent not individual characters but a group. I would not necessarily define a crowd as a chorus, though it can be.[15] Where there are elements of a piece of theatre that seem to draw on chorus techniques and processes, but do not result in a fully realized chorus, I may use the adjective 'choral', or discuss the elements of 'chorality' in the work. While this is obviously not definitive, I believe this terminology would be recognized and understood by the majority of practitioners. Let us take, for example, Declan Donellan's recent production of *Macbeth* for Cheek by Jowl (2010). He used the *ensemble* continually to create the visual dynamics of the piece (his actors were effectively his set, creating spatial dimensions to scenes) and that exhibited elements of *chorality*, but it was when he used the whole company, together, to play the witches, that he actually created a *chorus*. These labels are not always clear cut. When Shared Experience ensembles use their trademark technique of the whole company physically performing a scene change, has the ensemble momentarily become a chorus?

In a production where members of the ensemble play protagonist roles, but come in and out of the chorus, or join the chorus when their character is not 'on' (increasingly popular as it both expands the chorus size and gives a more equal relationship between all actors in the company[16]), I believe 'ensemble' would refer to the whole cast, 'chorus' would describe those functioning in the ascribed role of the chorus at any given moment. When an actor moves between playing a protagonist and joining the chorus, it can, in the transition, highlight the differing nature of group and individual identity, as the actor subjugates himself to the group. With many ensembles embracing the 'poor theatre' aesthetic, we are rarely, when watching physical theatre, working within the realms of Naturalism or Realism,[17] which means that, far from being asked to suspend disbelief when we see an actor make this transition, we are deliberately shown the exposed mechanics of the theatrical transition; drawing our attention to the different dramaturgical nature of the individual and the chorus (and the boundaries of both) in this way can become in itself a part of the thematic exploration into communality.

---

[15] Lecoq's comments on the difference are particularly useful at Lecoq (2000: 138).

[16] A good recent example would be Lucy Pittman Wallace's production of Seamus Heaney's *Burial at Thebes: A Version of Antigone* for Nottingham Playhouse (2005).

[17] A counter-example might be Katie Mitchell's *Iphigenia at Aulis* and *Trojan Women* at the National Theatre (2004, 2007), which maintained, and experimented with, elements of the fourth wall.

Fig. 20.1. Chorus of Berkoff's *Messiah*, 2003. Photographer: Geraint Lewis

The full-blown choruses that have grown out of this moment in British theatre have a relationship with Greek drama's dramaturgical structures, while often extending the possibilities of the form. Foley Sherman argues that Steven Berkoff (Lecoq trained), who has, throughout a long career, developed his notion of chorus in both Greek and non-Greek productions, lays the ground-work for the surge of physical theatre in the 1980s in London, and Berkoff's influence on the emergence of physical theatre should not be overlooked. Foley Sherman (another Lecoq graduate incidentally) makes an interesting examination of Berkoff's chorus trajectory from his *Agamemnon* (1973) to his final *Coriolanus* (1996);[18] Berkoff sustains throughout his career a commit-ment to 'rigorously trained ensembles executing exaggerated and precise movement sequences...coordinated speech and movement of unnamed characters',[19] whether or not the story he is tackling originates in a dramatur-gical form that includes chorus. For example, Berkoff saw chorus as the heart of his *Coriolanus*: 'My chorus for *Coriolanus* will be all men, a combination of soldiers, rebels, citizens, servants and messengers. A team will evolve like a *corps de ballet* and that is what it shall be . . . the heart of the produc-tion.' For me, the chorus of Berkoff's *Messiah* (2001) (Figure 20.1), which radically split critics, best exemplified the prodigious physical skill of his

---

[18] Berkoff first directed *Coriolanus* for New York Public Theatre (1988), then revisited it in Munich (1991), and then Leeds (1995) with himself in the title role.

[19] Foley Sherman (2010: 232).

choruses; they played a range of groups, including Roman centurions, Christ's disciples, Palestine's Jews, and morphed between them, defining each new group identity with their physicality. Again, the meta-theatrical questions about communality and group identity are posed by one group of actors embodying each of these conflicting groups and defining them through corporeal changes to the body; here, it is implied that in each body there is the corporeal potential to be part of any one of these conflicting ethnic groups.

Another (non-Greek) recent chorus that posed different questions about the form was Emma Rice's Chorus of the Unloved in Kneehigh's *Tristan and Yseult*,[20] described by Emma Rice as Cornwall's 'greatest and oldest story'. Rice comments:

The chorus took us through the piece, a band of 'love-spotters', the unloved. These are the people who look on in life, who are not chosen to play the starring role—these are at the heart of this production, because, if we have all known love, we have also known the opposite.[21]

This chorus comprised anorak-clad bird-spotters, watching the world through their binoculars (Figure 20.2). Lyn Gardner in the *Guardian* commented on how important they were, tonally, to the piece, 'because what could so easily just be all hearts and flowers becomes something much tougher, far more moving'.[22] The chorus grew out of the company's devising and storytelling style, to which both ensemble and chorus are fundamental. They have some formal debt to Greek tragedy, though the work is not related thematically or in content to Greek drama. Interestingly, they are not united by place, religion, or ethnicity, in terms of their group identity, but by an emotional experience—being 'unloved', an interesting comment on what can create and define commonality. When Tristan and Yseult joined the chorus, donning their trademark balaclavas at the end of the production, we understood that this was a community to which all of us, at some point in our lives, may well belong.

This chorus is typical of Rice and Kneehigh's work and style, and it was subsequent to this that Emma Rice moved on to tackle her first Greek myth, in a version of Euripides' *Bacchae* (2004[23]), using a skill set in chorus work thoroughly developed outside the *œuvre* of Greek tragedy and then applying it to it. The chorus members of her *Bacchae* were burly men, in tutus; the company certainly faced no 'problem' in using this element of the Greek

---

[20] Premiered at the Restormel Castle in Lostwithiel (2003) before transferring to the National Theatre (2005).

[21] Emma Rice's comments on the 2012 production taken from the Kneehigh website <www.kneehigh.co.uk> (accessed 14 January 2013).

[22] Lyn Gardner, reviewing in the *Guardian*, Thursday, 14 April 2005.

[23] *Tristan and Yseult* premiered in 2003 (see n. 20). Rice then worked on *The Bacchae* in 2004, before returning to work on *Tristan and Yseult* for the National Theatre transfer in 2005.

Fig. 20.2. Kneehigh's Chorus of the Unloved from *Tristan and Yseult,* 2004

form, as it was already a core part of its theatrical vocabulary. Reversing the narrative, we can see examples of practitioners who have developed their understanding of chorus directing Greek texts and then gone on to apply it to other work. Katie Mitchell's extensive work on Greek tragedy, in collaboration with movement director Struan Leslie, in her *Oresteia, Iphigenia at Aulis,* and *Trojan Women* at the National Theatre (2000, 2004, 2007), has clearly influenced the chorality of her later non-Greek theatre (and opera) productions and her collaborations with movement director Joseph Alford.

I discussed Rice's Chorus of the Unloved, at length, with Anthony Shuster, who played Tristan in the performances at the Minack Theatre, and one of the Chorus of the Unloved in the performances at the National Theatre, about the balance of individualism and uniformity in this chorus, which seemed to allow space for individual personalities but never to lose its choral identity. One of the things he flagged up was the importance of 'clown' in the creative process (again, in Lecoq's sense of the word). 'Clown' follows on from 'chorus' in Lecoq's pedagogic process and it is interesting to see the combination of techniques here. Although group decisions had been made about how the 'Unloved' might speak or move, it was then applied and nuanced with reference to the individual actor within the chorus: for example, all of the Unloved had timid and slightly grating voices, but his was a timid, grating, northern voice because it picked up on (and exaggerated) his own northern roots. Rice's chorus invites us to consider the balance of individuality to uniformity that can exist within a chorus before it ceases to be a chorus and becomes a group of individuals. Much of my own choral experimentation has explored the tension between individuality and uniformity: what tensions are created when one aspect of dramaturgy (voice *or* physicality *or* intention) unites us as a group, but another maintains individuality?[24] I heed Lecoq's warning against too much uniformity: 'There is always the risk of ending up with a militarized chorus, over-disciplined, clean and neat, in which everyone marches lifeless together.'[25]

When Suzy Willson created *The Red Ladies*,[26] she deliberately cast thirty women of different ages, ethnicities, and theatrical backgrounds and then clad them identically. She drew on the unique potential of the non-choreographed chorus to move as one without a leader to send her chorus onto the streets to interact with audiences, improvise, and respond to interventions. In a theatrical culture where site-specific work, guerrilla theatre, happenings, and audience interaction are extending ideas of what theatre can be and where theatre can take place, this process of creating a chorus allowed chorus work to take place in unrehearsed and unmediated scenarios. My production of Seamus Heaney's *Cure at Troy*, which between 1999 and 2005 toured to wildly different spaces, from the bankside at Deptford to the Theatre at Delphi, worked on the basis that the chorus had to be trained to move, think, respond together, and maintain its group identity in performance without inflexible choreography, to allow the chorus members to work freely, cohesively, and instinctively in innumerable different spaces (and, on one possibly misguided occasion, in promenade). We celebrated how empowering it was for a chorus to go on stage knowing it could make a collective decision in the moment without discussion. I have continued to use the same chorus techniques with most companies of actors I have worked with, regardless of whether chorus work will be a part of the end performance, because that ability to respond as a group, whatever happens in a live performance scenario, is invaluable.

---

[24] For experimentation with these ideas I thank the various casts of my production of Seamus Heaney's *Cure at Troy*, the Live Canon ensemble, the RADA students with whom I worked on *Alcestis*, and the cast of the 2010 Cambridge Greek Play, *Agamemnon*.

[25] Lecoq (2000: 141).

[26] I discuss this production in depth with Suzy Willson in Willson and Eastman (2010: 420 ff.).

However this proliferation of chorus as a process has clearly been director-led. Often texts have been used and edited according to the needs of the process (Katie Mitchell with Don Taylor's translations), collated in the devising process (Suzy Willson's use of found texts), used predominantly as inspiration (Complicité), created in the process (Kneehigh's use of multiple writers within the company), or created by the director (Steven Berkoff). The integration of text and physical theatre is a wider challenge in contemporary theatre, and there are many companies working to progress this (for example, the collaboration between Frantic Assembly's choreographers and writer Abi Morgan, well exemplified in their recent *Love Story* (Lyric Hammersmith, 2012)).

There is a different narrative to explore when we come to look at writers' responses to the chorus in the same period. Some prominent recent versions of Greek tragedy have either just written the chorus out or replaced it with a number of individual characters. Glyn Maxwell's recent *After Troy* (Oxford Playhouse, 2010), a version of Euripides' *Trojan Women* and *Hecuba*, implied an offstage chorus of women, but they did not appear on stage. Elements of the chorus's role were there in the songs and movement of the protagonists, their lyricism, some offstage singing, but there was no physical chorus on stage. Martin Crimp's *Cruel and Tender* (Young Vic, 2004) replaced the chorus with three individually named women in the Queen's entourage. When questioned about this choice during a talk at the Archive of Performances of Greek and Roman Drama (APGRD) at the University of Oxford, he commented: 'There's an absence of communality in Western European culture. Therefore what can chorus mean?'

It strikes me that exploring a chorus on stage is an excellent way to start to interrogate the nature of communality in Western Europe and what chorus 'can mean'; turning a chorus into three individuals sidesteps the question (I say that while believing it to be a politically brilliant play; it just ducks out on exploring any form of communality). While exploring chorus with a group of young people, between the ages of 15 and 18, in an outreach project in North London in 2006 on behalf of the Almeida Theatre entitled *Revolutionary Stages*, I discovered they felt themselves very much part of identifiable groups and communities: the conflict, and dramatic potential, was in the number of different communities—their family, their ethnicity, their religion, their friendship group—to which they felt beholden. Rather than an absence of communality, they were negotiating a plethora of competing communalities.

For British writers, there has been a struggle with finding an authentic British voice for writing and translating chorus. Many versions of Greek tragedy since the mid-1990s have tried to find a choral voice by revisiting the oral, musical, or ritualistic discourse of their indigenous cultures. The South African Farber Foundry's *Molora, a Version of the Oresteia* (2007) used a deeply traditional, rural Xhosa aesthetic; a number of Irish productions have turned to traditional Irish folk. British productions have struggled to find that authentic oral culture (few turning to the English folk tradition) and have often culturally 'borrowed' (I am thinking of the plethora of Greek tragedy productions with Balkan music for the chorus). Our traditional religious culture gives us Christian liturgy, and, while gospel has been used to give the chorus voice in a number of productions, perhaps most recently and notably David Greig's *Bacchae* for the National Theatre of Scotland (2008), that is, again, an imported, this time American, tradition.

There has also been a struggle, throughout the twentieth century, to find performable verse forms into which to translate Greek drama. David Wiles, in his survey of a number of twentieth-century translations, alludes to T. S. Eliot's claim that verse translators fail to escape associations with Shakespeare, whose iambic line defined verse drama, making everything subsequent feel archaic by association. He says of Ranjit Bolt's translations (which have frequently been used by the National Theatre): 'Rhyme failed to save Bolt's text from the danger that Eliot identified: redundant historical baggage—a problem that applies most emphatically to southern English actors and writers using a globalized R.P.'[27]

Perhaps the greatest success in writing performable lyric chorus that has escaped this baggage has come in the last two decades from a trio of writers who have all used their authentic northern English (Lancashire and Yorkshire) voices: Tony Harrison, Ted Hughes, and Blake Morrison (connected in that they have all had versions of Greek drama premiered by the northern voice ensemble Northern Broadsides).[28] They have combined their northern diction with pre-Shakespearian Anglo-Saxon verse forms.[29] Harrison and Morrison have, particularly, engaged with the oral dialect poetry tradition of Yorkshire and Lancashire in the eighteenth and nineteenth centuries[30] and, in this, found an authentic English oral, communal, tradition to draw on.

Tony Harrison, the pioneer of northern dialect Greek drama, wanted to reclaim Greek drama from RP, from the establishment, the educational elite, and the London stages and return it to the popular theatre, while asserting his right to write in his authentic voice and to give that voice to kings and gods, not just comedy servants. Yet alongside this political agenda was a *theatrical*

---

[27] Wiles (2005: 10).

[28] Northern Broadsides is a Halifax-based theatre company, founded in 1992 by Barrie Rutter to perform classic theatre repertoire in the actors' native northern accents. While it is a stretch to say that Hughes is using dialect, as a Yorkshireman he bequeathed his final play, *Alcestis*, to Northern Broadsides for posthumous production, saying his 'tuning fork' had always been in the Calder Valley. It was, as he intentioned, premiered in broad northern accents at the Viaduct Theatre, Halifax, in 2000.

[29] For example, Morrison uses a ten-syllable pentameter, with two stresses either side of the caesura, which is akin to northern alliterative poetry of the Middle Ages.

[30] A good starting place for exploring this poetic culture is Hollingsworth (1982).

passion to write text that demanded to be performed with the physical energy of the Greek (he works from the original Greek):

As a Northerner I am drawn to the physicality of Aeschylus's language. I relish its cragginess and momentum. At school I was never allowed to read verse out loud because of my Yorkshire accent. They said I was a barbarian, not fit to recite the treasures of our culture. And while my translation of Aeschylus isn't what you could call a deliberate revenge, it is most emphatically a rediscovery of the dignity of the accent.[31]

Stephe Harrop's study of physical performance and the language of translation examines the changes required in the body and the breath to perform northern dialect verse with more short vowels, more explosive consonants, and concludes that it necessitates a more dynamic, muscular, physical performance.[32] In contrast to many directors' experiments with physical chorus, which have subjugated text, here is a writer creating a text that demands a certain level of physical engagement from its performers.

At the heart of Harrison's work was the desire for an audience to hear its own community's voice or accent, reflected on the stage, to explore the communality of language between performer and audience:

It seemed to me that the common language was used in the theatre. It has to be in the theatre, the common bond of the theatre, especially in Greek theatre where the audience and the actor were lit by the common light of the sun, that this was ideal conditions to create a common language.[33]

This desire to reflect a community back upon itself in a chorus is taken one stage further when the members of the community are themselves invited to form the chorus on stage.

The 'community chorus', as it is currently termed in theatre practice, is a chorus composed of amateur actors, taken from an actual community with which a production wants to engage. There can be multiple intentions for this: a theatre wanting to engage with its neighbours in a participatory way; a theatre wanting to involve young people (or another demographic); a production wanting an authenticity to the community it portrays; an exploration into the nature of community itself; and perhaps there should be a cynical fifth—a cheap way to recruit a large chorus.

The first impulse was excellently exemplified by the recent Royal Opera House's *The Purfleet Opera: Ludd and Isis* project (2010). Upon building a large new production park at Thurrock that was going to dominate the town,

---

[31] *Sunday Times*, 29 November 1981.
[32] Harrop (2010: 235).
[33] Tony Harrison being interviewed by John Tusa for Radio 3. There is an audio recording at <http://www.bbc.co.uk/radio3/johntusainterview/harrison_transcript.shtml> (accessed 14 January 2012).

the company thought the best way to engage with its new neighbours was to invite them to create and participate in an opera about their own community. Crucially, many of the local people's stories were integrated into Stephen Plaice's libretto alongside its driving mythology. Involving a community chorus is often as much about recording and celebrating the oral stories of a marginalized community. The recent *Pandora* (Arcola Theatre, 2010) inter-wove the stories of members of the local Hackney community, and children from the area, with the Pandora myth. Interviews with the original contribu-tors were shown within the performance, creating a multimedia community chorus on television screens.

The recent *100% London* project at Hackney Empire (2012, created by the company Rimini Protokoll) gathered 100 people on stage who exactly repre-sented the demographic of London in percentages (according to age, ethnicity, marital status, home status, income bracket, and so on). The production then used these 100 Londoners to create a whole range of striking aesthetic illus-trations of the statistics the group represented, moving on to separating the 100 in response to challenging questions, experiences, and opinions. Not only was it visually stunning and highly entertaining; it was also a fascinating study in the relationship between individuality and chorality. The nature of the project demonstrated the differences within the community we might label 'London', yet, for me, the 100 people on stage never ceased to be a chorus throughout the duration of the performance. It was a remarkable affirmation that individuality within a chorus can coexist with commonality. On a larger scale, the integration of 20,000 volunteers into Danny Boyle's Olympic opening ceremony (London, 2012) may be the largest display of a community chorus performing a construction of national British identity that we are likely to see.

In the inaugural Sheffield Festival of Ancient Drama in 2012, Helen Slaney used a local community chorus from Sheffield in her *Prometheus*. Given that the original Greek chorus members were drawn from the community, and the experience of being involved in a theatrical production was a part of one's civic education, the inclusion of the community as chorus in contemporary pro-ductions may be seen as a cyclical return to the idea of theatrical participation as a civic act. It is not just a reflection on what we mean by community, it is a participatory act defining community.

Looking at contemporary British chorus work since the 1990s, we see three narratives drawing together. The first is the work of British directors, which has, over those twenty years, become increasingly dominated by Lecoq-style chorus practice as both a process and an end-form. Chorus is being widely used in theatre as an invaluable and enabling technique, not just in Greek drama; and we have a graduating generation of actors confident with chorus work, though not necessarily having linked it to Greek tragedy in their practice. We see the potential of the non-choreographed chorus to participate in improvised, site-specific, and interactive work. The second is the work of writers looking for a verse form in which to render Greek drama performable and for an authentic communal voice, rooted in an oral verse tradition. This has predominantly been found outside RP and engaged non-London, non-RP audiences with Greek drama as a popular rather than academic form. The third is the interaction with actual communities in community theatre, outreach, youth theatre, and participatory projects. All these broaden the reach and relevance of classical drama and reception in contemporary British theatre.

It seems British theatre has never been more equipped or able to deliver fully the chorus in a probing, dynamic, progressive, and theatrical way. Metatheatrical questioning of the very nature or validity of chorus invites us to ask essential questions about our notions of commonality and community and the relationship between the individual and the group. I end with a quote from Lecoq that cuts to the heart of that tension:

To speak through another's mouth, in a common choral voice, is to be, at one and the same time, grounded in the truth of a living character, and in touch with a dimension which transcends human reality. All of the actor's art is needed to establish a connecting link between these two apparently contradictory poles rather than being torn apart.[34]

Moreover, negotiating between the contradictory poles of individuality and chorality is both a theatrical and a social challenge; our continuing engagement with classical texts and the dramaturgy of the chorus is poised to form an ongoing part of our exploration of that tension.

---

[34] Lecoq (2000: 135).

References

Abbate, C. (1989). 'Wagner, "On Modulation", and *Tristan*', *Cambridge Opera Journal*, 1: 33–58.

Adam, J. (1902). *The Republic of Plato*. Cambridge.

Adler, T. (2005). 'Fissures beneath the Surface: Drama in the 1940s and 1950s', in D. Krasner (ed.), *A Companion to Twentieth-Century American Drama*. Oxford, 159–74.

Adorno, T. W. (2005). *In Search of Wagner*, trans. R. Livingstone. London and New York.

Allison, J. W. (1997). 'Homeric Allusions at the Close of Thucydides' Sicilian Narrative', *American Journal of Philology*, 118: 499–516.

Alonge, M. (2005). *The Palaikastro Hymn and the Modern Myth of Cretan Zeus* <http://www.princeton.edu/~pswpc/papers/authorAL/alonge/alonge.html> (accessed 11 January 2013).

Anon. (1920). *Das Deutsche Theater*, booklet of Deutsches Theater. Berlin.

Anon. (1934). *Deutsche Bühnenkorrespondenz*, cited in R. Stommer, *Die inszenierte Volksgemeinschaft. Die 'Thing-Bewegung' im Dritten Reich*. Marburg, 1985, 73.

Anon. (2006). *La Tragedie mahommetiste où l'on peut voir et remarquer l'infidélité commise par Mahumet, fils ayné du Roy des Othomans nomme Amurat, à l'endroit d'un sien amy et son fidelle serviteur, lequel Mahumet pour seul jouir de l'Empire fit tuer son petit frère par ce fidèle ami, et comment il le livra en la puissance de sa mère pour en prendre vengeance, chose de grande cruauté* [Rouen, 1612], in C. Biet (ed.), *Théâtre de la cruauté et récits sanglants en France (XVIe–XVIIe siècle)*. Paris, 603–43.

Armstrong, R. (2005). *A Compulsion for Antiquity: Freud and the Ancient World*. Ithaca, NY.

Aronson, A. (2000). 'American Theatre in Context: 1945—Present', in D. W. Wilmeth and C. Bigsby (eds), *The Cambridge History of American Theatre*. Cambridge, iii. 87–162.

Ast, F. (1808). *Grundriss der Philologie*. Landshut.

Athanassaki, L., and Bowie, E. (2011) (eds). *Archaic and Classical Choral Song: Performance, Politics and Dissemination*. Berlin.

Bacon, H. (1995). 'The Chorus in Greek Life and Drama', *Arion*, 3: 6–24.

Bagordo, A. (1998). *Die antiken Traktate über das Drama (mit einer Sammlung der Fragmente)*. Stuttgart and Leipzig.

Banducci, A. (1993). 'Staging a *tragédie en musique*: A 1748 Promptbook of Campra's *Tancrède*', *Early Music*, 21: 180–90.

Barker, A. (1984). *Greek Musical Writings*. Cambridge, vols i and ii.

Barone, P. (2004). *Schiller und die Tradition des Erhabenen*. Berlin.

Bartlet, M. E. C. (1992). 'The New Repertory at the Opéra during the Reign of Terror: Revolutionary Rhetoric and Operatic Consequences', in M. Boyd (ed.), *Music and the French Revolution*. Cambridge, 107–56.

Barton, C. (2002). 'Being in the Eyes: Shame and Sight in Ancient Rome', in D. Fredrick (ed.), *The Roman Gaze: Vision, Power and the Body*. Baltimore, 216–35.

Bartsch, S. (1994). *Actors in the Audience*. Cambridge, MA.

Battezzato, L. (2005). 'The New Music of the *Trojan Women*', *Lexis*, 23: 73–104.

Bauman, T., and McClymonds, M. P. (1995) (eds). *Opera and the Enlightenment*. Cambridge.

Baur, D. (1999). *Der Chor im Theater des 20. Jahrhunderts: Typologie des theatralen Mittels Chor*. Tübingen.

Beacham, R. (1999). *Spectacle Entertainments of Early Imperial Rome*. New Haven.

Beaumarchais, P., and Condorcet, J. (1785) (eds). *Œuvres complètes de Voltaire*. Kehl.

Beaumont, C. W. (1944). *The Ballet Called* Giselle. London.

Becker, H. (1981) (ed.). *Quellentexte zur Konzeption der europäischen Oper im 17. Jahrhundert*. Kassel.

Beckman, W. (1999). *Marx, the Young Hegelians and the Origins of Radical Social Theory: Dethroning the Self*. Cambridge.

Belfiore, E. (1984). 'A Theory of Imitation in Plato's *Republic*', *Transactions and Proceedings of the American Philological Association*, 114: 121–46.

Belfiore, E. (2006). 'Dancing with the Gods: The Myth of the Chariot in Plato's *Phaedrus*', *American Journal of Philology*, 127: 185–217.

Bell, C. (1919). *The New Republic*, 30 July: 415.

Benjamin, W. (1968 [1936]). 'The Work of Art in the Age of Mechanical Reproduction', in *Illuminations: Essays and Reflections*, ed. with intr. by H. Arendt, trans. H. Zohn. New York, 217–51.

Bennett, W. C. (1850). *Poems*. London.

Benton, C. (2002). 'Split Vision: The Politics of the Gaze in Seneca's *Troades*', in D. Fredrick (ed.), *The Roman Gaze: Vision, Power and the Body*. Baltimore, 31–56.

Bernot, D., and Cazeneuve, J. (1963). *Dances sacrées: Égypte ancienne, Israel, Islam, Asie centrale, Inde, Cambodge, Bali, Java, Chine, Japon*. Sources orientales, 6. Paris.

Betzwieser, T. (2000). 'Musical Setting and Scenic Movement: Chorus and "chœur dansé" in Eighteenth-Century Parisian Opéra', *Cambridge Opera Journal*, 12: 1–28.

Bierl, A. (2001). *Der Chor in der Alten Komödie: Ritual und Performativität (unter besonderer Berücksichtigung von Aristophanes' Thesmophoriazusen und der Phalloslieder fr. 851 PMG)*. Munich.

Bierl, A. (2009a). *Ritual and Performativity: The Chorus in Old Comedy*, trans. A. Hollmann. Washington.

Bierl, A. (2009b). 'Der neue Sappho-Papyrus aus Köln und Sapphos Erneuerung: Virtuelle Choralität, Eros, Tod, Orpheus und Musik' online at: <http://chs.harvard.edu/wa/pageR?tn=ArticleWrapper&bdc=12&mn=2122> (accessed 12 January 2013).

Bierl, A. (2011). 'Alcman at the End of Aristophanes' *Lysistrata*: Ritual Interchorality', in L. Athanassaki and E. Bowie (eds), *Archaic and Classical Choral Song: Performance, Politics and Dissemination*. Berlin, 415–36.

Biet, C. (1994). *Oedipe en monarchie: tragédie et théorie juridique à l'âge classique*. Paris.

Biet, C. (2006) (ed.). *Théâtre de la cruauté et récits sanglants en France (XVIe–XVIIe siècle)*. Paris.

Billings, J. (2013). 'Choral Dialectics: Hölderlin and Hegel', in R. Gagné and M. Hopman (eds), *Choral Mediations in Greek Drama*. Cambridge, 317–38.

Billings, J. (forthcoming). *The Genealogy of the Tragic: Greek Tragedy and German Philosophy*. Princeton.

Bloch, M. (1974). 'Symbols, Songs, Dance and Features of Articulation: Is Religion a Form of Traditional Authority?', *Archives Européennes Sociologiques*, 15: 55–81. Republished in M. Bloch, *Ritual, History and Power: Selected Papers in Anthropology*. London, 1989, 19–45.

Boeckh, A. (1808). *Graecae tragoediae principum, Aeschyli, Sophoclis, Euripidis, num ea, quae supersunt, et genuina omnia sint, et forma primitive servata, an eorum familiis aliquid debeat ex iis tribui*. Heidelberg.

Boeckh, A. (1843). *Des Sophokles Antigone griechisch und deutsch, herausgegeben von August Boeckh, nebst zwei Abhandlungen über diese Tragödie im Ganzen und über einzelne Stellen derselben*. Berlin.

Boeckh, A. (1874 [1843]). 'De primis in Sophoclis Oedipo Coloneo canticis', in F. Acherson, E. Bratuschek, and P. Eichholtz (eds), *August Boeckh's Gesammelte Kleine Schriften*. Leipzig, iv. 527–33.

Boeckh, A. (1877). *Encyclopädie und Methodologie der Philologischen Wissenschaften*, ed. Ernst Bratuschek. Leipzig.

Boetius, S. (2005). *Die Wiedergeburt der griechischen Tragödie auf der Bühne des 19. Jahrhunderts: Bühnenfassungen mit Schauspielmusik*. Tübingen.

Bonifazi, A. (2001). *Mescolare un cratere di canti: Pragmatica della poesia epinicia in Pindaro*. Alessandria.

Bosher, K., Macintosh, F., McConnell, J., and Rankine P. (2014) (eds). *Oxford Handbook to Greek Drama in the Americas*. Oxford.

Bouteille-Meister, C. (2011). 'Représenter le présent: Formes et fonctions de "l'actualité" dans le théâtre d'expression française à l'époque des conflits religieux (1554–1629)'. Unpublished thesis, Paris.

Bowie, E. (2006). 'Choral Performances', in D. Konstan and S. Said (eds), *Greeks on Greekness: Viewing the Greek Past under the Roman Empire*. Supplement to the Proceedings of the Cambridge Philological Society. Cambridge, 61–92.

Bowra, C. M. (1962). *Primitive Song*. London.

Boyle, N. (2000). *Goethe: The Poet and the Age*: ii. *Revolution and Renunciation, 1790–1803*. Oxford.

Boym, S. (2002). *The Future of Nostalgia*. New York.

Bradley, A. C. (1904). *Shakespearian Tragedy*. London.

Bradley, A. C. (1909). 'Hegel's Theory of Tragedy', in *Oxford Lectures on Poetry*. London, 69–98.

Bradley, L. (2006). *Brecht and Political Theatre: The Mother on Stage*. Oxford.

Braulich, H. (1969). *Max Reinhardt: Theater zwischen Traum und Wirklichkeit*. Berlin.

Brecht, B. (1988–2000). *Bertolt Brecht, Grosse kommentierte Berliner und Frankfurter Ausgabe*, ed. W. Hecht et al. 30 vols. Berlin and Frankfurt am Main.

Brécy, R. (1991). *La Chanson de la commune: Chansons et poèmes inspirés par la Commune de 1871*. Paris.

Brelich, A. (1969). *Paides e parthenoi*. Rome.

Bremer, J. M. (2000). 'Der dithyrambische Agon: Ein kompetitiver Gottesdienst oder gar keiner?', in A. Bagordo and B. Zimmermann (eds), *Bakchylides: 100 Jahre nach seiner Wiederentdeckung*. Munich, 59–67.

Bremmer, J. N. (1998). '"Religion", "Ritual" and the Opposition "Sacred vs. Profane": Notes towards a Terminological Genealogy', in F. Graf (ed.), *Ansichten griechischer Rituale: Geburtstags-Symposium für Walter Burkert*. Stuttgart and Leipzig, 9–32.

Brenet, M. (1884). *Grétry: Sa Vie et ses œuvres*. Paris.

Bryer, J. R., and Davison, R. A. (2005) (eds). *The Art of the American Musical*. New Brunswick, NJ.

Brisson, L., and Pradeau, J.-F. (2007). *Les Lois de Platon*. Paris.

Brockhaus, F. A. (1809). *Conversations-Lexicon*. Leipzig.

Brown, B. A. (1991). *Gluck and the French Theatre in Vienna*. Oxford.

Brown, J. (1763). *A Dissertation on the Rise, Union, and Power: The Progressions, Separations, and Corruptions of Poetry and Music*. London.

Brown, P., and Ograjenšek, S. (2010) (eds). *Ancient Drama in Music for the Modern Stage*. Oxford.

Brumoy, P. (1730). *Le Théâtre des Grecs*. 3 vols. Paris.

Brumoy, P. (1749). *Le Théâtre des Grecs*. Paris

Burkert, W. (1983). *Homo Necans*, trans. P. Bing. Berkeley and Los Angeles, and London).

Burnett, A. P. (1985). *The Art of Bacchylides*. Cambridge, MA.

Burnett, A. P. (1989). 'Performing Pindar's Odes', *Classical Philology*, 84: 283–93.

Butler, E. (1935). *The Tyranny of Greece over the German Imagination*. Cambridge.

Butler, M. R. (2006). 'Producing the Operatic Chorus at Parma's Teatro Ducale, 1759–1769', *Eighteenth-Century Music*, 3: 231–51.

Cahusac, L. de (1754). *La Danse ancienne et modern*. La Haye.

Calame, C. (1977a). *Les Chœurs de jeunes filles en Grèce archaïque*, i. *Morphologie, fonction religieuse et sociale*. Rome.

Calame, C. (1977b). *Les Chœurs de jeunes filles en Grèce archaïque*. ii. *Alcman*. Rome.

Calame, C. (1983). *Alcman: Introduction, texte critique, témoignages, traduction et commentaire*. Rome.

Calame, C. (1997). *Choruses of Young Women in Ancient Greece: Their Morphology, Religious Role, and Social Function*, trans. D. Collins and J. Orion. Lanham, MD.

Calame, C. (1999). 'Performative Aspects of the Choral Voice in Greek Tragedy: Civic Identity in Performance', in S. Goldhill and R. Osborne (eds), *Performance Culture and Athenian Democracy*. Cambridge, 125–53.

Calame, C. (2003). 'Fabrications du genre et identités politiques en comparaison: La Création poétique de Thésee par Bacchylide', *Études de lettres*, 3: 13–45.

Calame, C. (2009a). 'Apollo in Delphi and in Delos: Poetic Performances between Paean and Dithyramb', in L. Athanassaki, R. Martin, and J. F. Miller (eds), *Apolline Politics and Poetics*. Delphi, 169–97.

Calame, C. (2009b). *Poetic and Performative Memory in Ancient Greece: Heroic Gestures and Ritual Gestures in Time and Space*. Washington.

Calame, C. (2013). 'Choral Practices in Plato's *Laws*: Itineraries of Initiation?', in A.-E. Peponi (ed.), *Performance and Culture in Plato's Laws*. Cambridge.

Calder, W. M. (1975). 'The Size of the Chorus in Seneca's *Agamemnon*', *Classical Philology*, 70: 32–5.

Calvo-Merino, B., Glaser, D. E., Grèzes, J., Passingham, R. E., and Haggard, P. (2005). 'Action Observation and Acquired Motor Skills: An fMRI Study with Expert Dancers', *Cerebral Cortex*, 15: 1243–9.

Calzabigi, R. de (1994). *Scritti teatrali e letterari*, ed. A. L. Bellina. Rome.

Cameron, K. N. (1943). 'The Political Symbolism of *Prometheus Unbound*', *Publications of the Modern Language Association*, 58/3: 728–53.

Campbell, L. (1897). 'Sophocles and Shakespeare: Ars Tragica Sophoclea cum Shaksperiana Comparata. By Lionel Horton-Smith', *Classical Review* 11: 119–20.

Campe, J. H. (1804). *Wörterbuch der Deutschen Sprache*. Braunschweig.

Carey, C. (1991). 'The Victory Ode in Performance', *Classical Philology*, 86: 192–200.

Carey, C. (2011). 'Alcman: From Laconia to Alexandria', in L. Athanassaki and E. Bowie (eds.), *Archaic and Classical Choral Song: Performance, Politics and Dissemination*. Berlin, 437–60.

Carlson, M. (1978). *Goethe and the Weimar Theatre*. Ithaca, NY.

Carnegy, P. (2006). *Wagner and the Art of the Theatre*. New Haven and London.

Carter, A. (2005). *Dance and Dancers in the Victorian and Edwardian Music Hall*. Aldershot.

Carter, D. M. (2007). *The Politics of Greek Tragedy*. Bristol.

Carter, T. (1989). *Jacopo Peri (1561–1633): His Life and Works*. 2 vols. New York.

Carter, T., and Szweykowski, Z. (1994) (eds and trans). *Composing Opera: From* Dafne *to* Ulisse Errante. Kraków.

Castronovo, D. (1986). *Thornton Wilder*. New York.

Ceccarelli, P. (1998). *La pirrica nell'antichità greco-romana: Studi sulla danza armata*. Pisa and Rome.

Chagnon, N. (1968). *Yanomamö: The Fierce People*. New York.

Chantraine, P. (1999). *Dictionnaire étymologique de la langue grecque*, rev. edn. with supplement. Paris.

Chapman, J. V. (1988). 'Silent Drama to Silent Dream: Parisian Ballet Criticism, 1800–1850', *Dance Chronicle*, 11: 365–80.

Chapman, J. V. (1989). 'The Paris Opéra Ballet School, 1789–1827', *Dance Chronicle*, 12: 196–220.

Chazin-Bennahum, J. (1988). *Dance in the Shadow of the Guillotine*. Carbondale and Edwardsville, IL.

Citron, S. (1996). *The Wordsmiths: Oscar Hammerstein 2nd and Alan Jay Lerner*. London.

Clark, D. (1971). 'Introduction', in D. Clark (ed.), *The Twentieth Century Interpretations of Murder in the Cathedral*. Englewood Cliffs, NJ, 1–13.

Clark, J. (1984). *Bruno Schönlank und die Arbeitersprechchorbewegung*. Schriften des Fritz-Hüser-Instituts für deutsche und ausländische Arbeiterliteratur der Stadt Dortmund. Cologne.

Clark, M. (2001). 'Bodies at the Opéra', in R. Parker and M. A. Smart (eds), *Reading Critics Reading: Opera and Ballet Criticism in France from the Revolution to 1848*. Oxford, 237–53.

Clinton, K. (1992). *Myth and Cult: The Iconography of the Eleusinian Mysteries*. Stockholm.

Connor, W. (1985). 'The Razing of the House in Greek Society', *Transactions and Proceedings of the American Philological Association*, 115: 79–102.

Connor, W. (1987). 'Tribes, Festivals and Processions: Civic Ceremonial and Political Manipulation in Archaic Greece', *Journal of Hellenic Studies*, 107: 40–50.

Conway, R. S. (2004). 'Ridgeway, Sir William (1858–1926)', rev. A. M. Snodgrass, in *Oxford Dictionary of National Biography*. Oxford <http://www.oxforddnb.com/index/101035752/William-Ridgeway> (accessed January 2008).

Cook, A. B. (1914–40). *Zeus: A Study in Ancient Religion*, 3 vols. Cambridge.

Cooke, K. (1972). *A. C. Bradley and his Influence in Twentieth-Century Shakespeare Criticism*. Oxford.

Corneille, P. (1987). *Œuvres complètes III*, ed. G. Couton. Paris.

Cornford, F. M. (1914). *The Origin of Attic Comedy*. London.

Costa, C. D. N. (1973) (ed.). *Medea*. Oxford.

Craik, T. W. (1997) (ed.). *King Henry V*. Walton-on-Thames.

Crébillon, P.-J. (1819). *Œuvres de Crébillon, tome premier*. Paris.

Crescimbeni, G. M. (1730–1). *L'istoria della volgar poesia*. 3rd edn. Venice.

Cronk, N., Mason, H., Renwick, J., and Jory, D. (2001) (eds). *Oedipe*, in *Œuvres complètes de Voltaire*, A1. Oxford, 15–284.

Cross, R. C., and Woozley, A. D. (1964). *Plato's Republic: A Philosophical Commentary*. London.

Crotty, K. (1982). *Song and Action: The Victory Odes of Pindar*. Baltimore.

Crouzet, D. (1994). *La Nuit de la Saint Barthélémy: Une rêve perdu de la Renaissance*. Paris.

Csapo, E. (2008). 'Star Choruses: Eleusis, Orphism and New Musical Imagery and Dance', in M. Revermann and P. Wilson (eds), *Performance, Iconography, Reception: Studies in Honour of Oliver Taplin*. Oxford, 262–90.

Csapo, E., and Slater, W. (1995). *The Context of Ancient Drama*. Ann Arbor.

Curran, S. (1986). 'The Political Prometheus', *Studies in Romanticism*, 70: 273–81.

Dacier, A. (1692). *La Poëtique d'Aristote*. Paris.

Dahlhaus, C. (1989). *The Idea of Absolute Music*, trans. R. Lustig. Chicago.

Dale, A. M. (1969). *Collected Papers*. Cambridge.

D'Alembert, J. (1757). 'Genève', in *Encyclopédie ou Dictionnaire raisonné des sciences, des arts et des métiers*, vol. 7. Paris.

D'Alembert, J. (2003). 'Geneva', in *The Encyclopedia of Diderot & d'Alembert Collaborative Translation Project*, trans. N. S. Hoyt and T. Cassirer. Ann Arbor <http://hdl.handle.net/2027/spo.did2222.0000.150> (accessed 8 March 2012).

D'Alessio, G. B. (1994). 'First Person Problems in Pindar', *Bulletin of the Institute of Classical Studies*, 39: 117–39.

D'Alessio, G. B. (2004). 'Past Future and Present Past: Temporal Deixis in Greek Archaic Lyric', *Arethusa*, 37: 267–94.

D'Alessio, G. B. (2007). 'ἦν ἰδού: ecce Satyri (Pratina, *PMG* 708 = *TrGF* 4 F3): Alcune considerazioni sull'uso della deissi nei testi lirici e teatrali', in F. Perusino and M. Colantonio (eds), *Dalla lirica corale alla poesia drammatica: Forme e funzioni del canto corale nella tragedia e nella commedia greca*. Pisa, 95–128.

D'Alessio, G. B. (2009). 'Language and Pragmatics', in F. Budelmann (ed.), *The Cambridge Companion to Greek Lyric*. Cambridge, 114–29.

D'Angour, A. (1997). 'How the Dithyramb got its Shape', *Classical Quarterly*, 47: 331–51.

D'Angour, A. (2011). *The Greeks and the New: Novelty in Ancient Greek Imagination and Experience*. Cambridge.

Danneberg, L. (2007). 'Dissens, *ad-personam*-Invektiven und wissenschaftliches Ethos in der Philologie des 19. Jahrhunderts: Wilamowitz-Moellendorff *contra* Nietzsche', in R. Klausnitzer and C. Spoerhase (eds), *Kontroversen in der Literaturtheorie/ Literaturtheorie in der Kontroverse*. Bern, 93–147.

D'Aubignac, F. H. (2001). *La Pratique du théâtre*, ed. H. Baby. Paris.

Davis, M. A. (1990). 'Ratis Audax: Valerius Flaccus' Bold Ship', in A. J. Boyle (ed.), *The Imperial Muse: Ramus Essays on Roman Literature*. Bendigo, 46–73.

Davis, P. (1989). 'The Chorus in Seneca's *Thyestes*', *Classical Quarterly*, 39: 421–35.

Davis, P. (1993). *Shifting Song: The Chorus in Seneca's Tragedies*. Hildesheim.

Davis, R. (2010/11). 'Is Mr Euripides a Communist?: The Federal Theatre Project's 1938 Trojan Incident', *Comparative Drama*, 44/4–45/1: 457–76.

Dawe, R. E. (1996) (ed.). *Sophocles: The Classical Heritage*. New York.

Day, J. W. (2010). *Archaic Greek Epigram and Dedication: Representation and Reperformance*. Cambridge.

Dean, W. (1969). *Handel and the Opera Seria*. Berkeley and Los Angeles.

Deathridge, J. (2008). 'Wagner's Greeks, and Wieland's Too', in *Wagner Beyond Good and Evil*. Berkeley and Los Angeles, 102–9.

Deen, L. W. (1960). 'Heroism and Pathos in Hardy's *Return of the Native*', *Nineteenth-Century Fiction*, 15/3: 207–19.

Degauque, I. (2002) (ed.). *Oedipe: tragédie de Voltaire. Suivie de Oedipe travesti: parodie de Dominique*. Montpellier.

Depew, M. (2000). 'Enacted and Represented Dedications: Genre and Greek Hymn', in M. Depew and D. Obbink (eds), *Matrices of Genre: Authors, Canons, and Society*. Cambridge, MA, and London, 59–79.

De Polignac, F. (1995). *Cults, Territory, and the Origins of the City-State* [*La Naissance de la Cité Grecque*, rev. edn, Paris, 1984], trans. J. Lloyd. Chicago.

Des Croix, N.-C. (2006). *Les Portugais infortunés*. [Rouen 1608], in C. Biet (ed.), *Théâtre de la cruauté et récits sanglants en France (XVIe–XVIIe siècle)*. Paris, 711–804.

Dhuga, U. S. (2011). *Choral Identity and the Chorus of Elders in Greek Tragedy*. Lanham, MD.

Dickens, C. (1998). *A Tale of Two Cities*, ed. A. Sanders. Oxford.

Diderot, D., and D'Alembert, J. (1969) (eds). *Encyclopédie ou dictionnaire Raisonné*, facsimile reprint. 5 vols. New York.

Dodd, D. B., and Faraone, C. A. (2003) (eds). *Initiation in Ancient Greek Rituals and Narratives: New Critical Perspectives*. London.

Dolan, J. (2005). *Utopia in Performance: Finding Hope at the Theater*. Ann Arbor.

Donaldson, J. W. (1830). *The Theatre of the Greeks: Or the History, Literature or Criticism of the Grecian Drama*. 3rd edn. Cambridge.

Doni, G. B. (1763). *Trattati di musica*. Florence.

Dort, B. (1988). *La Représentation émancipée: Essai*. Arles.

Dougherty, C. (1994). 'Pindar's Second Paean: Civil Identity on Parade', *Classical Philology*, 89: 205–18.

Dreyfus, L. (2007). 'Beyond the Interpretation of Music', *Dutch Journal of Music Theory: Tijdschrift voor Muziektheorie*, 12: 253–72.

Dreyfus, L. (2009). 'Christopher Peacocke's "The Perception of Music"', *British Journal of Aesthetics*, 49: 293–7.

Dreyfus, L. (2010). *Wagner and the Erotic Impulse*. Cambridge, MA.

Droysen, G. (1959). *Ein tief gegründet Herz: Der Briefwechsel Felix Mendelssohn-Bartholdys mit Johann Gustav Droysen*, ed. C. Wehmer. Heidelberg.

Dubos, J.-B. (1719). *Réflexions critiques sur la poésie et sur la peinture*. 2 vols. Paris.

Dubos, J.-B. (1993), *Réflexions critiques sur la poésie et sur la peinture*. Geneva.

Dunbar, R. (1996). *Grooming, Gossip and the Evolution of Language*. London.

Dunbar, Z. (2011). 'Dionysian Reflections upon "A Chorus Line"', *Studies in Musical Theatre*, 4: 155–69.

Dunbar, Z. (2012). 'Music Theatre and Musical Theatre', in D. Wiles and C. Dymkowski (eds), *The Cambridge Companion to Theatre History*. Cambridge.

Durkheim, E. (1915). *The Elementary Forms of the Religious Life* [*Les Formes élémentaires de la vie religieuse*, Paris, 1912], trans. J. Ward Swain. London.

Dyer, T. (1846). 'On the Choral Dancing of the Greeks', *Classical Museum*, 3: 229–44.

Eagleton, T. (1990). *The Ideology of the Aesthetic*. Oxford.

Eagleton, T. (2003). *Sweet Violence: The Idea of the Tragic*. Oxford.

Easton, C. (1996). *No Intermissions: The Life of Agnes de Mille*. Boston.

Eatock, C. (2009). *Mendelssohn and Victorian England*. Farnham.

Edwards, C. (1997). 'Unspeakable Professions: Public Performance and Prostitution in Ancient Rome', in J. Hallett (ed.), *Roman Sexualities*. Princeton.

Ehrenreich, B. (2007). *Dancing in the Streets: A History of Collective Joy*. London.

Else, G. F. (1986). *Plato and Aristotle on Poetry: Edited with Introduction and Notes by Peter Burian*. Chapel Hill, NC.

Elsner, J. (2007). *Roman Eyes: Visuality and Subjectivity in Art and Text*. Princeton.

Engel, F. (1910). 'Review of the *Oresteia*', *Berliner Tageblatt*, 8 November.

Enright, W. J. (1899). 'Initiation Ceremonies of the Aborigines of Port Stephens', *Journal and Proceedings of the Royal Society of New South Wales*, 33: 115–24.

Esslin, M. (1959). *Brecht: A Choice of Evils. A Critical Study of the Man, his Work and his Opinions*. London.

Evans-Pritchard, E. E. (1928). 'The Dance', *Africa*, 1/4: 446–62.

Ewans, M. (1982). *Wagner and Aeschylus: The Ring and the Oresteia*. Cambridge.

Ewans, M. (2007). *Opera from the Greek: Studies in the Poetics of Appropriation*. Aldershot.

Fairclough, H. (1929). *Horace: Satires, Epistles and Ars Poetica, with an English Translation*, rev. edn. London.

Falkner, T. M. (1995). *The Poetics of Old Age in Greek Epic, Lyric, and Tragedy*. Norman, OK, and London.

Fantham, E. (1982) (ed.). *Seneca's Troades: A Literary Introduction with Text, Translation and Commentary*. Princeton.

Fantham, E. (2000). 'Production of Seneca's *Trojan Women*, Ancient and Modern', in G. Harrison (ed.), *Seneca in Performance*. London, 13–26.

Fantuzzi, M. (1993). 'Preistoria di un genere letterario: A proposito degli *Inni* V e VI di Callimaco', in R. Pretagostini (ed.), *Tradizione e innovazione nella cultura greca da Omero all'età ellenistica: Scritti in onore di Bruno Gentili*. Rome, 927–46.

Fechter, P. (1955). *Menschen auf meinen Wegen: Begegnungen gestern und heute.* Gütersloh.

Fergusson, F. (1996). 'Three Allegorists: Brecht, Wilder and Eliot', in M. Blank (ed.), *Critical Essays on Thornton Wilder*. New York, 61–71.

Ferrari, G. (2008). *Alcman and the Cosmos of Sparta*. Chicago and London.

Ferri, R. (2003) (ed.). *Octavia*. Cambridge.

Fetting, H. (1973). *Max Reinhardt über Schauspielkunst*. Material zum Theater, 32 [= Reihe Schauspiel, 11]. Berlin.

Fetting, H. (1974) (ed.). *Max Reinhardt: Schriften, Briefe, Reden, Aufzeichnungen, Interviews, Gespräche und Auszüge aus Regiebüchern*. Berlin.

Fink, B. (2009). 'So Far: A History of Rodgers & Hammerstein's *Allegro*', CD book notes in Rodgers and Hammerstein's *Allegro*, CD Masterworks Broadway. New York.

Finley, M. I. (1952). *Studies in Land and Credit in Ancient Athens, 500–200 BC: The Horos-Inscriptions*. New Brunswick, NJ; repr. New York, 1973.

Fischer-Lichte, E. (2004). 'Thinking about the Origins of Theatre in the 1970s', in E. Hall, F. Macintosh, and A. Wrigley (eds), *Dionysus since 69: Greek Tragedy at the Dawn of the Third Millennium*. Oxford, 329–60.

Fischer-Lichte, E. (2005). *Theatre, Sacrifice, Ritual: Exploring New Forms of Political Theatre*. London and New York.

Fischer-Lichte, E. (2008). *The Transformative Power of Performance: A New Aesthetic*, trans. S. I. Jain. London.

Fischer-Lichte, E. (2010). 'Politicizing Antigone', in S. E. Wilmer and A. Zukauskaite (eds.), *Interrogating Antigone in Postmodern Philosophy & Criticism*. Oxford, 329–52.

Fitch, J. G. (1981). 'Sense-Pauses and Relative Dating in Seneca, Sophocles and Shakespeare', *American Journal of Philology*, 102: 289–307.

Flashar, H. (1991). *Inszenierung der Antike: Das griechische Drama auf der Bühne der Neuzeit 1585–1990*. Munich.

Flashar, H. (2009). *Inszenierung der Antike: Das griechische Drama auf der Bühne*. Munich.

Foley, H. (1993). 'The Politics of Tragic Lamentation', in A. Sommerstein (ed.), *Tragedy, Comedy and the Polis*. Nottingham.

Foley, H. (2003). 'Choral Identity in Greek Tragedy', *Classical Philology*, 98: 1–30.

Foley Sherman, J. (2010). 'Steven Berkoff, Choral Unity and Modes of Governance', *New Theatre Quarterly*, 26: 232–47.

Forbes, A. K. (1878 [1856]). *Ras Mala; or, Hindoo Annals of the Province of Goozerat in Western India*. London.

Ford, A. (2004). 'Catharsis: The Power of Music in Aristotle's *Politics*', in P. Murray and P. Wilson, *Music and the Muses: The Culture of 'Mousike' in the Classical Athenian City*. Oxford, 309–36.

Fordin, H. (1995). *Getting to Know Him: A Biography of Oscar Hammerstein II*. New York.

Forsyth, E. (1994). *La Tragédie française de Jodelle à Corneille, 1553–1640: Le Thème de la vengeance*, rev. edn. with supplement. Paris.

Foster, D. H. (2010). *Wagner's Ring Cycle and the Greeks*. Cambridge.

Fowler, R. (1999). 'Moments and Metamorphoses: Virginia Woolf's Greece', *Comparative Literature*, 51/3: 217–42.

Freeman, R. S. (1981). *Opera without Drama: Currents of Change in Italian Opera, 1675–1725.* Ann Arbor.

Fülöp-Miller, R. (1927). *The Mind and Face of Bolshevism.* London.

Gagné, R., and Hopman, M. (2013) (eds). *Choral Mediations in Greek Tragedy.* Cambridge.

Gardel, P. (1790). *Télémaque dans l'île de Calypso.* Paris.

Gardiner, C. P. (1987). *The Sophoclean Chorus: A Study of Character and Function.* Iowa City.

Garfinkel, Y. (2003). *Dancing at the Dawn of Agriculture.* Austin.

Geary, J. (2006). 'Reinventing the Past: Mendelssohn's *Antigone* and the Creation of an Ancient Greek Musical Language', *Journal of Musicology*, 23: 187–226.

Geary, J. (2010). 'Incidental Music and the Revival of Greek Tragedy from the Italian Renaissance to German Romanticism', in P. Brown and S. Ograjenšek (eds), *Ancient Drama in Music for the Modern Stage.* Oxford, 47–66.

Geck, M. (1967). *Die Wiederentdeckung der 'Mathäuspassion' im 19. Jahhundert: Die zeitgenössischen Dokuments und ihre ideengeschichtliche Deutung.* Regensburg.

Gentges, I. (1931) (ed.). *Sprechchöre I.* Berlin.

Gernet, L. (1981). *The Anthropology of Ancient Greece* [*Anthropologie de la Grèce Antique*, Paris, 1968]. Baltimore.

Gilbert, W.S. (1994). *The Savoy Operas: The Complete Text of all the Gilbert and Sullivan Operas 1875–1896.* Ware, Herts.

Gildenhard, I., and Ruehl, M. (2003) (eds). *Out of Arcadia, Bulletin of the Institute Classical Studies* Supplement 79. London.

Gilkes, A. H. (1880). *School Lectures on the Electra of Sophocles and Macbeth.* London.

Girard, R. (1977). *Violence and the Sacred*, trans. P. Gregory. Baltimore.

Glixon, B., and Glixon, J. (2006). *Inventing the Business of Opera: The Impresario and his World in Seventeenth-Century Venice.* Oxford.

Goehr, L. (1998). *The Quest for Voice: On Music, Politics and the Limits of Philosophy.* Oxford.

Goehr, L. (2008). *Elective Affinities: Musical Essays on the History of Aesthetic Theory.* New York.

Golder, H. (1996). 'Making a Scene: Gesture, Tableau, and the Tragic Chorus', *Arion*, 4: 11–19.

Golder, H., and Scully, S. (1994/5) (eds). *The Chorus in Greek Tragedy and Culture* [=*Arion* 3].

Goldhill, S. (1996). 'Collectivity and Otherness—the Authority of the Tragic Chorus: Response to Gould', in M. S. Silk (ed.), *Tragedy and the Tragic.* Oxford, 244–56.

Goldhill, S. (2002). *Who Needs Greek? Contests in the Cultural History of Hellenism.* Cambridge.

Goldhill, S. (2007). *How to Stage Greek Tragedy Today.* Chicago and London.

Goldhill, S. (2008). 'Wagner's Greeks: The Politics of Hellenism', in M. Revermann and P. Wilson (eds), *Performance, Iconography, Reception: Studies in Honour of Oliver Taplin.* Oxford, 453–80.

Goldhill, S. (2011). *Victorian Culture and Classical Antiquity: Art, Opera, Fiction, and the Proclamation of Modernity.* Princeton.

Goldhill, S. (2012). *Sophocles and the Language of Tragedy.* New York.

Goldschmidt, W. R. (2006). *The Bridge to Humanity: How Affect Hunger Trumps the Selfish Gene.* New York.

Gorer, G. (1935). *Africa Dances.* London.

Görgemanns, H. (1985). 'Wilamowitz und die griechische Tragödie', in W. M. Calder III, H. Flashar, and T. Lindken (eds), *Wilamowitz nach 50 Jahren.* Darmstadt, 130–50.

Gossman, L. (1994). 'Philhellenism and Anti-Semitism: Matthew Arnold and his German Models', *Comparative Literature,* 46: 1–39.

Gould, J. (1996). 'Tragedy and Collective Experience', in M. S. Silk (ed.), *Tragedy and the Tragic.* Oxford, 217–43.

Graf, F. (1996). '"Pompai" in Greece : Some Considerations about Space and Ritual in the Greek Polis', in R. Hägg (ed.), *The Role of Religion in the Early Greek Polis.* Aström, 55–6.

Graf, F., and Iles Johnston, S. (2007). *Ritual Texts for the Afterlife.* London.

Granover, M. (1973). 'The Strength of Weak Ties', *American Journal of Sociology,* 78/6: 1360–80.

Gravina, G. (1973). *Scritti critici e teorici,* ed. A. Quondam. Bari.

Greenwood, E. (2006). *Thucydides and the Shaping of History.* London.

Gregor-Dellin, M., and Mack, D. (1978) (eds). *Cosima Wagner's Diaries,* trans. G. Skelton. London.

Griffin, R., and Matthew, F. (2004) (eds). *Fascism: Fascism and Culture.* Fascism: Critical Concepts in Political Science, 3. London and New York.

Griffith, M. (1995). 'Brilliant Dynasts: Power and Politics in the *Oresteia*', *Classical Antiquity,* 14: 62–129.

Griffith, M. (1998). 'The King and Eye: The Rule of the Father in Greek Tragedy', *Proceedings of the Cambridge Philological Society,* 44: 22–86.

Griffith, M., and Carter, D. M. (2011). 'Introduction', in D. M. Carter (ed.), *Why Athens: A Reappraisal of Tragic Politics.* Oxford, 1–16.

Griffiths, A. (1972). 'Alcman's *Partheneion*: The Morning After the Night Before', *Quaderni urbinati di cultura classica,* 14: 7–30.

Grimm, J., and Grimm, W. (1854) (eds). *Deutsches Wörterbuch.* Leipzig.

Grossmann, S. (1919). 'Review of the *Oresteia*', *Vossische Zeitung,* 29/30 December.

Grout, D. J. (1963). 'The Chorus in Early Opera', in A. Abert (ed.), *Festschrift Friedrich Blume zum 70. Geburtstag.* Kassel, 151–61.

Gruber, M. A. (2009). *Der Chor in den Tragödien des Aischylos: Affekt und Reaktion.* Tübingen.

Gründer, K. (1969) (ed.). *Der Streit um Nietzsches 'Geburt der Tragödie': Die Schriften von E. Rohde, R. Wagner, U. von Wilamowitz-Moellendorff.* Hildersheim,

Guest, I. (1986). *Gautier on Dance: Théophile Gautier Selected, Translated and Annotated.* London.

Guest, I. (1996). *The Ballet of the Enlightenment: The Establishment of the Ballet d'Action in France, 1770–1793.* London.

Guest, I. (2002). *Ballet under Napoleon.* Alton.

Guest, I. (2008). *The Romantic Ballet in Paris*. Alton.

Gurley, R. R. (1841). *Letter to the Hon. Henry Clay, President of the American Colonization Society, and Sir Thomas Fowell Buxton, Chairman of the General Committee of the African Civilization Society, on the Colonization and Civilization of Africa*. London.

Güthenke, C. (forthcoming). '"Lives" as Parameter: The Privileging of Ancient Lives as a Category of Research around 1900', in R. Fletcher and J. Hanink (eds), *Creative Lives: New Approaches to Ancient Intellectual Biography*.

Hagen, E. H., and Bryant, G. A. (2003). 'Music and Dance as a Coalition Signaling System', *Human Nature*, 14: 21–51.

Hall, E. (1996). *Aeschylus, Persians*. Warminster.

Hall, E. (2006). *The Theatrical Cast of Athens: Interactions between Ancient Greek Drama and Society*. Oxford.

Hall, E. (2007). 'The English-Speaking Aristophanes', in E. Hall and A. Wrigley (eds), *Aristophanes in Performance 421 BC–AD 2007*. Oxford, 66–92.

Hall, E. (2008). 'Is the Barcelona *Alcestis* a Latin Pantomime Libretto?', in E. Hall and R. Wyles (eds), *New Directions in Ancient Pantomime*. Oxford, 258–82.

Hall, E. (2010). 'British Refractions of India and the 1857 "Mutiny" through the Prism of Ancient Greece and Rome', in E. Hall and P. Vasunia (eds), *India, Greece & Rome 1757–2007*. BICS Supplement, 108: 33–48.

Hall, E. (2011). 'The Problem with Prometheus: Myth, Abolition and Radicalism', in E. Hall, R. Alston and J. McConnell (eds), *Ancient Slavery and Abolition*. Oxford, 209–46.

Hall, E. (2012*a*). *Adventures with Iphigenia in Tauris: A Cultural History of Euripides; Black Sea Tragedy*. New York.

Hall, E. (2012*b*). 'The Politics of Metrical Variety in the Classical Athenian Theatre', in D. Yatromanolakis (ed.), *Music and Politics in Ancient Greek Societies*. New York and London, 1–28.

Hall, E. (forthcoming). 'Greek Tragedy and North American Modernism', in K. Bosher, F. Macintosh, J. McConnell, and P. Rankine (eds), *Oxford Handbook to Greek Drama in the Americas*. Oxford.

Hall, E., and Macintosh, F. (2005). *Greek Tragedy and the British Theatre 1660–1914*. Oxford.

Hall, E., and Wyles, R. (2008) (eds). *New Directions in Ancient Pantomime*. Oxford.

Halliwell, S. (1986). *Aristotle's Poetics*. Chicago.

Halliwell, S. (1987). *The Poetics of Aristotle: Translation and Commentary*. London.

Halliwell, S. (1995). *Aristotle: Poetics*. Cambridge, MA.

Halliwell, S. (1998). *Aristotle's Poetics*. 2nd edn. London

Halmos, P. (1952). 'The Decline of the Choral Dance', in E. Josephson and M. Josephson (eds), *Man Alone: Alienation in Modern Society*. New York, 172–9.

Hambly, W. D. (1926). *Tribal Dancing and Social Development*. London.

Hamilton, J. T. (2008). *Music, Madness and the Unworking of Language*. New York.

Hammerstein, O. (1947). *Allegro*, in *The Rodgers and Hammerstein Theatre Library*, <https://www.rnh.com> (accessed 2 February 2012).

Hanning, B. R. (1973). 'Apologia per Ottavio Rinuccini', *Journal of the American Musicological Society*, 26: 240–62.

Hanning, B. R. (1980). *Of Poetry and Music's Power: Humanism and the Creation of Opera.* Ann Arbor.

Hanslick, E. (1854). *Vom Musikalisch-Schönen: Ein Beitrag zur Revision der Ästhetik der Tonkunst.* Berlin.

Hardie, A. (2004). 'Muses and Mysteries', in P. Murray and P. Wilson (eds), *Music and the Muses.* Oxford, 11–38.

Hardy, A. (2006). *Scédase ou l'hospitalité violée* in C. Biet (ed.) *Théâtre de la cruauté et récits sanglants en France (XVIe–XVIIe siècle).* Paris 335–90.

Harrison, A. R. W. (1968). *The Law of Athens, Family and Property.* Oxford.

Harrison, J. E. (1903). *Prolegomena to the Study of Greek Religion.* Cambridge.

Harrison, J. E. (1908–9). 'The Kouretes and Zeus Kouros: A Study in Pre-Historic Sociology', *Annual of the British School at Athens*, 15: 308–38.

Harrison, J. E. (1912). *Themis: A Study of the Social Origins of Greek Religion.* Cambridge.

Harrop, S. (2010). 'Physical Performance and the Languages of Translation', in E. Hall and S. Harrop (eds), *Theorizing Performance, Greek Drama, Cultural History and Critical Practice.* London, 232–40.

Hartigan, K. V. (1995). *Greek Tragedy on the American Stage: 1882–1994.* Westport, CT.

Haubold, J. (2000). *Homer's People: Epic Poetry and Social Formation.* Cambridge.

Heartz, D. (2004). *From Garrick to Gluck: Essays on Opera in the Age of Enlightenment.* New York.

Heath, M. (1988). 'Receiving the *kômos*: The Context and Performance of the Epinician', *American Journal of Philology*, 109: 181–95.

Heath, M., and Lefkowitz, M. (1991). 'Epinician Performance', *Classical Philology*, 86: 173–91.

Hegel, G. W. F. (1970). *Vorlesungen über die Ästhetik*, in *Werke*, vols. 13–15. Frankfurt.

Hegel, G. W. F. (1975). *Aesthetics: Lectures on Fine Art*, trans T. Knox. Oxford.

Heine, H. (1835). *De L'Allemagne.* Paris.

Hempel, D. (1997). *Friedrich Leopold Graf zu Stolberg (1750–1819): Staatsmann und politischer Schriftsteller.* Weimar.

Henderson, M. C. (2001). *Mielziner: Master of Modern Stage Design.* New York.

Hennenberg, F. (1984). *Brecht Liederbuch.* Frankfurt am Main.

Henrichs, A. (1995). 'Why Should I Dance?: Choral Self-Referentiality in Greek Tragedy', *Arion*, 3: 56–111.

Henrichs, A. (1996). 'Dancing in Athens, Dancing on Delos: Some Patterns of Choral Projection in Euripides', *Philologus*, 140: 48–62.

Herder, B. (1855). *Conversations-Lexikon.* Freiburg.

Herrick, M. (1946). *The Fusion of Horatian and Aristotelian Literary Criticism, 1531–1555.* Urbana, IL.

Heuner, U. (2002). '"Wir sprechen im Chor": Das chorische Theater Wilhelm Leyhausens', *Modernes Theater*, 17: 115–25.

Hill, D. E. (2000). 'Seneca's Choruses', *Mnemosyne*, 53: 561–87.

Hinderer, W. (2009). 'Die antike Tragödie als Herausforderung: Schillers *Braut von Messina*', in W. Hinderer, *Schiller und kein Ende: Metamorphoses und kreative Aneignungen.* Würzburg, 299–342.

Hinge, G. (2006). *Die Sprache Alkmans: Textgeschichte und Sprachgeschichte.* Wiesbaden.

Hollingsworth, B. (1982). *Songs of the People: Lancashire Dialect Poetry of the Industrial Revolution*. Manchester.

Homans, J. (2010). *Apollo's Angels: A History of Ballet*. London.

Hopman, M. (2009). 'Layered Stories in Aeschylus' *Persians*', in J. Grethlein and A. Rengakos (eds), *Narratology and Interpretation: Reading the Content of the Form*. Berlin, 357–76.

Hornblower, S. (2009). 'Greek Lyric and the Politics and Sociologies of Archaic and Classical Greek Communities', in F. Budelmann (ed.), *Cambridge Companion to Greek Lyric*. Cambridge, 39–57.

Horton-Smith, L. (1896). *Ars Tragica Sophoclea cum Shakesperiana Comparata*. London.

Howard, P. (1995). *Gluck: An Eighteenth-Century Portrait in Letters and Documents*. Oxford.

Hubbard, T. (2011). 'The Dissemination of Pindar's Non-Epinician Choral Lyric', in L. Athanassaki and E. Bowie (eds), *Archaic and Classical Choral Song: Performance, Politics and Dissemination*. Berlin, 347–64.

Hughes, C. (1940). 'Music of the French Revolution', *Science & Society*, 4: 193–210.

Hull, A. E. (1927). *Music: Classical, Romantic and Modern*. London.

Humboldt, W. (1816). *Aeschylus Agamemnon metrisch übersetzt*. Leipzig.

Humphreys, S. C. (1978). *Anthropology and the Greeks*. London.

Hurd, R. (1749). *Q. Horatii Flacci Ars Poetica: Epistola ad Pisones*. London.

Hutchinson, G. O. (2001). *Greek Lyric Poetry: A Commentary on Selected Larger Pieces*. Oxford.

Iliadis, M. (2011). 'The *Persians*: Two Performances (1889 and 1934)', in C. Hanratty and E. Ioannidou (eds), *Epidaurus Encounters, Greek Drama, Ancient Theatre and Modern Performance*. Berlin, 99–109.

Ingleheart, J. (2008). '*Et mea sunt populo saltata poemata saepe* (*Tristia* 2.519): Ovid and the Pantomime', in E. Hall and R. Wyles (eds), *New Directions in Ancient Pantomime*. Oxford.

Issacharov, M. (1981). 'Space and Reference in Drama', *Poetics Today*, 2: 211–24.

Jaccottet, A. F. (2003). *Choisir Dionysos: Les Associations dionysiaques ou la face cachée du dionysisme*. Zurich.

Jackson Knight, W. F. (1936). *Cumaean Gates: A Reference of the Sixth Aeneid to the Initiation Pattern*. Oxford.

Jacobs, M., and Warren, J. (1986) (eds). *Max Reinhardt: The Oxford Symposium*. Oxford.

Jacobshagen, A. (1997). *Der Chor in der französischen Oper des späten Ancien Régime*. Frankfurt.

Jahn, O. (1866). *Gesammelte Aufsätze über Musik*. Leipzig.

Jeanmaire, H. (1939). *Couroi et courètes: Essai sur l'éducation spartiate et sur les rites d'adolescence dans l'antiquité hellénique*. Lille.

Jebb, R. (1888). *Sophocles: The Antigone*. Cambridge.

Jenisch, D. (1786). *Agamemnon, ein Trauerspiel*. Berlin.

Joannidès, A. (1970). *La Comédie Française de 1680 à 1900*. Geneva. 1st edn. Paris, 1901.

Johnson, J. (1991). 'Music in Hegel's *Aesthetics*: A Re-Evaluation', *British Journal of Aesthetics*, 31/2: 152–62.

Jones, D. E. (1971). 'The Chorus', in D. R. Clark (ed.), *The Twentieth Century Interpretations of Murder in the Cathedral*. Englewood Cliffs, NJ, 79–81.

Jones, D. E., and Clark, D. R. (1971). 'Introduction', in D. R. Clark (ed.), *The Twentieth Century Interpretations of Murder in the Cathedral*. Englewood Cliffs, NJ, 1–13.

Jones, E. (forthcoming). *Lyric Physicality: Bodies and Objects in Archaic Greek Lyric Poetry*.

Jones, S. (2013). *Literature, Modernism and Dance*. Oxford

Jory, E. (1998). 'Pantomime Assistants', in T. W. Hillard and E. A. Judge (eds), *Ancient History in a Modern University*. Grand Rapids, MI.

Jory, E. (2008). 'The Pantomime Dancer and his Libretto', in E. Hall and R. Wyles (eds), *New Directions in Ancient Pantomime*. Oxford.

Judet de La Combe, P. (1999). 'Klassische Philologie als modern Kulturkritik. Wilamowitz und die Orestie (1900)', in C. König and E. Lämmert (eds), *Konkurrenten in der Fakultät. Kultur, Wissen und Universität um 1900*. Frankfurt, 248–59.

Kain, P. (1982). *Schiller, Hegel and Marx: State, Society and the Aesthetic Ideal of Ancient Greece*. Kingston and Montreal.

Kant, I. (1908). *Kritik der Urteilskraft*, in *Kants Gesammelte Schriften I.5*. Berlin, 165–485.

Kant, M. (2007). 'The Soul of the Shoe', in M. Kant (ed.), *The Cambridge Companion to Ballet*. Cambridge, 184–200.

Kavoulaki, A. (1999). 'Processional Performance and the Democratic Polis', in S. Goldhill and R. Osborne (eds), *Performance Culture*. Cambridge, 293–320.

Kelly, H. A. (1979). 'Tragedy and the Performance of Tragedy in Late Antiquity', *Traditio*, 35: 21–44.

Kelly, H. A. (1994). *Out of Control: The New Biology of Machines, Social Systems, and the Economic World*. New York.

Kindermann, H. (1935). 'Geist und Gestalt der deutschen Gegenwartsdichtung', *Zeitschrift für Deutsche Bildung*, 11: 192–202.

Kirstein, L. (1970). *Movement and Metaphor: Four Centuries of Ballet*. New York and Washington.

Kitto, H. D. F. (1950). *Greek Tragedy*. London.

Kitzinger, M. R. (2008). *The Choruses of Sophokles' Antigone and Philoktetes: A Dance of Words*. Leiden.

Klaar, A. (1911). 'Review of the *Oresteia*', *Vossische Zeitung*, 4 October.

Knapp, R. (2006). *The American Musical and the Formation of National Identity*. Oxford.

Knopf, J. (2001). *Brecht Handbuch*, i. *Stücke*. Stuttgart and Weimar.

Köchly, H. (1879). *Gottfried Hermann: Zu seinem hundertsten Geburtstage*. Heidelberg.

Kohn, T. D. (2004). 'Seneca's Use of Four Speaking Actors', *Classical Journal*, 100: 163–75.

Koller, H. (1954). *Die Mimesis in Der Antike: Nachahmung, Darstellung, Ausdruck*. Bern.

Koller, H. (1955). 'Ἐγκύκλιος παιδεία', *Glotta*, 34: 174–89.

Körner, J. (1928). 'Friedrich Schlegels "Philosophie der Philologie", mit einer Einleitung herausgegeben', *Logos*, 17: 1–72.

Kotzamani, M. A. (1997). 'Lysistrata, Playgirl of the Western World: Aristophanes on the Early Modern Stage'. Unpublished dissertation, the City University of New York.

Kovacs, D. (1998). *Euripides: Electra*. Cambridge, MA.

Kowalzig, B. (2004). 'Changing Choral Worlds: Song-Dance and Society in Athens and Beyond', in P. Murray and P. Wilson (eds), *Music and the Muses*. Oxford, 39–65.

Kowalzig, B. (2007a). *Singing for the Gods: Performances of Myth and Ritual in Archaic and Classical Greece*. Oxford.

Kowalzig, B. (2007b). '"And now all the world shall dance" (Eur. *Bacch.* 114): Dionysus' Choroi between Drama and Ritual', in E. Csapo and M. Miller (eds), *The Origins of Theater in Ancient Greece and Beyond*. Cambridge, 221–51.

Krausz, M. (1993) (ed.). *The Interpretation of Music. Philosophical Essays*. Oxford.

Kraut, R. (1997). *Aristotle Politics: Books VII and VIII*. Oxford.

Kreuzer, J. (2002) (ed.). *Hölderlin Handbuch: Leben-Werk-Wirkung*. Stuttgart and Weimar.

Krieger, E. (1986). 'Sprechchor', in M. Brauneck and G. Schneilin (eds), *Theaterlexikon: Begriffe und Epochen, Bühnen und Ensembles*. Hamburg, 802.

Kuntz, M. (1993). *Narrative Setting and Dramatic Poetry*. Leiden.

Kurke, L. (1991). *The Traffic in Praise: Pindar and the Poetics of Social Economy*. Ithaca, NY.

Kurke, L. (2005). 'Choral Lyric as "Ritualization": Poetic Sacrifice and Poetic *ego* in Pindar's Sixth Paian', *Classical Antiquity*, 24: 81–130.

Kurke, L. (2007). 'Visualizing the Choral: Epichoric Poetry, Ritual, and Elite Negotiation in Fifth-Century Thebes', in C. Kraus et al. (eds), *Visualizing the Tragic*. Oxford, 63–101.

Kurke, L. (2013). 'Imagining Chorality: Wonder, Plato's Puppets, and Moving Statues', in A.-E. Peponi (ed.), *Performance and Culture in Plato's Laws*. Cambridge.

Lada-Richards, I. (1999). *Initiating Dionysos: Ritual and Theatre in Aristophanes' Frogs*. Oxford.

Lada-Richards, I. (2007). *Silent Eloquence: Lucian and Pantomime Dancing*. London.

Lada-Richards, I. (2010), 'Dead but not Extinct: On Reinventing Pantomime Dancing in Eighteenth-Century England and France', in F. Macintosh (ed.), *The Ancient Dancer in the Modern World*. Oxford, 19–38.

Ladianou, K. (2005). 'The Poetics of "Choreia": Imitation and Dance in the "Anacreontea"', *Quaderni Urbinati di Cultura Classica*, 80: 47–58.

La Harpe, J.-F. (1781). *Philoctète*. Paris.

Latacz, J. (1997). 'Schiller und die griechische Tragödie', in H. Flashar (ed.), *Tragödie: Idee und Transformation*. Stuttgart, 235–57.

Lavecchia, S. (2000). *Pindari Dithyramborum Fragmenta*. Rome and Pisa.

Lawler, L. B. (1940). 'The Dance of the Πινακίδες', *Transactions of the American Philological Association*, 71: 230–8.

Lawler, L. B. (1941). 'Ἰχθύες χορευταί', *Classical Philology*, 6: 142–55.

Lawler, L. B. (1946a). 'Ὄρχησις φοβέρα', *American Journal of Philology*, 67: 67–70.

Lawler, L. B. (1946*b*). 'The Geranos Dance: A New Interpretation', *Transactions of the American Philological Association*, 77: 112–30.

Lawler, L. B. (1954). 'Phora, schêma, deixis in Greek Dance', *Transactions and Proceedings of the American Philological Association*, 85: 148–58.

Lawton, H. W. (1949) (ed. and trans.). *Handbook of French Renaissance Dramatic Theory*. Manchester.

Layard, J. (1936). 'Maze-Dances and the Ritual of the Labyrinth in Malekula', *Folklore*, 47: 123–70.

Layard, J. (1942). *Stone Men of Malekula: Vao*. London.

Leake, W. (1938). *Gilkes and Dulwich 1885–1914: A Study of a Great Headmaster*. London.

Lebègue, R. (1954). *La Tragédie française de la Renaissance*. 2nd edn. Brussels.

Lecoq, J. (2000). *The Moving Body*, trans. D. Bradby. London.

Lefkowitz, M. (1963). 'Τῶ καὶ ἐγώ : The First Person in Pindar', *Harvard Studies in Classical Philology*, 67: 177–253.

Lefkowitz, M. (1991). *First-Person Fictions: Pindar's Poetic I*. Oxford.

Lefranc de Pompignan, J.-J. (1770). *Tragédies d'Eschyle*. Paris.

Leigh Foster, S. (1996). *Choreography and Narrative: Ballet's Staging of Story and Desire*. Bloomington and Indianapolis.

Lennox, C. (1759). *The Greek Theatre of Father Brumoy*. 3 vols. London.

Leslie, S. (2010). 'Gesamtkunstwerk: Modern Moves and the Ancient Chorus', in F. Macintosh (ed.), *The Ancient Dancer in the Modern World*. Oxford, 411–19.

Lesure, F. (1984) (ed.). *Querelle des Gluckistes et des Piccinistes*. Geneva.

Lewes, G. H. (1845). 'Was Dancing an Element of the Greek Chorus?', *Classical Museum*, 2: 344–66.

Ley, G. (2007). *The Theatricality of Greek Tragedy: Playing Space and Chorus*. Chicago.

Leyhausen, W. (1934). *Wir sprechen im Chor: Was ist für den Sprechchor geeignet?* Berlin.

Leyhausen, W. (1948). *Aischylos: Die Perser, Prometheus, Agamemnon*. Berlin.

Lincoln, B. (1999). *Theorizing Myth: Narrative, Ideology and Scholarship*. Chicago.

Lloyd-Jones, H. (1994). *Sophocles: Electra*. Cambridge, MA.

Long, R. E. (2003). *Broadway, the Golden Years: Jerome Robbins and the Great Choreographer-Directors, 1940 to the Present*. New York.

Longepierre, H.-B. (1981). *Electre*. Paris.

Lonsdale, S. H. (1981). *Animals and the Origins of Dance*. London.

Lonsdale, S. H. (1993). *Dance and Ritual Play in Greek Religion*. Baltimore.

Lopez, J. (2003). *Theatrical Convention and Audience Response in Early Modern Drama*. Cambridge.

Lurje, M. (2004). *Die Suche nach der Schuld: Sophokles' Oedipus Rex, Aristoteles' Poetik und das Tragödienverständnis der Neuzeit*. Stuttgart.

McClung, B. D. (2007). *Lady in the Dark: Biography of a Musical*. Oxford.

McClymonds, M. P. (1980). *Niccolò Jomelli: The Last Years, 1769–1774*. Ann Arbor.

Macintosh, F. (1997). 'Tragedy in Performance: Nineteenth- and Twentieth-Century Productions', in P. E. Easterling (ed.), *Cambridge Companion to Greek Tragedy*. Cambridge, 284–323.

Macintosh, F. (2009*a*). *Sophocles' Oedipus Tyrannus*. Cambridge.

Macintosh, F. (2009*b*). 'The "Rediscovery" of Aeschylus for the Modern Stage', in J. Jouanna and F. Montanari (eds), *Eschyle à l'aube du théâtre occidental: Neuf exposés suivis de discussions*. Geneva, 435–68.

Macintosh, F. (2010) (ed.). *The Ancient Dancer in the Modern World: Responses to Greek and Roman Dance*. Oxford.

McLellan, D. (1969). *The Young Hegelians and Karl Marx*. London.

McMillin, S. (2006). *The Musical as Drama: A Study of the Principles and Conventions behind Musical Shows from Kern to Sondheim*. Princeton.

McNeill, W. H. (1995). *Keeping Together in Time: Dance and Drill in Human History*. Cambridge, MA.

Mahaffy, J. (1883). *A History of Classical Greek Literature*. 2nd edn. 2 vols. London.

Mallet, E.-F. (1753). 'Choeur', in Diderot and D'Alembert (eds), *Encyclopédie, ou dictionnaire raisonné des sciences, des arts et des métiers III*. Paris, 361.

Mann, T. (1937). *Freud, Goethe, Wagner*. New York.

Marchand, S. (1996). *Down from Olympus: Archaeology and Philhellenism in Germany, 1750–1970*. Princeton.

Marotti, F. (1974) (ed.). *Lo spettacolo dall' umanesimo al manierismo: Teoria e tecnica*. Milan.

Marshall, C. W. (2000). 'Location! Location! Location! Choral Absence and Dramatic Space in Seneca's *Troades*', in G. W. M. Harrison (ed.), *Seneca in Performance*. London, 27–51.

Martin, R. (2007). 'Outer Limits, Choral Space', in C. Kraus et al. (eds), *Visualizing the Tragic*. Oxford, 35–62.

Marx, P. (2006). *Max Reinhardt: Vom bürgerlichen Theater zur metropolitanen Kultur*. Tübingen.

Masson, P.-M. (1930). *L'opéra de Rameau*. Paris.

Mastronarde, D. (2010). *The Art of Euripides: Dramatic Technique and Social Context*. Cambridge.

Matt, S. (2007). 'You Can't Go Home Again: Homesickness and Nostalgia in US History', *Journal of American History*, 94: 469–97.

Maurice, T. (1806). *The Fall of the Mogul: A Tragedy, Founded on an Interesting Portion of Indian History, and Attempted Partly on the Greek Model*. London.

Mavromoustakos, P. (2004). 'Syngeneies eklektikes kai mi: I skinothesia tou archaiou dramatos kata ti dekaetia tou 1930', in *Scheseis tou Neoellinikou theatrou me to europaiko/Proceedings of the Second Greek Conference of Theatre Studies* (Athens), 291–302.

Mayer, R. (2002). *Seneca: Phaedra*. London.

Mayhew, R. (2011). *Aristotle Problems Books 1–19*. Cambridge, MA.

Mead, M. (1928). *Coming of Age in Samoa: A Psychological Study of Primitive Youth for Western Civilisation*. London.

Mégavand, M. (2003). 'Face à ce qui se dérobe: La Choralité à l'œuvre dans RWANDA 94', in C. Triau (ed.), *Choralités*. Brussels, 105–7 [= Special Issue, *Alternatives théâtrales*, 76–7].

Meltzoff, A. N., and Prinz, W. (2002) (eds). *The Imitative Mind: Development, Evolution, and Brain Bases*. Cambridge.

Menz, E. (1976). 'Sprechchor und Aufmarsch: Zur Entstehung des Thingspiels', in H. Denkler and K. Prümm (eds), *Die deutsche Literatur im Dritten Reich: Themen, Traditionen, Wirkungen.* Stuttgart, 330–46.

Merker, B. (2000). 'Synchronous Chorusing and Human Origins', in N. L. Wallin, B. Merker, and S. Brown (eds), *The Origins of Music.* Cambridge, MA, 315–32.

Metastasio, P. (1943–54). *Tutte le opere*, ed. B. Brunelli. Milan.

Meyerbeer, G. (2008). *The Complete Libretti.* In the original and in translations by R. Arsenty and Introductions by R. I. Letellier, Vol. V. Newcastle-upon-Tyne.

Michel, C. (2010). 'Programm und Fragment: Zu Gottfried Hermanns Briefwechsel mit Goethe (1820–1831)', in K. Sier and E. Wöckener-Gade (eds), *Gottfried Hermann (1772–1848). Internationales Symposium in Leipzig 11.–13. Oktober 2007.* Tübingen, 51–82.

Michelakis, P. (2002). *Achilles in Greek Tragedy.* Cambridge.

Miles, L. K., Nind, L. K., and Macrae, C. N. (2009). 'The Rhythm of Rapport: Interpersonal Synchrony and Social Perception', *Cognition*, 190: 585–9.

Miller, A. (1994). *The Theater Essays of Arthur Miller.* London.

Mithen, S. J. (2005). *The Singing Neanderthals: The Origins of Music, Language, Mind and Body.* London.

Mittenzwei, W. (1987). *Das Leben des Bertolt Brecht oder Der Umgang mit den Welträtseln.* Frankfurt.

Moggach, D. (2006) (ed.). *The New Hegelians: Politics and Philosophy in the Hegelian School.* Cambridge.

Molloy, M. E. (1996). *Libanius and the Dancers.* Hildesheim.

Montgomery, J., Benger, E., and Grahame, J. (1807). *Poems on the Abolition of the Slave Trade.* London.

Mordden, E. (1992). *Rodgers & Hammerstein.* New York.

Morgan, K. (1993). 'Pindar the Professional and the Rhetoric of the Kômos', *Classical Philology*, 88: 1–15.

Morrison, J. (1986). *Winckelmann and the Notion of Aesthetic Education.* Oxford.

Morrow, G. (1960). *Plato's Cretan City: A Historical Interpretation of the Laws.* Princeton.

Morshead, E. (1895). *The Ajax and Electra of Sophocles.* London.

Most, G. (1998). 'Karl Otfried Müller's Edition of Aeschylus' *Eumenides*', in W. M. Calder III and R. Schlesier (eds), *Zwischen Rationalismus und Romantik: Karl Otfried Müller und die antike Kultur.* Hildesheim, 349–73.

Most, G. (2004). '1805, Summer: Homer between Poets and Philologists', in D. Wellbery (ed.), *A New History of German Literature.* Cambridge, MA, 500–5.

Mouze, L. (2005). *Le Législateur et le poète: Une interprétation des Lois de Platon. Savoirs et systèmes de pensée.* Villeneuve d'Ascq.

Mukta, P. (1999). 'The "Civilising Mission": The Regulation and Control of Mourning in Colonial India', *Feminist Review*, 63, *Negotiations and Resistances*, 25–47.

Mullen, W. (1982). *Choreia: Pindar and Dance.* Princeton.

Müller, J. (1987). 'Choreographische Strategie: Zur Funktion der Chöre in Schillers Tragödie *Die Braut von Messina*', in H. Brandt (ed.), *Friedrich Schiller, Angebot und Diskurs: Zugänge—Dichtung—Zeitgenossenschaft.* Berlin, 431–48.

Müller, K. O. (1833). *Aischylus Eumeniden griechisch und deutsch.* Göttingen.

Müller, U., Wapnewski, P., and Deathridge, J. (1992) (eds). *Wagner Handbook.* Cambridge, MA.

Murata, M. (1981). *Operas for the Papal Court, 1631–1668.* Ann Arbor.

Murata, M. (1984). 'Classical tragedy in the history of early opera in Rome', *Early Music History*, 4: 101–34.

Murnaghan, S. (2011). '*Choroi achoroi*: The Athenian Politics of Tragic Choral Identity', in D. Carter (ed.), *Why Athens?: A Reappraisal of Tragic Politics.* Oxford, 245–68.

Murray, P. (1996). *Plato on Poetry.* Cambridge.

Naerebout, F. (1997). *Attractive Performances: Ancient Greek Dance: Three Preliminary Studies.* Amsterdam.

Naerebout, F. (2010). '"In Search of A Dead Rat": The Reception of Ancient Greek Dance in Late Nineteenth-Century Europe and America', in F. Macintosh (ed.), *The Ancient Dancer in the Modern World.* Oxford, 39–56.

Nagy, G. (1990). *Pindar's Homer: The Lyric Possession of an Epic Past.* Baltimore and London.

Nauen, F. (1971). *Revolution, Idealism and Human Freedom: Schelling, Hölderlin, Hegel and the Crisis of Early German Idealism.* The Hague.

Nehamas, A. (1999). 'Plato and the Mass Media', in *Virtues of Authenticity: Essays on Plato and Socrates.* Princeton, 279–302.

Nehamas, A., and Woodruff, P. (1995). *Plato: Phaedrus.* Indianapolis.

Nemirovitch-Dantchenko, V. (1937). *My Life in the Russian Theatre*, trans. K. Cournos. London.

Nietzsche, F. (1984 [1895]). *Die Geburt der Tragödie aus dem Geiste der Musik.* Munich.

Nietzsche, F. (1956). *The Birth of Tragedy and the Genealogy of Morals*, trans. F. Golffing. New York.

Nietzsche, F. (1993). *Birth of Tragedy out of the Spirit of Music.* London.

Nietzsche, F. (1994). *Die Geburt der Tragödie: Schriften zu Literatur und Philosophie der Griechen, hg. und erläutert von Manfred Landfester.* Frankfurt.

Nightingale, A. (2004). *Spectacles of Truth in Classical Greek Philosophy: Theoria in its Cultural Context.* Cambridge.

Nolan, F. (1979). *The Sound of Their Music: The Story of Rodgers and Hammerstein.* New York.

Noverre, J.-G. (1807). *Lettres sur les arts imitateurs en général et sur la danse en particulier.* 2 vols. Paris.

Noverre, J.-G. (1930). *Letters on Dancing and Ballets*, trans. C. W. Beaumont from the rev., enlarged edn at St Petersburg 1803. London.

Oergel, M. (2006). *Culture and Identity: Historicity in German Literature and Thought 1770–1815.* Berlin.

Oliver, A. R. (1947). *The Encyclopedists as Critics of Music.* New York.

Olsson, J. E. (1981). *Bertolt Brecht: Mutter Courage und ihre Kinder: Historisch-kritische Ausgabe.* Lund and Frankfurt am Main.

Ozouf, M. (1998). *Festivals and the French Revolution*, trans. A. Sheridan. Cambridge, MA.

Palisca, C. K. (1989). *The Florentine Camerata: Documentary Studies and Translations.* New Haven.

Palisca, C. K. (1994). *Studies in the History of Italian Music and Music Theory.* Oxford.

Palisca, C. K. (2006). *Music and Ideas in the Sixteenth and Seventeenth Centuries.* Urbana, IL.

Pangle, T. L. (1980). *The Laws of Plato: Translated with Notes and an Interpretive Essay.* New York.

Panno, G. (2007). *Dionisiaco e alterità nelle 'Leggi' di Platone: Ordine del corpo automovimento dell'anima nella città tragedia.* Milan.

Parakilas, J. (2003). 'The Chorus', in D. Charlton (ed.), *The Cambridge Companion to Grand Opera.* Cambridge, 76–92.

Parker, R. (2005). *Athenian Religion: A History.* Oxford.

Parker, R. (2011). *On Greek Religion.* Ithaca, NY.

Parret, H. (1998). 'Kant on Music and the Hierarchy of the Arts', *Journal of Aesthetics and Art Criticism*, 56/3: 251–64.

Pascal, J.-N. (2011). 'De la somme à l'encyclopédie: Parcours à travers un siècle d'éditions du *Théâtre des Grecs* (1730–1826)', *Anabases Traditions et Réceptions de l'Antiquité*, 14: 113–31.

Patin, M. (1841–3). *Études sur les tragiques grecs, Sophocle.* Paris.

Paulin, R. (1985). *Ludwig Tieck: A Literary Biography.* Oxford.

Peacocke, C. (2009). 'The Perception of Music: Sources of Significance', *British Journal of Aesthetics*, 49: 257–75.

Peponi, A.-E. (2004). 'Initiating the Viewer: Deixis and Visual Perception in Alcman's Lyric Drama', *Arethusa*, 37: 295–316.

Peponi, A.-E. (2009). '*Choreia* and Aesthetics in the *Homeric Hymn to Apollo*: The Performance of the Delian Maidens (lines 156–64)', *Classical Antiquity*, 28: 39–70.

Peponi, A.-E. (2013a). 'Dithyramb and the Problem of Choral Mimesis', in B. Kowalzig and P. Wilson (eds), *Dithyramb in Context.* Oxford, 353–67.

Peponi, A.-E. (2013b). 'Choral Anti-Aesthetics', in *Performance and Culture in Plato's Laws.* Cambridge, 212–39.

Peponi, A.-E. (2013c) (ed.). *Performance and Culture in Plato's Laws.* Cambridge.

Perlman, P. (1995). '*Invocatio* and *imprecatio*: The Hymn to the Greatest Kouros from Palaikastro and the Oath in Ancient Crete', *Journal of Hellenic Studies*, 115: 161–7.

Péron, J. (1987). 'Demi-chœurs chez Alcman: Parth. I, v. 39–59', *Grazer Beiträge*, 14: 35–53.

Perrault, C. (1692). *Parallèle des anciens et des modernes en ce qui régarde les arts et les sciences III.* Paris.

Perrucci, A. (1961). *Dell'arte rappresentativa premeditata ed al'improvviso*, ed. A. Bragaglia. Florence.

Perusino, F., and Colantonio, M. (2007) (eds). *Dalla lirica corale alla poesia drammatica: forme e funzioni del canto corale nella tragedia e nella commedia greca.* Pisa.

Petersen, U. (1974). *Goethe und Euripides: Untersuchungen zur Euripides-Rezeption in der Goethezeit.* Heidelberg.

Petraki, Z. (2008). 'The Soul Dances: Psychomusicology in Plato's *Republic*', *Apeiron*, 41: 147–70.

Petrey, S. (2001). 'Robert le Diable and Louis-Philippe the King', in R. Parker and M. A. Smart (eds), *Reading Critics Reading: The Opera and Ballet Criticism in France from the Revolution to 1848*. Oxford.

Pickard-Cambridge, A. (1962). *Dithyramb, Tragedy and Comedy*, 2nd edn. Oxford.

Pierer, H. A. (1849). *Universal-Lexikon*. Altenburg.

Pillau, H. (1981). *Die fortgedachte Dissonanz: Hegels Tragödietheorie und Schillers Tragödie: Deutsche Antworten auf die französische Revolution*, Munich.

Poe, J. P. (1969). 'An Analysis of Seneca's *Thyestes*', *Transactions of the American Philological Association*, 100: 355–76.

Poe, J. P. (1983). 'The Sinful Nature of the Protagonist of Seneca's *Oedipus*', in A. Boyle (ed.), *Seneca Tragicus: Ramus Essays in Senecan Drama*. Berwick.

Pois, R. A. (1995). 'The National Socialist *Volksgemeinschaft* Fantasy and the Drama of National Rebirth', in G. W. Gadberry (ed.), *Theatre in the Third Reich, The Prewar Years: Essays on Theatre in Nazi Germany*. Westport, CT, 17–31.

Poiss, T. (2010). 'Zur Idee der Philologie: Der Streit zwischen Gottfried Hermann und August Boeckh', in K. Sier and E. Wöckener-Gade, *Gottfried Hermann (1772–1848). Internationales Symposium in Leipzig 11.–13. Oktober 2007*. Tübingen, 143–63.

Porter, J. I. (2010). *The Origins of Aesthetic Thought in Ancient Greece: Matter, Sensation, and Experience*. Cambridge.

Potter, R. (1777). *The Tragedies of Aeschylus*. Norwich.

Potts, A. (1994). *Flesh and the Ideal: Winckelmann and the Origins of Art History*. New Haven.

Prader, F. (1996). 'The Bride of Messina', in R. Dawe (ed.), *Sophocles: The Classical Heritage*. New York, 137–57.

Pritchett, W. K. (1974). *The Greek State at War*, ii. Berkeley and Los Angeles.

Pym, A. (2010). *Exploring Translation Theories*. London and New York.

Race, W. (1997). *Pindar: Nemean Odes, Isthmian Odes, Fragments*. Cambridge, MA.

Racine, J. (1671). *Bérénice, Tragédie*. Paris.

Racine, J. (1999). *Œuvres complètes*, i. *Théâtre—Poésie*, ed. G. Forestier. Paris.

Rackham, H. (1932). *Aristotle: Politics*. Cambridge, MA.

Radcliffe-Brown, A. R. (1922). *The Andaman Islanders: A Study in Social Anthropology*. Cambridge.

Ralph, J. (1743). *The Case of our Present Theatrical Disputes, Fairly Stated, in which is Contained a Succinct Account of the Rise, Progress and Declension of the Ancient Stage*. London.

Rancière, J. (2004). 'The Politics of Literature', *Substance*, 33/1: 10–24.

Rancière, J. (2009). *The Emancipated Spectator*. London.

Rappaport, R. A. (1967). *Pigs for the Ancestors: Ritual in the Ecology of a New Guinea People*. New Haven.

Rappaport, R. (1999). *Ritual and Religion in the Making of Humanity*. Cambridge.

Reader, W. D. (1972). 'The Autobiographical Author as Fictional Character: Point of View in Meredith's "Modern Love"', *Victorian Poetry*, 10/2: 131–43.

Reichard, G. (1987). *August Wilhelm Schlegels 'Ion': Das Schauspiel und die Aufführungen unter der Leitung von Goethe und Iffland*. Bonn.

Revermann, M. (2008). 'Reception Studies of Greek Drama', *Journal of Hellenic Studies*, 128: 175–8.

Rheingold, H. (2003). *Smart Mobs: The Next Social Revolution.* Cambridge, MA.

Ridgeway, W. (1915). *The Dramas and Dramatic Dances of Non-European Races in Special Reference to the Origin of Greek Tragedy: With an Appendix on the Origin of Greek Comedy.* Cambridge.

Riemer, P., and Zimmermann, B. (1998) (eds). *Der Chor im antiken und modernen Drama.* Stuttgart.

Ringer, M. (1998). *Electra and the Empty Urn: Metatheater and Role Playing in Sophocles.* Chapel Hill, NC.

Ritter, J. (1982). *Hegel and the French Revolution: Essays on the* Philosophy of Right. Cambridge, MA.

Rizzolati, G., and Craighero, L. (2004). 'The Mirror-Neuron System', *Annual Review of Neuroscience,* 27: 169–92.

Robbins, E. (1994). 'Alcman's Partheneion: Legend and Choral Ceremony', *Classical Quarterly,* 44: 7–16.

Rochefort, G. (1782). *Electre.* Paris.

Rodgers, R. (2002). *Musical Stages.* New York.

Rodgers, R., and Hammerstein, O. (2009). *Allegro,* CD Masterworks Broadway. New York.

Rodighiero, A., and Scattolin, P. (2011) (eds). '. . . *un enorme individuo, dotato di polmoni soprannaturali': Funzioni, interpretazioni, e rinascite del coro drammatico greco.* Verona.

Rood, T. (1998). 'Thucydides and his Predecessors', *Histos,* 2: 230–67.

Rosand, E. (1991). *Opera in Seventeenth-Century Venice: The Creation of a Genre.* Berkeley and Los Angeles.

Rosenmeyer, P. A. (1992). *The Poetics of Imitation: Anacreon and the Anacreontic Tradition.* Cambridge.

Rosenmeyer, T. G. (1989). *Senecan Drama and Stoic Cosmology.* Berkeley and Los Angeles.

Rousseau, J.-J. (1969). *Dictionaire de Musique.* Hildesheim.

Rousseau, J.-J. (1987). *Discours sur les sciences et les arts/Lettre à d'Alembert sur les spectacles,* ed. with introduction by J. Varlrot. Paris.

Routledge, W. S., and Routledge, K. (1910). *With a Prehistoric People: The Akikiyu of British East Africa.* London.

Rudnytsky, P. (1987). *Freud and Oedipus.* New York.

Rühle, G. (2007). *Theater in Deutschland. 1887–1945; seine Ereignisse—seine Menschen.* Frankfurt am Main.

Russell, D., and Winterbottom, M. (1989) (eds). *Classical Literary Criticism.* Oxford.

Rutherford, I. (1997). 'Odes and Ends; Closure in Greek Lyric', in D. H. Roberts, F. M. Dunn, and D. Fowler (eds), *Classical Closure: Reading the End in Greek and Latin Literature.* Princeton, 43–61.

Rutherford, I. (2001). *Pindar's Paeans: A Reading of the Fragments with a Survey of the Genre.* Oxford.

Rutherford, I. (2003). 'The Prosodion; Approaches to a Lyric Genre', in F. Benedetti and S. Grandolini (eds), *Studi di filologia e tradizione greca in memoria di Aristide Colonna.* Naples and Perugia, 713–26.

Rutherford, I. (2004). '*Khoros heis ek têsde tês poleôs*: State-Pilgrimage and Song-Dance in Athens', in P. Murray and P. Wilson (eds), *Music and the Muses: The Culture of 'Mousike' in the Classical Athenian City.* Oxford, 67–90.

Rutherford, I. (2013*a*). 'Dithyrambos, Thriambos, Triumphus: Dionysian Discourse at Rome', in B. Kowalzig and P. Wilson (eds), *Dithyramb in Context.* Oxford, 409–23.

Rutherford, I. (2013*b*). 'Strictly Ballroom: Egyptian *mousike* and Plato's Comparative Poetics', in A.-E. Peponi (ed.), *Performance and Culture in Plato's Laws.* Cambridge, 67–83.

Sachs, C. (1937). *World History of the Dance.* New York.

Sallnow, M. J. (1987). *Pilgrims of the Andes: Regional Cults in Cusco.* Washington and London.

Sandbach, F. H. (1961). *Plutarch: Moralia Vol. IX.* Cambridge, MA.

Sandys, J. (1880). *The Bacchae of Euripides.* Cambridge.

Savage, R., and Sansone, M. (1989). '*Il corago* and the Staging of Early Opera: Four Chapters from an Anonymous Treatise *circa* 1630', *Early Music*, 17: 494–511.

Scaliger, J. C. (1561). *Poetices Libri Septem.* Lyons; repr. Stuttgart, 1964.

Schadewaldt, W. (1970). *Hellas und Hesperien: Gesammelte Schriften zur Antike und zur neueren Literatur*, ed. R. Thurow and E. Zinn. 2 vols. Zurich.

Schadewaldt, W. (1996). 'Ancient Tragedy on Stage' in R. Dawe (ed.), *Sophocles: The Classical Heritage.* New York, 283–308.

Schadewaldt, W. (2000). 'Richard Wagner and the Greeks', trans. D. C. Durst, *Dialogos*, 6: 108–40.

Schelling, F. W. J. (1859). 'Philosophie der Kunst', in *Schellings Sämmtliche Werke I.* Stuttgart, 357–736.

Schelling, F. (1989). *The Philosophy of Art*, trans. D. Stott. Minneapolis.

Schiesaro, A. (2003) *The Passions in Play: Thyestes and the Dynamics of Senecan Drama.* Cambridge.

Schiller, F. (1841). *The Bride of Messina: A Tragedy with Choruses*, trans. A. Lodge. London.

Schiller, F. (1986). 'Über den Gebrauch des Chors in der Tragödie', in F. Schiller, *Die Braut von Messina.* Stuttgart, 3–12.

Schiller, F. (1988–2004). *Werke und Briefe in zwölf Bänden.* 12 vols. Frankfurt.

Schiller, F. (1996). *Dramen IV*, ed. M. Luserke. Frankfurt.

Schiller, F. (2006). *The Bride of Messina and On the Use of the Chorus in Tragedy*, trans. A. Lodge, The Project Gutenberg EBook <http://www.gutenberg.org/files/6793/6793-h/6793-h.htm> (accessed 6 June 2012).

Schirmer, L. (2002). 'Einfach Klassisch! Theatralische Bemühungen um die Antike', *Museums-Journal. Berichte aus den Museen, Schlössern und Sammlungen in Berlin und Potsdam*, 1: 35–7.

Schlegel, A. (1846). *A Course of Lectures on Dramatic Art and Literature*, trans. J. Black. London.

Schlegel, A. W. (1894). *A Course of Lectures on Dramatic Art and Literature*, trans. J. Black. Rev. edn. London.

Schlegel, A. W. (1966). *Vorlesungen über dramatische Kunst und Literatur: Erster Teil*, in E. Lohner (ed.), *Kritische Schriften und Briefe*, v. Stuttgart.

Schlegel, A. W. (1989). *Vorlesungen über Ästhetik I (1798–1803)*, in E. Behler (ed.) *Kritische Ausgabe der Vorlesungen 1*. Paderborn.

Schlegel, F. (1958–). *Kritische Friedrich-Schlegel-Ausgabe*, ed. E. Behler. Paderborn.

Schleef, E. (1997). *Droge Faust Parzifal*. Frankfurt am Main.

Schlosser, J. G. (1784). *Prometheus in Fesseln*. Basel.

Schlösser, R. (1935). *Das Volk und seine Bühne: Bemerkungen zum Aufbau des deutschen Theaters*. Berlin.

Schmidt, C. (2010). *Tragödie als Bühnenform: Einar Schleefs Chor-Theater*. Bielefeld.

Schmidt, D. (2001). *On Germans and Other Greeks: Tragedy and the Ethical Life*. Bloomington.

Schneider, G. (1998). 'United States of America: Musical Theater', in S. J. Cohen (ed.), *International Encyclopedia of Dance*. Oxford and New York, 230–53.

Schopenhauer, A. (1958). *The World as Will and Representation*, trans. E. Payne. 2 vols. New York.

Scott, K. (1928). 'The Deification of Demetrius Poliorketes Part II', *American Journal of Philology*, 49: 217–39.

Seaford, R. (1986). 'Immortality, Salvation, and the Elements', *Harvard Studies in Classical Philology*, 90: 1–26.

Seaford, R. (1990), 'The Imprisonment of Women in Greek Tragedy', *Journal of Hellenic Studies*, 110: 76–90.

Seaford, R. (1994). *Reciprocity and Ritual: Homer and Tragedy in the Developing City-State*. Oxford.

Seaford, R. (1996). *Euripides: Bacchae*. Warminster.

Seaford, R. (2003*a*). 'Dionysos, Money, and Drama', *Arion*, 11: 1–19.

Seaford, R. (2003*b*). 'Aeschylus and the Unity of Opposites', *Journal of Hellenic Studies*, 123: 141–63.

Seaford, R. (2004). *Money and the Early Greek Mind*. Cambridge.

Seaford, R. (2005). 'Mystic Light in Aeschylus' *Bassarai*', *Classical Quarterly*, 55: 602–6.

Seaford, R. (2006). *Dionysos*. Routledge.

Seaford, R. (2012). *Cosmology and the Polis*. Cambridge.

Sears, A. (2008). 'The Coming of the Musical Play: Rodgers and Hammerstein', in W. A. Everett and P. R. Laird (eds), *The Cambridge Companion to the Musical*. Cambridge, 147–63.

Seaton, D. (2001). 'Mendelssohn's Dramatic Music', in D. Seaton (ed.), *The Mendelssohn Companion*. Westport, CT, 192–204.

Segal, C. P. (1993). *Euripides and the Poetics of Sorrow*. Durham, NC.

Sergl, A. (1998). 'Das Problem des Chors im deutschen Klassizismus: Schillers Verständnis der *Iphigenie auf Tauris* und seine *Braut von Messina*', *Jahrbuch der deutschen Schillergesellschaft*, 42: 165–94.

Serre, S. (2008). 'Monopole de l'art, art du monopole? L'opéra de Paris sous l'ancien régime', *Entreprise et Histoire*, 53: 80–90.

Shelley, P. B. (1822). *Hellas: A Lyrical Drama*, ed. H. B. Forman. London.

Shelley, P. B. (2003). *The Major Works*, ed. Z. Leader and M. O'Neill. Oxford.

Sheppard, J. (1920). *The Oedipus Tyrannus of Sophocles*. Cambridge.

Sier, K., and Wöckener-Gade, E. (2010) (eds). *Gottfried Hermann (1772–1848). Internationales Symposium in Leipzig 11.–13. Oktober 2007*. Tübingen.

Silk, M. S. (1996) (ed.). *Tragedy and the Tragic: Greek Theatre and Beyond*. Oxford.

Silk, M. S. (1998). '"Das Urproblem der Tragödie": Notions of the Chorus in the Nineteenth Century', in P. Riemer and B. Zimmermann (eds), *Der Chor im antiken und modernen Drama*. Stuttgart, 195–226.

Silk, M. S., and Stern, J. P. (1981). *Nietzsche on Tragedy*. Cambridge.

Simon, G. (2005). 'Chronologie Leyhausen, Wilhelm: Unter Mitwirkung von Dagny Guhr and Ulrich Schermaul', in *Quellen und Literatur aus dem GIFT-Archiv zum Thema 'Wer und was ist warum auf wessen Kosten deutsch?'* <http://homepages. uni-tuebingen.de/gerd.simon/ChrLeyhausen.pdf> (accessed 14 January 2013).

Sklenář, R. (2007–8). 'Seneca *Oedipus* 980–94: How Stoic a Chorus?', *Classical Journal*, 103: 183–94.

Slater, W. (2000). 'Gnomology and Criticism', *Greek, Roman and Byzantine Studies*, 41: 99–121.

Smith, E. (2002) (ed.). *King Henry V*. Cambridge.

Smith, M. (2000). *Ballet and Opera in the Age of* Giselle. Princeton.

Smith, R. E. F. (1977) (ed.). *The Russian Peasant in 1920 and 1984*. London.

Smither, H. (1977–2000). *A History of the Oratorio*. 4 vols. Chapel Hill, NC, and London.

Sokolowski, F. (1969). *Lois sacrées des cités grecques*. Paris.

Solerti, A. (1904–5) (ed.). *Gli albori del melodrama*. 3 vols. Milan, repr. Hildesheim, 1969.

Sommerstein, A. (1989). *Aeschylus: Eumenides*. Cambridge.

Sourvinou-Inwood, C. (1997). 'Reconstructing Change: Ideology and the Eleusinian Mysteries', in M. Golden and P. Toohey (eds), *Inventing Ancient Culture*. London, 132–64.

Sourvinou-Inwood, C. (2003). 'Aspects of the Eleusinian Cult', in M. Cosmopoulos (ed.), *Greek Mysteries*. London, 25–49.

Spencer, B., and Gillen, F. J. (1904). *The Northern Tribes of Central Australia*. London.

Spencer, P. (1985a) (ed.). *Society and the Dance*. Cambridge.

Spencer, P. (1985b). 'Dance as Antithesis in Samburu Discourse', in P. Spencer (ed.), *Society and the Dance*. Cambridge, 140–60.

Stanford, W., and McDowell, R. B. (1971). *Mahaffy: A Biography of an Anglo-Irishman*. London.

Stehle, E. (1997). *Performance and Gender in Ancient Greece: Nondramatic Poetry in its Setting*. Princeton.

Steinberg, M. (1991). 'The Incidental Politics to Mendelssohn's *Antigone*', in R. L. Todd (ed.), *Mendelssohn and his World*. Princeton, 137–57.

Steiner, G. (1961). *The Death of Tragedy*. London.

Steiner, G. (1984). *Antigones*. London.

Steiner, G. (1996). 'Tragedy, Pure and Simple', in M. S. Silk, *Tragedy and the Tragic: Greek Theatre and Beyond*. Oxford, 534–46.

Stempel, L. (2010). *Showtime*. New York.

Stephenson, R. H. (1995). *Goethe's Conception of Knowledge and Science*. Edinburgh.

Stern, T. (2009). *Documents of Performance in Early Modern England*. Cambridge.

Stites, R. (1989). *Revolutionary Dreams: Utopian Vision and Experimental Life in the Russian Revolution*. New York and Oxford.

Stocking, G. (1996) (ed.). *Volksgeist as Method and Ethic: Essays on Boasian Ethnography and the German Anthropological Tradition*. Madison.

Stommer, R. (1985). *Die inszenierte Volksgemeinschaft. Die 'Thing-Bewegung' im Dritten Reich*. Marburg.

Strathern, A. (1985). 'A Line of Boys: Melpa Dance as a Symbol of Maturation', in P. Spencer (ed.), *Society and the Dance*. Cambridge, 119–39.

Strauss, B. S. (1993). *Fathers and Sons in Athens: Ideology and Society in the Era of the Peloponnesian War*. Princeton.

Strohm, R. (1997). *Dramma per Musica: Italian Opera Seria in the Eighteenth Century*. New Haven.

Styan, J. (1982). *Max Reinhardt*. Cambridge.

Sulzer, J. G. (1771). 'Chor', in *Allgemeine Theorie der schönen Künste, Erster Theil*. Leipzig, 200–4.

Sutton, D. F. (1984). 'Seneca's *Hercules Furens*: One Chorus or Two?', *American Journal of Philology*, 105: 301–5.

Sutton, D. F. (1986). *Seneca on the Stage*. Leiden.

Swift, L. A. (2009). 'How to Make a Goddess Angry: Making Sense of the Demeter Ode in Euripides' *Helen*', *Classical Philology*, 104: 418–38.

Swift, L. A. (2010). *The Hidden Chorus: Echoes of Genre in Tragic Lyric*. Oxford.

Szegedy-Maszak, A. (1981). *The Nomoi of Theophrastus*. New York.

Szondi, P. (1961). *Versuch über das Tragische*. Frankfurt am Mein.

Szondi, P. (2002). *An Essay on the Tragic*, trans. P. Fleming. Stanford.

Tait, A. L. (1984). *Lunacharsky: Poet of the Revolution*. Birmingham.

Tambiah, S. J. (1985). *Culture, Thought, and Social Action: An Anthropological Perspective*. Cambridge, MA.

Tarrant, R. (1985) (ed.). *Seneca's Thyestes*. Atlanta.

Thackeray, W. M. (1888). *The History of Pendennis. The Complete Works of William Makepeace Thackeray in 13 Volumes*, Vol. 2. London.

Treadwell, N. (2008). *Music and Wonder at the Medici Court*. Bloomington.

Triau, C. (2003) (ed.). *Choralités*. Brussels [= Special Issue, *Alternatives théâtrales*, 76–7].

Trubotchkin, D. (2005). '*Agamemnon* in Russia', in F. Macintosh, P. Michelakis, E. Hall, and O. Taplin (eds), *Agamemnon in Performance 458BC–AD 2004*. Oxford, 255–73.

Tsantsanoglou, K. (2006). 'The Scholia on Alcman's Partheneion', *Hellenika* 56: 7–30.

Ugolini, G. (2003). '"Philologus inter Philologos": Friedrich Nietzsche, die klassische Philologie und die griechische Tragödie', *Philologus*, 147: 316–42.

Ulf, C. (2006). 'Anlässe und Formen von Festen mit überlokaler Reichweite in vor- und frügarchaischer Zeit: Wozu dient der Blick in ethnologisch-anthropologische Literatur?', in K. Freitag et al. (eds), *Kult—Politik—Ethnos (Historia Einzelschriften 189)*. Stuttgart, 17–41.

Usher, S. (1985). *Dionysius of Halicarnassus: The Critical Essays in Two Volumes*. Cambridge, MA.

Valdesolo, P., and DeSteno, D. (2011). 'Synchrony and the Social Tuning of Compassion', *Emotion*, 11: 262–6.

Van Aken, K. R. (2006). *Race and Gender in the Broadway Chorus*. Unpublished dissertation, University of Pittsburgh.

Van Gennep, A. (1909). *Les Rites de passage*. Paris.

Van Gennep, A. (1960). *The Rites of Passage* [*Les Rites de passage*, Paris, 1909], ed. and trans. M. Vizedom and G. Caffee. London.

Vanneschi, F. (1747). *Fetonte, Drama per il Teatro di S. M. B.* London.

Vasunia, P. (2007). *Zarathustra and the Religion of Ancient Iran: The Greek and Latin Sources in Translation*. Mumbai.

Vatry, A. R. (1733). 'Dissertation où l'on traite des avantages que la Tragédie ancienne retiroit de ses chœurs', in *Mémoires de litterature, tirez des registres de l'Académie Royale des Inscriptions et Belles Lettres*. Paris, viii. 199–210.

Vernant, J.-P. (1990). 'The Historical Moment of Tragedy in Greece: Some of the Social and Psychological Conditions', in J.-P. Vernant and P. Vidal–Naquet, *Myth and Tragedy in Ancient Greece*, trans. by J. Lloyd. New York, 23–8.

Vernant, J.-P. and Vidal-Naquet, P. (1990). *Myth and Tragedy in Ancient Greece*, trans. by J. Lloyd. New York.

Verrall, A. W. (1891). *The Student's Manual of Greek Tragedy*. London and New York.

Vicaire, P. (1960). *Platon: Critique Littéraire*. Paris.

Vidal-Naquet, P. (1981). 'Oedipe à Vicence et à Paris: Deux moments d'une histoire', *Quaderni di Storia*, 14: 3–29.

Visvardi, E. (forthcoming). *Dancing the Emotions: Pity and Fear in the Tragic Chorus*. Leiden.

Voltaire (1819). *Œuvres complètes de Voltaire*, ed. A. A. Renouard, iii. Paris.

Voltaire (1877). *Œuvres complètes de Voltaire*, ed. L. Moland, vi. Paris.

Voltaire (1992). *Œuvres complètes de Voltaire*, 31A. Voltaire Foundation. Oxford.

Voltaire (1998). *Œuvres complètes de Voltaire*, 5. Voltaire Foundation. Oxford

Voltaire (2001). *Œuvres Complètes de Voltaire*, 1A. Voltaire Foundation. Oxford

Wagner, R. (1892–9). *Richard Wagner's Prose Works*, trans. W. Ashton Ellis. 8 vols. London.

Wagner, R. (1911–14 [1873]). 'Das Bühnenfestspielhaus in Bayreuth', in *Sämtliche Schriften und Dichtungen*. Leipzig, ix. 322–44.

Wagner, R. (1983). 'Die Kunst und die Revolution', in *Dichtungen und Schriften,* vol. 5, ed. D. Borchmeyer. Bayreuth, 273–309.

Wagner, R. (1983 [1850]). *Oper und Drama*, in *Dichtungen und Schriften*, vol. 7, ed. D. Borchmeyer. Frankfurt am Main.

Wagner, R. (1983 [1851]). *Eine Mitteilung an meine Freunde*, in *Dichtungen und Schriften*, vol. 6, ed. D. Borchmeyer. Frankfurt am Main, 199–325.

Wagner, R. (1983 [1879]). *Über die Anwendung der Musik auf das Drama*, in *Dichtungen und Schriften*, vol. 9, ed. D. Borchmeyer. Frankfurt am Main, 324–42.

Warstat, M. (2004). *Theatrale Gemeinschaften: Zur Festkultur der Arbeiterbewegung 1918-1933*. Tübingen.

Warstat, M. (2005). 'Community Building within a Festival Frame: Working-Class Celebrations in Germany 1918-1933', *Theatre Research International*, 30: 262–73.

Weaver, B. (1949). '*Prometheus Bound* and *Prometheus Unbound*', *Proceedings of the Modern Language Association*, 64/1: 115–33.

Webb, R. (2008). *Demons and Dancers: Performance in Late Antiquity*. Cambridge, MA.

Webster, H. (1908). *Primitive Secret Societies*. New York.

Webster, T. B. L. (1970). *The Greek Chorus*. London.

Weinberg, B. (1970–4) (ed.). *Trattati di poetica e retorica del cinquecento*. 4 vols. Bari.

Weir Smyth, H. (1999). *Aeschylus: Libation Bearers*. Cambridge, MA.

Weiss, P. (1982). 'Metastasio, Aristotle and the *opera seria*', *Journal of Musicology*, 1: 385–94.

West, M. L. (1965). 'The Dictaean Hymn to the Kouros', *Journal of Hellenic Studies*, 85: 149–59.

Whittall, A. (1980). 'Leitmotif', in *Grove Music Online* <www.oxfordmusiconline. com> (accessed 12 January 2013).

Wiater, N. (2011). *The Ideology of Classicism: Language, History, and Identity in Dionysius of Halicarnassus*. Berlin.

Wilamowitz-Moellendorff, U. von (1889). *Euripides' Herakles*. 2 vols. Berlin.

Wilamowitz-Moellendorff, U. von (1907). *Einführung in die Griechische Tragödie*. Berlin.

Wilamowitz-Moellendorff, U. von (1969 [1872]). 'Zukunftsphilologie! Eine Erwidrung auf Friedrich Nietzsches "Geburt der Tragödie"', in K. Gründer (ed.), *Der Streit um Nietzsches "Geburt der Tragödie": Die Schriften von E. Rohde, R. Wagner, U. von Wilamowitz-Moellendorff*. Hildersheim, 27–55.

Wilamowitz-Moellendorff, U. von (1972). 'Die Autobiographie im Altertum', in *Kleine Schriften*. Berlin, vi. 120–7 [first published in *Internationale Wochenschrift für Wissenschaft, Kunst und Technik*, 1 (1907): 1105–1114].

Wilder, T. (2007). 'Preface to *Our Town*', in J. D. McClatchy (ed.), *Thornton Wilder: Collected Plays & Writings on Theater*. New York, 657–9.

Wiles, D. (1997). *Tragedy in Athens: Performance Space and Theatrical Meaning*. Cambridge.

Wiles, D. (2005). 'Sophoclean Diptychs: Modern Translations of Dramatic Poetry', *Arion*, 13: 9–26.

Wiles, D. (2011). *Theatre and Citizenship: The History of a Practice*. Cambridge.

Williams, S. (2003). 'The Spectacle of the Past in Grand Opera' in D. Charlton (ed.), *The Cambridge Companion to Grand Opera*. Cambridge, 58–78.

Willson, S., and Eastman, H. (2010). '*Red Ladies*: Who Are They and What Do They Want?', in F. Macintosh (ed.), *The Ancient Dancer in the Modern World*. Oxford, 420–30.

Willson, S., and Fussetti, G. (2002). 'The Pedagogy of the Poetic Body', in D. Bradby and M. Delgado (eds), *The Paris Jigsaw: Internationalism and the City's Stages*. Manchester, 93–112.

Wilmer, S.E., and Zukauskaite, A. (2010) (eds). *Interrogating Antigone in Postmodern Philosophy & Criticism*. Oxford.

Wilson, P. (2000). *The Athenian Institution of the Khoregia: The Chorus, the City, and the Stage*. Cambridge.

Wilson, P. (2003). 'The Politics of Dance: Dithyrambic Contest and Social Order in Ancient Greece', in D. J. Phillips and D. Pritchard (eds), *Sport and Festival in the Ancient Greek World*. Swansea, 163–96.

Wilson, P. (2007). 'Performance in the *Pythion*: The Athenian Thargelia', in P. Wilson (ed.), *The Greek Theatre and Festivals: Documentary Studies*. Oxford, 150–82.

Wiltermuth, S. S., and Heath, C. (2009). 'Synchrony and Cooperation', *Psychological Science*, 20: 1–5.

Winnington-Ingram, R. P. (1980). *Sophocles: An Interpretation*. Cambridge.

Winterer, C. (2002). *The Culture of Classicism: Ancient Greece and Rome in American Intellectual Life, 1780–1910*. Baltimore.

Wittgenstein, L. (1958). *Philosophical Investigations*, trans. G. E. M. Anscombe. 2nd edn. Oxford.

Wolster, P. (1786). 'Abhandlung über den Nutzen, den das alte Trauerspiel aus seinen Chören hatte', in *Theaterkalender auf das Jahr 1786*, 29–37.

Wood, C., and Sadler, G. (2000) (ed. and trans.). *French Baroque Opera: A Reader*. Aldershot.

Worth, K. (2004). 'Greek Notes in Samuel Beckett's Theatre Art', in E. Hall, F. Macintosh, and A. Wrigley (eds), *Dionysus since 69: Greek Tragedy at the Dawn of the Third Millennium*. Oxford, 265–83.

Wulf, J. (1989). *Kultur im Dritten Reich: Eine Dokumentation*. Frankfurt am Main and Berlin.

Wyndham, H. S. (1906). *The Annals of Covent Garden Theatre from 1732–1897*. 2 vols. London.

Wynne-Edwards, V. C. (1962). *Animal Dispersion in Relation to Social Behaviour*. Edinburgh.

Yatromanolakis, D., and Roilos, P. (2004) (eds). *Greek Ritual Poetics*. Washington.

Zanobi, A. (2008). 'The Influence of Pantomime on Seneca's Tragedies', in E. Hall and R. Wyles (eds), *New Directions in Ancient Pantomime*. Oxford.

Zarifi, Y (2010). 'Staneiwski's Secret Alphabet of Gestures: Dance, Body and Metaphysics', in F. Macintosh (ed.), *The Ancient Dancer in the Modern World*. Oxford, 389–410.

Zedler, J. H. (1731–50). *Grosses vollständiges Universal-lexicon aller Wissenschafften und Künste*. Halle.

Zimmerman, A. (2001). *Anthropology and Antihumanism in Imperial Germany*. Chicago.

Zimmermann, B. (2008). 'Seneca and Pantomime', trans. E. Hall, in E. Hall and R. Wyles (eds), *New Directions in Ancient Pantomime*. Oxford, 218–26.

Zimmermann, B. (2011). 'Teoria e utilizzo del coro in Friedrich Schiller', in A. Rodighiero and P. Scattolin (eds), '. . . *un enorme individuo, dotato di polmoni soprannaturali': Funzioni, interpretazioni, e rinascite del coro drammatico greco*. Verona, 291–305.

Ziolkowski, T. (2008). 'August Böckh und die "Sonnettenschlacht bei Eichstädt"', in F. Strack (ed.), *200 Jahre Heidelberger Romantik*. Heidelberg and Berlin, 207–23.

Zwierlein, O. (1966). *Die Rezitationsdramen Senecas*. Meisenheim.

Index